Paris

timeout.com/paris

Time Out Guides Ltd
Universal House
251 Tottenham Court Road
London W1T 7AB
United Kingdom
Tel: +44 (0)20 7813 3000
Fax: +44 (0)20 7813 6001
Email: guides@timeout.com
www.timeout.com

This edition first published in Great Britain in 2010 by Ebury Publishing.
A Random House Group Company
20 Vauxhall Bridge Road, London SW1V 2SA

Random House Australia Pty Ltd 20 Alfred Street, Milsons Point, Sydney, New South Wales 2061, Australia

Random House New Zealand Ltd 18 Poland Road, Glenfield, Auckland 10, New Zealand

Random House South Africa (Pty) Ltd Isle of Houghton, Corner Boundary Road & Carse O'Gowrie,
Houghton 2198, South Africa

Random House UK Limited Reg. No. 954009

For further distribution details, see www.timeout.com.

ISBN: 978-1-84670-168-9

A CIP catalogue record for this book is available from the British Library.

Printed and bound by Firmengruppe APPL, aprinta druck, Wemding, Germany.

The Random House Group Limited supports The Forest Stewardship Council (FSC), the leading international
forest certification organisation. All our titles that are printed on Greenpeace approved FSC certified paper
carry the FSC logo. Our paper procurement policy can be found at http://www.rbooks.co.uk/environment.

Time Out carbon-offsets its flights with Trees for Cities (www.treesforcities.org).

Contents

Introduction

It may not have made it into the natural hazards section of this guide, but it seems only fair to warn readers that there is now a recognised condition called 'Paris Syndrome', a state of shock brought on when the city of lights fails to twinkle. Considering that the French capital ranks as the most visited city in the world by quite some considerable margin, the reported 12 annual cases may seem rather trifling, but the very fact that such an affliction even exists reveals something – that no other destination in the world has quite such a weight of expectation attached to it. Whether it's Rollerblading through the streets on a Friday-night skate, maxing out the credit cards in the quirky boutiques of the northern Marais, slipping into Bofinger for a theatrical post-show *plateau de fruits de mer* or simply staring in awe at the towering sight of 2,500,000 rivets on the banks of the Seine, there's something so overwhelmingly exciting about Paris that it makes you feel truly alive. This is a city where even the clichés are cool.

Obviously, like the 12 poor souls above, some visitors will leave disappointed – perhaps unable to cope with the grumpy waiters, lumpy bolsters, unhelpful shop assistants or rude cab drivers, or caught out by the frightening price of a beer on the Champs-Elysées (someone was recently overheard complaining about their €23 bill for a pint of Amstel, which even by tourist rip-offs is going some). But for most, these traditional 'drawbacks' are all part of the charm of one of the world's most charming cities – good news for the estimated two million jobs in the city linked to tourism.

Naturally, no self-respecting leader would change such a successful formula, and charismatic mayor Bertrand Delanoë has chosen to hold the gherkins and instead accessorise with chic add-ons such as Vélib' and Paris-Plage, brilliant urban refinements that keep the capital up with the urban elite. And slowly but surely, Paris's pleasures are spreading beyond the Grands Boulevards, crossing the Périphérique and into the formerly forbidden lands of the *banlieue*. From art complexes to anatomy museums, 21st-century Paris no longer stops at the 20th arrondissement.

Dominic Earle, Editor

Paris in Brief

IN CONTEXT

Our In Context section details the fabled history that helps make Paris such a fascinating town. However, it also focuses on the 21st-century city, currently undergoing substantial changes. The central drive of these changes is to integrate Paris with its *banlieue*, and ten of the world's top architects have sketched out their visions of Grand Paris. We take a look into the future of the French capital.
► *For more, see pp15-50.*

SIGHTS

Tourists touting the *I-Spy Book of Paris Sights* head straight for the Louvre and the Eiffel Tower, and with good reason – you can't go wrong with either. But these two honeypot attractions aren't the sum total of the city's attractions: you'll also find everything from undiscovered museums to beautiful cemeteries, dazzling modern architecture to centuries-old cathedrals. They're all featured here.
► *For more, see pp51-152.*

CONSUME

Few cities retain such a towering culinary reputation, and despite the credit crunch Paris has seen some great new restaurant and café openings recently, which are reviewed here. Also in this section, you'll find a comprehensive guide to the fabulous shopping in the city and our picks for Paris's best hotels, with more than 100 properties detailed in full.
► *For more, see pp153-272.*

ARTS & ENTERTAINMENT

There's plenty to entertain visitors. The city's theatre scene is becoming more and more accessible to non-French speakers, and film is as popular as ever, with some wonderfully historic cinemas. Paris has exceptional opera and world music scenes, a thriving collection of galleries, and even *chanson* is managing to reinvent itself for today's audience.
► *For more, see pp273-346.*

ESCAPES & EXCURSIONS

For all the city's charms, it's worth considering an escape from the hubbub. You certainly won't need to travel far to find one: the grand, handsome Fontainebleau is only around an hour away, with historic Chantilly, bucolic Giverny (Monet's inspiration) and the genuinely astonishing palace of Versailles even closer. Got more time to explore? Hop on a TGV and head for Metz, Lyon or Montpellier.
► *For more, see pp347-362.*

Paris in 48 Hours

Day 1 From Marais Mansions to Midnight Munchies

9AM Start the day on the Right Bank with an awesome croissant from the hugely popular **Moisan** (*see p261*), an easy stroll from beautiful 17th-century place des Vosges. The Marais is abuzz with culture, shops, bars and, in its imposing *hôtels particuliers*, important cultural institutions: take your pick from the **Musée Carnavalet** (*see p101*), **Musée d'Art et d'Histoire du Judaïsme** (*see p100*) or the **Maison Européenne de la Photographie** (*see p103*). Shoppers, meanwhile, will find rich pickings in the streets leading off the main shopping thoroughfare of rue des Francs-Bourgeois.

NOON From the Marais, head across the Seine via the Pont de Sully to the **Institut du Monde Arabe** (*see p121*), which holds a fine collection of Middle Eastern art and a rooftop café with fabulous views down the Seine. (Other wonderful panoramas in Paris include the summit of the **Parc des Buttes-Chaumont** (*see p113*) and the **Sacré-Coeur** (*see p95*), although the latter is worth saving for dusk.) After a wander along the Left Bank to lunch in the back room at **La Palette** (*see p237*), a classic café, meander along the stone quays that border the Seine and leaf through tatty paperbacks at the riverside *bouquinistes* (*see p241*), before ducking into the **Musée d'Orsay** (*see p145*) for an Impressionist masterclass.

4PM From here, either hop on a boat tour or explore the islands. Snag an ice-cream from **Berthillon** (*see p58*) on the Ile St-Louis, before popping over to the Ile de la Cité to visit the **Mémorial des Martyrs de la Déportation** (*see p56*) and **Notre-Dame** (*see p56*).

9PM Evenings start with aperitifs. Join the sociable crowd on the terrace seats at **Le Bar du Marché** (*see p235*) and watch the Left Bank people-traffic pass by over a kir and a light supper. Then cross the river to hip newcomer the **Chacha Club** (*see p327*) in Les Halles. Post-dancefloor hunger pangs can be satiated at welcoming bistro **La Poule au Pot** (9 rue Vauvilliers, 1st, 01.42.36.32.96), open until 6am.

NAVIGATING THE CITY

Neatly contained within the Périphérique and divided by the Seine into left and right banks, Paris is a compact city. The city's 20 arrondissements (districts) spiral out, clockwise and in ascending order, from the Louvre. Each piece of this jigsaw has its own character.

The Paris métro is reliable, and local buses are frequent and cheap. However, the city is best seen from ground level, whether on foot or, courtesy of the Vélib' bike-hire scheme, on two wheels. For full details of transport, *see p364*.

SEEING THE SIGHTS

To skip the queues, try to avoid visiting major attractions at the weekend. Major museums are less busy during the week, especially if you take advantage of the late-night opening offered by many of the big museums. Pre-booking is essential before 1pm at the Grand Palais, and it's also possible to pre-book at the Louvre.

Day 2 Paintings, Park Life and Bistro Perfection

9AM If you'd like to see the **Louvre** (*see p59*), now's the time: early, before the crowds have descended (and preferably not on a weekend). Otherwise, cross the Pont des Arts and head south through the narrow Left Bank streets to the city's oldest church, **Eglise St-Germain-des-Prés** (*see p126*), followed by coffee at **Les Editeurs** (*see p236*). Then stroll down to the **Jardin du Luxembourg** (*see p129*), pull up two green chairs (using one as a footrest) and size up the park life. The adjacent **Musée National du Luxembourg** (*see p131*) hosts world-class art exhibitions.

NOON From here, hop on the métro to Jacques Bonsergent. Amble along the tree-lined Canal St-Martin, crossing over its romantic bridges to explore little shops and waterside cafés and maybe stopping at *cave à vins* **Le Verre Volé** (*see p234*) for a plate of charcuterie and cheese. On Sundays, traffic is outlawed from the quai de Valmy and the bar-lined quai de Jemmapes. There are plenty of boutiques in the area, alongside kitsch merchants **Antoine et Lili** (*see p253*). For a swift *demi* near the water, head to friendly **Chez Prune** (*see p233*), before catching the métro to Alma Marceau.

5PM Modern art lovers should make a point of visiting the wonderful collection at the **Musée d'Art Moderne de la Ville de Paris** (*see p86*); it's a neighbour to the **Palais de Tokyo** (*see p87*), a dynamic contemporary art space. From here, you can walk to the Champs-Elysées and take a night-time hike up the freshly renovated **Arc de Triomphe** (*see p85*) to see the lights of the avenue stretching into the city.

8PM Head back to the Palais de Tokyo and relax with an expertly shaken cocktail at the hip bar with its terrace overlooking the Seine. Then head up to Les Halles for supper at Grégory Lemarchand's hot new loft-style bistro, **Frenchie** (*see p187*), next to rue Montorgeuil. Still got energy? Our Nightlife chapter (*see p326*) awaits...

Note that most national museums are closed on Tuesdays, but all are free on the first Sunday of the month. Many municipal museums close on Mondays.

PACKAGE DEALS

The most economical way to visit a large number of museums is with a **Paris Museum Pass** (www.parismuseumpass. fr), which offers access to more than 60 museums and attractions. Participating attractions, which include the Louvre and the Musée d'Orsay, are denoted in our listings with PMP. Covering two days (€32), four days (€48) or six days (€64), passes are available from participating locations and tourist offices.

The Galeries Nationales du Grand Palais also now operate an annual pass. The **Sesame** (www.rmn.fr) grants free entry (with queue-jumping rights), shop discounts and various other privileges. The card costs €47 for an individual, €79 for a couple and €22 for 13-25s.

Paris in Profile

THE SEINE & ISLANDS

Ile de la Cité is the bullseye of the capital, where its history begins – home to the law courts, **Notre-Dame** and a dinky flower market. East from here, **Ile St-Louis** is one of the smartest addresses in the capital.

▶ *For more, see pp53-58.*

THE LOUVRE

The world's largest museum, the **Louvre** is home to some 35,000 works of art, from ancient Egypt to the 19th century. Crowds can be oppressive, especially around the *Mona Lisa*, but there's also plenty of space for contemplation.

▶ *For more, see pp59-65.*

OPERA TO LES HALLES

At the western end of this stretch, it's all large-scale consumerism and high-end culture; to the east are sleaze, buzz and **Les Halles**, home to the grim Forum des Halles mall. Heading south, the **Tuileries** gardens provide respite.

▶ *For more, see 66-81.*

CHAMPS-ELYSEES & WESTERN PARIS

The city's most famous thoroughfare, the **Champs-Elysées** has been transformed of late. At its western end, the **Arc de Triomphe** is also gleaming after a refurb. **Western Paris** is a civilised mix of important museums and grand residences.

▶ *For more, see pp82-90.*

MONTMARTRE & PIGALLE

Montmartre has one of the city's densest concentrations of tourists. After the views and the **Sacré-Coeur**, explore the romantic sidestreets. The popular image of **Pigalle** covers sex shops and neon, but the area is cleaning up its act.

▶ *For more, see pp91-96.*

BEAUBOURG & THE MARAIS

Beaubourg is home to the **Centre Pompidou**, which holds Europe's largest collection of modern art. The **Marais**, with ancient buildings and a street plan largely unmolested by Haussmann, is the heartland of Jewish and gay Paris.

▶ *For more, see pp97-103.*

BASTILLE & EASTERN PARIS

Bastille is not so much revolutionary as creative these days; now the area around the iconic place de la Bastille is well stocked with record shops, music venues and lively bars. Further east lies Paris's biggest park, the **Bois de Vincennes**.

▶ *For more, see pp104-108.*

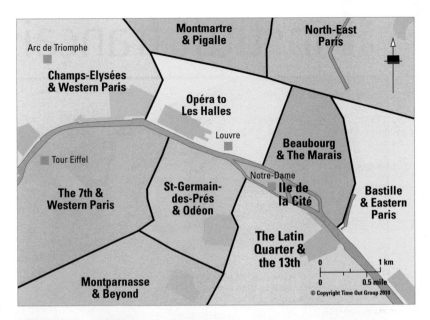

Montmartre & Pigalle

North-East Paris

Arc de Triomphe

Champs-Elysées & Western Paris

Opéra to Les Halles

Louvre

Tour Eiffel

Beaubourg & The Marais

The 7th & Western Paris

St-Germain-des-Prés & Odéon

Notre-Dame

Ile de la Cité

Bastille & Eastern Paris

The Latin Quarter & the 13th

Montparnasse & Beyond

0   1 km
0   0.5 mile
© Copyright Time Out Group 2010

NORTH-EAST PARIS
The drab **Gare du Nord** is many visitors' first taste of Paris. But east are **Belleville** and **Ménilmontant**, two of the city's most multicultural areas and now a real nightlife hub.
▶ *For more, see pp109-113.*

THE LATIN QUARTER & THE 13TH
Academic tradition persists in the **Latin Quarter**, home to the **Panthéon** and the **Sorbonne**. Further east, the vast ZAC Rive Gauche development project means the **13th** is on the up.
▶ *For more, see pp114-124.*

ST-GERMAIN-DES-PRES & ODEON
Intellectual heritage and some of the most expensive coffee in the city are to be found in **St-Germain-des-Prés** & **Odéon**, now best known for its fashion houses and luxury brands.
▶ *For more, see pp125-131.*

MONTPARNASSE & BEYOND
There's just enough of a good-time feel in **Montparnasse** at night to recall the area's artistic heyday in the '20s and '30s. South, **Parc Montsouris** offers relief from the urban sprawl.
▶ *For more, see pp132-138.*

THE 7TH & WESTERN PARIS
The 7th is home to many of Paris's finest museums and the **Eiffel Tower**, its most celebrated monument. Elsewhere, this is a rarefied area of smart shops and posh homes.
▶ *For more, see pp139-146.*

Institut Français is one of the oldest established of the 150 Instituts Français which exist throughout the world. Founded in 1910, it has an unrivalled reputation for its cultural programme and the quality of its classes, which explore both language and culture. The fact that the Institut Français is part of the French Ministry of Foreign Affairs' cultural network is a guarantee of the highest degree of professionalism and skill and it is also an accredited examination centre. All the tutors at the Institut Français are native French speakers who are trained in the latest methods for teaching French as a foreign language.

What's on offer

The Institut Français offers a wide range of classes and timetables to suit even the most hectic of diaries, it can cater for all those wishing to discover France through the medium of its language. Courses range from General French (once or several times a week) to specialised French in language, culture and business. Moreover its comprehensive exam preparation classes will get your French up to speed. Whether you're working towards a qualification in general, business or legal French, its experienced teaching staff will provide the support students need to help them pass their exams. Also on offer are one-to-one courses providing flexible, effective, and tailor-made solutions to your specific French language needs. Whatever the level, and whether on an individual or group basis the Institut Français can fine-tune a programme of study and arrange the most appropriate time, place and frequency of classes to meet your requirements. Corporate tuition is also available on a one-to-one basis or small groups, at the Institut Français or at your desk.

Location

The Institut Français, Language Centre is housed in charming listed buildings in the very heart of South Kensington and is a stone's throw from its Cultural Centre which houses the Ciné Lumière (UK's leading showcase for French cinema, screening a mix of new releases and classic films. All films are shown with English subtitles) and the largest French multi-media library in the UK.

Facilities

The Language Centre offers a language laboratory, video and audio visual equipment, the latest teaching aids and a direct satellite link to French TV enabling students to feast on French programmes with their coffee in the cafeteria. Moreover the multi-media library offers a wide variety of documentation for Francophiles and French language-learners of all levels. Everyone studying at the Language Centre is entitled to one year's free membership of the Institut Français Cultural Centre.

Time Out Paris

Editorial
Editor Dominic Earle
Copy Editor Ros Sales
Listings Editor Julien Sauvalle
Proofreader Marion Moisy
Indexer Jonathan Cox

Managing Director Peter Fiennes
Editorial Director Ruth Jarvis
Series Editor Will Fulford-Jones
Business Manager Dan Allen
Editorial Manager Holly Pick
Assistant Management Accountant Ija Krasnikova

Design
Art Director Scott Moore
Art Editor Pinelope Kourmouzoglou
Senior Designer Henry Elphick
Graphic Designers Kei Ishimaru, Nicola Wilson
Advertising Designer Jodi Sher

Picture Desk
Picture Editor Jael Marschner
Deputy Picture Editor Lynn Chambers
Picture Researcher Gemma Walters
Picture Desk Assistant Ben Rowe
Picture Librarian Christina Theisen

Advertising
Commercial Director Mark Phillips
International Advertising Manager Kasimir Berger
Head of French Advertising Sales Charlie Sokol

Marketing
Marketing Manager Yvonne Poon
Sales & Marketing Director, North America & Latin America Lisa Levinson
Senior Publishing Brand Manager Luthfa Begum
Art Director Anthony Huggins

Production
Group Production Director Mark Lamond
Production Manager Brendan McKeown
Production Controller Damian Bennett

Time Out Group
Chairman Tony Elliott
Chief Executive Officer David King
Group Financial Director Paul Rakkar
Group General Manager/Director Nichola Coulthard
Time Out Communications Ltd MD David Pepper
Time Out International Ltd MD Cathy Runciman
Time Out Magazine Ltd Publisher/MD Mark Elliott
Group IT Director Simon Chappell
Marketing & Circulation Director Catherine Demajo

Contributors
Introduction Dominic Earle. **History** Simon Cropper. **Paris Today** Rich Woodruff. **Architecture** Natasha Edwards. **Future City** Natasha Edwards. **Sightseeing** Simon Cropper (*Sweet Success* Anna Brooke; *Secret Museums* Alison Culliford; *Portrait of the Artist, Making an Exhibition, History of Cinema* Rich Woodruff). **Hotels** Alison Culliford (*Room With a View* Simon Cropper). **Restaurants** Rosa Jackson (*Secret Supper* Alison Culliford). **Cafés & Bars** Anna Brooke (*Perfect Mix* Alison Culliford). **Shops & Services** Alison Culliford; *Fashion* Katie Walker. **Calendar** Dominic Earle (*Pedal Power* Rich Woodruff). **Cabaret, Circus & Comedy** Anna Brooke. **Children** Anna Brooke. **Dance** Estelle Ricoux. **Film** Simon Cropper. **Galleries** Natasha Edwards. **Gay & Lesbian** Robert Vallier. **Music** *Classical & Opera* Stephen Mudge; *Rock, Roots & Jazz* Anna Brooke. **Nightlife** Julien Sauvalle. **Sport & Fitness** Rich Woodruff. **Theatre** Anna Brooke. **Escapes & Excursions** Dominic Earle (*Follow the Fizz* Anna Brooke). **Directory** Julien Sauvalle.

Maps john@jsgraphics.co.uk, except: pages 415-416.

Photography Oliver Knight, except: page 3 Ekaterina Krasnikova/Shutterstock; pages 4, 7, 8 (top, right), 8 (lower top, right), 8 (left, middle), 40, 68, 84, 99, 102, 108, 115, 127, 129, 147, 187, 204, 208, 211, 230, 231, 236, 269 (left), 280, 291, 306, 307, 311, 313, 322, 329, 352 Olivia Rutherford; pages 5 (lower left), 8 (top, left), 9 (bottom), 57 (top), 59, 62, 63 (bottom, left), 118, 200 Jean-Christophe Godet; page 16 Ullsteinbild/TopFoto; page 22 The Bridgeman Art Library; page 25 akg-images; pages 29, 315 (right) Getty Images; page 31 ABACA/PA Photos; page 46 AGA; page 48 Jean Nouvel; page 49 Castro Denissof Casi; page 50 Christian de Portzamparc; pages 53, 55, 57 (bottom), 61, 63 (right), 294, 342, 277 Heloise Bergman; pages 63 (top, left), 135, 185, 186, 201, 219, 242, 262, 344, 355 Karl Blackwell; page 113 Alison Culliford; page 143 J Manoukian; page 190 Ilepet/Shutterstock; page 191 Rob Greig; page 212 Eric Laignel; page 271 Kapu/Shutterstock; page 287 © Disney; page 297 Allstar/Cinetext/MIRAMAX; page 315 (left) The Art Archive/Musée George Sand et de la Vallée Noire La Châtre/Dagli Orti; page 318 Pierre Grosbois; page 332 Amaury Choay; page 337 Associated Press; page 357 Charlie Pinder; page 361 Marie Perrin/Lyon Tourism. The following images were provided by the featured establishments/artists: page 5 (bottom), 44, 134, 149, 166, 225, 232, 274, 279, 284, 292, 320, 325, 347, 358, 359.

The Editor would like to thank all contributors to previous editions of *Time Out Paris*, whose work forms the basis for parts of this book.

About the Guide

GETTING AROUND

The back of the book contains street maps of Paris, as well as overview maps of the city and its surroundings. The maps start on page 395; on them are marked the locations of hotels (**❶**), restaurants (**❶**), and cafés and bars (**❶**). The majority of businesses listed in this guide are located in the areas we've mapped; the grid-square references in the listings refer to these maps.

THE ESSENTIALS

For practical information, including visas, disabled access, emergency numbers, useful websites and local transport, please see the Directory. It begins on page 363.

THE LISTINGS

Addresses, phone numbers, websites, transport information, hours and prices are all included in our listings, as are selected other facilities. All were checked and correct at press time. However, business owners can alter their arrangements at any time, and fluctuating economic conditions can cause prices to change rapidly.

The very best venues in the city, the must-sees and must-dos in every category, have been marked with a red star (★). In the Sights chapters, we've also marked venues with free admission with a FREE symbol.

THE LANGUAGE

Many Parisians speak a little English, but a few basic French phrases go a long way. You'll find a primer on page 382, along with some help with restaurants on page 190.

PHONE NUMBERS

The area code for Paris is 01. Even if you're calling from within Paris, you'll always need to use the code. From outside France, dial your country's international access code (00 from the UK, 011 from the US) or a plus symbol, followed by the French country code (33), 1 for Paris (dropping the initial zero) and the eight-digit number. So, to reach the Louvre, dial +33.1.40.20.50.50. For more on phones, *see p379*.

FEEDBACK

We welcome feedback on this guide, both on the venues we've included and on any other locations that you'd like to see featured in future editions. Please email us at guides@timeout.com.

Time Out Guides

Founded in 1968, Time Out has grown from humble beginnings into the leading resource for anyone wanting to know what's happening in the world's greatest cities. Alongside our influential weeklies in London, New York and Chicago, we publish more than 20 magazines in cities as varied as Beijing and Beirut; a range of travel books, with the City Guides now joined by the newer Shortlist series; and an information-packed website. The company remains proudly independent, still owned by Tony Elliott four decades after he launched *Time Out London*.

Written by local experts and illustrated with original photography, our books also retain their independence. No business has been featured because it has advertised, and all restaurants and bars are visited and reviewed anonymously.

ABOUT THE EDITOR

Dominic Earle is a freelance travel writer. In addition to editing Time Out City Guides to Paris, Copenhagen and Stockholm, he has also contributed to publications including *The Guardian* and *The Independent*.

A full list of the book's contributors can be found opposite. However, we've also included details of our writers in selected chapters throughout the guide.

In Context

Gare du Nord. *See p110.*

History

Gauls, guillotines and grands projets.

TEXT: SIMON CROPPER

The earliest settlers seem to have arrived in Paris around 120,000 years ago. One of them lost a flint spear-tip on the hill now called Montmartre, and the dangerous-looking weapon is to be seen today in the Stone Age collection at the Musée des Antiquités Nationales. There was a Stone Age weapons factory under present-day Châtelet, and the redevelopment of Bercy in the 1990s unearthed ten neolithic canoes, five of which are now sitting high and dry in the Musée Carnavalet.

By 250 BC, a Celtic tribe known as the Parisii had put the place firmly on the map. The Parisii were river traders, wealthy enough to mint gold coins; the Musée de la Monnaie de Paris has an extensive collection of their small change. Their most important *oppidum*, a primitive fortified town, was located on an island in the Seine river, which is generally thought to have been what is today's Ile de la Cité. A superb strategic location and the capacity to generate hard cash were guaranteed to attract the attention of the Romans.

Simon Cropper lived in Paris for several years and writes about the city, food and cinema for Time Out.

'Seeing the walls of the city defended against him, no less a pillager than Attila the Hun was forced to turn back, and he was defeated soon afterwards.'

ROMAN PARIS

Julius Caesar arrived in southern Gaul as proconsul in 58 BC, and soon used the pretext of dealing with invading barbarians to stick his Roman nose into the affairs of northern Gaul. Caesar had a battle on his hands, but eventually the Paris region and the rest of Gaul were in Roman hands. Roman Lutetia (as Paris was known) was a prosperous town of around 8,000 inhabitants. As well as centrally heated villas and a temple to Jupiter on the main island (the remains of both are visible in the Crypte Archéologique), there were the sumptuous baths (now the Musée National du Moyen Age) and the 15,000-seater Arènes de Lutèce.

CHRISTIANITY

Christianity arrived in around 250 AD in the shape of Denis of Athens, who became the first bishop of Paris. Legend has it that when he was decapitated by Valerian on Mons Martis, the mount of the martyrs (today better known as Montmartre), Denis picked up his head and walked with it to what is now St-Denis, to be buried there. The event is depicted in Henri Bellechose's *Retable de Saint-Denis*, now exhibited in the Louvre.

Gaul was still a tempting prize. Waves of barbarian invaders began crossing the Rhine from 275 onwards. They sacked more than 60 cities in Gaul, including Lutetia, where the population was massacred and the buildings on the Montagne Ste-Geneviève were pillaged and burned. The bedraggled survivors used the rubble to build a rampart around the Ile de la Cité and to fortify the forum.

It was at this time that the city was renamed Paris. Protected by the Seine and the new fortifications, its main role was as a rear base for the Roman armies defending Gaul, and it was here in 360 that Julian was proclaimed emperor by his troops. Around 450, with the arrival of the Huns in the region, the people of Paris prepared once again to flee. They were dissuaded by a feisty woman named Geneviève, famed for her piety. Seeing the walls of the city defended against him, no less a pillager than Attila the Hun was forced to turn back, and he was defeated soon afterwards.

CLOVIS

In 464, Paris managed to resist another siege, this time by the Francs under Childeric. However, by 486, after a further blockade lasting ten years, Geneviève had no option but to surrender the city to Childeric's successor, Clovis, who went on to conquer most of Gaul and founded the Merovingian dynasty. He chose Paris as capital of his new kingdom, and it stayed that way until the seventh century, in spite of conflicts among his successors. Under the influence of his wife, Clotilde, Clovis converted to Christianity. He founded, and was buried in, the basilica of the Saints-Apôtres, later rededicated to Ste Geneviève when the saviour and future patron saint of Paris was interred there in 512. All that remains of the basilica today is a pillar in the grounds of the Lycée Henri IV; but there's a shrine dedicated to St Geneviève and some relics in the fine Gothic church of St-Etienne-du-Mont next door. Geneviève and Clovis had set a trend. The Ile de la Cité was still the heart of the city, but, under the Merovingians, the Left Bank was the up-and-coming area for fashion-conscious Christians, with 11 churches built here in the period (whereas there were only four on the Right Bank and one on the Ile de la Cité).

IN CONTEXT

Not everyone was sold on the joys of city living, though. From 614 onwards, the Merovingian kings preferred the *banlieue* at Clichy, or wandered the kingdom trying to keep rebellious nobles in check. By the time one of the rebels, Pippin 'the Short', decided to do away with the last Merovingian in 751, Paris was starting to look passé.

Pippin's son, Charlemagne, built his capital at Aix-la-Chapelle (now Aachen in Germany), and his successors, the Carolingian dynasty, moved from palace to palace, consuming the local produce. Paris, meanwhile, was doing nicely as a centre for Christian learning, and had grown to a population of 20,000 by the beginning of the ninth century. This was the high point in the political power of the great abbeys like St-Germain-des-Prés, where transcription of the Latin classics was helping to preserve much of Europe's Roman cultural heritage. Power in the Paris area was exercised by the counts of Paris.

PARIS FINDS ITS FEET
From 845, Paris had to fight off another threat – the Vikings. But after various sackings and seiges, the Carolingians were finally able to secure the city. The dynasty gave way to the Capetian dynasty in 987, when Hugues Capet was elected king of France. Under the Capetians, although Paris was now at the heart of the royal domains, the city did not yet dominate the kingdom. Robert 'the Pious', king from 996 to 1031, stayed more often in Paris than his father had done, restoring the royal palace on the Ile de la Cité, and Henri I (1031-60) issued more of his charters in Paris than in Orléans. In 1112, the abbey of St-Denis replaced St-Benoît-sur-Loire as principal monastery.

Paris itself still consisted of little more than the Ile de la Cité and small settlements under the protection of the abbeys on each bank. On the Left Bank, royal largesse helped to rebuild the abbeys of St-Germain-des-Prés, St-Marcel and Ste-Geneviève, although it took more than 150 years for the destruction wrought there by the Vikings to be repaired. The Right Bank, where mooring was easier, prospered from river commerce, and three boroughs grew up around the abbeys of St-Germain-l'Auxerrois, St-Martin-des-Champs and St-Gervais. Bishop Sully of Paris began building the cathedral of Notre-Dame in 1163.

The reign of Philippe-Auguste (1180-1223) was a turning point in the history of Paris. Before, the city was a confused patchwork of royal, ecclesiastical and feudal authorities. Keen to raise revenues, Philippe favoured the growth of the guilds, especially the butchers, drapers, furriers, haberdashers and merchants; so began the rise of the bourgeoisie.

He also ordered the building of the first permanent market buildings at Les Halles, and a new city wall, first on the Right Bank to protect the commercial heart of Paris, and later on the Left Bank. At the western end of the wall, Philippe built a castle, the Louvre, to defend the road from the ever-menacing Normandy, whose duke was also King of England.

A GOLDEN AGE
Paris was now the principal residence of the king and the uncontested capital of France. To accommodate the growing royal administration, the Palais de la Cité, site and symbol of power for the previous thousand years, was remodelled and enlarged. Work was begun by Louis IX (later St Louis) in the 1240s, and continued under Philippe IV ('le Bel'). This architectural complex, of which the Sainte-Chapelle and the nearby Conciergerie can still be seen, was inaugurated with great pomp at Pentecost 1313.

The palace was quickly filled with functionaries, so the king spent as much of his time as he could outside Paris at the royal castles of Fontainebleau and, especially, Vincennes. The needs of the plenipotentiaries left behind to run the kingdom were met by a rapidly growing city population, piled into rather less chic buildings.

Paris was also reinforcing its identity as a major religious centre: as well as the local clergy and dozens of religious orders, the city was home to the masters and students

IN CONTEXT

'Resolutely Catholic, Paris was the scene of some horrific violence against the Huguenots.'

of the university of the Sorbonne (established in 1253), who were already gaining a reputation for rowdiness. An influx of scholars from all over Europe gave the city a cultural and intellectual cachet it was never to lose.

By 1328, Paris was home to 200,000 inhabitants, making it the most populous city in Europe. However, that year was also notable for being the last of the medieval golden age: the dynasty of Capetian kings spluttered to an inglorious halt when Charles IV died without an heir. The English quickly claimed the throne for Edward III, the son of Philippe IV's daughter. Refusing to recognise his descent through the female line, the late king's cousin, Philippe de Valois, claimed the French crown as Philippe VI. So began the Hundred Years War between France and England – a war that in fact would go on for 116 years.

TROUBLES AND STRIFE

To make matters worse, the Black Death (bubonic plague) ravaged Europe from the 1340s onwards. Citizens not finished by the plague had to contend with food shortages, ever-increasing taxes, riots, repression, currency devaluations and marauding mercenaries. Meanwhile, in Paris, the honeymoon period for the king and the bourgeoisie was coming to an end. Rich and populous, Paris was expected to bear the brunt of the war burden; and as defeat followed defeat (notably the disaster at Crécy in August 1346), the bourgeoisie and people of the city were increasingly exasperated by the futility of the sacrifices they were making for the hideously expensive war. To fund the conflict, King Jean II tried to introduce new tax laws – without success. When the king was captured by the English at Poitiers in 1356, his problems passed to his 18-year-old son, Charles.

The Etats Généraux, consultant body to the throne, was summoned to the royal palace on the Ile de la Cité to discuss the country's woes. The teenage king was besieged with angry demands for reform from the bourgeoisie, particularly from Etienne Marcel, then provost of the local merchants. Marcel seized control of Paris and began a bitter power struggle with the crown; in 1357, fearing widespread revolt, Charles fled to Compiègne. But as he ran, he had Paris blockaded. Marcel called on the peasants, who were also raging against taxes, but they were quickly crushed. He then called on Charles 'the Bad' of Navarre, ally to the English, but his arrival in Paris made many of Marcel's supporters nervous. On 31 July 1358, Marcel was murdered, and the revolution was over. As a safeguard, the returning Charles built a new stronghold to protect Paris: the Bastille.

By 1420, following the French defeat at Agincourt, Paris was in English hands; in 1431, Henry VI of England was crowned King of France in Notre-Dame. He didn't last. Five years later, Henry and his army were driven back to Calais by the Valois king, Charles VII. Charles owed his power to Jeanne d'Arc, who led the victorious French in the Battle of Orléans, only to be betrayed by her compatriots, who decided she was getting too big for her boots. She was captured and sold to the English, who had her burned as a witch.

By 1436, Paris was once again the capital of France. But the nation had been nearly bled dry by war and was still divided politically, with powerful regional rulers across France continuing to threaten the monarchy. Outside the French borders, the ambitions of the Austrian Habsburg dynasty represented a serious threat. In this general atmosphere of instability, disputes over trade, religion and taxation were all simmering dangerously in the political background.

RENAISSANCE AND REFORMATION

In the closing decades of the 15th century, the restored Valois monarchs sought to reassert their position. A wave of building projects was the public sign of this effort, producing such masterpieces as St-Etienne-du-Mont, St-Eustache and private homes like the Hôtel de Cluny (which today houses the Musée National du Moyen Age) and the Hôtel de Sens, which now accommodates the Bibliothèque de Forney. The Renaissance in France had its peak under François I. As well as being involved in the construction of the magnificent châteaux at Fontainebleau, Blois and Chambord, François was also responsible for transforming the Louvre from a fortress into a royal palace.

Despite burning heretics by the dozen, François was unable to stop the spread of Protestantism, launched in Germany by Martin Luther in 1517. Resolutely Catholic, Paris was the scene of some horrific violence against the Huguenots, as supporters of the new faith were called. By the 1560s, the situation had degenerated into open warfare. Catherine de Médicis, the scheming Italian widow of Henri II, was the real force in court politics. It was she who connived to murder prominent Protestants gathered in Paris for the marriage of the king's sister on St Bartholomew's Day (23 August 1572). Catherine's main aim was to dispose of her powerful rival, Gaspard de Coligny, but the situation got out of hand, and as many as 3,000 people were butchered. Henri III attempted to reconcile the religious factions and eradicate the powerful families directing the conflict, but the people of Paris turned against him and he was forced to flee. His assassination in 1589 brought the Valois line to an end.

THE BOURBONS

The throne of France being up for grabs, Henri of Navarre declared himself King Henri IV, launching the Bourbon dynasty. Paris was not impressed. The city closed its gates against the Huguenot king, and the inhabitants endured a four-year siege by supporters of the new ruler. Henri managed to break the impasse by having himself converted to Catholicism (and is supposed to have said, '*Paris vaut bien une messe*' – Paris is well worth a mass).

Henri set about rebuilding his ravaged capital. He completed the Pont Neuf, the first bridge to span the whole Seine. He commissioned place Dauphine and the city's first enclosed residential square – the place Royale – now place des Vosges.

Henri also tried to reconcile his Catholic and Protestant subjects, issuing the Edict of Nantes in 1598, effectively giving each religion equal status. The Catholics hated the deal, and the Huguenots were suspicious. Henri was the subject of at least 23 attempted assassinations by fanatics of both persuasions. Finally, in 1610, a Catholic by the name of François Ravaillac fatally stabbed the king while he was in traffic on rue de la Ferronnerie.

TWO CARDINALS

Since Henri's son, Louis XIII, was only eight at the time of his father's death, his mother, Marie de Médicis, took up the reins of power. We can thank her for the Palais du Luxembourg and the 24 paintings she commissioned from Rubens, now part of the Louvre collection. Louis took up his royal duties in 1617, but Cardinal Richelieu, chief minister from 1624, was the man who ran France. Something of a schemer, he outwitted the king's mother, his wife (Anne of Austria) and a host of others. Richelieu helped to strengthen the power of the monarch, and he did much to limit the independence of the aristocracy.

The Counter-Reformation was at its height, and lavish churches such as the Baroque Val-de-Grâce were an important reassertion of Catholic supremacy. The 17th century was 'le Grand Siècle', a time of patronage of art and artists, even if censorship forced the brilliant mathematician and philosopher René Descartes into exile. The first national newspaper, *La Gazette*, hit the streets in 1631; Richelieu used it as a propaganda tool. The cardinal founded the Académie Française, which is still working, slowly, on the

IN CONTEXT

Heads Will Roll

The French Revolution – from conception to bloody execution.

In the winter of 1788-89, Louis XVI was losing his grip on his country's problems. Wars had left the state practically bankrupt; harvests had failed and food prices soared. Distress and discontent reigned, and with it came demands for an end to absolute monarchy and wider participation in government, particularly from the bourgeoisie.

Under pressure, Louis allowed the formation of an Assemblée Nationale, which began work on a national constitution. But behind the scenes, he began gathering troops to force it to disband; and on 12 July he dismissed the commoner's ally, finance minister Jacques Necker. On 14 July a crowd stormed the Bastille prison in response. Only seven prisoners were inside, but the symbolic victory was immense.

The establishment of the constitution forged ahead. Tax breaks for the nobility and clergy were abolished; Church property was seized. But the price of bread remained high. In October, a mob of starving women marched the 12 miles to Versailles and demanded that the king come to Paris. He promised to send them grain, an offer they rejected by decapitating some of his guards.

Louis transferred to the Tuileries. In the months that followed, the Jacobins – the more radical of the revolutionary elements – roused powerful Republican feeling. The king and his family attempted to flee Paris on 20 June 1791, but were apprehended.

On 14 September, Louis accepted the constitution. But other monarchies were plotting to reinstate him. In 1792, Austrian and Prussian troops invaded France. The Republicans, correctly, suspected Louis of conspiracy, and raised an army to capture him. He and his family were incarcerated by the radical Commune de Paris, headed by Danton, Marat and Robespierre.

Then came a massacre. Republicans invaded the prisons and murdered 2,000 so-called traitors. The monarchy was abolished on 22 September; the king was executed on 21 January 1793. Headed by Robespierre, the Jacobins vowed to wage terror against all dissidents. The Great Terror of 1794 saw the guillotine slice through 1,300 necks in six weeks.

Eventually there was no more stomach for killing. Robespierre and his cohorts attempted some democratic reform, but most people wanted them gone. On 28 July 1794, he was executed and the Reign of Terror collapsed. The biggest and bloodiest of revolutions was over.

dictionary of the French language that Richelieu commissioned from them in 1634. Richelieu died in 1642; Louis XIII followed suit a few months later. The new king, Louis XIV, was five years old. Anne of Austria became regent, with the Italian Cardinal Mazarin, a Richelieu protégé, as chief minister. Rumour has it that Anne and Mazarin may have been married. Mazarin's townhouse is now home to the Bibliothèque Nationale de France – Richelieu.

Endless wars against Austria and Spain had depleted the royal coffers and left the nation drained by exorbitant taxation. In 1648, the royal family was chased out of Paris by a popular uprising, 'la Fronde', named after the catapults used by some of the rioters. Parisians soon tired of the anarchy that followed. When Mazarin's army retook the city in 1653, the boy-king was warmly welcomed. Mazarin died in 1661 and Louis XIV, now 24 years old, decided he would rule France without the assistance of any chief minister.

SHINE ON, SUN KING

The 'Roi Soleil', or Sun King, was an absolute monarch. 'L'état, c'est moi' (I am the State) was his vision of power. To prove his grandeur, the king embarked on wars against England, Holland and Austria. He also refurbished and extended the Louvre, commissioned place Vendôme and place des Victoires, constructed the Observatory and laid out the *grands boulevards* along the line of the old city walls. The triumphal arches at Porte St-Denis and Porte St-Martin date from this time too. His major project was the palace at Versailles. Louis moved his court there in 1682.

Louis XIV owed much of his brilliant success to the work of Jean-Baptiste Colbert, who was nominally in charge of state finances, but eventually took control of all the important levers of the state machine. Colbert was the force behind the Sun King's redevelopment of Paris. The Hôtel des Invalides was built to accommodate the crippled survivors of Louis' wars, the Salpêtrière to shelter fallen women. In 1702 Paris was divided into 20 *quartiers* (not until the Revolution was it re-mapped into arrondissements). Colbert died in 1683, and Louis' luck on the battlefield ran out. Hopelessly embroiled in the War of the Spanish Succession, the country was devastated by famine in 1692. The Sun King died in 1715, leaving no direct heir. His five-year-old great-grandson, Louis XV, was named king, with Philippe d'Orléans as regent. The court moved back to Paris. Installed in the Palais-Royal, the regent set about enjoying his few years of power, hosting lavish dinners that degenerated into orgies. The state, meanwhile, remained chronically in debt.

THE ENLIGHTENMENT

Some of the city's more sober residents were making Paris the intellectual capital of Europe. Enlightenment thinkers such as Diderot, Montesquieu, Voltaire and Rousseau were active during the reign of Louis XV. Literacy rates were increasing – 50 per cent of French men could read, 25 per cent of women – and the publishing industry was booming.

The king's mistress, Madame de Pompadour, encouraged him to finance the building of the Ecole Militaire and the laying out of place Louis XV, known to us as place de la Concorde. The massive church of St-Sulpice was completed in 1776. Many of the great houses in the area bounded by rue de Lille, rue de Varenne and rue de Grenelle date from the first half of the 18th century. The private homes of aristocrats and wealthy bourgeois, these would become the venues for numerous salons, the informal discussion sessions often devoted to topics raised by Enlightenment questioning.

The Enlightenment spirit of rational humanism finally took the venom out of the Catholic–Protestant power struggle, and the increase in public debate helped to change views about the nature of the state and the place and authority of the monarchy. As Jacques Necker, Louis XVI's finance minister on the eve of the Revolution, put it, popular opinion was 'an invisible power that, without treasury, guard or army, gives its

IN CONTEXT

laws to the city, the court and even the palaces of kings'. Thanks to the Enlightenment, and an ever- growing burden of taxation on the poorest strata of society to prop up the wealthiest, that power would eventually overturn the status quo.

THE FRENCH REVOLUTION
The great beneficiary of the French Revolution, Napoleon Bonaparte, once remarked that lucky generals were to be preferred over good generals. The same applies to kings, and the gods of fortune certainly deserted Louis XVI in 1789, when bad weather and worse debts brought France to its knees. But few would have predicted that the next five years would see the execution of the king and most of the royal family, terror stalking the streets in the name of revolution, and the steady rise of a young Corsican soldier. For an account of the Revolution, *see p22* **Heads Will Roll**.

NAPOLEON
Amid the post-Revolutionary chaos, power was divided between a two-housed Assembly and a Directory of five men. The French public reacted badly to hearing of England's attempts to promote more popular rebellion; when a royalist rising in Paris needed to be put down, a young officer from Corsica was the man to do it – Napoleon Bonaparte.

Napoleon quickly became the Directory's right-hand man. When they needed someone to lead a campaign against Austria, he was the man. Victory saw France – and Napoleon – glorified. After a further, aborted, campaign to Egypt in 1799, Napoleon returned home to put down another royalist plot, made himself the chief of the newly governing three-man Consul – and by 1804 was emperor.

After failing to squeeze out the English by setting up the Continental System to block trade across the Channel, Napoleon waged massive wars against Britain, Russia and Austria. On his way to the disaster of Moscow, Napoleon gave France the *lycée* educational system, the Napoleonic Code of civil law, the Legion of Honour, the Banque de France, the Pont des Arts, the Arc de Triomphe, the Madeleine church (he re-established Catholicism as the state religion), La Bourse and rue de Rivoli. He was also responsible for the centralised bureaucracy that still drives the French mad.

As Russian troops – who had chased Napoleon's once-mighty army all the way from Moscow and Leipzig – invaded France, Paris itself came under threat. Montmartre, then named Montnapoléon, had a telegraph machine at its summit, one that had given so many of the emperor's orders and transmitted news of so many victories. The hill fell to Russian troops. Napoleon gave the order to blow up the city's main powder stores, and thus Paris itself. His officer refused. Paris accommodated carousing Russian, Prussian and English soldiers while Napoleon was sent to exile in Elba. A hundred days later, he was back, leading an army against Wellington and Blücher's troops in the mud of Waterloo, near Brussels. A further defeat saw the end of him. Paris survived further foreign occupation. The diminutive Corsican died on the South Atlantic prison island of St Helena in 1821.

ANOTHER ROUND OF BOURBONS
Having sampled revolution and military dictatorship, the French were now ready to give monarchy a second chance. The Bourbons got back in business in 1815, in the person of Louis XVIII, Louis XVI's elderly brother. Several efforts were made to adapt the monarchy to the new political realities, though the new king's Charter of Liberties was not a wholly sincere expression of how he meant to rule.

When another brother of Louis XVI, Charles X, became king in 1824, he decided that enough royal energy had been wasted trying to reconcile the nation's myriad factions. It was time for a spot of old-fashioned absolutism. But the forces unleashed during the Revolution, and the social divisions that had opened as a result, were not to be ignored – and the people were happy to respond with some old-fashioned rebellion.

IN CONTEXT

Gustav Eiffel (top) on the **Eiffel Tower**. *See p27.*

In the 1830 elections, the liberals won a hefty majority in the Chamber of Deputies, the legislative body. Charles's unpopular minister Prince Polignac, a returned émigré, promptly dissolved the Chamber, announced a date for new elections and curtailed the number of voters. Polishing off this collection of bad decisions was the 26 July decree abolishing the freedom of the press. The day after its issue, 5,000 print workers and journalists filled the streets and three newspapers went to press. When police tried to confiscate copies, they sparked a three-day riot, 'les Trois Glorieuses', with members of the disbanded National Guard manning the barricades. On 30 July, Charles dismissed Polignac, but it was too late. He had little choice but to abdicate, and fled to England. As French revolutions go, it was a neat, brief affair.

Another leftover from the *ancien régime* was now winched on to the throne – Louis-Philippe, Duc d'Orléans, who had some Bourbon blood in his veins. A father of eight who never went out without his umbrella, he was eminently acceptable to the newly powerful bourgeoisie. But the poor, who had risked their lives in two attempts to change French society, were unimpressed by the new king's promise to embrace a moderate and liberal version of the Revolutionary heritage.

THE NINETEENTH CENTURY

Philosopher Walter Benjamin declared Paris 'the capital of the 19th century', and he had a point. Though it was smaller than its global rival, London, in intellectual and cultural spheres it reigned supreme. On the demographic front, its population doubled to one million between 1800 and 1850. Most of the new arrivals were rural labourers, who had come to find work on the city's ever-expanding building sites. Meanwhile, the middle classes were doing well, thanks to the relatively late arrival of the industrial revolution in France, and the solid administrative structures inherited from Napoleon. The poor were as badly off as ever, only now there were more of them. The back-breaking hours worked in the factories would not be curbed by legislation: 'Whatever the lot of the workers is, it is not the manufacturer's responsibility to improve it,' said one trade minister. In Left Bank cafés, a new bohemian tribe of students derided the materialistic government. Workers' pamphlets and newspapers, such as *La Ruche Populaire*, gave voice to the starving, crippled poor. A wave of ill feeling was gradually building up against Louis-Philippe.

On 23 February 1848, hundreds of Parisians – men, women and students – moved along the boulevards towards a public banquet at La Madeleine. The king's minister,

'Prussian forces laid siege to the city. Paris held out, starving, for four brave months, its citizens picking rats from the gutter for food.'

François Guizot, had forbidden any direct campaigning by opposition parties in the forthcoming election, so the parties held banquets instead of meetings.

One diarist of the time noted that some of the crowd had stuffed swords and daggers underneath their shirts, but the demonstration was largely peaceful – until the troops stationed on the boulevard des Capucines opened fire, igniting a riot.

As barricades sprang up all over the city, a trembling Louis-Philippe abdicated and a liberal provisional government declared a republic. The virtual epidemic of poverty and unemployment was stemmed by creating national *ateliers*, but such 'radical' reforms made the right extremely nervous. A conservative government took power in May 1848, and shut down the *ateliers*. A month later, the poor were back in the streets. Some 50,000 took part in the 'June Days' protests, which were quite comprehensively crushed by General Cavaignac's troops. In total, about 1,500 Parisians died and some 5,000 were deported.

As the pamphleteer Alphonse Karr said of the revolution's aftermath, 'plus ça change, plus c'est la même chose' (the more things change, the more they stay the same). In December 1848, Louis Bonaparte – nephew of Napoleon – was elected president. By 1852, he had moved into the Tuileries palace and declared himself Emperor Napoleon III.

THE SECOND EMPIRE

The emperor appointed a lawyer as *préfet* to mastermind the reconstruction of Paris. In less than two decades, prefect Georges-Eugène Haussmann had created the most magnificent city in Europe. His goals included better access to railway stations, better water supplies, and a long list of new hospitals, barracks, theatres and *mairies*. It was a colossal project, and it transformed the capital with a network of wide, arrow-straight avenues that were more hygienic than the narrow streets they replaced.

Not everyone was happy. Haussmann's works destroyed thousands of buildings, including beautiful Middle Ages monuments; on the whole of Ile de la Cité only Notre-Dame and a handful of houses survived. Entire residential areas were wiped off the map, and only the owners of the buildings themselves were compensated; tenants were merely booted out. Writers and artists lamented the loss of the more quirky Paris they used to know, and criticised the unfriendly grandeur of the new city. But there was no going back.

At home, the city's rapid industrialisation saw the rise of Socialism and Communism among the disgruntled working classes, and Napoleon III gave limited rights to trade unions. Abroad, though, the now constitutional monarch was a disaster. After the relatively successful Crimean War of the mid 1850s, he tried in vain to impose the Catholic Maximilian as ruler of Mexico. The Franco-Prussian war was his next misadventure. France was soon defeated. At Sedan, in September 1870, 100,000 French troops were forced to surrender to Bismarck's Prussians; Napoleon III himself was captured, never to return.

The war continued, and back in Paris, a provisional government hastily took power. Elections gave conservative monarchists the majority, though the Paris vote was firmly Republican. Former prime minister Adolphe Thiers assumed executive power. Meanwhile, Prussian forces marched on Paris and laid siege to the city. Paris held out, starving, for four brave months, its citizens picking rats from the gutter for food.

Léon Gambetta, a young politician, escaped in style (by hot-air balloon) but failed to raise an army in the south. In January 1871, the provisional government signed a bitter armistice that relinquished the industrial heartlands of Alsace and Lorraine and agreed to pay a five-million-franc indemnity. German troops would stay on French soil until the bill was paid.

But with occupying army camps stationed around their city, Parisians considered the treaty a dishonour and remained defiant. Thiers ordered his soldiers to enter the city and strip it of its cannons, but the insurgents cut them short. The new government scuttled off to the haven of Versailles, and on 26 March Paris elected its own municipal body, the Commune, so called in memory of the spirit of 1792. The 92 members of the Commune hailed from the left and working classes; their agenda was liberal (schools would be secularised, debts suspended) but war-like (Germany must be defeated). Paris itself was given a little makeover: the column extolling Napoleonic glory on place Vendôme was pulled down, and statues of the great emperor were smashed all over town.

Thiers would not stand by and watch. Artillery fire picked at the Communards' sandbag barricades on the edges of Paris, and the suburbs fell by 11 April. In the sixth week of fighting, troops broke in through the Porte de St-Cloud and covered the springtime city in blood. The ill-equipped Communards faced a massacre: some 25,000 were killed in a matter of days. In revenge, around 50 hostages were taken and shot, including the Archbishop of Paris. The infamous *pétroleuses*, women wielding petrol bombs, burned off their anger, torching the Tuileries and the Hôtel de Ville. On the last day of *la semaine sanglante*, 28 May, 147 Communards were trapped and shot in Père-Lachaise cemetery, against the 'Mur des Fédérés', still an icon of the Commune struggle. The dead were buried in the streets, the prisons crammed with 40,000 Communards; thousands were deported, many to penal colonies in New Caledonia.

THE THIRD REPUBLIC
Thanks mainly to the huge economic boost provided by colonial expansion in Africa and Indo-China, the horrors of the Commune were soon forgotten in the self-indulgent materialism of the turn of the century and the Third Republic. The Eiffel Tower was built as the centrepiece of the 1889 Exposition Universelle. For the next Exposition Universelle, in 1900, the Grand Palais and Petit Palais, the Pont Alexandre III and the Gare d'Orsay (now the Musée d'Orsay) were built to affirm France's position as a world power, and the first line of the métro opened. The first film screening had been held (1895), and clubs like the Moulin Rouge were buzzing. The lurid life of Montmartre, depicted by Toulouse-Lautrec – and its cheap rents – would attract the world's artistic community.

THE GREAT WAR
On 3 August 1914, Germany declared war on France. Although the Germans never made it to Paris in World War I – German troops were stopped 20 kilometres (12 miles) short of the city thanks to the French victory in the Battle of the Marne – the artillery was audible. Paris, and French society as a whole, suffered terribly, despite ultimate victory.

The nations gathered at Versailles to make the peace, and established new European states. The League of Nations was formed. Artists responded to the horrors and absurdity of the conflict with Surrealism, a movement founded in Paris by André Breton, a doctor who had treated troops in the trenches and embraced Freud's theories of the unconscious. In 1924, Surrealism had a manifesto, a year later its first exhibition. Again, artists (and photographers) flocked to Paris. Montmartre was now too expensive, and Montparnasse became the hub of artistic life. The interwar years were a whirl of activity in artistic and political circles. Paris became the avant-garde capital of the world, recorded by Hemingway, F Scott Fitzgerald and Gertrude Stein, who had made the city their home.

IN CONTEXT

'The Vichy government was so eager to please the Germans, it organised anti-Semitic measures without prompting.'

Meanwhile, the Depression unleashed a wave of political violence, Fascists fighting Socialists and Communists for control. At the same time, many writers were leaving Paris for Spain to cover – and, indeed, to take part in – the Civil War. Across the German border, the contentious territories of Alsace-Lorraine – and the burden of the World War I peace agreements signed in Paris – became one of many bugbears held by the new chancellor, Adolf Hitler. As war broke out, France believed that its Maginot line would hold strong against the German threat. When the Nazis attacked France in May 1940, they simply bypassed the fortifications and came through the Ardennes.

WORLD WAR II

Paris was in German hands by June. The city fell without a fight. A pro-German government was set up in Vichy, headed by Marshall Pétain, and a young army officer, Charles de Gaulle, went to London to organise the Free French opposition. For Frenchmen happy to get along with the German army, the period of the Occupation presented few hardships and, indeed, some good business opportunities. Food was rationed, and tobacco and coffee went out of circulation, but the black market thrived. For people who resisted, there were the Gestapo torture chambers at avenue Foch or rue Lauriston. The Germans further discouraged uncooperative behaviour with executions: one victim, whose name now adorns a métro station, was Jacques Bonsergent, a student caught fly-posting and shot because he refused to reveal the names of his friends who escaped.

The Vichy government was so eager to please the Germans, it organised anti-Semitic measures without prompting. From the spring of 1941, the French authorities deported Jews to the death camps, frequently via the internment camp at Drancy. Prime Minister Pierre Laval argued that it was a necessary concession to his Third Reich masters. In July 1942, 12,000 Jewish French citizens were rounded up in the Vélodrome d'Hiver, a sports complex on quai de Grenelle, and then dispatched to Auschwitz.

THE LIBERATION

Paris survived the war practically unscathed, ultimately thanks to the bravery of one of its captors. On 23 August 1944, as the Allied armies of liberation approached the city, Hitler ordered his commander, Dietrich von Choltitz, to detonate the explosives that had been set all over town in anticipation of a retreat. Von Choltitz refused. On 25 August, French troops, tactfully placed at the head of the US forces, entered the city, and General de Gaulle led the parade down the Champs-Elysées. Writers and artists swept back into Paris to celebrate. Hemingway held court at the Ritz and Scribe hotels with the great journalists of the day, clinking glasses with veterans of the Spanish Civil War such as photographer Robert Capa and George Orwell. Picasso's studio was besieged by well-wishers.

However, the Liberation was by no means the end of France's troubles. De Gaulle was the hero of the hour, but relations between the interim government he commanded and the Resistance – largely Communist – were still tricky. Orders issued to *maquis* leaders in the provinces were often ignored. The Communists wanted a revolution, and de Gaulle suspected them of hatching plans to seize Paris prior to August 1944. Meanwhile, de Gaulle knew that he had to commit every available French soldier to the

IN CONTEXT

Going in Seine

It's 100 years since Paris's worst flooding – and it could happen again.

When the original, 19th-century Pont de l'Alma was replaced in the early 1970s by the wider, stronger version that you see today, one feature of the old bridge was retained: the Zouave statue that stands at the foot of the supporting pillar in midstream. Initially a straightforward emblem of French military success in the Crimean War, the Zouave became better known as a yardstick during the Seine's periodic floods. The fact that it was reinstated on the new bridge, alone of four statues that adorned the old one, is a measure of its stature in Paris folklore.

January 2010 was the centenary of the Zouave's dampest hour, when heavy rainfall and a badly timed thaw swelled the Seine to its highest level in recorded history, and the waters lapped around the stone soldier's neck. Hundreds of streets in central Paris were several feet deep in water, and their inhabitants were obliged to get around by boat: the vast photographic record of the disaster (a boon for photographers and postcard publishers) contains hundreds of scenes more reminiscent of Venice than Paris. Many residents had to get into and out of their buildings via a ladder and first-storey window.

As it turns out, the Zouave's new base is higher above the average water level than previously, so if the Seine does rise to its neck, the city will be in even more trouble than it was a century ago. The deluge of 1910 was a so-called 'hundred-year flood', which means, statistically speaking, that the next one is already overdue; and since the new bridge was installed, the waters have risen as far as his belt (in 1985). Today, flooding of the riverside expressways is a nearly annual event.

But worryingly, despite years of discussion by the city council and the government, Paris has no equivalent of London's Thames Barrier – although smaller barrages and reservoirs much further upstream have gone some way to alleviating the effects of high water runoff. So that just leaves the rather ominous 'in case of flooding' advice on the Mairie de Paris website, vague allusions to 'plans of action' and smart street maps shaded to show likely zones of flooded streets and electricity outage. In the meantime, the Zouave watches and waits.

march on Germany, or risk being sidelined by the other Allies after the war. He had to leave homeland security to the very people – the 'patriotic militias' – who were most likely to be at least sympathetic to the Communist cause; or, even more dubiously, gendarmes who had previously worked with the occupying power.

Recovery was slow. There were shortages of everything; indeed, many complained they had been better off under the Germans. Even in the ministries, paper was so scarce that correspondence had to be sent out on Vichy letterhead with the sender crossing out 'Etat Français' at the top and writing 'République Française' instead.

THE FOURTH REPUBLIC

On 8 May 1945, de Gaulle made a broadcast to the nation to announce Germany's surrender. Paris went wild, but the euphoria didn't last. There were strikes. And more strikes. Liberation had proved to be a restoration, not the revolution the Communists, now the most powerful political force in the land, had hoped for. The Communist Party was, in at least one respect, as pragmatic as everyone else: it did its utmost to turn parliamentary democracy to its advantage, to wit, getting as many of the top jobs as it could.

A general election was held on 21 October 1945. The Communists secured 159 seats, the Socialists got 146 and the Catholic Mouvement Républicain Populaire got 152. A fortnight later, at the Assemblée Nationale's first session, a unanimous vote was passed maintaining de Gaulle in his position as head of state – but he remained an antagonistic leader. His reluctance to take a firm grip on the disastrous economic situation alienated many intellectuals and industrialists who had once been loyal to him, and his characteristic aloofness only made the misgivings of the general populace worse. He, on the other hand, was disgusted by all the political chicanery. On 20 January 1946, de Gaulle resigned.

France, meanwhile, looked to swift industrial modernisation under an ambitious plan put forward by internationalist politician Jean Monnet. Although the economy and daily life remained grim, brash new fashion designer Christian Dior put together a stunning collection of strikingly simple yet luxurious clothes: the New Look. Such extravagance horrified many locals, but the fashion industry boomed. Meanwhile, the divisions in Paris between its fashionable and run-down working-class areas became more pronounced. The northern and eastern edges – areas revived only in the late 20th century by a taste for retro, industrial decor and cheap rent – were forgotten about.

Félix Gouin, the new Socialist premier, quickly nationalised the bigger banks and the coal industry. But the right wing was growing, and there was even a rise of royalist hopes. A referendum was held in May 1946 to determine the crucial tenet of the Fourth Republic's constitution: should the Assemblée Nationale have absolute or restricted power? The results were a narrow victory for people who, like de Gaulle, had insisted the Assemblée's power should be qualified. De Gaulle's prestige increased, but it was to be another 12 years, and a whole new constitution – the Fifth Republic – before he came back to power. He spent much of his '*passage du désert*' writing his memoirs.

THE ALGERIAN WAR AND MAY 1968

The post-war years were marked by the rapid disintegration of France's overseas interests and her rapprochement with Germany to create what would become the European Community. When revolt broke out in Algeria in 1956, almost 500,000 troops were sent in to protect national interests. A protest by Algerians in Paris on 17 October 1961 led to the deaths of hundreds of people at the hands of the city's police force. The extent of the violence was officially concealed for decades, as was the use of torture against Algerians by French troops. Algeria became independent in 1962.

Meanwhile, the slow, painful discoveries of collaboration in World War II, often overlooked in the rush to put the country back on its feet, were also being faced. The younger generation began to question the motives of the older one. De Gaulle's Fifth

Banlieue riots, 2005. *See p32.*

Republic was felt by many to be grimly authoritarian. In the spring of 1968, students unhappy with overcrowded university conditions took to the streets of Paris at the same time as striking Renault workers. These *soixante-huitards* sprang the greatest public revolt in French living memory. Many students were crammed into universities that had been cheaply expanded to accommodate them. Political discourse grew across the campuses, turning against the government's stranglehold on the media and President de Gaulle's poor grasp of the economy. Ministers did indeed at the time have a sinister habit of leaning on the leading newspaper editors of the day, and television was dubbed 'the government in your dining room'. Inflation was high, and the gap between the working classes and the bourgeoisie was becoming a chasm. Still, de Gaulle echoed many when he said the events of May 1968 were '*incompréhensible*'. The touchpaper was lit at overcrowded Nanterre university, on the outskirts of Paris, where students had been protesting against the war in Vietnam and the tatty state of the campus.

On 2 May, exhausted by the protests, the authorities closed the university down and threatened to expel some of the students. The next day, a sit-in was held in sympathy at the Sorbonne. Police were called to intervene, but made things worse, charging into the crowd with truncheons and tear gas. The city's streets were soon flooded with thousands of student demonstrators, now officially on strike. The trade unions followed, as did the lycées. By mid May nine million people were on strike. On 24 May, de Gaulle intervened. His speech warned of civil war and pleaded for people's support. It didn't go down well: riots broke out, with students storming the Bourse.

Five days later, as street violence peaked, de Gaulle fled briefly to Germany and Prime Minister Pompidou sent tanks to the edges of Paris. But the crisis didn't materialise. Pompidou conceded pay rises of between seven and ten per cent and increased the minimum wage; France went back to work. An election was called for 23 June, by which time the right had gathered enough momentum to gain a safe majority.

MITTERRAND
Following the presidencies of right-wingers Georges Pompidou and Valéry Giscard d'Estaing, the Socialist François Mitterrand took up the task in 1981. His *grands projets* had a big impact on Paris. Mitterrand commissioned IM Pei's Louvre pyramid, the Grande Arche de la Défense, the Opéra Bastille and the more recent Bibliothèque Nationale de France – François Mitterrand.

CHIRAC, BUSH AND IRAQ

France may still boast the world's fourth-largest economy, the nuclear deterrent and a permanent seat on the UN Security Council, but her influence on the world stage had been waning for years until President Chirac, flushed from re-election and well aware he was on to a PR winner, stood up in early 2003 to oppose the US-led invasion of Iraq. France's official disapproval of George Bush culminated in the threat to use her Security Council veto against any resolution authorising the use of force without UN say-so. Chirac's stance brought him popularity at home and abroad. But his domestic popularity couldn't last. His prime minister, Jean-Pierre Raffarin, and the centre-right government began attacking some of France's more prized national institutions with a programme of reforms, starting with the state pension system. This led to some of the largest nationwide protests France has seen since 1995, with striking métro staff, hospital workers, postmen, teachers and rubbish collectors creating havoc and bringing the capital to a virtual standstill. Planned restrictions on the uniquely Gallic, exceptionally generous system of unemployment benefit for out-of-work performing-arts professionals led to a further round of protests, as well as the cancellation of France's equivalents of Edinburgh and Glyndebourne, the Avignon and Aix summer cultural festivals. Then came the official mismanagement and aloofness that characterised the two-week heatwave of August 2003, during which as many as 14,000 elderly people died. The national mood stayed gloomy through 2004, and the clouds darkened further in 2005, as Paris surprisingly lost its Olympic bid.

Then, in October 2005, the accidental deaths of two North African teenagers in Clichy-sous-Bois sparked riots that spread through the *banlieue* like wildfire. Eventually Chirac declared an official state of emergency that was only lifted in January 2006. Then, in March, trouble flared once again, this time provoked by an unpopular new employment bill, the CPE – which, after three months of strikes and street protests, the government was forced to withdraw.

PRESIDENT BLING-BLING

Despite his provocations during the riots, Sarkozy was elected president in May 2007, beating the Socialist candidate Ségolène Royal. Aside from a few desultory Molotov cocktails hurled in place de la Bastille on the night of the election, the response on the Left to Sarkozy's victory was characterised more by bemusement than anger. For a few months, bemusement held sway in the population at large, especially when Sarkozy embarked on a very public whirlwind romance with *chanteuse* and ex-model Carla Bruni. But voters soon sickened of the unprecedented (and unpresidential) spectacle, and of Sarkozy's parallel courtship of several tycoons; by the time 'Président Bling-Bling' married Bruni in February 2008, his popularity had plummeted to less than 35 per cent; a televised skirmish at the Salon de l'Agriculture a few weeks later, in which he hissed '*pauvre con*' ('stupid twat') at a man in the crowd, was a further dent in his image.

Sarkozy remained a powerfully divisive figure in 2009 – and one not averse to Berlusconi-style manipulation: in the summer, the diminutive president's aides were rumbled for having chosen only short people to appear beside him at a public meeting. But it's his so-called Grand Paris scheme that is of greatest concern to the capital – a vast plan to recast the relationship of Paris with its suburbs, involving new building projects on a scale not seen since the time of Haussmann. If it goes ahead – the plans of the ten teams of international architects were unveiled in the spring – the city's administrative footprint will balloon to a size similar to that of Greater London, and large swathes of the urban fabric could be entirely remade. A new canal could be dug to connect Paris with the north of the country; and, most contentious of all, the city could get a crop of skyscrapers, a thing considered anathema until recently. Despite his opposition to the involvement (and politics) of Sarkozy, Mayor Bertrand Delanoë supports high-rise construction in the city – which means the face of Paris may soon change once again.

A city on the rise.

TEXT: RICH WOODRUFF

Paris Today

Imagine Paris stretching out along the Seine as far as the Channel port of Le Havre; or Paris's main train station located in the northern suburb of Aubervilliers; or a new forest planted over the flight path of Charles de Gaulle airport; or skyscrapers littering the cityscape. Such are the outlandish suggestions of some prize-winning international architects, commissioned by President Nicolas Sarkozy, for the future of the French capital.

Sarkozy presented his project for a Grand Paris ('Greater Paris') in April 2009, with many observers dubbing it the most ambitious plan for the capital since Baron Haussmann reshaped the city with his famed rectilinear boulevards in the mid 19th century. In many ways, the project typifies the kind of brash ambition that has already landed Sarkozy a pop-star wife. French presidents like to leave their mark on Paris. Pompidou bequeathed a cultural centre bearing his name, Chirac left behind the elegant Musée du Quai Branly, and Mitterrand pushed through a whole gamut of architectural *grands projets*, including the pyramid at the Louvre and the Opéra Bastille. For Sarkozy, though, a mere monument is not quite enough; he wants to transform the city's very fabric.

Rich Woodruff is a Paris-based journalist and video producer, specialising in cinema, culture, sport and travel.

Whatever your carbon footprint, we can reduce it

For over a decade we've been leading the way in carbon offsetting and carbon management.

In that time we've purchased carbon credits from over 200 projects spread across 6 continents. We work with over 300 major commercial clients and thousands of small and medium sized businesses, which rely upon our market-leading quality assurance programme, our experience and absolute commitment to deliver the right solution for each client.

Why not give us a call?

T: London (020) 7833 6000

'Ménilmontant and Belleville have become a hotbed for hip hybrid venues that combine bar, concert and exhibition spaces for local bobos.'

BRINGING IN THE BANLIEUE

The central drive of Sarkozy's initiative is to harmoniously integrate Paris with its surrounding suburbs – and thus to surmount the geographical, financial and cultural divisions that have long separated the two. Paris, unlike most major cities, has rigidly defined limits, and is administratively independent of its neighbouring *banlieue*, whose reputation for social problems was cemented by the infamous 2005 riots. Sarkozy's avowed aim is to create a united city where the *banlieue* ceases to exist as a separate entity.

In launching such a project, the right-wing Sarkozy has – quite knowingly – muscled in on the territory of Socialist Party Mayor Bertrand Delanoë. Since coming to power in 2001, the popular Delanoë has reshaped the city with his green-minded projects and cultural innovations, and has frequently upheld the idea of bringing Paris closer to its neighbouring communities. Several metro lines are being expanded outside the city limits, Vélib bike stations have been added in neighbouring communities, and a boat network has been launched to unite Seine-side suburbs with the east of Paris. City Hall has also signed co-operation agreements with a number of local boroughs, such as Ivry-sur-Seine, which has been working closely with Paris's 13th arrondissement on an exciting urban development project. This south-east area now boasts a major university and business centre, as well as a floating open-air swimming pool on the Seine and a new footbridge. Perhaps the clearest sign of City Hall's willingness to unite Paris with its *banlieue* is an initiative that consists of covering sections of the city's frequently congested Péripherique with landscaped gardens and sports fields, with the road running in a tunnel beneath. As well as improving the quality of life for local inhabitants, the project lessens the physical barrier with the suburbs – and sends a message that Paris is reaching out to local communities.

IN CONTEXT

Many of Paris's public spaces are now equipped with free Wi-Fi.

MAIRIE DE PARIS

* îledeFrance

Paris
Wi-Fi

CONSEILS D'UTILISATION

accédez ici à internet haut débit sans fil avec le pass Paris Wi-Fi offert par la Mairie de Paris et la Région Île-de-France

IN CONTEXT

Electric Avenue

Delanoë's eco-friendly car hire scheme gets the green light.

Emboldened by the runaway success of his Vélib bike hire initiative, Mayor Bertrand Delanoë is launching another green transport innovation: an eco-friendly car hire system. Dubbed 'Autolib', the new project will allow subscribers to pick up and drop off a car at any one of 1,400 designated stations, half of which will be located in Paris and half in the neighbouring suburbs. In Paris, some 200 stations will be built underground and the rest will be on the site of existing public parking places, further nudging Parisians towards giving up their own motors.

Despite some initial legal and financial stumbling blocks, the scheme is set to begin at the end of 2010 with a fleet of 4,000 green cars – Delanoë is adamant that the vehicles should be 100 per cent electric, with recharging stations at each Autolib station. The cars will seat four passengers and the top speed should be at least 80 kilometres per hour (50 miles per hour), allowing drivers to use the Périphérique and motorways just outside the city centre. Unlike the Vélib initiative, Autolib will require an obligatory monthly subscription fee, estimated at €15-€20, as well as a valid driving licence. The half-hourly rate, meanwhile, is likely to be around €4. Each vehicle will be tracked in real time, and when drivers have finished their hire period, they will be guided to the nearest available parking space.

To tie in with the launch of Autolib, Delanoë is planning to bring in a new transport pass, the Titre Intégral de Mobilité (TIM). This multi-purpose travel card would give access to the regular transport network, as well as Autolib, Vélib, taxis and parking outside Paris. A number of other transport projects could also be incorporated, including a circular rail network planned for the suburbs. In Paris itself, meanwhile, work is already under way on extending the tramway to the east and north of the city for 2012, while the Voguéo boat service on the Seine could soon include a host of new riverside stops in the city centre. For a city that once seemed to put the car above all else, Paris is certainly cleaning up its act.

'The mayor believes tower blocks represent the most efficient way to deliver on his promise of creating more social housing.'

THE FUTURE'S GREEN

Beyond these projects, Delanoë has concentrated his ample energy on reshaping Paris itself. While his eco-friendly policy-making has sometimes met with controversy, the city has undoubtedly become a more liveable place thanks to improved public transport (*see p36* **Electric Avenue**), anti-car measures and more green spaces. The mayor has also invested in technology: public parks, libraries and a splattering of big-name tourist locations are now equipped with free Wi-Fi access, and a project has been launched to equip 80 per cent of Paris buildings with an ultra-high speed fibre internet connection by 2010.

Despite the unsuccessful bid for the 2012 Olympics (Delanoë's most glaring mayoral failure), the city is also investing in a number of major sports projects. In line with the booming French swimming scene, spearheaded by Beijing Olympic 100 metres freestyle champion Alain Bernard, the city inaugurated its 38th swimming pool in 2009, and is currently renovating the long-abandoned art deco Piscine Molitor, which was first opened by Tarzan actor Johnny Weissmuller back in 1929. Other sports sites due for major upgrades include rugby's Stade Jean Bouin and Roland-Garros, site of the French tennis open.

CULTURE CLUB

Culture has thrived under Delanoë. Alongside the mayor's trademark festivals, the summertime Paris-Plage and popular Nuit Blanche nocturnal arts festival, Paris has developed a wealth of new initiatives for emerging artists and art forms. In 2008, the Maison des Métallos, a former trade union centre, reopened as a cutting-edge cultural showcase for up-and-coming artists; and an old funeral parlour was transformed into 104, a centre for contemporary creation. In 2010, the Théâtre de la Gaîté Lyrique will be reborn as a hub for digital arts and contemporary music. In the north-east, meanwhile, the formerly working-class areas of Ménilmontant and adjacent Belleville have become a hotbed for hip hybrid venues that combine bar, concert and exhibition spaces for local bobos (bourgeois bohemians). Celebrated designer Philippe Starck has even opened a stylish budget hotel in the neighbourhood.

Development projects of a more mainstream nature are also plentiful, including a new Jean Nouvel-designed classical music venue at Parc de la Villette for 2012; a much-needed revamp for the Musée de l'Homme, which is to be rebranded as a showcase for French anthropology; and a complete facelift for the much-maligned Les Halles gardens and subterranean shopping centre. The most long-awaited project, though, is undoubtedly the ultra-ambitious Cité de la Mode et du Design, whose opening date has been continually put back. Notwithstanding further setbacks, it should finally be open by early 2010. As a hub for the Paris fashion crowd, the complex promises to bring trendy designers and nocturnal thrill seekers to a previously lifeless Seine-side area near the Gare d'Austerlitz. Complete with a panoramic garden terrace, the complex will house the Institut Français de la Mode (French Fashion Institute), along with shops, restaurants and a riverside walkway. Some shops may even be open on Sundays, following the recent liberalisation of France's rigid Sunday trading laws.

Another of the capital's major architectural projects is the construction of the Cité Européenne du Cinéma, located in the northern suburb of St-Denis. Backed by maverick French film director Luc Besson, the massive site will house a nine-studio

IN CONTEXT

Time Out Travel Guides

France

Written by local experts

**Available at all good bookshops
and at timeout.com/shop**

PHOTO CREDIT: HÉLOISE BERGMAN

complex that promises to give the national film industry a massive boost when it opens in 2012. The other beneficiary of the initiative will be St-Denis itself, a suburb better known for poverty and violence.

This is one of a spate of high-profile developments to find suburban locations in the last few years. The Centre National de la Danse set up its headquarters in northern Pantin in 2004, the child-friendly Exploradome museum is being relocated to southern Vitry-sur-Seine, while a new contemporary art, cinema and music complex is planned for the Ile Seguin in south-west Boulogne-Billancourt. Parisians are even starting to explore cultural life outside their own 20 arrondissements. The savvy programming at the MAC/VAL art gallery, also in Vitry-sur-Seine, has successfully enticed the city's notoriously snobbish art clique into the *banlieue*, while studios like Les Laboratoires d'Aubervilliers and the Mains d'Oeuvres in St-Ouen are forging a creative niche within the contemporary art scene.

RECESSION BLUES

One high-profile consequence of the faltering economy has been the 'bossnapping' of a number of company CEOs, taken hostage by their own employees over redundancies. At the same time, that most quintessentially French form of protest, the strike, has become an even more dominant part of recession-hit Paris life. Universities, in particular, were paralysed by lengthy staff strikes and student blockades in protest over Sarkozy's proposed education reforms. And the recession has finally affected Paris property prices, which suffered their first downturn (by 2.1%) in over ten years during the first part of 2009. Previously, escalating house prices had been yet another factor forcing Parisians to re-evaluate their relationship with the *banlieue*. In their search for affordable property, families turned to the suburbs, where certain areas have registered a property price rise of 125 per cent over five years.

ON THE RISE

Another project hit by the credit crunch has been La Défense 2015, a long-term development plan for the business district to the west of Paris. The initiative is one of the founding cornerstones in Sarkozy's vision of a Greater Paris, aiming to attract inhabitants to La Défense by improving transport links and including some 1,400 flats within a series of new showcase towers designed by the likes of Norman Foster and Jean Nouvel. Even though delivery is now unlikely for 2015, the project should still give a much-needed boost to an area hardly known for its liveliness outside working hours.

If La Défense 2015 represents Sarkozy's answer to the Parisian accommodation crisis, Delanoë has his own plan. The mayor has set in motion a controversial project to erect high-rise buildings within Paris itself. For years, the subject has remained taboo thanks to a 1977 by-law that fixes maximum heights for Parisian buildings at 37 metres (121 feet) or ten storeys. Despite both public and political opposition (including dissent from his close partners, the Green Party), Delanoë has held firm with the plan, determined to revitalise a city so often accused of *muséification* or lack of dynamism. The mayor believes tower blocks represent the most efficient way to deliver on his promise of creating more social housing. At present, six sites have been identified on the city limits just inside the Péripherique to house 50-metre (164-foot, 15-storey) tower blocks, as well as 200-metre (656-foot) high buildings that would provide office space, shops and childcare centres.

The proposals for high-rise apartment towers by both Delanoë and Sarkozy are further proof that the capital's two political giants have similar long-term goals. For the time being, however, their efforts are uncoordinated, not least because Sarkozy sees Delanoë as something of a threat: as one of the few credible representatives of the muddled French left, the mayor is a potential candidate at the next presidential election. It seems safe to say that the city's historical and geographical divisions will not be overcome overnight.

IN CONTEXT

Architecture

A city of monumental ambitions.

TEXT: NATASHA EDWARDS

With its grandiose royal palaces and crowd-pulling opera houses, Paris has always been a showcase city, its rulers experts in pulling out the architectural stops when it comes to promoting image. Yet it is also one of Europe's most densely inhabited and lived-in capitals, which has given the city its inimitable mix of the monumental and the intimate. For all its apparent uniformity, due in large part to the prevalence of golden stone, Paris has never ceased to evolve and experiment, with aristocratic mansions, baroque churches and Haussmannian apartments existing happily alongside concrete avant-garde houses, industrial premises, the cast iron of the Eiffel Tower and the high-tech Centre Pompidou.

Natasha Edwards writes on French contemporary art, design, food and travel for Condé Nast Traveller, *the* Daily Telegraph, Elle Decoration *and the* Independent.

ROMANESQUE TO GOTHIC

Medieval Paris congregated on the Ile de la Cité and the Latin Quarter, following the broad lines of the Roman city. Although the clusters of medieval housing built around Notre-Dame were razed by Haussmann in the 19th century, much of the medieval street plan remains. A few churches survive as examples of simple Romanesque architecture, including the tower of **St-Germain-des-Prés** (*see p126*) and the well-preserved interior of **St-Julien-le-Pauvre** (*see p115*) – with its intricately carved capitals.

The Gothic trademarks of pointed arches, ogival vaulting and flying buttresses had their beginning at the **Basilique St-Denis** (*see p148*), started in the 12th century and completed in the 13th by master mason Pierre de Montreuil. **Notre-Dame** (*see p56*) continued the style with its sculpted façade, rich, delicate rose windows and fine, tendon-like buttresses (not to mention its characterful menagerie of gargoyles). Montreuil's **Sainte-Chapelle** (*see p58*), built 1246-48, represents the peak of Gothic design, reducing stonework to a minimum between the expanses of stained glass. The Flamboyant Gothic style that followed unleashed an orgy of decoration. **Eglise St-Séverin** (*see p115*), with its twisting spiral column, is particularly original. Civil architecture can be seen in the impressive vaulted halls of the **Conciergerie** (*see p56*). The **Tour Jean Sans Peur** (*see p81*) is a rare fragment of an early 15th-century mansion. The city's two finest medieval mansions are the Hôtel de Cluny (now the **Musée National du Moyen-Age**; *see p116*) in the Latin Quarter and the **Hôtel de Sens** (*see p103*) in the Marais. Although still distinctly Gothic in form and decoration, they set the pattern for Paris's later *hôtels particuliers*, with the main building set back behind a courtyard.

RENAISSANCE

Italianate town planning, with its ordered avenues, neat squares and public spaces, came late to Paris. It was instigated by François I, who installed Leonardo da Vinci at Amboise, brought over Primaticcio and Rosso to work on his palace at **Fontainebleau** (*see p351*), and began transforming the **Louvre** (*see p59*) with the Cour Carrée. The **Eglise St-Etienne du Mont** (*see p119*) and the massive **Eglise St-Eustache** (*see p81*) display a transitional style, adding the classical motifs of the Renaissance over an essentially Gothic structure. Aristocratic quarters were established in St-Germain-des-Prés and the newly developing Marais; the latter has the **Hôtel Carnavalet** (*see p101*) and the **Hôtel de Lamoignon** (24 rue Pavée, 4th), the finest examples of Renaissance mansions to be found in Paris, reflecting the erudition of their owners in the classical motifs and allegorical reliefs on the façades and a new, comfortable lifestyle with their large windows and grand first-floor salons.

THE ANCIEN REGIME

Henri IV took control of Paris in 1594 after a long siege. He found a city knee-deep in bodies and rubble, and promptly organised public building projects. Half-timbering was banned for façades, to be replaced by brick and stone, and bridges over the Seine were cleared of houses and shops. **Place Dauphine** (1st) and **place des Vosges** (*see p99*) reflected Henri's taste for classicism; the latter is irresistibly elegant, with symmetrical design, red-brick vaulted galleries and steeply pitched roofs, reflecting the influence of northern Renaissance style as well as Italy.

The *nouveaux riches* flocked to build mansions in the Marais and on the Ile St-Louis. Those in the Marais follow a symmetrical U-shaped plan, with the main residence at the rear of an elegant *cour d'honneur*; look through the entrance archways of the **Hôtel de Sully** (*see p100*) or the **Hôtel Salé** (*see p99*), where façades are richly decorated, in contrast with the face they present to the street.

The **Palais du Luxembourg** (*see p129*), built in the 1620s by Salomon de Brosse in Italianate style for Marie de Médicis, combines classic French *château* design with the more dramatic rustication of the Pitti Palace in Marie's native Florence. The 17th century was a high point in French power, and the monarchy desired buildings that reflected its

IN CONTEXT

grandeur. Great architects emerged under court patronage: de Brosse, François Mansart, Libéral Bruand and landscape architect André le Nôtre, who redesigned the Tuileries gardens, created the park and fountains at Versailles and planned the Champs-Elysées. The **Eglise du Val-de-Grâce** (*see p119*), designed by Mansart and finished by Jacques Lemercier, is a grand baroque statement designed to promote the Catholic Counter-Reformation, with its painted dome and barley sugar columns. Hospitals got the royal treatment: Libéral Bruand created the grand classical façades and polygonal chapel at the **Salpêtrière** (13th) and **Les Invalides** (*see p141*), with its grandiose galleried courtyard and domed double church. But even at **Versailles** (*see p354*), ultimate architectural symbol of royal absolutism in the mammoth scale and glittery reflections of the Hall of Mirrors, baroque never reached the decorative excesses of Italy or Austria.

Under Colbert, Louis XIV's chief minister, the creation of stage sets to magnify the Sun King's power proceeded apace. The Louvre grew as Claude Perrault created the sweeping west wing, triumphal arches at **Porte St-Denis** and **Porte St-Martin** commemorated military victories, while Hardouin-Mansart's sweeping, circular **place des Victoires** (*see p76*) and **place Vendôme** (*see p69*), an elegant octagon, were both designed to show off equestrian statues of the king.

ROCOCO AND NEO-CLASSICISM

In the early 18th century, the Faubourg St-Germain overtook the Marais as the city's most fashionable quarter, as the nobility built smart mansions with tall windows and elegant wrought ironwork, such as the **Hôtel Matignon**, today home of the French prime minister. However, the finest example of frivolous rococo decoration is the **Hôtel de Soubise** (60 rue des Francs-Bourgeois, 3rd), with panelling, plasterwork and paintings by celebrated decorators of the day, including Boucher, Restout and van Loo. In furniture-makers' **Faubourg St-Antoine**, a different sort of accommodation grew up, with workshops around long, narrow courtyards and lodgings up above.

Under Louis XV, a number of sumptuous buildings were commissioned, among them **La Monnaie** (now the **Musée de la Monnaie de Paris**; *see p127*), the **Panthéon** (*see p119*), the **Ecole de Droit** (place du Panthéon, 5th) and many new theatres. Soufflot's Panthéon, like Jacques-Ange Gabriel's neo-classical **place de la Concorde** (*see p72*), was inspired by the monuments of ancient Rome, as were the toll gates put up in 1785 by Nicolas Ledoux, famed for his almost minimalist geometrical style (still visible at Nation, Denfert-Rochereau and Parc Monceau) for the Mur des Fermiers Généraux.

THE 19TH CENTURY

The street fighting of the Revolution left Paris in a dilapidated state. Napoleon redressed this situation with a suitably grandiose vision to make Paris the most beautiful city in the world. He confiscated land from the aristocracy and the Church, and ordered a massive building spree. As well as five new bridges and 56 ornamental fountains, he built the **Eglise de la Madeleine** (*see p77*), a mock Greek temple in honour of the Grande Armée, plus a rash of self-aggrandising statues and arches, most notably the **Arc de Triomphe** (*see p85*) and the **Arc du Carrousel** (*see p69*).

In 1853 Bonaparte's nephew Louis Napoleon appointed Baron Haussmann as the *préfet* of Paris, with a brief to remake the city. A fearsome administrator rather than an architect, Haussmann faced problems of sanitation, sewage and traffic-clogged streets. He set about bringing order, cutting broad, long boulevards through the urban fabric. An estimated 27,000 houses were razed in the process. The Haussmannian apartment block has endured, setting an adaptable format that endured well into the 20th century, its utilitarian lines set off by mansarded roofs and rows of wrought-iron balconies. Haussmann also introduced English-style public parks, such as the **Buttes-Chaumont** (*see p113*), along with prisons, hospitals, train stations and sewers. Amid the upheaval, one building epitomised the grand style of the Second Empire: Charles Garnier's sumptuous **Palais Garnier** opera house (1862-75; *see p317*).

'When the Eiffel Tower was built in 1889, it was the tallest structure in the world.'

Haussmann could also be an innovator, persuading Baltard to build the new market pavilions at Les Halles in lacy iron rather than stone. Iron frames had already been used by Henri Labrouste in his lovely reading room at the **Bibliothèque Ste-Geneviève** (1844-50; 10 place du Panthéon, 5th), and they became increasingly common: stations such as Hittorff's **Gare du Nord** (1861-65; *see p110*) and Laloux's Gare d'Orsay (now **Musée d'Orsay**; *see p145*) are simply shells around an iron frame, producing spacious, light-filled interiors. The most daring iron construction of them all was, of course, the **Eiffel Tower** (*see p145*). When it was built in 1889, it was the tallest structure in the world. Stylistically, eclecticism ruled, from the neo-Renaissance **Hôtel de Ville** (*see p98*) to neo-Byzantine **Sacré-Coeur** (*see p95*).

EARLY 20TH CENTURY
An outburst of extravagance for the 1900 Exposition Universelle marked the beginning of the 20th century, notably the **Grand Palais** (*see p85*), with its massive glass and steel nave, and the **Petit Palais,** awash in sculptures, mosaics, marble and florid wrought iron, with design inspired by the Grand Trianon at Versailles. The **Train Bleu** brasserie in the Gare de Lyon (*see p205*) is an ornate example of the heavy, florid Beaux Arts style of this period. Art nouveau at its most fluid and flamboyant can be seen in Hector Guimard's instantly recognisable métro stations and his 1901 **Castel Béranger** (*see p90*).

All this was a long way from the roughly contemporary work of Henri Sauvage, who created a large social housing project in **rue des Amiraux** (18th), tiled artists' studio flats in **rue La Fontaine** (16th), and the more overtly art deco 1920s extension of **La Samaritaine** (19 rue de la Monnaie, 1st). Funded by philanthropists, social housing began to appear in the city, such as the Rothschilds' estate in **rue de Prague** (12th).

THE MODERN MOVEMENT
After World War I, two names stand out by virtue of their innovation and influence: Auguste Perret, architect of the **Théâtre des Champs-Elysées** (*see p318*), and Le Corbusier. A third architect, Robert Mallet-Stevens, is unrivalled for his elegance, best seen in his villas on rue Mallet-Stevens. Paris is one of the best cities in the world for Modern Movement houses and studios (many in the 16th and Montparnasse), but also in a more diluted form for town halls and schools built in the socially minded 1930s.

Perret stayed largely within a classical aesthetic, but was a pioneer in the use of reinforced concrete. Le Corbusier tried out his ideas in private houses, such as the **Villa La Roche** in the 16th (now **Fondation le Corbusier**). His **Pavillon Suisse** at the **Cité Universitaire** (*see p138*) and **Armée du Salut** hostel (12 rue Cantagrel, 13th) can be seen as a mid point between these villas and his Villes Radieuses mass housing schemes, which became so influential and so debasedacross Europe after 1945.

Meanwhile, the new love of chrome, steel and glass found its way into art deco cafés such as **La Coupole** (*see p214*). As in the 19th century, world fairs provided an excuse for grandiose state architecture, with a return to monumental classicism in the **Palais de la Porte Dorée**, built for the 1931 Exposition Coloniale, and the Palais de Chaillot and **Palais de Tokyo** (*see p87*), built for the 1937 Exposition Internationale.

POST-WAR PARIS
The aerodynamic aesthetic of the post-war era yielded the 1958 **UNESCO building** (*see p146*) by Bernard Zehrfuss, Pier Luigi Nervi and Marcel Breuer, and the beginnings of **La Défense** (*see p147*) with the same architects' **CNIT** building, then the largest

IN CONTEXT

Lost in Paris.

Plant Rooms

From public libraries to private houses, Paris is going green.

As Paris tries to meet new targets for sustainable development and renewable energy, solar panels and vegetal roofs have been sprouting up around the city, along with a wave of pioneering constructions intended to create prototypes for a green future. In the 18th arrondissement, the **ZAC Pajol** is a pioneering *éco-quartier* located on former SNCF sidings north of Gare de l'Est. The project is centred on the rehabilitated Halle Pajol, a massive 1920s iron-framed freight warehouse that is being transformed by Françoise-Hélène Jourda into a 330-bed youth hostel, public library, auditorium and interior garden. Jourda is focusing on the Halle as a skin creating a microclimate for the structures within, while 3,500 square metres of solar panels on the roof will form France's largest city centre solar power station when it comes into operation in 2013. Jourda, a pioneer of green architecture for more than 20 years, is also behind the region's first 'zero energy' office block on **rue de Landy** in St-Denis, where she aims to develop a new type of architecture that stands out from the usual office buildings nearby, minimising heat loss in a compact, wedge-shaped structure with zinc cladding and triple glazing.

In the 11th arrondissement, meanwhile, **rue Guénot** is set to become home to the city's first positive energy social housing, the result of a competition won by young architects Laurence Baudouin and Hélène Bergeron. Behind a six-storey white façade designed to blend into the local streetscape, the roof is treated as the source of energy for hot water and heating through solar panels, while also letting daylight into the core through a skylit lift shaft and stairwell. The 17 flats also make use of the building's aspect, with bedrooms placed on the east-facing side to get the morning sun, and living rooms with balconies situated on the west-facing courtyard side to benefit from the afternoon sun.

Even when it comes to eco-projects, Paris still retains its sense of fun. Nowhere is this more in evidence than round at R&Sie Architects' radical **I'm Lost in Paris** house, which sprouted in an undisclosed location somewhere in the 3rd arrondissement in 2008. A typically experimental concept by François Roche and Stéphanie Lavaux, the entire concrete structure is engulfed by 1,200 ferns, fed hydroponically with a mixture of rainwater and nutrients from 300 handblown glass beakers, which moderate the interior temperature and breathe oxygen into the atmosphere in a swathe of foliage – saving the planet and staying cool in one harmonious whole.

concrete span in the world. In the 1960s and '70s, tower blocks sprouted in the suburbs and new towns to replace the dismal *bidonvilles* (shanty towns) that had served as immigrant housing. Inside the city, redevelopment was limited, although new regulations allowed taller buildings; in 1960, the 67-metre-high (22 foot), 23-storey **33 rue Croulebarbe** in the 13th arrondissement, whose tubular steel structure allowed a large degree of prefabrication, marked Paris's first high-rise residential block, designed by Edouard Albert, setting the way for high-rise clusters at Les Olympiades (13th), the Fronts de Seine (15th) and in the 19th.

President Georges Pompidou embraced modernity too, disastrously in the case of the expressways along the Seine, and more benignly in the form of Piano and Rogers' high-tech **Centre Pompidou** (*see p98*), which opened in 1977 and was the first of the daring prestige projects that subsequently became a trademark of modern Paris. But after the construction of the controversial **Tour Montparnasse** (*see p137*), Pompidou's successor, Valéry Giscard d'Estaing, prevented the Paris horizon from rising any higher.

THE 1980S AND '90S

President François Mitterrand's *grands projets* dominated the 1980s and '90s, with Jean Nouvel's **Institut du Monde Arabe** (*see p121*), IM Pei's **Louvre Pyramid** (*see p59*) and Johan Otto Von Sprecklesen's **Grande Arche de la Défense** (*see p148*), as well as Carlos Ott's more dubious **Opéra Bastille** (*see p317*), Dominique Perrault's **Bibliothèque Nationale** (*see p124*) and Chemetov & Huidobro's **Bercy** finance ministry. Stylistically, the buzzword was 'transparency', from Pei's pyramid to Nouvel's **Fondation Cartier** (*see p134*), with its clever slices of glass. Christian de Portzamparc pursued a more eclectic postmodern style with his **Cité de la Musique** (*see p111*), a series of geometrical blocks set around a colourful internal street.

THE 21ST CENTURY

The age of the *grands projets* is over, although Jacques Chirac managed to squeeze one last legacy project into his reign with the completion of Nouvel's **Musée du Quai Branly** (*see p146*) in 2006, a highly colourful baroque structure. Younger architects are making their mark too: Manuelle Gautrand's **Citroën** showcase on the Champs-Elysées, for instance, cleverly plays on the firm's chevrons logo in a fine example of architecture as branding, and she is also behind the refurbishment of the **Théâtre de la Gaîté Lyrique** as a new multimedia arts centre.

The vast **Seine Rive Gauche** (*see p124*) development in the 13th arrondissement has at last taken shape, with a mixture of new-build and rehabilitated industrial buildings around the Bibliothèque Nationale for office, residential and university use, designed by an army of French and international architects, along with Jakob and MacFarlane's **Cité de la Mode et du Design** (*see p124*) and Dietmer Feichtinger's Simone de Beauvoir footbridge.

Other areas have also come up for a makeover: the 1970s **Forum des Halles** (*see p81*) is set for a new green canopy and re-landscaped gardens, and a new generation of skyscrapers rivalling each other in height and extravagant silhouettes soar at **La Défense** (*see p147*). Public housing projects range from small infilling schemes to large-scale projects such as Jakob and MacFarlane's polygonal concrete blocks along boulevard Sérusier in the 19th or the site at the former Hôpital Laennec in the 7th, where listed hospital buildings converted into offices by Benjamin Mouton are joined by new public housing and student accommodation by Valode et Pistre.

Meanwhile, the city also continues to benefit from exciting new cultural buildings. After the appearance of **104** (*see p111*) in the former municipal undertakers in 2008, Frank Gehry's cloudlike glass Fondation Louis Vuitton in the Bois de Boulogne (due to open 2011), Renzo Piano's egg-like **Fondation Pathé** (*see p123*), visible through the listed façade of the old Gaumont cinema on avenue des Gobelins, and Jean Nouvel's new Philharmonic concert hall at La Villette (due to open 2012) are all under way.

IN CONTEXT

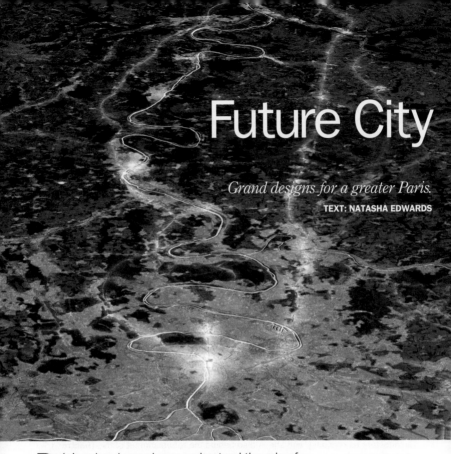

Future City

Grand designs for a greater Paris.

TEXT: NATASHA EDWARDS

Paris's rulers have always understood the role of architecture in the exercise of power. Long before François Mitterrand made his presidential mark on the capital in the 1980s with his Grands Projets – including the Opéra Bastille, Grande Arche de la Défense, Louvre Pyramid and Ministry of Finance – Colbert had glorified Louis XIV with the place Vendôme, place des Victoires and a series of triumphal arches. So it came as no surprise when President Nicolas Sarkozy opened the Cité de l'Architecture in November 2007 with a promise to 'return architecture to the heart of our political choices'. It was the starting point for a vast consultation process on the future of Paris. Months of debate and reams of paper later, the proposals put forward by the ten shortlisted architectural firms are both excitingly broad and frustratingly ambiguous. There are surprisingly few grand architectural statements: new train stations, yes; a new Palais Garnier, no. Instead the thinking behind the proposals focuses on Paris's future as a model city for the world in terms of usability and sustainability.

'Among concrete proposals are a circular métro floating above the Périphérique.'

The project brief set two distinct areas of research. On the one hand, entrants needed to examine the future of Paris in terms of its ability to compete with great world cities such as London, New York, Tokyo and Shanghai; on the other hand, they needed to look at making Paris an example for the sustainable, post-Kyoto city, tackling climate change and cutting greenhouse gas emissions. It's perhaps no surprise, then, that the proposals veer widely between the concrete and the highly conceptual, the prosaic and the futuristic, between those that cling to context and those that seem to ignore it completely. What has emerged is lots on transport, the saving and production of energy, a focus on the relationship between the city and nature, and a recurrent theme of the Seine. One thing that did not emerge was a precise definition of what the boundaries of 'Grand Paris' should be. Here we outline the ten proposals for the capital's future.

1. ROGERS STIRK HARBOUR & PARTNERS
'I have never come across another big city in which the heart is so disassociated from its limbs,' says Richard Rogers, who has tackled the lack of transport connections between the city centre and its sprawling outskirts, broken down the barrier of the Périphérique, and examined the notion of a future city that no longer simply absorbs imported produce and energy, but also limits waste and produces and recycles resources. Compactness is the key to the ecological future of the city in Rogers' mind, and he proposes hilltop parks between new tower blocks, as well as underground services and transport links, all in a literally green city created by green corridors along boulevards and temperature-mediating planted roofs.

2. ATELIER CHRISTIAN DE PORTZAMPARC
This is one of the most practical, realistically worked out schemes, based on detailed analysis of six 5x10km areas. Portzamparc views the existing conurbation as a place that wastes resources, and fixes social and cultural differences. His Grand Paris is not a uniform sprawl but a plantlike network of rhizomes (underground stems from which roots emerge). Dense, dynamic areas dedicated to commerce, industry, research or transport punctuate calmer, more residential areas. Among concrete proposals are a circular métro floating above the Périphérique, and a huge train station, Gare Europe Nord, at Aubervilliers. This would draw trains from all over northern Europe, allowing the rail tracks heading into Gare du Nord to be transformed into a new strip of parkland.

3. ATELIER CASTRO DENISSOF CASI
Roland Castro, known for his socially committed architecture and refurbishment of vast council estates, pleads for a 'Grand Paris of poets', where efficient high-speed public transport alternates with the gentle poetry of a *batobus* on the Seine, and talks of the 'need to create symbols' for the new metropolis. There's a distinctly sci-fi edge to his photo-montages of a skyscraper on the tip of the Ile St-Louis, a grand 'agora' resembling a Mayan temple at the confluence of the Seine and the Marne, something that looks like Sydney Opera House in the middle of Port de Gennevilliers, and a vision of La Corneuve transformed into something akin to Central Park.

4. AUC
The AUC group, led by Djamel Klouche, took a particularly abstract, academic approach in its historical analysis of 'a Parisian metropolis that is already there, inherited but non-identified'. Having looked at the diversity of what is already present, from the

IN CONTEXT

semi-rural village to the postwar surburb, its schema focuses on building clustered areas of housing, while also highlighting emblematic sites like the Louvre and complementing public transport links between clusters with electric cars.

5. AGENCE GRUMBACH & ASSOCIES

Antoine Grumbach talks not about 'Grand Paris' but a new linear conurbation, 'Seine Métropole', extending along the Seine all the way from Paris via Rouen to Le Havre, enabling inland Paris to become a port attached to the sea. This grand idea is apparently not new, but dates back to Napoleon. This is a Utopian think-big scheme, in which the river is a spine, punctuated by halts along its meanders. It would form a super-transport link for river, rail and road traffic, and at the same time a new alliance would be created between the city and the natural world. Says Grumbach: 'Through its geography and industrial savoir faire, the valley could encourage the birth of the third industrial revolution, that of green energy.'

6. ATELIERS JEAN NOUVEL

Ateliers Jean Nouvel, with Jean-Marie Duthilleul and Michel Cantal-Dupart, hopes to revive Paris's *genius loci*, or spirit of place, in a renunciation of what it calls the '20th-century martyrdom to functionalism', bringing about a renaissance of the city

Ateliers Jean Nouvel.

Atelier Castro Denissof Casi.

that 'symbolises light, culture, excellence, joie de vivre and wellbeing'. According to Duthilleul and Cantal-Dupart, everything is already there, nothing should be thrown away or replaced. Rather the plan aims to 'transform, mutate, recycle and augment' to profit from the city's potential and 'maximise possibilities'. Nouvel also aims for a reconciliation between rural and urban, emergency action for Paris's problem suburbs, developing the riverbanks, creating an ultra-rapid public transport network and constructing *haut-lieux* – tall buildings that form vertical ecological estates.

7. STUDIO 09
Italian planners Bernardo Secchi and Paola Viganò of Studio 09 have envisaged what they call 'the porous city', focusing both on water and significant landmarks, including train stations and historic monuments. As well as creating new wetlands on areas of unused or underused land to encourage biodiversity, the city would also be criss-crossed by a grid of fast public transport links connecting up to TGVs, tramways and the RER. This is seen as the answer to social inequality, and a means of escaping from simplistic clichés of a south west–north east divide.

8. EQUIPE LIN
For Finn Geipel and Giulia Andi's LIN team, Paris has become fossilised by its centralisation and the fact that it grew concentrically from its origins on the Ile de la Cité. Instead, they propose a 'multipolar' Grand Paris, where diverse areas of extreme density (historic town centres, heritage sites, university research campuses, manufacturing centres) alternate with less densely urbanised areas that are today considered suburban sprawl, but which would become new 'lightweight towns'. These would feature a mix of housing, small businesses, schools, urban agriculture, local shops and services, landscaped to function as a green lung producing food, wind and

'Lightweight towns would function as a green lung producing food, wind and solar energy.'

solar energy. In addition, a series of neglected riverbanks along the Seine, Marne, Oise and Essonne would be transformed into what LIN calls 'Seine Parc'. In short, Grand Paris would become 'an advanced laboratory for the post-Kyoto metropolis'.

9. GROUPE DESCARTES

Groupe Descartes, headed by Yves Lion, has come up with a highly conceptual project, made up of a grid of '20 large cities covering the whole Paris region', each with around 500,000 inhabitants. Quality of life would be improved by increasing personal space with larger accommodation – and planning restrictions would be lifted, allowing residents to extend their dwellings. Journey times between the new cities would be short, and improved public transport would reduce commuting time into the core by 30 minutes. Descartes aims to reconcile country and agriculture with the city, using the countryside around Paris as a resource to prevent climate change. The plan includes extending forests in the area, transforming N roads into landscaped boulevards and regenerating riverbanks.

10. MVRDV

Presenting his project in the form of four books, Dutch architect Winy Maas makes a plea for a city that is 'more optimistic, more ecological, more efficient and more... small'. He wants to produce what he dubs the 'Big Intensification Act' to create a Grand Paris that is 'one of the highest quality, greenest and most compact towns in the world'. MVRDV would increase the density of greater Paris to combat urban sprawl, covering over the Périphérique and increasing housing by adding storeys to existing buildings; liberating space for housing through an underground traffic infrastructure under the Periphérique and along the Seine; and investing in public transport, with new suspended métro lines.

Atelier Christian de Portzamparc

Sightseeing

Sacré-Coeur. *See p95.*

The sightseeing cruise of Paris : the best in 1H
www.vedettesdeparis.com

Location:
Right by the Eiffel Tower
Port de Suffren, 7th district + 00 33 (0)1 44 18 19 50
M° Bir-Hakeim & Trocadero; RER Champs de Mars

The Parisian sightseeing cruise has to be at the top of your list
of things to do when in the French capital.
Ideally located right by the Eiffel Tower, its charming boats
enhance the pleasure of a guided cruise on the River Seine.
Listed by the UNESCO World Heritage, the river banks offer
you some of the most appreciated and well-known
monuments such as the Eiffel Tower, the Louvre
and Notre Dame Cathedral amongst others.
Recorded multilingual commentary and a bar service on board.

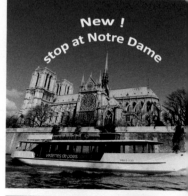

New !
stop at Notre Dame

Departures :
During the week: every 45 minutes from 11.30am to 6.45pm
Week end: every 30 minutes from 11.00am to 8.30pm

Sightseeing cruise: €11: Adult; €5: Children 5-12ys; free under 4ys

Exclusive : The Sparkling cruise
Sightseeing cruise + 1 Glass of Champagne for €16
The Pasta cruise
Sightseeing cruise + a light meal €18

New ! Get off at Notre Dame to visit île de la Cité ,
île St Louis then board again to end the cruise
and come back to the Eiffel Tower

Special offer
for Time Out readers
€3 OFF*
(On presentation of this guide)

PASTA PARTY

vedettes de paris

The Seine & Islands

Where it all began.

Like some mythical deity, Paris emerged from the waters of its river. The Seine was the transport route that brought settlers here in the first place, many millennia ago, and it gave them the economic wherewithal to stay put: it's no accident that the city's coat of arms consists of waves and a boat. As the city grew, so did the river's cultural importance, until it became what it still is today – the symbolic boundary between intellectual Left Bank Paris and the mercantile activities of the Right Bank.

| Map p406 | Restaurants p186 |
| Hotels p155 | |

In between the two sides, like a double bullseye, are the islands: the western Ile de la Cité, with its heavy payload of history, state machinery and religious grandeur; and the adjacent Ile St-Louis, once a mess of marshland and islets, and now one of the most exclusive residential districts in the city. Paris rippled out from the former, and splashes out in the upmarket boutiques of the latter; and the river still carries cargo, as well as cruise boats – and could, if President Sarkozy's 'Grand Paris' plan comes off, act as the defining thoroughfare in a newly energised economic region reaching all the way to the sea.

SIGHTS

ALONG THE SEINE

It's perhaps surprising that it took so long for the Seine to become a tourist magnet. For much of the 19th and 20th centuries, it was barely given a second thought by anyone who wasn't working on it or driving along its quayside roads. But in 1994, UNESCO added 12 kilometres of Paris riverbank to its World Heritage register. Floating venues such as **Batofar** (*see p328*) became super-trendy; and in the last ten years, it's been one new Seine-side attraction after another.

It's at its best in summer. Port de Javel and Jardin Tino-Rossi become open-air dancehalls; and there's the summer jamboree of Paris-Plage, Mayor Delanoë's inspired city beach that brings sand, palm trees, loungers and free entertainment to both sides of the Seine. After a few teething problems, the **Piscine Joséphine-Baker** (*see p340*) has revived the floating swimming pool concept that was so popular in the 19th and early 20th centuries.

Come on Sundays, and stretches of riverside roads will be closed for the benefit of cyclists and rollerskaters. And, of course, there's a wealth of boat tours (*see p367*).

What's more, the river itself is cleaning up its act. The recent crackdown on pollution had a big symbolic payoff recently when, for the first time since records began, a sea trout was caught in the Seine on the western outskirts of the city. The catch was significant because the sea trout is particularly fussy about the quality of the water in which it swims.

The bridges

From the honeyed arches of the oldest, the **Pont Neuf**, to the handsome, swooping lines of the newest, the **Passerelle Simone-de-Beauvoir**, the city's 37 bridges are among the best-known landmarks in the city, and enjoy some of its best views.

There was already a bridge on the site of the **Petit Pont** in the first century BC, when the

SIGHTS

Parisii Celts ran their river trade and toll-bridge operations. The Romans put up a cross-island thoroughfare in the form of a reinforced bridge to the south of Ile de la Cité, and another one north of it (where the **Pont Notre-Dame** now stands), thus creating a straight route all the way from Orléans through to Belgium.

Since then, the city's *ponts* have been bombed, bashed by buses and boats, weather-beaten and even trampled to destruction: in 1634, the Pont St-Louis collapsed under the weight of a religious procession. In the Middle Ages, the handful of bridges linking the islands to the riverbanks were lined with shops and houses, but the flimsy wooden constructions regularly caught fire or got washed away. The Petit Pont sank 11 times before councillors decided to ban building on top of bridges.

The Pont Neuf was inaugurated in 1607 and has been standing sturdy, gargoyles a-goggle, ever since. This was the first bridge to be built with no houses to obstruct the view of the river. It had a raised stretch of road at the edge to protect walkers from traffic and horse dung (the new-fangled 'pavement' soon caught on); the semicircular alcoves that now make handy pit stops for lovers were once filled with tooth-pullers, peddlers and *bouquinistes*.

The 19th century was boom time for bridge-building: 21 were built in all, including the city's first steel, iron and suspension bridges. The **Pont de la Concorde** used up what was left of the Bastille after the storming of 1789; the romantic **Pont des Arts** was the capital's first solely pedestrian crossing (built in 1803 and rebuilt in the 1980s). The most glitteringly exuberant bridge is the **Pont Alexandre III**, with its bronze and glass, garlanding and gilded embellishments. More practical is the **Pont de l'Alma**, with its Zouave statue that has long been a flood monitor: when the statue's toes get wet, the state raises the flood alert and starts to close the quayside roads; when he's up to his ankles in Seine, it's no longer possible to navigate the river by boat. This offers some

indication of how devastating the great 1910 flood was, when the plucky Zouave disappeared up to his neck (*see p29* **Going in Seine**).

The 20th century brought some spectacular additions. **Pont Charles-de-Gaulle**, for example, stretches resplendent like the wing of a huge aeroplane, and iron **Viaduc d'Austerlitz** (1905) is striking yet elegant as it cradles métro line 5. The city's newest crossing, the Passerelle Simone-de-Beauvoir, is a walkway linking the Bibliothèque Nationale to the Parc de Bercy in the 12th arrondissement.

ILE DE LA CITE

In the 1st & 4th arrondissements.

The Ile de la Cité is where Paris was born around 250 BC, when the Parisii, a tribe of Celtic Gauls, founded a settlement on this convenient bridging point of the Seine. Romans, Merovingians and Capetians followed, in what became a centre of political and religious power right into the Middle Ages: royal authority at one end, around the Capetian palace; the Church at the other, by Notre-Dame.

When Victor Hugo wrote *Notre-Dame de Paris* in 1831, the Ile de la Cité was still a bustling quarter of narrow medieval streets and tall houses: 'the head, heart and very marrow of Paris'. Baron Haussmann performed a marrow extraction when he supervised the expulsion of 25,000 people from the island, razing tenements and some 20 churches, and leaving behind large, official buildings – the law courts, the **Conciergerie**, Hôtel-Dieu hospital, the police headquarters and the cathedral. The lines of the old streets are traced into the parvis in front of **Notre-Dame**.

Perhaps the most charming spot on the island is the western tip, where Pont Neuf spans the Seine. Despite its name, it is in fact the oldest bridge in Paris, begun under the reign of Henri III and Catherine de Médicis in 1578 and taking 30 years to complete. Its arches are lined with grimacing faces, said to be modelled on some of the courtiers of Henri III. In 1991, the bridge (or, rather, a full-size facsimile of it) starred in Leos Carax's budget-busting film *Les Amants du Pont Neuf*.

Down the steps is a leafy triangular garden, square du Vert-Galant. You can take to the water here on the Vedettes du Pont Neuf. In the centre of the bridge is an equestrian statue of Henri IV; the original went up in 1635, was melted down to make cannons during the Revolution, and replaced in 1818. On the bridge's eastern side, place Dauphine, home to restaurants, wine bars and the ramshackle Hôtel Henri IV, was built in 1607, on what was then a sandy bar that

INSIDE TRACK
LITERARY LEANINGS

Baudelaire wrote part of *Les Fleurs du Mal* while living at the **Hôtel de Lauzun** at 17 quai d'Anjou; he and fellow poet Théophile Gautier also organised meetings of their dope-smokers' club here. A couple of centuries earlier, Racine, Molière and La Fontaine resided at the same address as guests of La Grande Mademoiselle, cousin of Louis XIV.

Piscine Joséphine-Baker. *See p53.*

flooded every winter. It was commissioned by Henri IV, who named it in honour of his son, the future King Louis XIII. The brick and stone houses, similar to those in place des Vosges (though subsequently much altered to accommodate sun terraces), look out over the quays and square. The third, eastern side was demolished in the 1860s, when the new Préfecture de Police was built. Known by its address, quai des Orfèvres, it was immortalised by Clouzot's film and Simenon's Maigret novels.

The towers of the Conciergerie dominate the island's north bank. Along with the Palais de Justice, it was originally part of the Palais de la Cité, residential and administration complex of the Capetian kings. It occupies the site of an earlier Merovingian fortress and, before that, the Roman governor's house. Etienne Marcel's uprising prompted Charles V to move the royal retinue to the Louvre in 1358, and the Conciergerie was assigned a more sinister role as a prison for people awaiting execution. The interior is worth a visit for its prison cells and the vaulted Gothic halls. On the corner of boulevard du Palais, the Tour de l'Horloge, built in 1370, was the first public clock in Paris.

Sainte-Chapelle, Pierre de Montreuil's masterpiece of stained glass and slender Gothic columns, stands among the nearby law courts. Enveloping the chapel, the Palais de Justice was built alongside the Conciergerie. Behind elaborate wrought-iron railings, most of the present buildings around the fine neo-classical entrance courtyard date from the 1780s reconstruction by Desmaisons and Antoine. After passing through security, you can visit the **Salle des Pas Perdus**, busy with plaintiffs and barristers, and sit in on cases in the civil and criminal courts. The Palais is still the centre of the French legal system.

Across boulevard du Palais, behind the Tribunal du Commerce, place Louis-Lépine is occupied by the Marché aux Fleurs, where horticultural suppliers sell flowers, cacti and exotic trees. On Sundays, they are joined by caged birds and small animals in the Marché aux Oiseaux. The Hôtel-Dieu, east of the market place, was founded in the seventh century. During the Middle Ages your chances of survival here were, at best, slim; today the odds are much improved. The hospital originally stood on the other side of the island facing the Latin Quarter, but after a series of fires in the 18th century it was rebuilt here in the 1860s.

Notre-Dame cathedral dominates the eastern half of the island. On the parvis in front of the cathedral is the bronze 'Kilomètre Zéro' marker, the point from which distances between Paris and the rest of France are measured. The **Crypte Archéologique** hidden under the parvis gives a sense of the island's multi-layered past, when it was a tangle of alleys, houses, churches and cabarets. Notre-Dame is still a place of worship, and holds its Assumption Day procession, Christmas Mass and Nativity scene on the parvis.

Sainte-Chapelle. *See p58.*

Walk through the garden by the cathedral to appreciate its flying buttresses. To the north-east, a medieval feel persists in the few streets untouched by Haussmann, such as rue Chanoinesse, rue de la Colombe and rue des Ursins, though the crenellated medieval remnant on the corner of rue des Ursins and rue des Chantres was redone in the 1950s for the Aga Khan. The capital's oldest love story unfolded in the 12th century at 9 quai aux Fleurs, where Héloïse lived with her uncle Canon Fulbert, who had her tutor and lover, the scholar Abélard, castrated. Héloïse was sent to a nunnery. Behind the cathedral, in a garden at the eastern end of the island, is the **Mémorial des Martyrs de la Déportation**, remembering people sent to Nazi concentration camps.

★ FREE Cathédrale Notre-Dame de Paris
Pl du Parvis-Notre-Dame, 4th (01.42.34.56.10/ www.cathedraledeparis.com). M° Cité/RER St-Michel. **Open** 8am-6.45pm Mon-Fri; 8am-7.15pm Sat, Sun. *Towers* Apr-Sept 10am-6.30pm daily *(June, Aug* until 11pm Sat, Sun). Oct-Mar 10am-5.30pm daily. **Admission** free. *Towers* €8; €5 reductions; free under-18s. PMP. **Credit** MC, V. **Map** p406 J7.
See right **Profile.**

★ La Conciergerie
2 bd du Palais, 1st (01.53.40.60.80). M° Cité/RER St-Michel Notre-Dame. **Open** Mar-Oct 9.30am-6pm daily. *Nov-Feb* 9am-5pm daily. **Admission** €6.50; €4.50 reductions; free under-18s (accompanied by an adult). *With Sainte-Chapelle* €11; €7.50 reductions. PMP. **Credit** MC, V. **Map** p408 J6.
The Conciergerie looks every inch the forbidding medieval fortress. However, much of the façade was added in the 1850s, long after Marie-Antoinette, Danton and Robespierre had been imprisoned here. The 13th-century Bonbec tower, built during the reign of St Louis, the 14th-century twin towers, César and Argent, and the Tour de l'Horloge all survive from the Capetian palace. The visit takes you through the Salle des Gardes, the medieval kitchens with their four huge chimneys, and the Salle des Gens d'Armes, an impressive vaulted Gothic hall built between 1301 and 1315 for Philippe 'le Bel'. After the royals moved to the Louvre, the fortress became a prison under the watch of the Concierge. The wealthy had private cells with their own furniture, which they paid for; others crowded on beds of straw. A list of Revolutionary prisoners, including a hairdresser, shows that not all victims were nobles. In Marie-Antoinette's cell, the Chapelle des Girondins, are her crucifix, some portraits and a guillotine blade.

La Crypte Archéologique
Pl Jean-Paul II, 4th (01.55.42.50.10). M° Cité/RER St-Michel Notre-Dame. **Open** 10am-6pm Tue-Sun. **Admission** €4; €2-€3 reductions; free under-14s. PMP. **Credit** (€15 minimum) MC, V. **Map** p406 J7.
Hidden under the forecourt in front of the cathedral is a large void that contains bits and pieces of Roman quaysides, ramparts and hypocausts, medieval cellars, shops and pavements, the foundations of the Eglise Ste-Geneviève-des-Ardens (the church where Geneviève's remains were stored during the Norman invasions), an 18th-century foundling hospital and a 19th-century sewer, all excavated since the 1960s. It's not always easy to work out exactly which wall, column or staircase is which – but you do get a vivid sense of the layers of history piled one atop another during 16 centuries.

FREE Mémorial des Martyrs de la Déportation
Sq de l'Ile de France, 4th (01.46.33.87.56). M° Cité/RER St-Michel Notre-Dame. **Open** Oct-Mar 10am-noon, 2-5pm daily. *Apr-Sept* 10am-noon, 2-7pm daily. **Admission** free. **Map** p406 J7.
This sober tribute to the 200,000 Jews, Communists, homosexuals and *résistants* deported to concentration camps from France in World War II stands on the eastern tip of the island. A blind staircase descends to river level, where simple chambers are

SIGHTS

Profile Cathédrale Notre-Dame de Paris

Paris's Gothic masterpiece.

Notre-Dame was commissioned in 1160 by Bishop Maurice de Sully, who wanted to rival the smart new abbey that had just gone up in St-Denis. It replaced the earlier St-Etienne basilica, built in the sixth century by Childebert I on the site of a Gallo-Roman temple to Jupiter. Notre-Dame was constructed between 1163 and 1334, and the amount of time and money spent on it reflected the city's growing prestige. Pope Alexander III may have laid the foundation stone; the choir was completed in 1182, the nave in 1208; the west front and twin towers went up between 1225 and 1250. Chapels were added to the nave between 1235 and 1250, and to the apse between 1296 and 1330. The cathedral was plundered during the French Revolution, and then rededicated to the cult of Reason. The original statues of the Kings of Judah from the west front were torn down by the mob (who believed them to represent the kings of France) and rediscovered only during the construction of a car park in 1977 (they're now in the Musée National du Moyen-Age).

By the 19th century, the cathedral was looking pretty shabby. Victor Hugo, whose novel *Notre-Dame de Paris* had been a great success, led the campaign for restoration. Gothic revivalist Viollet-le-Duc restored Notre-Dame to her former glory in the mid 19th century, although work has been going on ever since.

The west front remains a high point of Gothic art for the balanced proportions of its twin towers and rose window, and the three doorways with rows of saints and sculpted tympanums: the *Last Judgement* (centre), *Life of the Virgin* (left) and *Life of St Anne* (right). Inside, take a moment to admire the long nave with its solid foliate capitals and high altar with a marble Pietà by Coustou; the choir was rebuilt in the 18th century by Robert le Cotte, but is surrounded by medieval painted stone reliefs depicting the Resurrection (south) and Nativity (north).

To truly appreciate the masonry, climb up the towers. The route runs up the north tower and down the south. Between the two you get a close-up view of the gallery of chimeras – the fantastic birds and leering hybrid beasts designed by Viollet-le-Duc along the balustrade. After a detour to see the Bourdon (the massive bell), a staircase leads to the top of the south tower.

SIGHTS

BIG-SCREEN MOMENTS
Notre-Dame de Paris (1956)
In which Gina Lollobrigida, as Esmeralda, dances merrily on the parvis.

Amélie (2001)
The heroine's mother meets an unlucky end when a tourist falls on her from the cathedral heights.

lined with tiny lights and the walls are inscribed with verse. A barred window looks out at the Seine.

Sainte-Chapelle

*6 bd du Palais, 1st (01.53.40.60.80). M°
Cité/RER St-Michel Notre-Dame.* **Open** *Mar-
Oct 9.30am-6pm daily. Nov-Feb 9am-5pm daily.*
Admission €8; €5 reductions; free
under-18s (accompanied by an adult). PMP.
With Conciergerie €10; €8 reductions. **Credit**
MC, V. **Map** p408 J6.

Devout King Louis IX (St Louis, 1226-70) had a hobby of accumulating holy relics (and children: he fathered 11). In the 1240s he bought what was advertised as the Crown of Thorns, and ordered Pierre de Montreuil to design a suitable shrine. The result was the exquisite Flamboyant Gothic Sainte-Chapelle. With 15m (49ft) windows, the upper level, intended for the royal family and the canons, appears to consist almost entirely of stained glass. The windows depict hundreds of scenes from the Old and New Testaments, culminating with the Apocalypse in the rose window. *Photo p56.*

ILE ST-LOUIS

In the 4th arrondissement.

The Ile St-Louis is one of the most exclusive residential addresses in the city. Delightfully unspoiled, it has fine architecture, narrow streets and pretty views from the tree-lined

Berthillon.

quays, and still retains the air of a tranquil backwater, curiously removed from city life.

For hundreds of years, the island was a swampy pasture belonging to Notre-Dame, known as Ile Notre-Dame and used as a retreat for fishermen, swimmers and courting couples. In the 14th century Charles V built a fortified canal through the middle, thus creating the Ile aux Vaches ('Island of Cows'). Its real-estate potential wasn't realised until 1614, though, when speculator Christophe Marie persuaded Louis XIII to fill in the canal (present-day rue Poulletier) and plan streets, bridges and houses. The island was renamed in honour of the king's pious predecessor, and the venture proved a huge success, thanks to architect Louis Le Vau, who from the 1630s built fashionable new residences along the quai d'Anjou, quai de Bourbon and quai de Béthune, as well as the **Eglise St-Louis-en-l'Ile**. By the 1660s the island was full; its smart reception rooms were set at the front of courtyards to give residents riverside views.

Rue St-Louis-en-l'Ile – lined with fine historic buildings that now house quirky gift shops and gourmet food stores (many open on Sunday), quaint tearooms, stone-walled bars, restaurants and hotels – runs the length of the island. The grandiose **Hôtel Lambert** at no.2 was built by Le Vau in 1641 for Louis XIII's secretary, and has sumptuous interiors by Le Sueur, Perrier and Le Brun. At no.51 – **Hôtel Chenizot** – look out for the bearded faun adorning the rocaille doorway, which is flanked by stern dragons supporting the balcony. There's more sculpture on the courtyard façade, while a second courtyard hides craft workshops and an art gallery. Across the street, the **Hôtel du Jeu de Paume** at no.54 was once a tennis court; at no.31, famous ice-cream maker **Berthillon** still draws a crowd. At the western end there are great views of the flying buttresses of Notre-Dame from the terraces of the **Brasserie de l'Ile St-Louis** and the **Flore en l'Ile** café. At 6 quai d'Orléans, the **Adam Mickiewicz library-museum** (01.55.42.83.83, open 2-5pm Wed, 9am-noon Sat, hourly guided tours €5, free-€2 reductions) is dedicated to the Romantic poet, journalist and campaigner for Polish freedom.

FREE Eglise St-Louis-en-l'Ile

*19bis rue St-Louis-en-l'Ile, 4th (01.46.34.11.60/
www.saintlouisenlile.com). M° Pont Marie.* **Open**
9am-noon, 3-7pm Tue-Sun. **Admission** free.
Map p409 L7.

The island's church was built between 1664 and 1765, following plans by Louis Le Vau and later completed by Gabriel Le Duc. The baroque interior boasts Corinthian columns and a sunburst over the altar, and sometimes hosts classical music concerts.

The Louvre

An artistic and architectural masterpiece.

The world's largest museum is a city within the city, a vast, multi-level maze of galleries, passageways, staircases and escalators. It's famous for the artistic glories it contains within, but the very fabric of the museum is a masterpiece in itself – or rather, a collection of masterpieces modified and added to from one century to another. And because nothing in Paris ever stands still, the additions and modifications continue into the present day, with a major new Islamic Arts department set to open in 2010, and the franchising of the Louvre 'brand' via new outposts in Lens (www.louvrelens.fr) and Abu Dhabi. If any place demonstrates the importance of culture in French life, this is it.

ABOUT THE LOUVRE

Much like the building itself, the Louvre's collections were built up over the centuries. They encompass a rich visual history of the western world, from Ancient Egypt and Mesopotamia to the 19th century. Indeed, one of the most impressive things about the Louvre is the way it juxtaposes architecture and content. Look up from a case of Greek or Roman antiquities and you might see an 18th-century painted ceiling, or two doves by Braque. In the Egyptian section you'll find Louis XIV's bedchamber, complete with gilded bed, while Renaissance art is housed in the Grande Galerie, where the Sun King performed the 'scrofula ceremony', blessing the sick. In between exhibits, the Louvre's long windows afford stunning views of the building's façades, gardens and lovely interior courtyards.

INSIDE TRACK
PLAN YOUR ROUTE

Pick up a map at the information desk. The eight collections are colour-coded on it, and signs point the way to the most popular exhibits. Leaflets suggesting various thematic trails are also available. *Destination Louvre* (€7.50), from the Réunion des Musées Nationaux shop in the Carrousel du Louvre, is a good English-language guide.

Some 35,000 works of art and artefacts are on show, split into eight departments and housed in three wings: **Denon**, **Sully** and **Richelieu**. Under the atrium of the glass pyramid, each wing has its own entrance, though you can pass from one to another. Treasures from the Egyptians, Etruscans, Greeks and Romans each have their own galleries in the Denon and Sully wings, as do Middle Eastern and Islamic art. The first floor of Richelieu is taken up with European decorative arts from the Middle Ages up to the 19th century, including room after room of Napoleon III's lavish apartments.

The main draw, though, is the painting and sculpture. Two glass-roofed sculpture courts contain the famous Marly horses on the ground floor of Richelieu, with French sculpture below and Italian Renaissance pieces in the Denon wing. The Grand Galerie and Salle de la Joconde (home to the *Mona Lisa*), like a mini Uffizi, run the length of Denon's first floor with French Romantic painting alongside. Dutch and French painting occupies the second floor of Richelieu and Sully. Jean-Pierre Wilmotte's minimalist galleries in the Denon wing were designed as a taster for the Musée du Quai Branly, with art from Africa, the Americas and Oceania.

Mitterrand's Grand Louvre project expanded the museum two-fold. But the organisation and restoration of the Louvre is still a work in progress: check the website or lists in the Carrousel du Louvre to see which galleries are closed on certain days to avoid missing out on what you want to see.

The museum is also trying to strike a balance between highbrow culture and accessibility. Photography was banned in 2005 at the request of mainly French visitors, who complained that it interfered with their enjoyment; meanwhile, the link with Dan Brown's *Da Vinci Code* has been embraced with a dedicated audio guide. Laminated panels found throughout provide a surprisingly lively commentary, and the superb website is a technological feat unsurpassed by that of any of the world's major museums.

ADVANCE TICKETS AND ENTRY

IM Pei's glass pyramid is a wonderful piece of architecture, but it's not the only entrance to the museum – there are three others. Buying a ticket in advance means you can go in directly via the passage Richelieu off rue de Rivoli, or via the Carrousel du Louvre shopping mall (there are steps down either side of the Arc de Triomphe du Carrousel, at 99 rue de Rivoli or from the métro).

Advance tickets are valid for any day, and are available from the Louvre website or branches of **Fnac** and **Virgin Megastore** (for both, *see p271*). You can buy one from the Virgin in the Carrousel du Louvre and use it immediately. Another option is to buy a ticket at the Cour des Lions entrance (closed Fridays) in the south-west corner of the complex, convenient for the Italian collections. The Louvre is also accessible with the all-in **Paris Museum Pass**. Finally, don't forget that the Louvre is closed on Tuesdays.

OTHER TIPS

● The Louvre's website, much of which is in English, is an unbeatable resource. Every work on display is photographed, and you can search the Atlas database by room, artist or theme.
● Laminated cards in each room provide useful background information. Audioguides (€5; ID must be left) are available at the main entrances in the Carrousel du Louvre.
● Don't attempt to see more than two collections in one day. Your ticket is valid all day and you can leave and re-enter the museum as you wish.
● On Fridays after 6pm entry is free for the under-26s, but if you plan to make several visits, the Carte Louvre Jeunes (€15 per year under-26s, €30 per year under-30s) is worth getting.
● Some rooms are closed on a weekly basis – check on 01.40.20.53.17 or at www.louvre.fr.

LISTINGS INFORMATION

Louvre, Rue de Rivoli, 1st (01.40.20.50.50/ recorded information 01.40.20.53.17/disabled access 01.40.20.59.90/www.louvre.fr). M° Palais Royal Musée du Louvre. **Open** 9am-6pm Mon, Thur, Sat, Sun; 9am-10pm Wed, Fri. **Admission** *Permanent collections* €9 (incl entry to the Musée Delacroix but not shows at the Salle Napoléon);

€6 6-9.45pm Wed, Fri; free under-18s at all times, under-26s 6-9.45pm Fri, all 1st Sun of mth. PMP. *Exhibitions* €11. *Combined ticket* €14; €12 6-9.45pm Wed, Fri. **Credit** AmEx, MC, V. **Map** p403 G5.

REFRESHMENTS

Take your pick from **Richelieu**, **Denon** or **Mollien** cafés; the latter is just off the Mollien staircase and has a terrace. Under the pyramid, there's a sandwich bar and the smart, sophisticated **Grand Louvre** restaurant. The **Restorama**, in the Carrousel du Louvre, has self-service outlets. The terrace of **Café Marly** serves pricey brasserie fare and cocktails.

The collections

History of the Louvre

Sully: lower ground floor. Shown as dark brown on Louvre maps.
Here you can explore the medieval foundations of the Louvre, dating back to Philippe-Auguste's reign. Uncovered in 1985 during excavations for the Grand Louvre project, they include the remains of the moat that once surrounded the fort and the pillars of two drawbridges; the La Taillerie tower, with heart symbols cut into the stone by masons; and the outside of the dungeons. A well and a portion of ground have been left undisturbed, showing artefacts just as they were found, and a scale model shows the fortress at the time of Charles V. An exhibition in the Saint-Louis room – a guard room from the era of Philippe-Auguste, discovered in 1882 – recounts the history of the Louvre through rare archaeological finds, as well as an unfinished staircase and carved pillars.

Ancient Egypt

Denon: lower ground floor; Sully: lower ground, ground & 1st floors. Green on Louvre maps.
Announced by the pink granite Giant Sphinx (1898-1866 BC), the Egyptian department divides into two routes. The Thematic Circuit on the ground floor presents Nile culture (fishing, agriculture, hunting, daily and cultural life, religion and death). One of the big draws is the Mastaba of Akhethetep, a decorated burial chamber from Sakkara dating back to 2400 BC. Six small sphinxes, apes from Luxor and the lion-headed goddess Sekhmet recreate elements of temple complexes, while stone sarcophagi, mummies, amulets, jewellery and entrails form a vivid display on funeral rites. A display of Egyptian furniture (room 8, ground floor) dating from 1550 to 1069 BC contains pieces that look almost contemporary in design.

On the first floor the Pharoah Circuit is laid out chronologically, from the Seated Scribe and other stone figures of the Ancient Empire, via

SIGHTS

the painted figures of the Middle Empire, to the New Empire, with its animal-headed statues of gods and goddesses, hieroglyphic tablets and papyrus scrolls. Look for the statue of the god Amun protecting Tutankhamun, and the black diorite 'cube statues' of priests and attendants. The collection, one of the largest hoards of Egyptian antiquities in the world, has its origins in Napoleon's Egyptian campaign of 1798 and 1799, and the work of Egyptologist Jean-François Champollion, who deciphered hieroglyphics in 1824. The Coptic gallery, on the lower ground floor, houses textiles and manuscripts.

Oriental antiquities

Richelieu: lower ground & ground floors;
Sully: ground floor. Yellow on Louvre maps.
This section deals with Mesopotamia, Persia and the Levant from the fifth millennium BC to the first century AD. The huge Mesopotamian rooms contain glistening diorite sculptures from the Akkad dynasty and Gudea from the third millennium BC; in some cases, only the feet have survived intact. Make sure you don't miss the serene alabaster sculpture of Ebih-II, the superintendant of Mari (room 1b), and the earliest evidence of writing, in the form of fourth-century BC Sumerian tablets (room 1a). The Hammurabi Code, an essential document of Babylonian civilisation, is a black basalt stele recording 282 laws beneath reliefs of the king and the sun god; it's one of the oldest collections of laws in the history of mankind (room 3).

Next come two breathtaking palace reconstructions: the great court, c713 BC, from the palace of Sargon II at Khorsabad (in present-day Iraq), with its giant bearded and winged bulls and friezes of warriors and servants (room 4); and the palace of Darius I at Susa (now Iran), c510 BC, with its glazed-brick reliefs of archers, lions and griffins (room 12). The double-bull-headed column was one of 36 such gigantic supports at the palace. Entering the Iranian section, you find 5,000-year-old statues from Susa housed in the circular room 8, and a fine view of the Cour Napoléon. The Levantine section includes Cypriot animalistic vases and carved reliefs from Byblos.

Islamic arts

Richelieu: lower ground floor. Turquoise on
Louvre maps.
The Islamic decorative arts on show include early glassware, tenth- to 12th-century dishes decorated with birds and calligraphy, traditional Iranian blue-and-white wares, Iznik ceramics, intricate inlaid metalwork from Syria, tiles, screens, weapons and funerary steles. The highlight is three magnificent 16th-century kelims. In 2005 a Saudi prince, Prince Walid bin

Ancient Egypt.

Talal, gave over €17 million – one of the largest donations in French cultural history – for a new Islamic wing to be built as an extension to the southern wing. It's expected to open in the cour Visconti by 2010.

Greek, Roman & Etruscan antiquities

Denon: lower ground & ground floors; Sully: ground & 1st floors. Blue on Louvre maps.
The *Winged Victory of Samothrace*, a headless Greek statue dating from the second century BC, stands sentinel at the top of the grand staircase, giving an idea of its original dramatic impact on a promontory overlooking the Aegean sea. This huge department is made up of pieces amassed by François I and Cardinal Richelieu, plus the Borghese collection (acquired in 1808), and the Campana collection of thousands of painted Greek vases and small terracottas.

Endless dark rooms on the first floor harbour small bronze, silver and terracotta objects, but the really exciting stuff is on the ground floor. The grandiose, vaulted marble rooms are a fitting location for masterpieces such as the 2.3m (7.5ft) *Athena Peacemaker* and the *Venus de Milo* (room 12), and overflow with gods and goddesses, swords and monsters.

Also on the ground floor are artefacts from the Etruscan civilisation of south-central Italy, spanning the seventh century BC until submission to the Romans in the first century AD. The highlight is the painted terracotta Sarcophagus of the Cenestien Couple (c530-510 BC), which illustrates a smiling couple reclining at a banquet. Key Roman antiquities include a vivid relief of sacrificial animals, intricately carved sarcophagi, mosaic floors and the Boscoreale Treasure: magnificent silverwork

excavated at a villa near Pompeii. Pre-classical Greek art on the lower ground floor includes a large Cycladic head and Mycenean triad.

French painting

Denon: 1st floor; Richelieu: 2nd floor; Sully: 2nd floor. Red on Louvre maps.
There are around 6,000 of the most famous paintings in the world on show here, the most impressive being the huge 18th- to 19th-century canvases hanging in the Daru and Mollien rooms in the Denon wing, serving Classicism and Romanticism respectively. Here, art meets politics with David's enormous *Sacre de Napoléon*, Gros's propagandising *Napoléon Visitant le Champ de Bataille d'Eylau* and Delacroix's flag-flying *La Liberté Guidant le Peuple*. Géricault's beautiful but disturbing *Le Radeau de la Méduse* illustrates the grisly

true story of the abandoned men who resorted to cannibalism and murder after a famous shipwreck in 1816, while his generals on flame-eyed horses fuel the myth of the dashing French officer. Biblical and historical scenes rub shoulders with aristocracy and grand depictions of great moments in mythology. Ingres' *Grande Odalisque* is also found here, along with a new Ingres acquisition, a portrait of the Duc d'Orléans.

In the Richelieu wing you can find the earliest known non-religious French portrait, an anonymous depiction of French king Jean Le Bon (c1350); the *Pietà de Villeneuve-les-Avignon*, later attributed to Enguerrand Quarton; Jean Clouet's *Portrait of François I* (marking the influence of the Italian Renaissance on portraiture); and various works from the Ecole de Fontainebleau, including the anonymous

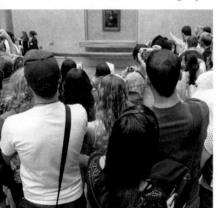

Diana the Huntress, an elegant nude who strangely resembles Diane de Poitiers, the mistress of Henri II. Poussin's religious and mythological subjects epitomise 17th-century French classicism, and are full of erudite references for an audience of cognoscenti. His works spill over into the Sully wing, where you'll also find Charles Le Brun's wonderfully pompous *Chancellier Séguier* and his four grandiose battle scenes, in which Alexander the Great is a suitable stand-in for Louis XIV.

The 18th century begins with Watteau's *Gilles* and the *Embarkation for Cythera*. Works by Chardin include sober still lifes, but also fine figure paintings. If you're used to the sugary images of Fragonard, don't miss the *Fantaisies*, which forgo sentimentality for fluent, broadly painted fantasy portraits, intended to capture moods rather than likenesses. Also in the Sully wing are sublime neo-classical portraits by David, Ingres' *La Baigneuse* and *Le Bain Turc*, portraits and Orientalist scenes by Chassériau, and landscapes by Corot.

French sculpture

Richelieu: lower ground & ground floors.
Light brown on Louvre maps.
French sculpture is displayed in and around the two covered courts created by the Grand Louvre scheme. A tour of the medieval regional schools takes in the *Virgins* from Alsace, 14th-century figures of Charles V and Jeanne de Bourbon that once adorned the exterior of the Louvre, and the late 15th-century tomb of Philippe Pot, an effigy of a Burgundian knight carried by eight mourners. Fine Renaissance memorials, fountains and portals include Jean Goujon's friezes from the Fontaine des Innocents.

In the Cour Marly, pride of place goes to Coustou's *Chevaux de Marly*, rearing horses being restrained by their grooms, plus two earlier equestrian pieces by Coysevox. Hewn from single blocks of marble, they were sculpted for the royal château at Marly-le-Roi before being moved to the Tuileries gardens, where copies now stand. In Cour Puget are the four bronze captives by Martin Desjardins, Clodion's rococo frieze and Pierre Puget's twisting, baroque *Milo of Croton*. Amid the 18th-century heroes and allegorical subjects, look out for Pigalle's *Mercury* and *Voltaire*.

Italian & Spanish painting

Denon: 1st floor. Red on Louvre maps.
Starting from the Sully end of the Denon wing, three rooms of fragile frescoes by Botticelli, Fra Angelico and Luini, and 13th- to 15th-century Florentine paintings on wood by Cimabue, Giotto, Fra Angelico and Lippi, open the Italian department, before you move into the long,

skylit Grande Galerie. To the right, the Salle des Sept Mètres has highlights of the Sienese school, including Simone Martini's *Christ Carrying the Cross* and Piero della Francesca's *Portrait of Sigismondo Malatesta*. Now that the *Mona Lisa* has moved, there is no need to bowl along the Grande Galerie at speed in your haste to see her, missing the wonders on either side.

Most notably, about a quarter of the way along on the left are Leonardo's *Virgin of the Rocks*, *Virgin and Child with Saint Anne* and *Saint-Jean Baptiste*, which form part of the Northern Italian section, along with Bellini's *Calvary* and *Portrait of a Man* and Raphael's *Portrait of Dona Isabel de Requesens*. The first turning on the right after the da Vincis leads into the Salle de La Joconde, whose toffee-coloured brushed concrete walls provide a suitably golden setting for Veronese's lavish *Wedding at Cana*, his *Crucifixion* and *Sainte Famille* and other Venetian masterpieces such as Lotto's *Adulterous Woman* and red-robed *Christ Carrying the Cross*, Tintoretto's *Suzanne Bathing* and Bassano's earthy canvases. Don't miss the exquisite Titians hidden behind the *Mona Lisa* on her stand-alone wall.

A trip back down the Passage de Mollien, containing 16th-century cartoons, frames Giorgio Vasari's *Annunciation*, revealing how much better it is to stand back and look at these paintings. In between the two in the Grande Galerie are Arcimboldo's famous *Four Seasons*, various Bronzinos and Caravaggios, plus works by Albani, Carracci and Reni. A small Spanish section takes in *Christ on the Cross Adored by Two Donors* by El Greco and his contemporary Jusepe de Ribera's *Club Foot*.

Graphic arts

Denon: 1st floor; Sully: 2nd floor.
Pink on Louvre maps.
The Louvre's huge collection of drawings includes works by Raphael, Michelangelo, Dürer, Holbein and Rembrandt. However, owing to their fragility, drawings are not shown as permanent exhibits. Four galleries (French and Northern schools on the 2nd floor; Italian and the latest acquisitions on the 1st) feature changing exhibitions. Other works can be viewed in the Salle de Consultation only upon written application to the management (01.40.20.51.94, fax 01.40.20.53.51).

Italian, Spanish & Northern sculpture

Denon: lower ground & ground floors.
Light brown on Louvre maps.

Michelangelo's *Dying Slave* and *Captive Slave* are the real showstoppers here, but other Renaissance treasures include a painted marble relief by Donatello, Adrien de Vriesse's bronze *Mercury and Psyche*, Giambologna's *Mercury* and the ethereal *Psyche Revived by Cupid's Kiss* by Antonio Canova. Benvenuto Cellini's *Nymph of Fontainebleau* relief is on the Mollien staircase.

Napoleon III's former stables were reopened in 2004 to house princely collections of statuary acquired by Richelieu and the Borghese and Albani families in the 17th and 18th centuries. The statues, either copies of classical works or restored originals, demonstrate the relationship between antique and modern sculpture. The height of the room also allows oversized works such as *Jupiter* and *Albani Alexander* to be displayed. Northern sculpture, on the lower ground floor, ranges from Erhart's Gothic *Mary Magdalene* to the neo-classical work of Thorvaldsen; pre-Renaissance Italian pieces include Donatello's clay relief *Virgin and Child*.

Northern schools

Richelieu: 2nd floor; Sully: 1st floor.
Red on Louvre maps.

Northern Renaissance works include Flemish altarpieces by Memling and van der Weyden, Bosch's fantastical, proto-surrealist *Ship of Fools*, Metsys' *The Moneylender and his Wife*, and the northern mannerism of Cornelius van Haarlem. The Galerie Médicis houses Rubens' Médicis cycle; Marie de Médicis, the widow of Henri IV, commissioned the 24 canvases for the Palais de Luxembourg in the 1620s. They blend historic events and classical mythology for the glorification of the queen, never afraid to put her best features on public display. Look out for Rubens' more personal portrait of his second wife, *Hélène Fourment and her Children*, plus van Dyck's *Charles I and his Groom* and David Teniers the Younger's peasant-filled townscapes.

Dutch paintings in this wing include early and late self-portraits by Rembrandt, his *Flayed Ox* and the warmly glowing nude *Bathsheba at her Bath*. There are Vermeer's *Astronomer* and *Lacemaker* amid interiors by De Hooch and Metsu, and the meticulously finished portraits and framing devices of Dou, plus works from the Haarlem school. German paintings in side galleries include portraits by Cranach, Dürer's *Self-Portrait* and Holbein's *Anne of Cleves*.

The rooms of Northern European and Scandinavian paintings include Caspar David Friedrich's *Trees with Crows*, the sober, classical portraits of Christian Købke, and pared-back views by Peder Balke. A fairly modest but high-quality British collection located on the first floor of the Sully includes landscapes by Wright of Derby, Constable and Turner, and portraits by Gainsborough, Reynolds and Lawrence.

Decorative arts

Richelieu: 1st floor; Sully: 1st floor.
Magenta on Louvre maps.

The decorative arts collection runs from the Middle Ages to the mid 19th century, and includes entire rooms decorated in the fashion of the day. Many of the finest medieval items came from the treasury of St-Denis, amassed by the powerful Abbot Suger, counsellor to Louis VI and VII, among them Suger's 'Eagle' (a porphyry vase), a serpentine plate surrounded by precious stones, and the sacred sword of the kings of France, dubbed 'Charlemagne's Sword' by the Capetian monarchs.

The Renaissance galleries display the *Hunts of Maximilien*, a dozen 16th-century tapestries depicting the months, zodiac and hunting scenes. Seventeenth- and 18th-century French decorative arts are shown in superb panelled rooms, and include characteristic brass and tortoiseshell pieces by Boulle. Displays then move on to French porcelain, silverware, watches and scientific instruments. Napoleon III's opulent apartments, used until the 1980s by the Ministry of Finance, have been preserved, with chandeliers and upholstery intact.

Next to the Denon wing, the Galerie d'Apollon reopened in 2004 after four years of restoration. A precursor to the Hall of Mirrors at Versailles, it was built for Louis XIV and is a showcase of talents from this golden age: architecture by Louis Le Vau, painted ceilings by Charles Le Brun and sculpture by François Girardon, the Marsy brothers and Thomas Regnaudin. Napoleon III then commissioned Delacroix to paint the central medallion, *Apollo Vanquishing the Python*, and now it houses the crown jewels and Louis XIV vases. Merry-Joseph Blondel's *Chute d'Icare* graces the ceiling of an anteroom of the adjacent Rotonde d'Apollon.

African, Asian, Oceanic & American arts

Denon: ground floor. White on Louvre maps.

A new approach to 'arts premiers' is seen in these eight rooms in the Pavillon des Sessions, prefiguring the Musée du Quai Branly. The spare, modern design allows each of the 100 key works to stand alone. The pure aesthetics of such objects as a svelte Zulu spoon with the breasts and buttocks of a woman, a sixth-century BC Sokoto terracotta head, a recycled iron sculpture of the god Gou that anticipates Picasso, and a pot-bellied, terracotta Chupicaro from Mexico can be appreciated in their own right. Computer terminals with mahogany benches offer visitors multimedia resources.

Opéra to Les Halles

Money makes this world go round.

In centuries gone by, these two adjoining central districts – bounded by the Grands Boulevards to the north and the river to the south – were the city's commercial and provisioning powerhouses, home to most of the newspapers, banks and major mercantile institutions. Nowadays, although there is still a strong financial slant thanks to the presence of the two stock exchanges and the Banque de France, the focus is on shopping: mass-market stuff in and around Les Halles, shading progressively into more exclusive and expensive brands the further one moves west, in particular on and just off rue St-Honoré.

Champs-Elysées & Western Paris	Montmartre & Pigalle	North-East Paris
	Opéra to Les Halles	
Tour Eiffel	Louvre	Beaubourg & The Marais
The 7th & Western Paris	St-Germain-des-Prés & Odéon	Notre-Dame
		Bastille & Eastern Paris
Montparnasse & Beyond	The Latin Quarter & the 13th	

Maps p401-402	**Restaurants** p193
Hotels p159	**Cafés & bars** p220

Les Halles itself was, famously, the city's wholesale food market until 1969, when the Second Empire iron-framed buildings that housed it were ripped out, and a thousand commentators gnashed their teeth in print. The soulless shopping centre that filled the gap in the 1970s has been one of the city's least liked features, and is itself doomed to destruction in the next few years, to be replaced by what promises to be a 21st-century glory of gardens, glass, and brighter, more open spaces.

TUILERIES & PALAIS-ROYAL

In the 1st arrondissement.

Once the monarchs had moved from the Ile de la Cité to spacious new quarters on the Right Bank, the Louvre and, later, the palaces of the **Tuileries** and **Palais-Royal** became the centres of royal power. **The Louvre** (*see pp59-63*) still exerts considerable influence today: first as a grandiose architectural ensemble, a palace within the city; and, second, as a symbol of the capital's cultural pre-eminence. What had been simply a fortress along Philippe-Auguste's city wall in 1190 was transformed into a royal residence with all the latest Gothic comforts by Charles V; François I turned it into a sumptuous Renaissance palace. For centuries it was a work in progress: everyone wanted to make their mark – including the most monarchical of presidents, François Mitterrand, who added IM Pei's glass pyramid, doubled the exhibition space and added the Carrousel du Louvre shopping mall, auditorium and food halls.

The palace has always attracted crowds: first courtiers and ministers; then artists; and, since 1793, when it was first turned into a museum, art-lovers – though the last department of the Finance Ministry moved out as late as 1991. Around the Louvre, other subsidiary palaces grew up: Catherine de Médicis commissioned Philibert Delorme to begin work on one in the Tuileries; and Richelieu built the Palais Cardinal, which later became the Palais-Royal.

On place du Louvre, opposite Claude Perrault's grandiose western façade of the Louvre, is **Eglise St-Germain-l'Auxerrois**, once the French kings' parish church and home to the only original Flamboyant Gothic porch in Paris, built in 1435. Mirroring it to the left of the belfry is the 19th-century first arrondissement *mairie*, with its fanciful rose window and classical porch. Next door is the stylish **Le Fumoir** (*see p220*), with a Mona Lisa of its own: amaretto, orange juice and champagne.

SIGHTS

Across rue de Rivoli from the Louvre, past the **Louvre des Antiquaires** antiques emporium (*see p268*), stands the understatedly elegant **Palais-Royal**, once Cardinal Richelieu's private mansion and now the Conseil d'Etat and ministry of culture. After a stroll in its quiet gardens, it's hard to believe that this was once the most debauched corner of Paris and the seedbed of the French Revolution.

In the 1780s, the Palais was a boisterous centre of Paris life, where aristocrats and the financially challenged inhabitants of the *faubourgs* rubbed shoulders. The coffee-houses in its arcades generated radical debate: here Camille Desmoulins called the city to arms on the eve of the storming of the Bastille; and after the Napoleonic Wars, Wellington and Field Marshal von Blücher lost so much money in the gambling dens that Parisians claimed they had won back their entire dues for war reparations. Only haute cuisine restaurant **Le Grand Véfour** (*see p189*), founded as

Secret Museums La Collection 1900

Maxim's makes the ideal setting for this display of art nouveau.

Couturier Pierre Cardin has owned belle époque restaurant Maxim's since 1981. The place is all flounces and furbelows, polished mahogany and elaborate stained glass, an over-the-top setting where European royalty and opera stars dine on dishes created a century ago. Now Cardin has added a museum of art nouveau, which he has been collecting since the age of 18. **La Collection 1900** (*see p69*) is accessible by guided tour only, led by enthusiasts such as Mañuel Villaverde-Cabrel, an art nouveau expert. 'This is the Marquise de Belbeuf driving her carriage, and here, in pink rabbit, the celebrated courtesan Emilienne d'Alençon,' he expounds as if they were his own best friends. These 19th-century courtesans were powerful women, amassing fortunes from their aristocratic clients and commanding A-list status at society dinners and galas.

There are rooms and rooms of exhibits, arranged so as to evoke a 19th-century courtesan's boudoir. Read Zola's *Nana* before your visit to grasp the full effect of the dreamy lake maidens sculpted in glistening faience, pewter vanity sets in the shape of reclining nudes, and beds inlaid with opium flowers to promote sleep. Dinner settings include Gustav Eiffel's own chunky tureens, just crying out for turtle soup, while a bed has been casually draped with a feather boa to suggest a recent assignation. Never has an art form been so redolent with erotic symbolism, and Maxim's, with its 'voluptuous perfume of drunkenness, luxury and gossip' makes the perfect setting to see art nouveau in all its overblown glory.

SIGHTS

Jardin des Tuileries. *See p71.*

Café de Chartres in the 1780s, survives from this era, albeit with decoration dating from a little later.

The **Comédie Française** theatre ('La Maison de Molière'; *see p345*) stands on the south-west corner. The company, created by Louis XIV in 1680, moved here in 1799. Molière himself is honoured with a fountain on the corner of rue Molière and rue de Richelieu. Brass-fronted **Café Nemours** on place Colette – Colette used to buy cigars from old-fashioned **A la Civette** nearby (157 rue St-Honoré, 1st, 01.42.96.04.99) – is another thespian favourite. In front of it, the métro entrance by artist Jean-Michel Othoniel, all glass baubles and aluminium struts, is a kitsch take on Guimard's celebrated art nouveau métro entrances.

Today, the stately arcades of the Palais-Royal house an eclectic succession of antiques dealers, philatelists, specialists in tin soldiers and musical boxes – and fashion showcases.

Here you'll find the recently opened European flagship of renowned New York designer **Marc Jacobs** (*see p247*), chic vintage clothes specialist **Didier Ludot** (*see p256*), and the elegant perfumery **Salons du Palais-Royal Shiseido** (*see p267*). Passing through the arcades to rue de Montpensier, the neo-rococo Théâtre du Palais-Royal and the centuries-old café **Entr'acte** (*see p220*), you'll find narrow, stepped passages that run between here and rue de Richelieu. On the other side of the palace towards Les Halles is galerie Véro-Dodat. Built by rich *charcutiers* during the Restoration period, it features wonderfully preserved neo-classical wooden shopfronts.

At the western end of the Louvre, by rue de Rivoli, are the **Musée des Arts Décoratifs**, the **Musée de la Mode et du Textile** and the **Musée de la Publicité**. All of these are administered independently of the Musée du Louvre, but were refreshed as part of the Grand Louvre scheme. Across place du Carrousel from the Louvre pyramid, the **Arc du Carrousel**, a mini-Arc de Triomphe, was built in polychrome marble for Napoleon from 1806 to 1809. The chariot on the top was originally drawn by the antique horses from San Marco in Venice, snapped up by Napoleon but returned in 1815. From the arch, the extraordinary axis along the **Jardin des Tuileries**, the Champs-Elysées up to the Arc de Triomphe and on to the Grande Arche de la Défense is plain to see.

The Jardin des Tuileries stretched as far as the Tuileries palace, until that was destroyed in the 1871 Paris Commune. The garden was laid out in the 17th century by André Le Nôtre and remains a pleasure area, with a funfair in summer; it also serves as an open-air gallery for modern art sculptures. Overlooking focal **place de la Concorde** is the **Musée de l'Orangerie**, reopened in May 2006 after a complete renovation; and the **Jeu de Paume**, built as a court for real tennis, now a centre for photographic exhibitions.

The stretch of rue de Rivoli running beside the Louvre towards Concorde was laid out by Napoleon's architects Percier and Fontaine from 1802 to 1811, and is notable for its arcaded façades. It runs in a straight line between place de la Concorde and rue St-Antoine, in the Marais; at the western end it's filled with tacky souvenir shops – though old-fashioned hotels remain, and there are also gentlemen's outfitters, bookshop **WH Smith** (*see p242*) and tearoom **Angelina** (*see p219*). The area was inhabited by English aristocrats, writers and artists in the 1830s and '40s after the Napoleonic Wars, sleeping at **Le Meurice** (*see p158*) and dining in the fancy restaurants of the Palais-Royal.

Place des Pyramides, at the junction of rue de Rivoli and rue des Pyramides, contains a gleaming gilt equestrian statue of Joan of Arc. One of four statues of her in the city, it's fêted as a proud symbol of French nationalism every May Day by supporters of the Front National.

Ancient rue St-Honoré, running parallel to rue de Rivoli, is one of those streets that changes style as it goes along: smart shops line it near place Vendôme, small cafés and inexpensive bistros predominate towards Les Halles. The baroque **Eglise St-Roch** is still pitted with bullet holes made by Napoleon's troops when they crushed a royalist revolt in 1795. With its old houses, adjoining rue St-Roch still feels wonderfully authentic; a couple of shops are built into the side of the church. Further up stands **Chapelle Notre-Dame de l'Assomption** (1670-76), now used by the city's Polish community, its dome so disproportionately large that locals have dubbed it *sot dôme* ('stupid dome'; a pun on 'Sodom').

Concept store **Colette** (*see p250*) brought some glamour to a once-staid shopping area, drawing a swarm of similar stores along in its wake. All are ideally placed for the fashionistas and film stars who touch down at **Hôtel Costes** (*see p157*). Opposite Colette is rue du Marché-St-Honoré, which once led to the covered Marché St-Honoré, since replaced by offices, in a square lined with trendy restaurants; to the north, rue Danielle-Casanova boasts 18th-century houses.

Further west along rue St-Honoré lies the wonderful, eight-sided **place Vendôme** and a perspective stretching from rue de Rivoli up to Opéra. At the end of the Tuileries, place de la Concorde, originally laid out for the glorification of Louis XV, is a masterclass in the use of open space, and spectacular when lit up at night. The winged Marly horses (only copies, the originals are in the Louvre) frame the entrance to the Champs-Elysées.

Smart rue Royale has tearoom **Ladurée** (*see p224*) and the famed restaurant **Maxim's** (3 rue Royale, 1st, 01.42.65.27.94), with a fabulous art nouveau interior. Rue Boissy d'Anglas proffers stylish shops and the trendy **Buddha Bar** (no.8, 1st, 01.53.05.90.00); and sporting luxuries at **Hermès** (*see p245*) on rue du Fbg-St-Honoré (a westward extension of rue St-Honoré), and high-end designs at **Yves Saint Laurent** (*see p250*), **Gucci** (no.2, 1st, 01.44.94.14.70), **Chloé** (no.54, 1st, 01.44.94.33.00) and others set the plush tone.

La Collection 1900

Maxim's, 3 rue Royale, 8th (01.42.65.30.47/ www.maxims-musee-artnouveau.com). M° Madeleine. **Open** *Guided tours (reservations essential)* 2pm Wed-Sun (English); 3.15pm, 4.30pm (French). **Admission** €15. **No credit cards. Map** p401 F4.
See p67 **Secret Museums**.

ᶠᴿᴱᴱ Eglise St-Germain-l'Auxerrois

2 pl du Louvre, 1st (01.42.60.13.96). M° Louvre Rivoli or Pont Neuf. **Open** 9am-7pm Mon-Sat; 9am-8.30pm Sun. **Admission** free. **Map** p406 H6.
The architecture of this former royal church spans several eras: the elaborate Flamboyant Gothic porch is the most striking feature. Inside, there's the 13th-century Lady Chapel and a canopied, carved bench by Le Brun made for the royal family in 1682. The church achieved notoriety on 24 August 1572, when its bell signalled the St Bartholomew's Day massacre.

★ ᶠᴿᴱᴱ Eglise St-Roch

296 rue St-Honoré, 1st (01.42.44.13.20). M° Pyramides or Tuileries. **Open** 9am-7pm daily. **Admission** free. **Map** p401 G5.
Begun in the 1650s in what was then the heart of Paris, this long church was designed chiefly by Jacques Lemercier; work took so long, the church was

SIGHTS

LE PARIS DES PARISIENS*

* The most Parisian journey

Sightseeing Cruise
Dinner Cruise
Lunch Cruise
Private Cruise

❄ ❄ ❄ ❄ ❄ ❄ ❄

At the foot of the Eiffel Tower

Bateaux Parisiens

Port de la Bourdonnais - 75 007 Paris
Tel. : + 33 1 766 414 45
www.bateauxparisiens.com

consecrated only in 1740. Famed parishioners and patrons are remembered in funerary monuments: Le Nôtre, Mignard, Corneille and Diderot are all here, as are busts by Coysevox and Coustou, Falconet's statue *Christ on the Mount of Olives* and Anguier's superb *Nativity*. Bullet marks from a 1795 shoot-out between royalists and conventionists still pit the façade.

★ FREE Jardin des Tuileries

Rue de Rivoli, 1st. M° Concorde or Tuileries. **Open** 7.30am-7pm daily. **Admission** free. **Map** p401 G5.
Between the Louvre and place de la Concorde, the gravelled alleyways of these gardens have been a chic promenade ever since they opened to the public in the 16th century; and the popular mood persists with the funfair that sets up along the rue de Rivoli side in summer. André Le Nôtre created the prototypical French garden with terraces and central vista running down the *Grand Axe* through circular and hexagonal ponds. When the Tuileries palace was burned down during the Paris Commune in 1871, the park was expanded. As part of Mitterrand's Grand Louvre project, fragile sculptures such as Coysevox's winged horses were transferred to the Louvre and replaced by copies, and the Maillol sculptures were returned to the Jardins du Carrousel; a handful of modern sculptures has been added, including bronzes by Laurens, Moore, Ernst, Giacometti, and Dubuffet's *Le Bel Costumé*. Replanting has restored parts of Le Nôtre's design and replaced damaged trees, and there's a gardeners' bookshop by place de la Concorde. *Photos p68.*

Jeu de Paume

1 pl de la Concorde, 8th (01.47.03.12.50/ www. jeudepaume.org). M° Concorde. **Open** noon-9pm Tue; noon-7pm Wed-Fri; 10am-7pm Sat, Sun (last entry 30mins before closing). **Admission** €7; €5 reductions. **Credit** MC, V. **Map** p401 F5.
The Centre National de la Photographie moved into this site in 2005. The building, which once served as a tennis court, has been divided into two white, almost hangar-like galleries. It is not an intimate space, but it works well for showcase retrospectives. A video art and cinema suite in the basement shows new digital installation work, as well as feature-length films made by artists. There's also a sleek café and a decent bookshop.
▶ *The Jeu de Paume's smaller site is the former Patrimoine Photographique at the Hôtel de Sully; see p100.*

★ Musée des Arts Décoratifs

107 rue de Rivoli, 1st (01.44.55.57.50/www.les artsdecoratifs.fr). M° Palais Royal Musée du Louvre or Pyramides. **Open** 11am-6pm Tue, Wed, Fri; 11am-9pm Thur; 10am-6pm Sat, Sun. Closed some hols. **Admission** (with Musée de la Mode & Musée de la Publicité) €8; €6.50 reductions; free under-18s. PMP. **Credit** MC, V. **Map** p402 H5.

Taken as a whole along with the Musée de la Mode et du Textile and Musée de la Publicité (for both, *see below*), this is one of the world's major collections of design and the decorative arts. Located in the west wing of the Louvre since its opening a century ago, the venue reopened in 2006 after a decade-long, €35-million restoration of the building and of 6,000 of the 150,000 items donated mainly by private collectors.
The major focus here is French furniture and tableware. From extravagant carpets to delicate crystal and porcelain, there is much to admire. Clever spotlighting and black settings show the exquisite treasures – including *châtelaines* made for medieval royalty and Maison Falize enamel work – to their best advantage. Other galleries are categorised by theme: glass, wallpaper, drawings and toys. There are cases devoted to Chinese head jewellery and the Japanese art of seduction with combs. Of most immediate attraction to the layman are the reconstructed period rooms, ten in all, showing how the other (French) half lived from the late 1400s to the early 20th century.

Musée de la Mode et du Textile

107 rue de Rivoli, 1st (01.44.55.57.50/www. lesartsdecoratifs.fr). M° Palais Royal Musée du Louvre or Pyramides. **Open** *Exhibitions* 11am-6pm Tue, Wed, Fri; 11am-9pm Thur; 10am-6pm Sat, Sun. **Admission** (with Musée des Arts Décoratif & Musée de la Publicité) €8; €6.50 reductions; free under-18s. PMP. **Credit** MC, V. **Map** p402 H5.
This municipal fashion museum holds Elsa Schiaparelli's entire archive and hosts exciting themed exhibitions. Dramatic black-walled rooms make a fine background to the clothes, and video screens and a small cinema space show how the clothes move, as well as interviews with the creators.

★ Musée de l'Orangerie

Jardin des Tuileries, 1st (01.44.77.80.07/ www.musee-orangerie.fr). M° Concorde. **Open** 9am-6pm Wed-Sun. **Admission** €7.50; €5.50 reductions; free under-18s. PMP. **Credit** MC, V. **Map** p401 F5.
The reopening of this Monet showcase a few years ago means the Orangerie is now firmly back on the tourist radar: expect long queues. The look is utilitarian and fuss-free, with the museum's eight, tapestry-sized *Nymphéas* (water lilies) paintings housed in two plain oval rooms. They provide a simple backdrop for the astonishing, ethereal romanticism of Monet's works, painted late in his life. Depicting Monet's 'jardin d'eau' at his house in Giverny, the *tableaux* have an intense, dreamy quality – partly reflecting the artist's absorption in the private world of his garden. Downstairs, the Jean Walter and Paul Guillaume collection of Impressionism and the Ecole de Paris is a mixed bag of sweet-toothed Cézanne and Renoir portraits, along with works by Modigliani, Rousseau, Matisse, Picasso and Derain. *Photos p72.*

SIGHTS

Musée de la Publicité

107 rue de Rivoli, 1st (01.44.55.57.50/www.les artsdecoratifs.fr). Mº Palais Royal Musée du Louvre or Pyramides. **Open** 11am-6pm Tue, Wed, Fri; 11am-9pm Thur; 10am-6pm Sat, Sun. **Admission** (with Musée des Arts Décoratifs & Musée de la Mode) €8; €6.50 reductions; free under-18s. PMP. **Credit** MC, V. **Map** p402 H5.

The upstairs element of the trio of museums in the Louvre west wing, the advertising museum has a distressed interior by Jean Nouvel. Only a fraction of the vast collection of posters, promotional objects and packaging can be seen at one time; vintage posters are accessed in the multimedia space.

★ FREE Palais-Royal

Pl du Palais-Royal, 1st. Mº Palais Royal Musée du Louvre. **Open** Gardens 7.30am-8.30pm daily. **Admission** free. **Map** p402 H5.

Built for Cardinal Richelieu by Jacques Lemercier, this building was once known as the Palais Cardinal. Richelieu left it to Louis XIII, whose widow Anne d'Autriche preferred it to the chilly Louvre and rechristened it when she moved in with her son, the young Louis XIV. In the 1780s the Duc d'Orléans, Louis XVI's fun-loving brother, enclosed the gardens in a three-storey peristyle and filled it with cafés, shops, theatres, sideshows and accommodation to raise money for rebuilding the burned-down opera. In stark contrast to Versailles, the Palais-Royal was a place where people of all classes could mingle, and its arcades became a trysting venue. Today, Daniel Buren's modern installation of black-and-white striped columns graces the main courtyard; the stately buildings around it house the Conseil d'Etat and ministry of culture.

FREE Place de la Concorde

1st/8th. Mº Concorde. **Map** p401 F5.

This is the city's largest square, its grand east-west perspectives stretching from the Louvre to the Arc de Triomphe, and north-south from the Madeleine to the Assemblée Nationale across the Seine. Royal architect Gabriel designed it in the 1750s, along with the two colonnaded mansions astride rue Royale; the west one houses the chic Hôtel de Crillon (*see p157*) and the Automobile Club de France, the other is the Naval Ministry. In 1792 the centre statue of Louis XV was replaced with the guillotine that would be used on Louis XVI, Marie-Antoinette and many more. The square was embellished in the 19th century with sturdy lampposts, the Luxor obelisk (from the Viceroy of Egypt), and ornate tiered fountains that represent navigation by water.

FREE Place Vendôme

1st. Mº Opéra or Tuileries. **Map** p401 G4.

Elegant place Vendôme got its name from a *hôtel particulier* built by the Duc de Vendôme that stood on the site. Opened in 1699, the eight-sided square was conceived by Hardouin-Mansart to show off an equestrian statue of the Sun King, torn down in 1792 and replaced in 1806 by the Colonne de la Grande Armée. Modelled on Trajan's Column in Rome and featuring a spiral comic strip illustrating Napoleon's military exploits, it was made from 1,250 Russian and Austrian cannons captured at the Battle of Austerlitz. During the 1871 Commune

Musée de l'Orangerie. *See p71.*

this symbol of 'brute force and false glory' was pulled down; the present column is a replica. Hardouin-Mansart only designed the façades, with their ground-floor arcade and giant Corinthian pilasters; the buildings behind were put up by nobles and speculators. Today the square houses sparkling jewellers, top fashion houses and the justice ministry. At no.12, you can visit the Grand Salon where Chopin died in 1849; its fabulous allegorical decoration dates from 1777 and has been restored as part of the new museum above the jewellers Chaumet (01.44.77.26.26).

THE BOURSE

In the 1st & 2nd arrondissements.

Far less frenzied than Wall Street, the city's traditional business district is squeezed between the elegant calm of the Palais-Royal and shopping hub the Grands Boulevards. Along rue du Quatre-Septembre, **La Bourse** (the stock exchange) is where financiers and stockbrokers beaver away in grandiose buildings. The Banque de France, France's national central bank, has occupied the 17th-century **Hôtel de Toulouse** since 1811, its long gallery still hung with Old Masters. Nearby, fashion and finance meet at stylish **place des Victoires**, designed by Hardouin-Mansart, forming an intimate circle of buildings today dedicated to fashion.

West of the square is shop-lined galerie Vivienne, the smartest of the covered passages

in Paris, adjoining galerie Colbert. Also look out for temporary exhibitions at the **Bibliothèque Nationale de France – Richelieu**. You can linger at the luxury food and wine merchant **Legrand** (*see p263*), or head along passage des Petits-Pères to admire the 17th- to 18th-century **Eglise Notre-Dame-des-Victoires**, the remains of an Augustine convent with a cycle of paintings around the choir by Carle van Loo.

Rue de la Banque leads to the Bourse, behind a commanding neo-classical colonnade. The area has a relaxed feel – it's dead at weekends – but animated pockets exist at places such as **Le Vaudeville** (29 rue Vivienne, 2nd, 01.40.20.04.62) and **Gallopin** (40 rue Notre-Dame-des-Victoires, 2nd, 01.42.36.45.38), busy brasseries frequented by stockbrokers and journalists. Rue des Colonnes is a quiet street lined with graceful porticoes and acanthus motifs dating from the 1790s; its design nemesis, the 1970s concrete-and-glass HQ of Agence France-Presse, the nation's biggest news agency, stands on the other side of busy rue du Quatre-Septembre. Although most newspaper offices have moved elsewhere, *Le Figaro* is still based in rue du Louvre.

★ Bibliothèque Nationale de France – Richelieu & Musée du Cabinet des Médailles
58 rue de Richelieu, 2nd (01.53.79.59.59/ www.bnf.fr). M° Bourse. **Open** *Galeries Mansart/Mazarine, exhibitions only 10am-*

SIGHTS

Walk Rest in Pieces

From Voltaire's heart to Sainte Geneviève's finger bone, Paris is full of grisly relics.

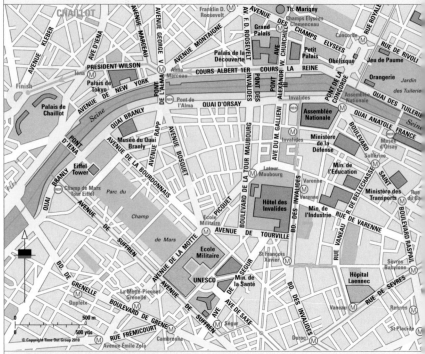

Paris has some of history's most influential characters buried on its soil; the Père-Lachaise cemetery alone shelters hundreds of writers, artists and politicians. But these are the lucky ones. Other famous figures did not always get to their final resting place in one piece. This itinerary uncovers some of the city's more macabre relics.

Start on place du Palais-Royal, 1st. Turn your back on the Louvre and walk into the **Comédie Française** (2 rue de Richelieu, 1st). In the foyer, look out for an old armchair inside a glass cage. It is believed to be the one from which Molière delivered his last lines at a performance of *Le Malade Imaginaire* in 1673. He died shortly after the curtain fell. In the same room, the statue of an old man regards theatregoers with a sarcastic smile. You may recognise Voltaire, the Enlightenment philosopher, immortalised here by sculptor Jean-Antoine Houdon. But this statue also serves as reliquary for the

philosopher's brain, sealed inside its pedestal. After Voltaire's death in 1778, his brain and heart were put in boiling alcohol to solidify them. His brain finally ended up at the Comédie in 1924.

In 1791, his heart was given to Napoleon III, who decided to keep it at the Imperial Library, now the **Bibliothèque Nationale – Richelieu**. Walk to the entrance at 58 rue de Richelieu, around the corner from the Comédie, and ask to see the *salon d'honneur*, an impressive oak-panelled room presided over by a statue of Voltaire identical to the one at the Comédie. The heart is enclosed in its wooden pedestal.

The next destination is on the Left Bank – an opportunity to test out the Vélib municipal bike scheme (*see p367*). There is a *borne* opposite the library, at 71 rue de Richelieu.

Head south and turn left into rue des Petits Champs. Cycle across place des Victoires and turn right into rue du Louvre.

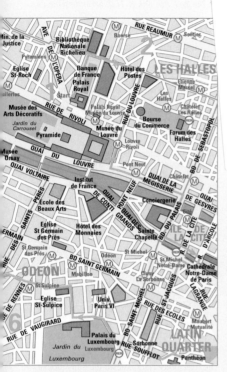

7pm Tue-Sat; noon-7pm Sun. *Cabinet des Médailles* 1-5.45pm Mon-Fri; 1-4.45pm Sat; noon-6pm Sun. **Admission** *Galeries/Cabinet des Médailles* free. **Credit** MC, V. **Map** p402 H4.

The history of the French Nation in the 1660s, when Louis couldn't be housed XIII townhouse Cardinal Mar the public many ne Neve

...Chapelle des Lazaristes, identifiable by its tall green doors next to no.95 rue de Sèvres, and climb up the stairs to the side of the altar. Here lies the fresh-looking corpse of Saint Vincent de Paul, patron saint of the poor. While his skeleton was preserved in its entirety, his face and hands were covered in wax and moulded to resemble the deceased, giving the disturbing impression that he passed away only minutes ago.

Pick up a Vélib at the *borne* on rue Vaneau and head north. Turn left into rue de Babylone and then right into boulevard des Invalides. Keep cycling towards the Seine, with the golden dome of **Les Invalides** (*see p141*) on your left – it's the last resting place of Napoleon. The emperor could easily win the title of most scattered cadaver in history. While his heart and innards are in Austria, you will need to travel to New York to get near his penis, bought at auction by a urologist for $3,800.

Next, from quai d'Orsay, cross the Pont Alexandre III and turn left on to cours Albert I. At place de l'Alma, take avenue du Président Wilson on your right. Carry on to place du Trocadéro. You can dispose of your bike at the Vélib *borne* on avenue d'Eylau, third right on the roundabout.

The **Musée de l'Homme** (17 place du Trocadéro, 16th, currently closed for refurbishment) is home to philosopher René Descartes' skull. The rest of his body is buried on the Left Bank, which makes the perfect start to another trek. But by now you will probably have had your share of gravestones for the day. Time to take a seat in the Café de l'Homme, order a coffee and enjoy one of the best views there is of the city. Chances are you've never felt more alive.

Follow the traffic down to the river, and turn left on to quai du Louvre. Carry on to Pont au Change. Once on the island, keep going south, and turn left on to quai du Marché Neuf. Go straight ahead until you're facing Notre-Dame cathedral. Drop your bike at the *borne* beside the square, on rue d'Arcole.

Head south across Pont au Double. On quai de Montebello, walk around the small park in front of you and take rue de la Bûcherie. Find rue St-Jacques at the end of rue de la Bûcherie and walk down to rue Soufflot. The columns of the **Panthéon** (*see p120*) should be clear to see on your left. The crypt gathers the shrines of over 70 illustrious Frenchmen, including Victor Hugo, Alexandre Dumas and our old friend Voltaire, whose carcass – or what remains of it – can finally rest in peace here.

A somewhat more sensational relic can be found in the **Eglise St-Etienne-du-Mont** (*see p119*), just around the corner from the

ational Library began in
...IV moved manuscripts that
...the Louvre to this lavish Louis
...formerly the private residence of
...rin. The library was first opened to
...n 1692, and by 1724 it had received so
...w acquisitions that the adjoining Hôtel de
...s had to be added.

Some of the original painted decoration by Romanelli and Grimaldi can still be seen in Galeries Mansart and Mazarine, now used for temporary exhibitions (and closed otherwise). The highlights, however, are the two circular reading rooms: the Salle Ovale, which is full of researchers, note-takers and readers, and the magnificent Salle de Travail, a temple to learning, with its arrangement of nine domes supported on slender columns clearly influenced by the Ottoman architecture of the Levant. The latter is now hauntingly empty, as most of its books have been moved to the Bibliothèque Nationale de France – François Mitterrand (see p124).

On the first floor is the Musée du Cabinet des Médailles, a modest two-room collection of coins and medals, including Greek, Roman and medieval examples. There is also a miscellany of other items, including Merovingian king Dagobert's throne, Charlemagne's chess set and small artefacts from the Classical world and ancient Egypt.

La Bourse

Palais Brongniart, pl de la Bourse, 2nd (01.49.27.14.70/http://palaisbourse.euronext. com). M° Bourse. **Open** Guided tours only; call 1 wk in advance. **Admission** €8.50; €5.50 reductions. **No credit cards. Map** p402 H4.
After a century at the Louvre, the Palais-Royal and rue Vivienne, in 1826 the Stock Exchange was transferred to the Bourse, a dignified testament to First Empire classicism designed at Napoleon's behest by Alexandre Brongniart. It was enlarged in 1906 to create a cruciform interior, where brokers buzzed around a central enclosure known as the *corbeille* ('basket' or 'trading floor'). Computers have made the design obsolete, but the pace remains frenetic.

FREE Place des Victoires

1st, 2nd. M° Bourse. **Map** p402 H5.
This circular square, the first of its kind, was designed by Hardouin-Mansart in 1685 to show off a statue of Louis XIV that marked victories against Holland. The original statue was destroyed after the Revolution (although the massive slaves from its base are now in the Louvre), and replaced in 1822 with an equestrian statue by Bosio. Among the occupants of the grand buildings that encircle the 'square' are fashion boutiques Kenzo and Victoire.

OPERA & GRANDS BOULEVARDS

In the 2nd, 8th, 9th & 10th arrondissements.

Opéra & Madeleine

Charles Garnier's wedding-cake **Palais Garnier** is all gilt and grandeur, as an opera house should be. Garnier was also responsible for the ritzy **Café de la Paix** (see p220) and the **InterContinental Paris Le Grand** (see p161) overlooking place de l'Opéra. Behind, in the basement of what is now the Hôtel Scribe, the Lumière brothers held the world's first public cinema screening in 1895. Outfitter **Old England** (no.12, 9th, 01.47.42.81.99), just opposite on boulevard des Capucines, with its wooden counters, Jacobean-style ceilings and old-style goods and service, could have served as their costume consultants. The **Olympia** concert hall (see p322), the celebrated host of the Beatles, Piaf and anyone in *chanson*, was knocked down, but rose again nearby. Over the road at no.35, pioneering portrait photographer Nadar opened a studio in the 1860s, frequented by the likes of Dumas père, Offenbach and Doré. In 1874, it hosted the first Impressionists' exhibition. Pedestrianised rue Edouard VII, laid out in 1911, leads to the octagonal square of the same name with Landowski's equestrian statue of the English monarch. Through an arch, another square contains the belle époque **Théâtre de l'Athénée-Louis Jouvet**.

The **Madeleine**, a monument to Napoleon's army, guards the end of the boulevard. At the head of rue Royale, its classical portico mirrors the Assemblée Nationale on the other side of place de la Concorde over the river, and the interior is a riot of marble and altars. Well worth a browse is extravagant delicatessen **Fauchon** (see p265) and other luxury food shops; here, too, is haute cuisine restaurant **Senderens** (see p197).

Landmark department stores **Printemps** (see p239) and the **Galeries Lafayette** (see p239), which opened just behind the Palais Garnier in the late 19th century, also merit investigation. Behind the latter stands the Lycée Caumartin, designed as a convent in the 1780s by Bourse architect Brongniart, and later one of the city's most prestigious schools. West along boulevard Haussmann is a small square containing the **Chapelle Expiatoire** dedicated to Louis XVI and Marie-Antoinette.

★ Chapelle Expiatoire

29 rue Pasquier, 8th (01.44.32.18.00). M° St-Augustin. **Open** 1-5pm Thur-Sat. **Admission** €5; €3.50 reductions; free under-18s. PMP. **Map** p401 F3.

The chapel was commissioned by Louis XVIII in memory of his executed predecessors, his brother Louis XVI and Marie-Antoinette. Their remains, along with those of 3,000 victims of the Revolution, including Camille Desmoulins, Danton, Malesherbes and Lavoisier, were found in 1814 on the spot where the altar stands. The year after, the bodies of Louis XVI and Marie-Antoinette were transferred to the Basilique St-Denis; the pair are now represented by marble statues, kneeling at the feet of Religion. Every January ardent (albeit unfulfilled) royalists gather here for a memorial service.

FREE Eglise de la Madeleine

Pl de la Madeleine, 8th (01.44.51.69.00/ www.eglise-lamadeleine.com). M° Concorde or Madeleine. **Open** 9.30am-7pm daily. **Admission** free. **Map** p401 G4.

The building of a church on this site began in 1764, and in 1806 Napoleon sent instructions from Poland for Barthélémy Vignon to design a 'Temple of Glory' dedicated to his Grand Army. After the emperor's fall, construction slowed and the building, by now a church again, was finally consecrated in 1845. The exterior is ringed by huge, fluted Corinthian columns, with a double row at the front, and a frieze of the Last Judgement just above the portico. Inside are giant domes, an organ and pseudo-Grecian side altars in a sea of multicoloured marble. The painting by Ziegler in the chancel depicts the history of Christianity, with Napoleon prominent in the foreground. It's a favourite venue for society weddings. *Photos p79.*

FREE Eglise St-Augustin

46 bd Malesherbes, 8th (01.45.22.23.12). M° St-Augustin. **Open** *Sept-June* 8.15am-7pm Mon-Fri; 8.30am-noon, 2.30-7.30pm Sat; 8.30am-12.30pm, 4-7.30pm Sun. *July, Aug* 10am-12.45pm, 4-7pm Tue-Fri; 10am-noon, 3-7.30pm Sat; 10am-noon, 3-7.30pm Sun. **Admission** free. **Map** p401 F3.

St-Augustin, designed between 1860 and 1871 by Victor Baltard, architect of the defunct Les Halles pavilions, is not what it seems. The domed, neo-Renaissance stone exterior is merely a shell: inside is an iron vault structure; even the decorative angels are cast in metal. Impressive paintings by Adolphe William Bouguereau hang in the transept.

Musée de la Franc-Maçonnerie

16 rue Cadet, 9th (01.45.23.43.97/www.godf.org). M° Cadet. **Open** 2-6pm Tue-Fri; 1-5pm Sat. Closed 2wks July, Aug, 1wk Sept. **Admission** €2; free under-12s. **No credit cards**. **Map** p402 H3.

Tucked away at the back of the French Masonic Great Lodge, this museum opened in 1973. It traces the history of French freemasonry, ranging from information on stonemasons' guilds to prints of masons General Lafayette and the 1848 revolutionary leaders Blanc and Barbès.

Musée de l'Opéra

Palais Garnier, 1 pl de l'Opéra, 9th (01.53.79.37.47/www.bnf.fr). M° Opéra. **Open** *Oct-June* 10am-5pm daily. *July-Sept* 10am-6pm Mon-Fri, Sun; 10am-5pm Sat. **Admission** €7; €5 reductions; free under-10s. **No credit cards**. **Map** p401 G4.

The Palais Garnier houses temporary exhibitions relating to current opera or ballet productions, along with a permanent collection of paintings, scores and bijou opera sets housed in period cases. The entrance fee includes a visit to the auditorium, if rehearsals permit.

FREE Musées des Parfumeries-Fragonard

9 rue Scribe, 9th (01.47.42.04.56) & 39 bd des Capucines, 2nd (01.42.60.37.14). M° Opéra. **Open** 9am-6pm Mon-Sat; 9am-5pm Sun. **Admission** free. **Map** p401 G4.

Two museums showcase the collection of perfume house Fragonard: five rooms at rue Scribe range from Ancient Egyptian ointment flasks to Meissen porcelain scent bottles; the second museum has bottles by Lalique and Schiaparelli.

★ Palais Garnier

1 pl de l'Opéra, 9th (08.92.89.90.90/www. operadeparis.fr). M° Opéra. **Open** 10am-6pm daily. *Guided tours in English (08.25.05.44.05)* July, Aug 11.30am & 2.30pm daily. Sept-June Wed, Sat & Sun. **Admission** €8; €4 reductions. *Guided tours* €12; €6-€10 reductions. **Credit** AmEx, MC, V. **Map** p401 G4.

The Palais Garnier is a monument to Second Empire high society. The comfortably upholstered auditorium seats more than 2,000 people – and the exterior is just as opulent, with sculptures of music and dance on the façade, Apollo topping the copper dome, and nymphs bearing torches. Carpeaux's sculpture *La Danse* shocked Parisians with its frank sensuality: in 1869, someone threw a bottle of ink over its marble thighs. The original is now safe in the Musée d'Orsay, where there's also a massive scale model of the building. The Grand Foyer, with its mirrors and parquet, coloured marble, moulded stucco, sculptures and paintings by Baudry, have all been magnificently restored. You can also visit the Grand Escalier, the auditorium with a false ceiling painted by Chagall in 1964, red satin and velvet boxes, and the library and museum – it was once the emperor's private salons, where he could arrive directly by carriage on the ramp at the rear of the building.

Quartier de l'Europe

Its streets named after European cities, the area from Gare St-Lazare towards place de Clichy was the Impressionists' quarter. In those days it epitomised modernity, with the station, which opened in 1837, serving the line from Paris to St-Germain-en-Laye (it was rebuilt in the 1880s). The long shabby commuter hub has had a revamp; a glass dome now disgorges travellers from the métro interchange. The adjoining **Hôtel Concorde St-Lazare** (*see p159*) was the city's first great station hotel, with a grandiose hallway built by Eiffel in 1889 for visitors to the Exposition Universelle as he was putting up his Tower. Monet, who lived nearby in rue d'Edimbourg, depicted the steam age in *La Gare St-Lazare* and *Pont de l'Europe*; Pissarro and Caillebotte painted views of the new boulevards, and Manet had a studio on rue de St-Petersbourg. Rue de Budapest remains a red-light district; rue de Rome has long been home to stringed-instrument makers. East of St-Lazare stands the **Eglise de la Trinité**.

FREE Eglise de la Trinité

Pl Estienne-d'Orves, 9th (01.48.74.12.77). M° Trinité. **Open** 7.15am-8pm Mon-Fri; 9am-8.30pm Sat, Sun. **Admission** free. **Map** p401 G3.
Noted for its tiered bell tower, this neo-Renaissance church was constructed between 1861 and 1867.
▶ *Composer Olivier Messiaen (1908-92) was organist at the church for over 30 years.*

The Grands Boulevards

Contrary to popular belief, the string of Grands Boulevards between Madeleine and République (des Italiens, Montmartre, Poissonnière, Bonne-Nouvelle, St-Denis, St-Martin) was not built by Baron Haussmann, but by Louis XIV in 1670, replacing the fortifications of King Philippe-Auguste's city wall. Their ramparts have left their traces in the strange changes of levels, with stairways climbing up to side streets at the eastern end. The boulevards burgeoned after the French Revolution, as residences, theatres and covered passages were put up on land taken from aristocrats and monasteries. To this day they offer a glimpse of the city's divergent personalities – a stroll from Opéra to République runs from luxury shops via St-Denis prostitutes – and the phrase *théâtre des boulevards* is still used for lowbrow theatre. Between boulevard des Italiens and rue de Richelieu is place Boïeldieu and the **Opéra Comique** (*see p318*), where Bizet's *Carmen* had its première in 1875.

The 18th-century Hôtel d'Angny, now the town hall of the ninth arrondissement, was once home to the infamous *bals des victimes*, where every guest had to have a relative who had lost his or her head to the guillotine. The **Hôtel Drouot** auction house is ringed by antiques shops, coin- and stamp-dealers and wine bar Les Caves Drouot, where auctiongoers and valuers congregate.

There are several grand *hôtels particuliers* on rue de la Grange-Batelière, which leads on one side down the curious passage Verdeau, occupied by antiques dealers, and on the other back to the boulevards via passage Jouffroy. With its grand, barrel-vaulted glass-and-iron roof, this is home to the lovely **Hôtel Chopin** (*see p161*), shop windows of doll's houses, antique walking sticks, art books and film posters, and the colourful entrance of the **Grévin** waxworks (*see p286*).

Over the boulevard, passage des Panoramas is the oldest remaining covered arcade in Paris. When it opened in 1800, panoramas – vast illuminated circular paintings – of Rome, Jerusalem, London and other cities drew large crowds. Today it contains tearoom **L'Arbre à Cannelle** (no.57, 2nd, 01.45.08.55.87), coin- and stamp-sellers, furniture-makers and old-fashioned printer **Stern** (no.47), established in 1840. The passage leads into a tangle of other little passages and the stage door of the **Théâtre des Variétés** (7 bd Montmartre, 2nd, 01.42.33.09.92), a pretty neo-classical theatre where Offenbach premièred *La Belle Hélène*.

Rue du Fbg-Montmartre is home to celebrated belle époque *bouillon* **Chartier** (no.7, 9th, 01.47.70.86.29), which serves up hundreds of meals a day to the budget-minded. The street is also part of a significant Jewish quarter, less well known than the Marais, that grew up in the 19th century. There are several kosher bakers, restaurants and France's largest synagogue at 44 rue de la Victoire (01.40.82.26.26), an opulent Second Empire affair completed in 1876. Cobbled Cité Bergère, constructed in 1825 with desirable residences, now houses budget hotels, though the pretty iron-and-glass *portes-cochères* remain. On rue Richer stands the art deco **Folies-Bergère** (no.32, 9th, 08.92.68.16.50), only sporadically used for cabaret revues. To the south of boulevard Bonne-Nouvelle lies **Sentier**, and to the north rue du Fbg-Poissonnière is a mixture of rag-trade outlets and *hôtels particuliers*.

Back on the boulevard is evidence of a move north of the Marais by trendsetting hubs, including **Rex** and chic **De la Ville Café** (*see p223*). East of here are Louis XIV's twin triumphal arches, the **Porte St-Martin** and **Porte St-Denis**, which were erected to commemorate his military victories.

★ Le Grand Rex

1 bd Poissonnière, 2nd (01.45.08.93.58/ reservations 08.92.68.05.96/www.legrandrex. com). M° Bonne Nouvelle. **Tour** *Les Etoiles du Rex* every 5mins 10am-7pm Wed-Sun; daily during school hols. **Admission** €9.80; €8 reductions. *Tour & film* €14.80; €12 reductions. **Credit** AmEx, MC, V. **Map** p402 J4.

SIGHTS

Eglise de la Madeleine. *See p77.*

Opened in 1932, this huge art deco cinema was designed by Auguste Bluysen with fantasy Hispanic interiors by US designer John Eberson. Go behind the scenes in the crazy 50-minute guided tour (*see p286*), which includes a presentation about the construction of the auditorium and a visit to the production room, complete with nerve-jolting Sensurround effects.

Hôtel Drouot

9 rue Drouot, 9th (01.48.00.20.20/www. drouot.fr). M° Richelieu Drouot. **Open** 11am-6pm Mon-Sat. **Auctions** 2pm Mon-Sat. **Map** p402 H3.

A spiky aluminium-and-marble concoction is the unlikely location for France's second largest art market – though it is now rivalled by Sotheby's and Christie's. Inside, escalators take you up to a number of small salerooms, where everything from medieval manuscripts and antique furniture to oriental arts, modern paintings, posters, jewellery and fine wines might be up for sale. Details of forthcoming auctions are published in the weekly *Gazette de l'Hôtel Drouot*, sold at various newsstands around the city. **Other locations** Drouot-Montaigne, 15 av Montaigne, 8th (01.48.00.20.80); Drouot-Montmartre, 64 rue Doudeauville, 18th (01.48.00.20.99).

FREE Porte St-Denis & Porte St-Martin

Rue St-Denis/bd St-Denis, 2nd/10th; 33 bd St-Martin, 3rd/10th. M° Strasbourg St-Denis. **Map** p402 K4.

These twin triumphal gates were erected in 1672 and 1674 at important entry points to the city as part of Colbert's strategy to glorify Paris and celebrate Louis XIV's victories on the Rhine. They are modelled on the triumphal arches of Ancient Rome. The Porte St-Denis is based on a perfect square with a single arch, bearing Latin inscriptions and decorated with military trophies and battle scenes. Porte St-Martin bears allegorical reliefs of Louis XIV's campaigns.

LES HALLES & SENTIER

In the 1st & 2nd arrondissements.

Les Halles is an ugly nexus of commerce and entertainment, with a massive RER-métro interchange as its centrepiece. The area is due for a makeover in the next few years, however.

For centuries, Les Halles was the city's wholesale food market. Covered markets were set up here in 1181 by King Philippe-Auguste; in the 1850s Baltard's spectacular cast-iron and glass pavilions were erected. In 1969 the market was relocated to the southern suburb of Rungis. Baltard's ten pavilions were knocked down (one was saved and now stands at Nogent-sur-Marne), leaving a giant hole. After a long political dispute, it

---

INSIDE TRACK JEAN JAURES

On the corner of rue Montmartre and rue du Croissant, take a look at the Café du Croissant where the charismatic leader of the Socialist party, Jean Jaurès, was assassinated in 1914. At 9.40pm on 31 July, the aptly named Raoul Villain leaned in through an open window of the café and aimed his revolver at the bearded Jaurès. One shot went wide, but the other hit Jaurès in the head, and he died within minutes.

---

was filled in the early 1980s by the miserably designed **Forum des Halles** underground shopping and transport hub, and the unloved Jardin des Halles.

East of the Forum, in the middle of place Joachim-du-Bellay, stands the **Renaissance Fontaine des Innocents**. The canopied fountain has swirling stone reliefs of water nymphs and titans by Jean Goujon (the ones you see today are copies; the originals are in the Louvre). It was inaugurated for Henri II's arrival in Paris in 1549 on the traditional royal route along rue St-Denis. It was moved and reconstructed here when the nearby Cimetière des Innocents, the city's main burial ground, was demolished in 1786, after flesh-eating rats started gnawing into people's living rooms; the bones were transferred to the catacombs.

Pedestrianised rue des Lombards is a beacon of live jazz, with **Sunset/Sunside**, **Baiser Salé** and **Au Duc des Lombards** (for all, *see p324-25*) from which to choose. In 1610, King Henri IV was assassinated by a Catholic fanatic named François Ravaillac on nearby rue de la Ferronnerie. Today, the street has become an extension of the Marais gay circuit.

The ancient, easternmost stretch of rue St-Honoré runs into the southern edge of Les Halles. The Fontaine du Trahoir stands at the corner with rue de l'Arbre-Sec. Opposite, the **Hôtel de Truden** (52 rue de l'Arbre-Sec) was built in 1717 for a rich wine merchant; in the courtyard on rue des Prouvaires, the market-traders' favourite **La Tour de Montlhéry** (*see p194*) serves up meaty fare through the night. Fashion chains line the commercial stretch of the rue de Rivoli south of Les Halles. Running towards the Seine, ancient little streets such as rue des Lavandiers-Ste-Opportune and rue Jean-Lantier show a different side of Les Halles. Between rue de Rivoli and the Pont Neuf is department store La Samaritaine, currently closed for safety reasons. Next door, a former section of it contains the chic **Kenzo** flagship store. From here, quai de la

Mégisserie, lined with horticultural suppliers and pet shops, leads towards Châtelet.

Looming over the northern edge of the Jardin des Halles is the massive **Eglise St-Eustache**, with Renaissance motifs inside and chunky flying buttresses outside. At the western end of the gardens is the circular, domed **Bourse de Commerce**. In front of it, an astrological column is all that remains from a grand palace belonging to Marie de Médicis that stood here.

The empire of French designer **Agnès b** (*see p253*) stretches along most of rue du Jour, with streetwise outlets such as **Kiliwatch** (*see p255*) clustered along the buzzing rue Tiquetonne. On rue Etienne-Marcel, the restored **Tour Jean Sans Peur** is a weird Gothic relic of the fortified medieval townhouse of Jean Sans Peur, duke of Burgundy.

Busy, pedestrianised rue Montorgueil is lined with grocers, delicatessens and pavement cafés. Some historic façades remain from when this was an area in which the well-heeled and the working class mingled: **Pâtisserie Stohrer** (no.51, 2nd, 01.42.33.38.20), founded in 1730 and credited with the invention of the sugary *puits d'amour*; **Le Rocher de Cancale** (no.78, 01.42.33.50.29); and, back towards Les Halles, the golden snail sign hanging in front of **L'Escargot Montorgueil** (no.38, 01.42.36.83. 51), a restaurant established in 1832.

Stretching north, bordered by boulevard de Bonne-Nouvelle to the north and boulevard Sébastopol to the east, lies Sentier, the historic garment district, and cocky rue St-Denis, which has long relied on strumpets and strip joints. The grime is unremitting along its northern continuation, rue du Fbg-St-Denis.

Rue Réaumur is lined with striking art nouveau buildings, constructed as industrial premises in the early 1900s. Between rue des Petits-Carreaux and rue St-Denis is the site of the medieval Cour des Miracles – a refuge where paupers would 'miraculously' regain use of their eyes or limbs. A disused aristocratic estate, it was a sanctuary for the underworld until it was cleared out in 1667.

Sentier's streets and passages buzz with porters shouldering linen bundles, as sweatshops churn out passable copies of catwalk creations. Streets such as rue du Caire, rue d'Aboukir and rue du Nil reflect the Egyptian craze that followed Napoleon's Egyptian campaign in 1798 and 1799 – look out too for the sphinx heads and mock hieroglyphics at 2 place du Caire.

FREE Bourse de Commerce

2 rue de Viarmes, 1st (01.55.65.55.65). M° Louvre Rivoli. **Open** *tour groups* 9am-6pm Mon-Fri. **Admission** free. **Map** p402 J5.
Housing the Paris chamber of commerce, this trade centre for coffee and sugar was built as a grain

market in 1767. The circular building was then covered by a wooden dome, replaced by an avant-garde iron structure in 1809. It is sadly underused.

FREE Eglise St-Eustache

Rue du Jour, 1st (01.42.36.31.05/www.saint-eustache.org). M° Les Halles. **Open** 9am-7.30pm daily. **Admission** free. **Map** p402 J5.
This massive, barn-like church, built between 1532 and 1640, has a Gothic structure but Renaissance decoration in its façade and Corinthian capitals. Among the paintings in the side chapels are a *Descent from the Cross* by Luca Giordano; contemporary pieces by John Armleder were added in 2000. Murals by Thomas Couture adorn the 19th-century Lady chapel. There is a magnificent 8,000-pipe organ, and free recitals are held at 5.30pm on Sundays.

FREE Forum des Halles

1st. M° Les Halles/RER Châtelet Les Halles. **Admission** free. **Map** p402 J5.
The labyrinthine mall and transport interchange extends three levels underground and includes the Ciné Cité multiplex cinema and the Forum des Images, as well as shops and the Forum des Créateurs, a section for young designers. Despite an open central courtyard, a sense of gloom prevails. All should change by 2012, with a new landscaping of the whole area.

Pavillon des Arts

Les Halles, 101 rue Rambuteau, 1st (01.42.33. 82.50). M° Châtelet. **Open** 11.30am-6.30pm Tue-Sun. **Admission** €5.50; €2.50-€4 reductions; free under-14s. **No credit cards. Map** p402 K5.
This gallery in Les Halles hosts exhibitions on anything from photography to local history.

★ Tour Jean Sans Peur

20 rue Etienne-Marcel, 2nd (01.40.26.20.28/ www.tourjeansanspeur.com). M° Etienne Marcel. **Open** *Nov-Mar* 1.30-6pm Wed, Sat, Sun. *Apr-Oct* 1.30-6pm Wed-Sun. Tour 3pm. **Admission** €5; €3 reductions; free under-7s. *Tour* €8. **No credit cards. Map** p402 J5.
This Gothic turret (1409-11) is the remnant of the townhouse of Jean Sans Peur, duke of Burgundy. He was responsible for the assassination of his rival Louis d'Orléans, which sparked the Hundred Years' War and saw Burgundy become allied to the English crown. Jean had this show-off tower added to his mansion to protect him from vengeance by the aggrieved widow and her husband's followers, known as the 'Armagnacs'. In 1419 he was assassinated by a partisan of the dauphin, the future Charles VII. You can climb the tower, which has rooms leading off the stairway. Carved vaulting halfway up depicts naturalistic branches of oak, hawthorn and hops, symbols of Jean Sans Peur and Burgundian power. The huge mansion originally spanned Philippe-Auguste's city wall.

SIGHTS

Champs-Elysées & Western Paris

Hang with the platinum set in the city's golden triangle.

There seems to be an unwritten law in France that no mention of the capital's most famous thoroughfare can be made in print or broadcast media without immediately calling it *'la plus belle avenue du monde'*. In truth, it's not especially beautiful and it heaves with cars and crowds – especially the section west of the Rond-Point – at pretty much any time of the day. The hordes aren't here for beauty, though. They're here for the shops, which the avenue, after years in the retail doldrums, now supplies in upmarket abundance.

The posh shopping going on along and around the Champs is entirely in keeping with the prevailing wealth and grandeur in the eighth arrondissement, and in the adjoining 16th and 17th. But fortunately, in the midst of all this rampant consumerism and airy affluence are a good number of museums covering such cerebral topics as architecture, human evolution and life on the ocean waves.

Map pp400-401	**Restaurants** p195
Hotels p162	**Cafés & bars** p224

Map pp400-401 · Restaurants p195 · Hotels p162 · Cafés & bars p224

CHAMPS-ELYSEES

In the 8th & 16th arrondissements.

The Champs-Elysées is, and has long been, a symbolic gathering place. Sports victories, New Year's Eve, displays of military might on 14 July – all are celebrated here. Over the past decade, the avenue has undergone a renaissance, thanks initially to a facelift instigated by Jacques Chirac.

Chi-chi shops and chic hotels have set up in the 'golden triangle' (avenues George V, Montaigne and the Champs): **Louis Vuitton** (*see p247*), **Chanel** (*see p244*) and **Jean-Paul Gaultier** (*see p245*), the **Marriott** (70 av des Champs-Elysées, 8th, 01.53.93.55.00) and **Pershing Hall** (*see p165*). The **Four Seasons George V** (*see p162*) has undergone a revamp, and fashionable restaurants such as **Spoon, Food & Wine** (12 rue de Marignan,

8th, 01.40.76.34.44) draw affluent and screamingly fashionable crowds. Crowds line up for the glitzy **Le Lido** cabaret (*see p281*), the now commercialised **Queen** nightclub (*see p333*) and numerous cinemas, or stroll down the avenue to floodlit **place de la Concorde** (*see p72*). The famous **Drugstore Publicis** (*see p241*) is where locals head to stock up on late-night wines and groceries.

This great spine of western Paris started life as an extension to the Tuileries, laid out by Le Nôtre in the 17th century. By the Revolution, the avenue had reached its full extent, but it was during the Second Empire that it became a focus for fashionable society, military parades and royal processions. Bismarck was so impressed when he arrived with the conquering Prussian army in 1871 that he had a replica, the Ku'damm, built in Berlin, and Hitler's troops made a point of marching down it in 1940, as did their Allied counterparts four years later.

The lower, landscaped reach of the avenue hides two theatres and elegant restaurants **Laurent** (41 av Gabriel, 8th, 01.42.25.00.39) and **Ledoyen** (1 av Dutuit, 8th, 01.53.05.10.01), housed in fancy Napoleon III pavilions. At the Rond-Point des Champs-Elysées, no.7 (now the Artcurial gallery bookshop and auction house) and no.9 give visitors some idea of the magnificent mansions that once lined the avenue. From here on, it's platinum cards and lanky women aplenty, as avenue Montaigne rolls out a full deck of fashion houses.

Models and magnates nibble on the terrace at fashionable restaurant **L'Avenue** (no.41, 8th, 01.40.70.14.91). You can admire the lavish **Hôtel Plaza Athénée** (*see p165*) and Auguste Perret's innovative 1911-13 **Théâtre des Champs-Elysées** concert hall (*see p318*), with an auditorium painted by Maurice Denis and lights by Lalique.

South of the avenue, the glass-domed **Grand Palais** and Petit Palais, both built for the 1900 Exposition Universelle and still used for major art exhibitions, create a magnificent vista across the elaborate Pont Alexandre III to Les Invalides. The rear wing of the Grand Palais, opening on to avenue Franklin-D-Roosevelt, contains the **Palais de la Découverte** science museum.

To the north lie more smart shops, antiques dealers and bastions of officialdom; on circular place Beauvau, wrought-iron gates herald the Ministry of the Interior. The 18th-century Palais de l'Elysée, the official presidential residence, is at 55-57 rue du Fbg-St-Honoré.

Nearby, with gardens extending to avenue Gabriel, are the palatial **British Embassy** and ambassadorial residence, which was once the Hôtel Borghèse.

The western end of the Champs-Elysées is dominated by the **Arc de Triomphe** towering above place Charles-de-Gaulle, also known as L'Etoile. Built by Napoleon, the arch was modified to celebrate the Revolutionary armies. From the top, visitors can gaze over the square (commissioned later by Haussmann), with 12 avenues radiating out in all directions.

South of the arch, avenue Kléber leads to the monumental buildings and terraced gardens of the panoramic Trocadéro, now housing the aquarium and cinema, **Cinéaqua**. The vast 1930s **Palais de Chaillot** dominates the hill and houses four museums, plus the **Théâtre National de Chaillot** (*see p346*).

To the west of Chaillot, on avenue du Président-Wilson, are two major museums: the **Musée d'Art Moderne de la Ville de Paris** and the **Palais de Tokyo Site de Création Contemporaine** are both inside the the **de Tokyo** building. Opposite is the **Musée Galliera**, used for fashion exhibitions, and up the hill at place d'Iéna are the Asian and oriental art collections of the **Musée National des Arts Asiatiques – Guimet**.

Towards the Champs-Elysées, the former townhouse of avant-garde patron Marie-Laure de Noailles has been given a cheeky revamp. It now houses the **Galerie-Musée Baccarat**.

SIGHTS

Galerie-Musée Baccarat. *See p85*.

SIGHTS

Arch Revival

The Arc is now a triumph inside and out.

The **Arc de Triomphe** (*see right*) is the city's second most iconic monument after the Eiffel Tower – older, shorter, but far more symbolically important: indeed, the island on which it stands, in the centre of the vast traffic junction of l'Etoile, is the nearest thing to sacred ground in all of secular France, indelibly associated as it is with two of French history's greatest men. The first was the man who had it built. Napoleon ordered the Arc de Triomphe's construction in 1809 as a monument to the achievements of his armies, but he never lived to see it finished: the arch was only completed in 1836 (although the emperor did view a full-size wood and canvas mock-up when he entered the city with his new wife Marie-Louise of Austria in 1810). Nonetheless, it bears the names of Napoleon's victories and key military subordinates, and is decorated on its flanks with a frieze of battle scenes and sculptures, including Rude's famous *Le Départ des Volontaires* (aka La Marseillaise).

The Arc has had martial associations ever since: victorious French troops paraded through it at the end of World War I, and the tomb of the Unknown Soldier lies under its centre, below an eternal flame that is relit in a solemn ceremony every evening. The man who relit it on 26 August 1944 is the Arc's other great figure, Charles de Gaulle, who followed the reignition ceremony with an iconic triumphal march through Paris; the text of his famous 1940 radio broadcast from London is immortalised in a bronze plaque in the ground.

Despite such grand associations, until recently the interior of the Arc was far less impressive, having changed little since the 1930s. As Jean-Paul Ciret, director of cultural development for France's national monuments, put it: 'The way we were showing the Arc to visitors was not worthy of an important landmark. There was no light inside, and the ceiling was dirty.' So in 2008, after a revamp by architect Christophe Girault and artist Maurice Benayouna, an impressive new museum opened with interactive screens and multimedia displays allowing visitors to look at other famous arches throughout Europe and the world, as well as screens exploring the Arc's tumultuous 200-year history, before heading up to the roof and taking in one of the finest views in the city.

★ Arc de Triomphe
Pl Charles-de-Gaulle (access via underpass), 8th (01.55.37.73.77). M° Charles de Gaulle Etoile. **Open** *Oct-Mar* 10am-10.30pm daily. *Apr-Sept* 10am-11pm daily. **Admission** €9; €5.50 reductions; free under-18s. PMP. **Credit** AmEx, MC, V. **Map** p400 C3.
See left **Arch Revival***.

FREE Cimetière de Passy
2 rue du Commandant-Schloesing, 16th (01.53.70.40.80). M° Trocadéro. **Open** *16 Mar-5 Nov* 8am-5.30pm Mon-Fri; 8.30am-5.30pm Sat; 9am-5.30pm Sun. *6 Nov-15 Mar* 8am-6pm Mon-Fri; 8.30am-6pm Sat; 9am-6pm Sun. **Admission** free. **Map** p400 B5.
Since 1874, this cemetery has been one of the most desirable Paris locations in which to be laid to rest. Here you'll find composers Debussy and Fauré, painters Manet and his sister-in-law Berthe Morisot, writer Giraudoux, along with various generals and politicians.

★ Cinéaqua
2 av des Nations Unies, 16th (01.40.69.23.23/ www.cineaqua.com). M° Trocadéro. **Open** 10am-8pm daily. **Admission** €19.50; €12.50-€15 reductions; free under-3s. **Credit** MC, V. **Map** p400 B5.
This aquarium and three-screen cinema is a wonderful attraction and a key element in the renaissance of the once moribund Trocadéro. Many people have baulked at the admission price, though.

★ Cité de l'Architecture et du Patrimoine
Palais de Chaillot, 1 pl du Trocadéro, 16th (01.58.51.52.00/www.citechaillot.fr). M° Trocadéro. **Open** 11am-7pm Mon, Wed, Fri-Sun; 11am-9pm Thur. **Admission** €8; €5 reductions; free under-18s. **Credit** MC, V. **Map** p400 B5.
Opened in 2007 in the eastern wing of the Palais de Chaillot, this architecture and heritage museum impresses principally by its scale. The expansive ground floor is filled with life-size mock-ups of cathedral façades and heritage buildings, and interactive screens place the models in context. Upstairs, darkened rooms house full-scale copies of medieval and Renaissance murals and stained-glass windows. The highlight of the modern architecture section is the walk-in replica of an apartment from Le Corbusier's Cité Radieuse in Marseille. Temporary exhibitions are housed in the large basement area.

FREE Fondation d'Enterprise Paul Ricard
12 rue Boissy d'Anglas, 8th (01.53.30.88.00/ www.fondation-entreprise-ricard.com). M° Concorde. **Open** 10am-7pm Mon-Fri. **Admission** free. **Map** p401 F4.

The Pastis firm promotes modern art with the Prix Paul Ricard, where young French artists are shortlisted by an independent curator for an annual prize.
▶ *The Prix Paul Ricard coincides with FIAC (see p279) each autumn.*

FREE Fondation Mona Bismarck
34 av de New-York, 16th (01.47.23.38.88/ www.monabismarck.org). M° Alma Marceau. **Open** 10.30am-6.30pm Tue-Sat. Closed Aug. **Admission** free. **Map** p400 C5.
The Fondation provides a chic setting for eclectic exhibitions, from Etruscan antiquities to folk art.

Fondation Pierre Bergé Yves Saint Laurent
3 rue Léonce-Reynaud, 16th (01.44.31.64.00/ www.fondation-pb-ysl.net). M° Alma Marceau. **Open** *Exhibitions* 11am-6pm Tue-Sun. Closed Aug. **Admission** €5; €3 reductions; free under-10s. **Credit** AmEx, MC, V. **Map** p400 D5.
When Yves Saint Laurent bowed out of designing in 2002, he reopened his fashion house as this foundation, exhibiting Picasso and Warhol paintings with the dresses they closely inspired. Every sketch and every *toile* has been carefully catalogued, and many of Saint Laurent's friends and clients have presented the designer with the dresses he created for them, stored in the upper floors at precisely 18 degrees centigrade and a hygrometric level of 50 per cent.

★ Galerie-Musée Baccarat
11 pl des Etats-Unis, 16th (01.40.22.11.00/ www.baccarat.fr). M° Boissière or Iéna. **Open** 10am-6pm Mon, Wed-Sat. **Admission** €5; €3.50 reductions; free under-18s. **Credit** *Shop* AmEx, DC, MC, V. **Map** p400 C4.
Philippe Starck has created a neo-rococo wonderland in the former mansion of the Vicomtesse de Noailles. From the red carpet entrance with a chandelier in a fish tank to the Alchemy room, decorated by Gérard Garouste, there's a play of light and movement that makes Baccarat's work sing. See items by designers Georges Chevalier and Ettore Sottsass, services made for princes and maharajahs, and monumental items made for the great exhibitions of the 1800s. *Photo p83.*
▶ *If you want to eat at the opulent Le Cristal Room restaurant (01.40.22.11.10), be warned that there's a long waiting list.*

Galeries Nationales du Grand Palais
3 av du Général-Eisenhower, 8th (01.44.13.17.17/ reservations 08.92.68.46.94/www.grandpalais.fr). M° Champs-Elysées Clemenceau. **Open** 10am-10pm Mon, Wed, Fri-Sun; 10am-8pm Thur; pre-booking compulsory before 1pm. **Admission** *Before 1pm with reservation* €12. *After 1pm without reservation* €10; €9 reductions; free under-13s. **Credit** MC, V. **Map** p401 E5.
Built for the 1900 Exposition Universelle, the Grand Palais was the work of three different architects,

each of whom designed a façade. During World War II it accommodated Nazi tanks. In 1994 the magnificent glass-roofed central hall was closed when bits of metal started falling off, although exhibitions continued to be held in the other wings. After major restoration, the Palais reopened in 2005.

Musée d'Art Moderne de la Ville de Paris

11 av du Président-Wilson, 16th (01.53.67.40.00/ www.mam.paris.fr). M° Alma Marceau or Iéna. **Open** 10am-6pm Tue-Sun. **Admission** *Temporary exhibitions* €4.50-€9; €2.50-€4.50 reductions; free under-13s. **No credit cards.** **Map** p406 H7.

This monumental 1930s building, housing the city's modern art collection, is particularly strong on the Cubists, Fauves, the Delaunays, Rouault and Ecole de Paris artists Soutine, Modigliani and van Dongen.

Musée de la Contrefaçon

16 rue de la Faisanderie, 16th (01.56.26.14.00). M° Porte Dauphine. **Open** 9am-12.30pm, 2-5.30pm Tue-Sun. **Admission** €4; €3 reductions; free under-12s. **No credit cards.** **Map** p400 A4.

This museum was set up by the French anti-counterfeiting association with the aim of deterring forgers – but playing spot-the-fake with brands such as Reebok, Lacoste and Vuitton is fun for visitors.

Musée Dapper

35bis rue Paul-Valéry, 16th (01.45.00.91.75/www. dapper.com.fr). M° Victor Hugo. **Open** 11am-7pm Mon, Wed-Sun. **Admission** €6; €4 reductions; free under-16s. **Credit** MC, V. **Map** p400 B4.

Named after the 17th-century Dutch humanist Olfert Dapper, the Fondation Dapper began as an organisation dedicated to preserving sub-Saharan art. Reopened in 2000, the venue created by Alain Moatti houses a performance space, bookshop and café. Each year it stages two African-themed exhibitions.

Musée Galliera

10 av Pierre-1er-de-Serbie, 16th (01.56.52.86.00). M° Iéna. **Open** *Exhibitions* 10am-6pm Tue-Sun. **Admission** (incl audio-guide) €7.50; €3.50 reductions; free under-14s. **Credit** MC, V. **Map** p400 D5.

This look at clothes through history takes an academic approach to its subject. Housed in a *hôtel particulier* built by Eiffel, the Galliera has a huge

---

INSIDE TRACK EAT UP

At the top of the Théâtre des Champs-Elysées is the sleek, glass-fronted **Maison Blanche** restaurant (01.47.23.55.99), with magnificent views across the Seine to the Eiffel Tower.

---

costume collection. It has links with the fashion industry, and its initiative with young designers shows innovative work.

★ Musée National des Arts Asiatiques – Guimet

6 pl d'Iéna, 16th (01.56.52.53.00/www.musee guimet.fr). M° Iéna. **Open** 10am-5.45pm Mon, Wed-Sun (last entry 5.15pm). **Admission** €6.50; €4.50 reductions, all Sun; free students, under-18s, all 1st Sun of mth. PMP. **Credit** *Shop* AmEx, DC, MC, V. **Map** p400 C5.

Founded by industrialist Emile Guimet in 1889 to house his collection of Chinese and Japanese religious art, and later incorporating oriental collections from the Louvre, the museum has 45,000 objects from neolithic times onwards. Lower galleries focus on India and South-east Asia, centred on stunning Hindu and Buddhist Khmer sculpture from Cambodia. Don't miss the Giant's Way, part of the entrance to a temple complex at Angkor Wat. Upstairs, Chinese antiquities include mysterious jade discs. Afghan glassware and Moghul jewellery also feature.

Musée National de la Marine

Palais de Chaillot, 17 pl du Trocadéro, 16th (01.53.65.69.69/www.musee-marine.fr). M° Trocadéro. **Open** 10am-6pm Mon, Wed-Sun. **Admission** *Main collection & temporary exhibitions* €9; €5-€7 reductions; free under-6s. *Main collection* €7; €5 reductions; free under-18s. PMP. **Credit** *Shop* MC, V. **Map** p400 B5.

French naval history is outlined in detailed models of battleships and Vernet's series of paintings of French ports (1754-65). There's also an imperial barge, built when Napoleon's delusions of grandeur were reaching their zenith in 1810.

FREE Palais de Chaillot

Pl du Trocadéro, 16th. M° Trocadéro. **Admission** free. **Map** p400 C5.

This immense pseudo-classical building was constructed by Azéma, Boileau and Carlu for the 1937 international exhibition, with giant sculptures of *Apollo* by Henri Bouchard, and inscriptions by Paul Valéry. It stands on the foundations of an earlier complex put up for the 1878 World Fair.

▶ *The Palais houses the Musée National de la Marine and the Musée de l'Homme (closed for renovation until 2012). In the east wing are the Théâtre National de Chaillot (see p346) and the Cité de l'Architecture et du Patrimoine (see p85).*

★ Palais de la Découverte

Av Franklin-D.-Roosevelt, 8th (01.56.43.20.21/ www.palais-decouverte.fr). M° Champs-Elysées Clemenceau or Franklin D. Roosevelt. **Open** 9.30am-6pm Tue-Sat; 10am-7pm Sun (last entry 30mins before closing). **Admission** €7; €4.50 reductions; free under-5s. *Planetarium* €3.50. **Credit** AmEx, MC, V. **Map** p401 E5.

Jardin de Bagatelle, **Bois de Boulogne**. *See p90.*

This science museum houses designs dating from Leonardo da Vinci's time to the present. Models, real apparatus and audiovisual material bring displays to life, and permanent exhibits cover astrophysics, astronomy, biology, chemistry, physics and earth sciences. The Planète Terre section highlights meteorology, and one room is dedicated to the sun. There are shows at the Planetarium too, and 'live' experiments take place at weekends and during school holidays.

Palais de Tokyo: Site de Création Contemporaine

13 av du Président-Wilson, 16th (01.47.23.54.01/ www.palaisdetokyo.com). M° Alma Marceau or Iéna. **Open** noon-midnight Tue-Sun. **Admission** €6; €4.50 reductions; free under-18s, art students. **Map** p400 B5.

When it opened in 2002, many thought the Palais' stripped-back interior was a design statement. In fact, it was a response to tight finances. The 1937 building has now come into its own as an open-plan space with a skylit central hall, hosting exhibitions and performances. Extended hours and a funky café have drawn a younger audience, and the roll-call of artists is impressive (Pierre Joseph, Wang Du and others). The name dates to the 1937 Exposition Internationale, but is also a reminder of links with a new generation of artists from the Far East.

MONCEAU & BATIGNOLLES

In the 8th & 17th arrondissements.

Parc Monceau, with its neo-antique follies and large lily pond, lies at the far end of avenue Hoche (the main entrance is on boulevard de Courcelles, the circular pavilion by Ledoux). Three museums capture the extravagance of the area when it was newly fashionable in the 19th century: the **Musée Jacquemart-André**, with its Old Masters, the **Musée Nissim de Camondo** (superb 18th-century decorative arts), and the **Musée Cernuschi** (Chinese art). There are some nice exotic touches too, such as the unlikely red lacquer **Galerie Ching Tsai Too** (48 rue de Courcelles, 8th), built in 1926 for a dealer in oriental art near the wrought-iron gates of Parc Monceau, and the onion domes of the Russian Orthodox **Alexander Nevsky Cathedral** on rue Daru. Built in the mid 19th century, when a stay in Paris was essential to the education of every Russian aristocrat, it is still at the heart of an émigré little Russia.

Famed for its stand during the 1871 Paris Commune, the Quartier des Batignolles to the north-east towards place de Clichy is more working class, housing the rue de Lévis market, tenements lining the deep railway canyon and square des Batignolles park, with the pretty **Eglise Ste-Marie-de-Batignolles** looking on to a semi-circular square. It's fast becoming trendy, with a restaurant scene to match.

★ FREE Alexander Nevsky Cathedral

12 rue Daru, 17th (01.42.27.37.34). M° Courcelles. **Open** times vary. **Admission** free. **Map** p400 D3.

All onion domes, icons and incense, this Russian Orthodox church was completed in 1861 in the neo-Byzantine Novgorod-style of the 1600s, by the tsar's architect Kouzmin, responsible for the Fine Arts Academy in St Petersburg.

Sweet Success

Urban apiculture in the heart of the Right Bank.

Paris is buzzing with more than just tourists these days thanks to avid apiarists like Nicolas Géant, founder of bee breeding company Nicomiel (www.nicomiel.com), who has just installed two new beehives smack bang in the middle of the Champs-Elysées on the roof of the Grand Palais. Géant expects his 100,000 bees to harvest some 100kg of Miel du Grand Palais per year (on sale in the Grand Palais shop). He follows in the footsteps of Jean Paucton, beekeeper at

the Opéra Garnier, whose rooftop hives have been producing Miel des Toits de l'Opéra since 1983 (on sale for €12.50 in Fauchon).

According to Géant, placing beehives on prominent Paris monuments isn't just a money-spinning gimmick. It draws attention to a more serious problem: that bees can no longer thrive in the countryside. 'Like numerous other pollinating insects, bees are being killed by pesticides and intensive farming,' says Géant. 'Around 400,000 French hives have disappeared every year between 1995 and 2007. Paris, on the other hand, is pesticide free, drips in bee-friendly acacia, chestnut and linden trees, and actively encourages apiculture in its parks. In fact, the Ile de France has more bee colonies than anywhere else in the country – around 300.'

But if bees are thriving in the cities, where's the problem? 'Because,' Géant adds, 'we need bees in the countryside where we grow our food. If they keep dying, we may see a worldwide food shortage.'

We can all support the cause by spreading the word – and Paris's honey on our toast. And, for budding beekeepers, the Société Centrale d'Apiculture (www.la-sca.net, 01.45.42.29.08) offers beekeeping lessons in the Jardin du Luxembourg (6th) and Parc Georges Brassens (15th) for €185 a year.

FREE Cimetière des Batignolles

8 rue St-Just, 17th (01.53.06.38.68). M° Porte de Clichy. **Open** *16 Mar-6 Nov* 8am-5.45pm Mon-Fri; 8.30am-5.45pm Sat; 9am-5.45pm Sun & public hols. *7 Nov-15 Mar* 8am-5.15pm Mon-Fri; 8.30am-5.15pm Sat; 9am-5.15pm Sun & public hols. **Admission** free.
Squeezed inside the Périphérique are the graves of poet Paul Verlaine, Surrealist André Breton, and Léon Bakst, costume designer of the Ballets Russes.

FREE Musée Cernuschi

7 av Velasquez, 8th (01.53.96.21.50/www. cernuschi.paris.fr). M° Monceau or Villiers. **Open** 10am-6pm Tue-Sun. **Admission** free. *Temporary exhibitions* €7.50-€9; €3.80-€6 reductions; free under-18s. **Map** p401 E2.
Since the banker Henri Cernuschi built a *hôtel particulier* by the Parc Monceau for the treasures he found in the Far East in 1871, this collection of Chinese art has grown steadily. The museum has been expanded to twice its size, and was reopened back in 2005 with a total exhibition area of 3,200sq m (34,500sq ft) and

1,000 exhibits. The fabulous displays range from legions of Han and Wei dynasty funeral statues to refined Tang celadon wares and Sung porcelain.

★ Musée Jacquemart-André

158 bd Haussmann, 8th (01.45.62.11.59/www. musee-jacquemart-andre.com). M° Miromesnil or St-Philippe-du-Roule. **Open** 10am-6pm daily. **Admission** €10; €7.50 reductions; free under-7s. **Credit** AmEx, MC, V. **Map** p401 E3.
Long terrace steps and a stern pair of stone lions usher visitors into this grand 19th-century mansion, home to a collection of equally stately *objets d'art* and fine paintings. The collection was assembled by Edouard André and his artist wife Nélie Jacquemart, using money inherited from his rich banking family. The mansion was built to order to house their art hoard, which includes Rembrandts, Tiepolo frescoes and various paintings by Italian masters Uccello, Mantegna and Carpaccio. The visit unfolds in style, from the richly decorated ground floor past a marble winter garden and up a double spiral staircase.

SIGHTS

▶ *The adjacent tearoom, with its fabulous tottering cakes, is a favourite with the smart lunch set.*

Musée Nissim de Camondo

63 rue de Monceau, 8th (01.53.89.06.50/www. lesartsdecoratifs.fr). M° Monceau or Villiers. **Open** 10am-5.30pm Wed-Sun. **Admission** €6; €4.50 reductions; free under-18s. PMP. **Credit** AmEx, MC, V. **Map** p401 E3.

Put together by Count Moïse de Camondo, this collection is named after his son Nissim, who was killed in World War I. Moïse replaced the family's two houses near Parc Monceau with this palatial residence and lived here in a style in keeping with his love of the 18th century. Grand first-floor reception rooms are filled with furniture by craftsmen of the Louis XV and XVI eras, silver services, Sèvres and Meissen porcelain, Savonnerie carpets and Aubusson tapestries.

FREE Parc Monceau

Bd de Courcelles, av Hoche, rue Monceau, 8th. M° Monceau. **Open** *Nov-Mar* 7am-8pm daily. *Apr-Oct* 7am-10pm daily. **Admission** free. **Map** p401 E2.

Surrounded by grand *hôtels particuliers* and elegant Haussmannian apartments, Monceau is a favourite with well-dressed children and their nannies. It was laid out in the 18th century for the Duc de Chartres in the English style, with a lake, lawns and a variety of follies: an Egyptian pyramid, a Corinthian colonnade, Venetian bridge and sarcophagi.

PASSY & AUTEUIL

In the 16th arrondissement.

West of l'Etoile, the extensive 16th arrondissement is the epitome of bourgeois respectability, with grandiose apartments and exclusive residences lining the private roads. It's also home to some seminal examples of modernist architecture, plus several of the city's most important museums.

When Balzac lived at no.47 rue Raynouard in the 1840s, Passy was a country village (it was absorbed into the city in 1860) where the rich came to take cures at its mineral springs – a history alluded to by rue des Eaux. The novelist's former abode, **Maison de Balzac**, is open to the public. The **Musée du Vin** is of interest if only for its setting in the cellars of the wine-producing Abbaye de Minimes, destroyed in the Revolution. Rue de Passy, formerly the village high street, and parallel rue de l'Assomption, are the focus of local life, with fashion shops and *traiteurs*, the department store **Franck et Fils** (80 rue de Passy, 16th, 01.44.14.38.00) and a pricey covered market.

The former Passy station is now restaurant **La Gare** (19 chaussée de la Muette, 16th, 01.42.15.15.31). Ladies who shop stop by the lovely art deco **La Rotonde** café (12 chaussée de la Muette, 16th, 01.45.24.45.45) or stock up on cakes at Japanese *pâtisserie* **Yamazaki** (6 chaussée de la Muette, 16th, 01.40.50.19.19).

West of the former high society pleasure gardens of the Jardin du Ranelagh you'll find the **Musée Marmottan**, with its superb collection of Monet's late water-lily canvases, other Impressionists and Empire furniture.

Next to the Pont de Grenelle stands the circular **Maison de Radio France**, the giant home of state broadcasting. You can attend concerts (*see p316*) or take a tour around its endless corridors. From here, in more upmarket Auteuil, you can head up rue Fontaine, the best place to find art nouveau architecture by Hector Guimard, of métro entrance fame. He also designed the less ambitious nos.19 and 21. At no.96 pay homage to Marcel Proust, who was born here.

Nearby, the **Fondation Le Corbusier** occupies two of the architect's avant-garde houses in square du Dr-Blanche. A little further up rue du Dr-Blanche sculptor Henri Bouchard himself commissioned the studio and house that is now the dusty **Atelier-Musée Henri Bouchard**. Much of the rest of Auteuil is private territory, with exclusive streets of residences off rue Chardon-Lagache; the studio of 19th-century sculptor Jean-Baptiste Carpeaux remains,

Castel Béranger. *See p90.*

SIGHTS

looking rather lost, at no.39 boulevard Exelmans. The top storey was later added by Guimard.

West of the 16th, across the Périphérique, sprawls the parkland of **Bois de Boulogne**. At porte d'Auteuil are the romantic **Serres d'Auteuil** and sports venues the **Parc des Princes**, home of football club Paris St-Germain (for both, *see p334*), and **Roland Garros** (*see p334*), host of the French Tennis Open. Another attraction will open in 2012: the **Fondation Louis-Vuitton**, to be housed in a new Frank Gehry glass construction.

★ FREE Bois de Boulogne
16th. M° Les Sablons or Porte Dauphine. **Admission** free.
Covering 865 hectares, the Bois was once the Forêt de Rouvray hunting grounds. It was landscaped in the 1860s, when artificial grottoes and waterfalls were created around the Lac Inférieur. The Jardin de Bagatelle (route de Sèvres à Neuilly, 16th, 01.40.67.97.00, *photo p87*) is famous for its roses, daffodils and water lilies, and contains an orangery that rings to the sound of Chopin in summer. The Jardin d'Acclimatation (*see p290*) is a children's amusement park, with a miniature train, farm, rollercoaster and boat rides. The Bois also boasts two racecourses (Longchamp and Auteuil), sports clubs and stables, and restaurants, including Le Pré Catelan (route de Suresnes, 16th, 01.44.14.41.00).

By day the Bois attracts picnickers and dog walkers, with a boating lake and nearby cycle hire, but by night it's transformed into a parade ground for transsexuals and swingers of every stripe.

Castel Béranger
14 rue La Fontaine, 16th. M° Jasmin.
Guimard's masterpiece of 1895-98 epitomises art nouveau in Paris. From outside you can see his love of brick and wrought iron, asymmetry and renunciation of harsh angles not found in nature. Green seahorses climb the façade, and the faces on the balconies are thought to be self-portraits, inspired by Japanese figures, to ward off evil spirits. *Photo p89.*

Fondation Le Corbusier
Villa La Roche, 8-10 square du Dr-Blanche, 16th (01.42.88.41.53/www.fondationlecorbusier.fr).
M° Jasmin. **Open** 1.30-6pm Mon; 10am-6pm Tue-Thur; 10am-5pm Fri, Sat. Closed Aug. **Admission** €2-€4; free under-14s. **No credit cards**.
Designed by Le Corbusier in 1923 for a Swiss art collector, this house shows the architect's ideas in practice, with its stilts, strip windows, roof terraces and balconies, built-in furniture and an unsuspected use of colour inside: sludge green, blue and pinky beige. A sculptural cylindrical staircase and split volumes create a variety of geometrical vistas; inside, Le Corbusier's own neo-Cubist paintings and furniture sit alongside pieces by Perriand. Adjoining Villa Jeanneret houses the foundation's library.

FREE Le Jardin des Serres d'Auteuil
3 av de la Porte d'Auteuil, 16th (01.40.71.75.23).
M° Porte d'Auteuil. **Open** *Winter* 10am-5pm daily. *Summer* 10am-6pm daily. **Admission** free.
These romantic glasshouses were opened in 1895 to cultivate plants for Paris parks and public spaces. Today there are seasonal displays of orchids and begonias. Look out for the steamy tropical pavilion, which is home to palms, birds and Japanese ornamental carp.

Maison de Balzac
47 rue Raynouard, 16th (01.55.74.41.80/www.paris.fr/musees). M° Passy. **Open** 10am-6pm Tue-Sun. **Admission** €4; €2-€3 reductions; free under-13s. **Credit** MC, V. **Map** p404 B6.
Honoré de Balzac rented this apartment in 1840 to escape his creditors. Converted into a museum, it has memorabilia spread over several floors. Mementos include first editions and letters, plus portraits of friends and the novelist's mistress Mme Hanska, with whom he corresponded for years before they married. Along with a 'family tree' of his characters that extends across several walls, you can see Balzac's desk and the monogrammed coffee pot that fuelled all-night work on *Comédie Humaine*.

★ Musée Marmottan – Claude Monet
2 rue Louis-Boilly, 16th (01.44.96.50.33/www.marmottan.com). M° La Muette.
Open 11am-6pm Mon, Wed-Sun (last entry 5.30pm); 11am-8pm Tue (last entry 8.30pm). **Admission** €9; €5 reductions; free under-8s. **Credit** MC, V.
Originally a museum of the Empire period left to the state by collector Paul Marmottan, this old hunting pavilion has become a famed holder of Impressionist art thanks to two bequests: the first by the daughter of the doctor of Manet, Monet, Pissarro, Sisley and Renoir; the second by Monet's son Michel. Its Monet collection, the largest in the world, numbers 165 works, plus sketchbooks, palette and photos. A special circular room was created for the breathtaking late water lily canvases; upstairs are works by Renoir, Manet, Gauguin, Caillebotte and Berthe Morisot, 15th-century primitives, a Sèvres clock and a collection of First Empire furniture.

Musée du Vin
Rue des Eaux, 16th (01.45.25.63.26/www.museeduvinparis.com). M° Passy. **Open** 10am-6pm Tue-Sun. **Admission** (with guidebook and glass of wine) €11.90; €9.90 reductions; free under-14s, diners in the restaurant. **Credit** *Shop, restaurant* AmEx, DC, MC, V. **Map** p404 B6.
Here the Confrères Bacchiques defend French wines from imports and advertising laws. In the cellars of an old wine-producing monastery are displays on the history of viticulture, with waxwork peasants, old tools, bottles and corkscrews. Visits finish with a wine tasting and, a paid extra, a meal.

SIGHTS

Montmartre & Pigalle

Tourists abound, but romance still rules on Paris's highest hill.

Back in the 1930s, literary geographers such as the celebrated *flâneur* Léon-Paul Fargue could still describe Montmartre as 'a pocket of provincial France lodged in Paris', but these days it's one of the most conspicuously tourist-heavy parts of the city. That's not to say it has entirely lost its soul, however: the district that was only made an official part of the city in 1860 is riddled with romantic narrow streets and the famous steep staircases of countless black and white photos, and it's easier than one might think to lose sight of the package holiday hordes. And although

Map pp401-402	**Restaurants** p198
Hotels p169	**Cafés & bars** p225

Montmartre's artistic star has faded, its appetite for after-dark revelry hasn't: there's a wealth of hip bars and cafés here, and at the bottom of the hill, in once-notorious Pigalle, the seediness of yesteryear's sex clubs and brothels is steadily being replaced by hot music venues and nightspots.

SIGHTS

MONTMARTRE

In the 18th arrondissement.

Perched on a hill (or *butte*), Montmartre is the highest point in Paris, its tightly packed houses spiralling round the mound below the dome of **Sacré-Coeur**. Despite the many tourists, it's surprisingly easy to fall under the spell of this unabashedly romantic district. Climb quiet stairways, peer down narrow alleys and into ivy-covered houses and quiet squares, and explore streets such as rue des Abbesses, rue des Trois-Frères and rue des Martyrs, with their cafés, boutiques and bohemian residents.

For centuries, Montmartre was a tranquil village. When Haussmann sliced through the city centre in the mid 19th century, working-class families started to move out, and migrants poured into an industrialising Paris from across France. The population of Montmartre swelled. The *butte* was absorbed into the city of Paris in 1860, but remained proudly independent. Its key role in the Commune in 1871, fending off government troops, is marked by a plaque on rue du Chevalier-de-la-Barre.

Artists moved into the area from the 1880s. Renoir found subject matter in the cafés and

guinguettes, and Toulouse-Lautrec patronised the local bars and immortalised its cabarets in his famous posters. Later, it was frequented by Picasso and artists of the Ecole de Paris.

You can start a wander from Abbesses métro station, one of only two in Paris (along with Porte Dauphine) to retain its original art nouveau metal-and-glass awning designed by Hector Guimard. Across place des Abbesses is art nouveau **St-Jean-de-Montmartre** church, a pioneering reinforced concrete structure with turquoise mosaics around the door. Along rue des Abbesses and adjoining rue Lepic, which winds its way up the hill, are food shops, boutiques, wine merchants and cafés, including the ever-popular **Le Sancerre** (*see p227*).

In the other direction from Abbesses, at 11 rue Yvonne-Le-Tac, is the Chapelle du Martyr. According to legend, St Denis picked up his head here after his execution in the third century (hence one plausible explanation of the name Montmartre – martyr's mount). Rue Orsel, with a typical local cluster of retro design, ethnic and second-hand clothes shops, leads to place Charles-Dullin, where a cluster of cafés overlook the respected Théâtre de l'Atelier (1 pl Charles-Dullin, 18th, 01.46.06.49.24, www.theatre-atelier.com).

Up the hill, the cafés of rue des Trois-Frères are a popular spot for an evening drink. The street leads into sloping place Emile-Goudeau, whose staircases, wrought-iron streetlights and old houses are particularly evocative of days gone by. The Bâteau Lavoir, a piano factory that stood at no.13, witnessed the birth of Cubism. Divided in the 1890s into a warren of studios for impoverished artists of the day, it was here that Picasso painted *Les Demoiselles d'Avignon* in 1906 and 1907, when he, Braque and Juan Gris were all residents. The building burned down in 1970, but has since been reconstructed.

On rue Lepic, which winds up the hill from rue des Abbesses, are the village's two remaining windmills: the **Moulin du Radet**, which was moved here in the 17th century from its hillock in rue des Moulins near the Palais-Royal; and the **Moulin de la Galette**, site of the celebrated dancehall depicted by Renoir (now in the Musée d'Orsay) and today a smart restaurant. Vincent van Gogh and his beloved brother Theo lived at no.54 from 1886 to 1888.

On tourist-swamped place du Tertre at the top of the hill, painters flog lurid sunset views of Paris or offer (sometimes aggressively) to draw your portrait; nearby **Espace Dalí** (11 rue Poulbot, 18th, 01.42.64.40.10, www.daliparis.com) has rather more illustrious art.

Cimetière de Montmartre.

Round here, so legend has it, the bistro concept was born in the early 1800s, when Russian soldiers shouted '*Bistro!*' ('Quickly!') to be served. Just off the square is **St-Pierre-de-Montmartre**, the oldest church in the district, with columns that have bent with age. Founded by Louis VI in 1133, it's an example of early Gothic, in contrast to its extravagant neighbour, the Sacré-Coeur basilica.

For all its kitsch and swarms of tourists, **Sacré-Coeur** is well worth the visit for its sheer 19th-century excess. Rather than the main steps, take the staircase down rue Maurice-Utrillo to pause on a café terrace on the small square at the top of rue Muller, or wander down through the adjoining park to the Halle St-Pierre. The old covered market is now used for shows of naïve art, but the surrounding square and streets, known as the **Marché St-Pierre**, are packed with fabric shops.

On the north side of place du Tertre in rue Cortot is the quiet 17th-century manor that houses the **Musée de Montmartre**, dedicated to the neighbourhood and its former famous inhabitants. Dufy, Renoir and Utrillo all used to have studios in the entrance pavilion. Nearby in rue des Saules is the Montmartre vineyard, planted by local artist Poulbot in 1933 in commemoration of the vines that once covered the area. The grape harvest here every autumn is a local highlight, celebrated with great pomp. Further down the hill, among rustic, shuttered houses, is the cabaret **Au Lapin Agile** (*see p281*). This old artists' meeting point got its name from André Gill, who painted the inn sign of a rabbit (the 'lapin à Gill').

A series of squares leads to rue Caulaincourt, crossing the **Cimetière de Montmartre** (enter on avenue Rachel, reached by stairs from rue Caulaincourt or place de Clichy). A stone's throw south of here is the pocket-sized *chanson* venue **Les Trois Baudets** (*see p323*), which saw the Paris debuts of Brel, Brassens, Vian, Gainsbourg, Gréco and others, and was relaunched under Mairie management in 2008. Winding down the back of the hill, avenue Junot is lined with exclusive residences, such as the avant-garde house built by Adolf Loos for poet Tristan Tzara at no.15, exemplifying his Modernist maxim: 'Ornament is crime.'

★ FREE Cimetière de Montmartre

20 av Rachel, access by staircase from rue Caulaincourt, 18th (01.53.42.36.30). M° Blanche or Place de Clichy. **Open** *6 Nov-15 Mar* 8am- 5.30pm Mon-Sat; 9am-5.30pm Sun & public hols. *16 Mar-5 Nov* 8am-6pm Mon-Sat; 9am-6pm Sun & public hols. **Admission** free. **Map** p401 G1.

Portrait of the Artist

Jean-Jacques Henner remembered.

During his lifetime, Jean-Jacques Henner (1829-1905) was one of France's most respected artists, winning multiple prizes and official state honours. While the Impressionists were revolutionising the rules of painting in the late 19th century, Henner was carving himself out a sturdy reputation as a talented landscape painter and exceptional portraitist.

Reopened in 2009 after four years of renovation work, the **Musée National Jean-Jacques Henner** (*see below*) traces the artist's life from his humble beginnings in Alsace to his rise as one of the most sought-after painters in Paris. Although he never lived here, the building was the home and studio of his contemporary, Guillaume Dubufe, and the interiors have been widely refurbished to recreate the feel of the period. A Chinese-style fireplace on the ground floor and Egyptian *mashrebeeyah* in the striking red-walled studio testify to the eclectic tastes of the time, while many of the furnishings belonged to Henner himself.

The closure of the museum has also allowed the paintings themselves to be cleaned and restored, a process not helped by Henner's predilection for incorporating unusual raw materials, such as the top of a cigar box. The spruced-up works are now spread across the museum's three compact floors in loosely chronological order. On the first floor, Alsatian landscapes and family portr[...] lifelo[...] annex[...] 1871 p[...] most fa[...] on displa[...] door. A sy[...] portrays a [...] in mourning [...] beyond the c[...]

Success t[...] [...] arts and, after winning the G[...] [...] de Rome in 1878, to Italy, where he painted a smattering of genre scenes and small luminous landscapes. What brought the artist most acclaim (and criticism), however, was his trademark nymph paintings. In the brightly lit top-floor studio, the walls are filled with canvases displaying pale-skinned, red-headed nudes tending their hair among wooded landscapes that resemble the Alsace of Henner's youth. The idealised soft, blurred outlines contrast with the realism of the female anatomy, while the composition recalls Italian Renaissance.

The revamped museum also includes a number of works from Henner's private collection (Heim, Flandrin, Monticelli) and a small room for temporary exhibitions, the first of which focuses on Goya's bull-fighting works. There's even a blog (www.henner-intime.fr), launching Henner firmly into the 21st century.

Truffaut, Nijinsky, Berlioz, Degas, Offenbach and German poet Heine are all buried here. So, too, are La Goulue, the first great cancan star and model for Toulouse-Lautrec, celebrated local beauty Mme Récamier, and the consumptive heroine Alphonsine Plessis, inspiration for Dumas's *La Dame aux Camélias* and Verdi's *La Traviata*. Flowers are still left on the grave of pop diva and gay icon Dalida, who used to live on nearby rue d'Orchampt.
▶ *For a walk around celebrity-filled Père-Lachaise cemetery, see p106.*

Musée d'Art Halle St-Pierre
2 rue Ronsard, 18th (01.42.58.72.89/www.halle saintpierre.org). M° Anvers. **Open** *Jan-July, Sept-Dec* 10am-6pm daily; *Aug* noon-6pm Mon-Fri. **Admission** €7.50; €6 reductions; free under-4s. **Credit** *Shop* MC, V. **Map** p402 J2.
The former covered market in the shadow of Sacré-Coeur specialises in *art brut, art outsider* and *art singulier* from its own and other collections.

Musée de Montmartre
12 rue Cortot, 18th (01.49.25.89.37/ www.museedemontmartre.fr). M° Anvers or Lamarck-Caulaincourt. **Open** 11am-6pm Wed-Sun. **Admission** €8; €4-€6 reductions; free under-12s. **Credit** *Shop* MC, V. **Map** p402 H1.
At the back of a garden, this 17th-century manor displays the history of the hilltop, with rooms devoted to composer Gustave Charpentier and a tribute to the Lapin Agile cabaret, with original Toulouse-Lautrec posters. There are paintings by Suzanne Valadon, who had a studio above the entrance pavilion, as did Renoir, Raoul Dufy and Valadon's son Maurice Utrillo.

NEW Musée National Jean-Jacques Henner
43 av de Villiers, 17th (01.47.63.42.73). M° Malesherbes. **Open** 11am-6pm Mon, Wed-Sun. **Admission** €5; €3 reductions. **Map** p401 E2. *See above* **Portrait of the Artist**.

SIGHTS

★ FREE Sacré-Coeur

*35 rue du Chevalier-de-la-Barre, 18th
(01.53.41.89.00/www.sacre-coeur-montmartre.
com). M° Abbesses or Anvers.* **Open** *Basilica*
6am-10.30pm daily. *Crypt & dome* Winter
10am-5.45pm daily. Summer 9am-6.45pm
daily. **Admission** free. *Crypt & dome* €5.
Credit MC, V. **Map** p402 J1.
Work on this enormous mock Romano-Byzantine
edifice began in 1877. It was commissioned after the
nation's defeat by Prussia in 1870, voted for by the
Assemblée Nationale and built from public subscription. Finally completed in 1914, it was consecrated
in 1919 – by which time a jumble of architects had
succeeded Paul Abadie, winner of the original competition. The interior boasts lavish mosaics.

La Goutte d'Or

The area north of Barbès Rochechouart
métro station was the backdrop for Zola's
L'Assommoir, his novel set among the district's
laundries and absinthe cafés. Today, heroin has
replaced absinthe as the means of escape.

La Goutte d'Or is primarily an African and
Arab neighbourhood, and can seem like a slice
of the Middle East or a state under perpetual
siege due to the frequent police raids. Down
rue Doudeauville, you'll find lively ethnic music
shops; rue Polonceau contains African grocers
and Senegalese restaurants. Mayor Delanöe has
tried to attract young designers to the area by
designating rue des Gardes 'rue de la mode',
and square Léon is the focus for La Goutte d'Or
en Fête in June, which brings together local
musicians. Some of them, such as Africando
and the Orchestre National de Barbès, have
become well known across Paris. A market sets
up under the métro tracks along boulevard de la
Chapelle on Monday, Wednesday and Saturday
mornings, with stalls of exotic vegetables and
rolls of African fabrics.

Further north, at porte de Clignancourt, is
the city's largest flea market, the **Marché aux
Puces de Clignancourt** *(see p249)*.

PIGALLE

In the 9th arrondissement.

In the 1890s, Toulouse-Lautrec's posters of
Jane Avril at the Divan Japonais, Chat Noir
and Moulin Rouge, and of *chanson* star Aristide
Bruant, immortalised Pigalle's cabarets and
were landmarks of art and advertising. At the
end of the 19th century, 25 of the 58 buildings
on rue des Martyrs were cabarets (a few, such
as the drag shows Michou and Madame Arthur,
remain today); others were *maisons closes*. But
it's still a happening street: Le Divan Japonais is
now **Le Divan du Monde** *(see p328)*, a club

Sacré-Coeur.

and music venue; a hip crowd packs into
La Fourmi *(see p226)* opposite; and up the
hill, there's a cluster of *atelier*-boutiques where
designers have set up their sewing machines
at the back of the shop.

Along the boulevard, behind its bright
red windmill, the **Moulin Rouge** *(see p281)*,
once the image of naughty 1890s Paris, is now
a cheesy tourist draw. Its befeathered dancers
still cancan and cavort across the stage, but are
no substitute for La Goulue and Joseph Pujol –
le pétomane who could pass wind melodically.
In stark contrast is the **Cité Véron** next door,
a cobbled alley with a small theatre and
cottagey buildings; writer and jazz musician
Boris Vian lived at 6bis between 1953 and
1958. The famous **Elysée Montmartre**
music hall *(see p328)* today has an array
of concerts and club nights, but the **Folies
Pigalle** *(see p328)* nightspot retains its
undeniable Pigalle flavour with its after-
parties and drag queens.

Musée de l'Erotisme

*72 bd de Clichy, 18th (01.42.58.28.73/www.
musee-erotisme.com). M° Blanche.* **Open**
10am-2am daily. **Admission** €8; €5 students.
Credit MC, V. **Map** p401 H2.
Seven floors of erotic art and artefacts amassed by
collectors Alain Plumey and Joseph Khalif. The
first three run from first-century Peruvian phallic
pottery through Etruscan fertility symbols to Yoni

INSIDE TRACK
DALIDA'S MONTMARTRE

During her 30-year career, Egyptian-born icon Dalida recorded more than 1,000 songs, scoring 45 gold records and two platinum albums, before committing suicide in the late 1980s. Much of the Dalida myth is rooted in Montmartre: she lived in the 'Castle of Sleeping Beauty', a four-storey house on rue d'Orchampt; place Dalida is graced by a bronze bust of the idol; and her grave in the Montmartre cemetery is a place of pilgrimage.

sculptures from Nepal; the fourth gives a history of Paris brothels; and the recently refurbished top floors host exhibitions of modern erotic art.

La Nouvelle Athènes

Just south of Pigalle and east of rue Blanche lies this often overlooked quarter, dubbed the New Athens when it was colonised by a wave of artists, writers and composers in the early 19th century. Long-forgotten actresses and *demi-mondaines* had mansions built here; some are set in tiny rue de la Tour-des-Dames, which refers to one of the many windmills owned by Couvent des Abbesses. To glimpse more of these miniature palaces, wander through the adjoining streets and passageways.

Just off rue Taitbout is square d'Orléans, a remarkable housing estate built in 1829 by the English architect Edward Cresy. These flats and studios attracted the glitterati of the day, including George Sand and her lover Chopin. In the house built for Dutch painter Ary Scheffer in nearby rue Chaptal, the **Musée de la Vie Romantique** displays Sand's mementos.

The **Musée Gustave Moreau** on rue de La Rochefoucauld is reason alone to visit, featuring the artist's apartment and magnificent studio. Fragments of bohemia can still be gleaned in the area, although the Café La Roche, where Moreau met Degas for drinks and rows, has been downsized to **Café Matisse** (57 rue Notre-Dame-de-Lorette, 9th, 01.53.16.44.58). Degas painted most of his memorable ballet scenes in rue Frochot, and Renoir hired his first proper studio at 35 rue St-Georges. A few streets away in Cité Pigalle, a collection of studios, is van Gogh's last Paris house (no.5), from where he moved to Auvers-sur-Oise. There is a plaque here, but nothing marks the building in rue Pigalle where Toulouse-Lautrec slowly drank himself to an early grave.

The area around the neo-classical **Eglise Notre-Dame-de-Lorette**, built in the form of a Greek temple, was built up in Louis-Philippe's reign and was famous for its courtesans or *lorettes*, elegant ladies named after their haunt of rue Notre-Dame-de-Lorette. In 1848, Gauguin was born at no.56; from 1844 to 1857, Delacroix had a studio at no.58. The latter then moved to place de Furstemberg in the sixth (now the Musée Delacroix). Rue St-Lazare contains some delightfully old-fashioned shops and bistros.

The lower stretch of rue des Martyrs is packed with tempting food shops, and a little further up the hill you should look out for the prosperous residences of the Cité Malesherbes and avenue Trudaine. The circular place St-Georges was home to the true Empress of Napoleon III's Paris: the Russian-born Madame Païva. She lived in the neo-Renaissance no.28, thought to be outrageous at the time of its construction. La Païva shot herself after a passionate affair with the millionaire cousin of Chancellor Bismarck.

★ Musée Gustave Moreau

14 rue de La Rochefoucauld, 9th (01.48.74.38.50/ www.musee-moreau.fr). M° Trinité. **Open** 10am-12.45pm, 2-5.15pm Mon, Wed-Sun. **Admission** €5; €3 reductions, all Sun; free under-18s. PMP. **Credit** MC, V. **Map** p401 G3.

This wonderful museum combines the small private apartment of Symbolist painter Gustave Moreau (1825-98) with the vast gallery he built to display his work – set out as a museum by the painter himself, and opened in 1903. Downstairs shows his obsessive collector's nature with family portraits, Grand Tour souvenirs and a boudoir devoted to the object of his unrequited love, Alexandrine Durem. Upstairs is Moreau's fantasy realm, which plunders Greek mythology and biblical scenes for canvases filled with writhing maidens, trance-like visages, mystical beasts and strange plants. Don't miss the trippy masterpiece *Jupiter et Sémélé* on the second floor.

▶ *Printed on boards that you can carry around the museum are the artist's lengthy, rhetorical and mad commentaries.*

FREE Musée de la Vie Romantique

Hôtel Scheffer-Renan, 16 rue Chaptal, 9th (01.55.31.95.67/www.vie-romantique.paris.fr). M° Blanche or St-Georges. **Open** 10am-6pm Tue-Sun. *Tearoom* May-Oct 11.30am-5.30pm Tue-Sun. **Admission** free. *Exhibitions* €7; €3.50 reductions; free under-14s. **Credit** AmEx, DC, MC, V. **Map** p401 G2.

When Dutch artist Ary Scheffer lived in this small villa, the area teemed with composers, writers and artists. Aurore Dupin, Baronne Dudevant (George Sand) was a guest at Scheffer's soirées, along with great names such as Chopin and Liszt. The museum is devoted to Sand, although the watercolours, lockets, jewels and plastercast of her right arm that she left behind reveal little of her ideas or affairs.

Beaubourg & the Marais

Galleries and good times in the heart of Gay Paree.

Whereas historic *quartiers* like Montmartre and St-Germain-des-Prés are well past their heyday, the Marais has been luckier, and for the last two decades has been one of the hippest parts of the city, stuffed with modish hotels, boutiques and restaurants – in no small part due to its popularity with the gay crowd. It's also prime territory for arts lovers, thanks to its generous quotient of museums, and its tightly knit street plan – largely untouched by Haussmann – makes it a charming place in which to get lost. The Marais' neighbour to the west is Beaubourg, whose focal point is the iconic Centre Pompidou, with the city's all-important Hôtel de Ville a stone's throw to the south.

Champs-Elysées & Western Paris	Montmartre & Pigalle	North-East Paris
	Opéra to Les Halles	
Tour Eiffel	Louvre	Beaubourg & The Marais
The 7th & Western Paris	St-Germain-des-Prés & Odéon	Notre-Dame
		Bastille & Eastern Paris
		The Latin Quarter & the 13th
Montparnasse & Beyond		

Map p406	**Restaurants** p199
Hotels p170	**Cafés & bars** p227

BEAUBOURG & HOTEL DE VILLE

In the 4th arrondissement.

Modern architecture in Paris took off with the **Centre Pompidou**, a benchmark of inside-out high-tech designed by Richard Rogers and Renzo Piano that's as much an attraction as the **Musée National de l'Art Moderne** within. The piazza outside attracts street performers and artists; the reconstructed **Atelier Brancusi**, left by the sculptor to the state, was moved here from the 15th arrondissement.

On the other side of the piazza, rue Quincampoix houses galleries, bars and cobbled passage Molière, with its old shopfronts and the **Théâtre Molière** (01.44.54.53.00). Beside the Centre Pompidou is place Igor-Stravinsky and the Fontaine Stravinsky – full of spraying kinetic fountains, and a colourful snake by the late artists Niki de Saint Phalle and Jean Tinguely – as well as the red-brick **IRCAM** music institute (*see p316*), also designed by Renzo Piano.

South of here stands the spiky Gothic **Tour St-Jacques**. Towards the river, on the site of the Grand Châtelet (a fortress put up in the 12th century to defend Pont au Change), place du Châtelet's Egyptian-themed fountain is framed by twin theatres designed by Davioud as part of Haussmann's urban improvements in the 1860s. They're now two of the city's main arts venues: the **Théâtre de la Ville** (*see p346*) and the **Théâtre du Châtelet** (*see p345*), an opera and concert hall.

Beyond Châtelet, the **Hôtel de Ville** (city hall) has been the symbol of municipal power since 1260. The equestrian statue out front is of 14th-century merchant leader and rebel Etienne Marcel. Revolutionaries made the Hôtel de Ville their base in the 1871 Commune, but it was set on fire by the Communards themselves and wrecked during savage fighting. It was rebuilt according to the original model, on a larger scale, in fanciful neo-Renaissance style, with knights in armour along the roof and statues of French luminaries dotted all over the walls. The square outside was formerly called place de Grève, after the nearby

SIGHTS

riverside wharf where goods were unloaded for market. During the 16th-century Wars of Religion, Protestant heretics were burned in the square, and the guillotine stood here during the Terror, when Danton, Marat and Robespierre made the Hôtel de Ville their own seat of government. Today the square hosts an ice rink every December, and screenings of major sports events. Across the road stands the Bazar de l'Hôtel de Ville department store, or **BHV** (*see p238*).

FREE Atelier Brancusi

Piazza Beaubourg, 4th (01.44.78.12.33/ www.centrepompidou.fr). Mº Hôtel de Ville or Rambuteau. **Open** 2-6pm Mon, Wed-Sun. **Admission** free. **Credit** AmEx, V. **Map** p406 K6.

When Constantin Brancusi died in 1957, he left his studio and its contents to the state, and it was later moved and rebuilt by the Centre Pompidou. His fragile works in wood and plaster, the endless columns and streamlined bird forms show how Brancusi revolutionised sculpture.

★ Centre Pompidou (Musée National d'Art Moderne)

Rue St-Martin, 4th (01.44.78.12.33/www.centre pompidou.fr). Mº Hôtel de Ville or Rambuteau. **Open** 11am-9pm (last entry 8pm) Mon, Wed, Fri-Sun (until 11pm some exhibitions); 11am-11pm Thur. **Admission** *Museum & exhibitions* €10 (€12 May-mid Aug); €8 reductions; free under-18s, 1st Sun of mth (museum only). PMP. **Credit** AmEx, DC, MC, V. **Map** p406 K6.

The primary colours, exposed pipes and air ducts make this one of the best-known sights in Paris. The then-unknown Italo-British architectural duo of Renzo Piano and Richard Rogers won the competition with their 'inside-out' boilerhouse approach, which put air-conditioning, pipes, lifts and the escalators on the outside, leaving an adaptable space within. The multi-disciplinary concept of modern art museum (the most important in Europe), library, exhibition and performance spaces, and repertory cinema was also revolutionary. When the centre opened in 1977, its success exceeded all expectations. After a two-year revamp, the centre reopened in 2000 with an enlarged museum, renewed performance spaces, vista-rich Georges restaurant and a mission to get back to the stimulating interdisciplinary mix of old. Entrance to the forum is free (as is the library, which has a separate entrance), but you now have to pay to go up the escalators.

The Centre Pompidou (or 'Beaubourg') holds the largest collection of modern art in Europe, rivalled only in its breadth and quality by MoMA in New York. Sample the contents of its vaults (50,000 works of art by 5,000 artists) on the website, as only a fraction – about 600 works – can be seen for real at any one time. There is a partial rehang each year.

For the main collection, buy tickets on the ground floor and take the escalators to level four for post-1960s art. Level five spans 1905 to 1960. There are four temporary exhibition spaces on each of these two levels (included in the ticket). Main temporary exhibitions take place on the ground floor, in gallery two on level six, in the south gallery, level one and in the new Espace 315, which is devoted to artists aged under 40.

On level five, the historic section takes a chronological sweep through the history of modern art, via Primitivism, Fauvism, Cubism, Dadaism and Surrealism up to American Color-Field painting and Abstract Expressionism. Masterful ensembles let you see the span of Matisse's career on canvas and in bronze, the variety of Picasso's invention, and the development of cubic orphism by Sonia and Robert Delaunay. Others on the hits list include Braque, Duchamp, Mondrian, Malevich, Kandinsky, Dali, Giacometti, Ernst, Miró, Calder, Magritte, Rothko and Pollock. Don't miss the reconstruction of a wall of André Breton's studio, combining the tribal art, folk art, flea-market finds and drawings by fellow artists that the Surrealist artist and theorist had amassed. The photography collection also has an impressive roll call, including Brassaï, Kertész, Man Ray, Cartier-Bresson and Doisneau.

Level four houses post-'60s art. Its thematic rooms concentrate on the career of one artist or focus on movements such as Anti-form or *arte povera*. Recent acquisitions line the central corridor, and at the far end you can find architecture and design. Video art and installations by the likes of Mathieu Mercier and Dominique Gonzalez-Foerster are in a room devoted to *nouvelle création*.

FREE Hôtel de Ville

29 rue de Rivoli, 4th (01.42.76.40.40/www. paris.fr). Mº Hôtel de Ville. **Open** 10am-7pm Mon-Sat. **Map** p406 K6.

Rebuilt by Ballu after the Commune, the palatial, multi-purpose Hôtel de Ville is the heart of the city administration, and a place in which to entertain visiting dignitaries. Free exhibitions are held in the Salon d'Accueil (open 10am-6pm Mon-Fri). The rest of the building, accessible by weekly guided tours (book in advance), has parquet floors, marble statues, crystal chandeliers and painted ceilings.

Tour St-Jacques

Square de La-Tour-St-Jacques, 4th. Mº Châtelet. **Map** p406 J6.

Loved by the Surrealists, this solitary Flamboyant Gothic belltower with its leering gargoyles is all that remains of the St-Jacques-La-Boucherie church, built for the powerful Butchers' Guild in 1508-22. The statue of Blaise Pascal at the base commemorates his experiments on atmospheric pressure, carried out here in the 17th century. A weather station now crowns the 52m (171ft) tower, not open to the public.

Place des Vosges.

THE MARAIS

In the 3rd & 4th arrondissements.

The narrow streets of the Marais contain aristocratic *hôtels particuliers*, art galleries, boutiques and stylish cafés, with beautiful carved doorways and early street signs carved into the stone. The Marais, or 'marsh', started life as a piece of swampy ground inhabited by a few monasteries, sheep and market gardens. This was one of the last parts of central Paris to be built up. In the 16th century, the elegant Hôtel Carnavalet and Hôtel Lamoignon sparked the area's phenomenal rise as an aristocratic residential district; Henri IV began building **place des Vosges** in 1605. Nobles and royal officials followed, building smart townhouses where literary ladies such as Mme de Sévigné held court. The area fell from fashion a century later; many of the narrow streets remained unchanged as mansions were transformed into workshops, crafts studios, schools, tenements, and even, on rue de Sévigné, a fire station.

Rue des Francs-Bourgeois, crammed with impressive mansions and original boutiques, runs like a backbone right through the Marais, becoming more aristocratic as it leaves the food shops of rue Rambuteau behind. Two of the most refined early 18th-century residences are **Hôtel d'Albret** (no.31), a venue for jazz concerts during the Paris Quartier d'Eté festival (*see p276*), and the palatial **Hôtel de Soubise** (no.60), the national archives. Begun in 1704 for the Prince and Princesse de Soubise, it has interiors by Boucher and Lemoine and currently hosts the **Musée de l'Histoire de France**, along with the neighbouring Hôtel de Rohan. There's also a surprising series of rose gardens.

Facing the Archives Nationales, the **Crédit Municipal** (no.55) acts as a sort of municipal pawnshop: people exchange goods for cash, and items never reclaimed are sold at auction. On the corner of rue Pavée is the Renaissance Hôtel Lamoignon, with a magisterial courtyard adorned with Corinthian pilasters. Built in 1585, it now contains the **Bibliothèque Historique de la Ville de Paris** (no.24, 01.44.59.29.40). Further up, the **Musée Carnavalet** runs across the Hôtel Carnavalet and the Hôtel le Peletier de St-Fargeau.

At its eastern end, rue des Francs-Bourgeois leads into the beautiful brick-and-stone place des Vosges. At one corner is the **Maison de Victor Hugo**, where the writer lived from 1833 to 1848. An archway in the south-west corner leads to the **Hôtel de Sully**, accommodating the Patrimoine Photographique. Designed in 1624, the building belonged to Henri IV's minister, the Duc de Sully.

Several other important museums are also found in sumptuous *hôtels*. The Hôtel Salé on rue de Thorigny, built in 1656, was nicknamed ('salty') after its owner, Fontenay, who collected the salt tax. Home to the **Musée National Picasso**, it is currently under restoration until 2012. Nearby, the pretty Hôtel Donon, built in 1598, contains the **Musée Cognacq-Jay** and has remarkable 18th-century panelled interiors, and the Hôtel Guénégaud contains the **Musée de la Chasse et de la Nature** hunting museum.

SIGHTS

SIGHTS

The Marais has also long been a focus for the Jewish community. Today, Jewish businesses are clustered along rue des Rosiers, rue des Ecouffes and rue Pavée, where there's a synagogue designed by Guimard. Originally made up mainly of Ashkenazi Jews, who fled the pogroms in eastern Europe at the end of the 19th century (many were later deported during World War II), the community expanded in the 1950s and '60s with a wave of Sephardic Jewish immigration after French withdrawal from North Africa.

The lower ends of rue des Archives and rue Vieille-du-Temple are the centre of café life and the hub of the gay scene. Bars such as the **Open Café** (see p308) draw gay crowds in the early evening. In their midst, the 15th-century **Cloître des Billettes** at 22-26 rue des Archives is the only surviving Gothic cloister in Paris.

Workaday rue du Temple is full of surprises. Near rue de Rivoli, **Le Noveau Latina** (see p298) specialises in Latin American films and holds tango balls in the room above. At no.41, an archway leads into the former Aigle d'Or coaching inn, now the **Café de la Gare** café-théâtre (see p283). Further north, at no.71, the grandiose Hôtel de St-Aignan, built in 1650, contains the **Musée d'Art et d'Histoire du Judaïsme**. The top end of rue du Temple and adjoining streets such as rue des Gravilliers are packed with costume jewellery, handbag and rag-trade wholesalers in what is the city's oldest Chinatown.

The north-west corner of the Marais hinges on the **Musée des Arts et Métiers**, a science museum with early flying machines displayed in the 12th-century chapel of the former priory of St-Martin-des-Champs, and the adjoining Conservatoire des Arts et Métiers. Across rue St-Martin on square Emile-Chautemps, the **Théâtre de la Gaîté Lyrique** is currently undergoing renovation, and will reopen in 2010 as a centre for contemporary music and the 'digital arts'.

Despite the Marais' rise to fashion, the less gentrified streets around the northern stretch of rue Vieille-du-Temple towards place de la République are awash with designers on the rise and old craft workshops. Rue Charlot, housing an occasional contemporary art gallery at the passage de Retz at no.9 (01.48.04.37.99/ www.passagederetz.com), is typical of the trend. At the top, the **Marché des Enfants-Rouges** (once an orphanage whose inhabitants were attired in red uniforms) is one of the city's oldest markets, founded in 1615.

★ FREE Espace Claude Berri

8 rue Rambuteau, 3rd (01.44.54.88.50/www. espace-claudeberri.com). M° Rambuteau. **Open** 11am-7pm Tue-Sat. Closed Aug. **Admission** free. **Map** p409 K6.
See p102 **Art House**.

Hôtel de Sully

62 rue St-Antoine, 4th (01.42.74.47.75/www. jeudepaume.org). M° St-Paul. **Open** noon-7pm Tue-Fri; 10am-7pm Sat, Sun. **Admission** €5; €2.50 reductions. **Credit** MC, V. **Map** p409 L7.
Along with the Jeu de Paume, the former Patrimoine Photographique forms part of the two-site home for the Centre National de la Photographie.

FREE Maison de Victor Hugo

Hôtel de Rohan-Guéménée, 6 pl des Vosges, 4th (01.42.72.10.16/www.musee-hugo.paris.fr). M° Bastille or St-Paul. **Open** 10am-6pm Tue-Sun. **Admission** free. *Exhibitions* prices vary. **Credit** MC, V. **Map** p409 L6.
Victor Hugo lived here from 1833 to 1848, and today the house is a museum devoted to the life and work of the great man. On display are his first editions, nearly 500 drawings and, more bizarrely, Hugo's home-made furniture.

★ Musée d'Art et d'Histoire du Judaïsme

Hôtel de St-Aignan, 71 rue du Temple, 3rd (01.53.01.86.60/www.mahj.org). M° Rambuteau. **Open** 11am-6pm Mon-Fri; 10am-6pm Sun. Closed Jewish hols. **Admission** €6.80; €4.50 reductions; free under-18s. **Credit** *Shop* MC, V. **Map** p409 K6.
It's fitting that a museum of Judaism should be lodged in one of the grandest mansions of the Marais, for centuries the epicentre of local Jewish life. It sprung from the collection of a private association formed in 1948 to safeguard Jewish heritage after the Holocaust. Pick up a free audio-guide in English to help you navigate through displays illustrating ceremonies, rites and learning, and showing how styles were adapted across the globe through examples of Jewish decorative arts. Photographic portraits of modern French Jews, each of whom tells his or her own story on the audio soundtrack, bring a contemporary edge. There are documents and paintings relating to the emancipation of French Jewry after the Revolution and the infamous Dreyfus case, from Zola's *J'Accuse!* to anti-Semitic cartoons. Paintings by the early 20th-century avant-garde include works by El Lissitsky and Chagall. The Holocaust is marked by Boris Taslitzky's stark sketches from Buchenwald and Christian Boltanski's courtyard memorial to the Jews who lived in the building in 1939, 13 of whom died in the camps.

Musée des Arts et Métiers

60 rue Réaumur, 3rd (01.53.01.82.00/ www.arts-et-metiers.net). M° Arts et Métiers. **Open** 10am-6pm Tue, Wed, Fri-Sun; 10am-9.30pm Thur. **Admission** €6.50; €4.50 reductions; free under-18s & 6-9.30pm Thur. PMP. **Credit** V. **Map** p402 K5.
The 'arts and trades' museum is, in fact, Europe's oldest science museum, founded in 1794 by the constitutional bishop Henri Grégoire, initially as a way

INSIDE TRACK
POMPIDOU IN THE PROVINCES

The Centre Pompidou's vaults contain some 50,000 works by 5,000 artists, but only a fraction – about 600 works – can be displayed at any one time. The obvious solution was to build another gallery, and the **Centre Pompidou Metz** (www.centre pompidou-metz.fr) is now finally set to open its doors in May 2010, just 82 minutes from Paris on the new TGV Est line. Designed by Shigeru Ban and Jean de Gastines, the building is every bit as architecturally groundbreaking as its big brother in Beaubourg, with three massive tunnel-style galleries, criss-crossed and stacked atop each other like Lego blocks, with huge windows at the ends offering natural light and views of the city.

to educate France's manufacturing industry in useful scientific techniques. Housed in the former Benedictine priory of St-Martin-des-Champs, it became a museum proper in 1819; it's a fascinating, attractively laid out and vast collection of treasures. Here are beautiful astrolabes, celestial spheres, barometers, clocks, weighing devices, some of Pascal's calculating devices, amazing scale models of buildings and machines that must have demanded at least as much engineering skill as the originals, the Lumière brothers' cinematograph, an enormous 1938 TV set, and still larger exhibits like Cugnot's 1770 'Fardier' (the first ever powered vehicle) and Clément Ader's bat-like, steam-powered Avion 3. The visit concludes in the chapel, which now contains old cars, a scale model of the Statue of Liberty, the monoplane in which Blériot crossed the Channel in 1909, and a Foucault pendulum.
▶ *Try to time your visit to coincide with one of the spellbinding demonstrations of the museum's old music boxes in the Théâtre des Automates.*

★ FREE Musée Carnavalet
23 rue de Sévigné, 3rd (01.44.59.58.58/www. carnavalet.paris.fr). Mº St-Paul. **Open** 10am-6pm Tue-Sun. **Admission** free. *Exhibitions* €7; €3.50-€5.50 reductions; free under-13s. **Credit** *Shop* AmEx, MC, V. **Map** p409 L6.
Here, 140 chronological rooms depict the history of Paris, from pre-Roman Gaul to the 20th century. Built in 1548 and transformed by Mansart in 1660, this fine house became a museum in 1866, when Haussmann persuaded the city to preserve its beautiful interiors. Original 16th-century rooms house Renaissance collections, with portraits by Clouet and furniture and pictures relating to the Wars of Religion. The first floor covers the period up to 1789, with furniture and paintings displayed in restored, period interiors;

neighbouring Hôtel Le Peletier de St-Fargeau covers the period from 1789 onwards. Displays relating to 1789 detail that year's convoluted politics and bloodshed, with prints and memorabilia, including a chunk of the Bastille. There are items belonging to Napoleon, a cradle given by the city to Napoleon III, and a reconstruction of Proust's cork-lined bedroom.

★ Musée de la Chasse et de la Nature
Hôtel Guénégaud, 62 rue des Archives, 3rd (01.53.01.92.40/www.chassenature.org). Mº Rambuteau. **Open** 11am-6pm Tue-Sun. **Admission** €6; €4.50 reductions; free under-18s. **Map** p409 K5.
A two-year overhaul turned the three-floor hunting museum from a musty old-timer into something really rather special. When it reopened in 2007, it had kept the basic layout and proportions of the two adjoining 17th-century mansions it occupies, but many of its new exhibits and settings seem more suited to an art gallery than a museum. The history of hunting and man's larger relationship with the natural world are examined in things like a quirky series of wooden cabinets devoted to the owl, wolf, boar and stag, each equipped with a bleached skull, small drawers you can open to reveal droppings and footprint casts, and a binocular eyepiece you can peer into for footage of the animal in the wild. A cleverly simple mirrored box contains a stuffed hen that is replicated into infinity on every side; and a stuffed fox is set curled up on a Louis XVI chair as though it were a domestic pet. Thought-provoking stuff.

FREE Musée Cognacq-Jay
Hôtel Donon, 8 rue Elzévir, 3rd (01.40.27.07.21/ www.paris.fr/musees). Mº St-Paul. **Open** 10am-6pm Tue-Sun. **Admission** free. **Map** p409 L6.
This cosy museum houses a collection put together in the early 1900s by La Samaritaine founder Ernest Cognacq and his wife Marie-Louise Jay. They stuck mainly to 18th-century French works, focusing on rococo artists such as Watteau, Fragonard, Boucher, Greuze and pastellist Quentin de la Tour, though some English artists (Reynolds, Romney, Lawrence) and Dutch and Flemish names (an early Rembrandt, Ruysdael, Rubens), plus Canalettos and Guardis, have managed to slip in. Pictures are displayed in panelled rooms with furniture, porcelain, tapestries and sculpture of the same period.

Musée de l'Histoire de France
Hôtel de Soubise, 60 rue des Francs-Bourgeois, 3rd (01.40.27.60.96/www.archivesnationales. culture.gouv.fr/chan/chan/musee). Mº Hôtel de Ville or Rambuteau. **Open** 10am-12.30pm, 2-5.30pm Mon, Wed-Fri; 2-5.30pm Sat, Sun. **Admission** €3; €2.30 reductions; free under-18s. **Credit** V. **Map** p409 K6.
Documents and artefacts covering everything from the founding of the Sorbonne to an ordinance about umbrellas are displayed in the recently renovated

SIGHTS

Hôtel de Soubise. Its rococo interiors feature paintings by François Boucher and Carle van Loo.

FREE **Place des Vosges**

4th. M° St-Paul. **Map** p409 L6.

Paris's first planned square was commissioned in 1605 by Henri IV and inaugurated by his son Louis XIII in 1612. With harmonious red-brick and stone arcaded façades and steeply pitched slate roofs, it differs from the later pomp of the Bourbons. Laid out symmetrically with carriageways through Pavillon de la Reine on the north side and Pavillon du Roi on the south, the other lots were sold off as concessions to officials and nobles (some façades are imitation brick). It was called place Royale prior to the Napoleonic Wars, when the Vosges was the first region to pay its war taxes. Mme de Sévigné, salon hostess and letter-writer, was born at no.1bis in 1626. At that time the garden hosted duels and trysts; now it attracts children from the nearby nursery school.

The St-Paul district

In 1559, Henri II was fatally wounded jousting on today's rue St-Antoine, marked by Pilon's marble *La Vierge de Douleur* in the **Eglise**

Art House

The late Claude Berri's impressive contemporary collection.

Claude Berri, who died in January 2009, was for many years best known as one of France's most successful film directors and producers – he directed the international arthouse hit *Jean de Florette* and produced France's second biggest box office success, *Bienvenue chez les Ch'tis*. But in 2008 the 74-year-old made a name for himself in another field, the world of contemporary art, when he opened the **Espace Claude Berri** (*see p100*) – a showcase for exhibitions by up-and-coming talent and Berri's own impressive collection.

The film mogul had been buying paintings and sculptures since the 1970s and by the time of his death boasted one of France's biggest collections. His first purchase was a Magritte, followed by works by Picasso, Dalí, Giacometti and Fernand Léger, but the bulk of his collection is made up of living artists. Robert Ryman was a favourite;

others featured include Richard Serra, Bruce Nauman, Dan Flavin, Daniel Buren, Jeff Wall, Christian Boltanski and Paul McCarthy.

Berri had long wanted to share his collection with the public. Back in 1991, he opened a small gallery space in Paris. This time around, he invested in premises in the Marais, a stronghold for art galleries and dealers. Dominated by a high, sloping skylight, the interiors were redesigned by Jean Nouvel, architect of both the Fondation Cartier and the Musée Quai Branly.

The aim of the space is to alternate themed exhibitions of works from Berri's private collection with solo shows organised around artists, critics or gallery owners – for one show, the whole ground floor was filled with giant, irreverent installations by Frenchman Gilles Barbier. Other exhibitions have been dedicated to Indian artists, and to trees in contemporary art.

SIGHTS

St-Paul-St-Louis. South of rue St-Antoine is the sedate residential area of St-Paul, lined with dignified 17th- and 18th-century façades. The linked courtyards of Village St-Paul house antiques sellers. On rue des Jardins-St-Paul is the largest surviving section of the fortified wall of Philippe-Auguste (www.philippe-auguste.com), complete with towers.

By St-Paul métro station on the corner of rue François-Miron and rue de Fourcy is the Hôtel Hénault de Cantorbe, renovated and given a minimalist modern extension as the **Maison Européenne de la Photographie**. Down rue de Fourcy towards the river, across a medieval formal garden, you can see the rear façade of the Hôtel de Sens, a rare medieval mansion built as the Paris residence of the Archbishops of Sens in the 15th century, with an array of turrets. It is home to the **Bibliothèque Forney** (1 rue du Figuier, 01.42.78.14.60, closed Mon & Sun) with its exhibitions of applied arts and graphic design.

Near Pont Sully are square Henri-Galli, with a rebuilt piece of the Bastille, and the **Pavillon de l'Arsenal**, built by a rich timber merchant to put on art shows, and home to displays relating to Paris architecture.

Winding rue François-Miron leads you back towards the Hôtel de Ville. At 17 rue Geoffroy-l'Asnier, the Mémorial du Martyr Juif Inconnu is being extended as part of the **Mémorial de la Shoah**, a museum, memorial and study centre devoted to the Holocaust that opened in 2005. As you pass no.26, note the Cité des Arts complex of artists' studios, and the ornate lion's head and giant shell motif on the doorway of the 17th-century Hôtel de Châlon-Luxembourg. Rue du Pont-Louis-Philippe contains jewellers, designer furniture and gift shops, and stepped rue des Barres boasts tearooms overlooking the chevet of the **Eglise St-Gervais-St-Protais**.

FREE Eglise St-Gervais-St-Protais

Pl St-Gervais, 4th (01.48.87.32.02). M° Hôtel de Ville. **Open** times vary. **Admission** free. **Map** p409 K6.

Gothic at the rear and classical at the front, this church also has an impressive Flamboyant Gothic interior, most of which dates from the 16th century. The nave gives an impression of enormous height, with tall columns that soar up to the vault. There are plenty of fine funerary monuments, especially the baroque statue of Chancellor Le Tellier.

FREE Eglise St-Paul-St-Louis

99 rue St-Antoine, 4th (01.42.72.30.32). M° St-Paul. **Open** 8am-8pm daily. **Admission** free. **Map** p409 L7.

This domed baroque Counter-Reformation church is modelled, like all Jesuit churches, on the Chiesa del Gesù in Rome. Completed in 1641, it features a single nave, side chapels and a three-storey façade featuring statues of Saints Louis, Anne and Catherine – all replacements. The provider of confessors to the kings of France, the Eglise St-Paul-St-Louis was richly endowed until Revolutionary iconoclasts pinched its treasures, including the hearts of Louis XIII and XIV. Afterwards, in 1802, it was converted back into a church, and today it houses Delacroix's *Christ in the Garden of Olives*.

Maison Européenne de la Photographie

5-7 rue de Fourcy, 4th (01.44.78.75.00/ www.mep-fr.org). M° St-Paul. **Open** 11am-8pm (last entry 7.30pm) Wed-Sun. **Admission** €6.50; €3.50 reductions; free under-8s, all 5-8pm Wed. **Credit** MC, V. **Map** p409 L6.

Probably the capital's best photography exhibition space, hosting retrospectives by Larry Clark and Martine Barrat, along with work by emerging photographers. The building, an airy mansion with a modern extension, contains a huge permanent collection.
► *The venue organises the biennial Mois de la Photo and the Art Outsiders festival of new media web art in September.*

★ FREE Le Mémorial de la Shoah

17 rue Geoffroy-l'Asnier, 4th (01.42.77.44.72/ www.memorialdelashoah.org). M° Pont Marie or St-Paul. **Open** 10am-6pm Mon-Wed, Fri-Sun; 10am-10pm Thur. *Research centre* 10am-5.30pm Mon-Wed, Fri, Sun; 10am-7.30pm Thur. **Admission** free. **Map** p409 K6.

Airport-style security checks mean queues, but don't let that put you off: the Mémorial du Martyr Juif Inconnu is an impressively presented and moving memorial to the Holocaust. Enter via the Wall of Names, where limestone slabs are engraved with the first and last names of each of the 76,000 Jews deported from France from 1942 to 1944 with, as an inscription reminds the visitor, the say-so of the Vichy government. The basement-level permanent exhibition documents the plight of French and European Jews through photographs, texts, films and individual stories: 'The French,' reads one label (captioning is also given in English), 'were not particularly interested in the fate of French Jews at this point.'

FREE Pavillon de l'Arsenal

21 bd Morland, 4th (01.42.76.33.97/www. pavillon-arsenal.com). M° Sully Morland. **Open** 10.30am-6.30pm Tue-Sat; 11am-7pm Sun. **Admission** free. **Credit** *Shop* MC, V. **Map** p409 L7.

The setting is a fantastic 1880s gallery with an iron frame and glass roof; the subject is the built history of Paris; the result is disappointing. The ground floor houses a permanent exhibition on the city's development, but space and funds are lacking to the extent that exhibits are limited to a few storyboards, maps and photos, and three city models set into the floor (done far more impressively at the Musée d'Orsay).

SIGHTS

Bastille & Eastern Paris

Politics to the fore at the city's revolutionary roundabout.

The famous fortress-cum-prison is long gone, but its role in the kick-off to the French Revolution makes this patch of Paris one of the most historic pieces of soil in the whole country. The spot is now a large roundabout (you can see a chunk of the foundations in the métro station underneath) that is usually choked with traffic – except when it's choked with mass demonstrations: thanks to the symbolism of 1789, Bastille is a political hotspot to this day. The streets immediately north and east are particularly strong on good yet affordable restaurants, and the

Maps pp406-407	**Restaurants** p203
Hotels p173	**Cafés & bars** p228

Bercy district has seen its star rise with the arrival a few years ago of the Cinémathèque Française, and the shops and cafés at Bercy Village.

BASTILLE & FURTHER EAST

In the 11th, 12th and 20th arrondissements.

Place de la Bastille has been a potent symbol of popular rebellion ever since 1789. The area was transformed in the 1980s with the arrival of the **Opéra Bastille** (*see p317*), along with fashionable cafés, restaurants and bars. The present-day square occupies the site of the long-vanished prison ramparts, and is dominated by Opéra's curved façade. Opened

INSIDE TRACK
PROMENADE PLANTEE

The railway tracks atop the **Viaduc des Arts** (*see p108*) were replaced in the late 1980s by a handsome promenade planted with roses, shrubs and rosemary. It continues at ground level through the Jardin de Reuilly and the Jardin Charles Péguy on to the Bois de Vincennes.

in 1989 on the bicentenary of Bastille Day, the venue remains controversial, criticised for its poor acoustics and design. South of the square is the Port de l'Arsenal marina, where the Canal St-Martin meets the Seine. The canal continues underground north of the square, running beneath boulevard Richard-Lenoir, site of a lively outdoor market on Sunday mornings.

Rue du Fbg-St-Antoine has been the heart of the furniture-makers' district for centuries. Furniture showrooms still line the street, though they've been joined by clothes shops and bars. Cobbled rue de Lappe typifies the shift, as the last remaining furniture workshops hold out against theme bars overrun at weekends by suburban youths. Pockets of bohemian resistance remain on rue de Charonne, however, with the **Pause Café** (*see p230*) and its busy terrace, bistro **Chez Paul** (no.13, 11th, 01.47.00.34.57) and dealers in colourful 1960s furniture. Rue des Taillandiers and rue Keller are a focus for record stores, streetwear shops and fashion designers.

Narrow street frontages hide cobbled alleys, lined with craftsmen's workshops or quirky

SIGHTS

bistros dating from the 18th century. Note the cours de l'Ours, du Cheval Blanc, du Bel Air (and hidden garden) and de la Maison Brûlée, the passage du Chantier on rue du Fbg-St-Antoine, the rustic-looking passage de l'Etoile d'Or and the passage de l'Homme, with wooden shopfronts on rue de Charonne. This area was originally located outside the city walls on the lands of the Convent of St-Antoine (parts of which survive as the Hôpital St-Antoine). In the Middle Ages, skilled furnituremakers not belonging to the city's restrictive guilds earned the neighbourhood a reputation for free thinking that was cemented a few hundred years later during the Revolution.

Further down rue du Fbg-St-Antoine is place d'Aligre, home to a rowdy, cheap produce market, a more sedate covered food hall and the only flea market within the city walls, where a handful of *brocanteurs* sell junk and old books. The road ends in the major intersection of place de la Nation, another grand square. It was originally called place du Trône, after a throne that was positioned here when Louis XIV and his bride Marie-Thérèse entered the city in 1660. After the Revolution, between 13 June and 28 July 1799, thousands were guillotined on the site, their bodies carted to the nearby Cimetière de Picpus. The square still has two of Ledoux's toll houses and tall Doric columns from the 1787 Mur des Fermiers-Généraux. In the centre stands Jules Dalou's sculpture *Le Triomphe de la République*, erected for the centenary of the Revolution in 1889. East of place de la Nation, broad cours de Vincennes has a market on Wednesday and Saturday mornings and kerb-crawlers by night.

North of place de la Bastille, boulevard Beaumarchais divides Bastille from the Marais. East of place Voltaire, on rue de la Roquette, which heads east towards the Ménilmontant area and **Père-Lachaise** cemetery, a small park and playground marks the site of the prison de la Roquette, where a plaque remembers the 4,000 Resistance members imprisoned here in World War II.

★ FREE Cimetière du Père-Lachaise

Bd de Ménilmontant, 20th (01.55.25.82.10). M° Père-Lachaise. **Open** *6 Nov-15 Mar* 8am-5.30pm Mon-Fri; 8.30am-5.30pm Sat; 9am-5.30pm Sun. *16 Mar-5 Nov* 8am-6pm Mon-Fri; 8.30am-6pm Sat; 9am-6pm Sun & hols. **Admission** free. **Map** p407 P5.

Père-Lachaise is the celebrity cemetery – it has almost anyone French, talented and dead that you care to mention. Not even French, for that matter. Creed and nationality have never prevented entry: you just had to have lived or died in Paris or have an allotted space in a family tomb. For a tour round the cemetery, *see p106* **Walk**.

La Maison Rouge – Fondation Antoine de Galbert

10 bd de la Bastille, 12th (01.40.01.08.81/ www.lamaisonrouge.org). M° Quai de la Rapée. **Open** 11am-7pm Wed, Fri-Sun; 11am-9pm Thur. **Admission** €7; €5 reductions; free under-13s. **Credit** MC, V. **Map** p406 M7.

Founded by collector Antoine de Galberg, and set in a former printworks, the Red House is an independently run space that alternates monographic shows of contemporary artists' work with pieces from different private art collections.

BERCY & DAUMESNIL

The **Viaduc des Arts** is a former railway viaduct along avenue Daumesnil; its row of glass-fronted arches enclose craft boutiques and workshops. Above sprout the blooms and bamboo of the **Promenade Plantée**, which continues through the Jardin de Reuilly and east to the **Bois de Vincennes**.

Eglise du Saint-Esprit is a copy of Istanbul's Hagia Sofia; the nearby **Cimetière de Picpus** contains the graves of many of the victims of the Terror, as well as American War of Independence hero General La Fayette.

Just before the Périphérique, the **Palais de la Porte Dorée** was built in 1931 for the Exposition Coloniale. It features striking, albeit politically incorrect, reliefs on the façade and two beautiful art deco offices. Originally the

Promenade Plantée.

SIGHTS

Walk Cimetière du Père-Lachaise

The last resting place of some of France's most illustrious corpses.

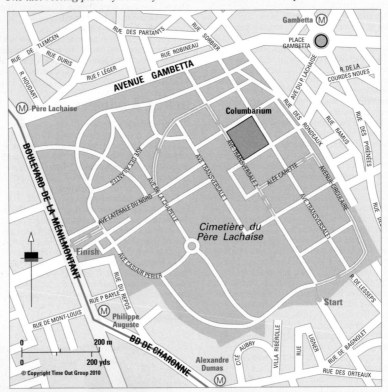

The Cimetière du Père-Lachaise, Paris's largest cemetery, is probably still best known to foreign visitors as the final resting place of one **James Douglas Morrison**, lead singer of the Doors. But ask a local what this 48-hectare site in the 20th arrondissement means to them, and they're more likely to mention the Mur des Fédérés or **Molière** than the Lizard King. On this walk, therefore, you'll pay tribute to the heroes and victims of French political history, and visit the tombs of some of France's greatest writers.

Rather than entering Père-Lachaise by the main entrance on boulevard Ménilmontant, start at the much more discreet gate set into the southern wall of the cemetery on rue de la Réunion, just off rue de Bagnolet. You join avenue

Circulaire, which hugs the cemetery wall. Turn right and then follow the path round until you reach the Mur des Fédérés in the south-east corner.

It was here, during the last week of May 1871, that the few remaining partisans of the **Paris Commune** (known as *fédérés* or communards) were lined up against a wall and summarily executed by troops loyal to the National Assembly at Versailles. A memorial procession to the wall, the Montée au Mur des Fédérés, takes place every year in May.

Across the path, in plot or 'division' No.97, stand a number of memorials to the victims of Nazism and Fascism. Next to an urn containing ashes from the crematorium at the Flossenburg concentration camp is a striking ziggurat commemorating people who were 'tortured, gassed, shot or hanged' at Mauthausen. And just behind this loom two enormous manacled hands hewn from stone, a deeply unsettling monument to the women who died at Ravensbruck. A little further along avenue Circulaire, on the same side, is the tomb of people who perished in 1962 at the hands of the police, not far from here at the Charonne métro station, after a demonstration in favour of Algerian independence.

Follow avenue Circulaire along the northern wall until you reach the Jardin du Souvenir. Turn left up avenue Carette, keeping an eye out on your right for the monumental sarcophagus housing the remains of **Oscar Wilde**, who died in Paris in 1900.

When you reach avenue Transversale no.2, turn left and walk down the hill, until you reach a bronze effigy of **Victor Noir**, a journalist who was shot by a cousin of Napoleon III in 1870. You'll notice that the effigy depicts Noir with a distinct enlargement in the region of the groin, and also that the area in question appears to have been rubbed down rather energetically: many *parisiennes* have believed that a little *frottage* with Victor would make them fertile.

Now retrace your steps in the direction of the crematorium and columbarium. On your left, in division 86, is the rough-hewn headstone of **Guillaume Appolinaire**. Across the path, **Marcel Proust** lies in an austere marble tomb with other members of his family.

Continue along avenue Transversale No.2, until you reach avenue des Thuryas. Turn left and walk down the hill into gently curving chemin Casimir Delavigne. About halfway down on the right is a bronze bust of **Honoré de Balzac**. The bust is accompanied by a bronze book and quill, upon which, on our most recent visit, an admirer had left an apple with a heart carved in it.

Walk straight on, down chemin Mont-Louis. Through the trees you'll catch a few tantalising glimpses of the Paris skyline as you head towards avenue Principale, and beyond that the main gate of the cemetery, and the din and traffic of boulevard Ménilmontant.

Musée des Colonies, then the Musée des Arts d'Afrique et d'Océanie (its collections now absorbed by the **Musée du Quai Branly**; *see p146*), it's the new home of the **Cité Nationale de l'Histoire de l'Immigration**. There's also an aquarium in the basement.

As recently as the 1980s, wine was unloaded from barges at Bercy, but after redevelopment this stretch of the Seine is now home to the vast Ministère de l'Economie et du Budget and, to the west, the **Palais Omnisports de Paris-Bercy** (*see p334*). To the east is the Bercy Expo exhibition and trade centre. In between lie the modern **Parc de Bercy** and the former American Center, built in the 1990s by Frank Gehry. It has now reopened as the Cinémathèque Française. At the eastern edge of the park is **Bercy Village**, where warehouses have been restored and opened as shops and cafés. Another conversion is the Pavillons de Bercy, with the **Musée des Arts Forains**, a collection of fairground rides and carnival salons.

★ FREE Bois de Vincennes

12th. Mº Château de Vincennes or Porte Dorée.
This is Paris's biggest park, created, like the Bois de Boulogne in the west, when the former royal hunting forest was landscaped by Alphand for Baron Haussmann. There are boating lakes, a Buddhist temple, a racetrack, restaurants, a baseball field (*see p336*) and a small farm (*see p288*). The park also contains the Cartoucherie theatre complex (*see p345*). The Parc Floral is a cross between a botanical garden and an amusement park. Amusements include Paris-themed crazy golf, with water drawn from the Seine, and an adventure playground. Next to the park stands the imposing Château de Vincennes, where England's Henry V died in 1422.
▶ *Jazz concerts take place in the Parc Floral on summer weekends; see p276.*

Cimetière de Picpus

35 rue de Picpus, 12th (01.43.44.18.54). Mº Daumesnil, Nation or Picpus. **Open** *15 Apr-14 Oct* 2-6pm Tue-Sun. *15 Oct-14 Apr* 2-4pm Tue-Sun. **Admission** €3. **No credit cards. Map** p407 Q8.
Redolent with revolutionary associations, French and American, this cemetery in a working convent is the resting place for the thousands of victims of the Revolution's aftermath, guillotined at place du Trône (now place de la Nation) between 14 June and 27 July 1794. At the end of a walled garden is a graveyard of aristocratic French families. In one corner is the tomb of General La Fayette, who fought in the American War of Independence and was married to the aristocratic Marie Adrienne Françoise de Noailles. Clearly marked are the sites of two communal graves, and you can see the doorway where the carts arrived. It was thanks to a maid who had seen the carts that the site was rediscovered,

SIGHTS

including the cemetery and adjoining convent, founded by descendants of the Noailles family. In the chapel, two tablets list the names and occupations of the executed: 'domestic servant' and 'farmer' figure alongside 'lawyer' and 'prince and priest'.

★ Cité Nationale de l'Histoire de l'Immigration

293 av Daumesnil, 12th (01.58.51.52.00/ www.histoire-immigration.fr). M° Porte Dorée. **Open** 10am-5.30pm Tue-Fri; 10am-7pm Sat, Sun. **Admission** €5; €3 reductions; free under-18s. *Aquarium* €4.50; €3 reductions. PMP. **No credit cards.**

Set in the stunning, colonial-themed Palais de la Porte Dorée (built in 1931 for the World Colonial Fair), the permanent collections here trace over 200 years of immigration history. There are thought-provoking images (film and photography), everyday objects (suitcases, accordions, sewing machines and so on) and artworks that symbolise the struggles immigrants had to face when integrating into French society. Don't miss the permanent exhibition area, Repères (bearings), that looks at why many immigrants chose France, the problems they faced upon arrival, and the way sport, work, language, religion and culture can ease integration. One of the most moving areas is the Galerie des Dons – a collection of personal memorabilia donated by individuals whose families came from foreign countries.

Cité Nationale de l'Histoire de l'Immigration.

▶ *At the end, head downstairs to the palace's aquarium, which displays a small collection of fish, turtles and crocodiles.*

FREE Eglise du Saint-Esprit

186 av Daumesnil, 12th (01.44.75.77.50/www. st-esprit.org). M° Daumesnil. **Open** 9.30am-noon, 3-7pm Mon-Fri; 9.30am-noon, 3-6pm Sat; from 9am Sun. **Admission** free. **Map** p407 P9.

Behind a red-brick exterior cladding, this unusual 1920s concrete church follows a square plan around a central dome, lit by a scalloped ring of windows. Architect Paul Tournon was directly inspired by the Hagia Sofia cathedral in Istanbul, though rather than mosaics, the inside is decorated with frescoes by Maurice Denis and others.

Musée des Arts Forains

53 av des Terroirs-de-France, 12th (01.43.40.16.22/www.pavillons-de-bercy.com). M° Cour St-Emilion. **Open** groups only, min 15 people, by appointment. **Admission** €12.50; €4 reductions. **No credit cards. Map** p407 P10.

Housed in a collection of Eiffel-era, iron-framed wine warehouses is a fantastical collection of 19th- and early 20th-century fairground attractions. The venue is hired out for functions on most evenings, and staff may well be setting the tables when you visit. Of the three halls, the most wonderful is the Salon de la Musique, where a musical sculpture by Jacques Rémus chimes and flashes in time with the 1934 Mortier organ and a modern-day digital grand piano playing *Murder on the Orient Express*. In the Salon de Venise you are twirled round on a gondola carousel; in the Salon des Arts Forains you can play a ball-throwing game that sets off a race of moustachioed waiters or brave the Vélocipède, a nightmarish carousel of penny farthings. The venue is open only to groups of 15 or more, but individuals can visit as part of a guided tour. Call ahead.

FREE Parc de Bercy

Rue de Bercy, 12th. M° Bercy or Cour St-Emilion. **Open** *Winter* 8am-5.30pm Mon-Fri; 9am-5.30pm Sat, Sun. *Summer* 8am-9pm Mon-Fri; 9am-9pm Sat, Sun. **Map** p407 N9/10.

Created in the 1990s, the Bercy park features a large lawn, a grid with square rose, herb and vegetable plots, an orchard, and gardens laid out to represent the four seasons.

FREE Le Viaduc des Arts

15-121 av Daumesnil, 12th (www.viaduc-des-arts.com). M° Gare de Lyon or Ledru-Rollin. **Map** p407 M8/N8.

Glass-fronted workshops in the arches beneath the Promenade Plantée provide showrooms for furniture and fashion designers, picture-frame gilders, tapestry restorers, porcelain decorators, and chandelier, violin and flute makers. Design industry body VIA holds exhibitions of work at Nos.29-35.

North-east Paris

Fashionably working class.

In the city's folklore, north-east Paris is working class Paris – and although patches of it are gentrifying and little actual industry remains, the area still has a distinctive rough and ready vibe. Many of the streets here are somewhat on the tatty side, but others are artsy and fashionable, especially those close to the Canal St-Martin; and large swaths of the north-east – for example rue du Fbg-St-Denis and the thoroughfares leading off it – are excitingly multi-ethnic, with thriving North African, Turkish and Caribbean enclaves. In the top right corner is La Villette (through which the German occupiers entered the city in 1940), with its science museums, wacky landscaped gardens and recently opened arts space in the former city undertaker's.

Map p403 & p407 **Restaurants** p206
Hotels p174 **Cafés & bars** p231

FBG-ST-DENIS TO GARE DU NORD

In the 10th arrondissement.

North of Porte St-Denis and Porte St-Martin, two of the oldest thoroughfares leading out of the city, rue du Fbg-St-Denis and rue du Fbg-St-Martin, traverse an area that was transformed in the 19th century by the railways, when it became the site of the Gare du Nord and Gare de l'Est. The grubby rue du Fbg-St-Denis is almost souk-like with its food shops, narrow passages and sinister courtyards. Garishly lit passage Brady is a surprising piece of India in Paris, full of restaurants, hairdressers and costume shops, whereas the art deco passage du Prado is more a continuation of the Sentier rag trade. The rue du Fbg-St-Martin follows the trace of the Roman road out of the city, and is full of children's clothes wholesalers, atmospheric courtyards and the ornate Mairie for the tenth. Rue des Petites-Ecuries ('Little Stables Street') was once known for saddlers, but now has shops, cafés and jazz venue **New Morning** (*see p325*), and is home to Turkish and Afro-Caribbean communities.

Rue de Paradis is known for its porcelain and glass outlets, and rue d'Hauteville shows traces of the area's grander days (notably the **Petit Hôtel Bourrienne**, at no.58, a Consulaire-style apartment open to the public). Opposite, the Cité Paradis is an alley of early industrial buildings. At the top of the street are the twin towers and terraced gardens of the **Eglise St-Vincent-de-Paul**. Behind, on rue de Belzunce, is Chez Casimir at no.6 (10th, 01.48.78.28.80). On boulevard Magenta, **Marché St-Quentin**, built in the 1860s, is one of the city's last few remaining cast-iron, covered market halls.

Boulevard de Strasbourg was cut through in the 19th century to create a vista up to the Gare de l'Est. At no.2, a neo-Renaissance creation houses the last fan-maker in Paris and the **Musée de l'Eventail**. Towards the station, Eglise St-Laurent (69 bd de Magenta, 119 rue du Fbg-St-Martin, 10th) is one of the city's oldest churches, an eclectic composition with a 12th-century tower, Gothic nave, baroque lady chapel, 19th-century façade and 1930s stained glass. Between the Gare de l'Est and **Canal St-Martin** are the restored **Couvent des Récollets** and Square Villemin park.

FREE Couvent des Récollets
148 rue du Fbg-St-Martin, 10th. M° Gare de l'Est. **Admission** free. **Map** p402 L3.

Founded as a monastery in the 17th century when still outside the city walls, this barracks, spinning factory and hospice was a military hospital from 1860 to 1968. Left empty, the convent was squatted by artists, Les Anges des Récollets, in the early 1990s. The buildings were renovated and reopened in 2004. One half, the Maison des Architectes, hosts a garden café and architectural debates. The other is the Centre International d'Accueil et d'Echanges des Récollets: 85 studios and duplexes for foreign 'creators' – artists and researchers (from painters to neurobiologists) – invited to stay here for extended periods. In rehabilitating the building, architect Frédéric Vincendon left traces of its history: the ghostly 17th-century stonework, 20th-century reinforced concrete columns and squatters' graffiti.

★ FREE Eglise St-Vincent-de-Paul

5 rue Belzunce, 10th (01.48.78.47.47). M° Gare du Nord. **Open** 2-7pm Mon; 8am-noon, 2-7pm Tue-Fri; 8am-noon, 2-7.30pm Sat; 9.30am-noon, 4.30-7.30pm Sun. **Admission** free. **Map** p402 K2.
Set at the top of terraced gardens, this church was begun in 1824 by Lepère and completed in 1844 by Hittorff. The twin towers, pedimented Greek temple portico and sculptures of the four evangelists along the parapet are in high classical mode. The interior has a splendid double-storey arcade of columns, murals by Flandrin and church furniture by Rude.

Gare du Nord

Rue de Dunkerque, 10th (08.91.36.20.20). M° Gare du Nord. **Map** p402 K2.
The grandest of the great 19th-century train stations (and Eurostar terminal since 1994) was designed by Hittorff between 1861 and 1864. A conventional stone façade, with Ionic capitals and statues representing towns served by the station, hides a vast iron-and-glass vault. The airy refurbishment of the suburban section by rue du Fbg-St-Denis makes the Eurostar's glass-topped digs look a little drab.

Musée de l'Eventail

2 bd de Strasbourg, 10th (01.42.08.90.20/www. annehoguet.fr). M° Strasbourg St-Denis. **Open** 2-6pm Mon-Wed (Mon-Fri during school hols).

Children's activities Wed afternoons. Closed Aug. **Admission** €6; €3-€4 reductions; free under-8s. **No credit cards**. **Map** p402 K4.
Anne Hoguet keeps the tradition of her ancestors alive in this arcane museum inside a 19th-century apartment, which has been a fan-maker's *atelier* since 1805. One room houses the tools of the trade; beside it is Hoguet's studio, where she works on fans for fashion and the stage. The former *salle d'exposition*, lined in blue silk, is where the collection of almost 1,000 historic fans is shown in glass cases and stored in cabinets.

Petit Hôtel Bourrienne

58 rue d'Hauteville, 10th (01.47.70.51.14). M° Bonne Nouvelle or Poissonnière. **Open** *Guided visits* 1-15 July, Sept noon-6pm daily. Rest of year by appointment Sat. **Admission** €7. **No credit cards**. **Map** p402 K3.
A rare example of the Consulaire style, this small *hôtel particulier* was built in 1789-98. It was occupied by Fortunée Hamelin, born (like her friend the Empress Josephine) in Martinique, and notorious for parading topless down the Champs-Elysées. A bedroom boudoir painted with tropical birds was her only decoration before the site was taken over by Louis Fauvelet de Bourrienne, Napoleon's private secretary. He had it decorated according to the latest fashion, making sure to keep his political options open (the dining room ceiling is painted with motifs favourable to monarchy and empire).

CANAL ST-MARTIN TO LA VILLETTE

In the 10th & 19th arrondissements

Canal St-Martin, built between 1805 and 1825, begins at the Seine at Pont Morland, disappears underground at Bastille, hides under boulevard

INSIDE TRACK
CANAL ST-MARTIN

If the Seine begins to pall, then take a trip up the city's second waterway, the Canal St-Martin, with **Canauxrama** (01.42.39.15.00,www.canauxrama.fr). The tree-lined canal is a pretty and characterful sight, and the trip even takes you underground for a stretch, where the tunnel walls are enlivened by a light show.

Richard-Lenoir, then emerges after crossing rue du Fbg-du-Temple, east of place de la République. Rue du Fbg-du-Temple itself is scruffy and cosmopolitan, lined with cheap grocers and discount stores, hidden courtyards and stalwarts of Paris nightlife: **Le Gibus** (*see p329*), bar-restaurant **Favela Chic** (*see p333*) and vintage dancehall **La Java** (*see p333*), as well as the **Palais des Glaces** (no.37, 10th, 01.42.02.27.17, www.palaisdesglaces.com), which programmes seasons of French comics.

The first stretch of the canal, lined with shady trees and crossed by iron footbridges and locks, has the most appeal. The quays are traffic-free on Sundays. Many canalside warehouses have been snapped up by artists and designers or turned into loft apartments. You can take a boat as far as La Villette.

East of here, the Hôpital St-Louis was commissioned in 1607 by Henri IV to house plague victims, and was built as a series of isolated pavilions in the same brick-and-stone style as place des Vosges, far enough from the town to prevent risk of infection. Behind the hospital, the rue de la Grange-aux-Belles housed the Montfaucon gibbet, put up in 1233, where victims were hanged and left to the elements. East of the hospital, the lovely cobbled rue Ste-Marthe and place Ste-Marthe have a provincial air, busy at night with multi-ethnic eateries.

North, on place du Colonel-Fabien, is the headquarters of the **Parti Communiste Français**, a modernist masterpiece built between 1968 and 1971 by Brazilian architect Oscar Niemeyer with Paul Chemetov and Jean Deroche. The canal disappears briefly again under place de Stalingrad, a locale best avoided after dark. The square was landscaped in 1989 to showcase the Rotonde de la Villette, one of Ledoux's grandiose 1780s toll houses that once marked the boundary of Paris; it now displays exhibitions and archaeological finds.

Here the canal widens into the Bassin de la Villette, and the new developments along the quai de Loire and further quai de la Marne, as well as some of the worst 1960s and '70s housing in the colossal blocks that stretch along rue de Flandres. At 104 rue d'Aubervilliers, the old municipal undertaker's has been turned into a multimedia art space, **104**.

At the eastern end of the basin is an unusual 1885 hydraulic lifting bridge, Pont de Crimée. Thursday and Sunday mornings add vitality with a market at place de Joinville. East of here, the Canal de l'Ourcq (created in 1813 to provide drinking water, as well as for freight haulage) divides: Canal St-Denis runs north towards the Seine, and Canal de l'Ourcq continues east through La Villette and the suburbs. Long the city's main abattoir district, still reflected in the Grande Halle de la Villette and in some of the

old meaty brasseries along boulevard de la Villette, the neighbourhood has been revitalised since the late 1980s by the postmodern **Parc de la Villette** complex, with the **Cité des Sciences et de l'Industrie** science museum and the **Cité de la Musique** concert hall.

★ FREE 104

104 rue d'Aubervilliers, 19th (01.53.35.50.00/ www.104.fr). M° Riquet. **Open** 11am-9pm Tue-Thur, Sun; 11am-11pm Fri, Sat. **Admission** free. *Exhibitions* €5; €3 reductions. **Credit** AmEx, MC, V.

It's more than a century since tourist-choked Montmartre was the centre of artistic activity in Paris. But now the north of Paris is again where the action is – albeit a couple of kilometres east of place du Tertre, in a previously neglected area of bleak railway goods yards and dilapidated social housing. 104, described as a 'space for artistic creation', occupies a vast 19th-century building on the rue d'Aubervilliers that used to house Paris's municipal undertakers. The site was saved from developers by Roger Madec, the mayor of the 19th, who's made its renovation the centrepiece of a massive project of cultural and urban renewal. There aren't any constraints on the kind of work the resident artists do – 104 is open to 'all the arts' – but they're expected to show finished pieces in one of four annual 'festivals'. And they're also required to get involved in projects with the public, the fruits of which are shown in a space next door.

★ La Cité des Sciences et de l'Industrie

La Villette, 30 av Corentin-Cariou, 19th (01.40.05.70.00/www.cite-sciences.fr). M° Porte de la Villette. **Open** 10am-6pm Tue-Sat; 10am-7pm Sun. **Admission** €8; €6 reductions; free under-7s. PMP. **Credit** MC, V. **Map** p403 inset.

This ultra-modern science museum pulls in five million visitors a year. Explora, the permanent show, occupies the upper two floors, whisking visitors through 30,000sq m (320,000sq ft) of space, life, matter and communication: scale models of satellites including the Ariane space shuttle, planes and robots, plus the chance to experience weightlessness, make for an exciting journey. In the Espace Images, try the delayed camera and other optical illusions, draw 3D images on a computer or lend your voice to the *Mona Lisa*. The hothouse garden investigates developments in agriculture and bio-technology.

▶ *The Cité des Enfants runs workshops for younger children. See the website for details.*

Musée de la Musique

Cité de la Musique, 221 av Jean-Jaurès, 19th (01.44.84.45.00/www.cite-musique.fr). M° Porte de Pantin. **Open** noon-6pm Tue-Sat; 10am-6pm Sun. **Admission** €8; €6.40 reductions; free under-18s, over-60s. PMP. **Credit** AmEx, MC, V. **Map** p403 inset.

SIGHTS

Alongside the concert hall, this innovative music museum houses a gleamingly restored collection of instruments from the old Conservatoire, interactive computers and scale models of opera houses and concert halls. Visitors are supplied with an audio guide in a choice of languages, and the musical commentary is a joy, playing the appropriate instrument as you approach each exhibit. Alongside the trumpeting brass, curly woodwind instruments and precious strings are more unusual items, such as the Indonesian gamelan orchestra, whose sounds influenced the work of Debussy and Ravel. Concerts in the amphitheatre use instruments from the collection.

★ FREE Parc de la Villette

Av Corentin-Cariou, 19th (01.40.03.75.75/www. villette.com). M° Porte de la Villette. Av Jean-Jaurès, 19th. M° Porte de Pantin. **Map** p403 inset. Dotted with red pavilions, or *folies*, the park was designed by Swiss architect Bernard Tschumi and is a postmodern feast (guided tours 08.03.30.63.06, 3pm Sun in summer). The *folies* serve as glorious giant climbing frames, as well as a first-aid post, burger bar and children's art centre. Kids shoot down a Chinese dragon slide, and an undulating suspended path follows the Canal de l'Ourcq. As well as the lawns, which are used for an open-air film festival in summer, there are ten themed gardens bearing evocative names such as the Garden of Mirrors, of Mists, of Acrobatics and of Childhood Frights. South of the canal are the Zénith (*see p319*), and the Grande Halle de la Villette – now used for trade fairs, exhibitions and September's jazz festival (*see p278*). It is flanked by the Conservatoire de la Musique and the Cité de la Musique, with rehearsal rooms, concert halls and the Musée de la Musique.

BELLEVILLE, MENILMONTANT & CHARONNE

In the 11th, 19th & 20th arrondissements.

When the city boundaries were expanded in 1860, Ménilmontant, Belleville and Charonne, once villages that provided Paris with fruit, wine and weekend escapes, were all absorbed. They were built up with housing for migrants, first from rural France and later from former colonies in North Africa and South-east Asia. The area encompasses one of the city's most beautiful parks, the romantic **Buttes-Chaumont**. Despite attempts to dissipate workers' agitation by splitting the village between the 11th, 19th and 20th administrative districts, Belleville became the centre of opposition to the Second Empire. Cabarets, artisans and workers typified 1890s Belleville; colonised by artists in the 1990s, today Belleville is a trendy hangout.

On boulevard de Belleville, Chinese and Vietnamese shops rub shoulders with Muslim and kosher groceries, and couscous and falafel eateries; a street market takes place here on Tuesday and Friday mornings.

North of here, along avenue Simon-Bolivar, is the Parc des Buttes-Chaumont. This is the most desirable part of north-east Paris, with Haussmannian apartments overlooking the park: to the east, near place de Rhin-et-Danube, is a small area of tiny, hilly streets lined with small houses and gardens, known by locals as the Quartier Mouzaïa.

Up on the slopes of the Hauts de Belleville, there are views over the city from rue Piat and rue des Envierges, which lead to the modern but charming **Parc de Belleville** with its Maison des Vents devoted to birds and kites. Below the park, rue Ramponneau mixes new housing and relics of old Belleville. At no.23 an old smithy has been transformed into La Forge, an artists' squat.

'Mesnil-Montant' used to be a few houses on a hill with vines and fruit trees – then came the bistros, bordellos and workers' housing. It became part of Paris in 1860 along with Belleville, and has a similar history. These days it's a thriving centre of alternative Paris, as artists and young professionals have moved in. Although side streets still have male-only North African cafés, rue Oberkampf is home to some of the city's most humming bars, many following the runaway success of the pivotal **Café Charbon** (*see p232*).

The area mixes 1960s and '70s housing projects with older dwellings, some gentrified, some derelict. Just below rue des Pyrénées, which cuts through the 20th, you can rummage around the rustic Cité Leroy or Villa l'Ermitage, cobbled cul-de-sacs of little houses and gardens, and old craft workshops. Rue de l'Ermitage has a curious neo-Gothic house at no.19 – and a bird's eye view from the junction with rue de Ménilmontant, right down the hill to the Centre Pompidou. On rue Boyer, **La Maroquinerie** (*see p321*) puts on an eclectic mix of literary events, political debate and live music, and at 88 rue de Ménilmontant, graffiti-covered art squat **La Miroiterie** opens house for art shows and the *magasin gratuit*, a free swap shop.

East of Père-Lachaise, the medieval **Eglise St-Germain-de-Charonne** is at the heart of what is left of the village of Charonne. Set at the top of steps next to its presbytery, it is the only church in Paris, except St-Pierre-de-Montmartre, still to have its own graveyard. Below here, centred on the old village high street of rue St-Blaise, is a prettified backwater of quiet tearooms and bistros, where old shops have been taken over by art classes.

Towards porte de Bagnolet, where rue de Bagnolet and rue des Balkans meet on the edge of a small park, the **Pavillon de l'Hermitage** is a small aristocratic relic built in the 1720s for

Françoise-Marie de Bourbon, the daughter of Louis XIV, when it was in the grounds of the Château de Bagnolet. A little further south at porte de Montreuil, cross the Périphérique for the Puces de Montreuil market (Mon, Sat, Sun).

FREE Eglise St-Germain-de-Charonne

Pl St-Blaise, 20th (01.43.71.42.04). Mº Porte de Bagnolet. **Admission** free. **Open** 9am-7pm.
The old village church of Charonne dates mainly from the 15th century, though one massive column and the bell tower remain from an earlier structure. The interior is almost square, with a triple nave and a simple organ loft. Two side altars have striking modern paintings (a crucifixion and a pietà) by Paul Rambié; a niche contains a wood statue of St Blaise.

FREE Musée Edith Piaf

5 rue Crespin-du-Gast, 11th (01.43.55.52.72). Mº Ménilmontant. **Open** *By appointment only* 1-6pm Mon-Wed. **Admission** free (donations welcome).
See below **Secret Museums**.

★ FREE Parc des Buttes-Chaumont

Rue Botzaris, rue Manin, rue de Crimée, 19th. Mº Buttes Chaumont. **Open** *Oct-Apr* 7am-8pm daily. *May-Aug* 7am-10pm daily. *Sept* 7am-9pm daily. **Map** p407 N2.
With its meandering paths and vertical cliffs, this lovely park was designed by Adolphe Alphand for Haussmann in the 1860s. A bridge (cheerfully named the Pont des Suicides) crosses the lake to an island crowned by a mini-temple.

Secret Museums Musée Edith Piaf

An intimate look at France's greatest singer.

The answerphone said it was closed for renovation, but when we arrived on the first week of reopening, the **Musée Edith Piaf**'s (*see above*) curator Bernard Marchois admitted he'd been on holiday. As he has every right to do, for this is a one-man, one-woman show. Les Amis d'Edith Piaf has 6,000 members, whose subscriptions go to buy memorabilia and keep the memory of the 'little sparrow' alive, but the museum is in Mr Marchois' home, a small apartment where Piaf lived at the age of 18, when she sang on the streets of Ménilmontant.

Phoning for an appointment is essential, and Mr Marchois gives you the codes for the building. You are greeted by strains of Piaf's music and a friendly little dog called Opium, perhaps a reference to the drug that contributed to the early death of Piaf at 47. The museum consists of two red-painted rooms crammed with letters, pictures, framed discs and personal objects belonging to the singer, and the first thing you'll see is a cardboard cut-out of the singer that shows her real size – only 1m 47cm (4ft 10in).

Mr Marchois doesn't speak English, though he has a photocopy of an article about the museum. It helps, therefore, to have seen the Marillon Cotillard film before you go, to allow you to piece together the scrapbook of Piaf's highly mythologised life. This will make sense of the boxing gloves belonging to her lover Marcel Cerdan, the tributes from many famous French artistes of the day, the photos of her aged four, just after she regained her sight, and again in

her 40s but looking about 70, her face puffed with alcohol and drug abuse. Her birth certificate shows that she was born not on the street but in a hospital, dispelling a myth that she allowed to perpetuate after a journalist misquoted her.

The museum's real treasures are two hand-written letters, one a chatty number written on her 28th birthday, and another more passionate pen to the actor Robert Dalban who she felt had betrayed her. These – and the well-worn, human-sized teddy bear cuddling a tiny monkey soft toy – are the only clues to the real Piaf, whose voice encapsulated that particular French melancholy, drama, stubbornness and heroism that made her the greatest singer the nation has ever known.

The Latin Quarter & the 13th

Education and renovation on the banks of the Seine.

To many first-time visitors – especially those from the States – the Latin Quarter can be a big disappointment. Countless books have led them to believe that the area is somehow the quintessence of Paris, and they come with their heads stuffed with expat writers – Orwell, Hemingway, Henry Miller – only to find a touristy jam of bad restaurants and uninspiring shops. Granted, many of the narrow, crooked streets (like the Marais, the Latin Quarter was another part of Paris largely untouched by Haussmann) are charming, and there are some real architectural glories, especially

| Map p406 | Restaurants p199 |
| Hotels p170 | Cafés & bars p234 |

ecclesiastical ones; but the crowds can make the experience of seeing them rather dispiriting. To the east of the Latin Quarter, the part of the 13th arrondissement known as the ZAC Rive Gauche, anchored by the four book-like towers of the Bibliothèque Nationale, is one of the city's fastest rising quarters.

ST-SEVERIN & ST-JULIEN-LE-PAUVRE

In the 5th arrondissement.

Boulevard St-Michel used to be synonymous with student rebellion; now it's a largely unprepossessing ribbon of fast-food joints and clothing shops, though **Gibert Joseph** (*see p241*) continues to furnish books and stationery to students. East of here, the semi-pedestrianised patch by the Seine has retained much of its medieval street plan. Rue de la Huchette and rue de la Harpe are now best known for their kebabs and pizzas, though there are 18th-century wrought-iron balconies and carved masks in the latter street. At the tiny **Théâtre de la Huchette** (*see p346*), Ionesco's absurdist drama *La Cantatrice Chauve* (*The Bald Soprano*) has been playing continuously since 1957. Also of interest are rue du Chat-qui-Pêche, supposedly the city's narrowest street, and rue de la Parcheminerie,

named after the parchment sellers and copyists who once lived here. Among the tourist shops stands the city's most charming medieval church, the **Eglise St-Séverin**, with leering gargoyles, spiky gabled side chapels and an exuberantly vaulted Flamboyant Gothic interior.

Across ancient rue St-Jacques is the **Eglise St-Julien-le-Pauvre**, built as a resting place for 12th-century pilgrims. Nearby rue Galande has old houses and the Trois Mailletz cabaret at no.56 (5th, 01.43.54.42.94). The medieval cellars of the **Caveau des Oubliettes** jazz club (*see p324*) were used as a prison after the French Revolution (*oubliette* is the French word for a pit into which prisoners were thrown, then forgotten). At no.42, arts cinema **Studio Galande** (*see p298*) draws goths for late-night screenings of the *Rocky Horror Picture Show* every Friday and Saturday. Just outside the church, in place Viviani, stands what is perhaps the city's oldest tree, a false acacia that was planted in 1602; it's now half-swamped by ivy and propped up by concrete buttresses.

The little streets between here and the eastern stretch of boulevard St-Germain are among the city's oldest: streets such as rue de Bièvre, which follows the course of the Bièvre river that flowed into the Seine in the Middle Ages, rue du Maître-Albert, and rue des Grands-Degrès, with traces of old shop signs painted on its buildings' façades. Remnants of the Collège des Bernardins, built for the Cistercian order, can be seen in rue de Poissy, where the 13th- to 14th-century gothic monks' refectory is being restored after service as firemen's barracks. Nearby are the **Eglise St-Nicolas-de-Chardonnet** (23 rue Bernardins, 5th, 01.44.27.07.90), associated with the schismatic Society of St Pius X and one of a small number of churches where you can hear the Tridentine Mass in Paris, and the art deco **Maison de la Mutualité** (24 rue St-Victor, 5th, 01.40.46.12.00), where you'll find everything from trade unions meetings to rock concerts.

At 47 quai de la Tournelle, the 17th-century Hôtel de Miramion now contains the **Musée de l'Assistance Publique**, devoted to the history of Paris hospitals. You'll find food for all budgets along quai de la Tournelle, starting with Michelin-starred haute-cuisine restaurant **La Tour d'Argent** (*see p211*), said to have been founded as an inn in 1582. After 60 years at the helm, owner Claude Terrail died in 2006, passing the restaurant to his son André. Nearby is the Tintin shrine, *café-tabac* **Le Rallye** (no.11, 5th, 01.43.54.29.65). Place Maubert, now a breezy morning marketplace (Tue, Thur, Sat), witnessed the hanging of Protestants during the 16th-century Wars of Religion. Just behind the square, the modern police station is home to an array of grisly criminal evidence in the **Musée de la Préfecture de Police**.

On the corner of boulevard St-Germain and boulevard St-Michel stand the striking ruins of the late second-century **Thermes de Cluny**, the Romans' main baths complex; the adjoining Gothic Hôtel de Cluny provides a suitable setting for the **Musée National du Moyen Age**, the national collection of medieval art. Adjoining boulevard St-Germain, its garden has been replanted with species portrayed in medieval tapestries, paintings and treatises.

FREE Eglise St-Julien-le-Pauvre

Rue St-Julien-le-Pauvre, 5th (01.43.54.52.16/ bookings 01.42.26.00.00). Mº Cluny La Sorbonne. **Open** 9.30am-1pm, 3-6.30pm daily. **Admission** free. **Map** p408 J7.

A former sanctuary for pilgrims en route to Compostela, this much-mauled church dates from the late 12th century, on the cusp of Romanesque and Gothic, and has capitals richly decorated with vines, acanthus leaves and winged harpies. Once part of a priory, it became the university church when colleges migrated to the Left Bank, and was the site of riotous university assemblies. Since 1889, it has been used by the Greek Orthodox Church.

★ FREE Eglise St-Séverin

3 rue des Prêtres-St-Séverin, 5th (01.42.34. 93.50). Mº Cluny La Sorbonne or St-Michel. **Open** 11am-7.30pm daily. **Admission** free. **Map** p408 J7.

Built on the site of the chapel of the hermit Séverin, itself set on a much earlier Merovingian burial ground, this lovely Flamboyant Gothic edifice was long the parish church of the Left Bank. It was rebuilt on various occasions to repair damage after ransacking by Normans and to meet the needs of the growing population. The church dates from the 15th century, though the doorway, carved with foliage, was added in 1837 from the demolished Eglise St-Pierre-aux-Boeufs on Ile de la Cité. The double ambulatory is famed for its forest of 'palm tree' vaulting, which meets at the end in a unique spiral column that inspired a series of paintings by Robert Delaunay. The bell tower, a survivor from one of the earlier churches on the site, has the oldest bell in Paris (1412). Around the nave are stained-glass windows dating from the 14th and 15th centuries (most of those in the side chapels are by 19th-century Chartres master Emile Hersh), and the choir apse has striking stained glass designed by artist Jean René Bazaine in the 1960s. Next door, around the former cemetery, is the only remaining charnel house in Paris.

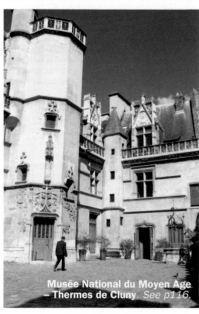

Musée National du Moyen Age – Thermes de Cluny. *See p116.*

SIGHTS

Rue Mouffetard. See p118.

Musée de l'Assistance Publique

Hôtel de Miramion, 47 quai de la Tournelle,
5th (01.40.27.50.05/www.aphp.fr). M° Maubert
Mutualité. **Open** 10am-6pm Tue-Sun. Closed
Aug. **Admission** €4; €2 reductions; free under-
13s. PMP. **No credit cards. Map** p406 K7.
The history of Paris hospitals, from the days when
they were receptacles for abandoned babies to the
dawn of modern medicine, is shown through paintings, prints, and a mock ward and pharmacy.

★ Musée National du Moyen Age – Thermes de Cluny

6 pl Paul-Painlevé, 5th (01.53.73.78.00/
www.musee-moyenage.fr). M° Cluny La
Sorbonne. **Open** 9.15am-5.45pm Mon, Wed-Sun.
Admission €8; €6 reductions, all on Sun;
free under-26s, all on 1st Sun of mth. PMP.
Credit *Shop* MC, V. **Map** p408 J7.
The national museum of medieval art is best known
for the beautiful, allegorical *Lady and the Unicorn*
tapestry cycle, but it also has important collections
of medieval sculpture and enamels. The building
itself, commonly known as Cluny, is also a rare
example of 15th-century secular Gothic architecture,
with its foliate Gothic doorways, hexagonal staircase jutting out of the façade and vaulted chapel. It
was built from 1485 to 1498 – on top of a Gallo-
Roman baths complex. The baths, built in characteristic Roman bands of stone and brick masonry,
are the finest Roman remains in Paris. The vaulted

frigidarium (cold bath), *tepidarium* (warm bath), *cal-*
darium (hot bath) and part of the hypocaust heating
system are all still visible. A themed garden fronts
the whole complex. Recent acquisitions include the
illuminated manuscript *L'Ascension du Christ* from
the Abbey of Cluny, dating back to the 12th century,
and the 16th-century triptych *Assomption de la*
Vierge by Adrien Isenbrant of Bruges. *Photo p115.*

FREE Musée de la Préfecture de Police

4 rue de la Montagne-Ste-Geneviève, 5th
(01.44.41.52.50/www.prefecture-police-paris.
interieur.gouv.fr). M° Maubert Mutualité. **Open**
9am-5pm Mon-Fri; 10am-5pm Sat. **Admission**
free. **No credit cards. Map** p406 J7.
The police museum is housed in a working *commis-*
ariat, which makes for a slightly intimidating entry
procedure. You need to walk boldly past the police
officer standing guard outside and up the steps to
the lobby, where you have to ask at the reception
booth to be let in – queuing, if necessary, with locals
there on other, but usually police-related, errands.
The museum is on the second floor; start from the
Accueil and work your way clockwise.
   None of the displays is labelled in English (though
there is a bilingual booklet), and a handful are not
labelled at all; but if you have basic French and
any sort of interest in criminology, this extensive
collection is well worth seeing. It starts in the early
17th century and runs to the Occupation, via the

founding of the Préfecture de Police by Napoleon in 1800. Exhibits include a prison register open at the entry for Ravaillac, assassin of Henri IV; a section on the Anarchist bombings of the 1890s; the automatic pistol used to assassinate President Doumer in 1932; a blood-chilling collection of murder weapons – hammers, ice picks and knives; sections on serial killers Landru and Petiot; and less dangerous items, such as a gadget used to snag banknotes from the apron pockets of market sellers.

THE SORBONNE, MONTAGNE STE-GENEVIEVE & MOUFFETARD

In the 5th arrondissement.

An influx of well-heeled residents in the 1980s put paid to the days of horn-rims, pipes and turtlenecks: accommodation here is now well beyond the reach of most students. The intellectual tradition persists, however, in the concentration of academic institutions around the Montagne Ste-Geneviève, and students throng the specialist bookstores and art cinemas on rue Champollion and rue des Ecoles.

The district's long association with learning began in about 1100, when a number of renowned scholars, including Pierre Abélard, began to live and teach on the Montagne, independent of the established cathedral school of Notre-Dame. This loose association of scholars came to be referred to as a 'university'. The Paris schools attracted students from all over Europe, and the 'colleges' – in reality student residences dotted round the area (some still survive) – multiplied, until the University of Paris was given official recognition with a charter from Pope Innocent III in 1215.

By the 16th century, the university – named the **Sorbonne**, after the most famous of its colleges – had been co-opted by the Catholic Church. A century later, Cardinal Richelieu rebuilt it. Following the Revolution, when it was forced to close, Napoleon revived the Sorbonne as the cornerstone of his new, centralised education system. The university participated enthusiastically in the uprisings of the 19th century; it was also a seedbed of the 1968 revolt, when it was occupied by protesting students. These days, it's decidedly less turbulent. Also on rue des Ecoles, the independent **Collège de France** was founded in 1530 by a group of humanists led by Guillaume Budé under the patronage of François I. The neighbouring **Brasserie Balzar** (no.49, 5th, 01.43.54.13.67) has been fuelling amateur philosophy for years.

From here, climb rue St-Jacques to rue Soufflot for the most impressive introduction to place du Panthéon. Otherwise, follow rue des

Carmes – with its baroque chapel, now used by the Syrian Church – and continue on rue Valette past the brick and stone entrance of the **Collège Ste-Barbe**, where Ignatius Loyola, Montgolfier and Eiffel studied. Alternatively, follow the serpentine rue de la Montagne-Ste-Geneviève; at the junction of rue Descartes, cafés and eccentric wine bistros overlook the sculpted 19th-century entrance to what was once the elite Ecole Polytechnique (since moved to the suburbs) and is now the research ministry. There's a small park here, and popular bistro **L'Ecurie** (2 rue Laplace, 5th, 01.46.33.68.49) – an old stable burrowed into medieval cellars.

Louis XV commissioned the huge, domed **Panthéon** to honour Geneviève, the city's patron saint, but it was converted during the Revolution into a secular temple for France's *grands hommes*. The surrounding place du Panthéon, also conceived by Panthéon architect Jacques-Germain Soufflot, is one of the city's great set pieces: looking on to it are the elegant fifth arrondissement town hall and, opposite, the law faculty. On the north side, the Ste-Geneviève university library (no.10, 5th, 01.44.41.97.97), built by Labrouste with an iron-framed reading room, contains medieval manuscripts. On the other side you'll find the historic **Hôtel des Grands Hommes** (no.17, 5th, 01.46.34.19.60, www.hoteldesgrandshommes.com), where Surrealist mandarin André Breton invented 'automatic writing' in the 1920s.

Pascal, Racine and the remains of Sainte Geneviève are all interred within **Eglise St-Etienne-du-Mont**, on the north-east corner of the square. Just behind it, within the illustrious and elitist Lycée Henri IV, is the Gothic-Romanesque **Tour de Clovis**, part of the former Abbaye Ste-Geneviève. Take a look

SIGHTS

landscape', and has held talks with the booksellers to encourage them to stock more improving merchandise; there are also plans to stimulate the trade with book festivals, organised tours of the stalls and the reinstatement of the annual literary prize awarded by the booksellers themselves. The *bouquinistes* may be up against the wall, but there's still life in those old boxes yet.

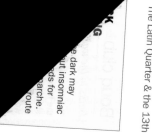

customers who can ... ... le of the book they're looking for), fear they're being squeezed out of business. Internet book dealers have taken a large slice of the rare and second-hand book market, and more and more of the green boxes are resorting to selling postcards and tourist souvenirs to survive.

In any other city, the law of the market-place might be given free rein. But this is Paris, and there's a reputation to maintain. The Mairie worries that the increasing number of displays of postcards, replica street signs and models of the Eiffel Tower will damage what it calls the city's 'cultural

through the entrance (open during termtime) and you'll also catch glimpses of the cloister and other monastic structures.

Further from place du Panthéon, along rue Clovis, is a chunk of Philippe-Auguste's 12th-century city wall. The exiled monarch James II once resided at 65 rue du Cardinal-Lemoine, in the severe buildings of the former Collège des Ecossais (now a school), founded in 1372 to house Scottish students; the king's brain was preserved here until carried off and lost during the French Revolution. Other well known ex-residents include Hemingway, who lived at 79 rue du Cardinal-Lemoine (note the plaque) and 39 rue Descartes in the 1920s, and James Joyce; the latter completed *Ulysses* while staying at 71 rue du Cardinal-Lemoine. Rimbaud lived in rue Descartes, and Descartes himself lived on nearby rue Rollin.

This area is still a mix of tourist picturesque and gentle village, where some of the buildings hide surprising courtyards and gardens. Pretty place de la Contrescarpe has been a famous rendezvous since the 1530s, when writers as renowned as Rabelais, Ronsard and Du Bellay frequented the Cabaret de la Pomme de Pin at no.1; it still has some lively cafés. When George Orwell stayed at 6 rue du Pot-de-Fer in 1928 and 1929 (he described his time here and his

work as a dishwasher in *Down and Out in Paris and London*), it was a place of astounding poverty; today, the street is lined with bargain bars and restaurants, and the restored houses along rue Tournefort bear little relation to the garrets of Balzac's *Le Père Goriot*.

Rue Mouffetard (*photo p116*), originally the road to Rome and one of the oldest streets in the city, winds south as a suite of cheap bistros, Greek and Lebanese tavernas and knick-knack shops thronged with tourists; the vibe described by Hemingway – 'that wonderful narrow crowded market street, beloved of bohemians' – has faded. The street market (Tue-Sat, Sun morning) on the lower half seethes on weekends, when it spills on to the square and around the cafés in front of the **Eglise St-Médard**. There's another busy market, more frequented by locals, at place Monge (Wed, Fri, Sun morning).

Back to the west of the Panthéon, head south beyond rue Soufflot and you'll notice that rue St-Jacques becomes prettier. Here you'll find several ancient buildings, including the elegant *hôtel* at no.151, good food shops, vintage bistro **Perraudin** (no.157, 5th, 01.46. 33.15.75) and the **Institut Océanographique** (no.195, 5th, 01.44.32.10.70, www.oceano.org/io), which has well-stocked aquariums much loved by children. Rue d'Ulm contains the elite

Ecole Normale Supérieure (no.45, 5th, 01.44.32.30.00, www.ens.fr), occupied in protest by the unemployed in January 1998; in an echo of 1968, students also joined in.

Turn off up hilly rue des Fossés-St-Jacques to discover place de l'Estrapade; in the 17th century the *estrapade* was a tall wooden tower from which deserters were dropped repeatedly until they died. Nearby, in rue des Irlandais, the Centre Culturel Irlandais hosts concerts, exhibitions, films, plays and spoken-word events promoting Irish culture. Back to the west of rue St-Jacques, rue Soufflot and broad rue Gay-Lussac (a hotspot of the May 1968 revolt), with their Haussmannian apartment buildings, lead to boulevard St-Michel and the Jardin du Luxembourg (*see p129*).

Further south along rue St-Jacques, in the potters' quarter of Roman Lutetia, is the least altered and most ornate of the city's baroque churches, the landmark **Eglise du Val-de-Grâce**. Round the corner, at 6 rue du Val-de-Grâce, is the former home of Alfons Maria Mucha, the influential Moravian art nouveau artist, best known for his posters of Sarah Bernhardt.

FREE Collège de France

11 pl Marcelin-Berthelot, 5th (01.44.27.12.11/ 01.44.27.11.47/www.college-de-france.fr). M° Cluny La Sorbonne or Maubert Mutualité/ RER Luxembourg. **Open** 9am-5pm Mon-Fri. **Admission** free. **Map** p408 J7.

Founded in 1530 with the patronage of François I, the college is a place of learning and a research institute. The present building dates from the 16th and 17th centuries; there's also a later annexe. All lectures are free and open to the public; some have been given by such eminent figures as anthropologist Claude Lévi-Strauss, philosopher Maurice Merleau-Ponty and mathematician Jacques Tits.

★ FREE Eglise St-Etienne-du-Mont

Pl Ste-Geneviève, 5th (01.43.54.11.79). M° Cardinal Lemoine/RER Luxembourg. **Open** 10am-7pm Tue-Sun. **Admission** free. **Map** p408 J8.

Geneviève, patron saint of Paris, is credited with having miraculously saved the city from the ravages of Attila the Hun in 451, and her shrine has been a site of pilgrimage ever since. The present church was built in an amalgam of Gothic and Renaissance styles between 1492 and 1626, and once adjoined the abbey church of Ste-Geneviève. The façade mixes Gothic rose windows with rusticated roman columns and reliefs of classically draped figures. The interior is wonderfully tall and light, with soaring columns and a classical balustrade. The stunning Renaissance rood screen, with its double spiral staircase and ornate stone strapwork, is the only surviving one in Paris, and

was possibly designed by Philibert Delorme. The decorative canopied wooden pulpit by Germaine Pillon dates from 1651, and is adorned with figures of the Graces and supported by a muscular Samson sitting on the defeated lion. Sainte Geneviève's elaborate neo-Gothic brass-and-glass shrine (shielding the ancient tombstone) is located to the right of the choir, surrounded by an assorted collection of reliquaries and dozens of marble plaques bearing messages of thanks. At the back of the church (reached through the sacristy), the catechism chapel constructed by Baltard in the 1860s has a cycle of paintings relating the saint's life story.

FREE Eglise St-Médard

141 rue Mouffetard, 5th (01.44.08.87.00). M° Censier Daubenton. **Open** 8am-noon, 2.30-7.30pm daily. **Admission** free. **Map** p406 J9.

The original chapel here was a dependency of the Abbaye Ste-Geneviève. The rebuilding towards the end of the 15th century created a somewhat larger, late Gothic structure best known for its elaborate vaulted ambulatory.

Eglise du Val-de-Grâce

Pl Alphonse-Laveran, 5th (01.43.29.12.31). RER Luxembourg or Port-Royal. **Open** noon-6pm Tue, Wed, Sat, Sun. **Admission** €5; €2.50 reductions; free under-6s. **No credit cards**. **Map** p406 H9.

Anne of Austria, the wife of Louis XIII, vowed to erect 'a magnificent temple' if God blessed her with a son. She got two. The resulting church and surrounding Benedictine monastery – these days a military hospital and the Musée du Service de Santé des Armées – were built by François Mansart and Jacques Lemercier. This is the most luxuriously baroque of the city's 17th-century domed churches, its ornate altar decorated with twisted barley-sugar columns. The swirling colours of the dome frescoes painted by Pierre Mignard in 1669 (which Molière himself once eulogised) are designed to give a foretaste of heaven. In contrast, the surrounding monastery offers the perfect example of François Mansart's classical restraint. Phone in advance if you're after a guided visit.

Musée du Service de Santé des Armées

Val de Grâce, pl Alphonse-Laveran, 5th (01.40.51.51.94). RER Luxembourg or Port Royal. **Open** noon-5pm Tue, Wed, Sat, Sun. **Admission** €5; €2.50 reductions; free under-6s. **No credit cards**. **Map** p406 J9.

Housed in the royal convent designed by Mansart, next door to a military hospital, this museum traces the history of military medicine via replicas of field hospitals and ambulance trains, and displays of antique medical instruments. The section on World War I demonstrates how the conflict propelled medical progress.

SIGHTS

★ Le Panthéon

Pl du Panthéon, 5th (01.44.32.18.00). M° Cardinal Lemoine/RER Luxembourg. **Open** 10am-6pm (until 6.30pm summer) daily. **Admission** €8; €6 reductions; free under-18s (if accompanied by an adult). PMP. **Credit** MC, V. **Map** p408 J8.

Soufflot's neo-classical megastructure was the architectural *grand projet* of its day, commissioned by a grateful Louis XV to thank Sainte Geneviève for his recovery from illness. But by the time it was ready in 1790, a lot had changed; during the Revolution, the Panthéon was rededicated as a 'temple of reason' and the resting place of the nation's great men. The austere barrel-vaulted crypt now houses Voltaire, Rousseau, Hugo and Zola. New heroes are installed but rarely: Pierre and Marie Curie's remains were transferred here in 1995; Alexandre Dumas in 2002. Inside are Greek columns and domes, and 19th-century murals of Geneviève's life by Symbolist painter Puvis de Chavannes, a formative influence on Picasso during the latter's blue period.

Mount the steep spiral stairs to the colonnade encircling the dome for superb views. A replica of Foucault's Pendulum hangs here; the original proved that the earth does indeed spin on its axis, via a universal joint that lets the direction of the pendulum's swing rotate as the earth revolves.

La Sorbonne

17 rue de la Sorbonne, 5th (01.40.46.22.11/ www.sorbonne.fr). M° Cluny La Sorbonne. **Open** *Tours* by appointment. Closed July & Aug. **Map** p408 J7.

Founded in 1253, the University of the Sorbonne was at the centre of the Latin Quarter's intellectual activity from the Middle Ages until 1968, when it was occupied by students and stormed by the riot police. The authorities then split the University of Paris into safer outposts, but the Sorbonne still houses the Faculté des Lettres. Rebuilt by Richelieu and reorganised by Napoleon, the present buildings date from the late 1800s, and have a labyrinth of classrooms and lecture theatres, as well as an observatory tower. The elegant dome of the 17th-century chapel dominates place de la Sorbonne; Cardinal Richelieu is buried inside. It's only open to the public for exhibitions or concerts.

AROUND THE JARDIN DES PLANTES

In the 5th arrondissement.

The quiet, easternmost part of the fifth arrondissement is home to yet more academic institutions, the Paris mosque and another Roman relic. Old-fashioned bistros on rue des Fossés-St-Bernard contrast with the forbidding 1960s architecture of the massive university campus of Paris VI and VII, the science faculty (known as Jussieu) built on what had been

the site of the important Abbaye St-Victor. Between the Seine and Jussieu is the strikingly modern, glass-faced **Institut du Monde Arabe**, which has a programme of concerts and exhibitions and a restaurant with a great view. The **Jardin Tino Rossi**, by the river, contains the slightly dilapidated **Musée de la Sculpture en Plein Air**; in summer this is a spot for dancing and picnicking.

Hidden among the hotels of rue Monge is the entrance to the **Arènes de Lutèce**, a Roman amphitheatre. The remains of a circular arena and its tiers of stone seating were discovered in 1869, when the street was being built. Excavation started in 1883, thanks to lobbying by Victor Hugo. Nearby rise the white minaret and green pan-tiled roof of the **Mosquée de Paris**, built in 1922. Its beautiful Moorish tearoom is a student haunt.

The mosque looks over the **Jardin des Plantes** botanical garden. Opened in 1626 as a garden for medicinal plants, it features an 18th-century maze and a winter garden bristling with rare species. It also houses the Muséum National d'Histoire Naturelle, with its brilliantly renovated **Grande Galerie de l'Evolution**, and a zoo, La Ménagerie, an unlikely by-product of the Revolution, when royal and noble collections of wild animals were impounded. Street names and the lovely animal-themed fountain on the corner of rue Cuvier pay homage to the many naturalists and other scientists who worked here. A short way away, at 11-13bis rue Geoffroy-St-Hilaire, the words 'Chevaux', 'Poneys' and 'Anes' are still visible on the façade of the old horse market.

FREE Arènes de Lutèce

Rue Monge, rue de Navarre or rue des Arènes, 5th. M° Cardinal Lemoine or Place Monge. **Open** *Summer* 9am-9.30pm daily. *Winter* 8am-5.30pm daily. **Admission** free. **Map** p406 K8.

This Roman arena, where wild beasts and gladiators fought, could seat 10,000 people. It was still visible during the reign of Philippe-Auguste in the 12th century, then disappeared under rubble. The site was rediscovered in 1869 and now incorporates a romantically planted garden. These days, it attracts skateboarders, footballers and boules players.

★ Grande Galerie de l'Evolution

36 rue Geoffroy-St-Hilaire, 2 rue Bouffon or pl Valhubert, 5th (01.40.79.56.01). M° Gare d'Austerlitz or Jussieu. **Open** *Grande Galerie* 10am-6pm Mon, Wed-Sun. *Other galleries* 10am-5pm Mon, Wed-Fri; 10am-6pm Sat, Sun. **Admission** *Grande Galerie* €9; €7 reductions; free under-4s. *Other galleries* (each) €7; €5 reductions; free under-4s. **No credit cards**. **Map** p406 K9.

SIGHTS

One of the city's most child-friendly attractions, this is guaranteed to bowl adults over too. Located within the Jardin des Plantes (*see below*), this beauty of a 19th-century iron-framed, glass-roofed structure has been modernised with lifts, galleries and false floors, and filled with life-size models of tentacle-waving squids, open-mawed sharks, tigers hanging off elephants and monkeys swarming down from the ceiling. The centrepiece is a procession of African wildlife across the first floor that resembles the procession into Noah's Ark. Glass-sided lifts take you up through suspended birds to the second floor, which deals with man's impact on nature and rewiring of evolution (crocodile into handbag). The third floor focuses on endangered and extinct species. The separate Galerie d'Anatomie Comparée et de Paléontologie contains over a million skeletons and a world-class fossil collection.

Institut du Monde Arabe

1 rue des Fossés-St-Bernard, 5th (01.40.51.38.38/ www.imarabe.org). M° Jussieu. **Open** *Museum* 10am-6pm Tue-Sun. *Library* 1-8pm Tue-Sat. *Café* noon-6pm Tue-Sun. *Tours* 3pm Tue-Fri; 3pm & 4.30pm Sat, Sun. **Admission** *Roof terrace, library* free. *Museum* €5; €4 reductions; free under-12s. PMP. *Exhibitions* varies. *Tours* €8. **Credit** MC, V. **Map** p406 K7.

A clever blend of high-tech and Arab influences, this Seine-side *grand projet* was constructed between 1980 and 1987 to a design by Jean Nouvel. Shuttered windows, inspired by the screens of Moorish palaces, act as camera apertures, contracting or expanding according to the amount of sunlight. A museum covering the history and archaeology of the Islamic Arab world occupies the upper floors: start at the seventh with Classical-era finds and work down via early Islamic dynasties to the present day. Unfortunately, the layout and arrangement are somewhat uninspired – objects in glass cases without much in the way of context. However, the Institut hosts several major, crowd-pleasing exhibitions throughout the year. What's more, there's an excellent Middle East bookshop on the ground floor and the views from the roof terrace (to which access is free) are fabulous.

▶ *Jean Nouvel's other landmark Paris buildings include the Musée du Quai Branly (see p146) and the Fondation Cartier (see p134).*

★ FREE Jardin des Plantes

36 rue Geoffroy-St-Hilaire, 2 rue Bouffon, pl Valhubert or 57 rue Cuvier, 5th. M° Gare d'Austerlitz, Jussieu or Place Monge. **Open** *Main garden* Winter 8am-dusk daily. Summer 7.30am-8pm daily. *Alpine garden* Apr-Sept

La Mosquée de Paris. *See p122.*

SIGHTS

8am-5.30pm daily. Closed Oct-Mar. *Ménagerie* Apr-Sept 9am-5pm daily. **Admission** *Alpine Garden* free Mon-Fri; €1 Sat, Sun. *Jardin des Plantes* free. *Ménagerie* €8; €6 reductions; free under-4s. **Credit** AmEx, MC, V. **Map** p406 L8.
Although small and slightly dishevelled, the Paris botanical garden – which contains more than 10,000 species and includes tropical greenhouses and rose, winter and Alpine gardens – is an enchanting place. Begun by Louis XIII's doctor as the royal medicinal plant garden in 1626, it opened to the public in 1640. The formal garden, which runs between two dead-straight avenues of trees parallel to rue Buffon, is like something out of *Alice in Wonderland*. There's also the Ménagerie (a small zoo) and the terrific Grande Galerie de l'Evolution (*see p120*). Ancient trees on view include a false acacia planted in 1636 and a cedar from 1734. A plaque on the old laboratory declares that this is where Henri Becquerel discovered radioactivity in 1896.

FREE Jardin Tino Rossi (Musée de la Sculpture en Plein Air)
Quai St-Bernard, 5th. M° Gare d'Austerlitz. **Open** 8am-dusk Mon-Fri; 9am-dusk Sat, Sun. **Admission** free. **Map** p406 L8.
This open-air sculpture museum by the Seine fights a constant battle against graffiti. Still, it's a pleasant enough, if traffic-loud, place for a stroll. Most of the works are second-rate, aside from Etienne Martin's bronze *Demeure I* and the Carrara marble *Fenêtre* by Cuban artist Careras.
► *From May to September, the gardens turn into an open-air dance studio, with informal classes in everything from hip hop to salsa; see p293.*

La Mosquée de Paris
2 pl du Puits-de-l'Ermite, 5th (01.45.35.97.33/ tearoom 01.43.31.38.20/baths 01.43.31.18.14/ www.mosquee-de-paris.net). M° Monge. **Open** *Tours* 9am-noon, 2-6pm Mon-Thur, Sat, Sun (closed Muslim hols). *Tearoom* 10am-11.30pm daily. *Restaurant* noon-2.30pm, 7.30-10.30pm daily. *Baths* (women) 10am-9pm Mon, Wed, Sat; 2-9pm Fri; (men) 2-9pm Tue, Sun. **Admission** €3; €2 reductions; free under-7s. *Tearoom* free. *Baths* €15-€35. **Credit** MC, V. **Map** p406 K9.
Some distance removed from the Arabic-speaking inner-city enclaves of Barbès and Belleville, this vast Hispano-Moorish construct is nevertheless the spiritual heart of France's Algerian-dominated Muslim population. Built from 1922 to 1926 with elements inspired by the Alhambra and the Bou Inania Medersa in Fès, the Paris mosque is dominated by a stunning green-and-white tiled square minaret. In plan and function it divides into three sections: religious (grand patio, prayer room and minaret, all for worshippers and not curious tourists); scholarly (Islamic school and library); and, via rue Geoffroy-St-Hilaire, commercial (café and domed hammam).

La Mosquée café (open 9am-midnight daily) is delightful – a modest courtyard with blue-and-white mosaic-topped tables shaded beneath green foliage and scented with the sweet smell of sheesha smoke (€6). Charming waiters distribute *thé à la menthe* (€2), along with syrupy, nutty North African pastries, sorbets and fruit salads. *Photo p121.*

LES GOBELINS & LA SALPETRIERE
In the 13th arrondissement.

Its defining features might be 1960s tower blocks, but the 13th arrondissement is also historic, especially in the area bordering the fifth. The **Manufacture Nationale des Gobelins**, home to the state weaving companies, continues a tradition founded in the 15th century, when tanneries, dyers and weaving workshops lined the Bièvre river. This putrid waterway became notorious, and the slums that grew up around it were depicted in Victor Hugo's *Les Misérables*.
The area was tidied up in the 1930s, when a small park, square René-Le-Gall, was laid out on the allotments used by tapestry workers. The river was built over, but local enthusiasts have since opened up a small stretch in the park. Nearby, through a gateway at 17 rue des Gobelins, you can spot the turret and first floor of a medieval house, recently renovated as apartments. The so-called Château de la Reine Blanche on rue Gustave-Geffroy is named after Queen Blanche of Provence, who had a château here; it was probably rebuilt in the 1520s for the Gobelin family. Blanche was also associated with a nearby Franciscan monastery, of which a fragmentary couple of arches survive on the corner of rue Pascal and rue de Julienne.
In the northern corner of the 13th, next to Gare d'Austerlitz, sprawls the huge Hôpital de la Pitié-Salpêtrière founded in 1656, with its striking **Chapelle St-Louis**.
The busy intersection of place d'Italie has seen a number of developments in recent years. Opposite the 19th-century town hall stands the Centre Commercial Italie 2, a bizarre high-tech confection. It houses a shopping centre but, sadly, no longer the Gaumont Grand Ecran Italie cinema. You'll also find a food market on boulevard Auguste-Blanqui (Tue, Fri, Sun).

FREE Chapelle St-Louis-de-la-Salpêtrière
47 bd de l'Hôpital, 13th (01.42.16.04.24). M° Gare d'Austerlitz. **Open** 8.30am-6pm Mon-Fri, Sun; 11am-6pm Sat. **Admission** free. **Map** p406 L9.
This austerely beautiful chapel, designed by Libéral Bruand and completed in 1677, features an octagonal dome in the centre and eight naves in which the

sick were separated from the insane, the destitute from the debauched. Around the chapel sprawls the vast Hôpital de la Pitié-Salpêtrière, founded on the site of a gunpowder factory (hence the name, derived from saltpetre) by Louis XIV to house rounded-up vagrant women. It became a centre for research into insanity in the 1790s, when renowned doctor Philippe Pinel began to treat some of the inmates as sick rather than criminal; Charcot later pioneered neuropsychology here, famously receiving a visit from Freud. Salpêtrière is today one of the city's main teaching hospitals, but the chapel is also used for contemporary art installations, notably during the Festival d'Automne (*see p278*), when its striking architecture provides a backdrop for artists such as Bill Viola, Anish Kapoor and Nan Goldin.

Manufacture Nationale des Gobelins

42 av des Gobelins, 13th (tours 01.44.08.53.49).
M° Les Gobelins. **Open** *Tours* 2pm, 3pm Tue-Thur. **Admission** €10; €6 reductions; free under-7s. **No credit cards. Map** p406 K10.

The royal tapestry factory was founded by Colbert when he set up the Manufacture Royale des Meubles de la Couronne in 1662; it's named after Jean Gobelin, a dyer who owned the site. It reached the summit of its renown during the *ancien régime*, when Gobelins tapestries were produced for royal residences under artists such as Le Brun. Tapestries are still made here and visitors can watch weavers at work. The tour (in French) through the 1912 factory takes in the 18th-century chapel and the Beauvais workshops.

History of Cinema

Pathé is opening up its archives.

As if film buffs weren't already spoiled for choice in Paris, they'll have another reason to get excited come 2011. The Fondation Jérôme Seydoux-Pathé is opening a showcase centre for its collection of film memorabilia and artefacts, including a space for temporary exhibitions.

Established in 1896, the Société Pathé Frères was one of the founding fathers of cinema, building its reputation on savvy technical innovations and the famed pre-film Pathé newsreels. Today, the company remains one of Europe's leading distributors, producers and cinema exhibitors, and the foundation's mission is to promote the history of cinema via the Pathé story. Its collection is composed of the company's archives for everything except film reels, and includes movie posters, journals, props, cameras, and all sorts of projectionists' paraphernalia.

To house such a prestigious collection, Pathé commissioned Renzo Piano, architect of the Centre Pompidou, to design a new building on the site of a former cinema near Place d'Italie. The only stipulation was that the building's old façade had to be conserved, as it was embellished with an elaborate sculpture by iconic artist Auguste Rodin. Piano's solution was to take visitors through the old entrance, across a short corridor, and into a brand new oval complex that will house the foundation's offices and collection. This five-storey building will be glass-fronted, with tinted panes used on certain floors to protect the archives. On the ground floor, a temporary exhibition space, including a small cinema, will host exhibitions based on the Pathé collection. Visitors will be treated to original posters, props and stills from landmark movies such as Marcel Carné's post-war classic *Les Enfants du Paradis*, as well as recent crowd-pleasers such as 2008's French box-office smash *Bienvenue chez les Ch'tis*.

The centre will also exhibit Pathé studio cameras and film projectors through the ages, while the top floor will feature a research library, accessible to the public by appointment only. Outside, visitors will be able to admire the building's audacious architecture from a small garden.

SIGHTS

CHINATOWN & THE BUTTE-AUX-CAILLES

South of rue de Tolbiac, the shop signs suddenly turn Chinese or Vietnamese, and even McDonald's is decked out *à la chinoise*. The city's main Chinatown runs along avenue d'Ivry, avenue de Choisy and into the 1960s tower blocks between. Whereas much of the public housing in and around Paris is pretty bleak, here a distinctly eastern vibe reigns, with restaurants, Vietnamese *pho* noodle bars and Chinese pâtisseries, hairdressers and purveyors of exotic groceries; not to mention the expansive **Tang Frères** supermarket (48 av d'Ivry, 13th, 01.45.70.80.00). There's even a Buddhist temple hidden in a car park beneath the tallest tower (av d'Ivry, opposite rue Frères d'Astier-de-la-Vigerie, 13th). Lion and dragon dances, and martial arts demonstrations, take place on the streets at **Chinese New Year** (*see p279*).

In contrast to Chinatown, the villagey Butte-aux-Cailles, occupying the wedge between boulevard Auguste-Blanqui and rue Bobillot, is a neighbourhood of old houses, winding streets, funky bars and restaurants. This area, home in the 19th century to many small factories, was one of the first to fight during the 1848 Revolution and the Paris Commune.

The Butte has preserved its rebellious character, with residents standing up to urban planners and commercial developers. This predominantly *soixante-huitard* resistance is concentrated in the cobbled rue de la Butte-aux-Cailles and rue des Cinq-Diamants. Here you'll find relaxed, inexpensive bistros such as **Le Temps des Cerises** (18 rue Butte-aux-Cailles, 13th, 01.45.89.69.48), run as a co-operative; **Chez Gladines** (30 rue des Cinq-Diamants, 13th, 01.45.80.70.10) and more upmarket **Chez Paul** (22 rue Butte-aux-Cailles, 13th, 01.45.89.22.11). The cottages built in 1912 in a mock-Alsatian style around a central green at 10 rue Daviel were among the earliest public-housing schemes in Paris. Just across rue Bobillot, the **Piscine Butte-aux-Cailles** (*see p340*) is a charming swimming pool.

Further south, you can explore passage Vandrezanne, the little houses and gardens of square des Peupliers, rue des Peupliers and rue Dieulafoy, and the flower-named streets of the Cité Florale. By the Périphérique, the **Stade Charléty** (17 av Pierre-de-Coubertin, 13th, 01.44.16.60.60) is that unlikely thing, a superb piece of stadium architecture.

Further east

The construction in the mid-1990s of the **Bibliothèque Nationale de France** breathed life into the desolate area, now known as the **ZAC Rive Gauche**, between Gare d'Austerlitz and the Périphérique. The ambitious, long-term ZAC project includes a new university quarter, new housing projects and a tramway providing links to the suburbs. The city's newest bridge, the pedestrian-only **Passerelle Simone-de-Beauvoir**, spans the Seine between the BNF and the Cinémathèque Française; the floating Piscine Josephine-Baker (*see p341*) is now a focus for the extended Paris-Plage entertainments; and Paris's latest big cultural venue, the much-delayed **Cité de la Mode et du Design** (**Docks en Seine**), is due to open in early 2010.

Further south-east, rue Watt is the lowest street in Paris (it runs below river level). At 12 rue Cantagrel is Le Corbusier's Cité de Réfuge de l'Armée de Salut hostel, a reinforced concrete structure built to house 1,500 homeless men.

Bibliothèque Nationale de France François Mitterrand

10 quai François-Mauriac, 13th (01.53.79.59.59/www.bnf.fr). M° Bibliothèque François Mitterrand. **Open** 2-7pm Mon; 9am-7pm Tue-Sat; 1-7pm Sun. **Admission** *1 day* €3.30. *1 year* €35; €18 reductions. **Credit** MC, V. **Map** p407 M10.

Opened in 1996, the new national library was the last and costliest of Mitterrand's *grands projets*. Its architect, Dominique Perrault, was criticised for his curiously dated design, which hides readers underground and stores the books in four L-shaped glass towers. He also forgot to specify blinds to protect books from sunlight; they had to be added afterwards. In the central void is a garden (filled with 140 trees, which were transported from Fontainebleau at enormous expense). The library houses over ten million volumes and can accommodate 3,000 readers. The research section, just below the public reading rooms, opened in 1998. Much of the library is open to the public: books, newspapers and periodicals are accessible to anyone over 18, and you can browse through photographic, film and sound archives in the audio-visual section.

▶ *The library is now accessible by Voguéo (www.vogueo.fr), a new scheduled boat service.*

Cité de la Mode et du Design (Docks en Seine)

28-36 quai d'Austerlitz, 13th. M° Chevaleret or Gare d'Austerlitz.

The striking bright green Cité de la Mode et du Design, designed by Jakob + MacFarlane, is due to open in 2010, containing restaurants and cafés, a concert and club venue, shops, the Institut Français de la Mode fashion and management school, and a riverside promenade. The most radical element is what the 'plug over' system – a framework of green steel tubing and screenprinted glass that clips on to the 1907 reinforced concrete warehouse beneath.

St-Germain-des-Prés & Odéon

Free thinkers and fashionistas on the south side of the Seine.

Like the Latin Quarter, St-Germain-des-Prés is another area that no longer quite lives up to its legend: these days, it's more sartorial than Sartrian. In the middle third of the 20th century the area was prime arts and intello territory, a place known as much for its high jinks as its lofty thinking: the haunt of Picasso, Giacometti, Camus, Prévert and, *bien sûr*, the Bonnie and Clyde of French philosophy, Jean-Paul Sartre and Simone de Beauvoir; the hotspot of the Paris jazz boom after World War II; and the heart of the Paris book trade. This is where the cliché of café terrace intellectualising was coined, but nowadays most of the local patrons of the Flore and the Deux Magots are in the fashion business, and couturiers have largely replaced publishers. Never mind: it's a smart and attractive part of the city to wander around in, and also has some very good restaurants.

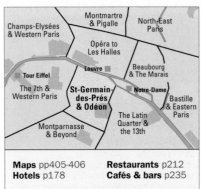

Champs-Elysées & Western Paris | Montmartre & Pigalle | North-East Paris

Opéra to Les Halles

Tour Eiffel | Louvre | Beaubourg & The Marais

The 7th & Western Paris | **St-Germain-des-Prés & Odéon** | Notre-Dame | Bastille & Eastern Paris

Montparnasse & Beyond | The Latin Quarter & the 13th

Maps pp405-406   **Restaurants** p212
Hotels p178   **Cafés & bars** p235

SIGHTS

FROM THE BOULEVARD TO THE SEINE

In the 6th arrondissement.

Hit by shortages of coal during World War II, Sartre shunned his cold flat on rue Bonaparte. 'The principal interest of the Café de Flore,' he noted at the time, 'was that it had a stove, a nearby métro and no Germans.' Although you can spend more on a few coffees here than on a week's heating these days, the **Café de Flore** (*see p236, photo p126*) remains an arty favourite, and hosts *café-philo* evenings in English. Its rival, **Les Deux Magots** (*see p236*), facing historic **Eglise St-Germain-des-Prés**, is frequented largely by tourists. Nearby is the celebrity favourite **Brasserie Lipp** (151 bd St-Germain, 6th, 01.45.48.53.91); art nouveau fans prefer **Brasserie Vagenende** (142 bd St-Germain, 6th, 01.43.26.68.18). The swish bookshop **La Hune** (*see p241*) provides sustenance of a more intellectual kind.

St-Germain-des-Prés grew up around the medieval abbey, the oldest church in Paris and site of an annual fair that drew merchants from across Europe. There are traces of its cloister and part of the abbot's palace behind the church on rue de l'Abbaye. Constructed in 1586 in red brick with stone facing, the palace prefigured the architecture of **place des Vosges**. Charming place de Furstemberg (once the palace stables) is home to the house and studio where the elderly Delacroix lived when painting the murals in St-Sulpice; it now houses the **Musée National Delacroix**. Wagner, Ingres and Colette lived on nearby rue Jacob; its elegant 17th-century *hôtels particuliers* now contain specialist book, design and antiques shops and a few pleasant hotels.

Further east, rue de Buci hosts a street market and upmarket food shops, and is home to cafés **Les Etages** (no.5, 6th, 01.46.34.26.26) and **Bar du Marché** (no.16, 6th, 01.43.26.55.15). **Hôtel La Louisiane** (60 rue de Seine, 6th, 01.44.32.17.17, www.hotellalouisiane.com) has hosted jazz stars Chet Baker and Miles Davis,

Café de Flore. *See p125.*

and Existentialist lovers Sartre and de Beauvoir. Rue de Seine, rue des Beaux-Arts and rue Bonaparte (Manet was born in the latter, at no.5, in 1832) are still packed with art galleries. It was in rue des Beaux-Arts, at the Hôtel d'Alsace, that Oscar Wilde complained about the wallpaper and then checked out for good. Now fashionably renovated, it has rechristened itself **L'Hôtel** (*see p178*). **La Palette** (*see p237*) and **Bistrot Mazarin** (42 rue Mazarine, 6th, 01.43.29.99.01, www.bistrotmazarin.com) are good pit stops with enviable terraces; rue Mazarine, with shops selling lighting, vintage toys and jewellery, also has Terence Conran's brasserie **L'Alcazar** (no.62, 6th, 01.53.10.19.99, www.alcazar.fr) and hip club **Wagg** (*see p330*).

On quai de Conti stands the neo-classical Hôtel des Monnaies, built at the demand of Louis XV by architect Jacques-Denis Antoine; formerly the mint (1777-1973), it's now the **Musée de la Monnaie**, a coin museum. Next door stands the domed **Institut de France**, cleaned to within an inch of its crisp, classical life. Opposite, the iron Pont des Arts footbridge leads directly to the Louvre. Further along, the city's main fine arts school, the **Ecole Nationale Supérieure des Beaux-Arts**, occupies an old monastery.

Ecole Nationale Supérieure des Beaux-Arts (Ensb-a)

14 rue Bonaparte, 6th (01.47.03.50.00/ www.ensba.fr). M° St-Germain-des-Prés. **Open** *Courtyard* 9am-5pm Mon-Fri.

Exhibitions 1-7pm Tue-Sun. **Admission** €4; €2 reductions. *Exhibitions* prices vary. **Credit** V. **Map** p408 H6.

The city's most prestigious fine arts school resides in what remains of the 17th-century Couvent des Petits-Augustins, the 18th-century Hôtel de Chimay, some 19th-century additions and some chunks of assorted French châteaux that were moved here after the Revolution (when the buildings briefly served as a museum of French monuments, before becoming the art school in 1816). The entrance is on quai Malaquais.

★ FREE Eglise St-Germain-des-Prés

3 pl St-Germain-des-Prés, 6th (01.55.42.81.33/ www.eglise-sgp.org). M° St-Germain-des-Prés. **Open** 8am-7.45pm Mon-Sat; 9am-8pm Sun. **Admission** free. **Map** p408 H7.

The oldest church in Paris. On the advice of Germain (later Bishop of Paris), Childebert, son of Clovis, had a basilica and monastery built here around 543. It was first dedicated to St Vincent, and came to be known as St-Germain-le-Doré ('the gilded') because of its copper roof, then later as St-Germain-des-Prés ('of the fields'). During the Revolution the abbey was burned and a saltpetre refinery installed; the spire was added in a clumsy 19th-century restoration. Still, most of the present structure is 12th century, and ornate carved capitals and the tower remain from the 11th. Tombs include those of Jean-Casimir, the deposed King of Poland who became Abbot of St-Germain in 1669, and of Scots nobleman William Douglas. Under the window in the second chapel is the funeral stone of philosopher-mathematician René Descartes; his remains have been here since 1819.

Institut de France

23 quai de Conti, 6th (01.44.41.44.41/ www.institut-de-france.fr). M° Louvre Rivoli or Pont Neuf. **Open** *Guided tours* Sat, Sun (01.44.41.43.32/www.monum.fr; call for times). **Admission** €8; €6 reductions. **No credit cards**. **Map** p408 H6.

INSIDE TRACK
SLICE OF HISTORY

In the 18th century, Dr Joseph-Ignace Guillotin first tested out his notorious device in the cellars of what is today the **Pub St-Germain** (17 rue de l'Ancienne-Comédie, 6th); the first victim was, reputedly, a sheep. Jacobin regicide Billaud-Varenne was among those who felt the steel of Guillotin's gadget; his former home at 45 rue St-André-des-Arts was the site of the first girls' *lycée* in Paris, the Lycée Fénelon, founded in 1883.

Eglise St-Germain-des-Prés.

This elegant domed building with two sweeping curved wings was designed as a school by Louis Le Vau and opened in 1684. The five academies of the Institut (Académie Française, Académie des Inscriptions et Belles-Lettres, Académie des Beaux-Arts, Académie des Sciences, Académie des Sciences Morales et Politiques) moved here in 1805. Inside is Mazarin's ornate tomb by Hardouin-Mansart, and the Bibliothèque Mazarine (open to over-18s with ID and two photos; €15/year). The Académie Française was founded by Cardinal Richelieu in 1635 with the aim of preserving the purity of French from corrupting outside influences (such as English).

FREE Musée de la Monnaie de Paris

11 quai de Conti, 6th (01.40.46.56.66/www.
monnaiedeparis.fr). M° Odéon or Pont Neuf.
Open 11am-5.30pm Tue-Fri; noon-5.30pm Sat,
Sun. Closed Aug. **Admission** free. **Credit**
Shop AmEx, MC, V. **Map** p408 H6.
Housed in the handsome neo-classical mint built in the 1770s, this high-tech museum tells the tale of global and local coinage from its pre-Roman origins, using sophisticated displays and audio-visual presentations. The history of the franc, from its wartime debut in 1360, is outlined in detail.

Musée National Delacroix

6 pl de Furstemberg, 6th (01.44.41.86.50/
www.musee-delacroix.fr). M° St-Germain-des-
Prés. **Open** *Sept-May* 9.30am-5pm Mon, Wed-
Sun. *June-Aug* 9.30am-5.30pm Mon, Wed-Sun.
Admission €5; free under-18s, all on 1st Sun
of mth. PMP. **Credit** MC, V. **Map** p408 H7.

Eugène Delacroix moved to this apartment and studio in 1857 in order to be near the Eglise St-Sulpice, where he was painting murals. This collection includes small oil paintings, free pastel studies of skies, sketches and lithographs, as well as his palette.

ST-SULPICE & THE LUXEMBOURG

In the 6th arrondissement.

Crammed with historic buildings and inviting shops, the quarter south of boulevard St-Germain between Odéon and Luxembourg epitomises civilised Paris. Just off the boulevard lies the covered market of St-Germain, now the site of a shopping arcade, auditorium, food hall and underground swimming pool. There are bars and bistros along rue Guisarde, nicknamed rue de la Soif ('thirst street') thanks to its carousers; it contains the late-night **Birdland** bar (no.8, 6th, 01.43.26.97.59) and a couple of notable bistros: **Mâchon d'Henri** (no.8, 6th, 01.43.29.08.70) and **Brasserie Fernand** (no.13, 6th, 01.43.54.61.47). Rue Princesse and rue des Canettes are a mix of budget restaurants and nocturnal haunts.

Pass the fashion boutiques, pâtisseries and antiquarian book and print shops and you come to **Eglise St-Sulpice**, a surprising 18th-century exercise in classical form with two unmatching turrets and a colonnaded façade. The square in front was designed in the 19th century by Visconti; it contains his

imposing, lion-flanked Fontaine des Quatre Points Cardinaux (a pun on cardinal points and the statues of Bishops Bossuet, Fénelon, Massilon and Flechier, none of whom was actually a cardinal). It's now the centrepiece for the **Foire St-Germain**, a summer arts fair.

Among shops of religious artefacts, the chic boutiques on place and rue St-Sulpice include **Yves Saint Laurent** (*see p250*), **Vanessa Bruno** (*see p254*) and milliner **Marie Mercié** (*see p257*). Prime shopping continues further west: clothes on rue Bonaparte and rue du Four, and accessory and fashion shops on rue du Dragon, rue de Grenelle and rue du Cherche-Midi. If you spot a queue in the latter, it's most likely for the bread at **Poilâne** (*see p261*). Across the street, at the junction of rue de Sèvres and rue du Cherche-Midi, César's bronze *Centaur* is the sculptor's tribute to Picasso.

The early 17th-century chapel of St-Joseph-des-Carmes – once a Carmelite convent, now hidden within the **Institut Catholique** (21 rue d'Assas, 6th, 01.44.39.52.00, www.icp.fr) – was the scene of the murder of 115 priests during the Terror in 1792. To the east lies wide rue de Tournon, lined by such grand 18th-century residences as the elegant Hôtel de Brancas (no.6), with figures of Justice and Prudence over the door. This street opens up to the **Palais du Luxembourg**, which now serves as the Senate, and the adjoining **Jardin du Luxembourg**.

Towards boulevard St-Germain is the neo-classical **Odéon, Théâtre de l'Europe** (*see p346*), built in 1779 and recently renovated. A house in the square in front was home to Revolutionary hero Camille Desmoulins, who incited the mob to attack the Bastille in 1789. It's now occupied by **La Méditerranée** (2 pl de l'Odéon, 6th, 01.43.26.02.30, www.la-mediterranee.com); the restaurant's menus and plates were designed by Jean Cocteau. Joyce's *Ulysses* was first published in 1922 by Sylvia Beach at the celebrated **Shakespeare & Co** (*see p242*) at 12 rue de l'Odéon. Next door is the venerable **Le Bar Dix** (*see p235*).

Further along the street, at 12 rue de l'Ecole-de-Médecine, is the neo-classical Université René Descartes (Paris V) medical school, and the **Musée d'Histoire de la Médecine**. The Club des Cordeliers, set up by Danton in 1790, devised revolutionary plots across the street at the **Couvent des Cordeliers** (no.15); the 14th-century refectory, all that remains of the monastery founded by St Louis, houses modern art exhibitions. Marat, one of the club's leading lights, was stabbed to death in the bathtub at his home in the same street; David depicted the moment after the crime in his iconic painting, the *Death of Marat*. This was the surgeons' district: observe the domed building at no.5, once the barbers' and surgeons' guild. Climb

rue André-Dubois to rue Monsieur-le-Prince to reach budget restaurant **Polidor** (no.41, 6th, 01.43.26.95.34), open since 1845.

FREE Eglise St-Sulpice

Pl St-Sulpice, 6th (01.42.34.59.98/www. paroisse-saint-sulpice-paris.org). M° St-Sulpice. **Open** 7.30am-7.30pm daily. **Admission** free. **Map** p408 H7.

It took 120 years and six architects to finish St-Sulpice. The grandiose façade, with its two-tier colonnade, was designed by Jean-Baptiste Servandoni. He died in 1766 before the second tower was finished, leaving one tower a good five metres shorter than the other. The trio of murals by Delacroix in the first chapel – *Jacob's Fight with the Angel, Heliodorus Chased from the Temple* and *St Michael Killing the Dragon* – create a suitably sombre atmosphere.

★ FREE Jardin & Palais du Luxembourg

Pl Auguste-Comte, pl Edmond-Rostand or rue de Vaugirard, 6th (01.44.54.19.49/www.senat.fr/ visite). M° Odéon/RER Luxembourg. **Open** *Jardin* summer 7.30am-dusk daily; winter 8am-dusk daily. **Map** p408 H8.

The palace itself was built in the 1620s for Marie de Médicis, widow of Henri IV, by Salomon de Brosse on the site of the former mansion of the Duke of Luxembourg. Its Italianate style was intended to remind her of the Pitti Palace in her native Florence. The palace now houses the French parliament's upper house, the Sénat (open only by guided visits).

Jardin du Luxembourg.

Cycle Paris Picnic

Fill your basket with Left Bank goodies.

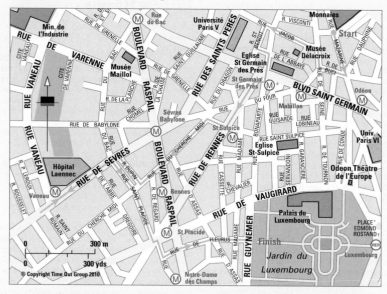

St-Germain may be more Louis Vuitton than Boris Vian these days, but there are still enough small galleries and bookshops to ensure that it retains a whiff of its bohemian past. Aside from art and books, the sixth arrondissement (and its neighbour the seventh) is also a great place to shop for food, since it has some of the finest artisanal bakeries and *traiteurs* in Paris.

And thanks to Vélib (www.velib.paris.fr), it's easier than ever to get around the *quartier* in order to stock up. What's more, the standard-issue bike is equipped with a basket that should carry all you'll need for a sumptuous picnic. This itinerary will probably take you the best part of two hours. Don't bother searching for a station each time you need to stop; just use the chain provided to lock your bike.

Detach your bike from the *borne* at 1 rue Jacques-Callot, 6th (Mº Mabillon) and cycle down rue Mazarine as far as the carrefour de Buci. Turn left into rue de Buci and carry on until the junction with rue de Seine. The stretch of rue de Seine between here and boulevard St-Germain is lined with butchers and greengrocers. Ignore the smell of roasting chickens (you'll be getting cooked

meat elsewhere), and just buy salad leaves and fruit. Then head back down rue de Seine towards the river. About halfway down, turn left into rue Jacob. Cross rue Bonaparte and take the next left into rue St-Benoît. Pause for a moment to look in the window of **Librairie St-Benoît-des-Prés** (2 rue St-Benoît, 6th, 01.40.20.43.42), which specialises in rare books, manuscripts, letters and autographs.

Continue down rue St-Benoît as far as place St-Germain-des-Prés, where you'll find three venerable St-Germain institutions: **Café de Flore** (*see p236*), **Les Deux Magots** (*see p236*) and **La Hune** bookshop (*see p241*). The Flore and the Deux Magots buzz more with tourists than writers these days, though the former is still a favoured haunt of enfant terrible Bernard-Henri Lévy. If you spot a man with a mane of black hair and a white shirt open to the navel poring over a notebook, it's probably BHL. Next door, La Hune, which opened in 1949, is a kind of holy shrine for that nearly extinct species, the Left Bank Intellectual.

But it's not books we're after, it's bread; so pick your way across boulevard St-Germain and follow rue Gozlin round into the rue de Rennes. This is a broad, busy main road lined with chain stores. There's not a great deal to distract as you bowl south for half a kilometre or so, until you reach rue du Vieux-Colombier on the right. You'll have to do battle with buses and taxis in this narrow cut-through, which leads to the altogether more charming rue du Cherche-Midi. On the left-hand side of the street, wedged in among the boutiques, jewellers and galleries, stands **Poilâne** (*see p261*), the renowned family bakers. You can expect to have to queue here for the famous Poilâne loaf – but it's worth it: dark, firm and distinctively flavoured. The tarts and the biscuits are wonderful too.

Having loaded the bread into your basket, carry on down rue du Cherche-Midi. Go straight across boulevard Raspail. Take the first right into rue Dupin. You'll eventually reach rue de Sèvres. Lock your bike up against the railings here and cross the road on foot to La Grande Epicérie, the food hall in Paris's oldest department store, **Le Bon Marché** (*see p239*). This is a gastronome's paradise. Make your way to the *traiteurs* in the centre of the hall and choose from a staggering array of cooked meats. While you're here, you can also pick up dressing for the salad and a bottle of wine (and a corkscrew if you don't already have one).

It just remains to buy some cheese, and for this you'll need to cycle a little further south down rue de Sèvres. You'll pass the wonderful art deco entrance to the Vaneau metro station on the right, with its green iron lattices and globe lanterns. A little further along on the same side of the street, on the corner of rue Pierre-Leroux, stands **Fromagerie Quatrehomme** (*see p262*). Run by Marie Quatrehomme, this place is famous across Paris for its comté fruité, beaufort and oozy st-marcellin.

Your basket will be near to overflowing. It's time to head for a picnic spot in the Jardin du Luxembourg. Turn round and cycle back up rue de Sèvres, then turn right into rue St-Placide. Shortly after you pass the St-Placide métro station, turn left into rue de Fleurus. The **Jardin du Luxembourg** (*see p129*) is ahead of you, on the far side of rue Guynemer. There's a Vélib station at 26 rue Guynemer. As is usual in Paris, the grass here is not for sitting on. Instead, find a bench in the shade and tuck in.

The mansion next door (Le Petit Luxembourg) is the residence of the Sénat's president. The gardens, though, are the real draw: part formal (terraces and gravel paths), part 'English garden' (lawns and mature trees), they are the quintessential Paris park. The garden is crowded with sculptures: a looming Cyclops (on the 1624 Fontaine de Médicis), queens of France, a miniature Statue of Liberty, wild animals, busts of Flaubert and Baudelaire, and a monument to Delacroix. There are orchards and an apiary. The Musée National du Luxembourg (*see below*) hosts prestigious exhibitions. Most interesting, though, are the people: a mixture of *flâneurs* and *dragueurs*, chess players and martial-arts practitioners, as well as children on ponies, in sandpits, on roundabouts and playing with the sailing boats on the pond.

▶ *For more child-friendly Paris parks, see p290.*

Musée d'Histoire de la Médecine
Université René Descartes, 12 rue de l'Ecole-de-Médecine, 6th (01.40.46.16.93/www.bium.univ-paris5.fr/musee). M° Odéon or St-Michel. **Open** *Mid July-Sept* 2-5.30pm Mon-Fri. *Oct-mid July* 2-5.30pm Mon-Wed, Fri, Sat. **Admission** €3.50; €2.50 reductions; free under-8s. **No credit cards. Map** p408 H7.
The history of medicine is the subject of the medical faculty collection. There are ancient Egyptian embalming tools, a 1960s electrocardiograph and a gruesome array of saws used for amputations. You'll also find the instruments of Dr Antommarchi, who performed the autopsy on Napoleon, and the scalpel of Dr Félix, who operated on Louis XIV.

★ Musée des Lettres et Manuscrits
8 rue de Nesle, 6th (01.40.51.02.25/www.musee deslettres.fr). M° Odéon. **Open** 1-8pm Tue-Fri; 10am-6pm Sat-Sun. Closed Nov. **Admission** €6; €4.50 reductions. **Credit** (€16 minimum) MC, V. **Map** p408 H7.
More than 2,000 documents and letters give an insight into the lives of the great and the good, from Magritte to Mozart. Einstein arrives at the theory of relativity on notes scattered in authentic disorder, Baudelaire complains about his money problems in a letter to his mother, and HMS *Northumberland*'s log-book records the day Napoleon boarded the ship to be taken to St Helena.

Musée National du Luxembourg
19 rue de Vaugirard, 6th (01.42.34.25.95/www. museeduluxembourg.fr). M° Cluny La Sorbonne or Odéon/RER Luxembourg. **Open** 10.30am-10pm Mon, Fri, Sat; 10.30am-7pm Tue-Thur; 9.30am-7pm Sun. **Admission** €11; €9 reductions; free under-10s. **Credit** MC, V. **Map** p408 H7.
When it opened in 1750, this small museum was the first public gallery in France. Its current steward-ship by the national museums and the French Senate has brought imaginative touches and some impres-sive coups. Book ahead to avoid queues.

SIGHTS

Montparnasse & Beyond

The rise and fall of 'Mount Parnassus'.

Yet another artists' quarter that has long since lost the character – and the characters – that made its name, Montparnasse is now conspicuously lacking in charm. Between the two world wars, it was the emblematic 'gay Paree' district of after-dark merriment and fruitful artistic exchange – and it was also remarkably cosmopolitan. A great number of its most prominent figures were expats (including its best chronicler, the Hungarian photographer Brassaï), and the late-night bars and artists' studios formed a bubble of cordial international relations that was irreparably popped in 1939. The local atmosphere soured further with the completion of the much-loathed Tour Montparnasse in the early 1970s, a dark monolith that casts an ominous spell on the whole quarter. Granted, this is rich territory for art museums – but with the exception of the Fondation Cartier, they're all about past glories.

Maps p404-405	**Restaurants** p214
Hotels p181	**Cafés & bars** p237

MONTPARNASSE

In the 6th & 14th arrondissements.

Artists Picasso, Léger and Soutine fled to 'Mount Parnassus' in the early 1900s to escape the rising rents of Montmartre. They were soon joined by Chagall, Zadkine and other refugees from the Russian Revolution, along with Americans such as Man Ray, Henry Miller, Ezra Pound and Gertrude Stein. Between the wars the neighbourhood was the epitome of modernity: studios with large windows were built by avant-garde architects; artists, writers and intellectuals drank and debated in the quarter's showy bars; and naughty pastimes – including the then risqué tango – flourished.

Sadly, the Montparnasse of today has lost much of its former soul, dominated as it is by the lofty **Tour Montparnasse** – the first skyscraper to be built in central Paris. The dismay with which its construction was greeted prompted a change in building regulations in the city. At its foot are a shopping centre, the **Red Light** (*see p328*) and **Mix Club** (*see p333*) nightclubs, and, in winter, an open-air ice rink. There are fabulous panoramic views from the café on the 56th floor.

The old Montparnasse station witnessed two events of historical significance. In 1898, a runaway train burst through its façade; and on 25 August 1944, the German forces surrendered Paris here. The station was rebuilt in the 1970s, a grey affair above which can be found the surprising Jardin Atlantique, a modest oasis of granite paths, trees and bamboo spread over a roof, the **Mémorial du Maréchal Leclerc** and the **Musée Jean Moulin**.

Rue du Montparnasse, appropriately for a street near the station that sends trains to Brittany, is dotted with crêperies. Nearby, strip joints have replaced most of the theatres on ever-saucy rue de la Gaîté, but boulevard

Cimetière du Montparnasse.
See p134.

Edgar-Quinet has pleasant cafés and a street market (Wed, Sat), plus the entrance to the **Cimetière du Montparnasse**. Boulevard du Montparnasse still buzzes at night, thanks to its many cinemas and dining spots: giant art deco brasserie **La Coupole** (*see p214*); opposite, classic café **Le Select** (*see p237*); **Le Dôme** (no.108, 14th, 01.43.35.25.81), now a top-notch fish restaurant and bar; and restaurant **La Rotonde** (no.105, 6th, 01.43.26.48.26). All were popularised by the literati between the wars, and now use this heritage to their advantage; Le Select seems the most authentic of the bunch. Nearby, on boulevard Raspail, stands Rodin's statue of Balzac, whose rugged rather than flattering appearance caused such a scandal that it was put in place only after the sculptor's death.

For a whiff of Montparnasse's artistic history, wander down rue de la Grande-Chaumière. Bourdelle and Friesz taught at the venerable **Académie de la Grande-Chaumière** (no.14, 01.43.26.13.72), frequented by Calder, Giacometti and Pompon among others (it still offers drawing lessons); Modigliani died at no.8 in 1920, ruined by tuberculosis, drugs and alcohol; nearby **Musée Zadkine** occupies the sculptor's old house and studio. Rue Vavin and rue Bréa, leading to the Jardin du Luxembourg, have become an

enclave of children's shops. Look out for no.6, the 1912 white-tiled apartment building where art nouveau architect Henri Sauvage lived.

Further east on boulevard du Montparnasse, literary café **La Closerie des Lilas** (no.171, 6th, 01.40.51.34.50) was a pre-war favourite with everyone from Lenin and Trotsky to Picasso and Hemingway; brass plaques on the tables indicate where each historic figure used to sit. Next to it is the lovely **Fontaine de l'Observatoire**, featuring bronze turtles and thrashing sea horses by Frémiet, and figures of the four continents by Carpeaux.

From here, the Jardins de l'Observatoire form part of the green axis between the Palais du Luxembourg and the royal observatory, the **Observatoire de Paris**. A curiosity next door is the Maison des Fontainiers, built over an expansive (now dry-ish) underground reservoir originally commissioned by Marie de Médicis to supply water to fountains around the city.

A relatively recent addition to boulevard Raspail is the glass and steel **Fondation Cartier pour l'Art Contemporain**. Designed by architect Jean Nouvel, it houses the jewellers' head offices and an exhibition space dedicated to contemporary art and photography.

West of the train station, the redevelopment of Montparnasse is also evident in the circular place de Catalogne, a piece of 1980s postmodern neo-classicism designed by Mitterrand's favourite architect, Ricardo Bofill, and the housing estates of rue Vercingétorix.

There are still traces of the old, arty Montparnasse for those willing to look for it: in impasse Lebouis, an avant-garde studio building has recently been converted into the **Fondation Henri Cartier-Bresson**; at 21 avenue du Maine, an ivy-clad alleyway of old studios contains the artist-run exhibition space Immanence, as well as the **Musée du Montparnasse**, housed in the former academy and canteen of Russian painter Marie Vassilieff; on rue Antoine-Bourdelle, the **Musée Bourdelle** includes another old cluster of studios, where sculptor Antoine Bourdelle, Symbolist painter Eugène Carrière and, briefly, Marc Chagall worked. Towards Les Invalides, on rue Mayet, craft and restoration workshops still hide in the old courtyards.

FREE Cimetière du Montparnasse

3 bd Edgar-Quinet, 14th (01.44.10.86.50). M° Edgar Quinet or Raspail. **Open** *16 Mar-5 Nov* 8am-6pm Mon-Fri; 8.30am-6pm Sat; 9am-6pm Sun. *6 Nov-15 Mar* 8am-5.30pm Mon-Fri; 8.30am-5.30pm Sat; 9.30am-5.30pm Sun. **Admission** free. **Map** p405 G9.

Formed by commandeering three farms (you can still see the ruins of a windmill by rue Froidevaux), the Montparnasse boneyard has literary clout: Beckett, Baudelaire, Sartre, de Beauvoir, Maupassant, Ionesco and Tristan Tzara all rest here. There are also artists, including Brancusi, Henri Laurens, Frédéric Bartholdi (sculptor of the Statue of Liberty) and Man Ray. The celebrity roll-call continues with Serge Gainsbourg, André Citroën and actress Jean Seberg. *Photo p133.*

★ Fondation Cartier pour l'Art Contemporain

261 bd Raspail, 14th (01.42.18.56.50/recorded information 01.42.18.56.51/www.fondation. cartier.fr). M° Denfert-Rochereau or Raspail.

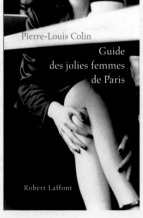

Open 11am-10pm Tue; 11am-8pm Wed-Sun.
Admission €6.50; €4.50 reductions; free under-
10s & under-18s 2-6pm Tue-Sun. Credit AmEx,
MC, V. Map p405 G9.
Jean Nouvel's glass and steel building, an exhibition
centre with Cartier's offices above, is as much a work
of art as the installations inside. Shows by artists
and photographers often have wide-ranging themes,
such as 'Birds' or 'Desert'. Live events around the
shows are called Nuits Nomades.

Fondation Dubuffet

*137 rue de Sèvres, 6th (01.47.34.12.63/www.
dubuffetfondation.com). M° Duroc.* Open 2-6pm
Mon-Fri. Closed Aug. Admission €4; free under-
10s. No credit cards. Map p405 E8.
You walk up a winding garden path to get to this
museum, founded by Jean Dubuffet, wine merchant
and master of *art brut*. The foundation ensures that
a fair body of his works is accessible to the public.
There's a changing display of Dubuffet's lively drawings, paintings and sculptures, as well as models of
the architectural sculptures from the *Hourloupe* cycle.
► *The foundation looks after the Closerie
Falbala, the 3D masterpiece of the Hourloupe
cycle, housed at Périgny-sur-Yerres, east of
Paris (viewings by appointment only, €8).*

★ Fondation Henri Cartier-Bresson

*2 impasse Lebouis, 14th (01.56.80.27.00/www.
henricartierbresson.org). M° Gaîté.* Open 1-6.30pm
Tue, Thur, Fri, Sun; 1-8.30pm Wed; 11am-6.45pm
Sat. Closed Aug & between exhibitions.
Admission €6; €3 reductions, all 6.30-8.30pm
Wed. No credit cards. Map p405 F10.
Opened in 2003, this two-floor gallery is dedicated to
the work of acclaimed photographer Henri Cartier-
Bresson. It consists of a tall, narrow *atelier* in a 1913
building, with a minutely catalogued archive, open to
researchers, and a lounge on the fourth floor screening films. In the spirit of Cartier-Bresson, who assisted
on three Jean Renoir films and drew and painted all
his life (some drawings are also found on the fourth
floor), the Fondation opens its doors to other disciplines with three annual shows. The convivial feel of
the Fondation – and its Le Corbusier armchairs – fos-
ters relaxed discussion with staff and other visitors.

FREE Mémorial du Maréchal Leclerc de Hauteclocque et de la Libération de Paris & Musée Jean Moulin

*Jardin Atlantique, 23 allée de la 2e DB (above
Gare Montparnasse), 15th (01.40.64.39.44/
www.ml-leclerc-moulin.paris.fr). M° Montparnasse
Bienvenüe.* Open 10am-6pm Tue-Sun. Admission
free. *Exhibitions* €4; €2-€3 reductions; free under-
13s. Credit *Shop* MC, V. Map p405 F9.
This double museum retraces World War II and the
Resistance through the Free French commander
Maréchal Leclerc and left-wing hero Jean Moulin.
Documentary material and film archives complement

Les Catacombes. *See p138.*

an impressive 270° slide show, complete with sound
effects, which tells the story of the Liberation of Paris.

FREE Musée-Atelier Adzak

*3 rue Jonquoy, 14th (01.45.43.06.98).
M° Plaisance.* Open usually 3-7pm Sat,
Sun (call in advance). Admission free.
The eccentric house, studio and garden built by the
late Roy Adzak, a British-born painter and sculptor
who died in 1987, harbour traces of the conceptual
artist's plaster body columns and dehydrations.
Now a registered British-run charity, it gives mostly
foreign artists a chance to exhibit in Paris.

FREE Musée Bourdelle

*16-18 rue Antoine-Bourdelle, 15th
(01.49.54.73.73/www.bourdelle.paris.fr). M°
Falguière or Montparnasse Bienvenüe.* Open
10am-6pm Tue-Sun. Admission free. *Exhibitions*
prices vary. Credit MC, V. Map p405 F8.
The sculptor Antoine Bourdelle (1861-1929), a pupil
of Rodin, produced a number of monumental works
including the modernist relief friezes at the Théâtre
des Champs-Elysées, inspired by Isadora Duncan
and Nijinsky. The museum includes the artist's

apartment and studios, which were also used by Eugène Carrière, Dalou and Chagall. A 1950s extension tracks the evolution of Bourdelle's equestrian monument to General Alvear in Buenos Aires, and his masterful *Hercules the Archer*. A new wing by Christian de Portzamparc houses bronzes, including various studies of Beethoven in different guises.

Set in one of the last surviving alleys of studios, this was home to Marie Vassilieff, whose own academy and cheap canteen welcomed poor artists, including famous names such as Picasso, Cocteau and Matisse. Trotsky and Lenin were also guests. Shows focus on present-day artists and the area's creative past.

Musée du Montparnasse
21 av du Maine, 15th (01.42.22.91.96/www. museedumontparnasse.net). M° Montparnasse Bienvenüe. **Open** 12.30-7pm Tue-Sun. **Admission** €5; €4 reductions; free under-12s. **No credit cards. Map** p403 F8.

Musée Pasteur
Institut Pasteur, 25 rue du Dr-Roux, 15th (01.45.68.82.83/www.pasteur.fr). M° Pasteur. **Open** 2-5.30pm Mon-Fri. Closed Aug. **Admission** €3; €1.50 reductions. **Credit** MC, V. **Map** p405 E9.

Parc Montsouris. *See p138.*

The flat where the famous chemist and his wife lived at the end of his life (1888-95) has not been touched; you can see their furniture and possessions, photos and instruments. An extravagant mausoleum on the ground floor houses Pasteur's tomb, decorated with mosaics depicting his scientific achievements.

Musée de la Poste

34 bd de Vaugirard, 15th (01.42.79.24.24/www. museedelaposte.fr). M° Montparnasse Bienvenüe. **Open** 10am-6pm Mon-Sat. **Admission** €5; €3.50 reductions; free under-26s. PMP. *Permanent & temporary exhibitions* €6.50; €5 reductions; free under-13s. **No credit cards. Map** p405 E9.
From among the uniforms, pistols, carriages, official decrees and fumigation tongs emerge snippets of history: during the 1871 Siege of Paris, hot-air balloons and carrier pigeons were used to get post out of the city, and *boules de Moulins*, balls crammed with hundreds of letters, were floated down the Seine in return, mostly never to arrive. The second section covers French and international philately.

★ FREE Musée Zadkine

100bis rue d'Assas, 6th (01.55.42.77.20/www. zadkine.paris.fr). M° Notre-Dame-des-Champs/ RER Port-Royal. **Open** 10am-6pm Tue-Sun. **Admission** free. *Exhibitions* €4; €2-€3 reductions; free under-13s. **Credit** (€15 minimum) MC, V. **Map** p408 G8.
Works by the Russian-born Cubist sculptor Ossip Zadkine are displayed around this tiny house and garden near the Jardin du Luxembourg. Zadkine's works cover musical, mythological and religious subjects, and his style varies with his materials. There are drawings and poems by Zadkine and paintings by his wife, Valentine Prax.

FREE Observatoire de Paris

61 av de l'Observatoire, 14th (01.40.51.22.21/ www.obspm.fr). Entry for visitors at 77 av Denfert-Rochereau, 14th. M° St-Jacques/RER Port-Royal. **Open** *Tours* 1st Sat of mth (except Aug) by written reservation only to: Service de la Communication (service des visites), Observatoire de Paris, 61 av de l'Observatoire, 75014 Paris. **Admission** free. **Map** p405 H10.
The Paris observatory was founded by Louis XIV's finance minister, Colbert, in 1667; it was designed by Claude Perrault (who also worked on the Louvre), with labs and an observation tower. The French meridian line drawn by François Arago in 1806 (which was used here before the Greenwich meridian was adopted as an international standard) runs north–south through the centre of the building. The dome on the observation tower was added in the 1840s..
► *You'll need to apply for an appointment at the Observatoire by letter, but check the website for openings linked to astronomical happenings – or visit on the Journées du Patrimoine (see p278).*

★ Tour Montparnasse

33 av du Maine, 15th (01.45.38.52.56/ www.tourmontparnasse56.com). M° Montparnasse Bienvenüe. **Open** *1 Oct-31 Mar* 9.30am-10.30pm daily. *1 Apr-30 Sept* 9.30am-11.30pm daily. **Admission** €10.50; €7.50-€4.50 reductions; free under-7s. **Credit** MC, V. **Map** p405 F9.
Built in 1974 on the site of the old station, this 209m (686ft) steel-and-glass monolith is actually shorter than the Eiffel Tower, but better placed for fabulous views of the city – including, of course, the Eiffel Tower itself. A lift whisks you up in 38 seconds to the 56th floor, where you'll find a display of aerial scenes of Paris, an upgraded café-lounge, a souvenir shop – and lots and lots of sky. On a clear day you can see up to 40km (25 miles). Another lift takes you all the way up to the roof. Classical concerts are held on the terrace.

DENFERT-ROCHEREAU & MONTSOURIS

In the 14th & 15th arrondissements.

In the run-up to the 1789 Revolution, the bones of six million Parisians were taken from the handful of overcrowded city cemeteries and wheelbarrowed to the **Catacombes**, a vast network of tunnels that stretches under much of Paris. The sections under the 13th and 14th arrondissements are open to the public; the gloomy Denfert-Rochereau entrance is next to one of the toll gates of the Mur des Fermiers-Généraux, built by Ledoux in the 1780s.

The bronze *Lion de Belfort* dominates the traffic-laden place Denfert-Rochereau, a favourite starting point for the city's countless political demonstrations. The regal beast was sculpted by Bartholdi, of Statue of Liberty fame, and is a scaled-down replica of one in Belfort that commemorates the brave defence by Colonel Denfert-Rochereau of the town in 1870. Nearby, the southern half of rue Daguerre is a sociable, pedestrianised market street (Tuesday to Saturday, Sunday mornings) brimming with cafés and food stores.

One of the big draws of the area is the **Parc Montsouris**, with lovely lakes, dramatic cascades and an unusual history. Surrounding the western edge of the park are a number of modest, quiet streets – including rue du Parc Montsouris and rue Georges-Braque – that used to be lined during the 1920s and '30s with charming villas and artists' studios by avant-garde architects Le Corbusier and André Lurçat. On the southern edge of the park sprawls the **Cité Universitaire** complex.

SIGHTS

SIGHTS

★ Les Catacombes
1 av du Colonel-Henri-Rol-Tanguy, 14th
(01.43.22.47.63/www.catacombes-de-paris.fr).
M°/RER Denfert Rochereau. **Open** 10am-5pm
Tue-Sun. **Admission** €8; €4-€6 reductions;
free under-14s. **Credit** (€15 minimum) MC, V.
Map p407 H10.
This is the official entrance to the 3,000km (1,864-mile) tunnel network that runs under much of the city. With public burial pits overflowing in the era of the Revolutionary Terror, the bones of six million people were transferred to the *catacombes*. The bones of Marat, Robespierre and their cronies are packed in with wall upon wall of their fellow citizens. A damp, cramped tunnel takes you through a series of galleries before you reach the ossuary, the entrance to which is announced by a sign engraved in the stone: 'Stop! This is the empire of death.' The tour lasts approximately 45 minutes and the temperature in the tunnels is 14°C. *Photo p135.*

FREE Cité Universitaire
17 bd Jourdan, 14th (01.44.16.64.00/
www.ciup.fr). RER Cité Universitaire.
The Cité Internationale Universitaire de Paris is an odd mix. Created between the wars in a mood of internationalism and inspired by the model of Oxbridge colleges, its 37 halls of residence across landscaped gardens were designed in a variety of supposedly authentic national styles. Some are by architects of the appropriate nationality (Dutchman Willem Dudok, for instance, designed the De Stijl-style Collège Néerlandais); others, such as the Khmer sculptures and bird-beak roof of the Asie du Sud-Est building, are merely pastiches. The Brits get what looks like a minor public school; the Maison Internationale is based on Fontainebleau; the Swiss and Brazilians get Le Corbusier. You can visit the sculptural white Pavillon Suisse (01.44.16.10.16, www.fondationsuisse.fr), which has a Le Corbusier mural on the ground floor. The spacious landscaped gardens are open to the public, and the newly renovated theatre stages drama and modern dance.

INSIDE TRACK TALL STOREYS

High-rise towers have been a Paris taboo ever since 1977, when a by-law was passed to fix maximum building heights at 37 metres or ten storeys. But now, Mayor Delanoë has unveiled plans for a series of new towers that will transform the city's skyline, and help him deliver on his promise to create more social housing. The first to go up will be the Projet Triangle, Porte de Versailles. Designed by Herzog & de Meuron, the 40-storey tower is due to open in 2014 and resembles an ultra-thin pyramid or shark's fin.

FREE Parc Montsouris
Bd Jourdan, 14th. RER Cité Universitaire.
Open 8am-dusk Mon-Fri; 9am-dusk Sat, Sun.
The most colourful of the capital's many parks, Montsouris was laid out for Baron Haussmann by Jean-Charles Adolphe Alphand. It includes a series of sweeping, gently sloping lawns, an artificial lake and cascades. On the opening day in 1878 the lake inexplicably emptied, and the engineer responsible committed suicide. *Photos p136.*

The 15th arrondissement

The expansive 15th arrondissement has little to offer tourists, though as a largely residential district it has plenty of good restaurants, street markets, and some good small shops, notably on rue du Commerce and rue Lecourbe. It's worth making a detour to visit **La Ruche** ('beehive'), designed by Eiffel as a wine pavilion for the 1900 Exposition Universelle and moved here to serve as artists' studios. Nearby is **Parc Georges Brassens**, opened in 1983, and at the porte de Versailles the sprawling **Paris-Expo** exhibition centre was created in 1923.

FREE Parc Georges Brassens
Rue des Morillons, 15th. M° Porte de Vanves or
Porte de Versailles. **Open** 8am-dusk Mon-Fri;
9am-dusk Sat, Sun. **Map** p404 D10.
Built on the site of the old Abattoirs de Vaugirard, Parc Georges Brassens prefigured the industrial regeneration of Parc André Citroën and La Villette. The gateways, crowned by bronze bulls, have been kept, as have a series of iron meat-market pavilions, which house a second-hand book market at weekends. The Jardin des Senteurs is planted with aromatic species, and a small vineyard yields 200 bottles of Clos des Morillons every year.

Paris-Expo
1 pl de la Porte de Versailles, 15th
(01.72.72.17.00/www.vipparis.com).
M° Porte de Versailles. **Map** p404 B10.
This vast exhibition centre, spread over different halls, hosts all manner of trade and art fairs. Many, such as the Foire de Paris (*see p275*) and art fair FIAC (*see p279*), are open to the public.

La Ruche
Passage de Dantzig, 15th (www.la-ruche.fr). M°
Convention or Porte de Versailles. **Map** p404 D10.
Have a peep through the fence or sneak in behind an unsuspecting resident to see the iron-framed former wine pavilion built by Gustave Eiffel for the 1900 Exposition Universelle, and later rebuilt by philanthropic sculptor Alfred Boucher to be let as studios for struggling artists. Chagall, Soutine, Brancusi, Modigliani, Lipchitz and Archipenko all spent periods here, and the 140 studios are still sought after by today's artists and designers.

The 7th & Western Paris

Home to old masters, new ministers and the city's greatest landmark.

The seventh arrondissement is one large workshop, dotted with the machinery of state and diplomacy: this is the home of France's parliament, several ministries and a gaggle of foreign embassies, as well as the French army's training establishment and the headquarters of UNESCO. Visually speaking, much of the district is formal and aloof, albeit smart, and there are few attractions to draw the visitor – with the sizeable exceptions, naturally, of the Invalides, the Musée d'Orsay, the Rodin museum and a certain A-shaped assembly of 19th-century iron lattice beside the river.

| Maps p404-405 | Restaurants p215 |
| Hotels p181 | Cafés & bars p234 |

THE FAUBOURG ST-GERMAIN

In the 7th arrondissement.

In the early 18th century, when the Marais went out of fashion, aristocrats built palatial new residences on the Faubourg St-Germain, the district developing around the site of the former city wall. It is still a well-bred part of the city, government ministries and foreign embassies colouring the area with flags and diplomatic plates. Many fine *hôtels particuliers* survive; glimpse their elegant entrance courtyards on rue de Grenelle, rue St-Dominique, rue de l'Université and rue de Varenne.

Just west of St-Germain, the 'Carré Rive Gauche' or 'Carré des Antiquaires' – the quadrangle enclosed by quai Voltaire, rue des Sts-Pères, rue du Bac and rue de l'Université – is filled with antiques shops. On rue des Sts-Pères, *chocolatier* **Debauve & Gallais** (no.30, 7th, 01.45.48.54.67), with its period interior, has been making chocolates since 1800. Rue du Pré-aux-Clercs, named after a field where students used to duel, is now a favourite with fashion insiders. There are still students to be found on adjoining rue St-Guillaume, home of the prestigious **Fondation Nationale des Sciences-Politiques** (no.27, 7th, 01.45.49.50.50), more commonly known as 'Sciences-Po'.

Rue de Montalembert is home to two of the Left Bank's most fashionable hotels: the **Hôtel Montalembert** (*see p182*) and the Hôtel du Pont-Royal, a gastronomic magnet ever since the addition of the trendy **Atelier de Joël Robuchon** (www.joel-robuchon.com). By the river, a Beaux-Arts train station – the towns once served still listed on the façade – houses the unmissable art collections of the **Musée d'Orsay**; outside on the esplanade are 19th-century bronze animal sculptures. Next door is the lovely 1780s Hôtel de Salm, once the Swedish embassy and now the **Musée National de la Légion d'Honneur et des Ordres de Chevalerie** (2 rue de la Légion d'Honneur, 7th, 01.40.62.84.25), devoted to France's honours system since Louis XI. The Legion of Honour was established by Napoleon in 1802. Across the street, a modern footbridge, the Passerelle Solférino, crosses the Seine to the Tuileries. The fancy Hôtel Bouchardon today houses the **Musée Maillol**. Right beside its curved entrance, the Fontaine des Quatre Saisons by Edmé Bouchardon features statues of the seasons surrounding allegorical figures of Paris above the rivers Seine and Marne.

Chapelle de la Medaille Miraculeuse.

You'll have to wait for the open-house **Journées du Patrimoine** (*see p278*) to see the decorative interiors and private gardens of other *hôtels*, such as the **Hôtel de Villeroy** (Ministry of Agriculture; 78 rue de Varenne, 7th), **Hôtel Boisgelin** (Italian Embassy; 51 rue de Varenne, 7th), **Hôtel d'Avaray** (Dutch ambassador's residence; 85 rue de Grenelle, 7th), **Hôtel d'Estrées** (Russian ambassador's residence; 79 rue de Grenelle, 7th) or **Hôtel de Monaco** (Polish Embassy; 57 rue St-Dominique, 7th). Among the most beautiful is the **Hôtel Matignon** (57 rue de Varenne, 7th), residence of the prime minister. Once used for French statesman Talleyrand for lavish receptions, it contains the biggest private garden in Paris. The Cité Varenne at no.51 is a lane of exclusive houses with private gardens.

Rue du Bac is home to the city's oldest and most elegant department store, **Le Bon Marché** ('the good bargain'), and to an unlikely pilgrimage spot, the **Chapelle de la Médaille Miraculeuse**. On nearby rue de Babylone, handy budget bistro **Au Babylone** (no.13, 7th, 01.45.48.72.13) has been serving up cheap lunches for decades, but the Théâtre de Babylone, where Beckett's *Waiting for Godot* was premiered in 1953, is long gone.

At the foot of boulevard St-Germain, facing place de la Concorde across the Seine, is the **Assemblée Nationale**, the lower house of the French parliament. Behind, elegant place du Palais-Bourbon leads into rue de Bourgogne, a rare commercial thoroughfare amid the official buildings, with some delectable pâtisseries and designer-furniture showrooms.

Nearby, the mid 19th-century **Eglise Ste-Clotilde** (12 rue Martignac, 7th, 01.44.18.62.60), with its skeletal twin spires, is an early example

of Gothic Revival. Beside the Assemblée is the Foreign Ministry, often referred to by its address, 'quai d'Orsay'. Beyond it, a long, grassy esplanade leads up to golden-domed Les Invalides. The vast military hospital complex, with its Eglise du Dôme and St-Louis-des-Invalides churches, all built by Louis XIV, epitomises the official grandeur of the Sun King as expression of royal and military power. It now houses the **Musée de l'Armée**, as well as Napoleon's tomb inside the Eglise du Dôme. Stand with your back to the dome to survey the cherubim-laden Pont Alexandre III and the **Grand** and **Petit Palais** over the river, all put up for the 1900 Exposition Universelle.

Just beside Les Invalides is the **Musée National Rodin**, occupying the charming 18th-century Hôtel Biron and its romantic gardens. Many of his great sculptures, including the *Thinker*, the *Burghers of Calais* and the swarming *Gates of Hell*, are displayed in the building and around the gardens – as are those of his mistress, Camille Claudel.

FREE Assemblée Nationale

33 quai d'Orsay, 7th (01.40.63.60.00/ www.assemblee-nationale.fr). M° Assemblée Nationale. **Map** p405 F5.

Like the Sénat, the Assemblée Nationale (also known as the Palais Bourbon) is a royal building adapted for republicanism. It was built between 1722 and 1728 for the Duchesse de Bourbon, daughter of Louis XIV and Madame de Montespan, who also put up the neighbouring Hôtel de Lassay for her lover, the Marquis de Lassay. The *palais* was modelled on the Grand Trianon at Versailles, with a colonnaded *cour d'honneur* opening on to rue de l'Université and gardens running down to the Seine. The Prince de Condé extended the palace, linked the two *hôtels* and laid

SIGHTS

out place du Palais-Bourbon. The Greek temple-style façade facing Pont de la Concorde (the rear of the building) was added in 1806 to mirror the Madeleine.

Flanking this riverside façade are statues of four great statesmen: L'Hôpital, Sully, Colbert and Aguesseau. The Napoleonic frieze on the pediment was replaced by a monarchist one after the restoration: between 1838 and 1841, Cortot sculpted the figures of France, Power and Justice. After the Revolution, the palace became the meeting place for the Conseil des Cinq-Cents. It was the forerunner of the parliament's lower house, which set up here for good in 1827. Visits are by arrangement through a serving *député* (if you're French) – or, after long queuing, during the Journées du Patrimoine (*see p278*).

★ FREE Chapelle de la Médaille Miraculeuse

Couvent des Soeurs de St-Vincent-de-Paul, 140 rue du Bac, 7th (01.49.54.78.88). M° Sèvres Babylone. **Open** 7.45am-1pm, 2.30-7pm daily. **Admission** free. **Map** p405 F7.

In 1830, saintly Catherine Labouré was said to have seen a vision of the Virgin, who told her to cast a medal that copied her appearance – standing on a globe with rays of light appearing from her outstretched hands. This kitsch chapel – murals, mosaics, statues and the embalmed bodies of Catherine and her mother superior – is one of France's most visited sites, attracting two million pilgrims every year. Reliefs in the courtyard tell the nun's story – and slot machines sell medals.

FREE Espace Fondation EDF

6 rue Récamier, 7th (01.53.63.23.45/www.edf.fr). M° Sèvres Babylone. **Open** noon-7pm Tue-Sun. **Admission** free. **Map** p405 G7.

This former electricity substation, converted by Electricité de France for PR purposes, is now used for varied, well-presented exhibitions examining the likes of garden designer Gilles Clément.

★ Les Invalides & Musée de l'Armée

Esplanade des Invalides, 7th (08.10.11.33.99/ www.invalides.org). M° La Tour Maubourg or Les Invalides. **Open** Apr-Sept 10am-6pm daily. Oct-Mar 10am-5pm daily. Closed 1st Mon of mth. **Admission** *Courtyard* free. *Musée de l'Armée & Eglise du Dôme* €8.50; €6.50 reductions; free under-18s. PMP. **Credit** MC, V. **Map** p405 E6.

Making an Exhibition

Paris's World Fairs have produced many of its finest buildings.

What do the Eiffel Tower, the Palais de Chaillot and the Grand Palais have in common? Beyond the obvious fact that they are major Paris monuments, these buildings share another key trait: they were all designed and built for the World Fair.

Best known these days simply as 'Expo', the World Fair was conceived as an international showcase for technological innovations and cultural exchange, with London welcoming the first edition in 1851. Between 1855 and 1937, Paris hosted the Exposition Universelle six times, with each successive show offering the city a plethora of new architectural landmarks.

Most structures were designed for a lifespan of just a few months and dismantled at the end of the Fair, but others have survived. The Grand Palais and Petit Palais were both built as exhibition halls for the 1900 World Fair, while the colonnaded Palais de Chaillot and Palais de Tokyo were erected for the 1937 Fair. The Champ de Mars was given a whole series of facelifts during the golden years of the Paris World Fairs. For some 50 years, its centrepiece was the Palais de l'Industrie, a huge arena-like hall constructed in 1855 to rival London's Crystal Palace. Most

famously, the Eiffel Tower was originally erected here as a temporary exhibit for the 1889 World Fair. it was spared subsequent dismantling thanks to the birth of radio communication: the tower's height made it a first-rate location for an antenna.

Less well-known vestiges of the Fairs are littered all around the city. La Ruche ('The Beehive') in the 15th arrondissement was designed as a wine rotunda by Gustave Eiffel in 1900 and subsequently became one of the city's most famous artists' studios, inhabited by the likes of Chagall, Modigliani and Brancusi. Many other monuments have been relocated – the Japanese Tower and Chinese Pavilion (1900) were transported all the way to Brussels, while the Chalet Suisse (1867) was rebuilt on the Ile Reuilly in the Bois de Vincennes and is now a well respected restaurant (www.lechaletdesiles.com).

In another corner of the Bois de Vincennes, the Jardin Tropical is a rather sadder Expo leftover. Built for the Exposition Coloniale of 1907, a showcase for France's colonial dominance, its once grandiose pavilions have since fallen into disrepair, and today the crumbling ruins are a rather forlorn tribute to a bygone era.

SIGHTS

Topped by its gilded dome – a glorious sight when illuminated after dusk – the Hôtel des Invalides was (and in part still is) a hospital. Commissioned by Louis XIV for wounded soldiers, it once housed as many as 6,000 invalids. Designed by Libéral Bruand (the foundations were laid in 1671) and completed by Jules Hardouin-Mansart, it's a magnificent monument to Louis XIV and Napoleon. Behind lines of cannons and bullet-shaped yews, the main (northern) façade has a relief of Louis XIV (Ludovicus Magnus) and the Sun King's sunburst. Wander through the main courtyard and you'll see grandiose two-storey arcades and a statue of Napoleon glaring down from the end; the dormer windows around the courtyards are sculpted to look like suits of armour.

The complex contains two churches – or, rather, a sort of double church: the Eglise St-Louis was for the soldiers, the Eglise du Dôme for the king. An opening behind the altar connects the two. The long, barrel-vaulted nave of the church of St-Louis is hung with flags captured from enemy troops. Since 1840 the baroque Eglise du Dôme has been dedicated to the worship of Napoleon, whose body was brought here from St Helena. On the ground floor, under a dome painted by de la Fosse, Jouvenet and Coypel, are chapels featuring monuments to Vauban, Foch and Joseph Napoleon (Napoleon's older brother and King of Naples, Sicily and Spain). Napoleon II (King of Rome) is buried in the crypt opposite his father the emperor. Two dramatic black figures holding up the entrance to the crypt, the red porphyry tomb, the ring of giant figures, and the friezes and texts eulogising the emperor's heroic deeds give the measure of the cult of Napoleon, cherished in France for ruling large swaths of Europe and for creating an administrative and educational system that endures to this day.

The Invalides complex also houses the enormous Musée de l'Armée, which is in effect several museums in one; allow a whole afternoon to visit it properly. Even if militaria are not your thing, the building is splendid, and there's some fine portraiture, such as Ingres' *Emperor Napoleon on his Throne*. The Antique Armour wing is packed full of armour and weapons that look as good as new, many displaying amazing workmanship, from the superb 16th-century suit made for François I to cabinets full of swords, maces, crossbows and muskets and arquebuses. The Plans-Reliefs section is a collection of gorgeous 18th- and 19th-century scale models of French cities, used for military strategy; also here is a stunning 17th-century model of Mont St-Michel, made by a monk from playing cards.

The World War I rooms bring the conflict into focus with uniforms, paintings, a scale model of a trench and, most sobering of all, white plastercasts of the hideously mutilated faces of two soldiers. The World War II wing covers the Resistance, the Battle of Britain and the war in the Pacific (there's a replica of Little Boy, the bomb dropped on Hiroshima), alternating artefacts with film footage. Also included in the entry price is the Historial Charles de Gaulle.

Musée Maillol

59-61 rue de Grenelle, 7th (01.42.22.59.58/ www.museemaillol.com). M° Rue du Bac. **Open** 11am-6pm (last admission 5.15pm) Mon, Wed-Sun. **Admission** €8; €6 reductions; free under-16s. **Credit** *Shop* AmEx, MC, V. **Map** p405 G7.

Dina Vierny was 15 when she met Aristide Maillol and became his principal model for the next decade, idealised in such sculptures as *Spring*, *Air* and *Harmony*. In 1995 she opened this delightful museum, exhibiting Maillol's drawings, engravings, pastels, tapestry panels, ceramics and early Nabis-related paintings, as well as the sculptures and terracottas that epitomise his calm, modern classicism. Vierny also set up a Maillol Museum in the Pyrenean village of Banyuls-sur-Mer. This Paris venue also has works by Picasso, Rodin, Gauguin, Degas and Cézanne, a whole room of Matisse drawings, rare Surrealist documents and works by naïve artists. Vierny has also championed Kandinsky and Ilya Kabakov, whose *Communal Kitchen* installation recreates the atmosphere of Soviet domesticity. Monographic exhibitions are devoted to modern and contemporary artists.

Musée National Rodin

Hôtel Biron, 79 rue de Varenne, 7th (01.44.18.61.10/www.musee-rodin.fr). M° Varenne. **Open** *Apr-Sept* 9.30am-5.45pm Tue-Sun (gardens until 6.45pm). *Oct-Mar* 9.30am-4.45pm Tue-Sun (gardens until 5pm). **Admission** €6; €5 reductions, all Sun; free under-18s, all 1st Sun of mth. PMP. *Exhibitions* €7; €5 18-25s. *Gardens* €1. **Credit** MC, V. **Map** p405 F6.

Musée National Rodin.

Secret Museums Musée Valentin Haüy

The history of braille explained.

VALENTIN HAÜY

1745 – 1822

SIGHTS

The tiny **Musée Valentin Haüy** (*see p146*) is devoted to the history of braille, a story intimately connected with the French Enlightenment just before the Revolution. Valentin Haüy, whose statue you will see as you pass the gates of the Institut National des Jeunes Aveugles, was an 18th-century linguist and philanthropist. He established France's first school for the blind, and it was here that Louis Braille became a star pupil some 34 years later.

The one-room museum is hidden at the end of the nondescript corridors of the Valentin Haüy Association, which offers educational services to the blind. The door opens on to glass-fronted cases of exhibits with, in the centre, a huge braille globe. You can explore on your own with the aid of French, English or braille explanatory texts, or allow the curator, Noêle Roy, to show you round. She will give a tour in English if preferred.

The first exhibit is a shocking print, depicting the fairground freak show that inspired Valentin Haüy to devote his life to educating not only the blind, but also the backward public who came to laugh at the likes of this blind orchestra forced to perform in dunce's hats. He wanted to prove that blind people had as great a capacity for learning and feeling as anyone else – in short, that they were human beings.

Next begins the tactile tour, with a chance to touch books printed by Haüy in embossed letters. After the Revolution, another philanthopist, Charles Barbier, tried to develop a universal writing system using raised dots, but it was difficult to read. Braille, the son of a harness-maker, arrived at the school as a ten-year-old in 1819, having been blind since the age of four after he accidentally stabbed himself in the eye with a stitching awl.

He spent his years at the school developing and perfecting his six-dot fingertip system. He was only 16 when he completed it, and went on to teach, write a treatise on arithmetic, and play the organ in two Paris churches. He died from tuberculosis at the age of 43. If it hadn't been for his childhood accident, this genius may never have had access to the education that led to his gift to humanity and his admission to the Pantheon.

The Rodin museum occupies the *hôtel particulier* where the sculptor lived in the final years of his life. The *Kiss*, the *Cathedral*, the *Walking Man*, portrait busts and early terracottas are exhibited indoors, as are many of the individual figures or small groups that also appear on the *Gates of Hell*. Rodin's works are accompanied by several pieces by his mistress and pupil, Camille Claudel. The walls are hung with paintings by Van Gogh, Monet, Renoir, Carrière and Rodin himself. Most visitors have greatest affection for the gardens: look out for the *Burghers of Calais*, the elaborate *Gates of Hell*, and the *Thinker*.
▶ *Rodin fans can also visit the Villa des Brillants at Meudon (19 av Rodin, Meudon, 01.41.14.35.00), where the artist worked from 1895.*

★ Musée d'Orsay

1 rue de la Légion-d'Honneur, 7th (01.40.49.48.14/ recorded information01.45.49.11.11/www.musee- orsay.fr). M° Solférino/RER Musée d'Orsay. **Open** 9.30am-6pm Tue, Wed, Fri-Sun; 9.30am-9.45pm Thur. **Admission** €9.50; €7 reductions; free under-18s, all 1st Sun of mth. PMP. **Credit Shop** MC, V. **Map** p405 G6.

The building was originally a train station, designed by Victor Laloux to coincide with the Exposition Universelle in 1900. Now it's a huge museum spanning the fertile art period between 1848 and 1914. It follows a chronological route, from the ground floor to the upper level and then to the mezzanine, showing links between Impressionist painters and their forerunners: here you'll find a profusion of paintings by Delacroix, Corot, Manet, Renoir, Pissarro, Gauguin, Monet, Caillebotte, Cézanne, Van Gogh, Toulouse-Lautrec and others. A central sculpture aisle takes in monuments and maidens by Rude, Barrye and Carrier-Belleuse, but the outstanding pieces are by Carpeaux. The sculpture terraces include busts by Rodin, heads by Rosso and bronzes by Bourdelle and Maillol.

WEST & SOUTH OF LES INVALIDES

The 7th & 15th arrondissements.

South-west of the Invalides is the huge **Ecole Militaire** (av de La Motte-Picquet, 7th), the military academy built by Louis XV to educate the children of penniless officers; it would later train Napoleon. The severe neo-classical building, designed by Jacques Ange Gabriel, is still used by the army and closed to the public.

From the north-western side of the Ecole Militaire begins the vast Champ de Mars, a market garden converted into a military drilling ground in the 18th century. It has long been home to the most celebrated Paris monument of all, the **Eiffel Tower**. At the south-eastern end of the Champ de Mars stands the Mur pour la Paix ('wall for peace'), erected in 2000 to articulate hopes for peace. South-east of the Ecole are the Y-shaped **UNESCO** building, built in 1958, and the modernist Ministry of Labour. Fashionable apartments line broad avenue Bosquet and avenue Suffren, though there's much architectural eclecticism in the area: look at the pseudo-Gothic and pseudo-Renaissance houses on avenue de Villars; Lavirotte's fabulous art nouveau doorway at 27 avenue Rapp; and the striking, box-shaped **Notre Dame de l'Arche de l'Alliance** church (81 rue d'Alleray, 15th, 01.56.56.62.56), which was completed in 1998. For signs of life, visit the Saxe-Breteuil street market. The upper reaches of rue Cler contain classy food shops.

★ Eiffel Tower

Champ de Mars, 7th (01.44.11.23.23/www.tour- eiffel.fr). M° Bir-Hakeim/RER Champ de Mars Tour Eiffel. **Open** *13 June-Aug* 9am-12.45am daily. *Sept-12 June* 9.30am-11.45pm daily. **Admission** *By stairs* (1st & 2nd levels, Sept-mid June 9.30am-6pm, mid June-Aug 9am-midnight) €4.50; €3-€3.50 reductions. *By lift* (1st & 2nd levels) €8; €4-€6.40 reductions; (3rd level) €13; €7.50-€9.90 reductions; free under-3s. **Credit** AmEx, MC, V. **Map** p404 C6.

No building better symbolises Paris than the Tour Eiffel. Maupassant claimed he left Paris because of it, William Morris visited daily to avoid having to see it from afar – and it was originally meant to be a temporary structure. The radical cast-iron tower was built for the 1889 World Fair and the centenary of the 1789 Revolution by engineer Gustave Eiffel. Eiffel made use of new technology that was already popular in iron-framed buildings. Construction took more than two years and used some 18,000 pieces of metal and 2,500,000 rivets. The 300m (984ft) tower stands on four massive concrete piles; it was the tallest structure in the world until overtaken by New York's Empire State Building in the 1930s. Vintage double-decker lifts ply their way up and down; you can walk as far as the second level. There are souvenir shops, an exhibition space, a café and even a post office on the first and second levels. The smart Jules Verne restaurant, on the second level, has its own lift in the north tower. At the top (third level), there's Eiffel's cosy salon and a viewing platform with panels pointing out what to see. Views can reach 65km (40 miles) on a good day, although the most fascinating perspectives are of the ironwork itself. At night, for ten minutes on the hour, 20,000 flashbulbs attached to the tower provide a beautiful effect. To avoid the queues, come late at night.
▶ *The Jules Verne restaurant is now run by Alain Ducasse; see p218.*

Musée des Egouts

Entrance opposite 93 quai d'Orsay, by Pont de l'Alma, 7th (01.53.68.27.81). M° Alma Marceau/RER Pont de l'Alma. **Open** 11am-4pm

SIGHTS

Wed-Sat (until 5pm May-Sept). Closed 3wks Jan. **Admission** €4.20; €3.50 reductions; free under-5s. **No credit cards**. **Map** p400 D5.

For centuries the main source of drinking water in Paris was the Seine, which was also the main sewer. Construction of an underground sewerage system began at the time of Napoleon. Today the Egouts de Paris constitutes a smelly museum; each sewer in the 2,100km (1,305-mile) system is marked with a replica of the street sign above. The Egouts can be closed after periods of heavy rain.

FREE **Musée Valentin Haüy**

5 rue Duroc, 7th (01.44.49.27.27/www.avh.asso.fr). Mº Duroc. **Open** 2.30-5pm Tue, Wed. **Admission** free. **Map** p405 E8.
See p144 **Secret Museums**.

FREE **UNESCO**

7 pl de Fontenoy, 7th (01.45.68.10.00/tours (book in advance) 01.45.68.03.59/www.unesco. org). Mº Ecole Militaire. **Open** 9.30am-6pm Mon-Fri. *Tours* 3pm Mon (in English 2.30pm Wed). **Admission** free. **Map** p405 D7.

The Y-shaped UNESCO headquarters, built in 1958, is home to a swarm of international diplomats. It's worth visiting for the sculptures and paintings – by Picasso, Arp, Giacometti, Moore, Calder and Miró – and for the Japanese garden, with its contemplation cylinder by minimalist architect Tadao Ando.

FREE **Village Suisse**

38-78 av de Suffren or 54 av de La Motte-Picquet, 15th (www.villagesuisse.com). Mº La Motte Picquet Grenelle. **Open** 10.30am-7pm Mon, Thur-Sun. **Map** p404 D7.

The mountains and waterfalls created for the Swiss Village at the 1900 Exposition Universelle are long gone, but the village lives on. Rebuilt as blocks of flats, the street level has been colonised by some 150 boutiques offering various high-quality, albeit pricey, antiques and collectibles.

Along the Seine

Downstream from the Eiffel Tower is the **Musée du Quai Branly**, the Chirac-sponsored museum of primitive arts which opened in 2006. A short way further on, the high-tech **Maison de la Culture du Japon** stands near Pont Bir-Hakeim on quai Branly. Beyond, the 15th arrondissement Fronts de Seine riverfront, with its tower-block developments, had some of the worst architecture of the 1970s inflicted upon it. This would-be brave new world of walkways, suspended gardens and tower blocks has no easily discoverable means of access. The adjacent Beaugrenelle shopping centre is more straightforward to get into, but remains dingy. Further west, things look up: the

sophisticated former headquarters of the Canal+ TV channel (2 rue des Cévennes, 15th), designed by American architect Richard Meier, is surrounded by fine modern housing; and the pleasant **Parc André Citroën**, created in the 1990s on the site of the former Citroën car works, runs all the way down to the Seine quayside, where you'll find the occasional cruise ship and summer partygoers.

FREE **Maison de la Culture du Japon**

101bis quai Branly, 15th (01.44.37.95.01/ www.mcjp.asso.fr). Mº Bir-Hakeim/RER Champ de Mars Tour Eiffel. **Open** noon-7pm Tue, Wed, Fri, Sat; noon-8pm Thur. Closed Aug. **Admission** free. **Map** p404 C6.

Constructed in 1996 by the Anglo-Japanese architectural partnership of Kenneth Armstrong and Masayuki Yamanaka, this opalescent glass-fronted Japanese cultural centre screens films and puts on exhibitions and plays. It also contains a library, an authentic Japanese tea pavilion on the roof, where you can watch the tea ceremony, and a well-stocked book and gift shop.

★ **Musée du Quai Branly**

37-55 quai Branly, 7th (01.56.61.70.00/ www.quaibranly.fr). RER Pont de l'Alma. **Open** 11am-7pm Tue, Wed, Sun; 11am-9pm Thur-Sat. **Admission** €8.50; €6 reductions; free under-18s. *Temporary exhibitions* €7; €5 reductions. **Credit** AmEx, DC, MC, V. **Map** p404 C6.

Surrounded by trees on the banks of the Seine, this museum, housed in an extraordinary building by Jean Nouvel, is a vast showcase for non-European cultures. Dedicated to the ethnic art of Africa, Oceania, Asia and the Americas, it joins together the collections of the Musée des Arts d'Afrique et d'Océanie and the Laboratoire d'Ethnologie du Musée de l'Homme, as well as contemporary indigenous art. Treasures include a tenth-century anthropomorphic Dogon statue from Mali, Vietnamese costumes, Gabonese masks, Aztec statues, Peruvian feather tunics, and rare frescoes from Ethiopia.

FREE **Parc André Citroën**

Rue Balard, rue St-Charles or quai Citroën, 15th. Mº Balard or Javel. **Open** 8am-dusk Mon-Fri; 9am-dusk Sat, Sun, public hols. **Map** p404 A9.

This park is a fun, postmodern version of a French formal garden, designed by Gilles Clément and Alain Prévost. It comprises glasshouses, computerised fountains, waterfalls, a wilderness and themed gardens featuring different coloured plants and even sounds. Stepping stones and water jets make it a garden for pleasure as well as philosophy. The tethered Eutelsat helium balloon takes visitors up for panoramic views. If the weather looks unreliable, call 01.44.26.20.00 to check the programme.

SIGHTS

Beyond the Périphérique

Paris and its suburbs are coming together at last.

The relationship between Paris and its suburbs has long been marked by unease, resentment and disdain, and although big change is afoot, the Boulevard Périphérique – the main ring road encircling the city's 20 arrondissements – will remain a symbolic frontier between 'inside' and 'outside'. Big chunks of the road itself, as unlovely as all city ring roads and a notorious hell for motorists, are set to be boxed over by gardens and other vote-winning urban amenities, but that's as nothing to what President Sarkozy has in mind for the suburbs themselves: a massive shake-up on a par with Haussmann's reshaping of central Paris, with a focus on beefed-up transport links across the greater Paris region and a major expansion of the city's administrative reach. The scheme, called 'Grand Paris', was launched in 2008, and it has the potential – so Sarkozy hopes – to put Paris on an economic footing with London. Watch this space.

SIGHTS

LIFE IN THE BANLIEUE

No one doubts the ambitiousness of Sarkozy's plan, but its power to sow discord has already become apparent. Mayor Delanoë has criticised it, arguing that Sarkozy's dream of creating a Greater Paris to rival the economic muscle of Greater London is inappropriate; and Sarkozy's appointment of a special minister to oversee the plan, Christian Blanc, has led the Socialist mayor and Paris politicians of other stripes to accuse Sarkozy of bypassing the city's power to decide its own future.

Delanoë is, in any case, right to feel slighted, since closing the social, cultural and economic divide between Paris and its suburbs has been one of his key policies. Tangible evidence of this has been improved transport links. The recently inaugurated T3 tramway now runs alongside the southern edge of the Périphérique, which divides Paris and the *banlieue*, and the eight-lane ring road itself has also had sections covered over and landscaped. Meanwhile, district councils of the outer boroughs are signing co-operation agreements with the

Mairie. One of the most recent, involving Ivry-sur-Seine, includes a plan for a local history museum to be built on a bridge across the river.

For many people, though, the suburbs still evoke memories of the violent 2005 riots. Much of the *banlieue* (especially the undesirable northern and eastern suburbs) remains poor and neglected: on certain estates, the fire brigade is attacked whenever it tries to extinguish blazes, attempts to reopen local shops are answered by chronic vandalism, and the police are afraid to enter some areas without back-up.

But there are also many respectable districts, with their own self-contained, provincial atmosphere quite different from that of the capital. Other signs that things are changing beyond the Périphérique include the arrival of **MAC/VAL**, the first permanent collection of contemporary art to open in suburban Paris.

LA DEFENSE

The skyscrapers and walkways of La Défense – named after a stand against the Prussians in 1870 – create a whole new world. The area has been a showcase for French business since the mid 1950s, when the CNIT hall was built to host trade shows, but it was the arrival of the **Grande Arche** that gave the district its most dramatic monument. Today, more than 100,000 people work here, and another 35,000 live in the blocks of flats on the southern edge, served by the inevitable mall, a huge multiplex and leisure complex. In summer 2007, Jean-Christophe Choblet, the creator of Paris-Plage, created a series of outdoor cultural events to encourage workers to socialise in the neighbourhood rather than take the usual commuter train home. On the central esplanade are fountains and sculptures by Miró and Serra. None of the skyscrapers is especially distinguished, although together they are an impressive sight.

La Grande Arche de La Défense

92044 Paris La Défense (01.49.07.27.55/www. grandearche.com). M° La Défense. **Open** *Apr-Sept* 10am-8pm daily. *Oct-Mar* 10am-7pm daily. **Admission** €10; €8.50 reductions; free under-6s. **Credit** MC, V.

Completed for the bicentenary of the Revolution in 1989, the Grande Arche was designed by Danish architect Johan Otto von Spreckelsen. Though it lines up neatly on the Grand Axe – from the Louvre, up the Champs-Elysées to the Arc de Triomphe – the building itself is skewed. A vertigo-inducing glass lift soars up through canvas 'clouds' to the roof, for a fantastic view over Paris.

▶ *Also here is the Musée de l'Informatique (08.20.21.02.30, www.museeinformatique.fr), which traces the story of computing with displays of old machines and multimedia displays.*

ST-DENIS & THE NORTH

North of Paris, the *département* of Seine St-Denis (and part of adjoining Val d'Oise) is the one that best fulfils the negative stereotype of the *banlieue*. It's a victim of its 19th-century industrial boom and the 20th-century housing shortage, when colossal estates went up in La Corneuve, Aulnay-sous-Bois and Sarcelles. It includes some of the poorest *communes* in all of France. Yet the *département* boasts a buzzing theatre scene, with the **MC93** in Bobigny (*see p346*), the **Théâtre Gérard-Philipe** (*see p346*) in St-Denis, and the Théâtre de la Commune in Aubervilliers, plus prestigious music festivals. Amid the sprawl stands one of the treasures of Gothic architecture: the **Basilique St-Denis**, final resting place for the majority of France's former monarchs.

Le Bourget, home to the city's first airport and still used for private business jets and an air fair, contains the **Musée de l'Air et de l'Espace** in its original passenger terminals and hangars. North-east of Paris, Pantin

arrived on the cultural scene with the opening in 2004 of the **Centre National de la Danse** (*see p346*) in a cleverly rehabilitated office block. North-west of St-Denis, Ecouen, noted for its beautiful Renaissance château, now the **Musée National de la Renaissance**, allows for a glimpse of a more rural past.

★ Basilique St-Denis

1 rue de la Légion-d'Honneur, 93200 St-Denis (01.48.09.83.54). M° St-Denis Basilique/tram 1. **Open** *Apr-Sept* 10am-6.15pm Mon-Sat; noon-6.15pm Sun. *Oct-Mar* 10am-5.15pm Mon-Sat; noon-5.15pm Sun. *Tours* 10.30am, 3pm Mon-Sat; 12.15pm, 3pm Sun. **Admission** €7; €4.50 reductions; free under-18s. PMP. **Credit** MC, V.

Legend has it that when St Denis was beheaded, he picked up his noggin and walked with it to Vicus Catulliacus (now St-Denis) to be buried. The first church, parts of which can be seen in the crypt, was built over his tomb in around 475. The present edifice was begun in the 1130s by Abbot Suger, the powerful minister of Louis VI and Louis VII. It is considered the first example of Gothic architecture, uniting the elements of pointed arches, ogival vaulting and flying buttresses. In the 13th century, master mason Pierre de Montreuil erected the spire and rebuilt the choir nave and transept. St-Denis was the burial place for all but three French monarchs between 996 and the end of the *ancien régime*, so the ambulatory is a museum of French funerary sculpture. It includes a fanciful Gothic tomb for Dagobert, the austere effigy of Charles V, and the sculpted Renaissance tomb of Louis XII and his wife Anne de Bretagne. In 1792 these tombs were desecrated, and the royal remains thrown into a pit.

★ FREE Musée de l'Air et de l'Espace

Aéroport de Paris-Le Bourget, 93352 Le Bourget Cedex (01.49.92.71.62/recorded information 01.49.92.70.00/www.mae.org). M° Gare du Nord, then bus 350/RER Le Bourget, then bus 152. **Open** *Apr-Sept* 10am-6pm Tue-Sun. *Oct-Mar* 10am-5pm Tue-Sun. **Admission** free. *With Concorde & Boeing 747* €6; €4 under-26s; free under-4s. PMP. **Credit** MC, V.

Set in the former passenger terminal at Le Bourget airport, the museum's collection begins with the pioneers, including fragile-looking biplanes and the command cabin of a Zeppelin airship. On the runway are Mirage fighters, a US Thunderchief, and Ariane launchers 1 and 5. A hangar houses the prototype Concorde 001 and wartime survivors. A scale models gallery opened in 2008.

Musée National de la Renaissance

Château d'Ecouen, 95440 Ecouen (01.34.38.38.50/ www.musee-renaissance.fr). Train Gare du Nord to Ecouen-Ezanville then bus 269 or walk. **Open** *15 Apr-Sept* 9.30am-12.45pm, 2-5.45pm Mon, Wed-Sun. *Oct-14 Apr* 9.30am-12.45pm,

SIGHTS

Musée de l'Air et de l'Espace.

2-5.15pm Mon, Wed-Sun. **Admission** €6.50; €5 reductions, all on Sun; free under-18s, all on 1st Sun of mth. **Credit** MC, V.

The Renaissance château completed in 1555 for Royal Constable Anne de Montmorency and wife Margaret de Savoie is the setting for a collection of 16th-century decorative arts (some sections are open only at certain times so it's a good idea to phone ahead). Best are the painted chimney pieces, decorated with biblical and mythological scenes.

VINCENNES & THE EAST

The more upmarket residential districts in the east surround the **Bois de Vincennes**, such as Vincennes, with its royal château, St-Mandé and Charenton-le-Pont. **Joinville-le-Pont** and **Champigny-sur-Marne** draw weekenders for the riverside *guinguette* dancehalls.

Château de Vincennes

Av de Paris, 94300 Vincennes (01.48.08.31.20/ www.chateau-vincennes.fr). M° Château de Vincennes. **Open** *May-Aug* 10am-6pm daily. *Sept-Apr* 10am-5pm daily. **Admission** *Short visit* €5; €3.50 reductions; free under-18s. *Long visit* €7.50; €4.80 reductions; free under-18s. **Credit** *Shop* MC, V.

An imposing curtain wall punctuated by towers encloses this medieval fortress, which is still home to an army garrison. The square keep was begun by Philippe VI and completed in the 14th century by Charles V, who added the curtain wall. Henry V died here in 1422, and Louis XIII used the château for hunting expeditions and had the Pavillon du Roi and Pavillon de la Reine built by Louis Le Vau, although

any decorative elements disappeared when they became barracks. Construction began on the chapel in 1380, but wasn't finished until the 16th century.

★ MAC/VAL

Pl de la Libération, 94404 Vitry-sur-Seine (01.43.91.64.20/www.macval.fr). M° Porte de Choisy then bus 183/RER C Gare de Vitry-sur-Seine then bus 180. **Open** noon-7pm Tue, Wed, Fri-Sun; noon-9pm Thur. **Admission** €5; €2.50 reductions; free under-26s, students, all on 1st Sun of mth. **Credit** AmEx, V.

Opened just days after the 2005 *banlieue* riots ended, this contemporary art mseum has earned a fearsome reputation for artistic savvy. Its permanent collection offers a stunning snapshot of French art from 1950 to the present, including installations by Gilles Barbier Jesús Rafael Soto and Christian Boltanski.

Musée Fragonard

7 av du Général de Gaulle, 94704 Maisons-Alfort (01.43.96.71.72/http://musee.vet-alfort.fr). M° Ecole Vétérinaire de Maisons-Alfort. **Open** 2-6pm Wed, Thur; 1-6pm Sat, Sun. Closed Aug. **Admission** €7; €5 reductions; free under-18s. **Credit** AmEx, V.

See p150 **Secret Museums**.

Pavillon Baltard

12 av Victor-Hugo, 94130 Nogent-sur-Marne (01.43.24.76.76/www.pavillonbaltard.fr). RER Nogent-sur-Marne. **Open** during exhibitions only.

When the market at Les Halles was demolished, someone had the nous to save one of its Baltard-designed iron-and-glass market pavilions (no.8, eggs and poultry) and relocate it here.

SIGHTS

Secret Museums Musée Fragonard

Old-school anatomy laid bare in Maisons-Alfort.

In 18th-century French medical schools, study aids were produced in one of two ways: they were either painstakingly sculpted in coloured wax, or made from the real things – organs, limbs, tangle vascular systems – all dried or preserved in formaldehyde.

Veterinary surgeon Honoré Fragonard (cousin of the famous rococo painter) was a master of the second method, and when Louis XV established a veterinary school in 1766 in Maisons-Alfort, Fragonard – its first director and professor of anatomy – set to work preparing thousands of anatomical samples.

Some of his most striking works are now on display at the **Musée Fragonard** (*see p149*). *Homme à la mandibule* is a flayed, grimacing man holding a jawbone in his right hand – an allusion to the story of Samson slaying the Philistines. *Tête humaine injectée* is a rather more sober human head whose blood vessels were injected with coloured wax, red for arteries and blue for veins. *Groupe de foetus humains dansant la gigue* is a nightmarish chorus line of three human foetuses, a scene that might have been imagined by Goya. And, most grandiose of all, *Cavalier de l'apocalypse* is a flayed man on the back of a flayed galloping horse, inspired, according to the museum's notes, by a painting by Dürer.

The museum reopened in 2008 after a 20-month renovation programme, and although the aforementioned *écorchés* (flayed specimens) are the most dramatic items, the rest of its 4,200 exhibits – largely from the animal kingdom, as you'd expect – are unusual, well presented and interesting. The *écorchés* will inevitably remind visitors of the controversial human anatomy exhibitions put on by Günther von Hagens – proof, if any were needed, that there's nothing new under the scalpel.

BOULOGNE & THE WEST

The capital's most desirable suburbs lie to the west. La Défense, Neuilly-sur-Seine, Boulogne-Billancourt, Levallois-Perret and, over the river, Issy-les-Moulineaux have become accepted business addresses for Parisians. Neuilly-sur-Seine is where President Nicolas Sarkozy cut his political teeth as mayor in the early 1990s.

Boulogne-Billancourt is the main town and a lively centre in its own right. In 1320, the Gothic Eglise Notre-Dame was begun in tribute to a miraculous statue of the Virgin that washed up at Boulogne-sur-Mer. By the 18th century, Boulogne was known for its wines and laundries, then, early in the 20th century, for its artist residents (Landowski, Lipchitz, Chagall, Gris), whereas Billancourt was known for car manufacturing, aviation and its film studios.

In the 1920s and '30s, Boulogne-Billancourt was proud of its modernity: Tony Garnier built the elegant new town hall on avenue André-Morizet; a new post office, apartments and schools all went up in the modern style; and private houses were built by the leading avant-garde architects of the day – Le Corbusier, Mallet-Stevens, Perret, Lurçat, Pingusson and Fischer – notably on rue Denfert-Rochereau and rue du Belvedère. The **Musée des Années 30** focuses on artists and architects who lived or worked in the town at the time. The innovative glass-fronted apartment block by Le Corbusier – including the flat where he lived from 1933 to 1965 – can be visited each Wednesday morning at 24 rue Nungesser et Coli (reserve ahead with the Fondation Le Corbusier on 01.42.88.41.53, www.fondationlecorbusier.asso.fr).

The former Renault factory has sat in the Seine like a beached whale ever since it closed in 1992. In 2000, billionaire François Pinault decided to convert it into a contemporary art museum. Finally, in May 2005, frustrated by the inertia of the Boulogne-Billancourt council and the lack of investment on the site, Pinault abandoned the idea. The Fondation François Pinault still went ahead – but in a very different location: a *palazzo* on Venice's Grand Canal. Across the Seine, villas in large gardens surround the **Parc de St-Cloud**, one of the loveliest areas of open space around Paris.

In the 19th century, riverside towns such as **Chatou**, **Asnières** and **Argenteuil**, accessible by train, became places of entertainment – for promenades, *guinguettes* and rowing on the Seine – as depicted in many Impressionist paintings.

At Rueil-Malmaison, the romantic **Château de Malmaison** was loved by Napoleon and Josephine. Josephine had a second château, **La Petite Malmaison** (229bis av Napoléon-Bonaparte, 01.47.49.48.15, by appointment only), built nearby. The empress is buried in the Eglise St-Pierre St-Paul in the old centre, as is her daughter Hortense de Beauharnais, Queen of Holland and mother of Napoleon III.

Suresnes, across the Seine from the Bois de Boulogne, has been a wine-producing village since Roman times, and still celebrates the Fête des Vendanges grape harvest every autumn. The 162-metre (532-foot) Mont Valérien was a place of pilgrimage. In 1841, a huge fortress was built here to defend Paris. It was occupied by the German army during World War II; French *résistants* were brought here at night to be shot. The fortress itself still belongs to the French army, and is the centre of its eavesdropping network. On the surrounding hill is the **American Cemetery** (190 bd de Washington), which contains the graves of American soldiers from World Wars I and II.

St-Germain-en-Laye is a smart suburb with a historic centre and a château. Henri II lived here with his wife Catherine de Médicis and his mistress Diane de Poitiers; it was here also that Mary Queen of Scots grew up, Louis XIV was born and the deposed James II lived for 12 years. Napoléon III turned the château into the **Musée des Antiquités Nationales**.

Château de Malmaison

Av du Château, 92500 Rueil-Malmaison (01.41.29.05.55/www.chateau-malmaison.fr). RER La Défense then bus 258. **Open** *Apr-Sept* 10am-12.30pm, 1.30-5.45pm Mon-Fri; 10am-12.30pm, 1.30-6.15pm Sat, Sun. *Oct-Mar* 10am-12.30pm, 1.30-5.15pm Mon, Wed-Fri; 10am-12.30pm, 1.30-5.45pm Sat, Sun. **Admission** €6-€8; €4.50-€6.50 reductions; free under-26s, all 1st Sun of mth. PMP. **Credit** AmEx, MC, V.
Napoleon and Josephine's love nest, bought by Josephine in 1799, was the emperor's favourite retreat during the Consulate (1800-03). After their divorce, Napoleon gave the château to his ex, who died here in 1814. The couple redesigned the entrance as a mil-

itary tent; you can see Napoleon's office, the billiard room and Josephine's tented bedroom. Today, the château is often used for wedding receptions.

★ FREE Mémorial de la France Combattante

Rue du Professeur-Léon-Bernard, 92150 Suresnes (01.47.28.46.35/tour reservations 01.49.74.35.87). Train to Suresnes-Mont-Valérien/RER La Défense then bus 160, 360 or tram 2. **Open** *Apr-Sept* 9am-noon, 2-7pm daily (guided tours 3pm, 4.30pm Sun, by reservation Mon-Sat). *Oct-Mar* 9am-noon, 2-5pm daily (guided tours 3pm Sun, by reservation Mon-Sat). **Admission** free.
Sixteen bronze relief sculptures by 16 artists represent France's struggle for liberation – from a Gaullist perspective. Behind an eternal flame, the crypt contains tombs of 16 heroes from 16 French battles in World War II. The memorial was built on the site where members of the Resistance were brought from prisons in Paris. A staircase from within the crypt leads visitors inside the curtain wall, then up around the hill to the chapel where prisoners were locked before execution, and down to the Clairière des Fusillés, the clearing where they were shot. The chapel walls were covered in the prisoners' last graffiti (of which only a small patch remains); it also contains five of the wooden firing posts. More than 1,000 men were shot here (women were deported). A monument by artist Pascal Convert lists the names of the victims, among them Communist politician Gabriel Péri.

Musée des Années 30

Espace Landowski, 28 av André-Morizet, 92100 Boulogne-Billancourt (01.55.18.53.00/www. annees30.com). Mº Marcel Sembat. **Open** 11am-6pm Tue-Sun. Closed 2wks Aug. **Admission** (incl Musée-Jardin Paul Landowski) €4.70; €3.60 reductions; free under-16s. **Credit** MC, V.
The Musée des Années 30 shows what a lot of second-rate art was produced in the 1930s, though there are decent modernist sculptures by the Martel brothers, graphic designs, and Juan Gris still lifes and drawings. The highlights are the designs by avant-garde architects Perret, Le Corbusier and Fischer.

Musée des Antiquités Nationales

Château St-Germain, pl Charles-de-Gaulle, 78105 St-Germain-en-Laye (01.39.10.13.00/ www.musee-antiquitesnationales.fr). RER St-Germain-en-Laye. **Open** 9am-5.15pm Mon, Wed-Sun. **Admission** €4.50; €3 reductions, all on Sun; free under-18s, all on 1st Sun of mth. **Credit** *Shop* MC, V.
This awe-inspiring museum traces France's rich archaeological heritage. The redesigned Neolithic galleries feature statue-menhirs, female figures and an ornate tombstone from Cys-la-Commune. Curiosities include the huge antlers from a prehistoric Irish deer and the 18th-century cork models of ancient sites.

SIGHTS

Consume

Christian Louboutin. *See p260*.

Hotels

Lay your head in a luxury palace or bag a boutique bargain.

Voted 'most charismatic city in the world' in a recent independent survey, Paris is upbeat about the future. Tourism figures may have suffered in 2008 but it didn't put the brakes on a host of new hotels that have flourished all over the capital. Whether they are part of the new trend for boutique hotels from the high-end chains, or independently owned, their defining mark is fabulous design and attention to detail. This year you can luxuriate in very fine surroundings without having to pay top dollar, and increasingly these 20- to 40-room boutiques have their own spas and bars, making well-being and conviviality part of the chic experience.

STAYING IN PARIS

Paris's luxury palaces continue to offer the ultimate dream hotel experience: at the **Crillon**, the **Bristol**, the **George V**, the **Plaza Athénée** and the **Ritz** uniformed flunkeys whisk you through revolving doors to an otherworldly domain of tinkling china, thick carpets and concierges for whom your wish is their desire, for a generous tip. By the end of 2010 there should be even more competition in the luxury sector with the completion of a new Shangri-La, a Mandarin Oriental and the complete makeover of the Royal Monceau by Philippe Starck.

Better value for money can be found at Paris's increasingly luxurious boutique hotels, several of which opened in 2009. For several hundred euros less a night than a palace, you can be soothed by fine linen, marble baths and a dreamy pool and hammam at **Le Metropolitan**, walk through silk taffeta curtains to your own terrace at **Le Petit Paris**, fall into a deep sleep at the pure white technological marvel that is the **Hôtel Gabriel**, and fraternise at the trendy cava bar of the Spanish-owned **Banke**. For those who like a bit more glitz, the sparkly **Diamond Opéra** and unabashedly sexy **Sublim Eiffel** use fibre optics to create your

own starry galaxy. All of these hotels have made the smooth move of abandoning petty pay-per-hour Wi-Fi in favour of providing it free, and Nespresso machines and iPod docks are making an appearance in bedrooms too.

Further down the scale, there is now a wide choice of moderately priced and even budget design hotels, especially in the trendy east and north-east of the city, such as the Starck-designed **Mama Shelter**, **Standard Design Hotel**, **Le Quartier Bastille** and **20 Prieuré**. And shoestring travellers should definitely check into the new **St Christopher's Inn** on the Canal d'Ourcq, whose façade is lit up like an art installation at night. But if Paris wouldn't be Paris for you without chintzy wallpaper, springy beds and a bathroom on the landing never fear: faithful stalwarts the **Esmeralda** and **Henri IV** are still going strong.

Hotels are graded according to an official star rating system designed to sort the deluxe from the dumps – but we haven't followed it in this guide, as the ratings merely reflect room size and amenities such as lifts or bars, rather than other important factors such as decor, staff or atmosphere. Instead, we've divided the hotels by area, then listed them in four categories, according to the standard prices (not including seasonal offers or discounts) for one night in a double room with en suite shower/bath. For **Deluxe** hotels, you can expect to pay more than €350; for properties in the **Expensive** bracket, €220-€350; for **Moderate** properties, allow €130-€219; while **Budget** rooms go for less than €130. For **gay hotels**, *see p312.*

> ❶ Red numbers given in this chapter correspond to the location of each hotel as marked on the street maps. *See pp400-409.*

Note that all hotels in France charge a room tax (*taxe de séjour*) of around €1 per person per night, although this is sometimes included in the rate. Children under 12 often stay for free when sharing a room with parents (check when booking), and small pets usually cost between €10 and €20 extra per night. Hotels are often booked solid and cost more during the major trade fairs (January, May, September), and it's hard to find a good room during Fashion Weeks (January, March, July and October). At quieter times, hotels can often offer special deals at short notice; phone ahead or check their websites.

THE ISLANDS

Expensive

★ Hôtel du Jeu de Paume

54 rue St-Louis-en-l'Ile, 4th (01.43.26.14.18/ www.jeudepaumehotel.com). M° Pont Marie. **Rates** €285-€315 double. **Credit** AmEx, DC, MC, V. **Map** p409 K7 ❶
With a discreet courtyard entrance, 17th-century beams, private garden and a unique timbered breakfast room that was once a real tennis court built under Louis XIII, this is a charming and romantic hotel. These days it is filled with an attractive array of modern and classical art, and has a coveted billiards table. A dramatic glass lift and catwalks lead to the guestrooms as well as two self-catering apartments, which are simple and tasteful, the walls hung with Pierre Frey fabric. *Bar. Gym. Internet (free, wireless). Room service. TV.*

Paris Yacht

Quai de la Tournelle, between Pont de Sully & Pont de la Tournelle, 5th (06.88.70.26.36/ www.paris-yacht.com). M° Maubert Mutualité. **Rates** (incl breakfast) €300 double. **No credit cards.** Map p409 K7 ❷
Paris Yacht has to be the city's quirkiest place to sleep – as long as you don't get seasick. Bobbing peacefully on the Left Bank opposite the Ile St-Louis and five minutes' walk from Notre-Dame, this two-cabin houseboat was built in 1933, and has been in service everywhere from Bastia to the Canal de Bourgogne. Now converted to accommodate up to four guests (welcomed with a bottle of champagne from the owners), the boat is equipped with everything from central heating to high-speed internet. During the summer, the terrace on the upper deck provides the perfect Seine-side setting for dinner. *Internet (free, wireless). TV.*

Moderate

Hôtel des Deux-Iles

59 rue St-Louis-en-l'Ile, 4th (01.43.26.13.35/ www.deuxiles-paris-hotel.com). M° Pont Marie. **Rates** €195 double. **Credit** AmEx, MC, V. **Map** p409 K7 ❸

Hôtel des Deux-Iles.

CONSUME

This peaceful 17th-century townhouse offers 17 soundproofed, air-conditioned rooms kitted out in toned down stripes, *toile de Jouy* fabrics and neo colonial-style furniture. Its star features are a tiny courtyard off the lobby and a vaulted stone breakfast area. All the rooms and bathrooms were freshened up in 2007 (fortunately saving the lovely blue earthenware tiles on the bathroom walls).
Concierge. Internet (free, wireless). Room service. TV.
▶ *The equally pleasant Hôtel le Lutèce (65 rue St-Louis-en-l'Ile, 01.43.26.23.52, www.paris-hotel-lutece.com) is run by the same team.*

Budget

Hospitel Hôtel Dieu
1 pl du Parvis-Notre-Dame, 4th (01.44.32.01.00/ www.hotel-hospitel.com). M° Cité or Hôtel de Ville. Rates €126 double. Credit MC, V. Map p408 J7 ❹
If the thought of sleeping in a working hospital doesn't put you off (half the rooms here are used by families of the Hôtel Dieu hospital's in-patients and staff), you can stay in one of 14 recently renovated, spotless rooms with colourful contemporary decor, right in the middle of Ile de la Cité in front of Notre-Dame. A medical smell is present but not strong, bathrooms are quite large, and you couldn't ask for a better sightseeing base.
Disabled-adapted rooms. Internet (free, wireless). No smoking throughout. Room service. TV.

Hôtel Henri IV
25 pl Dauphine, 1st (01.43.54.44.53/www.henri4 hotel.fr). M° Pont Neuf. Rates €45-€74 double (incl breakfast). Credit MC, V. Map p408 J6 ❺
On tree-lined, triangular Place Dauphine, surrounded by some of Paris's most expensive real estate on Ile de la Cité and a stone's throw from Notre-Dame, the Henri IV remains Paris's best value budget hotel. You therefore need to book well ahead to get a room. The rooms are simple and unadorned, but clean, and the three paupers' penthouses with balconies and rooftop views go first. Eleven of the 15 room have en suite bathrooms; the others offer very, very cheap rates.
No smoking throughout.

THE LOUVRE & PALAIS-ROYAL
Deluxe

Hôtel Costes
239 rue St-Honoré, 1st (01.42.44.50.00/ www.hotelcostes.com). M° Concorde or Tuileries. Rates €550-€750 double. Credit AmEx, DC, MC, V. Map p401 G5 ❻
Attitude definitely counts in this temple of notoriety – a place so trendy its website only contains contact details and an online boutique of its own *ultra-branché* products, and where innumerable A-listers

still gravitate to the low-lit bar after all these years. The Costes boasts one of the best pools in Paris, a sybaritic, Eastern-inspired affair with an underwater music system. Rooms are a modern take on Napoleon III, designed by Jacques Garcia.
Bars (2). Business centre. Concierge. Disabled-adapted rooms. Gym. Internet (free, wireless). No-smoking rooms. Parking (€30). Pool (indoor). Restaurant. Room service. Spa. TV.
▶ *The same management is responsible for the sleek Hôtel Costes K (81 av Kléber, 16th, 01.44.05.75.75), which has a fabulous spa.*

Hôtel de Crillon
10 pl de la Concorde, 8th (01.44.71.15.00/ www.crillon.com). M° Concorde. Rates €770-€950 double. Credit AmEx, DC, MC, V. Map p401 F4 ❼
The Crillon lives up to its *palais* reputation with decor strong on marble, mirrors and gold leaf. The Les Ambassadeurs restaurant has an acclaimed chef and a brand new kitchen with a glassed-in private dining area for groups of no more than six who wish to dine amid the bustle of the 80-strong kitchen staff. If you have euros to spare, opt for the Presidential Suite (the only one with a view over the American Embassy). The Winter Garden tearoom is a must.
Bar. Business centre. Concierge. Gym. Internet (free, wireless). No-smoking rooms. Parking (free). Restaurants (2). Room service. TV.

Hôtel Ritz
15 pl Vendôme, 1st (01.43.16.30.30/ ww.ritzparis.com). M° Concorde or Opéra. Rates €550-€870 double. Credit AmEx, DC, MC, V. Map p401 G4 ❽
Chic hasn't lost its cool at the grande dame of Paris hotels, where each of the 162 bedrooms (of which 56 are suites), from the romantic Frédéric Chopin to the glitzy Impérial, ooze sumptuousness. But then what else can one expect from a hotel that has proffered hospitality to Coco Chanel, the Duke of Windsor, Proust, and Dodi and Di? There are plenty of corners in which to strike a pose or quench a thirst, from Hemingway's elegant cigar bar to the Ancient Greece-themed poolside hangout.
Bars (3). Business centre. Concierge. Gym. Internet (€28/day, wireless; €25/day, high speed). No-smoking rooms. Parking (€47). Pool (indoor). Restaurants (2). Room service. Spa. TV.

Hôtel Sofitel le Faubourg
15 rue Boissy-d'Anglas, 8th (01.44.94.14.14/ www.sofitel.com). M° Concorde or Madeleine. Rates €305-€485 double. Credit AmEx, DC, MC, V. Map p401 F4 ❾
This hotel is close to all the major couture boutiques, which is no surprise, as it used to house the *Marie Claire* offices. The rooms have Louis XVI armchairs, large balconies, walk-in wardrobes and Roger &

CONSUME

Hôtel Westminster.

Gallet goodies in the bathrooms; for shopping widowers, there's a small gym and a hammam. It's quiet too: the street has been closed to traffic since 2001 because the American embassy is on the corner.

Bar. Business centre. Concierge. Disabled-adapted rooms. Gym. Internet (€16/day high speed). No-smoking rooms. Parking (€30). Restaurant. Room service. TV.

Other locations Sofitel Arc de Triomphe, 14 rue Beaujon, 8th (01.53.89.50.50); Sofitel Champs-Elysées, 8 rue Jean Goujon, 8th (01.40.74.64.64); Hôtel Scribe, 1 rue Scribe, 9th (01.44.71.24.24).

★ Le Meurice

228 rue de Rivoli, 1st (01.44.58.10.10/ www.lemeurice.com). M° Tuileries. **Rates** €665-€920 double. **Credit** AmEx, DC, MC, V. **Map** p401 G5 ⑩

With its extravagant Louis XVI decor, mosaic tiled floors and modish restyling by Philippe Starck, Le Meurice is looking grander than ever. All 160 rooms (kitted out with iPod-ready radio alarms) are done up in distinct historical styles; the Belle Etoile suite on the seventh floor provides panoramic views of Paris from its terrace. You can relax in the Winter Garden to the strains of regular jazz performances; for more intensive intervention, head over to the lavishly appointed spa with treatments by Valmont.

Bar. Business centre. Concierge. Disabled-adapted rooms. Gym. Internet (€30/day, wireless). No-smoking rooms. Restaurants (2). Room service. Spa. TV: DVD.

▶ *Don't miss dinner at the hotel's three Michelin-starred restaurant, which has chef Yannick Alléno at the helm; see p187.*

Le Westin

3 rue de Castiglione, 1st (01.44.77.11.11/ www.westin.com/paris). M° Tuileries. **Rates** (incl breakfast) €400-€580 double. **Credit** AmEx, DC, MC, V. **Map** p401 G5 ⑪

In the heart of shopping HQ, the Westin mixes belle époque features with pale limestone walls, beautiful vintage-style furniture (inspired by the 1930s and '40s), a neoclassical fountain and patio. Its sleek modern bedrooms, decked out with top-end gadgets and the award-winning Heavenly Bed, sport balcony views over the Tuileries gardens. The bathrooms are sumptuous, and some have their own balconies. There's an excellent restaurant, Le First, with a sleek, deep purple and pearly grey boudoir-like interior designed by Jacques Garcia.

Bar. Business centre. Concierge. Disabled-adapted rooms. Gym. Internet (€25/day, wireless). No-smoking rooms. Restaurant. Room service. Spa. TV.

Moderate

★ Hôtel Brighton

218 rue de Rivoli, 1st (01.47.03.61.61/www. esprit-de-france.com). M° Tuileries. **Rates** €197-€347 double. **Credit** AmEx, DC, MC, V. **Map** p401 G5 ⑫

CONSUME

With several rooms overlooking the Tuileries gardens, the Brighton is great value, so book well ahead for a room with a view. Recently restored, it has a classical atmosphere, from the high ceilings in the rooms to the faux-marble and mosaic downstairs.
Bar. Concierge. Disabled-adapted rooms. Internet (free, wireless). No-smoking rooms. Room service. TV.

Hôtel Mansart

5 rue des Capucines, 1st (01.42.61.50.28/ www.esprit-de-france.com). M° Madeleine or Opéra. **Rates** €165-€345 double. **Credit** AmEx, DC, MC, V. **Map** p401 G4 ⑬
This spacious hotel has real style, with a light, roomy lobby decorated with murals inspired by formal gardens. The 57 bedrooms feature pleasant fabrics, antiques and paintings; five of the rooms have an excellent view of place Vendôme.
Bar. Concierge. Internet (free, wireless). Room service. TV.

Hôtel des Tuileries

10 rue St-Hyacinthe, 1st (01.42.61.04.17/ www.hotel-des-tuileries.com). M° Tuileries. **Rates** €180-€240 double. **Credit** AmEx, DC, MC, V. **Map** p401 G5 ⑭
The fashion pack adores this 18th-century hotel (the staircase is listed), located in prime shopping territory. Done out with ethnic rugs, a smattering of animal prints, bright art and antique furniture, the 26 comfy bedrooms feel like they belong more in an eccentric family home than a central Paris hotel.
Concierge. Internet (€10/hr, shared terminal or wireless). TV.

Le Relais du Louvre

19 rue des Prêtres St-Germain-l'Auxerrois, 1st (01.40.41.96.42/www.relaisdulouvre.com). M° Pont Neuf or Louvre-Rivoli. **Rates** €170-€215 double. **Credit** AmEx, MC, V. **Map** p402 H6 ⑮
The cellar of this characterful hotel, with its antiques and wooden beams, was once used by revolutionaries to print anti-royalist literature. It also inspired Puccini's Café Momus in *La Bohème*. The rooms are decorated in floral fabrics, and the front ones look out on to St-Germain-l'Auxerrois church. There's also a self-contained apartment for four people.
Concierge. Internet (free). No-smoking rooms. TV.

Budget

Hotel Lion d'Or

5 rue de la Sourdière, 1st (01.42.60.79.04/www. hotel-louvre-paris.com). M° Tuileries. **Rates** €85-€135 double. **Credit** MC, V. **Map** p401 G5 ⑯
Simple, brightly coloured rooms and fully furnished studios (with kitchenettes) that can sleep up to five make the Golden Lion a popular choice for families and groups of friends.
Safety box (reception). TV (some rooms).

OPERA TO LES HALLES

Deluxe

Hôtel Ambassador

16 bd Haussmann, 9th (01.44.83.40.40/ www.hotelambassador-paris.com). M° Chaussée d'Antin or Richelieu Drouot. **Rates** €260-€360 double. **Credit** AmEx, DC, MC, V. **Map** p401 H4 ⑰
If you're looking for some vintage style but can't face another gilded Louis XIV interior, check into this historic, Haussmann-era hotel, which sets traditional furniture against contemporary decor in each of the 294 bedrooms. The low-lit Lindbergh Bar is named after the pilot who dropped in for a celebratory drink and cigar after his solo transatlantic flight in 1927. The hotel is ideally situated for shopping at the *grands magasins.*
Bar. Business centre. Concierge. Disabled-adapted rooms. Gym. Internet (€7/30mins, shared terminal; free, wireless). No-smoking rooms. Restaurant. Room service. TV.

Hôtel Concorde St-Lazare

108 rue St-Lazare, 8th (01.40.08.44.44/ www.concordestlazare-paris.com). M° St-Lazare. **Rates** €220-€330 double. **Credit** AmEx, DC, MC, V. **Map** p401 G3 ⑱
Guests here are cocooned in soundproofed luxury. The 19th-century Eiffel-inspired lobby with jewel-encrusted pink granite columns is a historic landmark: the high ceilings, walls and sculptures look much as they have for over a century. Rooms are spacious, with double entrance doors and exclusive Annick Goutal toiletries; the belle époque brasserie, Café Terminus, and sexy Golden Black Bar were designed by Sonia Rykiel. Guests have access to a nearby fitness centre.
Bar. Business centre. Concierge. Internet (€10/day, shared terminal; free, wireless). No-smoking rooms. Parking (€25). Restaurant. Room service. TV.

Hôtel Westminster

13 rue de la Paix, 2nd (01.42.61.57.46/www. warwickwestminateropera). M° Opéra/RER Auber. **Rates** €350-€630 double. **Credit** AmEx, DC, MC, V. **Map** p401 G4 ⑲
This luxury hotel near place Vendôme has more than a touch of British warmth about it, no doubt owing to the influence of its favourite 19th-century guest, the Duke of Westminster (after whom the hotel was named; the current Duke reportedly still stays here). The hotel fitness centre has a top-floor location, with a beautiful tiled steam room and views over the city, and the cosy bar features deep leather chairs, a fireplace and live jazz at weekends.
Bar. Concierge. Gym. Internet (€20/day, high speed or wireless). No-smoking rooms. Parking (€25). Restaurant. Room service. Spa. TV.

CONSUME

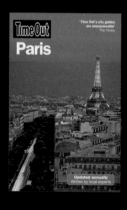
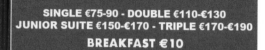

★ InterContinental Paris Le Grand

2 rue Scribe, 9th (01.40.07.32.32/www.paris.
intercontinental.com). M° Opéra. **Rates** €285-
€685 double. **Credit** AmEx, DC, MC, V.
Map p401 G4 ⑳
This 1862 hotel is the chain's European flagship – but,
given its size, perhaps 'mother ship' would be more
appropriate: this landmark establishment occupies
the entire block (three wings, almost 500 rooms) next
to the opera house; some 80 of the honey-coloured
rooms overlook the Palais Garnier. The space under
the vast *verrière* is one of the best oases in town, and
the hotel's restaurant and coffeehouse, the Café de
la Paix, poached its chef, Laurent Delarbre, from the
Ritz. For a relaxing daytime break, head to the I-Spa
for one of its seawater treatments.
Bar. Business centre. Concierge. Gym. Internet
(€24/day, high speed; free, wireless). No-smoking
rooms. Parking (€40). Restaurants (2). Room
service. Spa. TV.

Moderate

★ Hôtel Amour

8 rue Navarin, 9th (01.48.78.31.80/www.hotel
amourparis.fr). M° St-Georges. **Rates** €140-€275
double. **Credit** AmEx, MC, V. **Map** p402 H2 ㉑
Opened back in 2006, this boutique hotel is a real hit
with the in crowd. Each of the 20 rooms is unique,
decorated on the theme of love or eroticism by a
coterie of contemporary artists and designers such as
Marc Newson, M&M, Stak, Pierre Le Tan and Sophie
Calle. Seven of the rooms contain artists' installations,
and two others have their own private bar and a large
terrace on which to hold your own party. The late-
night brasserie has a coveted outdoor garden, and the
crowd is young and beautiful and loves to entertain.
Bar. Internet (free, wireless). No-smoking rooms
only. Restaurant.

Hôtel Arvor Saint Georges

8 rue Laferrière, 9th (01.48.78.60.92/www.
arvor-hotel-paris.com). M° St-Georges. **Rates**
€180-€220 double. **Credit** AmEx, DC, MC, V.
Map p402 H2 ㉒
Don't be put off by the slightly austere façade; the
owner intended it this way to contrast with the
homely atmosphere that reigns inside. Although
you're right in the middle of the city, the hotel has the
feel of a quiet country house. The decor is delicate and
uncluttered, and most of the 30 spacious rooms,
including six suites, overlook the rooftops (no.503 has
the best view of the Eiffel Tower). The small terrace
is the ideal spot to take a break from the Paris buzz.
Internet (free, wireless). No-smoking rooms. TV.

★ Hôtel Britannique

20 av Victoria, 1st (01.42.33.74.59/www.hotel-
britannique.fr). M° Châtelet, RER Châtelet-les-
Halles. **Rates** €190-€279 double. **Credit** AmEx,
MC, V. **Map** p408 J6 ㉓

Smiling staff in stripy waistcoats welcome you to
this adorable hotel, where guest areas and rooms are
cocooned in thick drapes, luscious carpets and a
mishmash of British colonial-style furniture that
make you feel like you've stepped into an English
country cottage. Enjoy deeply delicious pastries in
the warm, rustic breakfast room, or book a top floor
chambre and eat them on your plant-filled balcony
– a rare oasis of greenery for such a central and
reasonably priced hotel.
Bar. Concierge. Internet (high speed & wireless).
No-smoking rooms. TV.

Hôtel Langlois

63 rue St-Lazare, 9th (01.48.74.78.24/www.hotel-
langlois.com). M° Trinité. **Rates** €140-€150
double. **Credit** MC, V. **Map** p401 H3 ㉔
Built as a bank in 1870, this belle époque building
became the Hôtel des Croisés in 1896. In 2001, after
featuring in the Jonathan Demme film *Charade*, it
changed its name to Hôtel Langlois in honour of
the founder of the Cinémathèque Française. Its 27
spacious, air-conditioned bedrooms are decorated in
art nouveau style; the larger ones have delightful
hidden bathrooms.
Internet (free, wireless). Room service. TV.

Résidence Hôtel des Trois Poussins

15 rue Clauzel, 9th (01.53.32.81.81/www.
les3poussins.com). M° St-Georges. **Rates** €161-
€197 double; €160-€250 studio with kitchenette.
Credit AmEx, DC, MC, V. **Map** p401 H2 ㉕
Just off the beaten track in a pleasant *quartier*, and
within walking distance (uphill) of Montmartre, the
Résidence offers hotel accommodation in the traditional manner, and also has some rare self-catering
studios for people who'd rather cook than eat out.
Now completely redone, the decor is pleasantly traditional, with a preference for yellow.
Concierge. Disabled-adapted room. Internet (€4/hr,
wireless). Room service (nighttime only). TV.

Budget

Hôtel Chopin

10 bd Montmartre or 46 passage Jouffroy, 9th
(01.47.70.58.10/www.hotel-chopin.com). M°
Grands Boulevards. **Rates** €92-€106 double.
Credit MC, V. **Map** p402 J4 ㉖
Handsomely set in a historic, glass-roofed arcade
next door to the Grévin museum, the Chopin's orig-
inal 1846 façade adds to its old-fashioned appeal.
The 36 rooms are quiet and functional, done out in
either salmon and green or blue.
TV.

Hôtel du Cygne

3 rue du Cygne, 1st (01.42.60.14.16/www.
hotelducygne.fr). M° Etienne Marcel/RER
Châtelet Les Halles. **Rates** €90-€122 double.
Credit MC, V. **Map** p402 J5 ㉗

CONSUME

CONSUME

INSIDE TRACK THE A LA MODE

Hôtel le Bristol (see below), set on exclusive rue du Faubourg St-Honoré, has teamed up with its haute couture neighbours to offer Thés à la Mode – a lip-smacking afternoon tea (most Saturdays 3-5pm) accompanied by a top-end fashion show for just €55. Guests are fed tea, cakes, gourmet sandwiches and a parade of models dressed in new collections by brands such as Céline, Givenchy, Ungaro, Versace and Christian Lacroix.

This traditional hotel in a 17th-century building has 20 compact, cosy and simple rooms embellished with touches such as antiques and home-made furnishings. It's on a pedestrianised street in the bustling Les Halles district, so light sleepers might prefer the rooms overlooking the courtyard. The cheapest rooms have shared bathrooms.
Internet (free, wireless). TV.

Hôtel Madeleine Opéra

12 rue Greffulhe, 8th (01.47.42.26.26/www.hotel-madeleine-opera.com). M° Havre-Caumartin or Madeleine. **Rates** €95-€110 double. **Credit** MC, V. **Map** p401 G4 **㉓**
This bargain hotel is located just north of the Eglise de la Madeleine, in the heart of the city's theatre and *grands magasins* districts. Its sunny lobby sits behind a 200-year-old façade that was once a shopfront. The 23 rooms are a touch basic, but still nice enough, and breakfast is brought to your room every morning.
Internet (€5/45mins, wireless). Room service (morning). TV.

CHAMPS-ELYSEES & WESTERN PARIS

Deluxe

★ Four Seasons George V

31 av George V, 8th (01.49.52.70.00/www.four seasons.com/paris). M° Alma Marceau or George V. **Rates** €750-€1,095 double. **Credit** AmEx, DC, MC, V. **Map** p400 D4 **㉙**
There's no denying that the George V is serious about luxury: chandeliers, marble and tapestries; glorious flower arrangements; divine bathrooms; and ludicrously comfortable beds in some of the largest rooms in all of Paris. The Versailles-inspired spa includes whirlpools, saunas and a menu of treatments for an unabashedly metrosexual clientele; non-guests can now reserve appointments. It's worth every euro.
Bar. Business centre. Concierge. Disabled-adapted rooms. Gym. Internet (€22/24hrs, high speed). No-smoking rooms. Parking (€40). Pool (indoor). Restaurants (2). Room service. Spa. TV.

Hôtel le A

4 rue d'Artois, 8th (01.42.56.99.99/www.paris-hotel-a.com). M° Franklin D. Roosevelt or St-Philippe-du-Roule. **Rates** €365-€444 double. **Credit** AmEx, DC, MC, V. **Map** p401 E4 **㉚**
The black-and-white decor of this designer boutique hotel provides a fine backdrop for the models, artists and media types hanging out in the lounge bar area; the only splashes of colour come from the graffiti-like artworks by conceptual artist Fabrice Hybert. The 26 rooms all have granite bathrooms, and the starched white furniture slip covers, changed after each guest, make the smallish spaces seem larger than they are. The dimmer switches are a nice touch – as are the lift lights changing colour at each floor.
Bar. Concierge. Disabled-adapted rooms. Internet (€5/45mins, wireless). No-smoking rooms. Room service. TV.

Hôtel le Bristol

112 rue du Fbg-St-Honoré, 8th (01.53.43.43.00/www.hotel-bristol.com). M° Champs-Elysées Clémenceau. **Rates** €750-€900 double. **Credit** AmEx, DC, MC, V. **Map** p401 E4 **㉛**
Set on the exclusive rue du Faubourg St-Honoré, near luxury boutiques such as Christian Lacroix, Azzaro, Salvatore Ferragamo, Givenchy and Dolce & Gabbana, the Bristol is a supremely luxurious 'palace' hotel with a loyal following of fashionistas and millionaires drawn by the location, impeccable service, larger than average rooms and a three Michelin-starred restaurant with Eric Fréchon at the helm. The Bristol's new seven-storey wing opened in late 2009, with 22 new rooms and four suites, all with views of the Eiffel Tower.
Bar. Business centre. Concierge. Disabled-adapted rooms. Gym. Internet (high speed & wireless). No-smoking rooms. Parking (free). Pool (indoor). Restaurant. Room service. Spa. TV.

Hôtel Daniel

8 rue Frédéric-Bastiat, 8th (01.42.56.17.00/www.hoteldanielparis.com). M° Franklin D. Roosevelt or St-Philippe-du-Roule. **Rates** €420-€490 double. **Credit** AmEx, DC, MC, V. **Map** p401 E4 **㉜**
A romantic hideaway close to the monoliths of the Champs-Elysées, the city's new Relais & Châteaux property is decorated in chinoiserie and a palette of rich colours, with 26 rooms cosily appointed in *toile de Jouy* and an intricately hand-painted restaurant that feels like a courtyard. With meals at around €50 a head, the gastronomic restaurant Le Lounge, run by chef Denis Fetisson, is a good deal for this neighbourhood; the bar menu is served at all hours.
Bar. Concierge. Disabled-adapted rooms. Internet (free, wireless). No-smoking rooms. Parking (€25). Restaurant. Room service. TV.

Hôtel Fouquet's Barrière

46 av George V, 8th (01.40.69.60.00/www.
fouquets-barriere.com). Mº George V. **Rates**
€730-€950 double. **Credit** AmEx, DC, MC, V.
Map p400 D4 ⊛
This grandiose five-star hotel is built around the
famous fin-de-siècle brasserie Le Fouquet's. Five
buildings form the hotel complex, housing 107
rooms (including 40 suites), upmarket restaurant
Le Diane, the Sparis spa, an indoor swimming pool
and a rooftop terrace for hire. Jacques Garcia, of
Hôtel Costes and Westin fame, was responsible
for the interior design, which retains the Empire
style of the exterior while incorporating luxurious
modern touches inside – flat-screen TVs and mist-
free mirrors as standard in the marble bathrooms.
And, of course, it's unbeatable in terms of location
– right at the junction of avenue George V and
the Champs-Elysées.
Bar. Business centre. Concierge. Disabled-
adapted rooms. Gym. Internet (free, high speed
& wireless). No-smoking rooms. Parking (€45).
Pool (indoor). Restaurants (2). Room service.
Spa. TV.

CONSUME

Hôtel Banke. *See p169.*

1 - 5 p a s s a g e r u e l l e - P a r i s - 7 5 0 1 8 - F r a n c e
paris@kubehotel.com - www.kubehotel.com - t. +33 1 42 05 20 00

Hôtel Plaza Athénée

25 av Montaigne, 8th (01.53.67.66.65/www.
plaza-athenee-paris.com). M° Alma Marceau.
Rates €750-€860 double. **Credit** AmEx, DC,
MC, V. **Map** p400 D5 ㉞
This palace is ideally placed for power shopping at
Chanel, Louis Vuitton, Dior and other avenue
Montaigne boutiques. Material girls and boys will
enjoy the high-tech room amenities such as remote-
controlled air con, internet and video-game access
on the TV via infrared keyboard, and mini hi-fi.
Bar. Business centre. Concierge. Disabled-adapted
rooms. Gym. Internet (€15/hr, high speed &
wireless). No-smoking rooms. Parking (€25).
Restaurants (2; 4 in summer). Room service. TV.
▶ *Make time for a drink in the Bar du Plaza,*
a cocktail bunny's most outré fantasy, with
flattering lighting, high chairs for maximum leg-
crossing opportunities and ridiculous drinks.

Hôtel de Sers

41 av Pierre-1er-de-Serbie, 8th (01.53.23.75.75/
www.hoteldesers.com). M° Alma Marceau or
George V. **Rates** €550-€680 double. **Credit**
AmEx, DC, MC, V. **Map** p400 D4 ㉟
Behind this stately 19th-century façade, the Hôtel de
Sers calls itself a baby palace, displaying an ambitious mix of minimalist contemporary furnishings,
with a few pop art touches. Original architectural
details, such as the grand staircase and reception,
complete the picture. The large top floor apartment
affords dreamy views over Paris's rooftops.
Bar. Concierge. Disabled-adapted rooms. Gym.
Internet (free, high speed & wireless). No-
smoking rooms. Parking (€50). Restaurant.
Room service. TV.

★ Hôtel de la Trémoille

14 rue de la Trémoille, 8th (01.56.52.14.00/
www.hotel-tremoille.com). M° Alma-Marceau.
Rates €495-€660 double. **Credit** AmEx, DC,
MC, V. **Map** p400 D4 ㊱
Manager Olivier Lordonnois has pushed the
Trémoille to another level. The recent opening of a
new restaurant-bar-lounge and improved spa and fitness facilities have made it a serious competitor to the
other palaces nearby. The 93 rooms are decorated to
evoke no fewer than 31 different 'atmospheres', and
the bathrooms are filled with Molton Brown products.
A unique feature is the 'hatch', which enables room
service to deliver your meal without disturbing you.
Bar. Business centre. Concierge. Disabled-adapted
rooms. Gym. Internet (free, high speed). No-
smoking rooms. Restaurant. Room service.
Spa. TV.

Hôtel de Vigny

9-11 rue Balzac, 8th (01.42.99.80.80/www.
hoteldevigny.com). M° George V. **Rates** €440-
€520 double. **Credit** AmEx, DC, MC, V.
Map p400 D3 ㊲

One of only two Relais & Châteaux in the city, this
hotel has the feel of a private, plush townhouse.
Although it's just off the Champs-Elysées, the
Vigny pulls in a discerning, low-key clientele. Its
37 bedrooms and suites are decorated in tasteful
stripes or florals, with marble bathrooms. Enjoy
dinner in the art deco Baretto restaurant, or have a
cup of tea in the library.
Bar. Concierge. Internet (€7/hr, high speed).
No-smoking rooms. Parking (€23). Restaurant.
Room service. TV.

★ Jays Paris

6 rue Copernic, 16th (01.47.04.16.16/www.jays-
paris.com). M° Kléber or Victor Hugo. **Rates**
€420-€590 suite. **Credit** MC, V. **Map** p400 C4 ㊳
Introducing a new concept on the Paris hotel scene,
Jays is a luxurious *boutique-apart* hotel that trades
on a clever blend of antique furniture, modern
design and high-tech equipment. The marble staircase, lit entirely by natural light filtered through the
glass atrium overhead, gives an instant feeling of
grandeur, and leads to five suites, each with a fully
equipped kitchenette. A cosy salon is available to
welcome in-house guests and their visitors.
Bar. Concierge. Internet (free, high speed &
wireless). No smoking throughout. Parking (€15).
Room service. TV.

Pershing Hall

49 rue Pierre-Charron, 8th (01.58.36.58.00/
www.pershinghall.com). M° George V. **Rates**
€450-€540 double. **Credit** AmEx, DC, MC, V.
Map p400 D4 ㊳
The refreshing mix of 19th-century grandeur and
contemporary comfort makes Pershing Hall feel
quite large, but this luxury establishment is really a
cleverly disguised boutique hotel with just 26 rooms.
Fashionable locals frequent the stylish bar and
restaurant terrace. Designed by Andrée Putman, the
neat bedrooms emphasise natural materials, with
stained grey oak floors and fine mosaic-tiled bathrooms with geometric styling and copious towels.
Bar. Concierge. Gym. Internet (free, high speed;
pay as you go, wireless). No-smoking rooms.
Restaurant. Room service. Spa. TV.

THE BEST HOTEL BARS

For outré cocktails
Bar du Plaza at Hôtel Plaza Athénée.
See above.

For a taste of home
Duke's Bar at Hôtel Westminster.
See p159.

For hip with your half
Kube Rooms & Bar. *See p169.*

CONSUME

Le Sezz

6 av Frémiet, 16th (01.56.75.26.26/www.hotel sezz.com). M° Passy. **Rates** *€335-€470 double.* **Credit** AmEx, DC, MC, V. **Map** p404 B6 **40**

Le Sezz opened its doors in 2005 with 27 deluxe rooms and suites – the work of acclaimed French furniture designer Christophe Pillet. The understated decor represents a refreshingly modern take on luxury, with black parquet flooring, rough-hewn stone walls and bathrooms partitioned off with sweeping glass façades. The bar and public areas are equally chic.

Bar. Concierge. Internet (free wireless). No-smoking rooms. Parking (€20). Room service. Spa. TV.

Expensive

Hôtel Keppler

10 rue Keppler, 16th (01.47.20.65.05/www. hotelkeppler.com). M° George V or M°/RER Charles-de-Gaulle Etoile. **Rates** *€300-€490 double.* **Credit** AmEx, DC, MC, V. **Map** p400 C4 **41**

Room with a View

Exhibitionists are welcome at the Renaissance Paris Arc de Triomphe.

You can't miss it. The six-storey undulating glass façade on avenue Wagram is like no other part of the neighbourhood; at night, when it's all lit up, this very 21st-century building looks like a frozen waterfall.

Welcome to one of the city's newest hotels, the **Renaissance Paris Arc de Triomphe** (*see right*). It stands on the site of the Théâtre de l'Empire, a former theatre and TV studio that was severely damaged in a gas explosion in 2005, and had to be demolished – thus creating a rare construction opportunity within sight of the Arc de Triomphe. The design of the hotel was entrusted to star French architect Christian de Portzamparc, but the massively thick, curving pieces of his glass façade were beyond the manufacturing capability of France, and had to be made in Germany.

Bedrooms at the front of the hotel are flooded with natural light, of course; and exhibitionists can, by drawing back the ceiling-to-floor gauze curtains and

positioning themselves in the right part of the window's curve, undress and canoodle in full view not just of the street below and the buildings opposite, but also of their next door neighbours. All rooms are stylishly done out in pale greys, charcoals and dark wood, with Eames-style furniture and magenta cushions and throws.

Nice high-tech touches include an iPod dock on the bedside radio, glass-topped bedside surfaces that are illuminated from below, a wardrobe whose light switches on automatically as you approach, and a large flat-screen TV with Wi-Fi keyboard. The drinks cabinet includes a coffee machine.

Bathrooms are a glory of polished metal, tasteful tiles and gleaming glass and ceramics, with gourmet toiletries that include lemongrass soap and mint and thyme shampoo. Nor does the gourmet experience stop in the shower: the Makassar restaurant serves delicate and delicious Franco-Asian fusion food.

This newly renovated boutique hotel is a family-run treasure, decorated with striped wallpaper, funky mirrors, animal prints and various knick-knacks. None of the 39 rooms is huge, but all are cleverly thought through, so that lack of space is never an issue and the whole experience is pleasantly cosy. The top floor suites have their own (large) balcony – perfect for an alfresco breakfast – and views over Paris's rooftops towards the Eiffel Tower.
Bar. Concierge. Internet (wireless). Gym. No-smoking rooms. Room service. Sauna. TV.

Hôtel Pergolèse

3 rue Pergolèse, 16th (01.53.64.04.04/www. pergolese.com). M° Argentine. **Rates** €260-€290 double. **Credit** AmEx, DC, MC, V. **Map** p400 B3 ㊷

The Pergolèse was one of the first designer boutique hotels in town, but still looks contemporary a decade or so after being kitted out by Rena Dumas-Hermès with art deco-style furniture by Philippe Starck and rugs by Hilton McConnico. Rooms feature pale wood details and cool, white-tiled bathrooms.
Bar. Concierge. Internet (free, wireless). No-smoking rooms. Room service. TV.

★ Hôtel Regent's Garden

6 rue Pierre-Demours, 17th (01.45.74.07.30/ www.hotel-paris-garden.com). M° Charles de Gaulle Etoile or Ternes. **Rates** €289-€409 double. **Credit** AmEx, DC, MC, V. **Map** p400 C2 ㊸

This elegant hotel – built for Napoleon III's physician – features appropriately Second Empire high ceilings and plush upholstery, and a lounge overlooking a lovely walled patio. There are 39 large bedrooms, some with gilt mirrors and fireplaces. It's an oasis of calm just ten minutes from the Champs-Elysées, and the first hotel in Paris to receive an Ecolabel, for its recycling and energy- and water-saving efforts.
Concierge. Internet (€5/hr, shared terminal; free, wireless). No-smoking rooms. Parking (€14). Room service (daytime only). TV.

Hôtel Square

3 rue de Boulainvilliers, 16th (01.44.14.91.90/ www.hotelsquare.com). M° Passy/RER Avenue du Pdt Kennedy. **Rates** €380-€580 double. **Credit** AmEx, DC, MC, V. **Map** p404 A7 ㊹

Located in the upmarket 16th, this courageously modern hotel has a dramatic yet welcoming interior, and attentive service that comes from having to look after only 22 rooms. They're decorated in amber, brick or slate colours, with exotic woods, quality fabrics and bathrooms seemingly cut from one huge chunk of Carrara marble. View the exhibitions in the atrium gallery or mingle with the media types at the hip Zebra Square restaurant and DJ bar.
Bar. Concierge. Disabled-adapted rooms. Internet (free, wireless). No-smoking rooms. Parking (€25). Restaurant. Room service. TV.

★ Le Metropolitan

10 pl de Mexico, 16th (01.56.90.40.04/ www.radissonblu.com). M° Trocadero. **Rates** €278-€510 double. **Credit** AmEx, DC, MC, V. **Map** p400 B5 ㊺

This new 40-room offering from Radisson Blu is supremely sleek. The discreet entrance is only a few metres wide, but once inside the triangular structure opens out into surprising volumes, with a monumental art deco-style fireplace, and cream leather and black granite reminiscent of New York in the 1930s. The first floor contains a swank insiders' cocktail bar, but the biggest surprise of all is the breathtaking view of the Eiffel Tower from the front façade, best enjoyed through the huge oval window while lying on the four-poster bed of the sixth floor suite. All rooms exude *luxe, calme et volonté* with solid oak floors, linen curtains and baths or showers carved from black or cream marble. And below ground is a sublime swimming pool and hammam reserved for guests.
Bar. Concierge. Internet (free, wireless). No-smoking rooms. Parking (€30). Pool (indoor). Restaurant. Room service. TV.

Renaissance Paris Arc de Triomphe

39 av de Wagram, 17th (01.55.37.55.37/ www.marriott.com). M° Ternes. **Rates** €319-€389 double. **Credit** AmEx, DC, MC, V. **Map** p400 C3 ㊻

See left **Room with a View**.
Bar. Business centre. Concierge. Disabled-adapted rooms. Gym. Internet (€19.95/day, high speed). No-smoking rooms. Parking (€35). Restaurant. Room service. Spa. TV.

Moderate

Hôtel Elysées Ceramic

34 av de Wagram, 8th (01.42.27.20.30/ www.elysees-ceramic.com). M° Charles de Gaulle Etoile. **Rates** €220 double. **Credit** AmEx, DC, MC, V. **Map** p400 D3 ㊼

Situated between the Arc de Triomphe and place des Ternes, this comfortable hotel has one of Paris's finest art nouveau ceramic façades dating from 1904; inside, the theme continues with a ceramic cornice around the reception. All 57 rooms have been renovated in sophisticated chocolate or pewter tones with modern, art nouveau-inspired wallpaper and light fixtures. Outside is a terrace garden perfect for taking afternoon tea or evening cocktails.
Bar. Concierge. Internet (€10/hr, shared terminal; €8/hr, wireless). Room service (breakfast only). TV.

Opéra Diamond

4 rue de la Pépinière, 8th (01.44.70.02.00/ www.paris-hotel-diamond.com). M° St-Lazare. **Rates** €185-€430 double. **Credit** AmEx, DC, MC, V. **Map** p401 F3 ㊽

CONSUME

This sparkling newcomer to the Opéra/St-Lazare district lives up to its name with a night-sky decor made up of black granite resin punctuated with crystals and LEDs. The 30 rooms are equally splendid with Swarovski crystal touches to the furniture, black bathrooms and satin curtains that close to become a huge photomontage of a female nude crossed with architectural imagery. The Executive rooms on the fifth floor have iPod stations, Nespresso machines, and speakers in the bathrooms. A grassy courtyard with a fountain adds to the appeal. Unashamedly bling, but rather magical when night falls.
Bar. Concierge. Internet (free, wireless). No-smoking rooms. Room service. TV.

MONTMARTRE & PIGALLE
Deluxe

★ Hôtel Particulier Montmartre
23 av Junot, 18th (01.53.41.81.40/www.hotel-particulier-montmartre.com). M° Lamarck Caulaincourt. **Rates** €290-€590 suite. **Credit** MC, V. **Map** p401 H1 ➍➒
Visitors lucky (and wealthy) enough to manage to book a suite at the Hôtel Particulier Montmartre will find themselves in one of the city's hidden gems. Nestled in a quiet passage off rue Lepic, in the heart of Montmartre and opposite a mysterious rock known as the *Rocher de la Sorcière* (witch's rock), this sumptuous *Directoire*-style house is dedicated to art, with each of the five luxurious suites personalised by an avant-garde artist. The private garden conceived by Louis Bénech (famous for the Tuileries renovation) adds the finishing touch to this charming hideaway.
Concierge. Internet (free, wireless). No-smoking rooms. Room service. TV.

Expensive

Hôtel Banke
20 rue La Fayette, 9th (01.55.33.22.22/www.derbyhotels.com). M° Le Peletier. **Rates** €210-€315 double. **Credit** AmEx, MC, V. **Map** p401 H3 ➎➐
So called because the Haussmann-era building it occupies used to be a bank, the latest four-star addition to the Derby Hotels chain opened in spring 2009. It may well have the most eye-popping lobby in the city, a huge two-storey space done in outrageous belle époque style, all crimson, black pillars and gold leaf beneath a whopping glass roof. After such opulence, the rooms – the now familiar modern palette of muted tones and wood – are perhaps something of a let-down; but they are stylish and comfortably equipped. The mezzanine bar partakes of the lobby's *luxe*, and the Josefin restaurant serves nouvelle Med cuisine. The hotel even has its own art collection. *Photo p163.*
Bars (2). Concierge. Gym. Internet (free, wireless). Restaurants (2). Room service. Spa. TV.

Kube Hotel
1-5 passage Ruelle, 18th (01.42.05.20.00/www.kubehotel.com). M° La Chapelle. **Rates** €300-€400 double. **Credit** AmEx, DC, MC, V. **Map** p402 K1 ➎➊
The younger sister of the Murano Urban Resort (*see p170*), Kube is an edgier and more affordable hotel. Like the Murano, it sits behind an unremarkable façade in an unlikely neighbourhood – in this case, the ethnically diverse Goutte d'Or. The Ice Kube bar by Grey Goose serves up vodka glasses that, like the bar itself, are carved from ice; drinkers pay €38 to down four vodka cocktails in 30 minutes. Also on the menu, 'aperifood' and 'snackubes' by culinary designer Nicolas Guillard. The art brunch on Sundays introduces a different artist each month, with DJs and a buffet. To top off the futuristic style, access to the 41 rooms is by fingerprint technology. *Photo p170.*
Bars (2). Concierge. Disabled-adapted rooms. Gym. Internet (free, wireless). No-smoking rooms. Parking (€30). Restaurant. Room service. TV.

Terrass Hotel
12-14 rue Joseph-de-Maistre, 18th (01.46.06.72.85/www.terrass-hotel.com). M° Place de Clichy. **Rates** €280-€330 double. **Credit** AmEx, DC, MC, V. **Map** p401 H1 ➎➋
There's nothing spectacular about this classic hotel, but for people willing to pay top euro for the best views in town, it fits the bill. Ask for room 704 and you can lie in the bath and look at the Eiffel Tower. Julien Rocheteau, trained by Ducasse, is at the helm of gastronomic restaurant Diapason; in fine weather, opt for a table on the seventh-floor terrace, open from June to September.
Bar. Concierge. Disabled-adapted rooms. Internet (€3/hr, shared terminal; free, wireless). No-smoking rooms. Restaurant. Room service. TV.

Moderate

Hôtel Royal Fromentin
11 rue Fromentin, 9th (01.48.74.85.93/www.hotelroyalfromentin.com). M° Blanche or Pigalle. **Rates** €179 double. **Credit** AmEx, DC, MC, V. **Map** p401 H2 ➎➌
Wood panelling, art deco windows and a vintage glass lift echo the hotel's origins as a 1930s cabaret hall; its theatrical feel attracted Blondie and Nirvana. It's just down the road from the Moulin Rouge, and many of its 47 rooms overlook Sacré-Coeur. Rooms have been renovated in French style, with bright fabrics and an old-fashioned feel.
Bar. Concierge. Internet (free, shared terminal & wireless). No-smoking rooms. TV.

Timhotel Montmartre
11 rue Ravignan, 18th (01.42.55.74.79/www.timhotel.fr). M° Abbesses or Pigalle. **Rates** €130-€160 double. **Credit** AmEx, DC, MC, V. **Map** p401 H1 ➎➍

CONSUME

The location adjacent to picturesque place Emile-Goudeau makes this one of the most popular hotels in the Timhotel chain. It has 59 rooms, comfortable without being plush; try to bag one on the fourth or fifth floor for stunning views over Montmartre. Special offers are often available at quieter times of the year; ring for details.
Concierge. Internet (free, wireless). No-smoking rooms. TV.

Budget

Hôtel des Arts
5 rue Tholozé, 18th (01.46.06.30.52/www. arts-hotel-paris.com). Mº Abbesses or Blanche. **Rates** €95-€165 double. **Credit** MC, V. **Map** p401 H1 ⑤
The wagging tail of Caramel the black labrador welcomes guests to this Montmartre gem, pleasantly decorated in oriental rugs, wooden bookcases and Provençal-style furniture. The rooms here are simple but inviting, some affording pleasant views of the hidden roof gardens and windmills of the *Butte*. Art by local artists is displayed in the basement breakfast room.
Bar. Concierge. Internet (wireless).

Hôtel Eldorado
18 rue des Dames, 17th (01.45.22.35.21/ www.eldoradohotel.fr). Mº Place de Clichy. **Rates** €70-€80 double. **Credit** AmEx, DC, MC, V. **Map** p401 G1 ⑤
This eccentric hotel is decorated with flea market finds. The Eldorado's winning features include a wine bar, one of the best garden patios in town and a loyal fashionista following. The cheapest rooms have shared bathrooms and toilets.
Bar. Internet (free, wireless). Restaurant.

Hôtel Ermitage
24 rue Lamarck, 18th (01.42.64.79.22/ www.ermitagesacrecoeur.fr). Mº Lamarck Caulaincourt. **Rates** (incl breakfast) €96-€100 double. **No credit cards. Map** p402 J1 ⑤
This 12-room townhouse hotel stands on the calm, non-touristy north side of Montmartre, only five minutes from Sacré-Coeur. Rooms are large and endearingly overdecorated, with bold floral wallpaper; those higher up have fine views.
No-smoking rooms. Parking (€15). Room service (morning only).

BEAUBOURG & THE MARAIS
Deluxe

★ Murano Urban Resort
13 bd du Temple, 3rd (01.42.71.20.00/ www.muranoresort.com). Mº Filles du Calvaire or Oberkampf. **Rates** €350-€650 double. **Credit** AmEx, DC, MC, V. **Map** p409 L5 ⑤

Behind this unremarkable façade is a super cool and supremely luxurious hotel, popular with the fashion set for its slick lounge-style design, excellent restaurant and high-tech flourishes – including coloured light co-ordinators that enable you to change the mood of your room at the touch of a button. The handsome bar has a mind-boggling 140 varieties of vodka to sample, which can bring the op art fabrics in the lift to life and make the fingerprint access to the hotel's 43 rooms and nine suites (two of which feature private pools) a late-night godsend.
Bar. Concierge. Gym. Internet (free, wireless). No-smoking rooms. Parking (€35). Restaurant. Room service. TV.

Expensive

Hôtel Bourg Tibourg
19 rue du Bourg-Tibourg, 4th (01.42.78.47.39/ www.hotelbourgtibourg.com). Mº Hôtel de Ville. **Rates** €230-€260 double. **Credit** AmEx, DC, MC, V. **Map** p409 K6 ⑤
The Bourg Tibourg has the same owners as Hôtel Costes (*see p157*) and the same interior decorator – but don't expect this jewellery box of a boutique hotel to look like a miniature replica. Aside from its enviable location in the heart of the Marais and its fashion-pack fans, here it's all about Jacques Garcia's neo-Gothic-cum-Byzantine decor – impressive and imaginative. Scented candles, mosaic-tiled bathrooms and luxurious fabrics in rich colours create the perfect escape. There's no restaurant or lounge – posing is done in the neighbourhood bars.
Concierge. Disabled-adapted rooms. Internet (free, wireless). Room service. TV.

CONSUME

Kube Hotel. *See p169.*

★ Hôtel du Petit Moulin

*29-31 rue de Poitou, 3rd (01.42.74.10.10/
www.hoteldupetitmoulin.com). M° St-Sébastien
Froissart.* **Rates** €190-€350 suite. **Credit** AmEx,
DC, MC, V. **Map** p409 L5 ⑥⓪

Within striking distance of the hip shops around rue
Charlot, this turn-of-the-century façade masks what
was once the oldest *boulangerie* in Paris, lovingly
restored as a boutique hotel by Nadia Murano and
Denis Nourry. The couple recruited Christian Lacroix
for the decor, and the result is a riot of colour, trompe
l'oeil effects and a savvy mix of old and new. Each of
its 17 exquisitely appointed rooms is unique, and the
walls in rooms 202, 204 and 205 feature drawings and
scribbles taken from Lacroix's sketchbook.
*Bar. Concierge. Internet (€5/45mins, wireless).
Parking (free). Room service. TV.*

Les Jardins du Marais

*74 rue Amelot, 11th (01.40.21.20.00/www.
lesjardinsdumarais.com). M° Bastille.* **Rates**
€150-€455 double. **Credit** AmEx, DC, MC, V.
Map p409 L5 ⑥①

The centrepiece of this ultra-swish hotel is a vast
courtyard, filled with tables, potted plants and lampposts that wouldn't look out of place in Narnia. Inside,
it's smart and modern; the lobby looks tastefully
trendy in its steely black and white marble, with purple furnishings and Philippe Starck chairs. Rooms are
less daring, with traditional fabrics and furniture.
*Bar. Concierge. Disabled-adapted facilities.
Gym. Internet (wireless). No-smoking rooms.
Restaurant. Room service. TV.*
▶ *The in-house restaurant is a favourite with the
local media crowd.*

Moderate

★ Hôtel de la Bretonnerie

*22 rue Ste-Croix-de-la-Bretonnerie, 4th
(01.48.87.77.63/www.bretonnerie.com). M° Hôtel
de Ville.* **Rates** €135-€165 double. **Credit** MC, V.
Map p409 K6 ⑥②

With wrought ironwork, exposed stone and wooden
beams, the labyrinth of corridors in this 17th-century
hôtel particulier is full of atmosphere. Tapestries, rich
colours and the occasional four-poster bed give the 29
rooms individuality. Location is convenient too.
*Concierge. Disabled-adapted room. Internet (free,
wireless). TV.*

Hôtel Duo

*11 rue du Temple, 4th (01.42.72.72.22/www.
duoparis.com). M° Hôtel de Ville.* **Rates** €200-
€340 double. **Credit** AmEx, DC, MC, V.
Map p406 K6 ⑥③

An unbeatable location, designer decor, a gym with
sauna and a convivial cocktail bar make this a popular choice for laptop-wielding young professionals. Its
Jean-Philippe Nuel decor is so striking that passers-
by sometimes enquire about the price of the outsize
lampshades and mustard-coloured armchairs in the
huge lounge lobby, which also has a bamboo courtyard garden. Based on a palette of brown with con-
trasting turquoise, mustard, lime green, pink or blue,
each room is different and you can request a balcony,
beams, wallpaper, a bath, separate loo, and road or
courtyard preference. The suite, which sleeps four,
even has its own little courtyard off the bedroom.
*Bar. Concierge. Disabled-adapted rooms. Gym.
Internet (free, wireless). Sauna. TV.*

Hôtel St-Louis Marais

*1 rue Charles V, 4th (01.48.87.87.04/www.
saintlouismarais.com). M° Bastille or Sully
Morland.* **Rates** €115-€140 double. **Credit**
AmEx, DC, MC, V. **Map** p409 L7 ㉔

Built as part of a 17th-century Célestin convent, this
peaceful hotel had its bathrooms redone and Wi-Fi
access installed in 2005. Rooms are compact and
cosy, with wooden beams, tiled floors and simple,
traditional decor.

*Concierge. Internet (€5/hr, wireless). No-smoking
rooms. Parking (€20). Room service (breakfast
only). TV.*

Other locations Hôtel St-Louis Bastille,
114 bd Richard Lenoir, 11th (01.43.38.29.29);
Hôtel St-Louis Opéra, 51 rue de la Victoire,
9th (01.48.74.71.13).

Hôtel St-Merry

*78 rue de la Verrerie, 4th (01.42.78.14.15/
www.hotelmarais.com). M° Châtelet or Hôtel de
Ville.* **Rates** €160-€230 double. **Credit** AmEx,
MC, V. **Map** p406 K6 ㉕

The Gothic decor of this former presbytery attached
to the Eglise St-Merry is ideal for a Dracula set, with
wooden beams, stone walls and plenty of iron;
behind the door of room nine, an imposing flying
buttress straddles the carved antique bed. On the
down side, the building has no lift, and only the
suite has a TV.

*Concierge. Internet (€2/day, wireless). No-
smoking rooms. Room service. TV (suite only).*
Other locations Hôtel Saintonge Marais,
16 rue de Saintonge, 3rd (01.42.77.91.13).

Budget

Grand Hôtel Jeanne d'Arc

*3 rue de Jarente, 4th (01.48.87.62.11/
www.hoteljeannedarc.com). M° Chemin Vert
or St-Paul.* **Rates** €90-€116 double. **Credit**
MC, V. **Map** p409 L6 ㉖

The Jeanne d'Arc's strong point is its location on a
quiet road close to pretty place du Marché-Ste-
Catherine. A recent refurbishment has made the
reception area striking, with a huge mirror adding
the illusion of space. The bedrooms are colourful
and comfortable.

Internet (€1/hr, wireless). No-smoking rooms. TV.

Hôtel Paris France

*72 rue de Turbigo, 3rd (01.42.78.00.04/
www.paris-france-hotel.com). M° Temple.*
Rates €98-€129 double. **Credit** AmEx,
DC, MC, V. **Map** p402 L5 ㉗

A great central location, sweet lift, spruce staff and
clean, pleasant rooms are on offer here. The attic
has views of Montmartre and (if you lean out far
enough) the Eiffel Tower.

*Bar. Internet (free, wireless). No-smoking
rooms. TV.*

Hôtel du Septième Art

*20 rue St-Paul, 4th (01.44.54.85.00/www.paris-
hotel-7art.com). M° Pont Marie or St-Paul.* **Rates**
€95-€150 double. **Credit** AmEx, DC, MC, V.
Map p409 L7 ㉘

Ideally located in a lively part of the Marais, the
quaint façade hides a treasure trove of movie memorabilia, which takes up most of the reception space.
Exposed brick walls and devoted staff make for a
friendly, cosy atmosphere. The decor in the bedrooms isn't exactly groundbreaking, but everything
is clean and well equipped. There's no lift.

*Bar. Gym. Internet (€5/hr, shared terminal; free,
wireless). TV.*

BASTILLE & EASTERN PARIS

Luxury

Hôtel Marceau Bastille

*13 rue Jules César, 12th (01.43.43.11.65/www.
hotelmarceaubastille.com). M° Bastille.* **Rates**
€350-€450 double. **Credit** AmEx, DC, MC, V.
Map p409 M7 ㉙

This slick boutique hotel has 55 rooms divided into
two different styles: urban or *écolo* (eco-friendly),
some with a balcony. The bar-lounge, overlooking a
pleasant, bamboo-planted patio, is surrounded by a
gallery that exhibits works of contemporary artists.

*Bar. Concierge. Disabled-adapted rooms. Gym.
Internet (free, wireless). No-smoking rooms.
Room service (6pm-midnight). TV.*

Moderate

Le Quartier Bastille, Le Faubourg

*9 rue de Reuilly, 12th (01.43.70.04.04/www.
lequartierhotelbf.com). M° Faidherbe Chaligny
or Reuilly-Diderot.* **Rates** €145-€160 double.
Credit AmEx, DC, MC, V. **Map** p407 P7 ㉚

Close to the Bastille and the hip 11th arrondissement,
the Quartier Bastille (a branch of Franck Altruie's
chain of budget design hotels) flashes funky, neo-
1970s furniture and just the right amount of colour.
Rooms are minimalist but more than comfortable.

*Disabled-adapted rooms. Internet (free, wireless).
No-smoking rooms. Parking (€18). TV.*

★ Le Quartier Bercy Square

*33 bd de Reuilly, 12th (01.44.87.09.09/
www.lequartierhotelbs.com). M° Daumesnil
or Dugommier.* **Rates** €135-€160 double.
Credit AmEx, DC, MC, V. **Map** p407 P9 ㉛

You'd never think that lime green and brown stripes
would match bold silver and white replica 19th-
century wallpaper, but it does at this boutique hotel
(another of Franck Altruie's addresses) in the trendy
12th arrondissement. Rooms are small but inviting,
often using coloured light to create atmosphere.

*Bar. Internet (free, wireless). No-smoking
rooms. TV.*

CONSUME

Standard Design Hotel
29 rue Taillandiers, 11th (01.48.05.30.97/ www.standard-hotel.com). Mº Ledru Rollin. **Rates** €175-€250 double. **Credit** AmEx, DC, MC, V. **Map** p407 M6 **72**

The Standard's black and white interior, with the occasional splash of colour, is satisfyingly generic and a winner with visitors looking for a break from the sometimes heavy atmosphere of older, more traditional hotels. The rooms have all mod cons, the breakfast room awakens the senses with bold stripes, and you can roll into bed after a night out in Bastille's cool bars and restaurants.
Bar. Internet (free, wireless). No-smoking rooms. TV.

Budget

★ Mama Shelter
109 rue de Bagnolet, 20th (01.43.48.49.49/ www.mamashelter.com). Mº Alexandre Dumas, Maraîchers or Porte de Bagnolet. **Rates** €89-€399 double. **Credit** AmEx, DC, MC, V.

Philippe Starck's latest design commission is set a stone's throw east of Père Lachaise, and its decor appeals to the young-at-heart with Batman and Incredible Hulk light fittings, dark walls, polished wood and splashes of bright fabrics. Every room comes equipped with an iMac computer, TV, free internet access and a CD and DVD player; and when hunger strikes, there's a brasserie with a romantic terrace. If you're sure of your dates, book online and take advantage of the saver's rate.
Bar. Internet (free, wireless). No-smoking rooms. Restaurant. TV.

Le Pavillon Bastille
65 rue de Lyon, 12th (01.43.43.65.65/www. pavillonbastille.com). Mº Bastille. **Rates** €100-€140 double. **Credit** AmEx, DC, MC, V. **Map** p407 M7 **73**

The best thing about this hotel is its location between the Bastille opera and the Gare de Lyon. The 25 rooms may be small, but you're a stone's throw from the Viaduc des Arts, where an elevated garden has replaced the railroad's tracks and arty boutiques now occupy the arches.
Bar. Disabled-adapted room. Internet (free, wireless). No-smoking rooms. TV.

NORTH-EAST PARIS
Moderate

Le Général Hôtel
5-7 rue Rampon, 11th (01.47.00.41.57/ www.legeneralhotel.com). Mº République. **Rates** €215-€260 double. **Credit** AmEx, DC, MC, V. **Map** p402 L5 **74**

A fashionable find near the nightlife action of the 11th, Le Général was one of Paris's first boutique

bargains when it opened back in 2003. It is still notable for its remarkably moderate rates and sleek, neutral-toned interior.
Bar. Business centre. Concierge. Disabled-adapted rooms. Gym. Internet (free, wireless). No-smoking rooms. Sauna. TV.

Hôtel Gabriel
25 rue du Grand Prieuré, 11th (01.47.00.13.38/ www.gabrielparismarais.com). Mº République. **Rates** €160-€280 double. **Credit** AmEx, DC, MC, V. **Map** p402 M5 **75**
See right **Sleep Well**.
Bar. Concierge. Internet (free, wireless). No smoking throughout. Room service. TV.

Budget

Le 20 Prieuré Hôtel
20 rue du Grand Prieuré, 11th (01.47.00.74.14/ www.hotel20prieure.com). Mº République. **Rates** €95-€170 double. **Credit** AmEx, MC, V. **Map** p402 M5 **76**

In a road where budget sleeps are fast metamorphosing into hip hotels, this young, funky and affordable place benefits from particularly welcoming staff. Each room features a huge blow-up of a Paris landmark covering the entire wall behind the bed, giving you the illusion that you are sleeping halfway up the Eiffel Tower, or on Bir-Hakeim bridge as the métro speeds by (great for *Last Tango in Paris* fans). Bathrooms are mundane in comparison, but things brighten up again in the light-flooded breakfast room, with pop art portraits and a reworked 1970s look.
Concierge. Internet (free, wireless). No-smoking rooms. TV.

Hôtel Beaumarchais
3 rue Oberkampf, 11th (01.53.36.86.86/ www.hotelbeaumarchais.com). Mº Filles du Calvaire or Oberkampf. **Rates** €110-€130 double. **Credit** AmEx, MC, V. **Map** p409 L5 **77**

This contemporary hotel is in the Oberkampf area, not far from the Marais and Bastille. Its 31 rooms are brightly decorated with colourful walls, bathroom mosaics and wavy headboards; breakfast is served on the tiny garden patio or in your room.
Concierge. Internet (free, high speed & wireless). Room service. TV.

Hôtel Garden Saint-Martin
35 rue Yves Toudic, 10th (01.42.40.17.72/ www.hotel-gardensaintmartin-paris.com). Mº Jacques Bonsergent. **Rates** €68-€87 double. **Credit** MC, V. **Map** p402 L4 **78**

The shops, cafés and bars along the Canal St-Martin draw visitors to this hotel, where creature comforts are guaranteed at an excellent rate. No prizes will be won for the ordinary decor, but there is a very pleasant patio garden, and the staff are helpful.
Internet (free, wireless). No-smoking rooms. TV.

CONSUME

Sleep Well

Recharge your batteries overnight at the Hôtel Gabriel.

Hôtel Gabriel (*see left*), Paris's first 'detox hotel', is a shrine to quality kip and healthy living, offering a chilled respite for everyone from the terminally jetlagged to weekend clubbers. To test it out, we checked in after a heavy weekend of partying. On a hot August day the air-conditioned, pure white room seemed rather clinical, but at night the 'Glowing Room' came alive with dancing silhouettes on the cupboards and illuminated cubbyholes stocked with health-food snacks. The TV may be neatly hidden behind mirrored glass, but the room is not short on techno wizardry: there's a chrome mini-bar that unfolds from inside its white knobless cupboard; an iPod station for which you can borrow an iPod pre-programmed with anything from Goldfrapp to Shirley Bassey; free Wi-Fi, of course; and the *sine qua non* of sleep aids, the NightCove device, conceived by a sleep professor and designer Jean-Philippe Nuel.

This white box is easily programmed to emit sounds and light that stimulate melatonin: choose between sleep, nap or wake-up programmes such as the sound of rain, sloping electro sounds or tropical birdsong. When you do manage to wake up, there's a cold room-service menu including lobster salad delivered fresh from specialist boutique hotel caterers; a minimalist bathroom with Korres products made from natural ingredients in Greece; and a scrumptious breakfast of organic yoghurt, chocolate muesli and mini

croissants. If you're still feeling run down, then head downstairs for a detox massage by Franco-Japanese masseuse Mitchiko and her colleagues – potent enough to make the next glass of wine course through your veins in an alarming way. A partner gym, suggested jogging routes and green taxis complete the healthy vibe.

THE LATIN QUARTER & THE 13TH

Expensive

★ Le Petit Paris
214 rue St-Jacques, 5th (01.53.10.29.29/ www.hotelpetitparis.com). M° Maubert Mutualité/RER Luxembourg. **Rates** €240-€340 double. **Credit** AmEx, MC, V. **Map** p408 J8 ⑳
This brand new Latin Quarter venture is a dynamic exercise in taste and colour. The 20 rooms, designed by Sybille de Margerie, are arranged by era, running from the puce and purple of the medieval rooms to the wildly decadent orange, yellow and pink of the swinging '60s rooms, replete with specially commissioned sensual photographs of Paris monuments. Luxury abounds with finest silks, velvets and taffetas. Some of the rooms have small terraces, and

those with baths have a TV you can watch while soaking. An honesty bar in the lounge and ultra-modern jukebox encourage conviviality.
Bar. Concierge. Disabled-adapted room. Internet (free, wireless). No-smoking rooms. TV.

Moderate

★ Five Hôtel
3 rue Flatters, 5th (01.43.31.74.21/www. thefivehotel.com). M° Les Gobelins or Port Royal. **Rates** €202-€342 double. **Credit** AmEx, MC, V. **Map** p406 J9 ⑳
The rooms in this stunning boutique hotel may be small, but they're all exquisitely designed, with Chinese lacquer and velvety fabrics. Fibre optics built into the walls create the illusion of sleeping under a starry sky, and you can choose from four different fragrances to subtly perfume your room (the

hotel is entirely non-smoking). Guests staying in the suite have access to a private garden with a jacuzzi. *Concierge. Internet (free, wireless). No smoking throughout. TV.*

Hôtel la Demeure

51 bd St-Marcel, 13th (01.43.37.81.25/www. hotel-paris-lademeure.com). Mº Les Gobelins. **Rates** €170-€210 double. **Credit** AmEx, DC, MC, V. **Map** p406 K9 🔢
This comfortable, modern hotel on the edge of the Latin Quarter is run by a friendly father and son. It has 43 air-conditioned rooms with internet access, plus suites with sliding doors to separate sleeping and living space. The wrap-around balconies of the corner rooms offer lovely views of the city, and bathrooms feature either luxurious tubs or shower heads with elaborate massage possibilities.
Internet (€8/hr; free, wireless). No-smoking rooms. Parking (€17). TV.

★ Hôtel de la Sorbonne

6 rue Victor-Cousin, 5th (01.43.54.58.08/ www.hotelsorbonne.com). Mº Cluny La Sorbonne/ RER Luxembourg. **Rates** €100-€350 double. **Credit** AmEx, DC, MC, V. **Map** p408 J8 🔢
It's out with the old at this charming, freshly renovated hotel, whose new look is very much a modern take on art nouveau, with bold, designer wallpapers, floral prints, lush fabrics and quotes from French literature woven into the carpets. Rooms are all equipped with iMac computers.
Concierge. Internet (free, wireless). No-smoking rooms. TV.

Select Hôtel

1 pl de la Sorbonne, 5th (01.46.34.14.80/ www.selecthotel.fr). Mº Cluny La Sorbonne. **Rates** (incl breakfast) €169-€245 double. **Credit** AmEx, DC, MC, V. **Map** p408 J8 🔢
Located at the foot of the Sorbonne, this 68-room hotel delivers pure, understated chic with its clever blend of modern art deco features, traditional stone walls and wooden beams. The winter garden and airy common areas have recently been redone in a sleek, contemporary style.
Bar. Concierge. Internet (wireless). No-smoking rooms. Room service (until 10pm). TV.

Budget

Familia Hôtel

11 rue des Ecoles, 5th (01.43.54.55.27/ www.hotel-paris-familia.com). Mº Cardinal Lemoine or Jussieu. **Rates** (incl breakfast) €107-€137 double. **Credit** AmEx, DC, MC, V. **Map** p406 K8 🔢
This old-fashioned Latin Quarter hotel has balconies hung with tumbling plants and walls draped with replica French tapestries. Owner Eric Gaucheron extends a warm welcome, and the 30 rooms have

personalised touches such as sepia murals, cherrywood furniture and stone walls. The Gaucherons also own the Hôtel Minerve next door – book in advance for both.
Concierge. Internet (free, wireless). Parking (€20). TV.
Other locations Hôtel Minerve, 13 rue des Ecoles, 5th (01.43.26.26.04).

★ Hôtel les Degrés de Notre-Dame

10 rue des Grands-Degrés, 5th (01.55.42.88.88/ www.lesdegreshotel.com). Mº Maubert-Mutualité or St-Michel. **Rates** (incl breakfast) €115-€170 double. **Credit** MC, V. **Map** p406 J7 🔢
On a tiny street across the river from Notre-Dame, this vintage hotel is an absolute gem. Its ten rooms are full of character, with original paintings, antique furniture and exposed wooden beams (nos.47 and 501 have views of the cathedral). It has an adorable restaurant and, a few streets away, two studio apartments that the owner rents out to preferred customers only.
Bar. Internet (free, wireless). No-smoking rooms. Restaurant. Room service (noon-midnight). TV.

Hôtel du Panthéon

19 pl du Panthéon, 5th (01.43.54.32.95/ www.hoteldupantheon.com). Mº Cluny La Sorbonne or Maubert Mutualité/RER Luxembourg. **Credit** AmEx, DC, MC, V. **Map** p408 J8 🔢
The 36 rooms of this elegant hotel are beautifully decorated with classic French *toile de Jouy* fabrics, antique furniture and painted woodwork. Some enjoy impressive views of the Panthéon; others squint out on to a hardly less romantic courtyard, complete with chestnut tree.
Internet (free, wireless). No-smoking rooms. TV.

Hôtel Résidence Gobelins

9 rue des Gobelins, 13th (01.47.07.26.90/ www.hotelgobelins.com). Mº Les Gobelins. **Rates** €79-€94 double. **Credit** AmEx, MC, V. **Map** p406 K10 🔢
A tiny lift leads to colourful rooms, all equipped with satellite TV and telephone. The breakfast room overlooks a private garden, and there's free internet use available at the reception, and the hotel is entirely non-smoking.
Internet (free, shared terminal). No smoking throughout. TV.

Hôtel Résidence Henri IV

50 rue des Bernardins, 5th (01.44.41.31.81/ www.residencehenri4.com). Mº Cardinal Lemoine. **Rates** €90-€310 double. **Credit** AmEx, DC, MC, V. **Map** p406 K7 🔢
This belle-époque-style hotel has a mere eight rooms and five apartments, so guests are assured of the staff's full attention. Peacefully situated next to leafy square Paul-Langevin, it's just minutes

CONSUME

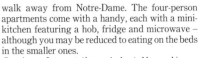

CONSUME

walk away from Notre-Dame. The four-person apartments come with a handy, each with a mini-kitchen featuring a hob, fridge and microwave – although you may be reduced to eating on the beds in the smaller ones.
Concierge. Internet (free, wireless). No-smoking rooms. TV.

ST-GERMAIN-DES-PRES & ODEON

Deluxe

★ L'Hôtel
13 rue des Beaux-Arts, 6th (01.44.41.99.00/ www.l-hotel.com). M° Mabillon or St-Germain-des-Prés. **Rates** €255-€640 double. **Credit** AmEx, DC, MC, V. **Map** p408 H6 ❻❾
Guests at the sumptuously decorated L'Hôtel these days are more likely to be models and film stars than the starving writers who frequented the place during Oscar Wilde's last days (the playwright died on the ground floor here in November 1900). Under Jacques Garcia's careful restoration, each room has its own special theme: Mistinguett's *chambre* retains its art deco mirror bed, while Oscar's tribute room is appropriately clad in green peacock murals.
Bar. Concierge. Internet (shared terminal; free, wireless). Pool (indoor). Restaurant. Room service (until 11pm). Sauna. TV.
▶ *Don't miss out on dinner in the fabulously decadent restaurant, run by talented chef Philippe Bélisse (see p205).*

Hôtel Lutetia
45 bd Raspail, 6th (01.49.54.46.46/www.lutetia-paris.com). M° Sèvres Babylone. **Rates** €240-€590 double. **Credit** AmEx, DC, MC, V. **Map** p405 G7 ❾❶
This historic Left Bank hotel is a masterpiece of art nouveau and early art deco architecture that dates from 1910. It has a plush jazz bar and lively brasserie. Its 250 rooms, revamped in purple, gold and pearl grey, maintain a 1930s feel. Big-name guests in years gone by have included Picasso, Josephine Baker and de Gaulle. It was also the Abwehr (German military intelligence) HQ during the Nazi occupation.
Bar. Business centre. Concierge. Gym. Internet (€18/day, high speed; free, wireless). No-smoking rooms. Restaurants (2). Room service. TV.

Villa d'Estrées
17 rue Gît-le-Coeur, 6th (01.55.42.71.11/ www.villadestrees.com). M° St-Michel. **Rates** €365-€405 double. **Credit** AmEx, DC, MC, V. **Map** p408 J7 ❾❶
Jewel colours, sumptuous fabrics, stripes and patterns are the hallmarks of this polished boutique hotel; there's nothing at all minimalist about Villa d'Estrées, which was designed by Jacques Garcia. Each of the ten rooms and suites is individually decorated, all with a nod to Empire style and a crisp, slightly masculine feel.
Bar. Concierge. Internet (free, wireless). No-smoking rooms. Restaurant. Room service (until 10pm). TV.

Artus Hotel. *See p180.*

Expensive

★ Hôtel de l'Abbaye Saint Germain

10 rue Cassette, 6th (01.45.44.38.11/www.
hotelabbayeparis.com). M° Rennes or St-Sulpice.
Rates (incl breakfast) €251-€367 double.
Credit AmEx, MC, V. **Map** p405 G7 ❸

A monumental entrance opens the way through a
courtyard into this tranquil hotel, originally part of
a convent. Wood panelling, well-stuffed sofas and
an open fireplace in the drawing room make for a
relaxed atmosphere, but, best of all, there's a surprisingly large garden where breakfast is served in the
warmer months. The 43 rooms and duplex apartment are tasteful and luxurious.
Bar. Concierge. Internet (€12/2hrs; free, shared
terminal). Room service. TV.

Le Placide

6 rue St-Placide, 6th (01.42.84.34.60/www.
leplacidehotel.com). M° Sèvres-Babylone, St-
Placide or Vanneau. **Rates** €300-€390 double.
Credit AmEx, DC, MC, V. **Map** p405 G7 ❸

With only ten rooms, the Placide is just about as
bijou as it gets. White, chrome and neutral tones
reign throughout (as does bark- or bamboo-
inspired wallpaper), broken only by the occasional
funky cushion. Rooms are spacious: all have large
bathrooms as well as their own sitting area. The
stylish ground-floor duplex has been designed
for disabled guests.
Bar. Concierge. Disabled-adapted rooms.
Internet (shared terminal; free, wireless).
Room service. TV.

★ Relais Saint-Germain

9 carrefour de l'Odéon, 6th (01.43.29.12.05/
www.hotel-paris-relais-saint-germain.com). M°
Odéon. **Rates** (incl breakfast) €285-€370 double.
Credit AmEx, DC, MC, V. **Map** p408 H7 ❹

The rustic, wood-beamed ceilings remain intact at
the Relais Saint-Germain, a 17th-century hotel
bought and renovated by much-acclaimed chef
Yves Camdeborde (originator of the *bistronomique*
dining trend) and his wife Claudine. Each of the 22
rooms has a different take on eclectic Provençal
charm, and the marble bathrooms are positively
huge by Paris standards.
Bar. Concierge. Internet (free, high speed &
wireless). No-smoking rooms. Restaurant.
Room service (until 10pm). TV.
▶ *Guests get first dibs on a highly sought-after*
seat in the 15-table Le Comptoir restaurant next
door; see p204.

La Villa

29 rue Jacob, 6th (01.43.26.60.00/www.villa-
saintgermain.com). M° St-Germain-des-Prés.
Rates €280-€370 double. **Credit** AmEx, DC,
MC, V. **Map** p408 H6 ❺

Refreshingly modern and stylish, the charismatic La
Villa features cool faux crocodile skin on the bedheads and crinkly taffeta over the taupe-coloured
walls. Wonderfully, your room number is projected
on to the floor outside your door; very useful for any
drunken homecomings.
Bar. Concierge. Internet (€5/30mins, high speed;
€12/hr, wireless). No-smoking rooms. Room
service (until midnight). TV.

Moderate

★ Artus Hotel

34 rue de Buci, 6th (01.43.29.07.20/www.artus hotel.com). M° Mabillon. **Rates** €195-€305 double (incl breakfast). **Credit** AmEx, DC, MC, V. **Map** p408 H7

The recently renovated Artus Hotel is the ideal spot for a classic taste of Paris – you couldn't be any closer to the heart of the Left Bank action if you tried. Inside the look is chic boutique, with 27 individually designed rooms and suites, ranging from cosy to capacious. Staff are eager to help and full of local tips. *Photo p178.*

Bar. Concierge. Internet (free, wireless). TV.

Le Clos Médicis

56 rue Monsieur-le-Prince, 6th (01.43.29.10.80/ www.closmedicis.com). M° Odéon/RER Luxembourg. **Rates** €215-€270 double. **Credit** AmEx, DC, MC, V. **Map** p408 H8

More like a stylish, private townhouse than a hotel, Le Clos Médicis is located by the Luxembourg gardens. Decor is refreshingly modern, with rooms done out with taffeta curtains and chenille bedcovers, and antique floor tiles in the bathrooms. The cosy lounge has a working fireplace.

Bar. Concierge. Internet (free, high speed & wireless). No-smoking rooms. TV.

Grand Hôtel de l'Univers

6 rue Grégoire-de-Tours, 6th (01.43.29.37.00/ www.hotel-paris-univers.com). M° Odéon. **Rates** €185-€280 double. **Credit** AmEx, DC, MC, V. **Map** p408 H7

Making the most of its 15th-century origins, this hotel features exposed wooden beams, high ceilings, antique furnishings and toile-covered walls. Manuel Canovas fabrics lend a posh touch, but there are also useful services such as a laptop for hire.

Bar. Concierge. Internet (€8/hr, shared terminal; free, wireless). No-smoking rooms. TV.

▶ *The same team runs the Hôtel St-Germain-des-Prés (36 rue Bonaparte, 6th, 01.43.26.00.19), which has a medieval-themed room and the sweetest attic in Paris.*

Hôtel du Globe

15 rue des Quatre-Vents, 6th (01.43.26.35.50/ www.hotel-du-globe.fr). M° Odéon. **Rates** €170 double. **Credit** MC, V. **Map** p408 H7

The Hôtel du Globe has managed to retain much of its 17th-century character – and very pleasant it is too. Gothic wrought-iron doors open into the florid corridors, and an unexplained suit of armour supervises guests from the tiny salon. The rooms with baths are somewhat larger than those with showers, and if you're an early booker you might even get the room with the four-poster bed (ask when reserving). *Internet (free, wireless). TV.*

Hôtel des Saints-Pères

65 rue des Sts-Pères, 6th (01.45.44.50.00/ www.espritfrance.com). M° St-Germain-des-Prés. **Rates** €175-€230 double. **Credit** AmEx, MC, V. **Map** p405 G7

Built in 1658 by one of Louis XIV's architects, this hotel has an enviable location near St-Germain-des-Prés's designer boutiques. It boasts a charming garden and a sophisticated, if small, bar. The most

CONSUME

Le Bellechasse.

coveted room is no.100, with its fine 17th-century ceiling by painters from the Versailles School; it also has an open bathroom, so you can gaze at scenes from the myth of Leda and the Swan while you scrub.
Bar. Concierge. Internet (free, wireless). TV.

Hôtel Villa Madame
44 rue Madame, 6th (01.45.48.02.81/www. hotelvillamadameparis.com). Mº St-Sulpice. **Rates** €220-€320 double. **Credit** AmEx, MC, V. **Map** p408 G7 ●
This newly revamped hotel (formerly the Regents) located in a quiet street is a lovely surprise, its courtyard garden used for breakfast in the summer months. Honey- and chocolate-coloured woods mix with warm-toned velvets to make the rooms (all with plasma screens) feel cosy and inviting; some even have small balconies with loungers.
Concierge. Disabled-adapted rooms. Internet (free, wireless). Room service (breakfast only). TV.

Budget

Hôtel de Nesle
7 rue de Nesle, 6th (01.43.54.62.41/www.hotel denesleparis.com). Mº Odéon. **Rates** €75-€110 double. **Credit** MC, V. **Map** p408 H6 ●
Only nine of the 20 rooms are en suite, but all are decorated with colourful murals, and many overlook a charming garden courtyard.
Internet (€15, shared terminal). Parking (€15).

MONTPARNASSE
Expensive

Hôtel des Académies et des Arts
15 rue de la Grande Chaumière, 6th (01.43.26.66.44/www.hotel-des-academies.com). Mº Notre-Dame des Champs, Raspail or Vavin. **Rates** €189-€294 double. **Credit** AmEx, DC, MC, V. **Map** p405 G8 ●
Reopened in early 2007 after a full refurbishment, this small boutique hotel scores highly on style. There are cosy salons, fireplaces and an extensive collection of art books. The 20 immaculate rooms are individually designed around four themes (Paris, Actor, Man Ray or Rulhmann), and offer wonderful views over the rooftops or down on to the spectacular Jérôme Mesnager mural in the courtyard.
Concierge. Disabled-adapted room. Internet (free, shared terminal & wireless). TV.

Moderate

★ Hôtel Aviatic
105 rue de Vaugirard, 6th (01.53.63.25.50/www. aviatic.fr). Mº Duroc, Montparnasse Bienvenüe or St-Placide. **Rates** €199-€299 double. **Credit** AmEx, DC, MC, V. **Map** p405 F8 ●

This historic hotel has masses of character, from the Empire-style lounge and garden atrium to the bistro-style breakfast room and polished marble floor in the lobby. New decoration throughout, in beautiful steely greys, warm reds, elegant, striped velvets and *toile de Jouy* fabrics, lends an impressive touch of glamour, and the service is consistently with a smile.
Concierge. Internet (€15/hr, wireless). Parking (€27). TV.
▶ *For lunch on the hop, staff will pack up a picnic so you can eat in the nearby Luxembourg gardens.*

Hôtel Delambre
35 rue Delambre, 14th (01.43.20.66.31/www. delambre-paris-hotel.com). Mº Edgar Quinet or Vavin. **Rates** €140-€160 double. **Credit** AmEx, MC, V. **Map** p405 G9 ●
Occupying a narrow slot in a small street between Montparnasse and St-Germain, this hotel was home to surrealist André Breton in the 1920s. Today it's modern and friendly, with cast-iron details in the 13 rooms and newly installed air-conditioning. The mini suite in the attic, comprising two separate rooms, is particularly pleasant and sleeps up to four.
Concierge. Disabled-adapted room. Internet (€9/hr, wireless). No-smoking rooms. TV.

Hôtel Istria Saint-Germain
29 rue Campagne-Première, 14th (01.43.20.91.82/www.hotel-istria-paris.com). Mº Raspail. **Rates** €190 double. **Credit** AmEx, DC, MC, V. **Map** p405 G9 ●
Behind this unassuming façade is the place where the artistic royalty of Montparnasse's heyday – the likes of Man Ray, Marcel Duchamp and Louis Aragon – once lived. The Istria Saint-Germain has been modernised since then, but it still has plenty of charm, with 26 bright, simply furnished rooms, a cosy breakfast room and a comfortable communal area.
Concierge. Disabled-adapted room. Internet (€6/hr, wireless). No-smoking rooms. Parking (€20). Room service. TV.
▶ *Film fans take note: the artists' studios next door featured in Godard's A Bout de Souffle.*

THE 7TH & WESTERN PARIS
Deluxe

★ Le Bellechasse
8 rue de Bellechasse, 7th (01.45.50.22.31/ www.lebellechasse.com). Mº Assemblée Nationale or Solférino/RER Musée d'Orsay. **Rates** (incl breakfast) €340-€390 double. **Credit** AmEx, MC, V. **Map** p405 F6 ●
A former *hôtel particulier*, the Bellechasse fell into the hands of Christian Lacroix, already responsible for the makeover of the Hôtel du Petit Moulin (*see p171*). It reopened in July 2007, duly transformed into a trendy boutique hotel. Only a few steps away from the Musée d'Orsay, it offers 34 splendid –

though rather small – rooms, in seven different decorative styles. It's advisable to book early, as the Bellechasse remains *the* hotel of the moment. *Bar. Internet (free, shared terminal & wireless). No-smoking rooms. TV.*

★ Le Montalembert
3 rue Montalembert, 7th (01.45.49.68.68/ www.montalembert.com). M° Rue du Bac. **Rates** €240-€500 double. **Credit** AmEx, DC, MC, V. **Map** p405 G6 ⓳

Grace Leo-Andrieu's impeccable boutique is a benchmark of quality and service. It has everything that *mode* maniacs (who flock here for Fashion Week) could want: bathrooms stuffed with Molton Brown toiletries, a set of digital scales and plenty of mirrors with which to keep an eye on their figure.

Stylish B&Bs

Chic chambres d'hôtes.

Think of bed and breakfast and you probably conjure up images of a cosy retreat in the countryside or by the coast. Few visitors consider B&B for a city break, but it's a growing trend in Paris with a wealth of choices available.

In 2005, the Mairie created the Charte Hôtes Qualité Paris, an initiative to encourage locals to offer B&B, and you can now search and book rooms all over the city via its website (www.hotesqualiteparis.fr).

Also worth a look is *Chambres d'hôtes à Paris* (€16, Hachette), a guide to B&B options in the city. Written by Pascale Desclos, the book picks out 100 of the best B&Bs, covering a vast range of styles, locations and prices. Prices start at €55 for two people, and almost a third of the featured rooms come in at under €80. Among the more opulent entries are an elegant suite in a Montmartre mansion house (€430 per night), and a spacious third-floor room with garden and balcony view of the Eiffel Tower (€380).

The city boasts plenty of quirky B&Bs too, none more so than **Le Loft** (www.chezbertrand.com). This eccentric apartment, on the ground floor of an old fireplace shop, features a circular double bed, kitchenette and, the *pièce de résistance*, a shiny red, open-topped Citroën 2CV sleeping 'two lovers', ideal for a bit of back-seat action. And if Bertrand's B&B gives you any design inspiration, the world's biggest flea market is just around the corner.

Decorated in pale lilac, cinnamon and olive tones, the entire hotel has Wi-Fi access, and each room is equipped with a flat-screen TV. Clattery two-person stairwell lifts are a nice nod to old-fashioned ways in a hotel that is otherwise *tout moderne.* *Bar. Concierge. Internet (free, shared terminal; €29/day, wireless). No-smoking rooms. Restaurant. Room service. TV: DVD.*

Expensive

Hôtel Duc de Saint-Simon
14 rue de St-Simon, 7th (01.44.39.20.20/ www.hotelducdesaintsimon.com). M° Rue du Bac. **Rates** €250-€285 double. **Credit** AmEx, DC, MC, V. **Map** p405 G6 ⓴

A lovely courtyard leads the way into this popular hotel situated on the edge of St-Germain-des-Prés. Of the 34 romantic bedrooms, four have terraces over a closed-off, leafy garden. It's perfect for lovers, though if you can do without a four-poster bed there are more spacious rooms than the Honeymoon Suite. *Bar. Concierge. Internet (free, shared terminal & wireless). No-smoking rooms. Room service. TV.*

Moderate

Hôtel La Bourdonnais
111-113 av de La Bourdonnais, 7th (01.47.05.45.42/www.hotellabourdonnais.com). M° Ecole Militaire. **Rates** €185-€220 double. **Credit** AmEx, DC, MC, V. **Map** p404 D7 ⑩

The Bourdonnais feels more like a traditional French bourgeois townhouse than a hotel, with 56 bedrooms decorated in rich colours, antiques and Persian rugs. The main lobby opens on to a jungle-like winter garden and patio, where guests take breakfast. *Concierge. Internet (€10/hr, shared terminal). Parking (€15). TV.*

Hôtel Lenox
9 rue de l'Université, 7th (01.42.96.10.95/www. lenoxsaintgermain.com). M° St-Germain-des-Prés. **Rates** €135-€230 double. **Credit** AmEx, DC, MC, V. **Map** p405 G6 ⑪

Its location may be in the seventh, but this venerable literary and artistic haunt is unmistakably part of St-Germain-des-Prés. The art deco-style Lenox Club Bar, open to the public, features comfortable leather club chairs and jazz instruments on the walls. Bedrooms, reached by an astonishing glass lift, have more traditional decor and city views. *Bar. Concierge. Internet (€10/hr, shared terminal & wireless). No-smoking rooms. Room service (from 5.30pm). TV.*

Sublim Eiffel
94 bd Garibaldi, 15th (01.40.65.95.95/ www.sublimeiffel.com). M° Sèvres-Lecourbe. **Rates** €159-€179 double. **Credit** AmEx, MC, V. **Map** p405 E8 ⑫

CONSUME

St Christopher's Inn. *See p184.*

Some Barry White on your iPod is essential for this luuurve hotel not far from the Eiffel Tower. Carpets printed with paving stones and manhole covers lead to the rooms, where everything has been put in place for steamy nights. It's all to do with the lighting effects, which include a starry Eiffel Tower or streetscene lights above the bed and sparkling LEDs in the showers, filtered by coloured glass doors. Lovers should head for the suite, with its jacuzzi, huge shower, bathrobes and DVDs, and book the Romance package (rose petals on the bed and champagne). All guests get the use of the mini-gym and hammam, and there is a massage room too. The bar adds a bit of jazz to a neighbourhood in need of some action.
Concierge. Bar. Gym. Hammam. Internet (free, wireless). Room service. TV.

Budget

Hôtel Eiffel Rive Gauche

6 rue du Gros-Caillou, 7th (01.45.51.51.51/ www.hotel-eiffel.com). M° Ecole Militaire. **Rates** €105-€155 double. **Credit** MC, V. **Map** p404 D6 **13**

The Provençal decor and warm welcome make this a nice retreat. For the quintessential Paris view at a bargain price, ask to stay on one of the upper floors: you can see the Eiffel Tower from nine of the 29 rooms. All feature Empire-style bedheads and modern bathrooms. Outside, there's a tiny, tiled courtyard with a bridge.
Concierge. Internet (€6/30mins, shared terminal; free, wireless). TV.

▶ *If this is fully booked, try sister hotel Eiffel Villa Garibaldi (48 bd Garibaldi, 15th, 01.56.58.56.58), which has equally reasonable rates.*

YOUTH ACCOMMODATION

Auberge Internationale des Jeunes

10 rue Trousseau, 11th (01.47.00.62.00/ www.aijparis.com). M° Ledru-Rollin. **Rates** (incl breakfast, per person) €17-€38. **Credit** AmEx, MC, V. **Map** p407 N7 **14**

Cleanliness is a high priority at this large, 120-bed hostel close to Bastille and within easy distance of the Marais. Rooms accommodate between two and four people, and the larger ones have their own shower and toilet. With the lowest hostel rates in central Paris, the place does tend to fill up fast in summer, but advance reservations can be made. Although the hostel is open all hours without any late-night curfew, the rooms are closed for cleaning every day between 10am and 3pm. Under-35s only.
Internet (€6/hr, shared terminal). Microwave.

Auberge Jules-Ferry

8 bd Jules-Ferry, 11th (01.43.57.55.60/ www.hihostels.com). M° République. **Rates** (incl breakfast & linens, per person) €23. **Credit** MC, V. **Map** p402 M4 **15**

This friendly IYHF hostel has 100 beds in rooms for two to six. There's no need – indeed, no way – to make advance bookings. There's no curfew, though rooms are closed between 10am and 2pm.
Internet (€6/hr, shared terminal).

BVJ Paris/Quartier Latin

44 rue des Bernardins, 5th (01.43.29.34.80/ www.bvjhotel.com). M° Maubert Mutualité. **Rates** (incl breakfast, per person) €29 dorm; €33 double. **No credit cards. Map** p406 J7 **116**
The BVJ hostel has 121 beds with homely tartan quilts in clean but bare modern dorms (accommodating up to ten), and rooms with showers. There's also a TV lounge and a work room in which to write up your journal.
Internet (€4/hr, shared terminal).
Other locations BVJ Paris/Louvre, 20 rue Jean-Jacques-Rousseau, 1st (01.53.00.90.90).

★ MIJE

6 rue de Fourcy, 4th (01.42.74.23.45/www.mije. com). M° St-Paul. **Rates** (incl breakfast, per person; €2.50 obligatory membership) €30 dorm (18-30s); €36 double. **No credit cards. Map** p409 L6 **117**
MIJE runs three 17th-century Marais residences – one is a former convent – that provide the most attractive hostel sleeps in Paris. Its plain, clean rooms have snow-white sheets and sleep up to eight people; all have a shower and basin. The Fourcy address has its own restaurant (evenings only). The curfew is at 1am unless you arrange otherwise with reception.
Internet (€6/hr, shared terminal).
Other locations (same phone) 12 rue des Barres, 4th; 11 rue du Fauconnier, 4th.

St Christopher's Inn

159 rue de Crimée, 19th (01.40.34.34.40/www.st-christophers.co.uk/paris-hostels). M° Crimée, Jaurès, Laumière or Stanlingrad. **Rates** per person €28-€38 dorm; €47-€54.50 double. **Credit** AmEx, MC, V. **Map** p403 N1 **118**
If you don't mind bunking up with others, you could try this Paris branch of the English youth hostel chain housed in a former boat hangar on the ever-gentrifying Canal de l'Ourcq. The decor in the bedrooms has a sailor's cabin feel, with round, colourful mirrors, bubble-pattern wallpaper and 1950s-inspired cabin furniture. The hostel really comes into its own in its bar Belushi's, where the usual backpack brigade are joined by Parisians bent on taking advantage of the canalside setting, satellite sports, lunchtime brasserie and some of the cheapest drinks in the capital. *Photo* p183.
Bar. Internet (free, wireless). No-smoking rooms. Restaurant.

BED & BREAKFAST

Alcove & Agapes

Le Bed & Breakfast à Paris, 8bis rue Coysevox, 18th (01.44.85.06.05/www.bed-and-breakfast-in-paris.com).
This B&B booking service offers over 100 *chambres d'hôtes* (€80-€320 for a double, including breakfast;

three-, four- and five-bed rooms available too) with hosts who range from artists to grannies. Extras can include anything from dinner to cooking classes or tours of Paris.

Good Morning Paris

43 rue Lacépède, 5th (01.47.07.28.29/www.good morningparis.fr).
This company has 100 rooms in the city. Prices range from €69 to €109 for doubles, and €106 for an apartment that sleeps two to four people. There's a minimum stay of two nights.

APART-HOTELS & FLAT RENTAL

A deposit is usually payable on arrival. Small ads for private short-term lets run in the fortnightly anglophone mag *FUSAC* (01.56.53.54.54, www.fusac.fr); or check out www.frenchconnections.co.uk, which has a selection of furnished apartments for four or more people, and www.apartmentservice.com.

Citadines Apart'hotel

Central reservations 01.41.05.79.79/www. citadines.com. **Rates** €110-€615. **Credit** AmEx, DC, MC, V.
The 16 modern Citadines complexes across Paris tend to attract a mainly business clientele. Room sizes vary from slightly cramped studios to quite spacious two-bedroom apartments.

Paris Address

Central reservations 01.43.20.91.57/www. parisaddress.com. **Rates** €80-€400. **Credit** AmEx, DC, MC, V.
Paris Address has over 280 apartments for rent in the heart of Paris and offers a friendly reception service – a great alternative to staying in a hotel.

Paris Appartements Services

20 rue Bachaumont, 2nd (01.40.28.01.28/ www.paris-apts.com). M° Sentier. **Open** 9am-6pm Mon-Fri. *Key pick-up* 24hrs. **Rates** (min 5 nights) €100-€214. **Credit** AmEx, MC, V.
This organisation specialises in short-term rentals, offering furnished studios and one-bedroom flats in the first to fourth arrondissements.

Swell Apartments

11 rue Duhesme, 18th (+44 (0)7725 056 421/ www.swell-apartments.co.uk). M° Lamarck Caulincourt. **Rates** €113-€131 (min 3 nights). **Credit** MC, V. **Map** p401 H1
Don't be put off by the tatty entrance; this one-bedroom flat on the north side of Montmartre (sleeping two) is lovely inside. The bedroom, with duck-egg blue and white walls, has a crystal chandelier and marble fireplace. The cosy lounge has elegant furniture.

CONSUME

Restaurants

Loosen your belt – eating still tops the bill in credit-crunch Paris.

While the rest of the world tightens its purse strings as the credit crunch bites, restaurants continue to thrive in Paris. While restaurant-going has recently gone down by an estimated 25 per cent in both Britain and the United States, Parisians seem reluctant to deprive themselves of this particular pleasure. Wander through the streets of St-Germain, the Marais, Canal St-Martin or Pigalle any night of the week and you'll be hard-pressed to find a table, while the most popular restaurants continue to fill up several weeks to several months ahead.

EATING IN PARIS

The ongoing health of restaurants is good news for visitors, who will find that in most cases prices have remained stable or gone down while chefs make a greater effort to provide good value. Contributing to that is the lowering of the TVA (VAT) for restaurants from 19.6 per cent to 5.5 per cent. In return for this tax break, restaurant owners agreed to reduce their prices on at least seven of ten key menu items, such as the *plat du jour*, children's menu, dessert and coffee. If many restaurateurs seem to have conveniently forgotten this part of the bargain, others have co-operated – in this case, the old and new prices are clearly marked on the menu.

A surprising number of new restaurants are thriving in the difficult economic climate, showing that Parisians will always appreciate good food at fair prices. A notable example is **Frenchie**, a brick-walled bistro run by a young French chef who previously worked with Jamie Oliver. His limited-choice set menu, which often surprises with unexpected flavour combinations, keeps the locals coming back for two dinner sittings every night. The past year has also seen the opening of the city's first raw food restaurant, **Cru**, which has a stunning courtyard terrace. For the fashion-minded, the apartment-restaurant **Derrière** is the latest place to be seen digging into a help-yourself terrine of chocolate mousse.

Since the smoking ban came into effect, Parisians have gradually been growing more health-conscious. This shows in the popularity of cafés such as **Rose Bakery** and the new **Cantine Merci**, where a plate of crunchy salads topped with sprouts and served with carrot juice might replace the traditional *steak-frites* washed down with red wine. But the French continue to love their classic grub, which can be found in slightly updated form (think snails in puff pastry with oyster mushrooms and romaine lettuce) at the latest neo-bistros such as **Jadis** and **Le Miroir**. And wine bars have become some of the best places to eat in the city, with **Racines** (where the biodynamic vegetables come from the garden of star chef Alain Passard) and **Le Baratin** leading the way.

Except for the very simplest restaurants, it's wise to book ahead. This can usually be done on the same day as your intended visit, although really top-notch establishments require bookings weeks or even months in advance and confirmation the day before.

All listings have been checked at the time of going to press but are liable to change. Many venues close for their annual break in August, and some also close at Christmas. Restaurants are presented by area. For more restaurant reviews, refer to *Time Out Paris Eating & Drinking*, available at www.timeout.com/shop.

About the author
Rosa Jackson *writes about Paris for publications around the world, and runs a custom food itinerary service (www.edible-paris.com).*

> ❶ Blue numbers given in this chapter correspond to the location of each restaurant on the street maps. *See pp400-409.*

CONSUME

Kaï. See p189.

With our reviews, we give the average price for a standard main course chosen from the à la carte menu. If 'Main courses' is not listed, only prix fixe options are available. 'Prix fixe' indicates the price of the venue's set menu at lunch and/or dinner. All bills include a service charge, but an additional tip of a few euros (for the whole table) is polite unless you're unhappy with the service. Budget eateries are marked €.

THE ISLANDS

Brasserie de l'Ile St-Louis

*55 quai de Bourbon, 4th (01.43.54.02.59). M°
Pont Marie.* **Open** noon-midnight Mon, Tue, Thur-Sun. Closed Aug. **Main courses** €20.
Credit MC, V. **Map** p409 K7 **❶ Brasserie**
Happily, this old-fashioned brasserie soldiers on while exotic juice bars on the Ile St-Louis come and go. The terrace has one of the best summer views in Paris and is invariably packed; the dining room exudes shabby chic. Nicotined walls make for an authentic Paris mood, though nothing here is gastronomically gripping: a well-dressed *frisée aux lardons* and a more successful pan of warming tripes.

Mon Vieil Ami

*69 rue St-Louis-en-l'Ile, 4th (01.40.46.01.35/
www.mon-vieil-ami.com). M° Pont Marie.* **Open**
noon-2.30pm, 7-11.30pm Wed-Sun. Closed 3wks
Jan & 1st 3wks Aug. **Main courses** €15-€22.
Prix fixe €41. **Credit** AmEx, DC, MC, V.
Map p409 K7 **❷ Bistro**

Antoine Westermann from the Buerehiesel in Strasbourg has created a true foodie destination here. Starters such as tartare of finely diced raw vegetables with sautéed baby squid on top impress with their deft seasoning. Typical of the mains is a cast-iron casserole of roast duck with caramelised turnips and couscous. Even the classic room has been successfully refreshed with black beams, white Perspex panels and a long *table d'hôte* down one side.

THE LOUVRE & PALAIS-ROYAL

★ L'Ardoise

*28 rue du Mont-Thabor, 1st (01.42.96.28.18/
www.lardoise-paris.com). M° Concorde or
Tuileries.* **Open** noon-2.30pm, 6.30-11pm
Tue-Sat; 6.30-11pm Sun. Closed 1st 3wks Aug.
Main courses €19. **Prix fixe** €33. **Credit**
MC, V. **Map** p401 G5 **❸ Bistro**
One of the city's finest modern bistros, L'Ardoise attracts gourmets eager to sample Pierre Jay's reliably delicious cooking. A wise choice might be six oysters with warm chipolatas and a pungent shallot dressing; equally attractive are a gamey hare pie with an escalope of foie gras nestling in its centre. A lightly chilled, raspberry-scented Chinon is a perfect complement. Unusually, it's open on Sundays.

Chez La Vieille

*37 rue de l'Arbre-Sec, 1st (01.42.60.15.78).
M° Louvre Rivoli.* **Open** noon-2.30pm, 7.30-
9.45pm Mon, Tue, Thur, Fri; noon-2.30pm

Wed. Closed Aug. **Main courses** €25.
Prix fixe *Lunch* €26. **Credit** AmEx, MC, V.
Map p406 J5 **❹ Bistro**

The rustic ground floor of this bistro bursts with well-rounded regulars, whereas upstairs is plain and bright. A wondrous ad-lib selection of starters might include hot *chou farci* and home-made *terrine de foie gras*. Equally impressive is *foie de veau*, coated in a pungent reduction of shallots and vinegar and served with potato purée. Puddings follow the same cornucopian principle as the starters. Opening hours are limited and booking ahead is essential, but the lunchtime prix fixe is a bargain.

Chez Vong

10 rue de la Grande-Truanderie, 1st (01.40.26.09.36/www.chez-vong.com). Mᵒ Etienne Marcel or Les Halles. **Open** noon-2.30pm, 7-11.30pm Mon-Sat. Closed 3wks Aug. **Main courses** €20. **Prix fixe** *Lunch* €24. **Credit** AmEx, DC, MC, V. **Map** p402 J5 **❺ Chinese**

The staff at this cosy Chinese restaurant take pride in its excellent cooking. From the greeting at the door to the knowledgeable, trilingual service (Cantonese, Mandarin and French), each part of the experience is thoughtfully orchestrated. Any doubts about authenticity are extinguished with the arrival of the beautifully presented dishes. Expertly cooked spicy shrimp glistens in a smooth, characterful sauce of onions and ginger, and *ma po* tofu melts in the mouth, its spicy and peppery flavours melding with those of the fine pork mince.

Les Fines Gueules

43 rue Croix-des-Petits-Champs, 1st (01.42.61. 35.41). Mᵒ Bourse or Sentier. **Open** 2.30-4pm, 7.30-11pm daily. **Main courses** €16. **Credit** MC, V. **Map** p402 H5 **❻ Bistro/wine bar**

At first glance, Les Fines Gueules might seem like an ordinary corner café, but a closer look at the menu reveals unusual attention to ingredients at this mini wine bar/bistro. Even if you've never heard of Hugo (Desnoyer, star butcher and supplier to some of the city's finest restaurants) or Jean-Luc (Poujauran, a celebrity Paris baker), you can taste the difference when the pedigree steak tartare arrives with a salad of baby leaves dressed in truffle oil. There are just a few seats around the bar, but upstairs is a buzzy dining room that attracts a mix of smoochy couples and business suits. A good selection of 'natural' and organic wines comes by the glass and the bottle.

★ Frenchie

5 rue du Nil, 2nd (01.40.39.96.19/www.frenchie-restaurant.com). Mᵒ Sentier. **Open** 8-11pm Tue; noon-2.30pm, 8-11pm Wed-Sat. **Main courses** €16. **Prix fixe** €19-€33. **Credit** MC, V. **Map** p402 J4 **❼ Bistro**

Grégory Lemarchand honed his craft with Jamie Oliver in London before opening this loft-style bistro next to the market street rue Montorgueil. It has been an instant hit thanks to the bold flavours of dishes such as gazpacho with calamari, squash blossoms and plenty of herbs; braised lamb with roasted aubergine and spinach; and coconut tapioca with strawberry sorbet. Be sure to book several days ahead.

Le Meurice. *See p189.*

CONSUME

Located in the heart of the LatinQuarter,
the Bouillon Racine combines art nouveau charm
and exceptionally tasty food.

Open daily noon-11pm (last order)

3 rue Racine, 6th. M° Odéon.
Tel: 01.44.32.15.60
Email.bouillon.racine@wanadoo.fr
www.bouillonracine.com

Le Grand Véfour

17 rue de Beaujolais, 1st (01.42.96.56.27/www.relaischateaux.com). M° Palais Royal Musée du Louvre. **Open** 12.30-1.30pm, 8-9.30pm Mon-Thur; 12.30-1.30pm Fri. Closed 1wk Apr, Aug, 1wk Dec. **Main courses** €74. **Prix fixe** *Lunch* €88. **Credit** AmEx, DC, MC, V. **Map** p402 H5 ❽ **Haute cuisine**

Opened in 1784 (as the Café de Chartres), this is one of the oldest and most historic restaurants in Paris. An à la carte meal begins with a fantasia suite of delicacies: tiny frogs' legs, for example, arranged within a circle of sage sauce; a first course of creamed Breton sea urchins served in their spiny shells with a quail's egg and topped with caviar. Fish dishes may be a touch overcooked, and the adventurous desserts are not always successful, but you'll forgive all after a glass of vintage armagnac.

Kaï

18 rue du Louvre, 1st (01.40.15.01.99). M° Louvre Rivoli. **Open** noon-2pm, 7-10.30pm Tue-Sat; 7-10.30pm Sun. Closed 1wk Apr & 3wks Aug. **Main courses** €27. **Prix fixe** *Lunch* €38. *Dinner* €65, €110. **Credit** AmEx, MC, V. **Map** p402 H5 ❾ **Japanese**

This restaurant has developed a following among fashionable diners. The 'Kaï-style' sushi is a zesty take on a classic: marinated and lightly grilled yellowtail is pressed on to a roll of *shiso*-scented rice. Not to be outdone, the grilled aubergine with miso, seemingly simple, turns out to be a smoky, luscious experience. A generous main of breaded pork lacks the finesse and refinement of the starters, but is still satisfying. Thoroughly French desserts come courtesy of celebrity pastry chef Pierre Hermé. *Photo p186.*

★ Le Meurice

Hôtel Meurice, 228 rue de Rivoli, 1st (01.44.58.10.55/www.meuricehotel.com). M° Tuileries. **Open** 7-10.30am, 12.30-2pm, 7.30-10pm Mon-Fri; 7-11am Sat, Sun. Closed 2wks Feb & Aug. **Main courses** €100. **Prix fixe** *Breakfast €36-€65.* *Lunch* €78. *Dinner* €220. **Credit** AmEx, DC, MC, V. **Map** p401 G5 ❿ **Haute cuisine**

Yannick Alléno, chef here since 2003, has really hit his stride and is doing some glorious, if rather understated, contemporary cooking. Alléno has a light touch, teasing the flavour out of every leaf, frond, fin or fillet. Turbot is sealed in clay before cooking and then sauced with celery cream and a coulis of flat parsley. Bresse chicken stuffed with foie gras and served with truffled *sarladais* potatoes is breathtakingly good. A fine cheese tray comes from Quatrehomme; the pastry chef amazes with his millefeuille. Jacket required for men. *Photo p187.*

★ Restaurant du Palais-Royal

110 galerie Valois, 1st (01.40.20.00.27/www.restaurantdupalaisroyal.com). M° Bourse, Musée du Louvre or Palais Royal. **Open** noon-2pm,

THE BEST AL FRESCO TABLES

For terrace chic
Restaurant du Palais-Royal. *See below.*

For an eyeful of the Eiffel
Au Bon Accueil. *See p216.*

For courtyard crudivores
Cru. *See p201.*

7-10pm Mon-Sat. Closed 19 Dec-10 Jan. **Main courses** €28. **Prix fixe** €60. **Credit** AmEx, DC, MC, V. **Map** p401 H5 ⓫ **Bistro**

There can be few more magical places to dine on a summer evening than the terrace of this restaurant. Inside is memorable too: you sit in a red dining room alongside the commissars of arts and letters who work at the ministry of culture a few doors down. Risotto is a speciality and the Black, Black and Lobster is tremendous; rice simmered in rich squid ink is served al dente, topped with tender but fleshy pink lobster, sun-dried tomato and spring vegetables. Don't miss out on the *baba au rhum*.

★ Thaïm

46 rue de Richelieu, 1st (01.42.96.54.67). M° Bourse or Palais Royal. **Open** noon-3pm, 7-11.30pm Mon-Fri; 7-11pm Sat. **Main courses** €10. **Prix fixe** *Lunch* €16. *Dinner* €25-€28. **Credit** MC, V. **Map** p402 H5 ⓬ **Thai**

Steering well away from Thai clichés, Thaïm has an elegant decor of dark wood and plum fabrics, and a brief menu that changes often, keeping the regulars coming back. Particularly good value is the three-course lunch menu, which might bring crisp fried parcels filled with spiced vegetables, an aromatic green fish curry (there is a choice of fish, meat or poultry every day), and sweet coconut-pumpkin soup. There is an extensive choice of teas, including a delicious iced ginger-coconut version.

Zen

8 rue de l'Echelle, 1st (01.42.61.93.99/www.restaurant-zen.fr.cc). M° Louvre Rivoli. **Open** noon-3pm, 7-10.30pm daily. Closed Aug. **Main courses** €12. **Prix fixe** *Lunch* €10-€18. *Dinner* €20-€50. **Credit** MC, V. **Map** p401 H5 ⓭ **Japanese**

There's no shortage of Japanese restaurants in this neighbourhood, but the recently opened Zen is refreshing in a couple of ways. First, there is no pale wood in sight; the colour scheme here is sharp white, green and yellow for a cheerful effect. Second, the menu has a lot to choose from – bowls of ramen, sushi and chirashi, hearty dishes such as chicken with egg on rice or tonkatsu – yet no detail is neglected. A perfect choice if you're spending a day at the Louvre – you can be in and out in 30 minutes.

CONSUME

Decoding the Menu

From cassoulet to clafoutis.

MEALS (REPAS)
petit déjeuner breakfast. **déjeuner** lunch. **dîner** dinner. **souper** late dinner, supper.

PREPARATION (LA PREPARATION)
en croûte in a pastry case. **farci** stuffed. **au four** baked. **flambé** flamed in alcohol. **forestière** with mushrooms. **fricassé** fried and simmered in stock, usually with creamy sauce. **fumé** smoked. **garni** garnished. **glacé** frozen or iced. **gratiné** topped with breadcrumbs or cheese and grilled. **à la grècque** vegetables served cold in the cooking liquid with oil and lemon juice. **grillé** grilled. **haché** minced. **julienne** (vegetables) cut into matchsticks. **lamelle** very thin slice. **mariné** marinated. **pané** breaded. **en papillote** cooked in a packet. **parmentier** with potato. **pressé** squeezed. **râpé** grated. **salé** salted.

COOKING TYPE (LA CUISSON)
cru raw. **bleu** practically raw. **saignant** rare. **rosé** (of lamb, duck, liver, kidneys) pink. **à point** medium rare. **bien cuit** well done.

BASICS (ESSENTIELS)
ballotine stuffed, rolled-up piece of meat or fish. **crème fraîche** thick, slightly soured cream. **épices** spices. **feuilleté** 'leaves' of (puff) pastry. **fromage** cheese. **fruits de mer** shellfish. **galette** round flat cake of flaky pastry, potato pancake or buckwheat savoury crêpe. **gelée** aspic. **gibier** game. **gras** fat. **légume** vegetable. **maison** of the house. **marmite** small cooking pot. **miel** honey. **noisette** hazelnut; small, round portion of meat. **noix** walnut. **noix de coco** coconut. **nouilles** noodles. **oeuf** egg; – **en cocotte** baked egg; – **en meurette** egg poached in red wine; – **à la neige** *see île flottante*. **parfait** sweet or savoury mousse-like mixture. **paupiette** slice of meat or fish, stuffed and rolled. **timbale** dome-shaped mould, or food cooked in one. **tisane** herbal tea. **tourte** covered pie or tart, usually savoury.

MEAT (VIANDE)
agneau lamb. **aloyau** beef loin. **andouillette** sausage made from pig's offal. **bavette** beef flank steak. **biche** venison. **bifteck** steak. **boudin noir/blanc** black (blood)/white pudding. **boeuf** beef; – **bourguignon** beef cooked Burgundy style, with red wine, onions and mushrooms; – **gros sel** boiled beef with vegetables. **carbonnade** beef stew with onions and stout or beer. **carré d'agneau** rack of lamb. **cassoulet** stew of white haricot beans, sausage and preserved duck. **cervelle** brains. **châteaubriand** thick fillet steak. **chevreuil** young roe deer. **civet** game stew. **cochon de lait** suckling pig. **contre-filet** sirloin steak. **côte** chop; – **de boeuf** beef rib. **croque-madame** sandwich of toasted cheese and ham topped with an egg. **croque-monsieur** sandwich of toasted cheese and ham. **cuisses de grenouille** frogs' legs. **daube** meat braised in red wine. **entrecôte** beef rib steak. **escargot** snail. **estouffade** meat that's been marinated, fried and braised. **faux-filet** sirloin steak. **filet mignon** tenderloin. **foie** liver; – **de veau** calf's liver. **gigot d'agneau** leg of lamb. **hachis parmentier** shepherd's pie. **jambon** ham; – **cru** cured raw ham. **jarret** ham shin or knuckle. **langue** tongue. **lapin** rabbit. **lard** bacon. **lardon** small cube of bacon. **lièvre** hare. **marcassin** wild boar. **merguez** spicy lamb/beef sausage. **mignon** small meat fillet. **moelle** bone marrow; **os à la –** marrowbone. **navarin** lamb and vegetable stew. **onglet** cut of beef, similar to *bavette*. **pavé** thick steak. **petit salé** salt pork. **pied** foot (trotter). **porc** pork. **porcelet** suckling pig. **pot-au-feu** boiled beef with vegetables. **queue de boeuf** oxtail. **ragoût** meat stew. **rillettes** potted pork or tuna. **ris de veau** veal sweetbreads. **rognons** kidneys. **rôti** roast. **sang** blood. **sanglier** wild boar. **saucisse** sausage. **saucisson sec** small dried sausage. **selle** (*d'agneau*) saddle (of lamb). **souris d'agneau** lamb knuckle. **tagine** slow-cooked North African stew. **tartare** raw minced steak (also tuna or salmon). **tournedos** small slices of beef fillet, sautéed or grilled. **travers de porc** pork spare ribs. **veau** veal.

CONSUME

POULTRY (VOLAILLE)

aiguillettes (*de canard*) thin slices (of duck breast). **blanc** breast. **caille** quail. **canard** duck; **confit de** – preserved duck. **coquelet** baby rooster. **dinde** turkey. **faisan** pheasant. **foie gras** fattened goose or duck liver. **gésiers** gizzards. **magret** duck breast. **oie** goose. **perdrix** partridge. **poulet** chicken. **suprême** (*de poulet*) fillets (of chicken) in a cream sauce.

FISH & SEAFOOD (POISSONS & FRUITS DE MER)

anguille eel. **bar** sea bass. **belon** smooth, flat oyster. **bisque** shellfish soup. **bouillabaisse** Mediterranean fish soup. **brochet** pike. **bulot** whelk. **cabillaud** fresh cod. **carrelet** plaice. **colin** hake. **coquille** shell. **coquilles St-Jacques** scallops. **crevettes** prawns (UK), shrimp (US). **crustacé** shellfish. **daurade** sea bream. **eglefin** haddock. **escabèche** sautéed and marinated fish, served cold. **espadon** swordfish. **fines de claire** crinkle-shelled oysters. **flétan** halibut. **hareng** herring. **homard** lobster. **huître** oyster. **langoustine** Dublin Bay prawns, scampi. **limande** lemon sole. **lotte** monkfish. **maquereau** mackerel. **merlan** whiting. **merlu** hake. **meunière** fish floured and sautéed in butter. **moules** mussels; – **à la marinière** cooked with white wine and shallots. **morue** dried, salted cod; **brandade de** – cod puréed with potato. **oursin** sea urchin. **palourde** type of clam. **poulpe** octopus. **raie** skate. **rascasse** scorpion fish. **rouget** red mullet. **St-Pierre** John Dory. **sandre** pike-perch. **saumon** salmon. **seiche** squid. **truite** trout.

VEGETABLES (LEGUMES)

aligot mashed potatoes with melted cheese and garlic. **asperge** asparagus. **céleri** celery. **céleri rave** celeriac. **cèpe** cep mushroom. **champignon** mushroom; – **de Paris** button mushroom. **chanterelle** small, trumpet-like mushroom. **choucroute** sauerkraut; – **garnie** with cured ham and sausages. **ciboulette** chive. **citronelle**

lemongrass. **coco** large white bean. **cresson** watercress. **échalote** shallot. **endive** chicory (UK), Belgian endive (US). **épinards** spinach. **frisée** curly endive. **frites** chips (UK), fries (US). **gingembre** ginger. **girolle** small, trumpet-like mushroom. **gratin dauphinois** sliced potatoes baked with milk, cheese and garlic. **haricot** bean; – **vert** green bean. **mâche** lamb's lettuce. **morille** morel mushroom. **navet** turnip. **oignon** onion. **oseille** sorrel. **persil** parsley. **pignon** pine nut. **poivre** pepper. **poivron** red or green (bell) pepper. **pomme de terre** potato. **pommes lyonnaises** potatoes fried with onions. **riz** rice. **truffes** truffles.

FRUIT (FRUITS)

ananas pineapple. **cassis** blackcurrants; blackcurrant liqueur. **citron** lemon; – **vert** lime. **fraise** strawberry. **framboise** raspberry. **groseille** redcurrant; – **à maquereau** gooseberry. **myrtille** bilberry, blueberry. **pamplemousse** grapefruit. **pomme** apple. **prune** plum. **pruneau** prune. **quetsche** damson.

DESSERTS & CHEESE (DESSERTS & FROMAGE)

bavarois moulded cream dessert. **beignet** fritter or doughnut. **chèvre** goat; goat's cheese. **clafoutis** batter filled with fruit. **crème brûlée** creamy custard dessert with caramel glaze. **crème chantilly** sweetened whipped cream. **fromage blanc** smooth cream cheese. **glace** ice-cream. **île flottante** whipped egg white floating in vanilla custard. **réglisse** liquorice. **tarte aux pommes** apple tart. **tarte tatin** warm, caramelised apple tart cooked upside down.

SOUPS & SAUCES (SOUPES & SAUCES)

aïoli garlic mayonnaise. **anchoïade** spicy anchovy and olive paste. **béarnaise** sauce of butter and egg yolk. **blanquette** 'white' stew made with eggs and cream. **potage** soup. **velouté** stock-based white sauce; creamy soup. **vichyssoise** cold leek and potato soup.

CONSUME

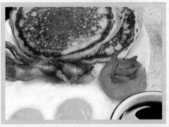

OPERA TO LES HALLES

€ Bioboa

3 rue Danielle-Casanova, 1st (01.42.61.17.67).
Mº Pyramides. **Open** 10am-6pm Mon-Sat. **Main courses** €11.50. **Prix fixe** €10-€15. **Credit** V.
Map p401 G4 ⓮ **Organic**

The fact that this place describes itself as a 'food spa' shows how it's embracing the organic ('bio' in French) revolution. There's a high-concept air about the place: white designer chairs and tables; a beautiful bird fresco that winds through it; and a mammoth fridge overflowing with expensive mineral waters, exotic smoothies and colourful takeaway salads for the fabulously busy. A healthy feast here might consist of soft-boiled eggs with sweet roasted autumn vegetables, or a juicy tofu burger with organic ketchup – one of Bioboa's staples.

★ € Bistrot Victoires

6 rue de la Vrillière, 1st (01.42.61.43.78).
Mº Bourse. **Open** noon-3pm, 7-11pm daily.
Main courses €11. **Credit** MC, V. **Map** p402 H5 ⓯ **Bistro**

Bistros with vintage decor serving no-nonsense food at generous prices are growing thin on the ground in Paris, so it's no surprise that this gem is packed to the gills with bargain-loving office workers and locals every day. The *steak-frites* are exemplary, featuring a slab of entrecôte topped with a smoking sprig of thyme, but *plats du jour* such as *blanquette de veau* (veal in cream sauce) are equally comforting. The wines by the glass can be rough, but the authentic buzz should make up for any flaws.

La Bourse ou la Vie

12 rue Vivienne, 2nd (01.42.60.08.83). Mº Bourse. **Open** noon-10pm Mon-Fri. Closed 1wk Aug & 1wk Dec. **Main courses** €10-€20. **Credit** AmEx, MC, V. **Map** p402 H4 ⓰ **Bistro**

After a career as an architect, the round-spectacled owner of La Bourse ou la Vie has a new mission in life: to revive the dying art of the perfect *steak-frites*. The only decision you'll need to make is which cut of beef to order with your chips, unless you pick the cod. Choose between ultra-tender *coeur de filet* or a huge, surprisingly tender *bavette*. Rich, creamy pepper sauce is the speciality here, but the real surprise is the chips, which gain a distinctly animal flavour from the suet in which they are cooked.

★ Chez Miki

5 rue de Louvois, 2nd (01.42.96.04.88). Mº Bourse. **Open** noon-2.30pm, 7-10.30pm Tue-Fri; 7-10.30pm Sat, Sun. **Main courses** €15. **Prix fixe** €30, €35. **Credit** MC, V. **Map** p402 H4 ⓱ **Japanese**

There are plenty of Japanese restaurants to choose from along nearby rue Ste-Anne, but none is as original – nor as friendly – as this tiny bistro run entirely by women, next to the square Louvois. The speciality here is bento boxes, which you compose yourself from a scribbled blackboard list (in Japanese and French). For €15 you can choose two small dishes – marinated sardines and fried chicken wings are especially popular – and a larger dish, such as grilled pork with ginger. Don't miss the inventive desserts, which might include lime jelly spiked with alcohol.

Drouant

18 pl Gaillon, 2nd (01.42.65.15.16/www.drouant.com). Mº Pyramides or Quatre Septembre. **Open** noon-2.30pm, 7pm-midnight daily. **Main courses** €20-€30. **Prix fixe** *Lunch* €43-€60. *Dinner* (10.30pm-midnight) €55-€60. **Credit** AmEx, DC, MC, V. **Map** p401 H4 ⓲ **Brasserie**

Star chef Antoine Westermann has whisked this landmark 1880 brasserie into the 21st century with bronze-coloured banquettes and butter-yellow fabrics. Westermann has dedicated this restaurant to the art of the hors d'oeuvre: they're served in themed sets of four ranging from the global (Thai beef salad with brightly coloured vegetables, coriander, and a sweet and spicy sauce) to the nostalgic (silky leeks in vinaigrette). The bite-sized surprises continue with the main course accompaniments – four of them for each dish – and the multiple mini-desserts.
▶ *Westermann also runs the successful Ile St-Louis bistro Mon Vieil Ami (see p186).*

Au Gourmand

17 rue Molière, 1st (01.42.96.22.19/www.augourmand.fr). Mº Palais Royal or Pyramides. **Open** 7.30-10pm Mon, Sat; 12.30-2pm, 7.30-10pm Tue-Fri. **Main courses** €26. **Prix fixe** *Lunch* €20. *Dinner* €30, €37. **Credit** MC, V. **Map** p401 H5 ⓳ **Bistro**

Ochre walls and red velvet curtains give this restaurant an almost too grown-up feel, but it's worth looking beyond that to the inventive fare coming out of the kitchen. Vegetables from celebrity market gardener Joël Thiébault star alongside meat in dishes such as juicy pork cheek wrapped in caul fat under a heap of colourful spring vegetables. Vegetarians can also find contentment here, perhaps in a thick slice of grilled aubergine topped with diced cucumber, tomato and ricotta. But a disastrous rum-spiked avocado mousse for dessert shows the chef's creativity with vegetables does have its limitations.

€ Higuma

32bis rue Ste-Anne, 1st (01.47.03.38.59). Mº Pyramides. **Open** 11.30am-10pm daily. **Main courses** €8. **Prix fixe** €10.50-€12.50. **Credit** MC, V. **Map** p401 H4 ⓴ **Japanese**

Higuma's no-nonsense food and service makes it one of the area's most popular destinations. On entering, customers are greeted by plumes of aromatic steam emanating from the open kitchen-cum-

CONSUME

bar, where a small team of chefs ladle out giant bowls of noodle soup piled with meat, vegetables or seafood. You can slurp at the counter or sit at a plastic-topped table.

★ Liza

14 rue de la Banque, 2nd (01.55.35.00.66/www. restaurant-liza.com). M° Bourse. **Open** 12.30-2pm, 8-10.30pm Mon-Thur; 12.30-2pm, 8-11pm Fri; 8-11pm Sat; noon-4pm Sun. **Main courses** €25. **Prix fixe** *Lunch* €16, €21. **Credit** AmEx, MC, V. **Map** p402 H4 ㉑ **Lebanese**

Liza Soughayar's restaurant showcases the style and superb food of contemporary Beirut. Lentil, fried onion and orange salad is delicious, as are the *kebbe* (minced seasoned raw lamb) and grilled halloumi cheese with home-made apricot preserve. Main courses such as minced lamb with coriander-spiced spinach and rice are light, flavoursome and well presented. Try one of the excellent Lebanese wines to accompany your meal, and finish with the halva ice-cream with carob molasses.

L'Office

3 rue Richer, 9th (01.47.70.67.31). M° Bonne Nouvelle. **Open** 8-10.30pm Tue, Wed, Sat; noon-2.30pm Thur, Fri. **Prix fixe** *Lunch* €12.50. *Dinner* €25. **Credit** MC, V. **Map** p402 J3 ㉒ **Bistro**

Brother-in-law to the chef-owner at Frenchie (*see p187*), Alsatian-born Nicolas Scheidt is making a name of his own in a neighbourhood not known for its bistros. Wallpaper-decorated pillars, big mirrors and hanging lights give the dining room a modern

spirit that's reflected in the food. Not everything works perfectly but there are flashes of brilliance, as in a salad of squid, cherry tomatoes and olives, or the slow-cooked guinea hen. Good to know about in this area, even if the bill is a bit steep.

Racines

8 passage des Panoramas, 2nd (01.40.13.06.41). M° Bourse or Bonne Nouvelle. **Open** noon-midnight Mon-Fri. **Main courses** €15. **Credit** MC, V. **Map** p402 J4 ㉓ **Wine bar**

The 19th-century passage des Panoramas contains an eclectic collection of shops and restaurants – among them this wildly popular wine bar opened by the former owners of La Crèmerie in St-Germain. The menu is limited to superb-quality cheese and charcuterie plates, plus a couple of hot dishes, perhaps pork cheeks stewed in red wine or braised lamb, and a few comforting desserts. Many of the intense-tasting wines are biodynamic, and despite the rather hectic atmosphere lingering over an extra glass or two is cheerfully tolerated.

★ La Tour de Montlhéry (Chez Denise)

5 rue des Prouvaires, 1st (01.42.36.21.82). M° Les Halles/RER Châtelet Les Halles. **Open** noon-3pm, 7.30pm-5am Mon-Fri. Closed 15 July-15 Aug. **Main courses** €24. **Credit** MC, V. **Map** p402 J5 ㉔ **Bistro**

At the stroke of midnight, this place is packed, jovial and hungry. Savoury traditional dishes, washed down by litres of the house Brouilly, are

Granterroirs.

the order of the day. Les Halles was the city's wholesale food market, and game, beef and offal still rule here. Diners devour towering rib steaks served with marrow and a heaped platter of chips, among the best in town. Brave souls can also try *tripes au calvados*, grilled *andouillette*, or perhaps go for a stewed venison, served with celery root and home-made jam.

CHAMPS-ELYSEES & WESTERN PARIS

Alain Ducasse au Plaza Athénée
Hôtel Plaza Athénée, 25 av Montaigne, 8th (01.53.67.65.00/www.alain-ducasse.com). M° Alma Marceau. **Open** 7.45-10.15pm Mon-Wed; 12.45-2.15pm, 7.45-10.15pm Thur, Fri. Closed mid July-mid Aug & 2wks Dec. **Main courses** €80-€135. **Prix fixe** €260-€360. **Credit** AmEx, DC, MC, V. **Map** p400 D5 **㉕ Haute cuisine**
The sheer glamour factor would be enough to recommend this restaurant, Alain Ducasse's most lofty Paris undertaking. The dining room ceiling drips with 10,000 crystals. An *amuse-bouche* of a single langoustine in a lemon cream with a touch of Iranian caviar starts the meal off beautifully, but other dishes can be inconsistent: a part-raw/part-cooked salad of autumn fruit and veg in a red, Chinese-style sweet-and-sour dressing, or Breton lobster in an overwhelming sauce of apple, quince and spiced wine. Cheese is predictably delicious, as is the *rum baba comme à Monte-Carlo*.

Astrance
4 rue Beethoven, 16th (01.40.50.84.40). M° Passy. **Open** 12.15-1.30pm, 8-9.30pm Tue-Fri. Closed 1wk Feb, 4wks Aug, 1wk Oct & 1wk Dec. **Prix fixe** *Lunch* €70. *Dinner* €190. **Credit** AmEx, DC, MC, V. **Map** p404 B6 **㉖ Haute cuisine**
When Pascal Barbot opened Astrance, he was praised for creating a new style of Paris restaurant – refined, yet casual and affordable. A few years later, this small, slate-grey dining room feels just like an haute cuisine restaurant. Most customers, having reserved at least a month ahead, give free rein to the chef with the 'Menu Astrance'. Barbot has an original touch, combining foie gras with slices of white mushrooms and a lemon condiment, or sweet lobster with candied grapefruit peel, a grapefruit and rosemary sorbet, and raw baby spinach. Wines by the glass are reasonably priced.

Le Bistrot Napolitain
18 av Franklin D. Roosevelt, 8th (01.45.62.08.37). M° St-Philippe-du-Roule. **Open** noon-2.30pm, 7.15-10.30pm Mon-Fri. Closed 1wk July, Aug & 1wk Dec. **Main courses** €25. **Credit** MC, V. **Map** p401 E4 **㉗ Italian**
This chic Italian bistro is as far from a tourist joint as it is possible to be. On weekday lunchtimes it is full of suave Italianate businessmen. Generosity defines the food – not just big plates, but lashings of the ingredients that others skimp on, such as the slices of tangy parmesan piled high over rocket on the tender beef carpaccio. The pizzas are very good: the Enzo comes with milky, almost raw *mozzarella di bufala* and tasty tomatoes. For pasta you can choose between dried and fresh, with variations such as fresh saffron tagliatelle.

★ Granterroirs
30 rue de Miromesnil, 8th (01.47.42.18.18/ www.granterroirs.com). M° Miromesnil. **Open** 9am-8pm Mon-Fri. *Food served* noon-3pm Mon-Fri. Closed 3wks Aug. **Main courses** €21. **Prix fixe** €39, €49. **Credit** MC, V. **Map** p401 F3 **㉓ Bistro**
This *épicerie* with a difference is the perfect remedy for anyone for whom the word '*terroir*' conjures up visions of grease-soaked peasant food. Here, the walls heave with more than 600 enticing specialities from southern France, including Périgord foie gras, charcuterie from Aubrac and a fine selection of wines. Great gift ideas – but why not sample some of the goodies by enjoying the midday *table d'hôte* feast? Come in early to ensure that you can choose from the five succulent *plats du jour* (such as marinated salmon with dill on a bed of warm potatoes).

€ Le Hide
10 rue du Général-Lanrezac, 17th (01.45.74.15.81/www.lehide.fr). M° Charles de Gaulle Etoile. **Open** noon-3pm, 7.30-10.30pm Mon-Fri; 7.30-10.30pm Sat. **Main courses** €16. **Prix fixe** €22, €29. **Credit** MC, V. **Map** p400 C3 **㉓ Bistro**
Ever since it opened, this snug bistro has been packed with a happy crowd of bistro-lovers who appreciate Japanese-born chef Hide Kobayashi's superb cooking and good-value prices. Expect dishes such as duck foie gras terrine with pear-and-thyme compôte to start, followed by tender *faux-filet* steak in a light foie gras sauce or skate wing with a lemon-accented *beurre noisette*. Desserts are excellent: perfect tarte tatin comes with crème fraîche from Normandy. Good, affordable wines explain the merriment, including a glass of the day for €2.

Maxan
37 rue de Miromesnil, 8th (01.42.65.78.60/ www.rest-maxan.com). M° Miromesnil. **Open** noon-2.30pm Mon; noon-2.30pm, 7.30-10.30pm Tue-Fri; 7.30-10.30pm Sat. Closed Aug. **Prix fixe** €30, €40. **Credit** MC, V. **Map** p401 F3 **㉚ Bistro**
This is a welcome new-wave bistro in an area where eating options tend to be fashion haunts, grand tables or tourist traps. Owner-chef Laurent Zajac uses quality seasonal ingredients, giving them a personal spin in dishes such as scallops with curry spices and artichoke hearts, classic veal sweetbreads

CONSUME

with wild asparagus, and an exotic take on *île flot-tante*. Popular with ministry of interior types at lunch, quieter by night.

Pierre Gagnaire

6 rue Balzac, 8th (01.58.36.12.50/www.pierre-gagnaire.com). M° Charles de Gaulle Etoile or George V. **Open** noon-1.30pm, 7.30-9.30pm Mon-Fri, Sun. Closed 1wk Apr & Aug. **Main courses** €105. **Prix fixe** *Lunch* €95, €245. *Dinner* €245. **Credit** AmEx, MC, V. **Map** p400 D3 ⓛ **Haute cuisine**

At Pierre Gagnaire most starters alone cost over €90, which seems to be the price of culinary experimentation. The €90 lunch menu is far from the experience of the *carte*: the former is presented in three courses, whereas the latter involves four or five plates for each course. Even the *amuse-bouches* fill the table: an egg 'raviole', ricotta with apple, fish in a cauliflower jelly, and glazed monkfish. The best thing about the lunch menu is that it includes four very indulgent desserts: clementine, raspberry and vanilla, chocolate, and passion fruit.

Rech

62 av des Ternes, 17th (01.45.72.29.47/www.rech.fr). M° Ternes. **Open** noon-2pm, 6.30-10pm Yue-Sat. Closed 3wks Aug. **Main courses** €28. **Prix fixe** *Lunch* €30. *Dinner* €53. **Credit** AmEx, MC, V. **Map** p400 C2 ⓛ **Bistro**

Alain Ducasse's personal touches are everywhere in this art deco seafood restaurant, which he took over in spring 2007, from the Japanese fish prints on the walls of the upstairs dining room to the blown glass candleholders on the main floor tables. The kitchen turns out the kind of precise, Mediterranean-inspired cooking you would expect from Ducasse: glistening sardine fillets marinated with preserved lemon, silky lobster ravioli and octopus carpaccio painted with pesto. As the fish dishes are light, you can justify indulging in a perfectly aged camembert and the XL éclair, an event in itself.

★ Restaurant L'Entredgeu

83 rue Laugier, 17th (01.40.54.97.24). M° Porte de Champerret. **Open** noon-2pm, 7.30-11pm Tue-Sat. Closed 1wk Apr, 1st 3wks Aug & 1wk Dec. **Prix fixe** *Lunch* €22, €30. *Dinner* €30. **Credit** DC, MC, V. **Map** p400 C2 ⓛ **Bistro**

Reading the menu here will make you seriously doubt your capacity for pudding. But have no fear. The heartiness of the dishes belies refined, perfectly gauged cooking, served in civilised portions. The table turnover is fast, but this is not a place to linger smoochily in any case – you'll be too busy marvelling at the sharp *gribiche* sauce cutting through the milky crisp-battered oysters, the depth and aroma of the saffron-infused fish soup, the perfect layered execution of the caramelised pork belly, and the delicate desserts. The wine list is creative and assured.

Senderens

9 pl de la Madeleine, 8th (01.42.65.22.90/www.senderens.fr). M° Madeleine. **Open** noon-3pm, 7.30-11.30pm daily. Closed 3wks Aug. **Main courses** €39. **Prix fixe** €110-€150 (with wine). **Credit** AmEx, DC, MC, V. **Map** p401 G4 ⓛ **Haute cuisine**

Alain Senderens reinvented his art nouveau institution (formerly Lucas Carton) a few years ago with a *Star Trek* interior and a mind-boggling fusion menu. Now, you might find dishes such as roast duck foie gras with a warm salad of black figs and liquorice powder, or monkfish steak with Spanish mussels and green curry sauce. Each dish comes with a suggested wine, whisky, sherry or punch (to match a rum-doused *savarin* with slivers of ten-flavour pear), and although these are perfectly chosen, the mix of flavours and alcohols can prove overwhelming at times.

★ Stella Maris

4 rue Arsène-Houssaye, 8th (01.42.89.16.22). M° Charles de Gaulle Etoile. **Open** noon-2.30pm, 7.30-10.30pm Mon-Fri; 7.30-10.30pm Sat. Closed 2wks Aug. **Main courses** €50. **Prix fixe** *Lunch* €49, €65. *Dinner* €70, €99, €130. **Credit** AmEx, DC, MC, V. **Map** p400 D3 ⓛ **Haute cuisine**

Tateru Yoshino has divided his life between Paris and Tokyo for many years. Trained by Robuchon and Troisgros, he turns out food that is resolutely French. The service is at times faltering, but charmingly so, and the space is beautiful. You might float your way through foie gras with carrots, truffles and pistachio oil, pan-fried sea bass with saffron risotto, and a perfectly lopsided Grand Marnier soufflé. The exquisite, powdery blandness of the tasting menu going-home present, *cake aux marrons glacés*, brings it all softly, dreamily, back next morning at breakfast. Expensive but wonderful.

La Table Lauriston

129 rue de Lauriston, 16th (01.47.27.00.07/www.restaurantlatablelauriston.com). M° Trocadéro. **Open** noon-2.30pm, 7-10.30pm Mon-Fri; 7-10.30pm Sat. Closed 3wks Aug & 1wk Dec. **Main courses** €23. **Prix fixe** *Lunch* €25. *Dinner* €40, €61. **Credit** AmEx, MC, V. **Map** p400 B5 ⓛ **Bistro**

Serge Barbey's dining room has a refreshingly feminine touch. The emphasis here is firmly on good-quality ingredients, skilfully prepared to show off their freshness. In spring, stalks of asparagus from the Landes are expertly trimmed to avoid any trace of stringiness and served with the simplest *vinaigrette d'herbes*. More extravagant is the *foie gras cuit au torchon*, in which the duck liver is wrapped in a cloth and poached in a bouillon. Skip the crème brûlée, which you could have anywhere, and order a dessert with attitude instead: the giant *baba au rhum*.

CONSUME

Taillevent

15 rue Lamennais, 8th (01.44.95.15.01/www.
taillevent.com). Mº George V. **Open** 12.15-
1.30pm, 7.15-9.30pm Mon-Fri. Closed Aug. **Main**
courses €75. **Prix fixe** *Lunch* €80, €140, €190.
Dinner €140, €190. **Credit** AmEx, DC, MC, V.
Map p400 D3 ❸ **Haute cuisine**

Prices here are not as shocking as in some restaurants at this level; there's a €80 lunch menu.
Rémoulade de coquilles St-Jacques is a technical feat,
with slices of raw, marinated scallop wrapped in a
tube shape around a finely diced apple filling, encir-
cled by a mayonnaise-like *rémoulade* sauce. An
earthier and lip-smacking dish is the trademark
épeautre – an ancient wheat – cooked 'like a risotto'
with bone marrow, black truffle, whipped cream and
parmesan, and topped with sautéed frog's legs.
Ravioli au chocolat araguani is a surprising and
wonderful dessert.

MONTMARTRE & PIGALLE

Le Ch'ti Catalan

4 rue de Navarin, 9th (01.44.63.04.33). Mº
Notre-Dame-de-Lorette. **Open** noon-3pm, 7.30-
11pm Mon-Fri; 7.30-11pm Sat. **Main courses**
€15. **Credit** MC, V. **Map** p402 H2 ❸ **Bistro**

It's unconventional, to say the least, to pair ingredients such as endives, bacon and eel, commonly
found in the north of France, with the sunny flavours
of French Catalan cooking. But that's what two

friends have done in this ochre-painted bistro. The
amazing thing is, it works. *Anchoïade* – red peppers
with tangy anchovies – is fresh and tasty; tender
pork cheeks served in a casserole with melting white
beans are succulent; and the *gueule noire* (black face)
– crushed spice biscuits with crème fraîche and egg
– refers to the slang for miners in northern France.

Le Miroir

94 rue des Martyrs, 18th (01.46.06.50.73).
Mº Abbesses. **Open** noon-3pm, 7-11pm Tue-
Sat; noon-3pm Sun. **Main courses** €15.
Prix fixe *Lunch* €18. **Credit** MC, V.
Map p402 H2 ❸ **Bistro**

This friendly modern bistro is a welcome addition
to a neighbourhood where good-value restaurants
are scarce. Big mirrors, red banquettes and a glass
ceiling at the back give it character, while the very
professional food and service reflect the owners'
haute cuisine training. Expect dishes such as a salad
of whelks with white beans, crisp-skinned duck and
chanterelle mushrooms, and a *petit pot de crème*
vanille with little chocolate cakes.

Le Moulin de la Galette

83 rue Lepic, 18th (01.46.06.84.77/www.
lemoulindelagalette.eu). Mº Notre-Dame-de-
Lorette. **Open** noon-2.45pm, 7.30-11pm Tue-Fri.
Closed Aug. **Main courses** €25. **Prix fixe**
Lunch €17, €25. *Dinner* €50. **Credit** AmEx, MC,
V. **Map** p402 H1 ❹ **Bistro**

Le Ch'tl Catalan.

The Butte Montmartre was once dotted with windmills, and this survivor houses a chic modern restaurant with a few tables in the cobbled courtyard. It's hard to imagine a more picturesque setting in Montmartre, but the kitchen makes an effort nonetheless, coming up with dishes such as foie gras with melting beetroot cooked in lemon balm and juniper or suckling pig alongside potato purée. Desserts, such as figs caramelised with muscovado sugar, look like a painter's tableau. If you're on a budget, stick to the set menus and order carefully from the wine list.

★ € Pétrelle

34 rue Pétrelle, 9th (01.42.82.11.02/www. petrelle.fr). M° Anvers. **Open** 8-10pm Tue-Sat. Closed 4wks July/Aug & 1wk Dec. **Main courses** €25. **Prix fixe** €29. **Credit** MC, V. **Map** p402 J2 ㊶ **Bistro**

Jean-Luc André is as inspired a decorator as he is a cook, and the quirky charm of his dining room has made it popular with fashion designers and film stars. But behind the style there's some serious substance. André seeks out the best ingredients from local producers, and the quality shines through. The €29 no-choice menu is very good value for money (marinated sardines with tomato relish, rosemary-scented rabbit with roasted vegetables, deep purple poached figs) – or you can splash out with luxurious à la carte dishes such as tournedos Rossini.

€ Rose Bakery

46 rue des Martyrs, 9th (01.42.82.12.80). M° Notre-Dame-de-Lorette. **Open** 9am-7pm Tue-Fri; 10am-5pm Sat, Sun. Closed 2wks Aug & 1wk Dec. **Main courses** €14. **Credit** AmEx, MC, V. **Map** p402 H2 ㊷ **British**

This English-themed café run by a Franco-British couple stands out for the quality of its ingredients – organic or from small producers – as well as the too-good-to-be-true puddings: carrot cake, sticky toffee pudding and, in winter, a chocolate-chestnut tart. The DIY salad plate is crunchily satisfying, but the thin-crusted *pizzettes*, daily soups and occasional risottos are equally good choices. Don't expect much beyond scones in the morning except at weekends, when brunch is served to a packed-out house. The dining room is minimalist but welcoming.

BEAUBOURG & THE MARAIS

★ L'Ambassade d'Auvergne

22 rue du Grenier-St-Lazare, 3rd (01.42.72.31.22/ www.ambassade-auvergne.com). M° Arts et Métiers. **Open** noon-2pm, 7.30-10pm daily. **Main courses** €18. **Prix fixe** €30, €40, €55, €65. **Credit** AmEx, MC, V. **Map** p409 K5 ㊸ **Bistro**

This rustic-style *auberge* is a fitting embassy for the hearty fare of central France. An order of cured ham comes as two hefty, plate-filling slices, and the salad bowl is chock-full of green lentils cooked in

Marché. See p203.

goose fat, studded with bacon and shallots. The *rôti d'agneau* arrives as a pot of melting chunks of lamb in a rich, meaty sauce with a helping of tender white beans. Dishes arrive with the flagship *aligot*, the creamy, elastic mash-and-cheese concoction. Among the regional wines (Chanturgue, Boudes, Madargues), the fruity AOC Marcillac makes a worthy partner.

€ Breizh Café
109 rue Vieille-du-Temple, 3rd (01.42.72.13.77/ www.breizhcafe.com). Mº Filles du Calvaire. **Open** noon-11pm Wed-Sun. Closed 3wks Aug. **Main courses** €10. **Credit** MC, V. **Map** p409 L5 **Crêperie**
With its modern interior of pale wood and its choice of 15 artisanal ciders, this outpost of a restaurant in Cancale, Brittany, is a world away from the average crêperie experience, you might start with a plate of creuse oysters from Cancale before indulging in an inventive buckwheat *galette* such as the Cancalaise, made with potato, smoked herring from Brittany and herring roe. The choice of fillings is fairly limited, but the ingredients are of high quality – including the use of Valrhona chocolate with 70% cocoa solids in the dessert crêpes.

★ € Cantine Merci
111 bd Beaumarchais, 3rd (01.42.77.78.92). Mº St-Sébastien Froissart. **Open** noon-3pm Mon-Sat. **Main courses** €8-€18. **Credit** MC, V. **Map** p409 L5 **Café**
The new fairtrade concept store Merci is all about feeling virtuous even as you indulge, and its basement canteen is a perfect example. Fresh and colourful salads, soup and risotto of the day, an organic salmon plate, and the *assiette merci*

(perhaps chicken kefta with two salads) make up the brief, Rose Bakery-esque menu, complete with invigorating teas and juices. Rustic desserts add just the right handmade touch.

★ € Chez Hanna
54 rue des Rosiers, 4th (01.42.74.74.99). Mº St-Paul. **Open** noon-midnight daily. **Main courses** €10. **Credit** MC, V. **Map** p409 K6 **Jewish**
By noon on a Sunday there is a queue outside every falafel shop along rue des Rosiers. The long-established L'As du Fallafel, a little further up the street, still reigns supreme, whereas Hanna remains something of a locals' secret, quietly serving up falafel and shawarma sandwiches to rival any in the world. A pitta sandwich bursting with crunchy chickpea-and-herb balls, tahini sauce and vegetables costs €4 if you order from the takeaway window, €8 if you sit at one of the tables in the buzzy dining room overlooking the street. Either way, you really can't lose.

Chez Julien
1 rue du Pont Louis-Philippe, 4th (01.42.78.31.64). Mº Pont Marie. **Open** noon-3pm, 7-11pm Mon-Sat. **Main courses** €25. **Credit** MC, V. **Map** p409 K6 **Bistro**
Thierry Costes discreetly took over this vintage bistro overlooking the Seine in spring 2007. The zebra banquette near the loo upstairs is most reminiscent of the Costes style, but the 1920s dining room is also unmistakably chic with plum walls, a big chandelier and red banquettes, and the terrace outside now stretches across the cobbled pedestrian street. The food is predictable and pricey – crab salad, steak with shoestring fries, roast Bresse chicken with mini-potatoes – but it's hard not to enjoy this slice of Paris life.

CONSUME

★ € Chez Omar

47 rue de Bretagne, 3rd (01.42.72.36.26). Mº Arts et Métiers or Temple. **Open** noon-2.30pm, 7-10.30pm Mon-Sat; 7-10.30pm Sun. **Main courses** €16. **No credit cards. Map** p409 L5 ㊽ North African

The once-fashionable Omar doesn't take reservations, and the queue can stretch the length of the zinc bar and through the door. Everyone is waiting for the same thing: couscous. Prices range from €11 (vegetarian) to €24 (*royale*); there are no tagines or other traditional Maghreb mains, only a handful of French classics (duck, fish, steak). Overstretched waiters slip through the crowds with mounds of semolina, vats of vegetable-laden broth and steel platters heaving with meat, including the stellar *merguez*. Even on packed nights, there's an offer of seconds – gratis – to encourage you to stay a little while longer.

Other locations Café Moderne, 19 rue Keller, 11th (01.47.00.53.62).

Cru

7 rue Charlemagne, 4th (01.40.27.81.84/www.restaurantcru.fr). Mº St-Paul. **Open** noon-3pm, 6.30pm-midnight Tue-Sun. **Main courses** €14-€27. **Prix fixe** *Lunch* €19. **Credit** MC, V. **Map** p406 L7 ㊾ Bistro

Opening a raw-food restaurant is a gamble, so the owners of Cru cheat here and there, offering root vegetable 'chips' and a few *plancha* dishes. Still, the extensive menu has plenty for the crudivore, such as some unusual carpaccios (the veal with preserved lemon is particularly good) and intriguing 'red' and 'green' plates, variations on the tomato and cucumber. The food is perfectly good, but the real reason to come here is the gorgeous courtyard terrace lurking behind this quiet Marais street.

★ Derrière

69 rue des Gravilliers, 3rd (01.44.61.91.95). Mº Arts et Métiers. **Open** noon-3pm, 7.30-11pm Tue-Fri; 7.30-11pm Sat. **Main courses** €15-€20. **Prix fixe** *Lunch* €25. **Credit** MC, V. **Map** p406 K5 ㊿ Bistro

Mourad Mazouz, the man behind Momo and Sketch in London, has hit on another winning formula with this apartment-restaurant in the same street as his North African restaurant 404 and bar Andy Wahloo. The cluttered-chic look by decorator Bambi Sloan mixes contemporary fixtures and antique furniture, such as the beat-up armchairs in the smoking room hidden behind a wardrobe door upstairs. It attracts a young, hip crowd that appreciates the high-calorie comfort food: roast chicken with buttery mashed potatoes, macaroni gratin with taramasalata, and chocolate mousse.

Le Gaigne

12 rue Pecquay, 4th (01.44.59.86.72/www.restaurantlegaigne.fr). Mº Rambuteau. **Open** 12.15-2.30pm, 7.30-10.30pm Tue-Thur; 12.15-2.30pm, 7.30-11pm Fri, Sat. **Main courses** €24. **Prix fixe** *Lunch* €16, €22. *Dinner* €39, €54. **Credit** AmEx, MC, V. **Map** p409 K6 (51) Bistro

It's a familiar story: young chef with haute cuisine credentials opens a small bistro in an out-of-the-way street. Here, the restaurant is even tinier than usual

CONSUME

Le Bistro Paul Bert. *See p204.*

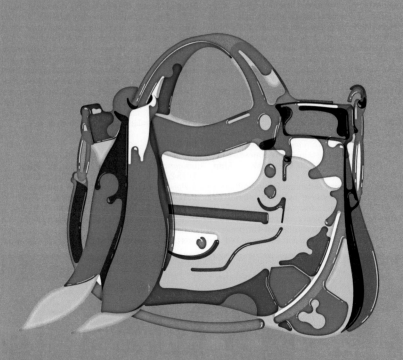

Ask New York City about New York City fabulous

nycgo.com

with only 20 seats and the cooking is unusually inventive. Chef Mickaël Gaignon has worked with Pierre Gagnaire, and it shows in dishes such as *l'oeuf bio* – three open eggshells filled with creamed spinach, carrot and celeriac – or roast monkfish with broccoli purée and a redcurrant emulsion. The dining room is pleasantly modern and staff are eager to please.

Le Hangar
12 impasse Berthaud, 3rd (01.42.74.55.44).
M° Rambuteau. **Open** noon-2.30pm, 7.30-11pm Tue-Sat. Closed Aug. **Main courses** €17.
No credit cards. Map p409 K5 **52 Bistro**
It's worth making the effort to find this bistro by the Centre Pompidou, with its terrace tucked away in a hidden alley and excellent cooking. A bowl of tapenade and toast is supplied to keep you going while choosing from the comprehensive *carte*. It yields, for starters, tasty and grease-free *rillettes de lapereau* (rabbit) alongside perfectly balanced pumpkin and chestnut soup. Main courses include pan-fried foie gras on a smooth potato purée made with olive oil.

Le Petit Marché
9 rue de Béarn, 3rd (01.42.72.06.67). M° Chemin Vert. **Open** noon-3pm, 7.30pm-midnight Mon-Fri; noon-4pm Sat, Sun. **Main courses** €17.
Prix fixe *Lunch* €20.50. **Credit** AmEx, MC, V.
Map 409 L6 **53 Bistro**
Petit Marché's menu is short and modern with Asian touches. Raw tuna is flash-fried in sesame seeds and served with a Thai sauce, making for a refreshing starter; crispy-coated deep-fried king prawns have a similar oriental lightness. The main vegetarian risotto is rich in basil, coriander, cream and al dente green beans. Pan-fried scallops with lime are precision-cooked and accompanied by a good purée and more beans. There's a short wine list. *Photo p200.*

BASTILLE & EASTERN PARIS

★ € A la Biche au Bois
45 av Ledru-Rollin, 12th (01.43.43.34.38).
M° Gare de Lyon. **Open** 7-11pm Mon; noon-2pm, 7-11pm Tue-Fri. Closed 4wks July-Aug & Christmas wk. **Main courses** €15.
Prix fixe €25. **Credit** AmEx, DC, MC, V.
Map p407 M8 **54 Bistro**
However crowded it gets here, it doesn't matter because everyone always seems so happy with the food and the convivial atmosphere. It's impossible not to be enthusiastic about the more than generous portions offered with the €24.90 prix fixe menu. Mains might include tasty portions of wild duck in blackcurrant sauce, partridge with cabbage or wild venison stew. If you can still do dessert, go for one of the home-made tarts laden with seasonal fruits. The wine list has a reputation as one of the best-value selections in town. Book in advance, but expect to wait anyway.

Bofinger. *See p204.*

Le Train Bleu.

★ Le Bistrot Paul Bert

18 rue Paul-Bert, 11th (01.43.72.24.01).
Mº Charonne or Faidherbe Chaligny. **Open**
noon-2pm, 7.30-11pm Tue-Thur; noon-2pm,
7.30-11.30pm Fri, Sat. Closed Aug. **Main
courses** €21. **Prix fixe** *Lunch* €16. *Dinner*
€34. **Credit** MC, V. **Map** p407 N7 ⑤⑤ Bistro
This heart-warming bistro gets it right almost down
to the last crumb. A starter salad of *ris de veau* illustrates the point, with lightly browned veal sweetbreads perched on a bed of green beans and baby
carrots with a sauce of sherry vinegar and deglazed
cooking juices. A roast shoulder of suckling pig and
a thick steak with a raft of golden, thick-cut *frites*
look inviting indeed. Desserts are superb too, including what may well be the best *île flottante* in Paris.
If you're in the area at lunchtime, bear in mind that
the prix fixe menu is remarkable value. *Photo p201.*

Bofinger

5-7 rue de la Bastille, 4th (01.42.72.87.82/
www.bofingerparis.com). Mº Bastille. **Open**
noon-3pm, 6.30pm-1am daily. **Main courses**
€22. **Prix fixe** €27. **Credit** AmEx, DC, MC, V.
Map p409 L7 ⑤⑥ Brasserie
Bofinger draws big crowds for its authentic art
nouveau setting and its brasserie atmosphere.
Downstairs is the prettiest place in which to eat, but
the upstairs room is air-conditioned. An à la carte
selection might start with plump, garlicky escargots
or a well-made langoustine terrine, followed by an
intensely seasoned salmon tartare, a generous (if
unremarkable) cod steak, or calf's liver accompanied

by cooked melon. Alternatively, you could have the
foolproof brasserie meal of oysters and fillet steak,
followed by a pungent plate of munster cheese and
bowl of cumin, washed down by the fine Gigondas
at €35.50 a bottle. *Photo p203.*

€ L'Encrier

55 rue Traversière, 12th (01.44.68.08.16).
Mº Gare de Lyon or Ledru-Rollin. **Open** noon-
2.15pm, 7.30-11pm Mon-Fri; 7.30-11pm Sat.
Closed Aug & Christmas wk. **Main courses**
€14. **Prix fixe** *Lunch* €14. *Dinner* €19, €23.
Credit MC, V. **Map** p407 M7 ⑤⑦ Bistro
Through the door and past the velvet curtain, you
find yourself face to face with the kitchen – and a
crowd of locals, many of whom seem to know the
charming boss personally. Start with fried rabbit
kidneys on a bed of salad dressed with raspberry
vinegar, perhaps, an original and wholly successful combination, and follow with goose *magret* with
honey – a welcome change from the usual duck
version and served with crunchy, thinly sliced
sautéed potatoes. To end, share a chocolate cake,
or try the popular profiteroles. The fruity Chinon
is a classy red.

La Gazzetta

29 rue de Cotte, 12th (01.43.47.47.05/www.
lagazzetta.fr). Mº Ledru-Rollin. **Open** noon-
2.30pm, 8-11pm Tue-Sat. Closed Aug. **Main
courses** €25. **Prix fixe** *Lunch* €16, €20.
Dinner €38, €50. **Credit** AmEx, DC, MC, V.
Map p407 N7 ⑤⑧ Bistro

Opened by the team behind bar Le Fumoir, La Gazzetta has a similarly moody feel, with dim lighting, a long zinc bar and retro decor. Chef Petter Nilssen is Swedish, but made his name in the south of France, and his food shows a Scandinavian influence in dishes such as bonito in a sweet-salty marinade with caraway, borage leaves, radish and pomelo, or new potatoes from the island of Noirmoutier off the Atlantic coast with seaweed butter and dill. The €38 menu is a good bet, with five courses and not too many decisions to make.

★ Le Souk

1 rue Keller, 11th (01.49.29.05.08). M° Bastille or Ledru-Rollin. **Open** 7.30-11.30pm Tue-Fri; 11.30am-2.30pm, 7.30pm-12.30am Sat; 11.30am-2.30pm, 7.30pm-11.30am Sun. **Main courses** €18. **Prix fixe** €27. **Credit** DC, MC, V. **Map** p407 N7 ⑳ **North African**

Potted olive trees mark the entrance to this lively den of Moroccan cuisine. Start with savoury *b'stilla*, a pasty stuffed with duck, raisins and nuts, flavoured with orange-blossom water and sprinkled with cinnamon and powdered sugar. Don't fill up, though, as the first-rate tagines and couscous are enormous. The *tagine canette* (duckling stewed with honey, onions, apricots, figs and cinnamon, then showered with toasted almonds) is terrific. For dessert, try the excellent millefeuille with fresh figs, while sweet mint tea is poured in a long stream by a *djellaba*-clad waiter.

La Table de Claire

30 rue Emile-Lepeu, 11th (01.43.70.59.84). M° Charonne. **Open** noon-2pm, 8-10.30pm Wed-Sat. **Main courses** €10. **Prix fixe** *Lunch* €13, €16. *Dinner* €31. **Credit** MC, V. **Map** p407 P6 ㊿ **Bistro**

With black-and-white tiled floors, a Formica bar and modern light fixtures and paintings, La Table de Claire has the look of a vintage bistro but the atmosphere of a living room, animated by the genial, curly-haired Serge. Claire's food is equally homely, though with a sophisticated touch: think foie gras with baby potatoes and pearl onion jam. The monthly *chef d'un soir* nights, when the owners' talented friends prepare their own recipes, have become a popular event.

Le Train Bleu

Gare de Lyon, pl Louis-Armand, 12th (01.43.43.09.06/www.le-train-bleu.com). M° Gare de Lyon. **Open** 11.30am-3pm, 7-11pm daily. **Main courses** €30. **Prix fixe** *Lunch* €49. *Dinner* €62, €96. **Credit** AmEx, DC, MC, V. **Map** p407 M8 ㊱ **Brasserie**

This listed dining room – with vintage frescoes and big oak benches – exudes a pleasant air of expectation. Don't expect cutting-edge cooking, but rather fine renderings of French classics. Lobster served on walnut oil-dressed salad leaves is a generous, beautifully prepared starter, as is the pistachio-studded *saucisson de Lyon* with a warm salad of small

Flipping Tasty

Head to Montparnasse for pancake heaven.

If you picture the crêpe as the soggy letdown of French cuisine, then a trip down rue Montparnasse and rue Odessa on a weekend night could change your mind. According to the organisation Paris Breton there are some 300,000 Bretons living in Paris, and Montparnasse, close to the railway station that brought them here, is their *quartier*, with queues down the street for the 15 or so crêperies.

In its finest manifestation, the buckwheat pancake, or *galette de sarrasin*, is a crisp, melt-in-the-mouth envelope for an imaginative selection of fillings that go far beyond the egg and ham staple. At the **Crêperie du Manoir Breton** (*see p214*), the Périgord is filled with *magret de canard*, creamed prunes and caramelised pear; the Landaise is smartly presented with a round of foie gras and caramelised pear on top; and the Roquefort is laden with the Ardèchois blue cheese, crème fraîche and walnuts. At the **Crêperie du Pont-Aven**

(*see p214*), with its attractive red interior dating back to 1920, the Gwazenn comes with scallops, mushrooms and cream; and the Pont-Aven is filled with salmon, leeks and cream; there are even several eel variations if you're feeling adventurous.

But the star crêperie of the area, and the one with the longest queues, is the prettily decorated **Josselin** (*see p214*), where the speciality is the Couple – two layers of galette with the filling in the middle. The savoury galette is followed by the dessert Crêpe de Froment, which comes in three varieties: classic (honey and lemon or wonderful caramel beurre salé); flambéed with calvados; or a fantasy creation oozing with chocolate, banana, ice cream and whipped cream. Wash it all down with bowls of cider, of which the brut is far better than the sweet. You'll be surprised how full you feel at the end and the bill should come to no more than €20 a head, a buckwheat bargain by Paris standards.

CONSUME

ratte potatoes. Mains of veal chop topped with a cap of cheese, and *sandre* (pike-perch) with a 'risotto' of *crozettes* are also pleasant. A few reasonably priced wines would be welcome.

Unico

15 rue Paul-Bert, 11th (01.43.67.68.08/ www.resto-unico.com). M° Faidherbe-Chaligny. **Open** 12.30-2.30pm, 8-10.30pm Tue-Sat. **Main courses** €20. **Credit** MC, V. **Map** p407 N7 ⑫ **Argentinian**

Architect Marcelo Joulia and photographer Enrique Zanoni were wise enough to retain the vintage 1970s decor of this former butcher's shop when they opened their temple to Argentinian beef. Orange tiles and matching light fixtures provide the backdrop for the fashionable, black-dressed crowd that comes here for thick slabs of meat grilled over charcoal and served with a selection of sauces. If you find yourself hesitating, opt for the *lomo* (fillet) with *chimichurri*, a mild salsa – and don't forget to wash it down with Argentinian wine, a rarity in Paris.

★ Au Vieux Chêne

7 rue du Dahomey, 11th (01.43.71.67.69/ www.vieuxchene.fr). M° Faidherbe-Chaligny. **Open** noon-2pm, 8-10.30pm Mon-Fri. Closed 1wk July & 2wks Aug. **Main courses** €20. **Prix fixe** *Lunch* €13.50, €17. *Dinner* €28, €33. **Credit** MC, V. **Map** p407 N7 ⑬ **Bistro**

Although everyone loves the the zinc-capped bar by the entrance, and the tiled floor, what makes this bistro so special is its desire to please. A starter of langoustines encased in fine crunchy angel hair and garnished with slices of fresh mango is delicious and refreshing, and chilled tomato soup is garnished with mint, a ball of tomato sorbet and a drizzle of olive oil. Stéphane Chevassus is a gifted game cook too, as proved by the tender roast pigeon sautéed with Chinese cabbage.

NORTH-EAST PARIS

★ € Le Baratin

3 rue Jouye-Rouve, 20th (01.43.49.39.70). M° Pyrénées. **Open** 12.15-3pm, 8-11pm Tue-Fri; 8-11pm Sat. **Main courses** €15. **Prix fixe** *Lunch* €15. **Credit** MC, V. **Map** p403 N3 ⑭ **Bistro**

Star pastry chef Pierre Hermé visits this cheerful little bistro and wine bar high up in Belleville at least every two weeks to fill up on Raquel Carena's homely cooking with the occasional exotic twist. Typical of her style, which draws on her native Argentina, are tuna carpaccio with cherries, roast Basque lamb with new potatoes and spinach, and hazelnut pudding. If the food weren't so fantastic, it would still be worth coming for the mostly organic wines. Le Baratin attracts gourmands from all over Paris – so be sure to book.

€ A la Bière

104 av Simon-Bolivar, 19th (01.42.39.83.25). M° Colonel Fabien. **Open** noon-3pm, 7pm-1.30am daily. **Main courses** €11. **Prix fixe** €13.50. **Credit** V. **Map** p403 M2 ⑮ **Brasserie**

A la Bière looks like one of those nondescript corner brasseries, but what makes it stand out is an amazingly good-value €13.40 prix fixe full of fine bistro favourites. White tablecloths and fine kirs set the tone; starters of thinly sliced pig's cheek with a nice French dressing on the salad, and a home-made rabbit terrine exceed expectations. The mains live up to what's served before: charcoal-grilled entrecôte with hand-cut chips, and juicy Lyonnais sausages with potatoes drenched in olive oil, garlic and parsley. This is one of the few bargains left in Paris.

Le Cambodge

10 av Richerand, 10th (01.44.84.37.70/www. lecambodge.fr). M° Goncourt or République. **Open** noon-2.30pm, 8-11.30pm Mon-Sat. Closed 1 Aug-15 Sept, 24 Dec-1 Jan. **Main courses** €13. **Credit** MC, V. **Map** p402 L4 ⑯ **Cambodian**

The system at Le Cambodge is simple: you write your order on a piece of paper, including preferences such as 'no coriander', 'no peanuts' or 'extra rice', and after a short wait the dishes appear. Two favourites are the *bobun spécial*, a hot and cold mix of sautéed beef, noodles, salad, bean sprouts and imperial rolls, and *ban-hoy*, a selection of the same ingredients to be wrapped in lettuce and mint leaves and dipped in a sauce. They also serve soups, salads and curries, including stewed pork in a fragrant coconut sauce.

★ Le Chateaubriand

129 av Parmentier, 11th (01.43.57.45.95). M° Goncourt. **Open** noon-2pm, 8-11pm Tue-Fri; 8-11pm Sat. Closed 3wks Aug, 1wk Dec. **Prix fixe** *Lunch* €19. *Dinner* €40. **Credit** AmEx, MC, V. **Map** p403 M4 ⑰ **Bistro**

Self-taught Basque chef Iñaki Aizpitarte runs this stylish bistro. Come at dinner to try the cooking at its most adventurous, as a much simpler (albeit cheaper) menu is served at lunch. Dishes have been deconstructed down to their very essence and put back together again. You'll understand if you try starters like chunky steak tartare with a quail's egg, or asparagus with tahini foam and little splinters of sesameseed brittle. The cooking's not always so cerebral – Aizpitarte's Spanish goat's cheese with stewed apple jam is brilliant. Be sure to book a few days ahead.

★ € Dong Huong

14 rue Louis-Bonnet, 11th (01.43.57.18.88). M° Belleville. **Open** noon-10.30pm Mon, Wed-Sun. Closed 2wks Jan & 3wks Aug. **Main courses** €7. **Credit** MC, V. **Map** p403 N4 ⑱ **Vietnamese**

The excellent food at this Vietnamese noodle joint attracts a buzzy crowd. The delicious *bành cuôn*, steamed Vietnamese ravioli stuffed with minced

CONSUME

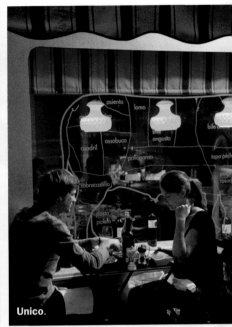

Unico.

Bread & Roses. *See p212.*

meat, mushrooms, bean sprouts, spring onions and deep-fried onion, are served piping hot. *Com ga lui*, chicken kebabs with tasty lemongrass, though not as delicate, come with tasty rice. *Bò bùn chà giò* (noodles with beef and small *nem* topped with onion strips, spring onion and crushed peanuts) makes a meal in itself. For dessert, the mandarin, lychee and mango sorbets are tasty and authentic.

€ La Madonnina

10 rue Marie-et-Louise, 10th (01.42.01.25.26). Mº Goncourt or Jacques Bonsergent. **Open** noon-2.30pm, 8-10.30pm Mon-Thur; noon-2.30pm,
8-11pm Fri; 8-11pm Sat. Closed 2wks Aug.
Main courses €14. **Prix fixe** *Lunch* €10.50, €15. **Credit** MC, V. **Map** p402 L4 ⑥⑨ Italian
La Madonnina flirts with kitsch so skilfully that it ends up coming off as cool. With its candles, mustard yellow walls and red-checked tablecloths, it's the perfect place for a romantic night out. La Madonnina describes itself as a *trattoria napoletana,* but most of the dishes are pan-southern Italian. The short menu changes monthly; don't miss the home-made pastas, such as artichoke and ricotta ravioli. The *cassata,* an extremely sweet Sicilian version of cheesecake, is authentic and unusual to see on menus outside Italy.

INSIDE TRACK
HAUTE FOR LESS

Alain Ducasse does not offer a special lunchtime menu at his restaurant, the Plaza Athénée (see p194), but **Aux Lyonnais** (32 rue St-Marc, 2nd, 01.42.96.65.04, www.auxlyonnais.com), his acclaimed bistro, offers a lunch menu for €26 – the cost of dessert at his three-star place.

THE LATIN QUARTER & THE 13TH

Atelier Maître Albert

1 rue Maître-Albert, 5th (01.56.81.30.01/ www.ateliermaitrealbert.com). M° Maubert Mutualité or St-Michel. **Open** noon-2.30pm, 6.30-11.30pm Mon-Wed; noon-2.30pm, 6.30pm-1am Thur, Fri; 6.30pm-1am Sat; 6.30-11.30pm Sun. **Main courses** €25. **Prix fixe** *Lunch* €23, €29. *Dinner* €30. **Credit** AmEx, DC, MC, V. **Map** p406 K7 **70** Bistro

This Guy Savoy outpost in the fifth arrondissement has slick decor designed by Jean-Michel Wilmotte. The indigo-painted, grey marble-floored dining room with open kitchen and rôtisseries on view is attractive, but it does mean that the place is very noisy at night. The short menu lets you have a Savoy classic or two to start with, including oysters in seawater *gelée*, perhaps, or more inventive dishes such as the ballotine of chicken, foie gras and celeriac in a chicken-liver sauce. Next up could be tuna served with tiny iron casseroles of dauphinois potatoes, accompanied by cauliflower in béchamel sauce.

L'Avant-Goût

26 rue Bobillot, 13th (01.53.80.24.00/www. lavantgout.com). M° Place d'Italie. **Open** noon-2pm, 7.45-10.45pm Tue-Sat. **Main courses** €16.50. **Prix fixe** *Lunch* €14. *Dinner* €31. **Credit** MC, V. Bistro

Self-taught chef Christophe Beaufront has turned this nondescript street on the edge of the villagey Butte-aux-Cailles into one of the city's foodie destinations. Typical of Beaufront's cooking is his *pot-au-feu de cochon aux épices*, a much-written-about dish that has been on his menu for years. He now presents the pork, sweet potato and fennel garnished with deep-fried ginger on a plate with a glass of bouillon to drink on the side. It's good, if not earth-shaking; however, a starter of piquillo pepper stuffed with smoked haddock rillettes does illustrate his talent.

▶ *Beaufront's food is available to take away at the épicerie across the street, complete with cast-iron cooking pots (to be returned).*

€ Le Bambou

70 rue Baudricourt, 13th (01.45.70.91.75). M° Olympiades or Tolbiac. **Open** noon-3.30pm, 7-10.30pm Tue-Sun. **Main courses** €10. **Prix fixe** €15, €26. **Credit** MC, V. Vietnamese

The Vietnamese fare here is a notch above what is normally served in Paris. Seating is elbow to elbow and, should you come on your own, the waiter will draw a line down the middle of the paper tablecloth and seat a stranger on the other side. That stranger might offer pointers on how to eat certain dishes, such as the no.42: grilled marinated pork to be wrapped in lettuce with beansprouts and herbs and eaten by hand, dipped into the accompanying sauce (no.43 is the same thing, but with pre-soaked rice paper wrappers).

Le Buisson Ardent

25 rue Jussieu, 5th (01.43.54.93.02/www. lebuissonardent.fr). M° Jussieu. **Open** noon-2pm, 7.45-10pm Mon-Fri; 7.45-10pm Sat. Closed Aug. **Main courses** €17. **Prix fixe** *Lunch* €14, €18. *Dinner* €25, €30. **Credit** MC, V. **Map** p406 K8 **71** Bistro

This bistro's square front dining room with its red banquettes and painted glass panels dating from 1923 has a quintessentially Paris charm, especially when compared to the surrounding kebab shops. There is plenty for adventurous eaters on chef Stéphane Maubuit's menu, such as pan-fried squid with chorizo and quinoa or white bean and pig's ear salad with pan-fried foie gras, but he also does conventional dishes (chestnut velouté with spice bread croûtons) very well. Desserts are less remarkable, but this is one of the area's best finds for the price.

★ Itinéraires

5 rue de Pontoise, 5th (01.46.33.60.11). M° Maubert Mutualité. **Open** noon-2pm, 8-11pm Tue-Fri; 8-11pm Sat. **Main courses** €22. **Prix fixe** *Lunch* €21, €28. *Dinner* €29, €34. **Credit** MC, V. **Map** p406 K7 **72** Bistro

Chef Sylvain Sendra played to a full house every night at his little bistro Le Temps au Temps near the Bastille before moving to this larger space near Notre Dame. The sleek space brings together all the elements that make for a successful bistro today: a long *table d'hôtes*, a bar for solo meals or quick bites, and a reasonably priced, market-inspired menu. Not everything is a wild success, but it's hard to fault a chef who so often hits the mark, in dishes such as squid-ink risotto with clams, *botargo* (dried mullet roe) and tomato.

L'Ourcine

92 rue Broca, 13th (01.47.07.13.65). M° Glacière or Les Gobelins. **Open** noon-2pm, 7-10.30pm Tue-Thur; noon-2.30pm, 7-11pm Fri, Sat. Closed 4wks July-Aug. **Prix fixe** *Lunch* (Tue-Fri) €24. *Dinner* €32. **Credit** MC, V. **Map** p406 J10 **73** Bistro

CONSUME

WHEREVER CRIMES AGAINST HUMANITY ARE PERPETRATED.

Across borders and above politics.
Against the most heinous abuses
and the most dangerous oppressors.
From conduct in wartime
to economic, social, and cultural rights.
Everywhere we go,
we build an unimpeachable case
for change and advocate action
at the highest levels.

HUMAN RIGHTS WATCH TYRANNY HAS A WITNESS

WWW.HRW.ORG

HUM
RIGH
WAT

This restaurant near Gobelins is a wonderful destination for anyone who really loves Basque and Béarnais cooking. Start with *pipérade*, succulent chorizo or a spread of sliced beef tongue with piquillo peppers; then try the sautéed baby squid with parsley, garlic and Espelette peppers, or the *piquillos* stuffed with puréed cod and potato. Service is friendly, and an appealing atmosphere is generated by a growing band of regulars. The wine list is quite short but does offer several pleasant southwestern bottles. The homely desserts include *gâteau basque*.

Le Pré Verre

8 rue Thénard, 5th (01.43.54.59.47/www. lepreverre.com). M° Maubert Mutualité. **Open** noon-2pm, 7.30-10.30pm Tue-Sat. Closed 3wks Aug & 2wks Dec. **Main courses** €18. **Prix fixe** *Lunch* €13.50. *Dinner* €28.50. **Credit** MC, V. **Map** p408 J7 **74** **Bistro**

Philippe Delacourcelle knows how to handle spices like few other French chefs. He also trained with the late Bernard Loiseau, and learned the art of French pastry at Fauchon. Salt cod with cassia bark and smoked potato purée is a classic: what the fish lacks in size it makes up for in rich, cinnamon-like flavour and crunchy texture, and smooth potato cooked in a smoker makes a startling accompaniment. Spices have a way of making desserts seem esoteric rather than decadent, but the roast figs with olives are an exception to the rule.

★ Ribouldingue

10 rue St-Julien-le-Pauvre, 5th (01.46.33.98.80). M° St-Michel. **Open** noon-2pm, 7-11pm Mon-Sat. **Prix fixe** €29. **Credit** MC, V. **Map** p408 J7 **75** **Bistro**

This bistro facing St-Julien-le-Pauvre church is the creation of Nadège Varigny, who spent ten years working with Yves Camdeborde before opening a restaurant inspired by the food of her childhood in Grenoble. It's usually full of people, including critics and chefs, who love simple, honest bistro fare, such as *daube de boeuf* or seared tuna on a bed of melting aubergine. And if you have an appetite for offal, go for the gently sautéed brains with new potatoes or veal kidneys with a perfectly prepared potato gratin. For dessert, try the fresh ewe's cheese with bitter honey.

★ € Rouammit & Huong Lan

103 av d'Ivry, 13th (01.45.85.19.23). M° Corvisart. **Open** noon-3pm, 7-11pm Tue-Fri; noon-4pm Sat, Sun. Closed 1wk Aug. **Main courses** €8. **Credit** MC, V. **Prix fixe** (Tue-Fri) €8.90, €10.80, €11.90. **Laotian**

Fans of South-east Asian food eventually learn to seek out Laotian holes-in-the-wall in Paris rather than splurge on flashier Thai restaurants. A perfect example is this Chinatown joint, easy to spot thanks to the queue outside the door. The food is cheap and

La Coupole. *See p214.*

delicious, and the service friendly. Among the highlights are *lap neua*, a tongue-tickling, chilli-spiked salad made with slivers of beef and tripe; *khao nom kroc*, Laotian ravioli filled with shrimp; and sweet, juicy prawns stir-fried with Thai basil. Even the sticky rice is exceptional.

La Tour d'Argent

15 quai de la Tournelle, 5th (01.43.54.23.31/ www.latourdargent.com). M° Pont Marie or Cardinal Lemoine. **Open** 7.30-10.30pm Mon; 12.30-2.30pm, 7.30-10.30pm Tue-Sat. Closed 3wks Aug. **Main courses** €80-€130. **Prix fixe** *Lunch* €65. *Dinner* €160. **Credit** AmEx, DC, MC, V. **Map** p406 K7 **76** **Haute cuisine**

This Paris institution is regaining its lustre following the death of aged owner Claude Terrail in 2006. In the kitchen, Breton-born Stéphane Haissant has brought a welcome creative touch to the menu, bringing in creative dishes such as a giant langoustine dabbed with kumquat purée and surrounded by lightly scented coffee foam. But he also shows restraint, as in duck (the house speciality) with cherry sauce and a broad bean flan. Following in his father's footsteps, Terrail's soft-spoken son André now does the rounds, making sure that the diners are happy.

ST-GERMAIN-DES-PRES & ODEON

Le 21

21 rue Mazarine, 6th (01.46.33.76.90).
Mº Odéon. **Open** noon-2pm, 8-10.30pm
Tue-Sat. **Main courses** €30. **Credit** MC, V.
Map p408 H6  **Bistro**

This clubby restaurant in St-Germain-des-Prés is
a big hit with a *beau monde* crowd of antiques
dealers, book editors and politicians. Chef Paul
Minchelli's original minimalist style has evolved
towards more homely preparations, as seen in a
delicious sauté of flaked cod, potatoes, onions and
green peppers, or squid in a squid ink sauce with
black rice. To keep the waistline-watching regulars
happy, a few of his old classics are also still offered,
including grilled red mullet. Don't miss the chocolate fondant cake for dessert, and don't be shy about
asking for help with the pricey wine list.

Bread & Roses

7 rue de Fleurus, 6th (01.42.22.06.06/www.
breadandroses.fr). Mº St-Placide. **Open** 8am-8pm
Mon-Sat. Closed Aug & 1wk Dec. **Main courses**
€18. **Credit** AmEx, MC, V. **Map** p405 G8
Bakery/café

Come for a morning croissant and you might find
yourself staying on for lunch, so tempting are the
wares at this Anglo-influenced *boulangerie/épicerie/*
café. Giant wedges of cheesecake sit alongside
French pastries, and huge savoury puff-pastry tarts
are perched on the counter. Attention to detail shows

even in the authentically pale taramasalata, which
is matched with buckwheat-and-seaweed bread.
Prices reflect the quality of the often organic ingredients, but that doesn't seem to deter any of the moneyed locals, who order towering birthday cakes here
for their snappily dressed offspring. *Photos p208.*

Le Comptoir

Hôtel Le Relais Saint-Germain, 9 carrefour
de l'Odéon, 6th (01.43.29.12.05). Mº Odéon.
Open noon-6pm, 8.30pm-midnight (last orders
9pm) Mon-Fri; noon-11pm Sat, Sun. Closed 3wks
Aug. **Main courses** €15. **Prix fixe** *Dinner*
(Mon-Fri) €50. **Credit** AmEx, DC, MC, V.
Map p408 H7 **Brasserie**

Yves Camdeborde runs the bijou 17th-century Hôtel
Le Relais Saint-Germain, whose art deco dining
room, modestly dubbed Le Comptoir, serves
brasserie fare from noon to 6pm and on weekend
nights, and a five-course prix fixe feast on weekday
evenings. The single dinner sitting lets the chef
take real pleasure in his work. On the daily menu,
you might find dishes like rolled saddle of lamb
with vegetable-stuffed 'Basque ravioli'. The catch?
The prix fixe dinner is booked up as much as six
months in advance.

★ L'Epigramme

9 rue de l'Eperon, 6th (01.44.41.00.09).
Mº Odéon. **Open** noon-2.30pm, 7-11.30pm
Tue-Sat; noon-2pm Sun. **Prix fixe** *Lunch* €22.
Dinner €28. **Credit** MC, V. **Map** p408 H7
Bistro

Jules Verne. *See p218.*

CONSUME

The recently opened L'Epigramme is a pleasantly bourgeois dining room with terracotta floor tiles, wood beams, a glassed-in kitchen and comfortable chairs. Like the decor, the food doesn't aim to innovate but sticks to tried and true classics with the occasional twist. Marinated mackerel in a mustardy dressing on toasted country bread gets things off to a promising start, but the chef's skill really comes through in main courses such as perfectly seared lamb with glazed root vegetables and intense jus. It's rare to find such a high standard of cooking at this price, so be sure to book.

La Ferrandaise

8 rue de Vaugirard, 6th (01.43.26.36.36/www. laferrandaise.com). M° Odéon/RER Luxembourg. **Open** noon-2.30pm, 7-10.30pm Tue-Thur; noon-2.30pm, 7pm-midnight Fri; 7pm-midnight Sat. **Main courses** €14. **Prix fixe** *Lunch* €15, €32. *Dinner* €32, €44. **Credit** MC, V. **Map** p408 H7 ❶ Bistro

This bistro has quickly established a faithful following. In the modern bistro tradition, the young, northern French chef serves solid, classic food with a twist. A platter of excellent ham, sausage and terrine arrives as you study the blackboard menu, and the bread is crisp-crusted, thickly sliced sourdough. Two specialities are the potato stuffed with escargots in a camembert sauce, and a wonderfully flavoured, slightly rosé slice of veal. Desserts might include intense chocolate with rum-soaked bananas and a layered glass of mango and meringue. Wines start at €14.

Huîtrerie Régis

3 rue de Montfaucon, 6th (01.44.41.10.07). M° Mabillon. **Open** 11am-midnight Tue-Sun. Closed mid July-Sept. **Main courses** €32. **Prix fixe** €21.50, €30. **Credit** MC, V. **Map** p408 H7 ❷ Oyster bar

Paris oyster fans are often obliged to use one of the city's big brasseries to get their fix of shellfish, but what if you just want to eat a reasonably priced platter of oysters? Enter Régis and his 14-seat oyster bar. The tiny room feels pristine and the tables are properly laid. Here you can enjoy the freshest oysters from Marennes for around €25 a dozen. The bread and butter is fresh and wines are well chosen. Hungry souls can supplement their feast with a slice of home-made apple tart or the cheese of the day.

Lapérouse

51 quai des Grands-Augustins, 6th (01.56.79.24.31/www.laperouse.fr). M° St-Michel. **Open** noon-2.30pm, 7.30-10pm Mon-Fri; 7.30-10pm Sat. Closed 1wk Jan & Aug. **Main courses** €40. **Prix fixe** *Lunch* €45, €105. *Dinner* €105. **Credit** AmEx, DC, MC, V. **Map** p408 J6 ❸ Brasserie

One of the most romantic spots in Paris, Lapérouse was formerly a clandestine rendezvous for French politicians and their mistresses; the tiny private dining rooms upstairs used to lock from the inside. Chef Alain Hacquard does a modern take on classic French cooking: his beef fillet is smoked for a more complex flavour; a tender saddle of rabbit is cooked in a clay crust, flavoured with lavender and rosemary and served with ravioli of onions. The only snag is the cost, especially of the wine – a half-bottle of Pouilly-Fuissé is nearly €35.

★ Le Restaurant

L'Hôtel, 13 rue des Beaux-Arts, 6th (01.44.41.99.01/www.l-hotel.com). M° St-Germain-des-Prés. **Open** 12.30-2pm, 7.30-10pm Tue-Sat. **Main courses** €39. **Prix fixe** *Lunch* €42, €85. *Dinner* €95, €115. **Credit** AmEx, DC, MC, V. **Map** p408 H6 ❹ Haute cuisine

Since being taken over by Oxford-based Cowley Manor, L'Hôtel has rechristened its restaurant (formerly Le Belier) and put the talented Philippe Bélisse in charge of the kitchen. You can choose from a short seasonal menu with dishes such as pan-fried tuna, John Dory or suckling pig. But for the same price you can also enjoy the marvellous four-course *menu dégustation* or, even better, the *menu surprise*. Highlights of the autumn menu were the wild Breton crab stuffed with fennel, avocado and *huile d'Argan*, and a main course of pigeon on a bed of beetroot.

La Taverna degli Amici

16 rue du Bac, 6th (01.42.60.37.74). M° Assemblée Nationale or Solférino. **Open** noon-2.30pm, 7.30-11pm Mon-Fri; 7.30-11pm Sat. Closed Aug & 1wk Dec. **Main courses** €16. **Prix fixe** *Lunch* €18. **Credit** MC, V. **Map** p401 G6 ❺ Italian

The ideal spot for a quick business lunch or a big, rumbustious dinner with friends. Occupying two floors, the yellow-walled rooms are well lit and airy. Run by the exceptionally friendly Notaro family, who own, manage and cook, the restaurant is constantly bustling. Don't miss the mixed bruschette, which includes three vegetable toppings, such as grilled courgettes marinated in olive oil, lemon and parsley. Pastas feature fresh, tasty toppings, such as their most popular dish, penne with *caccioricotta* (made with ewe's milk) and rocket. Most of the regulars finish with home-made tiramisu.

Le Timbre

3 rue Ste-Beuve, 6th (01.45.49.10.40/www.restaurantletimbre.com). M° Vavin. **Open** noon-2pm, 7.30-10.30pm Tue-Sat. Closed Aug & 1wk Dec. **Main courses** €17. **Prix fixe** *Lunch* €26. *Dinner* (Sat) €30. **Credit** MC, V. **Map** p405 G8 ❻ Bistro

Chris Wright's restaurant, open kitchen included, might be the size of the average student garret, but this Mancunian aims high. Typical of his cooking is

CONSUME

a plate of fresh green asparagus elegantly cut in half lengthwise and served with dabs of anise-spiked sauce and balsamic vinegar, and a little crumbled parmesan. Main courses are also pure in presentation and flavour – a thick slab of pork, pan-fried but not the least bit dry, comes with petals of red onion that retain a light crunch.

MONTPARNASSE & BEYOND

★ La Cerisaie

70 bd Edgar Quinet, 14th (01.43.20.98.98).
M° Edgar Quinet or Montparnasse. **Open**
noon-2pm, 7-10pm Mon-Fri. Closed Aug &
1wk Dec. **Main courses** €15. **Prix fixe**
Lunch €13, €19. *Dinner* €22, €27. **Credit** MC,
V. **Map** p405 G9 ❺ Bistro

Nothing about La Cerisaie's unprepossessing red façade hints at the talent that lurks inside. With a simple starter of white asparagus served with preserved lemon and drizzled with bright green parsley oil, chef Cyril Lalanne proves his ability to select and prepare the finest produce. On the daily changing blackboard menu you might find *bourride de maquereau*, a thrifty take on the garlicky southern French fish stew, or *cochon noir de Bigorre*, an ancient breed of pig that puts ordinary pork to shame. *Baba à l'armagnac*, a variation on the usual rum cake, comes with stunningly good chantilly.

La Coupole

102 bd du Montparnasse, 14th (01.43.20.14.20/
www.flobrasseries.com/coupoleparis). M° Vavin.
Open 8am-1am Mon-Fri; 8.30am-1am Sat,
Sun. **Main courses** €36. **Prix fixe** €17, €27.
Credit AmEx, DC, MC, V. **Map** p405 G9 ❻
Brasserie

INSIDE TRACK SHOW TIME

The promise of busty babes slinking across the stage still attracts throngs of tourists and businessmen to Paris's glamour cabarets, but many also book in for dinner as well. One of the best places to go for supper and a show is **Le Lido** (*see p281*), which combines a classy, high-tech 1,000-seater art deco-style dining room with the city's most contemporary revue, featuring costumes worthy of a catwalk, breathtaking fountains and fabulous *entr'acte* acts. An added bonus is that Philippe Lacroix's dishes – if you can afford it, splurge on the four-course Premier menu (€280, show included), which features foie gras, tender lobster, an excellent slab of Charolais steak and a gooey chocolate slice to finish.

La Coupole still glows with some of the old glamour. The people-watching remains superb, inside and out, and the long ranks of linen-covered tables, professional waiters, 32 art deco columns painted by different artists of the epoch, mosaic floor and sheer scale of the operation still make coming here an event. The set menu offers unremarkable steaks, foie gras, fish and autumn game stews, but the real treat is the shellfish, displayed along a massive counter. Take your pick from the *claires*, *spéciales* and *belons*, or go for a platter brimming with crabs, oysters, prawns, periwinkles and clams. *Photo p211.*

€ Crêperie du Manoir Breton

18 rue d'Odessa, 14th (01.43.35.40.73). M°
Edgar Quinet. **Open** noon-11pm daily. **Main**
courses €6-€10. **Credit** MC, V. **Map** p405 G9
❸ Crêperie

See p205 **Flipping Tasty.**

€ Crêperie du Pont-Aven

54 rue du Montparnasse, 14th (01.43.22.23.74/
www.creperie-de-pont-aven.com). M° Edgar
Quinet. **Open** noon-3pm, 6pm-midnight Mon-Fri;
noon-midnight Sat, Sun. **Main courses** €3-€10.
Credit MC, V. **Map** p405 G9 ❹ Crêperie

See p205 **Flipping Tasty.**

€ Josselin

67 rue du Montparnasse, 14th (01.43.20.93.50).
M° Edgar Quinet. **Open** noon-11pm Tue-Sun.
Main courses €5-€8. **No credit cards.**
Map p405 G9 ❺ Crêperie

See p205 **Flipping Tasty.**

L'Opportun

64 bd Edgar Quinet, 14th (01.43.20.26.89).
M° Edgar Quinet. **Open** noon-3pm, 7-11.30pm
Mon-Sat. **Main courses** €19. **Prix fixe**
(until 10pm) €21. **Credit** AmEx, DC, MC, V.
Map p405 G9 ❻ Bistro

Owner-chef Serge Alzérat is passionate about Beaujolais, dubbing his convivial cream and yellow restaurant a centre of 'beaujolaistherapy' and a place for 'the prevention of thirst'. He's also an advocate for good, honest Lyonnais food. Thus his menu is littered with the likes of *sabodet* (thick pork sausage) with a purée of split peas, duck skin salad, *tête de veau* (a favourite of ex-president Chirac, whose photo graces the walls) and meat – lots of it. *Fromage* fans should skip dessert and try the st-marcellin by master cheesemaker Hervé Mons.

Le Plomb du Cantal

3 rue de la Gaîté, 14th (01.43.35.16.92).
M° Gaîté. **Open** noon-midnight Mon-Fri, Sat,
Sun. **Main courses** €15. **Prix fixe** *Lunch*
€19. **Credit** MC, V. **Map** p405 G9 ❻ Bistro

This lively homage to the Auvergne may suffer from its 1980s decor, but with food like this, who cares? *Aligot* (potato puréed with fresh tomme

Le Lido. See box (below left).

cheese) and *truffade* (potatoes sautéed with tomme) are scraped out of copper pots on to plates at the table, the shoestring fries arrive by the saucepan-load, and the omelettes are made with three eggs, 300g of potatoes, and, if you're really hungry, a supplement of tomme. The roast chestnut-based *salade corrézienne* is delicious and, like all salads here, too enormous to finish. Wines are generally good and the service is friendly.

THE 7TH & WESTERN PARIS

Le 144 Petrossian
18 bd de La Tour-Maubourg, 7th (01.44.11.32.32/ www.petrossian.fr). M° La Tour Maubourg.
Open noon-2.30pm, 7.30-10.30pm Tue-Sat.
Main courses €35. **Prix fixe** *Lunch* €29, €90.
Dinner €45, €90. **Credit** AmEx, DC, MC, V.
Map p401 E5 **㉔ Russian**
Young Senegalese-French chef Rougui Dia directs the kitchen of this famed caviar house. You'll find Russian specialities such as blinis, salmon and caviar (at €39 an ounce) from the Petrossian boutique downstairs, but Dia has added preparations and spices from all over the world. You might start with a divine risotto made with carnaroli rice, codfish caviar and crisp parmesan. In similar Med-meets-Russia vein are main courses of lamb 'cooked for eleven hours' on a raisin-filled blini, and roast sea bream with a terrific lemon-vodka sauce. At dinner wines start at €40.

Afaria
15 rue Desnouettes, 15th (01.48.56.15.36).
M° Convention. **Open** noon-2pm, 7-11pm
Tue-Sat. **Prix fixe** *Lunch* €19. *Dinner* €27.
Credit MC, V. **Map** p404 C10 **㉟ Bistro**
Instead of the usual starter, main course and dessert categories, Basque-born chef Julien Duboué has divided his menu into sections such as 'les sudistes' for southern French-inspired cooking, and 'les petits appetits' for lighter dishes. Several dishes are for sharing, in particular a caveman-sized duck *magret* with balsamic fig vinegar, served on a terracotta roof tile with potato gratin perched on a bed of twigs. Other creations such as oysters with bulgur, houmous and preserved lemon show that Duboué is not just another Basque bistro chef, but a traveller who happily borrows ingredients from around the world.

L'Agassin
8 rue Malar, 7th (01.47.05.94.27). M° Ecole Militaire. **Open** noon-2.30pm, 7-11pm Tue-Sat. Closed Aug. **Prix fixe** *Lunch* €23, €34.
Dinner €34. **Credit** AmEx, DC, MC, V.
Map p405 D6 **㊱ Bistro**
André Le Letty left Anacréon – a bistro in the 13th – to open this restaurant in the heart of aristocratic Paris. It's a curious mix of contemporary and classic, with occasional old-fashioned touches in the cooking (with the likes of skate in butter and

caper sauce served with steamed potatoes) but a modern spirit. Several dishes come with supplements of €2 to €10, but these are often worth the extra cost – the *girolle* mushrooms in season are beautifully firm and juicy. The prune *clafoutis* is unusually light, with armagnac ice-cream making the perfect accompaniment.

★ L'Ami Jean
27 rue Malar, 7th (01.47.05.86.89). M° Ecole Militaire. **Open** noon-2pm, 7pm-midnight Tue-Sat. Closed Aug. **Main courses** €20. **Prix fixe** €32. **Credit** MC, V. **Map** p405 D6 ⑰ Bistro

This long-running Basque address is an ongoing hit thanks to chef Stéphane Jégo. Excellent bread from baker Jean-Luc Poujauran is a perfect nibble when slathered with a tangy, herby *fromage blanc* – as are starters of sautéed baby squid on a bed of ratatouille. Tender veal shank comes de-boned with a lovely side of baby onions and broad beans with tiny cubes of ham, and house-salted cod is soaked, sautéed and doused with an elegant vinaigrette. There's a great wine list, and some lovely Brana *eau de vie* should you decide to linger.

★ L'Arpège
84 rue de Varenne, 7th (01.47.05.09.06/www. alain-passard.com). M° Varenne. **Open** noon-2.30pm, 8-10.30pm Mon-Fri. **Main courses** €70. **Prix fixe** *Lunch* €135. *Dinner* €360. **Credit** AmEx, DC, MC, V. **Map** p405 F6 ⑱ Haute cuisine

Assuming you can swallow an exceptionally high bill – it's €42 for a potato starter, for example – chances are you'll have a spectacular time at chef Alain Passard's Left Bank establishment. His attempt to plane down and simplify the haute experience – the chrome-armed chairs look like something from the former DDR – seems a misstep; but then something edible comes to the table, such as tiny smoked potatoes served with a horseradish mousseline. A main course of sautéed free-range chicken with a roasted shallot, an onion, potato *mousseline* and pan juices is the apotheosis of comfort food. Desserts are elegant.

€ Le Bistro
17 rue Pérignon, 15th (01.45.66.84.03). M° Ségur. **Open** 8am-10pm daily. **Main courses** €11. **Credit** MC, V. **Map** p405 E8 ⑲ Bistro

At first glance there is nothing to distinguish this corner bistro from hundreds of other cafés in Paris. In the front room, with its wood-panelled ceiling are a plastic-topped bar and a few bare tables with black banquettes, and in the back is a larger room with red-and-white checked tablecloths. Then you see the plates going by, each one – from the goat's cheese salad to the *pavé de rumsteak* – loaded with golden fried potato rounds or hand-cut chips. This is the kind of neighbourhood bistro you had almost given up hope of finding in Paris.

★ Au Bon Accueil
14 rue de Monttessuy, 7th (01.47.05.46.11/www. aubonaccueilparis.com). M° Alma Marceau. **Open** noon-2.30pm, 7.30-10.30pm Mon-Fri. Closed 2wks Aug. **Main courses** €20. **Prix fixe** *Lunch* €27. *Dinner* €31. **Map** p404 D6 ⑩⓪ Bistro

Jacques Lacipière runs Au Bon Accueil, and Naobuni Sasaki turns out the beautiful food. Perhaps most impressive is his elegant use of little-known fish such as grey mullet and meagre (*maigre*), rather than the usual endangered species. The €27 lunch menu might highlight such posh ingredients as *suprême de poulet noir du Cros de la Géline*, free-range chicken raised on a farm run by two former cabaret singers. But the biggest surprise comes with desserts, worthy of the finest pastry shops. In summer book a table on the pavement terrace with its view of the Eiffel Tower.

Les Cocottes
135 rue St-Dominique, 7th (www.leviolon dingres.com). M° Ecole Militaire/RER Pont de l'Alma. **Open** noon-2.30pm, 7-10.30pm Mon-Sat. **Main courses** €15. **Credit** MC, V. **Map** p404 D6 ⑩① Bistro

Christian Constant has found the perfect recipe for pleasing Parisians at his new bistro: a flexible menu of salads, soups, *verrines* (light dishes served in jars) and *cocottes* (served in cast-iron pots), all at bargain prices – for this neighbourhood. Service is swift and the food satisfying, though the *vraie salade César Ritz*, which contains hard-boiled egg, shouldn't be confused with US-style Caesar salad. Soups such as an iced pea velouté are spot-on, and *cocottes* range from sea bream with ratatouille to potatoes stuffed with pig's trotter.

D'Chez Eux
2 av de Lowendal, 7th (01.47.05.52.55/www. chezeux.com). M° Ecole Militaire. **Open** noon-3pm, 7-10.30pm Tue-Sat. Closed Aug. **Main courses** €30. **Prix fixe** *Lunch* €37, €43. **Credit** MC, V. **Map** p405 E7 ⑩② Bistro

Arm yourself with stamina for a meal at this jovial south-western *auberge*, which looks touristy with its red-and-white checked tablecloths but attracts *bons vivants* from the neighbourhood, including the likes of Jacques Chirac. First come the help-yourself lyonnais-style 'salads' (cooked beetroot, lentils, celeriac rémoulade, ratatouille, etc), before hearty main dishes such as cassoulet or calf's liver with sherry vinegar, which are tasty and generous if not exactly refined. The heaving dessert cart (think chocolate mousse and rice pudding) will ensure that you waddle out overfed but happy.

Gaya Rive Gauche
44 rue du Bac, 7th (01.45.44.73.73/www. pierre-gagnaire.com). M° Rue du Bac. **Open** noon-2.30pm, 7.30-10.45pm Mon-Fri. **Main courses** €30. **Credit** AmEx, MC, V. **Map** p405 G6 ⑩③ Seafood

Secret Supper

Get yourself invited to a dinner party with a difference.

A cross between a private dinner party and a restaurant, 'clandestine restaurants' are springing up around Paris, offering the chance to meet strangers while you enjoy fine food.

There is no more insider lunch address in Paris than **Lunch in the Loft** (www.lunch intheloft.com, €50 per head): the exact location is revealed only once you sign up for the party for eight at the home of Claude Cabri, which just happens to be near one of the city's most famous food markets.

An artist who loves to cook, Claude widened her sphere of guests a year ago when she started emailing food bloggers under the mysterious name of 'Miss Lunch'. The surprise of who you might meet around the table is part of the fun, though you can check in advance if other guests will be primarily French- or English-speaking. Our party included an Anglo-American couple living in Paris, an Australian couple on holiday and a Franco-Italian vet who had procured one of the rare ingredients – an essence of mustard only available in Italian pharmacies. After the *apéro* of prosecco and grissini, Claude disappeared behind the curtain that separates the kitchen from the dining table, popping her head round every now and then to join in a conversation or elaborate on what her partner Eric was bringing to the table. Our autumn menu included an aubergine terrine and a home-made foie gras soaked in brine, smoked and encased in peppercorns, accompanied by a tangy pear 'mostarda'. Blackberries gathered in the grounds of a château combined with ceps for an unusual lasagne, accompanied by the last of the chosen wines, a Languedoc that echoed the blackberry flavours. The meal finished with a fig tart and coffee, a good four hours after we'd arrived.

A more professional atmosphere can be found at the **Hidden Kitchen** (www. hkmenus.com, €80 per head) in the Haussmannian apartment of young American chef Brad Perkins and his partner Laura Adrian. At their dinner parties, 12 guests sit down to a candlelit ten-course meal accompanied by four carefully chosen wines. The quality of the food was astounding, particularly the poached egg with sweet pea sauce and crispy pancetta, a recipe Brad had managed to prise out of a Basque chef; and the deep red beetroot salad that followed the stuffed pork roulade main course. With its higher priced fare and restaurant credentials (Brad used to cook at the Dahlia Lounge in Seattle), the Hidden Kitchen attracts mainly American foodies on vacation. True gastronomes should not miss it, but you'll probably have more fun chez Claude.

CONSUME

Superchef Pierre Gagnaire runs this comparatively affordable fish restaurant. The menu enumerates ingredients without much clue as to how they are put together, though the helpful waiters will explain if you don't like a surprise. But then surprises are what Gagnaire is famous for. The Fats Waller, for instance, turns out to be a soup of grilled red peppers with a bloody mary sorbet in the centre and daubs of quinoa, basmati rice and Chinese spinach. For the mains, diners are treated like sophisticated children – everything has been detached from the bone or carapace. Light desserts complete the successful formula.

Le Gorille Blanc

*11bis rue Chomel, 7th (01.45.49.04.54). M°
Sèvres-Babylone.* **Open** noon-2.30pm, 7-10.30pm
Mon-Fri; 7-10.30pm Sat. **Main courses** €18.
Prix fixe *Lunch* €19.50. **Credit** AmEx, MC, V.
Map p405 G7 ⓘ **Bistro**
There are not many inspiring places to eat near Le Bon Marché, so this bistro is quite a find. Crisp-skinned duck confit with sautéed potatoes is a sure bet here, but the kitchen also turns out sprightly fish dishes such as tapenade-coated sea bream fillet wrapped in filo pastry and served with tomato and aubergine confit. Desserts are simple but tasty.

Le Grand Pan

*20 rue Rosenwald, 15th (01.42.50.02.50).
M° Convention.* **Open** 12.30-2.30pm, 7.30-
11pm Mon-Fri; 7.30-11pm Sat. **Main courses**
€40. **Prix fixe** *Lunch* €30. **Credit** MC, V.
Map p405 D10 ⓘ **Bistro**
Young chef Benoît Gauthier trained with Christian Etchebest at the nearby Le Troquet, and he's come up with a clever formula that surfs the current Paris preference for great produce simply cooked. At dinner, a complimentary starter of soup is served – maybe courgette or white bean – and then you choose from the selection of grilled meats and lobster, many of which are designed for two people. Everything comes with a delicious mountain of home-made chips and green salad. Desserts run to homely choices like strawberry crumble or rice pudding with caramel sauce.

Jadis

*208 rue de la Croix-Nivert, 15th
(01.45.57.73.20). M° Convention or Porte de
Versailles.* **Open** noon-2.30pm, 7.30-9.30pm
Mon-Sat. **Main courses** €20. **Prix fixe** €32.
Credit MC, V. **Map** p404 C9 ⓘ **Bistro**
The residential 15th arrondissement has more than its fair share of great bistros, and Jadis confirms the trend. In this grey-painted dining room with red curtains and striped Basque napkins, young chef Guillaume Delage serves a gently updated take on classic French cuisine (Jadis means 'in days gone by'). The pared-down presentation of dishes such as snails in puff pastry with oyster mushrooms and romaine lettuce lets each element speak for itself. Don't miss the wonderful cheese trolley or the deconstructed desserts.

★ Jules Verne

*Pilier Sud, Eiffel Tower, 7th (01.45.55.61.44/
www.lejulesverne-paris.com). M° Bir Hakeim or
RER Tour Eiffel.* **Open** 12.15-1.30pm, 7-9.30pm
daily. **Main courses** €75. **Prix fixe** *Lunch* €85,
€165 (Sat, Sun). *Dinner* €200. **Credit** AmEx, DC,
MC, V. **Map** p404 C6 ⓘ **Haute cuisine**
You have to have courage to take on an icon like the Eiffel Tower, but superchef and entrepreneur Alain Ducasse has done just that in taking over the Jules Verne, perched in its spectacular eyrie above the city. He has transformed the cuisine and brought in his favourite designer, Patrick Jouin. Meanwhile, Ducasse protégé Pascal Féraud updates French classics, combining all the grand ingredients you'd expect with light, modern textures and sauces. Try dishes like lamb with artichokes, turbot with champagne zabaglione, and a fabulous ruby grapefruit soufflé. Reserve well ahead, and come for lunch if you want to make the most of the views. *Photo p212.*

Les Ombres

*27 quai Branly, 7th (01.47.53.68.00/
www.lesombres-restaurant.com). M° Alma-
Marceau.* **Open** noon-2.30pm, 7-10.30pm
daily. **Main courses** €35. **Prix fixe** *Lunch*
€38. *Dinner* €95. **Credit** AmEx, MC, V.
Map p404 D5 ⓘ **Bistro**
The full-on view of the Eiffel Tower at night would be reason enough to come to this glass-and-iron restaurant on the top floor of the Musée du Quai Branly, but young chef Arnaud Busquet's food also demands that you sit up and take notice. The influence of Joël Robuchon – a mentor to Busquet's mentor – shows in dishes such as thin green asparagus curved into a nest with tiny *lardons* and topped with a breaded poached egg, ribbons of parmesan and meat *jus*. There is a reasonable prix fixe at lunch.

Il Vino

*13 bd de La Tour-Maubourg, 7th (01.44.11.72.00/
www.ilvinobyenricobernardo.com). M° La Tour-
Maubourg.* **Open** noon-2pm, 7pm-midnight daily.
Prix fixe *Lunch* €50, €75. *Dinner* €95. **Credit**
AmEx, DC, MC, V. **Map** p401 E5 ⓘ **Italian**
Enrico Bernardo, youngest-ever winner of the World's Best Sommelier award, runs this restaurant where, for once, food plays second fiddle to wine. You are presented with nothing more than a wine list. Each of 15 wines by the glass is matched with a surprise dish, or the chef can build a meal around the bottle of your choice. Best for a first visit is one of the blind tasting menus for €75, €100 or (why not?) €1,000. The impeccably prepared food shows a strong Italian influence.

Cafés & Bars

Back to the old school.

Just as it looked as if Paris would be totally swamped with trendy New York-style watering holes, in came the credit crunch and out popped the idea of capitalising on the funky period features present in Paris's cafés. **Chez Jeanette** in the 10th pioneered the idea a couple of years ago (keeping all of its 1940s gear and winning a Fooding prize for it); but zinc bars, marble floors and red banquettes across the city are heaving sighs of relief as they too doggedly stay in place, while walls, lighting, sound systems and loos get spruced up around them. And of course, if it's real old-world Paris you're after, there's still a handful of landmark addresses, like **La Palette** with its original art deco tiles and frescoes, and **Le Cochon à l'Oreille**, an atmospheric remnant of Les Halles' heyday – you have to look hard to find them, though.

DRINKING IN PARIS

The traditional boundaries between bar, club, restaurant and dancehall are blurring. Hybrid spaces such as **La Bellevilloise** (a former Paris co-operative) and **La Maroquinerie** (previously a leather factory) house restaurant, bar, music venue and exhibition space all under one roof, and **L'Entrepôt** fulfils dual roles as a bastion of culture and coffee south of Montparnasse.

Urban regeneration still seems to be pulling punters northwards, beyond the Canal St-Martin in the tenth (home to fashionable boho bars and satisfying brunch spots) into the now ultra-trendy 19th, along the Canal de l'Ourcq. Those looking for a real 'neighbourhood' feel, meanwhile, should head into the 20th, where hidden gems like the St-Blaise district and the ever-gentrifying eastern edge of Nation are now home to fun, authentic addresses like **Chez Prosper**, **Les Pères Populaires** and the hip **Café Noir** on rue St-Blaise.

Other Right Bank hotspots include the Marais (and its north-west overspill around Etienne Marcel and Arts et Métiers métro

> ❶ Green numbers given in this chapter correspond to the location of each café or bar on the street maps. *See pp400-409.*

stations); the village-like area in and around Abbesses in Montmartre; and Les Batignolles, west of Place de Clichy, where rue des Dames draws the boho overspill from Montmartre into its wealth of cafés and bars. Over on the Left Bank, St-Germain-des-Prés and Montparnasse continue to trade on a proud literary heritage, and the Butte-aux-Cailles, in the 13th, has some of the last surviving cheap student haunts.

Wine in three colours is ubiquitous, and coffee comes as a strong espresso unless otherwise requested. The sturdy brasserie and noble bistro provide food with formality akin to a restaurant, so if you're just there for a drink, you'll pay more for the social nicety of aproned and waistcoated service. You can usually run a tab, and tipping is optional (service is always included in the bill).

THE LOUVRE & PALAIS-ROYAL

★ Angelina
226 rue de Rivoli, 1st (01.42.60.82.00).
M° Tuileries. **Open** 9am-7pm daily.
Credit MC, V. **Map** p401 G5 ❶
Angelina is home to Paris's most lip-smackingly scrumptious desserts – all served in the faded grandeur of a belle époque salon just steps from the Louvre. The hot chocolate is pure decadence; try the speciality 'African', a velvety potion so thick that you need a spoon to consume it. Epicurean delights include the Mont Blanc dessert, a ball of meringue

covered in whipped cream and sweet chestnut, and, for those with a waistline to watch, a brand new sugar- and butter-free *brioche aux fruits rouges*. The place heaves at weekends, so be prepared to queue.

Le Café des Initiés

3 pl des Deux-Ecus, 1st (01.42.33.78.29).
M° Louvre Rivoli or Les Halles. **Open** 7.30am-2am Mon-Fri; 9am-2am Sat, Sun. **Credit** AmEx, MC, V. **Map** p402 H5 **②**
Friendly staff and a central location have turned this designer hangout into a top spot for a trendy tipple, especially after work – cocktails are just €5 between 5pm and 8pm. The main room is lined with aerodynamic red banquettes, a long zinc bar provides character, and sleek, black, articulated lamps peer down from the ceiling. When hunger strikes, homely favourites such as shoulder of lamb baked in honey or tartare of salmon never fail to please.

Café Marly

93 rue de Rivoli, cour Napoléon, 1st
(01.49.26.06.60). M° Palais Royal Musée du
Louvre. **Open** 8am-2am daily. **Credit** AmEx, DC, MC, V. **Map** p401 H5 **③**
In the arcaded terrace overlooking the Louvre's glass pyramid, this classy, Napoleon III-style hangout (reached through the passage Richelieu, the entrance for advance Louvre ticket holders) is in an unrivalled location. One would expect nothing else from the ubiquitous Costes brothers – it's just a shame about the beer prices: it's €6 for a Heineken, so you might as well splash out €12 on a chocolate martini or a Shark, made of vodka, lemonade and grenadine. Most wines are under €10 a glass, and everything is impeccably served by razor-sharp staff. Brasserie fare and sandwiches are on offer too.

L'Entr'acte

47 rue de Montpensier, 1st (01.42.97.57.76).
M° Pyramides or Palais Royal Musée du Louvre.
Open noon-midnight daily. **Credit** MC, V.
Map p402 H5 **④**
A little detour off avenue de l'Opéra, down an 18th-century staircase, and you find an unexpected congregation spread across the pavement: half are here for this little bar near the Comédie Française, half for the adjoining Sicilian pizzeria. There's food to be had

at L'Entr'acte too – €10 plates of cheese and charcuterie, standard pastas and so on – but most come to enjoy an early evening glass of house Bourgueil. The interior is tiny, with an equally poky basement, but there's free Wi-Fi and even laptop loans.

Le Fumoir

6 rue de l'Amiral-de-Coligny, 1st
(01.42.92.00.24/www.lefumoir.fr). M° Louvre
Rivoli. **Open** 11am-2am daily. Closed 2wks Aug. **Credit** AmEx, MC, V. **Map** p402 H6 **⑤**
There aren't many places around the Louvre that can compete with this elegant local institution: neo-colonial fans whirr lazily and oil paintings adorn the walls. A sleek crowd sips martinis or reads papers at the long mahogany bar (originally from a Chicago speakeasy), giving way to young professionals in the restaurant and pretty things in the library. It feels a wee bit try-hard and resolutely well behaved, but the cocktails get tongues wagging soon enough, and food is consistently top notch.

★ La Garde Robe

41 rue de l'Arbre-Sec, 1st (01.49.26.90.60).
M° Louvre Rivoli. **Open** noon-3pm, 6-10.30pm Wed-Sat. **Credit** MC, V. **Map** p402 J5 **⑥**
This tiny wine bar (its name means wardrobe), where bottles line the walls like books in a library, is perfect for an end-of-the-day snifter, preferably accompanied by one of the platters of delicious parma ham, cheese or oysters. Organic and bio-dynamic wines stand their ground next to vintages from around the world.

OPERA TO LES HALLES

Le Brébant

32 bd Poissonnière, 9th (01.47.70.01.02).
M° Grands Boulevards. **Open** 7.30am-6am daily. **Credit** MC, V. **Map** p402 J4 **⑦**
The change that continues to sweep the Grands Boulevards is embodied in this prominent, round-the-clock bar-bistro. There's a permanently busy terrace below a colourful, stripy awning, and the cavernous, split-level interior has a cool neo-industrial feel. Prices are steep, so push the boat out and opt for an expertly made fruit daiquiri, or a Bonne Nouvelle of Bombay Sapphire gin and Pisang Ambon. There are rarer bottled beers too – Monaco, Picon and sundry brews from Brabant. A board advertises a decent range of proper eats: *burger-frites* (€15) and so on.

★ Café de la Paix

12 bd des Capucines, 9th (01.40.07.36.36/
www.cafedelapaix.fr). M° Opéra. **Open** 7am-midnight daily. **Credit** AmEx, DC, MC, V.
Map p401 G4 **⑧**
Lap up every detail – this is once-in-a-holiday stuff. Whether you're out on the historic terrace or looking up at the ornate stucco ceiling, you'll be sipping

---

THE BEST BANQUETTES

For old-school loungers
Chez Jeanette. *See p233.*

For budget boozers
Au Rendez-vous des Amis. *See p266.*

For stressed mothers
Poussette Café. *See p226.*

Café de la Paix.

in the footsteps of the likes of Oscar Wilde, Josephine Baker, Emile Zola, and Bartholdi and the Franco-American Union (as they sketched out the Statue of Liberty). Let the immaculate staff bring you a kir (€12) or, for an afternoon treat, the vanilla mille-feuille – possibly the best in Paris.

★ Le Cochon à l'Oreille
15 rue Montmartre, 1st (01.42.36.07.56).
M° Les Halles. **Open** 11am-2am Mon-Sat.
No credit cards. Map p402 J5 **9**
Some old bistros have the setting, others get the food. This little piggy (*cochon*) does a good job with both: the antique public telephone, the imposing zinc counter and the cosy wooden booths are charming reminders of Les Halles' heyday as the city's celebrated food market – note the tiles that depict scenes of the market in all its chaotic splendour. Food-wise, expect hearty, meaty dishes like stuffed pork on a bed of lentils and *confit de canard*, best accompanied by one of the 50 wines on the list. Enjoyed your meal? Write about it in the notebooks tucked away in little nooks.

De la Ville Café
34 bd de Bonne-Nouvelle, 10th (01.48.24.48.09/
www.delavillecafe.com). M° Bonne Nouvelle.
Open 11am-2am Mon-Sat; noon-2am Sun.
Credit MC, V. **Map** p402 J4 **10**
De la Ville has brought good news to Bonne-Nouvelle. A major expansion and refurbishment (it used to be a *maison close*) have upped the ante, bringing the in-crowd to this otherwise ignored quarter. Inside, the distressed walls and industrial-baroque feel remain, but the curvy club section at the back has become very cool. After 10pm on Fridays, Saturdays and some Thursdays DJs splice into the night.
▶ *The café was opened by the crew behind Café Charbon, see p231.*

Dédé la Frite
135 rue Montmartre, 2nd (01.40.41.99.90).
M° Sentier or Bourse. **Open** 8am-2am daily.
Credit MC, V. **Map** p402 J4 **11**
Suits from the nearby Bourse flock here for after-work cocktails (€7) and beers (€4), before giving in to the tempting aromas emanating from the kitchen: Dédé's frites at just €3 a tray are legendary and the rest of the food, reminiscent of an American diner (burgers, fries, ketchup on the bar), is an absolute bargain too. The place looks cool as well, with distressed walls, long bar, bright colours. After hours, when the alcohol flows and the munchies have been satisfied, the music is cranked up and the party really starts.

★ Harry's New York Bar
5 rue Daunou, 2nd (01.42.61.71.14/www.
harrys-bar.fr). M° Opéra. **Open** 10am-4am daily.
Credit AmEx, DC, MC, V. **Map** p401 G4 **12**

The city's most stylish American bar is an institution beloved of expats, visitors and hard-drinking Parisians (there are over 300 whiskies). The white-coated bartenders mix some of the most sophisticated cocktails in town, from the trademark bloody mary and white lady (both invented here, so they say) to the Pétrifiant, an aptly named elixir of half a dozen spirits splashed into a beer mug. They can also whip up personalised creations that will have you swooning in the downstairs piano bar, where Gershwin composed *An American in Paris*, and where jazz concerts are held most Thursday and Friday nights.

La Jungle
56 rue d'Argout, 2nd (01.40.41.03.45/www.la-jungle.com). M° Sentier. **Open** 10am-2am Mon-Fri; 4pm-2am Sat, Sun. **Credit** AmEx, MC, V.
Map p402 J5 **13**
Exoticism reigns at La Jungle, a former bordello that nowadays entertains the city's party animals with live afro-jazz on Wednesdays and Fridays (€2 extra on drinks), DJs on Saturdays, and jazz and blues on Sundays. Come here to enjoy exotic cocktails (€6), dishes with a Cameroonian bent and Flag beer from Senegal.

Le Tambour
41 rue Montmartre, 2nd (01.42.33.06.90/).
M° Sentier. **Open** 8am-6am daily. **Credit** MC,
V. **Map** p402 J5 **14**
Decked out with vintage public transport paraphernalia, slatted wooden banquettes and bus stop-sign bar stools, the Tambour has a split personality: there's the daytime Tambour, frequented by pretty much everybody; and the nighttime Tambour, a well-loved nighthawk's bar where the chatty regulars give the 24-hour clock their best shot and post-partygoers pile in for *steak-frites* at 3am (food is served until 4am).

Le Truskel
10 rue Feydeau, 2nd (01.40.26.59.97/
www.myspace.com/truskel_paris). M° Bourse.
Open 8pm-5am Mon-Fri; 6.15pm-5am Sat.
Closed Aug. **Credit** MC, V. **Map** p402 H4 **15**
The formula is quite simple at this pub-cum-club: an excellent selection of beers slakes your thirst, while an extensive repertoire of Britpop – sometimes live (ex-Pulp man and Paris resident Jarvis Cocker has been known to splice the night here, as has Pete Doherty and Franz Ferdinand) – assaults your ears. As a cheeky touch, a bar bell rings for no reason whatsoever, causing first-time visitors from the UK to down their drinks in one and dive for the bar.

Zenzoo
13 rue Chabanais, 2nd (01.42.96.27.28/www.zen-zoo.com). M° Quatre-Septembre. **Open** 11am-11pm Mon-Sat. Closed Aug. **Credit** MC, V.
Map p401 H4 **16**

CONSUME

Between 2.30pm and 7pm this tiny Taiwanese restaurant doubles as a 'tea bar', the only place in Paris that serves China's famous tapioca cocktails – sometimes known as 'bubble tea', they are served with an extra-wide straw to suck up the little tapioca balls at the bottom. The sensation may seem strange at first, but the tastes are great; among the flavours are mango, coconut and kumquat. Up the road at No.2, a spin-off boutique sells excellent oolong flower teas.

CHAMPS-ELYSEES & WESTERN PARIS

Charlie Birdy

124 rue La Boétie, 8th (01.42.25.18.06/ www.charliebirdy.com). Mº Franklin D. Roosevelt. **Open** 11am-5am daily. **Credit** AmEx, V. **Map** p401 E4 ⓯

Take a New York loft and meld it with a colonial English gentleman's club and you're looking at Charlie Birdy – a large 'pub' with a live music programme of jazz, soul and funk that's worth listening to. If you're in a hurry, stay away – the service can be aggravatingly slow. But if you take your time choosing from the 50-strong cocktail menu, sink into a comfy chesterfield and let the evening wash over you, it'll be worth it. Between 4pm and 8pm Monday to Friday cocktails are half-price.

Le Dada

12 av des Ternes, 17th (01.43.80.60.12). Mº Ternes. **Open** 7am-2am Mon-Sat; 7am-10pm Sun. **Credit** AmEx, MC, V. **Map** p400 C3 ⓰

Perhaps the hippest café in this stuffy part of town, Le Dada is best known for its well-placed, sunny terrace. Inside, the wood-block carved tables and red walls provide a warm atmosphere for a crowd that tends towards the well-heeled, well-spoken and, well, loaded. That said, the atmosphere is friendly; if terracing is your thing, you could happily spend a summer's day here – just bring along your Prada shades.

L'Endroit

67 pl du Dr-Félix-Lobligeois, 17th (01.42.29.50.00). Mº La Fourche or Rome. **Open** 8am-2am Mon-Wed, Sun; 8am-5.30am Thur-Sat. **Credit** MC, V. **Map** p401 F1 ⓳

You can't be a better spot in the old Batignolles village, with views over neo-classical Ste-Marie-des-Batignolles church, a cool thirtysomething crowd, decent wines, cocktails a go-go and excellent food that won't break the bank (€12 lunchtime menu).

Flute l'Etoile

19 rue de l'Etoile, 17th (01.45.72.10.14/ www.flutebar.com). Mº Ternes. **Open** 5pm-2am Tue-Sat; 6am-10pm Sun. **Credit** AmEx, MC, V. **Map** p400 C3 ⓴

With a menu of some 23 different champagnes and designer decor (slick wooden panelling, blue walls

and red velvet), Paris's first champagne lounge may be miniscule, but it certainly looks the part. Indeed the only indication that it's not French (it's American) is the sneaky appearance of a Californian sparkler on the champagne list. For drinkers wishing to sample different vintages without buying a whole glass (from €9), the small tasting glasses (from €5) are a thoughtful touch. And for anyone bored by plain old bubbly, cocktails such as champagne sangria and Rossini-Tini (champagne, raspberry juice, liqueur and Grey Goose vodka) make sophisticated alternatives.

Impala Lounge

2 rue de Berri, 8th (01.43.59.12.66). Mº George V. **Open** noon-2am Mon, Sun; noon-5am Tue-Sat. **Credit** AmEx, MC, V. **Map** p400 D4 ㉑

Dubbed the 'African Bar' by regulars, this wannabe-hip spot hams up the colonial with zebra skins, masks and a throne hewn from a tree trunk. Beer, wine, tea and standard favourites can all be had, but best are the cocktails, one of which claims to boost a waning libido with its mystery mix of herbs and spices. DJs rock Sunday afternoon away, and the snack-and-mains menu often includes ostrich.

★ Ladurée

75 av des Champs-Elysées, 8th (01.40.75.08.75/ www.laduree.fr). Mº George V or Franklin D. Roosevelt. **Open** 9am-11.30pm Mon-Thur; 9am-12.30am Fri; 10am-12.30am Sat; 10am-11.30pm Sun. **Credit** AmEx, DC, MC, V. **Map** p400 D4 ㉒

Decadence permeates this elegant tearoom, from the 19th century-style interior and service to the labyrinthine corridors that lead to the toilets. While you bask in the warm glow of bygone wealth, indulge in tea, pastries (the pistachio pain au chocolat is heavenly) and, above all, the hot chocolate. It's a rich, bitter, velvety tar that will leave you in the requisite stupor for any lazy afternoon.

▶ *The original branch at 16 rue Royale (8th, 01.42.60.21.79) is famed for its macaroons.*

Libre Sens

33 rue Marbeuf, 8th (01.53.96.00.72). Mº Franklin D. Roosevelt. **Open** 9am-3am daily. **Credit** MC, V. **Map** p400 D4 ㉓

Unusually for this part of town, Libre Sens is reasonably priced and down to earth. The design is slick, with low lighting and comfortable seating; particularly attractive are the large booths that accommodate groups and couples, the electric blue bar and the fine range of cognacs. Parisians love this place for a drink after work – happy hour (between 6.30pm and 8.30pm) includes champagne and cocktails from €7.

Sir Winston

5 rue de Presbourg, 16th (01.40.67.17.37). Mº Charles de Gaulle Etoile. **Open** 9am-3am Mon-Wed, Sun; 9am-4am Thur-Sat. **Credit** AmEx, V. **Map** p400 C4 ㉔

CONSUME

A bit of an anomaly, this. Grand and imperial, with a bit of Baroque thrown in for good measure, and located within sight of high-end glitz, Sir Winston does a nice line in jazz and gospel brunches on a Sunday. Colonial knick-knacks, chesterfields and chandeliers make up the decor, with Winnie himself framed behind a sturdy bar counter. A battalion of whiskies stands guard beside him, and the wine list is equally *recherché*. Where this place falters is in its somewhat sissy cocktail menu. A Sir Winston Breezer of Bacardi, melon liqueur, pineapple and banana juice? Harrumph!

MONTMARTRE & PIGALLE

Le Café Arrosé
123 rue Caulincourt, 18th (01.42.57.14.30).
M° Lamarck Caulaincourt. **Open** 8am-2am
Mon-Sat, 8am-7pm Sun. **Credit** MC, V.
Map p402 J1 ㉕
On the north side of the hill, this *resto-café* doesn't feature anything hugely different from most other bistros (red banquettes, menus on blackboards, 1930s tiled floor, zinc bar and contemporary art on the walls), yet there is something inexplicably

---

Perfect Mix
Bringing cocktail culture to Paris.

There was a time, not so long ago, when a request for a martini in a Paris bar would be greeted with 'rosso or bianco?' Worse still, you could be invited to an evening '*autour d'un cocktail*', only to be handed a glass of warm white wine instead. But thankfully this dismal state of affairs has finally been put right – and a lot of the credit should go to Romée, Pierre and Olivier, founders of the Experimental Cocktail Club.

Childhood friends from the South of France, these 27-year-old entrepreneurs realised that what Paris needed was a cocktail bar worthy of the name. Not a hotel bar where a drink will set you back €30, but a small and intimate speakeasy, unpretentious yet exacting in the art of cocktail mixing.

In 2007 they drew back the velvet curtains on a semi-secret venue off rue Montorgueil, and the **Experimental Cocktail Club** (37 rue Saint Sauveur, 2nd, 01.45.08.88.09, open 6pm-2am Mon-Wed, 6pm-3am Thur, 6pm-4am Fri, Sat) was born. These days there's a bouncer on the door, less to check your dress sense than to ask smokers to keep the noise down. Inside, the atmosphere ranges from cosy to thronging depending on the time and day, but even when it's busy you can be sure that your drink will start with a conversation. 'I always like to ask people what they *don't* like to start the ball rolling,' says Pierre.

A whisky sour created by mixologist Carina is a potent, zingy concoction of Laphroaig, Rittenhouse rye, maple syrup and fresh orange juice. Rarer treats include the wonderfully pure and aromatic Nikka Japanese whisky – the Experimental's second venue, the **Curio Parlour** (16 rue des Bernardins, 5th, 01.44.07.12.47, open 6pm-2am Tue, Wed, Sun, 6pm-3am Thur,

Experimental Cocktail Club.

6pm-5am Fri, Sat), contains the only Nikka bar outside Japan – and the 138° proof Bitter Truth, which is aged for 24 years. The tequila selection, Olivier's speciality, is equally rarified. 'Eighty per cent of what we offer is outside the mainstream,' he says. 'We want people to dare to be different.'

As well as whisky tastings, the trio put on themed costume parties, which started with the Hendrick's-sponsored Fantastic and Ridiculous Monday of the Unusual Cucumber and Rose Society, and took on a life of their own. Become a member of the Facebook groups to be updated on events.

Andy Whaloo.

pleasant about the ambience. Perhaps it's the smiley staff, decent wine list and mouthwatering food (from €12 for a main).

Les Caves Populaires

22 rue des Dames, 17th (01.53.04.08.32). *M° Place de Clichy.* **Open** 8am-2am Mon-Sat; 11am-2am Sun. Closed 2wks Aug. **Credit** MC, V. **Map** p401 G2
An old soak props up the bar with his *petit rouge*, while others play chess and groups of bobos (bourgeois bohemians) revel in the cheap prices – from €2.50 for a glass of quaffable wine, €3 for a beer and €7 for a cheese or charcuterie platter. It's a charming place and vaguely reminiscent of a wooden chalet, hence its second name, Les Caves du Châlet.

La Fourmi

74 rue des Martyrs, 18th (01.42.64.70.35). *M° Pigalle.* **Open** 8am-2am Mon-Thur; 8am-4am Fri, Sat; 10am-2am Sun. **Credit** MC, V. **Map** p402 H2
Set on the cusp of the ninth and 18th arrondissements, La Fourmi is an old bistro that has been converted for today's tastes, with picture windows lighting the spacious, roughshod interior, cool staff (and customers) and excellent music. The classic zinc bar counter is crowned by industrial lights, which helps you to see what you're reading as you rifle through the piles of flyers deciding where to go on to next; this is as good a place as any to find out what's happening in town.

Poussette Café

6 rue Pierre Sémard, 9th (01.78.10.49.00/ *www.lepoussettecafe.com).* *M° Poissonnière or Cadet.* **Open** 10.30am-6.30pm Tue-Sat. **Map** p402 J3
Fed up with the impracticalities of pushing her pram (*poussette*) into the local café, mother of two Laurence Constant designed her own parent- and child-friendly establishment. This upmarket *salon de thé* caters for the harassed parent (herbal teas, smoothies, quiches and salads) and demanding baby (purées, solids and cuddly toys).
▶ *You can sign up for magic shows and parenting workshops via the café's website.*

Au Rendez-vous des Amis

23 rue Gabrielle, 18th (01.46.06.01.60/www. *rdvdesamis.com).* *M° Abbesses.* **Open** 8.30am-2am daily. **Credit** MC, V. **Map** p402 H1
Considering its proximity to the honeypot that is Sacré Coeur, this café/bar is still cheap, making it popular with locals and foreign students, and the odd tourist. During happy hour (8pm to 10pm), a kir or glass of wine will set you back a very reasonable €2.70. There are cosy nooks round the back with plenty of upholstered spots to choose from.

★ Rouge Passion

14 rue Jean-Baptiste Pigalle, 9th (www.rouge-passion.fr). *M° St Georges or Pigalle.* **Open** noon-2.30pm Mon; noon-2.30pm, 7pm-midnight Tue-Sat. **Credit** MC, V. **Map** p401 G2

Two bright upstarts (Anne and Sébastien) determined to make their mark on Paris's bar scene are behind this venture – and they're going about it the right way. Offering a long list of wines (from just €3), free *assiettes apéros* (peanuts, olives and tapenades on toast) and decor that is perfect vintage chic, the formula is spot on. A small but mouthwatering selection of hot dishes, salads, cheese and *saucisson* platters (set lunch menu €20, mains from €15) help soak up the wine. Look out for the tasting classes, given by a guest sommelier.

Le Sancerre

35 rue des Abbesses, 18th (01.42.58.08.20). M° *Abbesses.* **Open** 7am-2am Mon-Thur; 7am-4am Fri, Sat; 9am-2am Sun. **Credit** MC, V. **Map** p402 H1 ③①

This popular Montmartre rock bar is home to a frenzied mix of alcohol-fuelled transvestites, tourists, lovers and bobo locals, who all come for the cheap beer (under €4), trashy music and buzzy terrace. The decor inside is dark and scruffy, the service undeniably slow and the food (omelettes, *steak-frites*) nothing special; yet there is something irresistibly refreshing about the no-frills approach that makes this bar stand out from the multitude of try-hard cafés in the area.

BEAUBOURG & THE MARAIS

★ Andy Whaloo

69 rue des Gravilliers, 3rd (01.42.71.20.38). *M° Arts et Métiers.* **Open** 4pm-2am Tue-Sat. **Credit** AmEx, MC, V. **Map** p409 K5 ③②

Andy Whaloo, created by the people behind its neighbour 404 and London's Momo and Sketch, is Arabic for 'I have nothing'. Bijou? This place brings new meaning to the word. The formidably fashionable crowd fights for coveted 'seats' on upturned paint cans; from head to toe, it's a beautifully designed venue, crammed with Moroccan artefacts and a spice rack of colours. It's quiet early on, with a surge around 9pm, and the atmosphere heats up as the night gets longer.

L'Apparemment Café

18 rue des Coutures St-Gervais, 3rd *(01.48.87.12.22). M° St-Sébastien Froissart.* **Open** noon-2am Mon-Fri; 4pm-2am Sat; 12.30pm-midnight Sun. **Credit** MC, V. **Map** p409 K6 ③③

The 'Apparently' feels more like a communal living room than a café. The low lighting, cosy nooks and board games (Trivial Pursuit and Taboo, both in French) make for an excellent place to while away an afternoon. Staff even organise the occasional fortune-telling evening. The location is perfect for shoppers too, being just off the rue Vieille-du-Temple. Lunches consist of simple DIY platters of meats, cheeses and salads, but at €15 for the basic version they're a bit rudimentary for the price. Eating is obligatory during busy periods, when it's definitely advisable to book.

Le Baromètre

17 rue Charlot, 3rd (01.48.87.04.54). M° Arts *et Métiers.* **Open** 8am-11pm Mon-Sat. **Credit** MC, V. **Map** p409 L5 ③④

This unpretentious wine bar is popular with the area's artisans. Lunchtimes are heaving, so unless you're after the sit-down *menu du jour* (€13) served at the back, you're better off coming for a lazy afternoon. Order a plate of cheese or the house speciality, bacon and andouillette gratin, and choose from a 20-strong list of wines by the glass, most under €3.50.

L'Estaminet

39 rue de Bretagne, 3rd (01.42.72.28.12/ *www.aromes-et-cepages.com). M° Temple.* **Open** 9am-8pm Tue-Sat; 9am-2pm Sun. **Credit** MC, V. **Map** p409 L5 ③⑤

L'Estaminet is tucked away in the Marché des Enfants-Rouges, a charming neighbourhood market and one of the city's oldest. The café has a warm interior, with a grandfather clock in the corner and guests eating €13 *plats du jour* off Limoges porcelain. Wines from around €4 a glass.

★ L'Etoile Manquante

34 rue Vieille-du-Temple, 4th (01.42.72.48.34/ *www.cafeine.com). M° Hôtel de Ville or St-Paul.* **Open** 9am-2am daily. **Credit** MC, V. **Map** p409 K6 ③⑥

The hippest of Xavier Denamur's merry Marais bars. Cocktails are punchy, traditional tipples just as good, and the salads and snacks are reasonably priced and tasty – but it's the design and buzz that are the main draws. The decor is trendy but comfortable, embellished with interesting art. As in all Denamur's places, no visit is complete without a trip to the toilets: here, an electric train shuttles between cubicles, starlight beams down from the ceiling, and a hidden camera films you washing your hands. Just watch the small screen on the wall behind you.

Lizard Lounge

18 rue du Bourg-Tibourg, 4th (01.42.72.81.34/ *www.cheapblonde.com). M° Hôtel de Ville.* **Open** noon-2am daily. **Credit** MC, V. **Map** p409 K6 ③⑦

An anglophone favourite deep in the Marais, this loud and lively (hetero) pick-up joint provides lager in pints (€6), plus cocktails (€7) and a viewing platform for beer-goggled oglers. Bare brick and polished woodwork are offset by the occasional lizard and a housey soundtrack. Bargain boozing (cocktails €5) kicks off at 5pm; from 8pm to 10pm there's another happy hour in the sweaty cellar bar (complete with miniscule dancefloor); on Mondays it lasts all day. A popular weekend brunch of bacon, sausages and eggs benedict caters to the homesick.

Le Loir dans la Théière

3 rue des Rosiers, 4th (01.42.72.90.61). M° St- *Paul.* **Open** 11.30am-7pm Mon-Fri; 10am-7pm Sat, Sun. **Credit** V. **Map** p409 L6 ③⑧

CONSUME

Le Loir is named after the unfortunate dormouse who gets dunked in the pot at the Mad Hatter's tea party in *Alice In Wonderland*. Its squishy sofas are the perfect complement to its comfort food: it specialises in baked goods, and the famed lemon meringue and chocolate fondant are divine. At weekends it's packed out with tourists in search of brunch; long queues of people looking enviously at your plate, plus occasionally patchy service, can mar the experience. Come early (before noon) or be prepared to queue.

La Perle

78 rue Vieille-du-Temple, 3rd (01.42.72.69.93).
M° Chemin Vert or St-Paul. **Open** 6am-2am
Mon-Fri; 8am-2am Sat, Sun. **Credit** MC, V.
Map p409 L6 ❸❾

The Pearl achieves a rare balance between all-day and late-night venue, and also has a good hetero/homo mix. In the morning it draws early risers; lunchtime is for a business crowd; the afternoon reels in retired locals, and in the evening screenwriters rub elbows with young dandies, keeping one eye on the mirror and an ear on the electro-rock. The menu runs from omelettes to *salade marine*. Expect a DJ later on.

Le Petit Fer à Cheval

30 rue Vieille-du-Temple, 4th (01.42.72.47.47/
www.cafeine.com). M° St-Paul. **Open** 9am-2am
daily. **Credit** MC, V. **Map** p409 K6 ❹⓿

Even a miniature Shetland pony would be pushed to squeeze his hoof into this *fer à cheval* (horseshoe) – the adorable little café, in business for more than 100 years, has one of France's smallest bars. Tucked in behind the glassy façade is a friendly dining room lined with reclaimed métro benches; if you want scenery, the tables out front overlook the bustle of rue Vieille-du-Temple. As with its sister bar L'Etoile Manquante (*see p227*), the loos are worth the detour – they look as if they've been pummelled out of a defunct Dalek, with metal panels and strange knobs everywhere.

Stolly's

16 rue Cloche-Perce, 4th (01.42.76.06.76/
www.cheapblonde.com). M° Hôtel de Ville or
St-Paul. **Open** 4.30pm-2am daily. **Credit** MC, V.
Map p409 K6 ❹❶

This seen-it-all drinking den has been serving a mainly anglophone crowd for nights immemorial. The staff make the place what it is, and a summer terrace eases libation, as do the long happy hours; but don't expect anyone at Stolly's to faff about with food. There's football on TV and a plastic shark to compensate.

Wini June

16 rue Dupetit-Thoars, 3rd (01.44.61.76.41).
M° Temple. **Open** 6pm-2am daily. **Credit**
MC, V. **Map** p409 L5 ❹❷

Wini June's virtual living room has become a favourite haunt of Paris fashionistas and designers, who lounge on the Empire-style or contemporary furnishings. Wine (served in crystal glasses) is accompanied by a selection of nibbles proffered by the attentive staff. The pint-sized terrace is an outdoor version of the interior, flanked with bamboo.

BASTILLE & EASTERN PARIS

Le Baron Rouge

1 rue Théophile-Roussel, 12th (01.43.43.14.32).
M° Ledru-Rollin. **Open** 10am-3pm, 5-10pm Tue-
Thur; 10am-10pm Fri, Sat; 10am-3pm Sun.
Credit AmEx, MC, V. **Map** p407 N7 ❹❸

It sells wine, certainly – great barrels of the stuff are piled high and sold by the glass at very reasonable prices. But the Red Baron is not just a wine bar – it's more like a local chat room, where regulars congregate to yak over their *vin*, or perhaps one of the few draught beers, and maybe a snack of sausages or oysters. Despite its lack of seating (there are only four tables), it's a popular pre-dinner spot, so arrive early and don't expect much elbow room; drinkers often spill out on to the pavement – joining the smokers.

Café Titon

34 rue Titon, 11th (09.53.17.94.10/
www.cafetiton.com). M° Faidherbe-Chaligny
or Rue des Boulets. **Open** 8am-2am Mon-Sat.
Credit MC,V. **Map** 407 P7 ❹❹

The funky Titon is Paris's only Franco-German café – and certainly the only place in town to flog *currywurst* (German sausage in curry sauce) and chips for just €5.50. It even turns into a *biergarten* during Germany's Oktoberfest. Its Parisian side doesn't get forgotten, though, with *croques*, *tartines*, an unbeatable lunch menu (€9.80 for a main and a *café*) and scrumptious cocktails (€6.90 for a margarita).

★ Chez Prosper

7 av du Trône, 11th (01.43.73.08.51).
M° Nation. **Open** 8.30am-1am daily.
Credit MC, V. **Map** p407 Q8 ❹❺

Chez Prosper welcomes punters all day long with that simplest of gestures: a smile. Yes, even when squeezing past people queuing for a spot on the sun terrace, the waiters are positively beaming. The traditional dining/drinks area – tiled floor, large mirrors, wooden furniture – is run with military precision, and orders arrive promptly. The *steak-frites* and *croques* (served on Poîlane bread) are hearty, and the naughty Nutella tiramisu is worth crossing town for.

China

50 rue de Charenton, 12th (01.43.46.08.09/
www.lechina.eu). M° Bastille or Ledru Rollin.
Open 6pm-2am Mon-Sat; noon-2am Sun. Closed
Aug. **Credit** AmEx, MC, V. **Map** p407 M7 ❹❻

This sexy take on a 1930s Shanghai gentleman's club, with red walls, leather chesterfields and the longest bar in Paris, serves some of the finest cocktails in town (including its signature singapore sling). The Cantonese cuisine is pricey, so skip dinner and head upstairs to the cigar bar (if you're romantically inclined) or downstairs to the cellar for weekly jazz, pop and world music concerts (website has details).

★ Les Furieux
74 rue de la Roquette, 11th (01.47.00.78.44/ www.lesfurieux.fr). Mᵒ Bastille or Voltaire. **Open** 4pm-2am Tue-Thur; 4pm-5am Fri, Sat; 7pm-2am Sun. **Credit** MC, V. **Map** p407 M6 ⑰

Just when it looked like 'lounge attitude' would contaminate every bar on rue de la Roquette, Les Furieux fought back with a healthy dose of rock and metal, padded red walls, faux-leather banquettes, black paint, and rotating exhibitions of photography on the walls. Locals flock here for the happy hour (6pm to 8pm), when cocktails with rockin' names like Grunge, Scud, and, er, Boris are half price. Diehards can pay tribute to Paris's hedonistic heyday with 12 different absinthes.

Le Houla Oups!
4 rue Basfroi, 11th (01.40.24.18.80/ www.myspace.com/lehoulaoups). Mᵒ Ledru-Rollin or Voltaire. **Open** 9am-2am Mon-Fri; 6pm-2am Sat. **Credit** MC, V. **Map** p407 N7 ⑱

Just off the main Roquette drag, this hip little den of rock – French rock to be precise – makes up in energy what it lacks in size. There are regular exhibitions,

live concerts, film nights (usually horror or genre movies), DJs and even auction evenings. During happy hour (6pm to 8pm) beer costs just €3 a pint. To keep in the loop, send an email to houlaoups@gmail.com asking to be put on the mailing list.

Le Motel
8 passage Josset, 11th (01.58.30.88.52). Mᵒ Ledru-Rollin. **Open** 6pm-1.45am Tue-Sun. Closed Aug. **Credit** MC, V. **Map** p407 M7 ⑲

Le Motel is the latest addition to the city's growing indie scene. It has a simple formula: cheap drinks and excellent music. During happy hour (6pm to 9pm) a pint of *blonde* costs €3.50 and cocktails €3. With DJs almost every night, the music ranges from cutting-edge indie to contemporary neo-folk and rock classics, with the odd Motown hit thrown in for good measure. Friendly twentysomethings cluster around faux Louis XVI armchairs or try their luck in the Sunday pop quiz.

L'Opa
9 rue Biscornet, 12th (01.46.28.12.90/www.opa-paris.com). Mᵒ Bastille. **Open** 8pm-2am Tue-Thur; 9pm-6am Fri, Sat. **Credit** V. **Map** p407 M7 ⑳

Late opening and Eric Perier's diverse range of nightly entertainment – DJs (weekends), videos, live acts (Tuesday to Thursdays) and the odd open mic event – are the attractions here, along with free admission and reasonable drinks prices. A couple of comfortable sofas take the edge off the loft-like, institutional interior, with a modest stage in one corner and an upstairs chill-out space and separate bar.

CONSUME

L'Alimentation Générale. *See p231.*

CONSUME

Chez Jeanette. *See p233.*

Pause Café

41 rue de Charonne, 11th (01.48.06.80.33).
Mº Ledru-Rollin. **Open** 8am-2am Mon-Sat;
9am-8pm Sun. **Credit** MC, V. **Map** p407 M7 ⑤
Featured in Cedric Klapisch's 1996 film *Chacun Cherche son Chat*, which was shot on location in the neighbourhood, the Pause Café has managed to prolong its moment of glory thanks to its large terrace on the corner of rues Charonne and Keller. Inside, the modern salons benefit from a smattering of primary colours with ornately plastered ceilings and plenty of light. Having been immortalised on celluloid, the friendly staff occasionally let fame go to their heads: service can be excruciatingly slow at times. The food – French café fare with an Asian twist – is not bad, but you might be waiting for a while; best to order a well-mixed cocktail to pass the time.

Les Pères Populaires

46 rue de Buzenval, 20th (01.43.48.49.22/
www.myspace.com/perespopulaires). Mº Buzenval
or Avron. **Open** 8am-2am daily. **Credit** MC, V.
Map p407 Q7 ⑤
On the far side of Nation, could this funky number be the cheapest bar in Paris? Wine is a mere €2 a glass, beer is €2.40 (€4.50 for a pint) and flavoured rums cost €4. To get an idea of the look of the place, think 1970s canteen-cum-retro classroom and you'll come close. During the day, the local freelance media crowd and a handful of musicians squat the tables for the free Wi-Fi; at night DJs spin electro sounds and a party atmosphere reigns.

Le Petit Bar

7 rue Richard Lenoir, 11th (no phone). Mº
Voltaire. **Open** 5pm-2am daily. **No credit cards. Map** p407 N6 ⑤
You couldn't invent this place if you tried: local soaks, immigrant South Americans, twentysomething students, Brits and retired war veterans all pop in for a taste of the most surreal experience in town, courtesy of the elderly Madame Polo, her fluffy cat and here canaries. Madame P is surely the last living link to a forgotten Paris and proof that in this age of excessive health and safety concerns, there are still places here that manage to slip through the net. A word of warning: don't drink out of the glasses – Madame Polo isn't too keen on cleaning. We recommend you opt instead for a €3 bottle of beer.

Le Temps des Cérises

31 rue de la Cerisaie, 4th (01.42.72.08.63).
Mº Bastille. **Open** 9am-9pm Mon-Fri. **Credit** MC, V. **Map** p409 L7 ⑤
Not to be confused with several other cafés of the same name, this one-room *bistro à vins* has changed very little over the years. Faded net curtains, Duralex tumblers behind the zinc bar and prices that begin at €2.50 for a *vin* or beer are all reminiscent of a bygone age. The blackboard wine list is limited but the selection is always well chosen, and food is old-fashioned and hearty (think beef stew and *blanquette de veau*). The general banter is football-centred, so get ready to rumble with the natives about PSG.

NORTH-EAST PARIS

L'Alimentation Générale

*64 rue Jean-Pierre-Timbaud, 11th
(01.43.55.42.50/www.alimentation-generale.net).
M° Parmentier.* **Open** 5pm-2am Wed, Thur,
Sun; 5pm-4am Fri, Sat. **Credit** AmEx, MC, V.
Map p403 M4

The 'Grocery Store' is rue Jean-Pierre-Timbaud's
answer to La Mercerie (*see p233*): a big old space filled
with junk. Cupboards of kitsch china and lampshades
made from kitchen sponges are an inspired touch.
The beer is equally well chosen – Flag, Sagres, Picon
and Orval by the bottle – and the unusual €8 house
cocktail involves basil and figs. DJs rock the joint:
expect a €5 cover price for big names or live bands
(including open-mic nights). Oh yes – and it has the
most brazen toilet walls this side of town. *Photo p229.*

★ Ave Maria

*1 rue Jacquard, 11th (01.47.00.61.73).
M° Parmentier.* **Open** 6.30pm-2am daily.
No credit cards. Map p403 M5

Unlike some places that eschew good food for alcohol and a funky interior, colourful Ave Maria scores
highly for all three. The kitsch interior is decked out
in a canopy of chinoiserie parasols and a vast collection of Hindu gods. Music, a combination of reggae, funk, soul and dub, is cool but unobtrusive.
Strangers sharing wooden benches devour exotic
dishes from the Brazilian-inspired menu, which combines meat, spices, lentils, rice and fruit. Cocktails
are equally quirky and start at just €4.50.

Bar Ourcq

*68 quai de la Loire, 19th (01.42.40.12.26/
http://barourcq.free.fr). M° Laumière.* **Open**
Winter 3pm-midnight Wed, Thur; 3pm-2am
Fri, Sat; 3-10pm Sun. *Summer* 5-9.30pm Wed-
Fri, Sun; 3pm-2am Sat. **No credit cards.**
Map p403 N1

This was one of the first hip joints to hit the Canal
de l'Ourcq, with an embankment broad enough to
accommodate *pétanque* games (ask at the bar) and
a cluster of deckchairs. It's a completely different
scene from the crowded bustle along Canal St-
Martin – more discerning and less self-satisfied. The
cabin-like interior is cosy, and drinks are listed in a
hit parade of prices, starting with €2.50 for a *demi*
or glass of red. Pastas at €9, exhibitions and a regular DJ spot keep the cool clientele sated. Closed on
rainy weekdays in summer.

La Bellevilloise

*19 rue Boyer, 20th (01.46.36.07.07/www.
labellevilloise.com). M° Gambetta.* **Open**
7pm-2am Wed, Thur; 6pm-2am Fri; 11am-1am
Sat, Sun. **Credit** V. **Map** p403 P4

The Bellevilloise is the latest incarnation of a building that once housed the capital's very first workers'
co-operative. Now it competently multitasks as a bar,
restaurant, club and exhibition space, hosting regular music and music festivals on the top level (where
there's a fake lawn with deckchairs and a massage
area). Enjoy brunch in the Halle aux Oliviers or decent
views of the *quartier* from the charming terrace;
downstairs the club-cum-concert venue has launched
some of Paris's most exciting new bands, and on '80s
nights you can hardly move for the thirtysomethings
living it up like they were 20 again.

Café Charbon

*109 rue Oberkampf, 11th (01.43.57.55.13/
www.nouveaucasino.net). M° Parmentier or
Ménilmontant.* **Open** 9am-2am Mon, Tue,
Sun; 9am-4am Wed- Sat. **Credit** MC, V.
Map p403 N5

The bar contained within this beautifully restored
belle époque building sparked the Oberkampf

INSIDE TRACK
COFFEE ETIQUETTE

A word about coffee in France. If you ask
for *un café*, you'll be given an espresso.
Ask for it '*serré*' if you prefer it more
concentrated, and '*allongé*' if you're
craving an American-style coffee. A
crème is made with milk, but good,
frothy cappuccino is rare. If you just want
a dash of frothy milk in your espresso,
ask for a '*noisette*'. And if you want
a skinny decaf? Head to Starbucks.

nightlife boom. Its booths, mirrors and adventurous music policy put trendy locals at ease, capturing the essence of café culture spanning each end of the 20th century. After more than 15 years, the formula still works – and is copied by nearby bars.

▶ *The management run the popular Nouveau Casino nightclub next door (see p329) and the groovy De la Ville Café (see p223) in the 10th.*

Café Chéri(e)

44 bd de la Villette, 19th (01.42.02.02.05/ http://cafecherie.blogspot.com). M° Belleville. **Open** 8am-2am daily. **Credit** MC, V. **Map** p403 M3 ⑥⓪

This splendid DJ bar is also an all-day café – but it doesn't compromise any of the cool that keeps it well ahead of the pack after dark. Music comes from all over, and runs from electro, rock, funk, hip hop,

indie, dance and jazz to golden oldies and ghetto-inspired grooves. The interior sparkles with wit and invention – note the marvellous mural alluding to the personal sacrifices made for a life of coupledom. There's a front terrace if you need a smoke or conversational respite from the BPM.

▶ *There's music from Thursdays to Saturdays after 10pm; see p327.*

Le Café Noir

15 rue St-Blaise, 20th (01.40.09.75.80/ www.cafenoirparis.com). M° Alexandre Dumas or Porte de Bagnolet. **Open** 9am-midnight Mon-Sat. **Credit** MC, V.

In the St-Blaise district (the former village of Charonne annexed to Paris in 1860), with views on to the village church, this gorgeous high-ceilinged café, decorated with old cafetières, draws in artists,

---

Let's Do Drunch

It's dinner meets lunch, of course.

After a late night on the tiles, Paris's early afternoon Sunday brunches have always been a godsend. The only hitch is that you had to be out of bed by 2pm to catch last orders around 4pm. But now loafers can celebrate the arrival of 'Le Drunch', which means that partied out Parisians can now head out for curative cuisine even later on Sundays. The trend is catching on across the city, but here are four surefire drunch joints to help dispel the Sunday afternoon blues.

First up is **Mini Palais** (3 av Winston-Churchill, 8th, 01.42.56.42.42, www.mini palais.com, open 6-11pm Sun), set inside the Grand Palais in what were once the palace's reception rooms. You'd be hard pushed to find a more majestic setting – the restaurant's imposing colonnaded balcony has views of the palace's glass roof and the current exhibition. Mini was the first restaurant to jump on the drunch bandwagon, and offers a special menu of creamy soups, cold meat platters, a chariot of squidgy desserts and hot drinks for €28.

For a chic, cocktail-oriented drunch, head for the panoramic **Bar du Concorde La Fayette** (3 pl du Général-Koenig, 01.40.68.50.68, www.concorde-lafayette. com, open 3pm-1am Sun) on the 33rd floor of the Concorde Lafayette hotel. The views over the west of the city across the Bois de Boulogne and Eiffel Tower are truly uplifting, especially when accompanied by a margarita (€12) and a plate of finger sandwiches (€8) or a prawn platter (€9).

If nothing but American fast food will satisfy, opt for an all-day breakfast (eggs, pancakes and bacon for €7.95) at **Breakfast in America** (17 rue des Ecoles, 5th, 01.43. 54.50.28, www.breakfast-in-america.com, open 4-11pm Sun), or tuck into the gorgeously juicy BIA Burger (with onions, pepper, cheddar and BBQ sauce) for €9.95.

Alternatively, head off the beaten track to Nation, where **Chez Prosper** (*see p228*) has been letting us drunch on copious salads covered in fried potatoes, tandoori chicken, salmon or cheesy *tartines* (on Poilâne bread) for years without even realising it.

Bar du Concorde La Fayette.

workers and an up-beat crowd of local trendies for a spot of coffee and a *verre de vin* throughout the day. At mealtimes expect inventive French cuisine, with the likes of foie gras speckled with speculoos biscuits, magret of duck with cardamom and vanilla, and pineapple and mango trifle.

Le Café des Sports

94 rue de Ménilmontant, 20th (01.46.36.48.18/ www.myspace.com/lecafedessports). M° Gambetta. **Open** 11am-1.30am Mon-Fri; noon-1.30am Sat, Sun. Closed Aug. **Credit** MC, V. **Map** p403 P4 ⓺
Le Café des Sports' fine and eclectic music pro-gramme ranges from electro (Saturdays), to pop or *chanson* (Tuesdays and Thursdays) to world dub. Beer and wine are fabulously cheap (just €2 from 6pm to 8pm) and there's even sometimes free cous-cous or tapas with your drink on a Monday evening. Unlike its sprawling neighbours, Le Café des Sports has just one room to call home. DJs play in the space around the back.

★ Chez Jeanette

47 rue du Fbg-St-Denis, 10th (01.47.70.30.89). M° Strasbourg St-Denis or Château d'Eau. **Open** 8am-2am daily. **Map** p402 K3 ⓺
When she sold her café back in March 2007, Jeanette handed over to the young team from Chez Justine because they promised not to change a thing. The monstrous 1940s dust-coated lights, leaky loos, tobacco-stained wallpaper depicting the Moulin Rouge and PVC-covered banquettes have finally been cleaned up, and the café has become one of Paris's hippest spots for an aperitif. There's a *plat du jour* at lunch and plates of cheese and charcuterie at night; at 8pm, the fluorescent lights go off and candlelight takes over, to a cheer. *Photos p230.*

Chez Prune

36 rue Beaurepaire, 10th (01.42.41.30.47). M° Jacques Bonsergent. **Open** 8am-2am Mon-Sat; 10am-2am Sun. **Credit** AmEx, MC, V.
Map p402 L4 ⓺
Chez Prune is an excellent lunch spot, and still one of the best places to spend an evening on the Canal St-Martin. The local bobo HQ, this traditional café, with high ceilings and low lighting, sticks to a sim-ple formula: groups of friends crowd around the cosily ordered banquettes, picking at moderately priced cheese or meat platters. Mostly, though, they come for a few leisurely drinks or an *apéro* before heading to one of the late night venues in the area.

Le Cinquante

50 rue de Lancry, 10th (01.42.02.36.83). M° Jacques Bonsergent. **Open** *Sept-July* 5.30pm-2am daily. *Aug* 5.30pm-2am Tue-Sun.
No credit cards. Map p402 L3 ⓺
Just down from the Canal St-Martin, the bare brick, Formica and framed '50s ads of this funky venue attract an inner circle of regulars. These days it's

established enough to produce its own T-shirts and customised bar stools. Reasonable prices – half-litre pitchers of sauvignon, Brouilly and Chablis in the €10 range – attract a mixed bag of tastes and gen-erations. The two rooms behind the main bar are set aside for dining (affordable classics) and music (gen-erally acoustic). Sunday is open-mic night.

La Gouttière

96 av Parmentier, 11th (01.43.55.46.42). M° Parmentier. **Open** 8am-2am Mon-Fri; 3pm-2am Sat. **Credit** V. **Map** p403 M4 ⓺
Far enough (five minutes) from rue Oberkampf to feel off the beaten track, the Gutter is not out-and-out lib-ertine, but you're on the right lines. Certainly, a come-what-may approach to music, drinking and eye contact abounds in the crowded venue. Decor, assum-ing you can see it, consists of a few LP covers and the kind of colour scheme often put to good use in adven-ture playgrounds. Reasonably priced lunches (food is a French and North African mix), the occasional live band, chess and card games complete the picture.

★ Le Mange Disque

58 rue de la Fontaine-au-Roi, 11th (01.58.30.87.07/www.mangedisque.net). M° Goncourt. **Open** 11am-3pm, 5pm-2am Tue-Sat. Closed Aug. **No credit cards. Map** p403 M4 ⓺
There's another Mange Disque in town, but it's not to be confused with this remarkably cool bar, which shows what you can do with a little art, a fine taste in music, the most mundane of furniture and the right connections. If you want to launch a CD, intro-duce a DJ or simply imbue your bash with cool, do it here. Savvy owner Hubert has brought in choice wines from little-known producers in south-west France, but only charges €3 a glass; likewise, the snacks cost under €10. Stacks of vinyl are left out for browsing, and with the constant traffic of events and launches, no two evenings are the same.

La Maroquinerie

23 rue Boyer, 20th (01.40.33.35.05/ www.lamaroquinerie.fr). M° Gambetta. **Open** 6pm-2am daily. Closed Aug.
Credit MC, V. **Map** p403 P4 ⓺
La Maroquinerie's former life as a leather factory is little in evidence these days. It's now a bright café and bar in competition with La Bellevilloise (*see p231*), with a coveted downstairs concert venue that hosts the odd literary debate and a wealth of cool music acts. The food is excellent – you can eat your way through the menu quite reasonably for around €25 – and wine sourced from across France starts at €3 a glass. The interior, with exposed brick, is cosy, and in summer chirpy locals invade the shaded terrace.

La Mercerie

98 rue Oberkampf, 11th (01.56.98.14.10). M° Parmentier. **Open** 5pm-2am daily.
Credit MC, V. **Map** p403 N5 ⓺

CONSUME

Opposite the landmark Charbon (*see p231*) the spacious Mercerie has cleaned up its act: after years of full-on grunge it has succumbed to the draw of shabby chic – or, to put it another way, a fashionable level of dishevelment. This was probably wise, as the novelty of sticky tables was beginning to wear thin, and the move has been appreciated by the party freaks who still cross town for its loud, eclectic music, live DJ programme, and cheapo happy hour (7pm to 9pm), when you can cane the house vodkas in flavours such as apricot, mango and honey. The back area, with its tea lights, provides intimacy if that's where your evening's headed.

Mon Chien Stupide
1 rue Boyer, 20th (01.46.36.25.49).
M° Gambetta. **Open** 6pm-2am Tue-Sun.
Credit MC, V. **Map** p403 P4 ⑥⑨
As the action moves relentlessly eastwards from Oberkampf, the once-distant outposts of Gambetta and Bagnolet appear on the radar of the discerning bar-hopper. Colourful and humorous, My Stupid Dog is a bar for grown-ups: an undercurrent of jazzy sounds drifts along nicely, cheese platters are accompanied by a quality selection of wines, and contemporary art freckles the walls. It's commendably unsympathetic to canines – note the 'Dog Paste' sign by the bar.

Au Passage
1bis passage St-Sébastien, 11th (01.43.55.07.52/
www.restaurant-aupassage.com). M° St-Sébastien
Froissart. **Open** 9am-10pm daily. **Credit** MC, V.
Map p409 M5 ⑦⓪
Tucked down a long, narrow alleyway off rue Amelot, opposite the back entrance of Pop In, you don't just happen upon Au Passage, you come because you've heard about the cheap lunchtime menus (€12.50) and the colourful local artists and wannabe *marginaux* (all almost as colourful as their teeth, stained with a glass too many of *vin rouge*). There's art on the far wall, some retro cookbooks, and a feeling that entire decades could pass without anyone really noticing.

★ Au P'tit Garage
63 rue Jean-Pierre-Timbaud, 11th
(01.48.07.08.12). M° Parmentier. **Open**
6pm-2am daily. **Credit** AmEx, MC, V.
Map p403 M4 ⑦①
As sweetly tuned as Chuck Berry's cherry-red '53, this quite marvellous rock 'n' roll bar is the pick of the bunch on rue Jean-Pierre-Timbaud. Not that the owners have fitted it with Americana or waitresses on rollerskates; the L'il Garage is as basic as the real car-fit business a few doors down the road. Stuffing bursts out of the bar stools and skip-salvage chairs accompany wobbly tables of ill-matched colours. Regulars cluster around the twin decks at the bar, while music-savvy Frenchettes giggle and gossip at the back.

Le Verre Volé
67 rue de Lancry, 10th (01.48.03.17.34/
www.leverrevole.fr). M° Jacques Bonsergent.
Open 10.30am-2.30pm, 7pm-2am Tue-Sun.
Closed Aug. **Credit** MC, V. **Map** p402 L4 ⑦②
This organic-only *cave à vins* doubles up as a miniscule wine bar and restaurant. Although wine (around €4 per glass) is the focus, you're obliged to eat; a hearty sausage and mash will set you back around €15 (other mains cost up to €20). Purists who would prefer a simple snack to complement their *bon vin* should opt for a plate of charcuterie and cheese at €12. It's good to know that staff will sell you a bottle of wine (and open it) for you to drink by the canal.

THE LATIN QUARTER & THE 13TH

★ Le Crocodile
6 rue Royer-Collard, 5th (01.43.54.32.37/
www.lecrocodile.fr). RER Luxembourg. **Open**
10pm-late Mon-Sat. Closed Aug. **Credit** MC, V.
Map p408 J8 ⑦③
Ignore the apparently boarded-up windows at Le Crocodile; if you're here late, then it's open. Friendly young regulars line the sides of this small, narrow bar and try to decide what to drink – not easy, given the length of the cocktail list: at last count there were 317 varieties. The generous €6-per-cocktail happy hour (Monday to Thursday before midnight) will allow you to start with a champagne *accroche-coeur*, followed up with a Goldschläger (served with gold leaf) before moving on to one of the other 316.

Le Merle Moqueur
11 rue de la Butte aux Cailles, 13th (no phone).
M° Place d'Italie. **Open** 5pm-2am daily.
No credit cards.
Amid semi-faded pseudo-tropical decor and '80s music, the Teasing Blackbird – a Butte-aux-Cailles institution – tantalises students and nostalgists with its splendid selection of rums (over 20) and a long list of cocktails. The atmosphere gets raucous after 10pm – get in early to grab one of the three tables.

Le Pantalon
7 rue Royer-Collard, 5th (no phone). RER
Luxembourg. **Open** 5.30pm-2am Mon-Sat.
No credit cards. Map p408 J8 ⑦④
A local café that seems familiar yet is utterly surreal. It has the standard fixtures, including the old soaks at the bar – but the regulars and staff are enough to tip the balance firmly into eccentricity. Friendly and funny French grown-ups and foreign students chat in a variety of languages; drinks are cheap enough to make you tipsy without the worry of a cash hangover.

Le Requin Chagrin
10 rue Mouffetard, 5th (01.44.07.23.24).
M° Place Monge. **Open** 4pm-2am daily.
Credit MC, V. **Map** p406 J8 ⑦⑤

CONSUME

Café de Flore.

The 'depressed shark' hasn't lost its bite. Students and beer guzzlers of all ages still cram in for the ten *bières* on tap and the five-hour happy hour (4-9pm), when drinks are a steal at just €2.50. You'll find the usual Left Bank suspects: groups of friends, blokes trying to get laid and *intellos* from the nearby universities who still stimulate their brains during down time with chess and quoits.

Sputnik
14 rue de la Butte aux Cailles, 13th (01.45.65.19.82/www.sputnik.fr). M° Place d'Italie.
Open 2pm-2am Mon-Sat; 4pm-midnight Sun.
Credit MC, V.
A hip young crowd gathers in this rock-oriented bar, which doubles as a sports bar during important football and rugby fixtures, and trebles as an internet café at other times. Ever-changing art exhibitions add interest to the walls, and live music once a month draws an indie crowd. Fancy falling in love? Try the €8 love potion cocktail Philtre d'Amour, which is made from gin, Malibu, pineapple and strawberries.

ST-GERMAIN-DES-PRES & ODEON

★ Le Bar Dix
10 rue de l'Odéon, 6th (01.43.26.66.83/ www.le10bar.com). M° Odéon. **Open** 6pm-2am daily. **No credit cards. Map** p408 H7 ⑦⑥

Generations of students have glugged back jugs of the celebrated home-made sangria (€3 a glass during happy hour) while squeezed into the cramped upper bar, tattily authentic with its Jacques Brel record sleeves, Yves Montand handbills and pre-war light fittings. Spelunkers and hopeless romantics negotiate the hazardous stone staircase to drink in the cellar bar, with its candlelight and century-old advertising murals. Can someone please come and slap a preservation order on the place?

★ Le Bar du Marché
75 rue de Seine, 6th (01.43.26.55.15).
M° Mabillon or Odéon. **Open** 8am-2am
daily. **Credit** MC, V. **Map** p408 H7 ⑦⑦
The market in question is the Cours des Halles, the bar a convivial corner café opening on to the pleasing bustle of St-Germain-des-Prés. Simple dishes like a ham omelette or a plate of herrings are in the €7 range, and Brouilly or muscadet is €4-€5 a glass – all proffered by waiters dressed in matching dungarees. It couldn't be anywhere else in the world. Locals easily outnumber tourists, confirming Rod Stewart's unusually astute observation that Paris gives the impression that no one is ever working.

Café de Flore
172 bd St-Germain, 6th (01.45.48.55.26/ www.cafe-de-flore.com). M° St-Germain-des-Prés.
Open 7.30am-1.30am daily. **Credit** AmEx, DC, MC, V. **Map** p408 H6 ⑦⑧

Bourgeois locals crowd the terrace tables at lunch, eating club sandwiches with knives and forks as anxious waiters frown at couples with pushchairs or single diners occupying tables for four. This historic café, former HQ of the Lost Generation intelligentsia, attracts tourists and, yes, celebrities from time to time. But a *café crème* is €4.60, and the omelettes and croque-monsieurs are best eschewed in favour of the better dishes on the menu (€15-€25). There are play readings on Mondays and philosophy debates on the first Wednesday of the month, at 8pm, in English.

★ Chez Georges

11 rue des Canettes, 6th (01.43.26.79.15). Mº Mabillon. **Open** noon-2am Tue-Sat. Closed Aug. **Credit** MC, V. **Map** p408 H7 ⑳
One of a dying breed of *cave-bars* in the Latin Quarter, Chez Georges is beloved of students, professionals and local eccentrics. Regulars pop in during the day to sip wine over a game of chess, and at night the *cave* fills up with people dancing to *chanson*, pop and even the odd bar mitzvah tune. The heat is mascara-melting and it's not for the claustrophobic, but it's a great way to meet new people.

Les Deux Magots

6 pl St-Germain-des-Prés, 6th (01.45.48.55.25/ www.lesdeuxmagots.com). Mº St-Germain-des-Prés. **Open** 7.30am-1am daily. **Credit** AmEx, DC, MC, V. **Map** p408 H7 ⑳

If you stand outside Les Deux Magots, you have to be prepared to photograph tourists wanting proof of their encounter with French philosophy. The former haunt of Sartre and de Beauvoir now draws a less pensive crowd that can be all too *m'as-tu vu*, particularly at weekends. The hot chocolate is still good, though, and served in generous portions. Visit on a weekday afternoon when the editors return, manuscripts in hand, to the inside tables, leaving enough elbow room to engage in some serious discussion.

Les Editeurs

4 carrefour de l'Odéon, 6th (01.43.26.67.76/ www.lesediteurs.fr). Mº Odéon. **Open** 8am-2am daily. **Credit** AmEx, MC, V. **Map** p408 H7 ㉛
It's no surprise to see row upon row of books in the bright, modern interior of Les Editeurs. A café with literary leanings, it sits on the lovely carrefour de l'Odéon, a crossroads that leads to the Luxembourg gardens. Bask in the glory of literary greats as portraits of authors and their editors look down on you. Brunch on Saturday and Sunday is good value at €25.50; in the evening, main courses come in between €17 and €26, and sandwiches are €14.50 throughout the day.

★ J'Go

Rue Clément, 6th (01.43.26.19.02/www.lejgo. com). Mº Mabillon or Odéon. **Open** 11am-midnight daily. **Credit** MC, V. **Map** p408 H7 ㉜

La Palette.

As its name suggests, J'Go (pronounced gigot) is all about lamb – well, meat of various kinds, actually: a buzzing Toulouse-style wine bar in the Marché St-Germain by day, it becomes a *rôtisserie* at meal times, serving its speciality spit-roasted lamb from Quercy, black pig from Bigorre, and whole roasted chickens. The €36 set menu is well worth the splurge, offering a whole jar of pâté, a giant bowl of salad, and lamb with creamy stewed *haricots blancs*. If you'd rather stick to wine and tapas, sidle up to one of the great wooden barrels, choose your poison (blindly if necessary – at €4 a glass all wines are good) and share a plate of charcuterie or foie gras *tartines* (€10).

★ La Palette

43 rue de Seine, 6th (01.43.26.68.15).
Mº Odéon. **Open** 9am-2am Mon-Sat. Closed Aug. **Credit** MC, V. **Map** p408 H6 🔞

La Palette is the café-bar of choice for the very beau Beaux-Arts students who study at the venerable institution around the corner, and young couples who steal kisses in the wonderfully preserved art-deco back room decorated with illustrations. It ain't cheap – a glass of Chablis sets you back €6, a demi €4.50 – but you're paying for the prime location once frequented by such luminaries as Jim Morrison, Picasso and Ernest Hemingway. Grab a spot on the leafy terrace if you possibly can – there's formidable competition for seats.

Le Rostand

6 pl Edmond-Rostand, 6th (01.43.54.61.58).
RER Luxembourg. **Open** 8am-2am daily.
Credit MC, V. **Map** p408 H8 🔞

Le Rostand has a truly wonderful view of the Jardin du Luxembourg from its classy interior, decked out with oriental paintings, a long mahogany bar and wall-length mirrors. It's a terribly well-behaved place; consider arriving draped in furs or sporting the latest designer eyewear if you want to fit in with the well-heeled clientele. Whiskies and cocktails are pricey, as is the brasserie menu, but the snack menu serves delicious omelettes and *croques* for around €8 (salad €4 extra). Perfect for a civilised drink after a stroll round the gardens.

MONTPARNASSE

Le Café Tournesol

9 rue de la Gaîté, 14th (01.43.27.65.72). Mº Gaîté.
Open 8.30am-1.30am Mon-Sat; 9.30am-1.30am Sun. **Credit** AmEx, MC, V. **Map** p405 G9 🔞

The Tournesol is young, vibrant and the best of the cafés on rue de la Gaïté. There's outdoor seating in the shadow of the Tour Montparnasse, and an exposed brick interior with a soul, funk and electro soundtrack. A croque-monsieur will set you back €6, a steak €12.50, and a demi of Stella €3. An abstract tableau presides over a well-organised back space, where there's plenty of seating for groups.

L'Entrepôt

7-9 rue Francis de Pressensé, 14th
(01.45.40.07.50/www.lentrepot.fr). Mº Pernéty.
Open 9am-midnight daily. **Credit** MC, V.
Map p405 F10 🔞

L'Entrepôt, housed in a former warehouse, is a wonderful multitasker and has enough to keep you keen all week. There's a café where literary readings are held, a restaurant with a plant-clad terrace (a godsend in the summer), and a bar on the ground floor with live music most Thursdays, Fridays, Saturdays and Mondays – mainly jazz, rap and *chanson*. There's also an arthouse cinema and exhibition space upstairs.

Le Select

99 bd du Montparnasse, 6th (01.45.48.38.24).
Mº Vavin. **Open** 7am-2am Mon-Thur, Sun; 7am-4am Fri, Sat. **Credit** MC, V. **Map** p405 G8 🔞

For a decade between the wars, the junction of boulevards Raspail and du Montparnasse was where Man Ray, Cocteau and Lost Generation Americans hung out in the vast, glass-fronted cafés. Eight decades on, Le Select is the best of what have inevitably become tourist haunts. Sure, its pricey menu is big on historical detail and short on authenticity, but by and large it manages to hold on to its heyday with dignity.

THE 7TH & WESTERN PARIS

Le Café du Marché

38 rue Cler, 7th (01.47.05.51.27). Mº Ecole
Militaire. **Open** 7am-midnight Mon-Sat; 7am-5pm Sun. **Credit** MC, V. **Map** p405 D6 🔞

This well-loved address is frequented by trendy locals, shoppers hunting down a particular type of cheese and tourists who've managed to make it this far from the Eiffel Tower. Le Café du Marché really is a hub of neighbourhood activity. Its *pichets* of decent house plonk always go down a treat, and mention must be made of the food – such as the huge house salad featuring lashings of foie gras and parma ham.

Café Thoumieux

4 rue de la Comète, 7th (01.45.51.50.40). Mº La
Tour Maubourg. **Open** noon-2am Mon-Fri; 5pm-2am Sat. Closed 3wks Aug. **Credit** AmEx, MC, V. **Map** p405 E6 🔞

Café Thoumieux is a laid-back destination for cocktails, tapas and big-screen sport. Banquettes snake around the room, and spiky Aztec-pattern lamps light up the faces of the pretty young locals who have made this place their own. The flavoured vodkas are delicious, with unusual flavours including vanilla, caramel and banana; just watch out for the treacherous, extra-high bar stools (the banquettes are definitely the safest option to avoid accidents) and the monstrous, pebble-dashed sink in the toilets – it's real.

CONSUME

Shops & Services

Push open the door to retail heaven.

With the looming prospect of relaxed Sunday trading laws, Paris shopping has never been in better shape. Where else in the world can you find so many independent boutiques and specialist shops, right in the middle of some of the most picturesque areas of the city? Whether it's tasting cheeses for a dinner party, getting measured up for a bra or selecting hand-made gloves or a one-off piece of vintage clothing, shopping in Paris is a sensual pleasure based around quality, not quantity. Although chain stores have made their mark, it's still a long way removed from the grim uniformity of so many provincial high streets.

HOW TO SHOP

Different areas of the city have different specialities. There are clusters of antiques shops in the seventh arrondissement, and second-hand and rare book outlets in the fifth; crystal and porcelain manufacturers still dot rue de Paradis in the tenth; furniture craftsmen as well as children's clothes shops inhabit rue du Fbg-St-Antoine; bikes and cameras are clustered on boulevard Beaumarchais; and the world's top jewellers can be found on place Vendôme. The historic covered passages in the second and ninth are also fun places in which to shop, with chic stores such as cosmetics line **By Terry** mixed in with philatelists and booksellers.

Family-run food shops have thankfully not been eroded by supermarket culture, and tend to cluster in 'market streets' such as rue des Martyrs and rue Mouffetard, as well as around the many covered and open-air food markets. Here everything from a vintage bottle of armagnac to a single praline chocolate is lovingly presented, served and wrapped. Informed discussion is still very much part of the purchasing process, and beautiful, old-style shops, unchanged for decades, add to the pleasure.

About the authors

Alison Culliford moved to France in 2001 and is a regular contributor to Time Out's Paris guides. Katie Walker is a fashion designer and writer who divides her time between London and Paris.

Green, organic and ethical have also suddenly become sexy concepts to the French. Even luxury brands have embraced them, seen at the first sustainable luxury trade fair, called 1.618, at the Palais de Tokyo in May 2009. The not-for-profit concept store **Merci** and the eco fashion store **House of Organic** offer guilt-free clothes shopping, and **Designpack Gallery** recycles packaging into funky and ingenious objects for the home.

Shops are generally open from 10am to 7pm Monday to Saturday, with specialist boutiques closing for an hour at lunch. Some are closed on Monday mornings. Sunday opening is found in the Marais, on the Champs-Elysées, at Bercy Village and in the Carrousel du Louvre, although this may change – President Sarkozy is currently trying to extend Sunday trading. Many shops on the Champs-Elysées stay open until midnight, and Thursday is late closing at department stores.

General

DEPARTMENT STORES

BHV (Bazar de l'Hôtel de Ville)

52-64 rue de Rivoli, 4th (01.42.74.90.00/DIY hire 01.42.74.97.23/www.bhv.fr). M° Hôtel de Ville. **Open** 9.30am-7.30pm Mon, Tue, Thur, Fri; 9.30am-8pm Sat; 9.30am-9pm Wed. **Credit** AmEx, MC, V. **Map** p406 J6.

Homeware heaven: there's even a Bricolage Café with internet access. Upper floors have a good range of men's outdoor wear, upmarket bed linen, toys, books, household appliances – and a large space devoted to every type of storage utility.

★ Le Bon Marché

24 rue de Sèvres, 7th (01.44.39.80.00/www. bonmarche.fr). M° Sèvres Babylone. **Open** 10am-8pm Mon-Wed, Sat; 10am-9pm Thur, Fri. **Credit** AmEx, DC, MC, V. **Map** p405 G7.

The city's oldest department store, opened in 1848, is also its most swish and user-friendly, thanks to an extensive redesign by LVMH. Luxury boutiques, Dior and Chanel among them, take pride of place on the ground floor; escalators designed by Andrée Putman take you up to the fashion floor, which has an excellent selection of global designer labels, from Lanvin to Claudie Pierlot. Designer names also abound in Balthazar, the prestigious men's section.
► *For top-notch nibbles, try the adjoining Grande Epicerie food hall (01.44.39.81.00, www.lagrande epicerie.fr, 8.30am-9pm Mon-Sat).*

Galeries Lafayette

40 bd Haussmann, 9th (01.42.82.34.56/ fashion shows 01.42.82.30.25/fashion advice 01.42.82.35.50/www.galerieslafayette.com). M° Chaussée d'Antin/RER Auber. **Open** 9.30am-8pm Mon-Wed, Fri, Sat; 9.30am-9pm Thur. **Credit** AmEx, DC, MC, V. **Map** p401 H3.

The store has been undergoing a massive renovation programme of late, with the opening in 2008 of Espace Luxe on the first floor, featuring luxury prêt-à-porter and accessories and nine avant-garde designers, and the unveiling of a vast new shoe department in the basement featuring some 150 brands. The men's fashion space on the third floor, Lafayette Homme, has natty designer corners and a 'Club' area with internet access. On the first floor, Lafayette Gourmet has exotic foods galore, and a vast wine cellar.
► *Lafayette Maison over the road has five floors of home furnishings and interior design products.*
Other locations Centre Commercial Montparnasse, 14 rue du Départ, 14th (01.45.38.52.87).

★ Printemps

64 bd Haussmann, 9th (01.42.82.50.00/www. printemps.com). M° Havre Caumartin/RER Auber. **Open** 9.35am-8pm Mon-Wed, Fri, Sat; 9.35am-10pm Thur. **Credit** AmEx, DC, MC, V. **Map** p401 G3.

In the magnificently appointed Printemps you'll find everything you didn't even know you wanted and English-speaking assistants to help you find it. But fashion is where it really excels; an entire floor is devoted to shoes, and the beauty department stocks more than 200 brands. In all, there are six floors of men's and women's fashion. In Printemps de la Mode, French designers sit alongside all the big international designers. The Fashion Loft offers

a younger but equally stylish take on current trends. Along with furnishings, Printemps de la Maison stocks everything from tableware to design classics.
► *For fast refuelling, Printemps has a tearoom, sushi bar and Café Be, an Alain Ducasse bakery.*

Tati

4 bd de Rochechouart, 18th (01.55.29.52.20/ www.tati.fr). M° Barbès Rochechouart. **Open** 10am-7pm Mon-Fri; 9.30am-7pm Sat. **Credit** MC, V. **Map** p402 J2.

Expect to find anything from T-shirts to wedding dresses, as well as bargain children's clothes and household goods at this discount heaven. It's unbeatably cheap, but don't expect high quality.
Other locations throughout the city.

SHOPPING MALLS

Bercy Village

Cour St Emilion, 12th (08.25.16.60.75/www. bercyvillage.com). M° Cour St-Emilion. **Open** 11am-9pm daily. **Credit** AmEx, DC, MC, V. **Map** p407 P10.

This retail and leisure development housed in old wine warehouses is a relaxed place to shop. Squarely aimed at tourists and out-of-towners, the shops include Agnès b, Nature et Découvertes, Andaska and Pacific Adventure sports shops, L'Occitane, Oliviers & Co and Résonances for gifts, and Omnisens spa and Sephora for beauty. There are also cafés, restaurants, a park and a multiplex.

Le Bon Marché

CONSUME

THE LUXURY
DEPARTMENT STORE
DESTINATION

PRINTEMPS
P A R I S

FIND ALL TOP INTERNATIONAL LABELS UNDER ONE ROO

BALENCIAGA, BOTTEGA VENETA, BURBERRY, CARTIER, CHANEL, CHRISTIAN
DIOR, DE BEERS, DOLCE&GABBANA, GUCCI, LONGCHAMP, MIU MIU, PRADA
VAN CLEEF & ARPELS, YVES SAINT LAURENT...

PRINTEMPS | HAUSSMANN, 64 BOULEVARD HAUSSMANN
75009 PARIS Tél : 33 (0)1 42 82 57 87

Drugstore Publicis

*133 av des Champs-Elysées, 8th (01.44.43.79.00/
www.publicisdrugstore.com). M° Charles de Gaulle
Etoile.* **Open** 8am-2am Mon-Fri; 10am-2am Sat,
Sun. **Credit** MC, V. **Map** p400 D4.

A 1960s legend, Drugstore Publicis was clad with
neon swirls by architect Michele Saee following a
renovation in 2004; a glass-and-steel café stretches
out on to the pavement. On the ground floor there's
a newsagent, pharmacy, bookshop and upmarket
deli full of quality olive oils and elegant biscuits.
The basement is a macho take on Colette, keeping
selected design items and lifestyle mags, and replacing high fashion with fine wines and a cigar cellar.

Forum des Halles

*Rue Pierre-Lescot & rue Rambuteau, 1st
(01.44.76.96.56/www.forumdeshalles.com)
M° Les Halles/RER Châtelet Les Halles.*
Open 10am-8pm Mon-Sat. **Map** p402 J5.

The Forum des Halles is Paris's biggest and least
pleasant shopping mall, although a facelift due
for completion in 2012 should improve matters.
Extending three levels underground, it incorporates
métro stations, multiplex, gym, swimming pool and
numerous restaurants, and is truly labyrinthine.
High street retailers dominate: Mango, Zara, Kookaï,
H&M, Bershka, Naf-Naf, Bodum, Habitat, Sephora,
Yves Rocher and a flagship Fnac are all here.

La Galerie du Carrousel
du Louvre

*99 rue de Rivoli, 1st (01.43.16.47.10/www.
carrouseldulouvre.com). M° Palais Royal
Musée du Louvre.* **Open** 10am-10pm daily.
Credit AmEx, MC, V. **Map** p406 J6.

This massive underground centre – open every day
of the year – is home to more than 35 shops, mostly
big-name chains vying for your attention and cash.
The Petit Prince boutique and Réunion des Musées
Nationaux shops are great if you're in the hunt for
some last-minute gifts.

La Vallée Village

*3 cours de la Garonne, 77700 Serris
(01.60.42.35.00/www.lavalleevillage.com).
Eurostar/TGV Marne La Vallée-Chessy-Parc
Disneyland/RER Val d'Europe.* **Open** 10am-7pm
Mon-Sat; 11am-7pm Sun. Closed 1 Jan, 1 May,
25 Dec. **Credit** AmEx, MC, V.

Now directly linked to London via the Eurostar,
La Vallée Village, near Disneyland Paris, is discount
shopping heaven. Its 90 stores feature all the usual
suspects – Armani, Hilfiger and Burberry – as well
as French brands Agnès b, Zadig & Voltaire and
Antik Batik.

▶ *If you want to shop in style, avoid the RER
and splurge on a VIP Shopping Out of the City
trip, complete with limousine, champagne and
goodie bags. From €750 for a group of four;
reservations 01.64.25.90.50.*

Specialist
BOOKS & MAGAZINES

Bouquinistes

*Along the quais, especially quai de Montebe[llo],
quai St-Michel, 5th. M° St-Michel.* **Open** times
vary from stall to stall, generally Tue-Sun.
No credit cards. Map p406 J7.

The green, open-air boxes along the *quais* are one
of the city's institutions. Most sell second-hand
books – rummage through boxes packed with
ancient paperbacks for something existential. *See
also p118* **Bouq Club**.

Gibert Joseph

*26 bd St-Michel, 6th (01.44.41.88.88/www.gibert
joseph.com). M° St-Michel.* **Open** 10am-8pm Mon-
Sat. **Credit** MC, V. **Map** p408 J7.

Formed back in 1929, this string of bookshops is normally packed out with students.

▶ *Further up bd St-Michel (nos.30, 32 & 34)
are branches specialising in stationery, CDs,
DVDs and art materials.*

★ La Hune

*170 bd St-Germain, 6th (01.45.48.35.85). M° St-
Germain-des-Prés.* **Open** 10am-11.45pm Mon-
Sat; 11am-7.45pm Sun. **Credit** AmEx, MC, V.
Map p405 G7.

This Left Bank institution boasts a global selection
of art and design books, and a magnificent collection of French literature and theory.

English-language

Abbey Bookshop

*29 rue de la Parcheminerie, 5th (01.46.33.75.00/
www.alevdesign.com/abbey). M° St-Michel.*
Open 11am-7pm Mon-Sat. **No credit cards.**
Map p408 J7.

Celebrating 20 years in business, the tiny Abbey
Bookshop is the domain of Canadian renaissance
man Brian Spence, who organises weekend hikes
as well as dressing up in doublet and hose for a spot
of 17th-century dancing. The tiny, narrow shop
stocks old and new works, a specialised Canadian
section, and highbrow subjects down the rickety

THE BEST BOOKSHOPS

For a good old rummage
Bouquinistes. *See above.*

For English classics
Shakespeare & Company. *See p242.*

For kids' capers
Red Wheelbarrow. *See p242.*

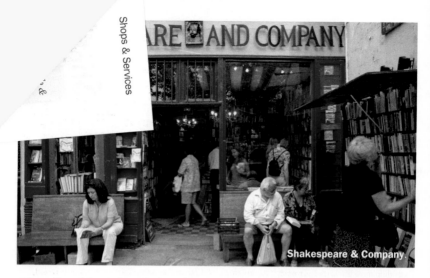

Shakespeare & Company

staircase. Several thousand more books are in storage, and he can normally order titles for collection within two days.

Galignani
224 rue de Rivoli, 1st (01.42.60.76.07/ www.galignani.com). M° Tuileries. **Open** 10am-7pm Mon-Sat. **Credit** MC, V. **Map** p401 G5.
Opened in 1802, this was the first English-language bookshop in mainland Europe. Today it stocks fine art books, French and English literature, philosophical tomes and magazines.

I Love My Blender
36 rue du Temple, 3rd (01.42.77.50.32/www. ilovemyblender.fr). M° Hôtel de Ville. **Open** 10am-7.30pm Tue-Sat. **Credit** AmEx, MC, V. **Map** p409 K6.
Christophe Persouyre left a career in advertising to share his passion for English and American literature: all the books he stocks were originally penned in English, and here you can find their mother-tongue and translated versions.

Red Wheelbarrow
22 rue St-Paul, 4th (01.48.04.75.08/www.thered wheelbarrow.com). M° St-Paul. **Open** 10am-6pm Mon; 10am-7pm Tue-Sat; 2-6pm Sun. **Credit** MC, V. **Map** p407 L7.
Penelope Fletcher Le Masson and Abigail Altman run this friendly literary bookshop in the Marais, which also has an excellent children's section.

★ Shakespeare & Company
37 rue de la Bûcherie, 5th (01.43.25.40.93). M° St-Michel. **Open** 10am-11pm Mon-Sat; 11am-11pm Sun. **Credit** MC, V. **Map** p408 J7.

Unequivocally the best bookshop in Paris, the historic and ramshackle Shakespeare & Company is always packed with expat and tourist book-lovers. There is a large second-hand section, antiquarian books next door, and just about anything you could ask for new.

Village Voice
6 rue Princesse, 6th (01.46.33.36.47/ www.villagevoicebookshop.com). M° Mabillon. **Open** 2-7.30pm Mon; 10am-7.30pm Tue-Sat; noon-6pm Sun. **Credit** AmEx, DC, MC, V. **Map** p405 H7.
New fiction, non-fiction and literary magazines in English, plus literary events and poetry readings.

WH Smith
248 rue de Rivoli, 1st (01.44.77.88.99/www. whsmith.fr). M° Concorde. **Open** 9am-7pm Mon-Sat; 12.30-7pm Sun. **Credit** AmEx, MC, V. **Map** p401 G5.
With 70,000 English-language titles and extensive magazine shelves, this is a home from home for Brits craving a fix of their native periodicals; the first floor has books, DVDs and audiobooks.

CHILDREN
Fashion

Children's fashion is clustered on rue Bréa (6th), rue Vavin (6th) and rue du Fbg-St-Antoine (12th). **Monoprix** (www.monoprix.fr) is a good source of inexpensive children's clothes, with some branches stocking Petit Bateau basics. For chic at a snip, try the **Bonpoint** (42 rue de l'Université, 7th, 01.40.20.10.55) and **Cacharel**

(114 rue d'Alésia, 14th, 01.45.42.53.04) stock shops; it may be last season's stuff, but your five-year-old is never going to know.

Bonton

82 rue de Grenelle, 7th (01.44.39.09.20/www. bonton.fr). Mᵒ Rue du Bac. **Open** 10am-7pm Mon-Sat. Closed 2wks Aug. **Credit** AmEx, DC, MC, V. **Map** p405 F6.

At this concept store for kids and trendy parents, T-shirts and trousers come in rainbow colours, and at pretty steep prices. Furniture and accessories are also available, as is a children's hairdresser.

Other locations 118 rue Vieille-du-Temple, 3rd (01.42.72.34.69).

▶ *In addition to the abovementioned branches, the Bonton Bazar store (122 rue du Bac, 7th, 01.42.22.77.69) offers cute kids' homeware for bedroom, bathroom, kitchen and 'library'.*

★ Finger in the Nose

17 rue Saintonge, 3rd (01.42.71.43.40/www. fingerinthenose.com). Mᵒ St-Sébastien Froissart. **Open** 11am-7pm Tue-Sat. **Credit** AmEx, MC, V. **Map** p409 L5.

As the name suggests, there is nothing twee about the kidswear from this Norwegian designer. In the Marais boutique blackboard walls with chalk slogans and drawings set off tough rebel urban wear for six- to 16-year-olds, including bright red Puffas, mod check jumpers, rock'n'roll T-shirts and jeans.

Jacadi

116 rue d'Alésia, 14th (01.40.44.51,87/ www.jacadi.fr). Mᵒ Alésia. **Open** 11am-7pm Mon; 10am-7pm Tue-Sat. **Credit** MC, V. **Map** p405 E10.

Jacadi's well-made clothes for babies and children – pleated skirts, smocked dresses, dungarees and Fair Isle knits – are a hit with well-to-do parents. The rue d'Alésia store is the largest.

Other locations throughout the city.

★ Papillon pour Bonton

84 rue de Grenelle, 7th (01.42.84.42.43). Mᵒ Rue du Bac. **Open** 10am-7pm Mon-Sat. **Credit** MC, V. **Map** p405 G6.

Bonton's new venture is all about nostalgia, with hand-knits, cashmere and alpaca, dinky stripes and Liberty prints in the shades of a hand-tinted photograph (old rose, grey, aubergine, sage). Pretty buttons accompany the fine finish that Bonton is famous for, and christening robes and pyjamas complete the collection, displayed in an old perfume shop amid flowery wallpaper and hunting trophies. Pure *Bagpuss*.

★ Du Pareil au Même

120-122 rue du Fbg-St-Antoine, 12th (01.43.43.96.01/www.dpam.com). Mᵒ Ledru-Rollin. **Open** 10am-7pm Mon-Sat. **Credit** AmEx, MC, V. **Map** p407 N7.

Bright, cleverly designed basics for children aged three months to 14 years, at low prices. The Bébé branch, with fashionable accessories and clothing for kids up to two years, is a good source of gifts. **Other locations** throughout the city.

Petit Bateau

26 rue Vavin, 6th (01.55.42.02.53/www.petit-bateau.com). Mᵒ Vavin. **Open** 10am-7pm Mon-Sat. **Credit** AmEx, MC, V. **Map** p405 G8.

Widely renowned in the city and beyond for its comfortable, well-made cotton T-shirts, vests and other separates, Petit Bateau carries an equally coveted teen range.

Other locations throughout the city.

★ Six Pieds Trois Pouces

223 bd St-Germain, 7th (01.45.44.03.72/ www.sixpiedstroispouces.com). Mᵒ Solférino. **Open** 10.30am-7pm Mon-Fri; 10am-7pm Sat. **Credit** AmEx, DC, MC, V. **Map** p405 F6.

The excellent array of children's and teens' shoes runs from Start-rite and Aster to Timberland and New Balance, alongside the shop's own brand.

Other locations 85 rue de Longchamp, 16th (01.45.53.64.21); 78 av de Wagram, 17th (01.46.22.81.64).

Zef

15 rue Debelleyme, 3rd (01.42.76.09.65/ www.zef.eu). Mᵒ St-Sébastien Froissart. **Open** 11am-7.30pm Mon-Sat. **Credit** AmEx, DC, MC, V. **Map** p409 L5.

Zef's designer is the daughter of fashion photographer Paolo Reversi. The trendy children's separates have a classic Italian look, in soft muted colours with adorable details like elbow patches on the jackets. Boots, sheepskin gilets and hats are part of the look.

Other locations 32 rue de Richelieu, 1st (01.42.60.61.04); 55bis rue des Sts-Pères, 6th (01.42.22.02.93; babies and toddlers 01.42.22.45.22).

Toys & books

Traditional toyshops abound; department stores (*see p238*) go overboard at Christmas. For a selection of children's books in English, try **WH Smith** (*see left*).

Arche de Noé

70 rue St-Louis-en-l'Ile, 4th (01.46.34.61.60). Mᵒ Pont Marie. **Open** 10.30am-1pm, 2-7pm daily. **Credit** AmEx, MC, V. **Map** p409 K7.

'Noah's Ark' is a great place for Christmas shopping, with traditional wooden toys from eastern Europe, games, jigsaws and finger puppets.

Fnac Junior

19 rue Vavin, 6th (08.92.35.06.66/www.eveilet jeux.com). Mᵒ Vavin. **Open** 10am-7.30pm Mon-Sat. **Credit** AmEx, MC, V. **Map** p405 G8.

CONSUME

Fnac carries books, toys, DVDs, CDs and CD-Roms for the under-12s. Storytelling and other activities (Wed, Sat) take place for three-year-olds and up. **Other locations** throughout the city.

★ Au Nain Bleu

5 bd Malesherbes, 8th (01.42.65.20.00/www. aunainbleu.com). M° Madeleine. **Open** Mon; 10am-7pm Tue-Sat. **Credit** AmEx, MC, V. **Map** p401 F4.

The city's best toyshop, decorated like a circus tent, draws gasps of wonder from children. Wooden doll's houses, pirate ships and gorgeous dolls are made to last more than one generation.

Village Joué Club

3-5 bd des Italiens, 2nd (01.53.45.41.41/ www.joueclub.fr). M° Richelieu Drouot. **Open** 10am-8pm Mon-Sat. **Credit** AmEx, MC, V. **Map** p402 H4.

Village Joué Club, the largest toy store in Paris, is spread out in and around passage des Princes.

FASHION

All the world's big-name designers have their own-label stores in Paris. In addition to international fashion juggernauts Mango, H&M and Zara, the high street has its fair share of Gallic cheapies: think **Etam**, Jennyfer and Pimkie. The highest density is in the **Forum des Halles** (*see p241*), on nearby rue de Rivoli, between the métro stations of Châtelet and Louvre Rivoli, and around Galeries Lafayette and Printemps.

Designer

Azzedine Alaïa

7 rue de Moussy, 4th (01.42.72.19.19). M° Hôtel de Ville. **Open** 10am-7pm Mon-Sat. **Credit** AmEx, DC, MC, V. **Map** p409 K6.

Ringing the doorbell gains you entry to the factory-style showroom in the same building as Alaïa's headquarters and apartment, where the Tunisian creator continues to astound with his originality. Stunning haute couture creations are in the back room, and sexy shoes bordering on fetish are scattered among the mannequins and rails.

★ Balenciaga

10 av George V, 8th (01.47.20.21.11/www. balenciaga.com). M° Alma Marceau or George V. **Open** 10am-7pm Mon-Sat. **Credit** AmEx, DC, MC, V. **Map** p400 D5.

With Nicolas Ghesquière at the helm, the Spanish fashion house is ahead of Japanese and Belgian designers in the hip stakes. Floating fabrics contrast with dramatic cuts, producing a sophisticated urban style that the fashion *haut monde* can't wait to slip into. Bags and shoes are also available.

▶ *Check out Balenciaga Edition, a range of couture designs from the 1950s and '60s reworked for the current collection.*

Balmain

44 rue François 1er, 8th (01.47.20.57.58/ www.balmain.com). M° George V. **Open** 10.30am-7pm Mon-Sat. **Credit** AmEx, DC, MC, V. **Map** p400 D4.

A large portrait of the late Pierre Balmain surveys the scene at his eponymous shop in the middle of the Triangle d'Or. What would he have made of the clothes around him? Long gone are the afternoon dresses with perfectly positioned waists, full skirts and trapezoidal necklines. While the clothes are still astonishingly expensive and exquisitely finished, the racks are these days lined with bondage trousers, studded jackets and animal print drainpipes. There hasn't been such a good display of grungy, punk glamour since Kensington Market closed its doors.

Carlos Miele

380 rue St-Honoré, 1st (01.42.97.53.66/ www.carlosmiele.com.br). M° Concorde. **Open** 10am-7pm Mon-Sat. **Credit** AmEx, MC, V. **Map** p402 H5.

The Brazilian designer favoured by Sandra Bullock, Heidi Klum and J Lo brings luxury with a conscience to the rue St-Honoré. He works with several co-operatives in *favelas* and with Amazonian Indians, honing traditional techniques like crochet, knotting, embroidery and featherwork.

★ Chanel

31 rue Cambon, 1st (01.42.86.26.00/www. chanel.com). M° Concorde or Madeleine. **Open** 10am-7pm Mon-Sat. **Credit** AmEx, DC, MC, V. **Map** p401 G4.

Fashion legend Chanel has managed to stay relevant, thanks to Karl Lagerfeld. Coco opened her first boutique in this street, at no.21, in 1910, and the tradition continues in this elegant interior. Lagerfeld has been designing for Chanel since 1983, and keeps on revamping the classics – the little black dress and the Chanel suit – with great success.

Other locations 42 av Montaigne, 8th (01.47.23.74.12); 25 rue Royale, 8th (01.44.51.92.93); 21 rue du Fbg-St-Honoré, 8th (01.53.05.98.95).

Comme des Garçons

54 rue du Fbg-St-Honoré, 8th (01.53.30.27.27). M° Concorde or Madeleine. **Open** 11am-7pm Mon-Sat. **Credit** AmEx, DC, MC, V. **Map** p401 F4.

Rei Kawakubo's design ideas and revolutionary mix of materials have influenced fashions of the past two decades, and are showcased in this fibreglass store.

▶ *Comme des Garçons Parfums (23 pl du Marché-St-Honoré, 1st, 01.47.03.15.03) provides a futuristic setting for the brand's fragrances.*

CONSUME

Dior

26-30 av Montaigne, 8th (01.40.73.73.73/
www.dior.com). M° Franklin D. Roosevelt.
Open 10am-7pm Mon-Sat. **Credit** AmEx, DC,
MC, V. **Map** p400 D5.
The Dior universe is here on avenue Montaigne,
from the main prêt-à-porter store and jewellery,
menswear and eyewear to Baby Dior.
Other locations throughout the city.

Gaspard Yurkievich

38 rue Charlot, 3rd (01.42.77.42.48/www.
gaspardyurkievich.com). M° Filles du Calvaire.
Open 11am-7pm Tue-Sat. **Credit** MC, V.
Map p402 L5.
The first boutique of this native Parisian fashion
missile. Hot men's and women's designs and a dangerous line of shoes are all on display.

Givenchy

28 rue du Fbg-St-Honoré, 8th (01.42.68.31.00/
www.givenchy.com). M° Madeleine or Concorde.
Open 10am-7pm Mon-Sat. **Credit** AmEx, DC,
MC, V. **Map** p401 F4.
In 2008, Givenchy opened this new flagship store for
men's and women's prêt-à-porter and accessories.
It incorporates surreal rooms within rooms – cut-out
boxes lined with white, black or mahogany panelling
– providing an art gallery setting for Givenchy's cutting-edge, sculptural and monochrome designs.

Hermès

24 rue du Fbg-St-Honoré, 8th (01.40.17.47.17/
www.hermes.com). M° Concorde or Madeleine.
Open 10.30am-6.30pm Mon-Sat. **Credit** AmEx,
DC, MC, V. **Map** p401 F4.

Hervé Léger.

The fifth generation of the family directs the Hermès
empire from this 1930s building. Originally – and
still – a saddler, it is no also-ran in the fashion stakes,
with Jean-Paul Gaultier at the reins. Most of its
clients, however, are tourists after a horsey scarf.

Hervé Léger

24 rue Cambon, 1st (01.42.60.02.00/www.
herveleger.com). M° Concorde. **Open** 10am-7pm
Mon-Sat. **Credit** AmEx, DC, MC, V. **Map** p401 G4.
A couple of decades ago Hervé Léger's silhouette-
cinching bandage dresses were as evocative of the
era as supermodels Linda, Christy, Naomi and
Cindy. But somewhere in the mid-'90s women lost
their love of Lycra, longing for the more conventional figure-flattering techniques of bias cut and tailoring. In the past few seasons, however, updated
reinterpretations of Léger's style, by the likes of
Christopher Kane and Marios Schwab, have been
nothing short of a fashion phenomenon. Less modified versions, sold by the Léger label itself (now
owned and designed by Max Azria of BCBG fame),
have been less critically acclaimed, but celebrities
just adore them.

★ Isabel Marant

16 rue de Charonne, 11th (01.49.29.71.55/
www.isabelmarant.tm.fr). M° Ledru-Rollin.
Open 10.30am-7.30pm Mon-Sat. **Credit** AmEx,
MC, V. **Map** p407 M7.
Marant's style is easily recognisable in her ethno-
babe brocades, blanket-like coats and decorated
sweaters. It's a favourite among young trendies.
Other locations 47 rue Saintonge, 3rd
(01.42.78.19.24); 1 rue Jacob, 6th (01.43.26.04.12).

★ Jay Ahr

2-4 rue du 29 Juillet, 1st (01.42.96.95.23/
www.jayahr.com). M° Tuileries. **Open** 11am-
7pm Mon-Sat. **Credit** AmEx, MC, V.
Map p401 G5.
Former jewellery designer Jonathan Riss opened this
shop as a fashion stylist in 2004, and struck gold
with simple, figure-flaunting, '60s-inspired dresses.
Think plunging necklines and Bianca Jagger in her
heyday, with Ali McGraw and Anita Pallenberg in
the mix. There are no price tags on the dresses, so
you have to ask; they start at around €500.

Jean-Paul Gaultier

6 rue Vivienne, 2nd (01.42.86.05.05/www.
jeanpaulgaultier.com). M° Bourse. **Open**
10.30am-7pm Mon-Fri; 11am-7pm Sat.
Credit AmEx, DC, MC, V. **Map** p402 H4.
Having celebrated his 30th year in the fashion business, Gaultier is still going strong. His boudoir boutique with its peach taffeta walls stocks men's and
women's ready-to-wear and the reasonably priced
JPG Jeans lines.
Other locations 44 av George V, 8th
(01.44.43.00.44).

CONSUME

▶ *The haute couture department (01.72.75.83.00) is strictly by appointment only, and is located above the store.*

John Galliano

384-386 rue St-Honoré, 1st (01.55.35.40.40/ www.johngalliano.com). M° Concorde or Madeleine. **Open** 11am-7pm Mon-Sat. **Credit** AmEx, DC, MC, V. **Map** p401 G4.

It's hard to imagine how he manages it all, but Dior chief Galliano still has his own range and a reputation as one of the UK's most original designers. You can admire the small but diverse collection of flamboyant and feminine delights through the showcase window, or from the Louis XVI-style chairs inside.

Kenzo

1 rue du Pont Neuf, 1st (01.40.28.11.80/www. kozen.com). M° Pont Neuf. **Open** 11am-7.30pm Mon-Sat. **Credit** AmEx, DC, MC, V. **Map** p402 J6.

Kenzo has long been a friend of Paris, having dressed the city itself in its various extravagant publicity campaigns. The flagship store has three floors of men's and women's fashion, and is crowned with the Bulle Kenzo spa and Philippe Starck-designed Kong restaurant on the fifth floor.

Other locations throughout the city.

Lanvin

22 rue du Fbg St-Honoré, 8th (01.44.71.31.73/ www.lanvin.com). M° Concorde or Madeleine. **Open** 10.30am-7pm daily. **Credit** AmEx, DC, MC, V. **Map** p401 F4.

The couture house that began in the 1920s with Jeanne Lanvin has been reinvented by the talented and indefatigable Albert Elbaz. In October 2007 he unveiled this, the revamped showroom that set new aesthetic standards for luxury fashion retailing. Lanvin has an exhibition room devoted to her in the Musée des Arts Décoratifs, and this apartment-boutique comes close, incorporating original furniture from the Lanvin archive that has been restored. All this would be nothing, of course, if the clothes themselves were not exquisite.

Lefranc.ferrant

22 rue de l'Echaudé, 6th (01.44.07.37.96/www. lefranc-ferrant.fr). M° St-Germain-des-Prés. **Open** 11am-7pm Tue-Sat and by appointment. **Credit** AmEx, MC, V. **Map** p408 H7.

The opening of this boutique has been eagerly awaited by keen followers of the talented Paris duo Béatrice Ferrant and Mario Lefranc. Their trademark is a surreal approach to tailoring, as in a strapless yellow evening gown made like a pair of men's trousers – complete with flies. Prices are in the €1,000 range and they love to undertake bespoke commissions.

Other location 149 Galerie de Balois, 1st (01.58.62.20.78).

★ Louis Vuitton

101 av des Champs-Elysées, 8th (08.10.81.00.10/ www.vuitton.com). M° George V. **Open** 10am-8pm Mon-Sat; 11am-7pm Sun. **Credit** AmEx, DC, MC, V. **Map** p400 D4.

The 'Promenade' flagship sets the tone for Vuitton's global image, from the 'bag bar', bookstore and new jewellery department to the women's and men's ready-to-wear. Contemporary art, videos by Tim White Sobieski and a pitch-black elevator by Olafur Eliasson complete the picture. Accessed by lift, the Espace Vuitton hosts temporary art exhibits – but the star of the show is the view over Paris.

Other locations 6 pl St-Germain-des-Prés, 6th; 22 av Montaigne, 8th.

Marc Jacobs

56 galerie de Montpensier, 1st (01.55.35.02.60/ www.marcjacobs.com). M° Palais Royal Musée du Louvre. **Open** 11am-8pm Mon-Sat. **Credit** AmEx, DC, MC, V. **Map** p402 H5.

By choosing the Palais-Royal for his first signature boutique in Europe, Marc Jacobs brought new life – and an influx of fashionistas – to these elegant cloisters. Stocking womenswear, menswear, accessories and shoes, it has already become a place of pilgrimage for the designer's legion of admirers, who are snapping up his downtown New York style.

Martin Grant

10 rue Charlot, 3rd (01.42.71.39.49/www.martin grantparis.com). M° Temple. **Open** 10am-6pm Mon-Fri. Closed 3wks Aug. **Credit** MC, V. **Map** p406 K6.

This high-end shop is tucked away in a second-floor Marais apartment. If you're a stickler for steady cuts, pure textiles and unfussy designs, Australian designer Martin Grant's interpretation of couture is for you.

Martin Margiela

23 & 25bis rue de Montpensier, 1st (womenswear 01.40.15.07.55/menswear 01.40.15.06.44/www.maisonmartinmargiela. com). M° Palais Royal Musée du Louvre. **Open** 11am-7pm Mon-Sat. **Credit** AmEx, DC, MC, V. **Map** p402 H5.

The first Paris outlet for the JD Salinger of fashion is a pristine, white, unlabelled space. His collection for women (Line 1) has a blank label but is recognisable by external white stitching. You'll also find Line 6 (women's basics) and Line 10 (menswear), plus accessories for men and women and shoes.

Other locations 13 rue de Grenelle, 7th (01.45.49.06.45).

Miu Miu

219 rue St-Honoré, 1st (01.58.62.53.20/www. miumiu.com). M° Tuileries. **Open** 11am-7pm Mon; 10am-7pm Tue-Sat. **Credit** AmEx, DC, MC, V. **Map** p401 G5.

CONSUME

Prada's younger sister has this rue St-Honoré store as its main boutique, selling its quirky women's fashions, shoes and bags.
Other locations 16 rue de Grenelle, 7th (01.53.63.20.30).

★ Paul & Joe

64 rue des Sts-Pères, 7th (01.42.22.47.01/ www.paulandjoe.com). M° Rue du Bac or St-Germain-des-Prés. **Open** 10am-7pm Mon-Sat. **Credit** AmEx, DC, MC, V. **Map** p405 G6.
International fashionistas have taken a real shine to Sophie Albou's retro-styled creations. The latest collection dresses leggy young things in a superb range of winter shorts, colourful mini dresses and voluminous trousers, with their intellectual paramours in slouchy woollens, tailored jackets and chunky boots.
Other locations *Men* 56 rue Vieille-du-Temple, 3rd (01.42.72.42.06); 62 rue des Sts-Pères, 7th (01.42.22.98.98). *Women* 46 rue Etienne-Marcel, 2nd (01.40.28.03.34); 2 av Montaigne, 8th (01.47.20.57.50).

Paule Ka

223 rue St-Honoré, 1st (01.42.97.57.06/ www.pauleka.com). M° Tuileries. **Open** 11am-7pm; 10am-7pm Tue-Sat. **Credit** AmEx, DC, MC, V. **Map** p401 G4.
Serge Cajfinger's '60s couture-influenced collections continue to gather a loyal following. With the opening of his rue St-Honoré boutique, he now has a foot in each of the city's fashion districts.
Other locations 20 rue Malher, 4th (01.40.29.96.03); 192 bd St-Germain, 6th (01.45.44.92.60); 45 rue François 1er, 8th (01.47.20.76.10).

Paul Smith

3 rue du Fbg-St-Honoré, 8th (01.42.68.27.10/ www.paulsmith.co.uk). M° Concorde. **Open** 10.30am-7pm Mon-Sat. **Credit** AmEx, DC, MC, V. **Map** p401 F4.
A 'so British' atmosphere is cultivated with '40s wallpaper, antiques, old books and bric-a-brac, much of it for sale along with the colourful shirts and knitwear in which Smith excels. Collections for men, women and children, along with eyewear and accessories, are all gathered in this elegant Haussmann apartment.

Prada

10 av Montaigne, 8th (01.53.23.99.40/www. prada.com). M° Alma Marceau. **Open** 11am-7pm Mon; 10am-7pm Tue-Sat. **Credit** AmEx, DC, MC, V. **Map** p400 D5.
The high priestess of European chic, Miuccia Prada's elegant stores pull in fashion followers of all ages. Handbags of choice are complemented by the coveted ready-to-wear range.

Other locations 5 rue de Grenelle, 6th (01.45.48.53.14); 6 rue du Fbg-St-Honoré, 8th (01.58.18.63.30).

Rick Owens

130 galerie de Valois, 1st (01.40.20.42.52/ www.owenscorp.com). M° Palais Royal Musée du Louvre. **Open** noon-7pm Mon; 10am-7pm Tue-Sat. **Credit** AmEx, DC, MC, V. **Map** p402 H5.
The LA designer and rock star favourite brings his glamour-meets-grunge style to the Palais-Royal, with hoods, zips and asymmetrical wrappings for men and women. It's not for animal lovers – the upstairs has a dedicated mink section.

★ Robert Normand

149-150 galerie de Valois, 1st (www.robert normand.com). M° Palais Royal Musée du Louvre. **Open** 1-7pm Mon; 10.30am-7pm Tue-Sat. **Credit** AmEx, DC, MC, V. **Map** p402 H5.
Normand is a new addition to the Palais-Royal. The designer, who has collaborated with Lanvin, Pucci and Christophe Lemaire, launched his own label in 2000 – an exuberant combination of pop art patterns with gangsta cuts, satin puffballs in peacock colours and blousons made of the kind of baroque fabrics favoured by African potentates.

Rue du Mail

5 rue du Mail, 2nd (01.42.60.19.20/www. ruedumail.com). M° Bourse. **Open** noon-5pm Mon-Fri. **Credit** AmEx, MC, V. **Map** p402 J4.
Martine Sitbon's sexy new collection is a hit with Cate Blanchett, Sofia Coppola, Scarlett Johansson et al. Swooping V necklines, flirty hemlines, black satin and fruity chiffons define the look.

★ Sonia Rykiel

175 bd St-Germain, 6th (01.49.54.60.60/www. soniarykiel.com). M° St-Germain-des-Prés or Sèvres Babylone. **Open** 10.30am-7pm Mon-Sat. **Credit** AmEx, DC, MC, V. **Map** p405 G6.
The queen of St-Germain celebrated the 40th birthday of her flagship store with a glamorous black and smoked glass refit perfect for narcissists: tons of mirrors reflect the flowing gowns of her current '70s throwback look. Menswear is across the street, and two newer boutiques stock the younger, more affordable Sonia by Sonia Rykiel range (59 rue des Sts-Pères, 6th, 01.49.54.61.00) and kids' togs (4 rue de Grenelle, 6th, 01.49.54.61.10).
▶ *For something on the wild side, the main shop also stocks a range of designer sex toys.*
Other locations throughout the city.

Stella McCartney

114-121 galerie du Valois, Jardin du Palais-Royal, 1st (01.47.03.03.80/www.stellamccartney. com). M° Palais Royal Musée du Louvre. **Open** 10.30am-7pm Mon-Sat. **Credit** AmEx, DC, MC, V. **Map** p402 H5.

Profile Marché aux Puces de St-Ouen

There's plenty of treasure among the tat at Paris's biggest flea market.

Covering seven hectares, with 3,000 traders and up to 180,000 visitors each weekend, the Marché aux Puces de St-Ouen is generally thought to be the biggest flea market in the world. If this conjures up images of a sprawling field filled with broken bed frames, faded curtains and sofas with the stuffing coming out, you're in for a surprise (and are better off going to the Montreuil version). The fleas left long ago, and since 1885 what started as a rag-and-bone shantytown outside the city limits has been organised into a series of enclosed villages, some entirely covered and others with open-air streets and covered boutiques for the antiques dealers. South of this sprawls the canvas-covered part where African tat, joss sticks, fake Converse trainers and cheap batteries are perused by crowds of teenagers – best avoided unless you're after that kind of thing.

In recent years rents have shot up. The result is that much of the Puces is more like a museum than a flea market, and restaurants are swiftly replacing antiques dealers who can no longer make ends meet. But once you get under its skin, the Puces still offers an intoxicating blend of the sublime and the ridiculous. Repeat visits pay off and the more you banter with the sellers (preferably in French) the more bargains will reveal themselves, especially in the couple of streets that still sell unrestored objects.

The main street is rue des Rosiers, and off this runs Marché Malassis (toys, vintage cameras and furniture), Marché Dauphine (furniture, ceramics), Marché Biron (expensive lighting, furniture and objets) and Marché Vernaison (more varied, with fashion, a gilding shop, books,

prints and kitchenware). The open-air Marché Paul Bert (one of the two markets owned by the Duke of Westminster) has some beautiful 19th- and 20th-century furniture, though you'll need to bargain hard. But if you are looking for genuine bargains and unrenovated things Marché Lecuyer is the place to head: as the home of house-clearance specialists, it's the closest thing you'll find to a reclamation yard and many of the traders have warehouses that they may open for you if you are searching for something in particular.

TOP TIPS

● Enter the market from Garibaldi métro rather than Porte de St-Ouen – a longer trek on line 13 but you avoid the crowds and new tat.

● Visit on a Monday morning, a cold, wet or snowy day, or in mid August – you're more likely to pick up a bargain.

● If you like the look of something, don't pick it up or touch it. This already shows the dealer that you want it. Be prepared to walk away if you really want that good deal.

● Bring cash with you (but keep an eye on your wallet). Some only take it, and for others it's a good bargaining tool. There is only one cashpoint and there is always a queue.

PLACES TO EAT

Le Soleil
109 av Michelet, St-Ouen (01.40. 10.08.08). High quality bistro.

Relais des Brocs
24 rue Jean Valles, St-Ouen (01.40.10. 14.66). Excellent *moules-frites* and steaks.

CONSUME

McCartney is crazy about the 'clash of history, fashion and contemporary art' at the Palais-Royal, where she has opened her sumptuous boutique overlooking the gardens. Thick carpets, maplewood and metal sculptures create a rarified setting for women's prêt-à-porter, bags, shoes, sunglasses, lingerie, perfume and skincare.

Yohji Yamamoto

25 rue du Louvre, 1st (01.42.21.42.93/www. yohjiyamamoto.co.jp). M° Les Halles or Sentier. **Open** 10.30am-7pm Mon-Sat. **Credit** AmEx, DC, MC, V. **Map** p405 G7.

One of the few true pioneers working in fashion today, Yamamoto is a master of cut and finish, both strongly inspired by the kimono and traditional Tibetan dress. His dexterity with form makes for unique shapes and styles, largely black. But when he does colour, it's a blast of brilliance.

▶ *Find the men's boutique at 25 rue du Louvre, 1st (01.45.08.82.45).*

Other location 4 rue Cambon, 1st (01.40.20.00.71).

Yves Saint Laurent

6 pl St-Sulpice, 6th (01.43.29.43.00/www.ysl. com). M° St-Sulpice. **Open** 11am-7pm Mon; 10.30am-7pm Tue-Sat. **Credit** AmEx, DC, MC, V. **Map** p408 H7.

The memory of the founding designer, who died in 2008, lives on in this elegant boutique, which was splendidly refitted in red in the same year. You'll find menswear at no.12 (01.43.26.84.40).

Other locations *Men* 32 rue du Fbg-St-Honoré, 8th (01.53.05.80.80); 12 pl St-Sulpice, 6th (01.43.26.84.40). *Women* 38 rue du Fbg-St-Honoré, 8th (01.42.65.74.59).

Boutique & concept

★ AB33 and N°60

33 & 60 rue Charlot, 3rd (01.42.71.02.82/ 01.44.78.91.90). M° Filles du Calvaire. **Open** 11am-8pm Tue-Sun. **Credit** AmEx, MC, V. **Map** p409 L5.

Delicate in summer, cosy in winter, the pretty, unstructured clothes in AB33 may not make the wish list of any sultry, groomed Parisienne, but would be perfect for her up-from-the-country Bardot-esque cousin. Owner Agathe Buchotte sells Forte, Forte, Kristina Ti and Philip Lim at this address, and in her second shop, up the road at No.60, edgier labels like McQ and Anglomania, plus a selection of slogan cotton totes with silly jokes about the recession.

Anikalena Skärström

16 rue du Pont aux Choux, 3rd (01.44.59.32.85/ www.anikalena.com). M° St-Sébastien Froissart. **Open** 11am-7pm Mon-Fri; noon-7pm Sat. Closed 2wks Aug. **Credit** MC, V. **Map** p402 J2.

Clean lines and streamlining are the guiding aesthetic for Anikalena's collections of sporty, sexy day and evening dresses and separates, with the occasional wow piece like the grass-green suede coat of 2008. A word to the wise: make sure you check the finish.

April 77

49 rue de Saintonge, 3rd (01.40.29.07.30/ www.april77.fr). M° Filles du Calvaire. **Open** 11am-7pm Tue-Sat. **Credit** MC, V. **Map** p402 J2.

The cult skinny jeans brand has acquired its own boutique, designed by Steven Thomas, to show off their collection inspired by the mid-'80s music scene.

Base One

47bis rue d'Orsel, 18th (01.73.75.37.10/www. baseoneshop.com). M° Anvers. **Open** 12.30-8pm Tue-Sat; 3.30-8pm Sun. Closed 2wks Aug. **Credit** MC, V. **Map** p402 J2.

Clubland duo Princesse Léa and Jean-Louis Faverole squeeze items from little-known local and international designers (Shai Wear, Li-Lei, Drolaic, OK47), plus small, established brands (Fenchurch, Motel, Consortium) into their boutique. Massive gold piggy banks from Present Time add un-Parisian bling.

Les Belles Images

74 rue Charlot, 3rd (01.42.76.93.61/www. myspace.com/lesbellesimages). M° Filles du Calvaire. **Open** 11am-7.30pm Tue-Sat. **Credit** MC, V. **Map** p402 L5.

A retro '60s vibe reigns at this boutique (women's and men's), where owner Sandy Bontout showcases items from current collections of obscure and big-name French and international labels, such as Ambali separates, Walk that Walk shoes and editor's picks from Veronique Leroy and Vivienne Westwood.

★ Colette

213 rue St-Honoré, 1st (01.55.35.33.90/www. colette.fr). M° Pyramides or Tuileries. **Open** 11am-7pm Mon-Sat. **Credit** AmEx, DC, MC, V. **Map** p401 G4.

The renowned and much-imitated one-stop concept and lifestyle store features a highly eclectic selection of must-have accessories, fashion, sneakers, books, media, shiny new gadgets, and hair and beauty brands själ, Kiehl's and uslu airlines, all in a swanky new space.

Dolls

56 rue de Saintonge, 3rd (01.44.54.08.21). M° Filles du Calvaire. **Open** 11am-3pm, 3.30-7.30pm Tue-Sat. Closed 2wks Aug. **Credit** DC, MC, V. **Map** p401 G4.

This hot new address for the Marais style crowd concentrates on a few well-chosen brands: Valentine Gaulthier (France), By Malene Birger (Denmark), Sass & Bide (Australia), NDC shoes (Belgium) and Citizens of Humanity jeans.

CONSUME

★ L'Eclaireur

*3ter rue des Rosiers, 4th (01.48.87.10.22/www.
leclaireur.com). M° St-Paul.* **Open** 11am-7pm Mon-
Sat. **Credit** AmEx, DC, MC, V. **Map** p409 L6.
Housed in a dandified warehouse, L'Eclaireur stocks
designs by Comme des Garçons, Martin Margiela,
Dries van Noten, Carpe Diem and Junya Watanabe.
Among its exclusive finds, check out smocks by
Finnish designer Jasmin Santanen. At the secretive
rue Hérold branch you have to ring the doorbell to
enter. A new space in rue Boissy d'Anglas, near
Concorde, sells chic fashions for men and women.
▶ *Men are catered for separately at L'Eclaireur
Homme (12 rue Malher, 4th, 01.44.54.22.11).*
Other locations 10 rue Hérold, 1st
(01.40.41.09.89); 10 rue Boissy d'Anglas, 8th
(01.53.43.03.70); 26 av des Champs-Elysées, 8th
(01.45.62.12.32).

Galerie Simone

*124 rue Vieille-du-Temple, 3rd (01.42.74.21.28).
M° St-Sébastien Froissart.* **Open** noon-7.30pm
daily. **Credit** AmEx, DC, MC, V. **Map** p409 L5.
Simone Gaubatz sources and cultivates talented
young designers from around the world, displaying
their most eye-catching creations on mannequins in
this gallery-style space.

Jack Henry

*25 rue Charlot, 3rd (01.42.78.93.51/www.jack
henry.fr). M° Filles du Calvaire.* **Open** 11am-
7.30pm Tue-Sun. **Credit** AmEx, MC, V.
Map p409 L5.
The work of this Paris-trained American designer
has real intellectual heft to it, but you only have to
touch the silky soft cotton and wool jersey from
Japan to want his finely crafted, beautifully conceived tunics, skirts and jackets. Luxurious leather
bags and jewellery from designers including
Théodora Gabrielli, alias Dorothée, who patiently
creates new pieces while serving in the shop, are also
on display.

Joseph

*147 bd St-Germain, 6th (01.55.42.77.55/www.
joseph.co.uk). M° St-Germain-des-Prés.* **Open**
11am-7pm Mon, Sat; 10.30am-7pm Tue-Fri.
Credit AmEx, DC, MC, V. **Map** p405 G6.
Taking a cue from its London store, Joseph has
opened a multi-brand shop with pieces by the likes
of Balmain and Lanvin, as well as accessories by
Bijoux de Sophie and handbags by Jérôme Dreyfuss.

Kitsuné

*52 rue de Richelieu, 1st (01.42.60.34.28/www.
kitsune.fr). M° Palais Royal Musée du Louvre
or Pyramides.* **Open** 11am-7.30pm Mon-Sat.
Credit MC, V. **Map** p402 H4.
The London/Paris style collective has finally got its
own boutique, which offers the entire catalogue of
music compilations, as well as branded clothing that

takes a back-to-basics approach using quality producers. You'll find Scottish cashmere, Japanese jeans
and Italian shirts, together with items made in collaboration with Pierre Hardy, Scheisser underwear
and James Heeley.

Kokon To Zai

*48 rue Tiquetonne, 2nd (01.42.36.92.41/www.
kokontozai.co.uk). M° Etienne Marcel.* **Open**
11.30am-7.30pm Mon-Sat. **Credit** AmEx, DC,
MC, V. **Map** p402 J5.
Always a spot-on spotter of the latest creations, this
tiny style emporium is sister to the Kokon To Zai in
London. The neon-lit club feel of the mirrored interior matches the dark glamour of the designs.
Unique pieces straight off the catwalk share space
with creations by Marjan Peijoski, Noki, Raf Simons,
Ziad Ghanem and new Norwegian designers.

★ LE66

*66 av des Champs-Elysées, 8th (01.53.53.33.80/
http://le66paris.blogspot.com). M° George V.* **Open**
11am-8pm Mon-Fri; 11.30am-8.30pm Sat; 2-8pm
Sun. **Credit** AmEx, DC, MC, V. **Map** p400 D4.
Eschewing the glass cabinet approach of Colette, this
fashion concept store is youthful and accessible, with
an ever-changing selection of hip brands including
Puma Black Label. Assistants, who are also the buyers and designers, make for a motivated team. The
store takes the form of three transparent modules,
the first a book and magazine store run by Black
Book of the Palais de Tokyo, and the second two
devoted to fashion. It even has its own vintage store,
in collaboration with Come On Eline and Kiliwatch.

Marc by Marc Jacobs

*19 pl du Marché-Saint-Honoré, 1st
(01.40.20.11.30/www.marcjacobs.com).
M° Tuileries.* **Open** 9am-6pm Mon-Sat.
Credit AmEx, DC, MC, V. **Map** p401 G4.
The new store for Jacobs' casual, punky line has
fashionistas clustering like bees round a honeypot,
not least for the fabulously inexpensive accessories
that make great gifts or add instant spice to a tired
outfit. A skateboard table and giant pedalo in the
form of a swan are the centrepieces of the store,
which stocks men's and women's prêt-à-porter,
shoes and special editions.

Margo Milin

*1 rue Charles François Dupuis, 3rd (06.61.77.
14.76/www.margomilin.com). M° République
or Temple.* **Open** 11.30am-7pm Mon-Sat; 2-5pm
Sun. **No credit cards. Map** p401 G4.
Looking like a model herself, St Martin's graduate
Marguerite Milin studied theatrical design and produces kimono-influenced wrap-around jumpers and
party dresses that play with a contrast of textures
and pattern versus plain. A fun, girly atmosphere is
always found in the boutique, as customers take
turns in the tiny changing room.

CONSUME

Inconspicuous Consumption

Guilt-free shopping at Merci, where all profits go to charity.

There's a buzz about the boulevard Beaumarchais. Here, at the eastern end of the Marais, Marie-France Cohen and her husband Bernard, erstwhile owners of childrenswear brand Bonpoint, have opened **Merci** (*see right*), Paris's latest shopping sensation housed in an elaborately reconfigured 19th-century fabric factory.

There are three ways to enter Merci, each one theatrical. The central entrance takes visitors through a quiet courtyard, home to the shop's emblem, a bright red Fiat Cinquecento; the side entrances lead shoppers through dark, quiet ante rooms – one a florist full of wild cow parsley and echinacea, the other a literary café with second-hand books from floor to ceiling like a snug reading room.

Inside the shop proper, there's a glorious mish-mash of merchandise. Three loft-like floors full of nooks and crannies heave with furniture, jewellery, stationery, fashion, household products, childrenswear and a haberdashery. The cross-selling doesn't stop at mixing what you wear with what you eat with (or sew with) – in an attempt to say that good design is more important than the monetary value or aspirational status of something, Merci deliberately showcases the old with the new, the everyday with the fancy and the inexpensive with the pricey. So you'll find a vintage baseball jacket or Burberry mac next to contemporary designs from Stella or Les Prairies de Paris;

a bodega beaker alongside a Philippe Starck goblet in Baccarat crystal; a Syrian stool made from tyres next to a Swedish stool designed for the National Museum in Stockholm; and enamel espresso cups on a vintage army campaign table.

That's not all. In a move that takes the recent trend for retailer responsibility to a new level, Merci gives all its profits to charity, specifically to its own foundation that currently helps deprived children in Madagascar. This generosity has inspired suppliers to give something too. Some have made exclusive pieces – Drucker, manufacturer of the prolific café chair, has dispensed with its usual navy, claret and moss green, and made a series of cute candy-coloured wicker chairs instead. Others have produced limited editions or re-editions – Helmut Lang has reprised a classic tuxedo jacket with a reduced wholesale price. And others, like publisher Gallimard, just plain donate.

All this promise of inconspicuous consumption and charitable donation in a sumptuous setting makes Merci a Bobo (bourgeois bohemian) magnet. So whether the sight of an artfully scruffy but clearly well-heeled customer waxing lyrical over a plastic ice bucket makes you think 'wonderful!' or something else beginning with 'w', what's for sure is that this most generous of general stores makes for great people watching too.

★ Maria Luisa
7 rue Rouget de L'Isle, 1st (01.47.03.96.15).
M° Concorde. **Open** 10.30am-7pm Mon-Sat.
Credit AmEx, DC, MC, V. **Map** p401 G4.
Venezuelan Maria Luisa Poumaillou was one of the
city's first stockists of Galliano, McQueen and the
Belgians, and has an eye for rising stars. She has
now pooled all the womenswear – previously split
up into small boutiques – in this new minimalist
flagship, featuring labels such as Charles Anastase,
Jill Sander and Ohne Titel. She also has a store
within Printemps (*see p239*).
▶ *Poumaillou's menswear store can be found at*
38 rue du Mont-Thabor, 1st (01.42.96.47.81).

Merci
111 bd Beaumarchais, 3rd (01.42.77.00.33/
www.merci-merci.com). M° St-Sébastien
Froissart. **Open** 10am-7pm Mon-Sat.
Credit AmEx, MC, V. **Map** p409 L5.
See left **Inconspicuous Consumption**.

★ Les Prairies de Paris
23 rue Debelleyme, 3rd (01.40.20.44.12/www.
lesprairiesdeparis.com). M° St-Sébastien
Froissart. **Open** 10.30am-7pm Mon-Sat.
Credit AmEx, MC, V. **Map** p409 L5.
Laeticia Ivanez opened this installation space/
boutique in the Marais in July 2008. The whole of
the ground floor is given over to art shows, gigs and
happenings, with an original Peter Colombo leather
chair placed centre left. Downstairs the '60s theme
continues, with a cocoon-like setting in which to
commune with the disco-glam separates and cute
children's collection.
Other locations 6 rue du Pré aux Clercs, 7th
(same nummber).

Set Galerie
7 rue d'Uzès, 2nd (01.40.16.56.49/www.
stephaneplassier.com). M° Grands Boulevards.
Open 11am-7pm Mon-Sat. **Credit** AmEx,
MC, V. **Map** p402 H1.
Multitalented Stéphane Plassier already has a name
for himself as an interior designer, branding consultant and *metteur en scène*. Now he's opened his own
concept store above the design control room of his
business. Fashion lines include Dessus-Dessous
(underwear), Beautiful Jacket (jackets for men)
and Set in Black, a range of black dresses. The
converted industrial space also hosts a brilliant collection of books and objects, including a section
devoted to religious kitsch.

Shine
15 rue de Poitou, 3rd (01.48.05.80.10). M° Filles
du Calvaire. **Open** 11am-7.30pm Mon-Sat; 2-7pm
Sun. **Credit** AmEx, MC, V. **Map** p407 M7.
See By Chloe, Marc by Marc Jacobs and Acne Jeans,
plus Repetto shoes and Véronique Branquino, are
among the goodies in this glossy showcase.

Surface 2 Air
68 rue Charlot, 3rd (01.44.61.76.27/www.
surface2airparis.com). M° St-Sébastien Froissart.
Open 11am-7.30pm Mon-Sat. **Credit** MC, V.
Map p409 L5.
This non-concept concept store also acts as an art
gallery and graphic design agency. The cult clothing
selection takes in Alice McCall's sassy frocks, Fifth
Avenue Shoe Repair jeans and printed dresses by
Wood Wood. For men, labels include Marios, Wendy
& Jim and F-Troupe.

Womenswear

★ Agnès b
2, 3, 6 & 19 rue du Jour, 1st (men
01.42.33.04.13/women 01.45.08.56.56/
www.agnesb.com). M° Les Halles. **Open** *Oct-*
Apr 10am-7pm Mon-Sat. *May-Sept* 10am-
7.30pm Mon-Sat. **Credit** AmEx, MC, V.
Map p402 J5.
Agnès b rarely wavers from her design vision: pure
lines in fine quality cotton, merino wool and silk.
Best buys are shirts, pullovers and cardigans that
keep their shape for years. Her mini-empire of men's,
women's, children's, travel and sportswear shops is
compact; see the website for details.
Other locations throughout the city.

Antoine et Lili
95 quai de Valmy, 10th (01.40.37.41.55/
www.antoineetlili.com). M° Jacques Bonsergent.
Open 11am-7pm Mon, Sun; 11am-8pm Tue-
Fri; 10am-8pm Sat. **Credit** AmEx, DC, MC, V.
Map p402 L3.
Antoine et Lili's fuchsia-pink, custard-yellow and
apple-green shopfronts are a new raver's dream. The
bobo designer's clothes, often in wraparound styles,
adapt to all sizes and shapes. The Canal St-Martin
'village' comprises womenswear, a kitsch home decoration boutique and childrenswear.
Other locations throughout the city.

ba&sh
22 rue des Francs-Bourgeois, 3rd
(01.42.78.55.10/www.ba-sh.com). M° Jacques
Bonsergent. **Open** 11am-7pm Mon, Sun; 11am-
8pm Tue-Fri; 10am-8pm Sat. **Credit** AmEx,
DC, MC, V. **Map** p402 L3.
This fresh, Paris-based label created by Barbara
Boccara and Sharon Krief now has 350 outlets
around the world, including five Paris boutiques.
You'll find dresses, skirts and blouses with ethnic
touches on one side and drapey jersey on the other.
Other locations throughout the city.

COS
4 rue des Rosiers, 4th (01.44.55.37.70/www.
cosstores.com). M° St-Paul. **Open** 10.30am-
7.30pm Mon-Sat. **Credit** AmEx, MC, V.
Map p402 J5.

CONSUME

H&M's upmarket brand Collection of Style (COS) now has a Paris outpost, designed by William Russell, in rue des Rosiers, causing some consternation among those who'd rather have kept this a chain-free zone.

Firmaman

200 bd Perèire, 17th (01.44.09.71.32/www. firmaman.com). M° Porte Maillot. **Open** 11am-7pm Tue-Sat. **Credit** AmEx, DC, MC, V. **Map** p400 B2.

Realising that pregnant women have long been scouring regular boutiques for a more fashionable maternity look, Marguerite Pineau Valencienne has chosen appropriate clothes from the likes of Isabel Marant, Bash and Citizens of Humanity, displayed alongside maternity wear by Blossom, Pietro Brunelli and Virginie Castaway. The city's first maternity concept store, it also has lingerie, well-being products and gifts for new mums, dads and babies.

★ Iro

53 rue Vieille-du-Temple, 4th (01.42.77.25.09/ www.iro.fr). M° St-Paul. **Open** 10.30am-7.30pm Mon-Sat. **Credit** AmEx, MC, V. **Map** p409 K6.

Fashion editors have tipped designers Laurent and Arik Bitton for stardom with what they call 'basic deluxe': skinny knits, skinny jeans, babydoll dresses and the 'perfecto' mini leather jacket. With a background in music, the brothers know how to hit just the right note between trendy and fashion victim, for a French silhouette.

Other locations 68 rue des Sts-Pères, 7th (01.45.48.04.06).

Manoush

217 rue St Honoré, 1st (01.40.20.04.44/ www.manoush.com). M° Tuileries. **Open** 10am-7pm Mon-Sat. **Credit** AmEx, DC, MC, V. **Map** p400 D4.

Manoush, which means 'gypsy' in French slang, has proved more than a flash-in-the-pan leftover from the boho craze of 2005 and now has four boutiques touting designer Frédérique Trou-Roy's kitsch and kooky vision.

Other locations throughout the city.

Vanessa Bruno

25 rue St-Sulpice, 6th (01.43.54.41.04/www. vanessabruno.com). M° Odéon. **Open** 10.30am-7.30pm Mon-Sat. **Credit** AmEx, DC, MC, V. **Map** p408 H7.

Mercerised cotton tanks, flattering trousers and feminine tops have a Zen-like quality that stems from Bruno's stay in Japan, and they somehow manage to flatter every figure type. She also makes great bags; the ample Lune was created to mark ten years in the business.

Other locations 12 rue de Castiglione, 1st (01.42.61.44.60); 100 rue Vieille-du-Temple, 3rd (01.42.77.19.41).

Zadig & Voltaire

42 rue des Francs-Bourgeois, 3rd (01.44.54.00.60/www.zadig-et-voltaire.com). M° Hôtel de Ville or St-Paul. **Open** 10.30am-7.30pm Mon-Sat; 1.30-7.30pm Sun. **Credit** AmEx, DC, MC, V. **Map** p409 K6.

Z&V's relaxed, urban collection is a winner. Popular separates include cotton tops, shirts and faded jeans; its winter range of cashmere jumpers is superb.

▶ *The more upmarket Zadig & Voltaire De Luxe is at 18 rue François 1er (01.40.70.97.89).*

Other locations throughout the city.

Menswear

Shops in **Streetwear & clubwear** (*see right*) stock more casual clothes; many brands listed in **Designer** (*see p244*) also cater for men.

APC

38 rue Madame, 6th (01.42.22.12.77/www. apc.fr). M° St-Placide. **Open** 11am-7.30pm Mon-Sat. **Credit** AmEx, MC, V. **Map** p405 G8.

The look here is simple but stylish: think perfectly cut basics in muted tones. Hip without trying too hard, its jeans are a big hit with denim aficionados – the skinny version nearly caused a stampede when they came out.

▶ *APC also stocks a great womenswear collection.*

Other locations 5 rue de Marseille, 10th (01.42.39.84.46); 112 rue Vieille-du-Temple, 3rd (01.42.78.18.02).

★ La Chemiserie

21 rue d'Uzès, 2nd (01.42.36.47.80/www. cacharel.fr). M° Grands Boulevards. **Open** 11am-7.30pm Mon-Sat. **Credit** AmEx, DC, MC, V. **Map** p402 J4.

Cacharel is behind this concept shirt store in a loft-style space. Cool, masculine and nonchalant, the shirts, which start at €45, have that Gallic panache for which the brand is famous, and are joined by a small selection of suits, velvet and cord blazers and cashmere scarves.

▶ *In the same street, check out the jackets and underwear at Set Galerie (see p253).*

★ Christophe Lemaire

28 rue de Poitou, 3rd (01.44.78.00.09/www. christophelemaire.com). M° St-Sébastien Froissart. **Open** 1-7pm Mon; 12.30-7.30pm Tue-Fri; 11am-7.30pm Sat. **Credit** AmEx, DC, MC, V. **Map** p409 L6.

Creative director for Lacoste for seven years, Lemaire opened his own boutique in an old pharmacy. It's decorated like a fantasy apartment: the salon, in '70s gold and glitz, stocks his own-label menswear and womenswear in high-tech Japanese textiles, and leads into a soundproofed music room with a wall of old speakers where you can buy collectable Lacoste and Lemaire's own fave CDs. Next door the seductive 'Japanese salon' holds the jeans range. You can also buy the vintage lighting on display here.

Eglé Bespoke

26 rue du Mont-Thabor, 1st (01.44.15.98.31/ www.eglebespoke.com). M° Concorde. **Open** 11am-7pm Mon-Sat & by appointment. **Credit** MC, V. **Map** p401 G5.

Two young entrepreneurs are reviving bespoke for a new generation in this tiny shop. Custom shirts start from €119 and can be delivered in a week or so; they will also make or copy shirts for women and produce made-to-order jeans for both sexes. Laser-printed buttons are perfect for stamping your beloved's shirt with a saucy message.

Jacenko

38 rue de Poitou, 3rd (01.42.71.80.38). M° St-Sébastien Froissart. **Open** 11am-7.30pm Tue-Sat; 2-7pm Sun. **Credit** MC, V. **Map** p402 J5.

A tasteful little boutique whose owner has a faultless eye for shirts, jackets, woollens and accessories that are dandy but not downright gay. McQ, Viktor & Rolf, Givenchy and John Smedley all appear.

Madelios

23 bd de la Madeleine, 1st (01.53.45.00.00/ www.madelios.com). M° Madeleine. **Open** 10am-7pm Mon-Sat. **Credit** AmEx, DC, MC, V. **Map** p401 G4.

A one-stop shop for men's fashion, with two floors and more than 100 labels. Suits by Kenzo, Paul Smith and Givenchy, plus shoes and accessories.

Nodus

22 rue Vieille-du-Temple, 4th (01.42.77.07.96/ www.nodus.fr). M° Hôtel de Ville or St-Paul. **Open** 10.45am-2pm, 3-7.30pm Mon-Sat; 1-7.30pm Sun. **Credit** AmEx, DC, MC, V. **Map** p409 K6.

Under the wooden beams of this cosy men's shirt specialist are neat rows of striped, checked and plain dress shirts, stylish silk ties with subtle graphic designs, and silver-plated crystal cufflinks.
Other locations throughout the city.

Pull-In Underwear

8 rue Française, 2nd (01.42.36.91.06/www.pull-in.com). M° Etienne Marcel. **Open** 10am-7.30pm Mon-Sat. **Credit** AmEx, MC, V. **Map** p402 H5.

Hailing from south-west France, Pull-In is the official underwear supplier to the French rugby team. The ultra-trendy brand makes swimwear, but its boxers in wacko patterns have now supplanted Calvin Kleins as *the* visible waistband for Gallic hip hoppers.

★ Purple Ice

15 rue Marie Stuart, 2nd (01.40.26.87.27/www. purpleiceboutique.com). M° Etienne Marcel. **Open** 11.30am-7.30pm Tue-Sun. **Credit** MC, V. **Map** p402 J5.

You'd be forgiven for assuming Romain Couapel was obsessed by Prince. He has, after all, called his shop Purple Ice, written the sign in the same '80s rock font as *Purple Rain*, and painted the walls and floor in the colour Prince called his own. But he doesn't seem that bothered by the diminutive rock guitar legend; he's more interested in the visual qualities than the back story. This attitude is mirrored in the good-looking, diverse clothes on sale: streetwear jeans by Real Real Genuine next to designer bags by JC de Castelbajac, and Vêtements de Famille's thoroughly modern take on the French Breton shirt next to Pearl Diver's retro Hawaiian shirts made in Japan.

Streetwear & clubwear

American Apparel

31 pl du Marché-St-Honoré, 1st (01.42.60.03.72/ www.americanapparel.net). M° Opéra, Pyramides or Tuileries. **Open** 10am-8pm Mon-Wed, Fri, Sat; 10am-10pm Thur; noon-7pm Sun. **Credit** AmEx, DC, MC, V. **Map** p401 G4.

Paris has acquired a taste for American Apparel's sweatshop-free, unisex cotton basics.
Other locations throughout the city.

Clery Brice

11 rue Pierre-Lescot, 1st (01.45.08.58.70/www. myspace.com/clerybrice). M° Les Halles/RER Châtelet Les Halles. **Open** 11am-12.30pm, 1.30-8pm Mon-Sat. **Credit** MC, V. **Map** p402 J5.

Here you pay lofty prices to get limited editions of the coolest trainers six months before the rest of the world even finds out they should be wearing them.

Ekivok

39 bd de Sébastopol, 1st (01.42.21.98.71/ www.ekivok.com). M° Les Halles/RER Châtelet Les Halles. **Open** 11am-7.30pm Mon-Sat. **Credit** MC, V. **Map** p402 J5.

In Ekivok's graffiti-covered boutique you'll find major brands Bullrot, Carhartt, Hardcore Session and Juicy Jazz for men, and Golddigga, Punky Fish, Skunk Funk, Emilie the Strange and Hardcore Session for women, plus Eastpak accessories.

Kiliwatch

64 rue Tiquetonne, 2nd (01.42.21.17.37//http:// espacekiliwatch.fr). M° Etienne Marcel. **Open** 2-7pm Mon; 11am-7.30pm Tue-Sat. **Credit** AmEx, MC, V. **Map** p402 J5.

The trailblazer of the rue Etienne-Marcel revival is filled with hoodies, casual shirts and washed-out jeans. Brands such as Gas, Edwin and Pepe Jeans accompany pricey, good-condition second-hand garb.

Royal Cheese

24 rue Tiquetonne, 2nd (01.42.33.50.83/www. royalcheese.com). M° Etienne Marcel. **Open** 11am-1pm, 2-8pm Mon-Fri; 11am-8pm Sat. **Credit** AmEx, DC, MC, V. **Map** p402 J5.

CONSUME

Clubbers hit Royal Cheese to snaffle up hard-to-find imports: Stüssy, Cheap Monday and Lee for the boys; Insight, Sessun, Edwin and Lazy Oaf for the girls. Prices are hefty: Japanese jeans cost €200.
Other locations 3 rue Mandar, 2nd (01.44.82.04.85).

★ Y-3

47 rue Etienne-Marcel, 3rd (01.45.08.82.45/ www.y-3.com). Mº Bourse. **Open** 11am-7pm Mon-Sat. **Credit** AmEx, MC, V. **Map** p402 J5.
The first Paris boutique for this successful collaboration between Yohji Yamamoto and Adidas gives regular sportswear a kick, with high-tech fabrics, oversized pockets and elegant design.

Used & vintage

See also p268 **Antiques & flea markets**.

Adrenaline

30 rue Racine, 6th (01.44.27.09.05/www. adrenaline-vintage.com). Mº Odéon. **Open** 11am-7pm Mon-Sat. **Credit** AmEx, MC, V. **Map** p408 H7.
This *dépôt-vente* specialises in vintage luggage and handbags. Iconic Vuitton suitcases and Kelly and Birkin bags command enormous prices, but there are some slightly more affordable pieces and a small collection of '60s couture.

La Belle Epoque

10 rue de Poitou, 3rd (06.80.77.71.32). Mº St-Sébastien Froissart. **Open** 1.30-6.30pm Tue-Sat. **Credit** MC, V. **Map** p409 L5.
Ex-model and theatrical costumier Philippe will happily spend many hours rhapsodising about the joys of vintage. In the shop you'll find everything from the blue velours Grace Jones ensemble by Yves Saint Laurent to a selection of inexpensive '70s shirts and fake fur coats.

Come On Eline

16-18 rue des Taillandiers, 11th (01.43.38.12.11). Mº Ledru-Rollin. **Open** Sept-July 11am-8.30pm Mon-Fri; 2-8pm Sun. Aug 2-8pm Mon-Fri. **Credit** DC, MC, V. **Map** p407 M7.
The owners of this three-floor vintage wonderland have an eye for what's funky, from cowboy gear to 1960s debutantes frocks, though prices are high.

Didier Ludot

20-24 galerie de Montpensier, 1st (01.42.96.06.56/www.didierludot.com). Mº Palais Royal Musée du Louvre. **Open** 10.30am-7pm Mon-Sat. **Credit** AmEx, DC, MC, V. **Map** p402 H5.
Didier Ludot's temples to vintage haute couture appear in Printemps, Harrods and New York's Barneys. The prices are steep, but the pieces are stunning: Dior, Molyneux, Balenciaga, Pucci, Féraud

and, of course, Chanel, from the 1920s onwards. Ludot also curates exhibitions, using the exclusive shop windows around the Palais-Royal as a gallery.
► *Didier Ludot stocks his own line of vintage little black dresses, also available at La Petite Robe Noire (125 galerie de Valois, 1st, 01.40.15.01.04).*

Free 'P' Star

8 rue Ste-Croix-de-la-Bretonnerie, 4th (01.42.76.03.72/www.freepstar.com). Mº St-Paul. **Open** noon-11pm Mon-Sat; 2-10pm Sun. **Credit** MC, V. **Map** p409 K6.
Late-night shopping is fun at this Aladdin's cave of retro glitz, ex-army wear and glad rags that has provided fancy dress for many a Paris party.

★ Gabrielle Geppert

31 & 34 galerie Montpensier, 1st (01.42.61.53. 52/www.gabriellegeppert.com). Mº Palais Royal Musée du Louvre. **Open** 10am-7.30pm Mon-Sat. **Credit** AmEx, DC, MC, V. **Map** p402 H5.
If Didier Ludot is too intimidating, visit Gabrielle Geppert's shop, where much fun can be had rummaging in the back room or trying on the outrageous collection of '70s sunglasses (about €380 a pop, but they will get you into any party worth going to). A new exclusive room dedicated to accessories by the likes of Hermès and Manolo Blahnik can be opened on request, and she also carries a range of original costume jewellery by Elisabeth Ramuz.

★ Marie Louise de Monterey

1 rue Charles-François-Dupuis, 3rd (01.48.04.83.88/www.marielouisedemonterey. com). Mº Temple. **Open** noon-7pm Tue-Sat. **Credit** MC, V. **Map** p409 L5.
Australian Maria Vrisakis has a great eye for vintage that echoes current fashion trends, and her crisply ironed pieces are displayed in a refreshingly airy and uncluttered space. There is an adorable babywear collection and vintage Prada shoes in Cinderella sizes.

Studio W

6 rue du Pont-aux-Choux, 3rd (01.44.78.05.02). Mº St-Sébastien Froissart. **Open** 2-7.30pm Tue-Sat. **Credit** MC, V. **Map** p409 L5.
Aesthete William Moricet's tiny shop is simply exquisite, from the vintage Courrèges and Yves Saint Laurent couture on mannequins to the glossy golden retriever who lounges among crocodile and patent leather shoes and bags.

Yukiko

97 rue Vieille-du-Temple, 3rd (01.42.71.13.41/ www.yukiko-paris.com). Mº St-Sébastien Froissart. **Open** 11am-1pm, 2-7.30pm Tue-Sat. **Credit** AmEx, MC, V. **Map** p409 L6.
Yukiko's exquisite shop is a world away from the jumble sale vibe of some second-hand clothes dens in Paris. An impressive range of vintage luxury

CONSUME

Maison Fabre.

brand accessories, her own line of simple, sexy dresses and the decor of the shop itself are all carefully colour co-ordinated, the result a harmony of burnished gold and milky pearl on salmon pink or chestnut silk against pretty pale green walls.

FASHION ACCESSORIES & SERVICES

Eyewear

★ Alain Mikli
74 rue des Sts-Pères, 7th (01.45.49.40.00/www. mikli.fr). Mº Sèvres Babylone or St-Sulpice. **Open** 10am-7pm Mon-Sat. **Credit** AmEx, DC, MC, V. **Map** p405 G7.
Cult French designer Mikli uses cellulose acetate, a blend of wood and cotton sliced from blocks. At his flagship Starck-designed boutique, frames are laid out in a glass counter like designer sweeties. **Other locations** throughout the city.

Anne et Valentin
4 rue Ste-Croix-de-la-Bretonnerie, 4th (01.40.29.93.01/www.anneetvalentin.com). Mº Hôtel de Ville or St-Paul. **Open** noon-8pm Tue-Sat. Closed 12-22 Aug. **Credit** AmEx, DC, MC, V. **Map** p409 K6.
This modish French eyewear firm occupies a cosy three-floor Marais boutique. A&V design chic unisex frames: light titanium models have names like Tarzan and Truman; coloured acetate frames have inventive details and colour combinations.

Hats & gloves

★ Maison Fabre
128 galerie de Valois, 1st (01.42.60.75.88/ www.maisonfabre.com). Mº Palais Royal Musée du Louvre. **Open** 11am-7pm Mon-Sat. **Credit** AmEx, MC, V. **Map** p402 H5.
This glovemaker from Millau, which was founded in 1924, has capitalised on its racy designs from the sports car eras of the 1920s and '60s, opening a sexy little boutique. Classic gloves made from the softest leather (€100) come in 20 wild colours. Then there are the variations: crocodile, python, coyote, fur-trimmed, fingerless. But the ultimate lust object is the patent leather 'Auto' glove fastened with a massive button – somewhere between the cool of *The Avengers* and the kook of *Austin Powers*.

Maison Michel
65 rue Ste-Anne, 2nd (01.42.96.89.77/www. michel-paris.com). Mº Pyramides. **Open** by appointment. **Credit** MC, V. **Map** p401 H4.
One of the specialist businesses saved from extinction by Chanel, Maison Michel has been making hats since 1936 and supplies haute couture designers and the Paris opera. They can create the perfect panama or a flamboyant creation for the races, and also launched a prêt-à-porter range in 2006 with a range of sexy, shiny, '60s-inspired cloches and caps.

★ Marie Mercié
23 rue St-Sulpice, 6th (01.43.26.45.83). Mº Odéon. **Open** 11am-7pm Mon-Sat. **Credit** AmEx, MC, V. **Map** p408 H7.
Mercié's creations make you wish you lived in an era when hats were de rigueur. Step out in one shaped like curved fingers (complete with shocking-pink nail varnish and pink diamond ring) or a beret like a face with red lips and turquoise eyes. Ready-to-wear starts at €30; *sur mesure* takes ten days.

Jewellery

Dotted in and around place Vendôme, the key *joailliers* define the luxurious spirit of Paris. The Marais is home to a number of fashion and costume jewellery boutiques.

Boucheron
26 pl Vendôme, 1st (01.42.61.58.16/www. boucheron.com). Mº Opéra. **Open** 10.30am-7pm Mon-Sat. **Credit** AmEx, DC, MC, V. **Map** p401 G4.
Boucheron was the first to set up shop on place Vendôme, attracting celebrity custom from the nearby Ritz hotel. Owned by Gucci, the grand jeweller produces stunning pieces, using traditional motifs with new accents: take, for example, its fabulous chocolate-coloured gold watch. **Other location** 33 rue du Fbg-St-Honoré, 8th (01.44.51.95.20).

★ Cartier
13 rue de la Paix, 2nd (01.58.18.23.00/www. cartier.com). Mº Opéra. **Open** 10.30am-7pm Mon-Sat. **Credit** AmEx, DC, MC, V. **Map** p401 G4.

CONSUME

Christian Louboutin. See p260.

See p260.

CONSUME

This iconic French jeweller and watchmaker has impressive landmark headquarters. Downstairs, pearls, panthers and the Trinity ring jostle for attention among historic pieces commissioned by crowned heads; the upper salons house perfumer Mathilde Laurent's bespoke scents.
Other locations throughout the city.

Chanel Joaillerie
18 pl Vendôme, 1st (01.55.35.50.05/www.chanel. com). M° Opéra or Tuileries. **Open** 11am-7pm Mon-Sat. **Credit** AmEx, DC, MC, V. **Map** p401 G4.
Chanel launched its fine jewellery in the 1990s, reissuing the single collection – big on platinum and diamonds – that Coco herself designed some 60 years previously. The current line reinterprets the motifs – camellias, stars and comets – to create a collection of contemporary classics.

Dior Joaillerie
8 pl Vendôme, 1st (01.42.96.30.84/www. dior.com). M° Opéra or Tuileries. **Open** 11am-7pm Mon, Sat; 10.30am-7pm Tue-Fri. **Credit** AmEx, DC, MC, V. **Map** p401 G4.
The unabashed bling of Victoire de Castellane's designs is responsible for the fad of semi-precious coloured stones and runaway success of the 'Mimi Oui', a ring with a tiny diamond on a slim chain. **Other locations** 28 av Montaigne, 8th (01.47.23.52.39).

KarryO'
62 rue des Sts-Pères, 6th (01.45.48.94.67/www. karryo.com). M° St-Germain-des-Prés. **Open** 11am-7pm Mon-Sat. **Credit** MC, V. **Map** p405 G7.

Paris socialites come here to source their vintage jewellery, as well as modern gems by owner Karine Berrebi. Her adjacent gallery, Unique, features one-of-a-kind finds, from jewels and decorative objects to Hermès bags and the occasional Schiaparelli fur.

★ Marie-Hélène de Taillac
8 rue de Tournon, 6th (01.44.27.07.07/ www.mariehelenedetaillac.com). M° Mabillon. **Open** 11am-7pm Mon-Sat. **Credit** MC, V. **Map** p408 H7.
Marie-Hélène de Taillac is a fine jeweller. But unlike her colleagues across the Seine, her diamonds and emeralds in simple, unpretentious settings work well with jeans and don't make her customers look like ancestral portraits. This combination of precious stones and modern styling has made her hugely popular with the fashion elite. No doubt they also adore her Left Bank shop – a Tom Dixon-designed space in Marie-Hélène's trademark luminous pale blue and pillar box red, complete with a technicolour painting of Jaipur (where her studio is based) by Jean-Philippe Delhomme of Barneys New York ad fame.

Viveka Bergström
23 rue de la Grange aux Belles, 10th (01.40.03.04.92/www.viveka-bergstrom.com). M° Colonel Fabien. **Open** 1-7pm Tue-Fri; noon-7pm Sat. **Credit** AmEx, MC, V. **Map** p402 L3.
The daughter of Saab's aeroplane designer in the 1950s, Viveka Bergström makes slinky tassel necklaces, oversized beaten gold rings and brooches, and conversation starters like the angel-wing bracelet and a necklace featuring a map of Paris.

Lingerie & swimwear

For swimwear, *see also p271* **Sport & fitness**.

★ Alice Cadolle

4 rue Cambon, 1st (01.42.60.94.22/www.cadolle. com). M° Concorde or Madeleine. **Open** 11am-7pm Mon-Sat. Closed Aug. **Credit** AmEx, MC, V. **Map** p401 G4.

Five generations of lingerie-makers are behind this boutique, founded by Hermine Cadolle, who claimed to be the inventor of the bra. Great-great-granddaughter Poupie Cadolle continues the tradition in a cosy place devoted to a luxury ready-to-wear line of bras, panties and corsets.
▶ *For a special treat, Cadolle Couture (255 rue St-Honoré, 1st, 01.42.60.94.94) will create indulgent bespoke lingerie (by appointment only).*

Erès

2 rue Tronchet, 8th (01.47.42.28.82/www. eres.fr). M° Madeleine. **Open** 10am-7pm Mon-Sat. **Credit** AmEx, DC, MC, V. **Map** p401 G4.

Erès's beautifully cut swimwear has embraced a sexy '60s look complete with buttons on the low-cut briefs. The top and bottom can be purchased in different sizes, or you can buy one piece of a bikini.
Other locations 4bis rue du Cherche-Midi, 6th (01.45.44.95.54); 40 av Montaigne, 8th (01.47.23.07.26); 6 rue Guichard, 16th (01.46.47.45.21).

Etam Lingerie

139 rue de Rennes, 6th (01.45.44.16.88/www. etam.com). M° Montparnasse-Bienvenüe. **Open** 10am-8pm Mon-Sat. **Credit** AmEx, DC, MC, V. **Map** p401 G4.

Etam, which started out in lingerie in 1916, has now opened the largest lingerie store in Europe. It may be quantity over quality, but who can resist the 'bar à culottes' or the 'hot and spicy corner'?

★ Fifi Chachnil

231 rue St-Honoré, 1st (01.42.61.21.83/www. fifichachnil.com). M° Tuileries. **Open** 11am-7pm Mon-Sat. **Credit** AmEx, MC, V. **Map** p401 G4.

Chachnil has a new approach to frou-frou underwear in the pin-up tradition. Her chic mixes – deep red silk bras with boudoir pink bows, and pale turquoise girdles with orange trim – will have ladies and their male admirers purring in delight. The transparent black babydoll negligées with an Empire-line bust are classic saucy retro.
Other locations 68 rue Jean-Jacques-Rousseau, 1st (01.42.21.19.98).

Princesse Tam-Tam

52 bd St-Michel, 6th (01.40.51.72.99/www. princessetamtam.com). M° Cluny La Sorbonne.

THE BEST SHOE SHOPS

For dancing feet
Repetto. *See p260.*

For trainer envy
Clery Brice. *See p255.*

For cutting-edge creations
Moss. *See p260.*

Open 1.30-7pm Mon; 10am-7pm Tue-Sat. **Credit** AmEx, MC, V. **Map** p408 J7.

This inexpensive underwear and swimwear brand now has traffic-stopping promotions. Bright colours and sexily transparent and sporty gear are in.
Other locations throughout the city.

Sabbia Rosa

73 rue des Sts-Pères, 6th (01.45.48.88.37). M° St-Germain-des-Prés. **Open** 10am-7pm Mon-Sat. **Credit** AmEx, MC, V. **Map** p405 G7.

Let Moana Moatti tempt you with feather-trimmed satin mules, or satin, silk and chiffon negligées in fine shades of tangerine, lemon, mocha or pistachio. All sizes are medium, others are made *sur mesure*; prices are just the right side of stratospheric.

Vannina Vesperini

4 rue de Tournon, 6th (01.56.24.32.72/www. vanninavesperini.com). M° Odéon. **Open** 11am-7pm Mon-Sat. **Credit** AmEx, MC, V. **Map** p408 J7.

Only the finest silk satin is used for this designer's underwear, camisoles and sophisticated nightwear. The new boutique has a made-to-measure *atelier*.

Yoba

11 rue du Marché-St-Honoré, 1st (01.40.41.04.06/www.yobaparis.com). M° Tuileries. **Open** 11am-8pm Mon-Fri; noon-8pm Sat. **Credit** MC, V. **Map** p401 G5.

One for the liberated ladies, this smart boutique stocks items from wispy lingerie to cheeky sex toys.

Shoes & bags

An entire floor of footwear, including designer labels, can be found at **Printemps** (*see p239*). Rue du Dragon, rue de Grenelle and rue du Cherche-Midi form the backbone of an area that is a must for shoe and accessory addicts.

Bruno Frisoni

34 rue de Grenelle, 6th (01.42.84.12.30/www. brunofrisoni.fr). M° Rue du Bac. **Open** 10.30am-7pm Tue-Sat. **Credit** AmEx, V. **Map** p405 G7.

Innovative Frisoni's shoes have a cinematic, pop edge: modern theatrics for the unconventional.

CONSUME

CONSUME

Christian Louboutin

19 rue Jean-Jacques-Rousseau, 1st (01.42.36.05.31/www.christianlouboutin.com). M° Palais Royal Musée du Louvre. **Open** 10.30am-7pm Mon-Sat. Closed 3wks Aug. **Credit** AmEx, MC, V. **Map** p402 J5.
Every fashionista, WAG and shoe fiend worth her salt owns or hankers after a pair of Louboutin's trademark red-soled creations. Each design is displayed to maximum advantage in an individual frame. There's a made-to-measure service. *Photos p258.*
Other locations 38 rue de Grenelle, 7th (01.42.22.33.07); 68 rue du Fbg-St-Honoré (01.42.68.37.65).

★ Hervé Chapelier

1bis rue du Vieux-Colombier, 6th (01.44.07.06.50/www.hervechapelier.fr). M° St-Germain-des-Prés or St-Sulpice. **Open** 10.15am-7pm Mon-Sat. **Credit** AmEx, MC, V. **Map** p407 G7.
Bag yourself a classic, chic, hard-wearing, bicoloured tote at Hervé Chapelier. Sizes and prices range from a dinky purse at €22 to a weekend bag at €130.
Other locations throughout the city.

Iris

28 rue de Grenelle, 7th (01.42.22.89.81/www.iris-shoes.it). M° Rue du Bac or St-Sulpice. **Open** 10.30am-7pm Mon-Sat. **Credit** AmEx, MC, V. **Map** p405 F7.
This white boutique stocks shoes by Marc Jacobs, John Galliano, Proenza-Schouler and Viktor & Rolf.

Jamin Puech

61 rue de Hauteville, 10th (01.40.22.08.32/www.jamin-puech.com). M° Poissonnière. **Open** 11am-7pm Mon-Fri; noon-7pm Sat. **Credit** AmEx, DC, MC, V. **Map** p402 K3.
The complete collection of Isabelle Puech and Benoît Jamin's dazzling handbags is displayed in a bohemian setting complete with antler-horn chairs.
Other locations throughout the city.

★ K Jacques

16 rue Pavée, 4th (01.40.27.03.57/www.kjacques.fr). M° St-Paul. **Open** 10am-6.45pm Mon-Sat; 2-6.45pm Sun. **Credit** MC, V. **Map** p409 L6.
See right **Elemental Chic.**

Moss

22 rue de Grenelle, 7th (01.42.22.01.42). M° Rue du Bac or St-Sulpice. **Open** 10.30am-7pm Mon-Sat. **Credit** AmEx, MC, V. **Map** p405 F7.
The three sisters who run this boutique pride themselves on sourcing cutting-edge shoes, that can be hard to find elsewhere, such as creations by former Celine stylist Avril Gau and signature designs by Laurence Dacade, Duccio del Duca and Hartian Bourdin. You'll also find scarves by Octavio Pizzaro and jewellery by Karry O', the fourth sister.

Peggy Huyn Kinh

9-11 rue Coëtlogon, 6th (01.42.84.83.82/www.phk.fr). M° St-Sulpice. **Open** 11am-7pm Mon-Sat. **Credit** AmEx, MC, V. **Map** p405 G7.
Once creative director at Cartier, Peggy Huyn Kinh now makes bags of boar skin and python, as well as silver jewellery.

★ Pierre Hardy

156 galerie de Valois, 1st (01.42.60.59.75/www.pierrehardy.com). M° Palais Royal Musée du Louvre. **Open** 11am-7pm Mon-Sat. **Credit** AmEx, DC, MC, V. **Map** p402 H5.
This classy black-and-white shoebox is home to Hardy's range of superbly conceived footwear – with a price tag to match – for men and women.
Other location 9-11 pl du Palais Bourbon, 7th (01.45.55.00.67).

★ Repetto

22 rue de la Paix, 2nd (01.44.71.83.12/www.repetto.com). M° Opéra. **Open** 9.30am-7.30pm Mon-Sat. **Credit** AmEx, MC, V. **Map** p401 G4.
This ballet shoe-maker struck gold when it decided to reissue its dance shoes with pavement soles. The prowly *ballerines* and showbiz dance boots in black, metallic and spangly finishes are fun, stylish and exceptionally comfortable. They are sold alongside the full range of real balletwear; you can try out your *pointes* on a red carpet with a *barre* if you want to show off.
Other locations 51 rue du Four, 6th (01.45.44.98.65).

Rodolphe Menudier

14 rue de Castiglione, 1st (01.42.60.86.27/www.rodolphemenudier.com). M° Concorde or Tuileries. **Open** 11am-7pm Mon; 10am-7pm Tue-Sat. **Credit** AmEx, MC, V. **Map** p401 G5.
This boutique makes the perfect backdrop for Menudier's racy designs. Open, silver-handled drawers display his stilettos in profile, as well as outrageous thigh-high boots with Plexiglass soles; more demure customers can opt for a pair of pumps.

Roger Vivier

29 rue du Fbg-St-Honoré, 8th (01.53.43.00.85/www.rogervivier.com). M° Concorde or Madeleine. **Open** 11am-7pm Mon-Sat. **Credit** AmEx, DC, MC, V. **Map** p401 F4.
The fashion editors' shoeman of choice, Vivier is credited with inventing the stiletto.

FOOD & DRINK

You could spend a lifetime sampling the breads, pastries, chocolate and cheeses available in Paris. Open-air markets continue to beckon with their fresh, seasonal produce, and **Galeries Lafayette** and **Le Bon Marché** (for both, *see p239*) have luxury food halls.

Bakeries

★ Arnaud Delmontel
39 rue des Martyrs, 9th (01.48.78.29.33/www.
arnaud-delmontel.com). M° St-Georges. **Open**
7am-8.30pm Mon, Wed-Sun. **No credit cards.**
Map p402 H2.
With its crisp crust and chewy crumb shot through
with irregular holes, Delmontel's Renaissance bread
is one of the finest in Paris. He puts the same skill into
his unsurpassable almond croissants.
Other locations 57 rue Damrémont, 18th
(01.42.64.59.63).

L'Autre Boulange
43 rue de Montreuil, 11th (01.43.72.86.04).
M° Faidherbe Chaligny or Nation. **Open** 7.30am-
1.30pm, 4-7.30pm Mon-Fri; 7.30am-1.30pm Sat.
Closed Aug. **Credit** MC, V. **Map** p407 P7.
Michel Cousin bakes up to 23 different types of
organic loaf in his wood-fired oven – varieties
include the *flutiot* (rye bread with raisins, walnuts
and hazelnuts) and a spiced cornmeal bread.

Le Boulanger de Monge
123 rue Monge, 5th (01.43.37.54.20/www.
leboulangerdemonge.com). M° Censier
Daubenton. **Open** 7am-8.30pm Tue-Sun.
Credit MC, V. **Map** p406 K9.
Dominique Saibron uses spices to give inimitable
flavour to his organic sourdough *boule*. Every day
about 2,000 bread-lovers visit this boutique, which
also produces one of the city's best baguettes.

Moisan
5 pl d'Aligre, 12th (01.43.45.46.60/www.
painmoisan.fr). M° Ledru-Rollin. **Open** 7am-
8pm Tue-Sat; 7am-2pm Sun. **No credit cards.**
Map p407 N7.
Moisan's organic bread, *viennoiseries* and rustic
tarts are outstanding. At this branch, situated by
the market, there's always a healthy queue.
Other locations throughout the city.

★ Du Pain et des Idées
34 rue Yves Toudic, 10th (01.42.40.44.52/
www.dupainetdesidees.com). M° Jacques
Bonsergent. **Open** 6.45am-8pm Mon-Fri.
No credit cards. Map p402 L4.
Christophe Vasseur won the Gault-Millau prize for
Best Bakery. Among his specialities are Le Rabelais
– *pain brioché* with saffron, honey and nuts; and Le
Pagnol aux Pommes, a bread studded with royal
gala apple (skin on), raisins and orange flower water.

★ Poilâne
8 rue du Cherche-Midi, 6th (01.45.48.42.59/
www.poilane.com). M° Sèvres Babylone or
St-Sulpice. **Open** 7.15am-8.15pm Mon-Sat.
Credit (€20 minimum) AmEx, DC, MC, V.
Map p405 G7.

Apol
queue
tarts a
Other
(01.45.7.

Chees

The sign *ma*
merchants wh
farms and age th...

Elementa

Superior sandals at ... Jacques.

Those who love clothes and understand
style appreciate that if you're up close
to Mother Nature, you have to ditch
the follies of the fashion spread for
something more fit for purpose. But what
they also realise is that such restraint
doesn't have to mean dowdy clothes. The
fashionable in a field rely on 'elemental
chic' brands, whose collections usually
have some high-tech or artisanal origin
and strike the right balance between form
and function, but in terms of price point,
heritage and celebrity endorsement,
bear a reassuring resemblance to the
designer brands they wear back in town.
So, for example, you might catch the
fash pack in Moncler in the mountains,
Barbour in the countryside, and if
paparazzi shots of Kate Moss on holiday
are anything to go by, **K Jacques** (*see
left*) sandals at the beach.

Set up in Saint-Tropez in 1933 by
Jacques Keklikian and his wife, the
K Jacques workshop started life stitching
together basic leather sandals for visitors
to the Med resort. The Homère (or
Homer), a Greco Roman-style sandal with
five horizontal straps across the foot,
was, and still is, the signature piece –
Picasso loved them, and over the years
they've counted the likes of Colette and
Bridget Bardot among their fans.

Now the company, run by grandson
Bernard, offers a range of around 60
styles that subtly reflect the trends of the
last 70 years, but remain, in essence,
simple, hard-wearing sandals. Examples
of each and every style are squeezed into
the Marais outpost, where makeshift
seating, wooden floors and cramped
dimensions make the attempt to find
the perfect pair about as comfortable
as getting changed in a beach hut.

Les Caves Augé.

...u lait cru
...unpasteurised

...t, 17th (01.46.22.50.45/www.
...eosse.com). M° Ternes. **Open** 9am-
...1pm Tue-Thur; 9am-1pm, 4.30-7pm Fri,
...**Credit** MC, V. **Map** p400 C2.
...eople cross town for these cheeses – wonderful
farmhouse camemberts, delicate st-marcellins, a
choice of *chèvres* and several rarities.

Fromagerie Dubois et Fils

80 rue de Tocqueville, 17th (01.42.27.11.38).
M° Malesherbes or Villiers. **Open** 9am-1pm,
4-8pm Tue-Fri; 8.30am-7.45pm Sat; 9am-1pm Sun.
Closed 1st 3wks Aug. **Credit** AmEx, MC, V.
Map p401 E2.
Superchef darling Dubois stocks 80 types of goat's
cheese, plus prized, aged st-félicien.

★ Fromagerie Quatrehomme

62 rue de Sèvres, 7th (01.47.34.33.45). M° Duroc
or Vaneau. **Open** 8.45am-1pm, 4-7.45pm Tue-
Thur; 8.45am-7.45pm Fri, Sat. **Credit** MC, V.
Map p405 F8.
Marie Quatrehomme runs this *fromagerie*. Justly
famous for her beaufort and st-marcellin, she also
sells specialities such as goat's cheese with pesto.
Other locations 9 rue du Poteau, 18th
(01.46.06.26.03).

Marie-Anne Cantin

12 rue du Champ-de-Mars, 7th (01.45.50.43.94/
www.cantin.fr). M° Ecole Militaire or Latour
Maubourg. **Open** 2-7.30pm Mon; 8.30am-7.30pm
Tue-Sat; 8.30am-1pm Sun. **Credit** AmEx, MC, V.
Map p404 D6.
Cantin, a defender of unpasteurised cheese and sup-
plier to many posh Paris restaurants, offers aged
chèvres and amazing morbier, mont d'or and comté.

Chocolate

Cacao et Chocolat

29 rue de Buci, 6th (01.46.33.77.63/www.cacao
etchocolat.com). M° Mabillon. **Open** 10.30am-
2pm, 3-7.30pm daily. **Credit** AmEx, DC, MC, V.
Map p405 H7.
This shop recalls chocolate's Aztec origins, with its
choice of spicy fillings (honey and chilli, nutmeg,
clove and citrus), chocolate masks and pyramids.
Other locations 63 rue St-Louis-en-l'Ile, 4th
(01.46.33.33.33); 36 rue Vieille-du-Temple, 4th
(01.42.71.50.06).

Christian Constant

37 rue d'Assas, 6th (01.53.63.15.15). M° Rennes
or St-Placide. **Open** 9.30am-8.30pm Mon-Fri;
9am-8pm Sat, Sun. **Credit** MC, V. **Map** p405 G8.

A master chocolate-maker and *traiteur*, Constant
scours the globe for new ideas. His *ganaches* are subtly flavoured with verbena, jasmine or cardamom.

Jacques Génin

133 rue de Turenne, 3rd (01.45.77.29.01/
www.jacquesgenin.com). M° Filles de Calvaire.
Open 11am-9pm Mon-Sat. **Credit** MC, V.
Map p409 L5.
Voted the 'best *chocolatier* in the world' by critic Mort
Rosenblum, Jacques Génin's creations could previously only be tasted in top restaurants. But now his
impressive boutique allows you to taste *sur place*
or take a bag home. The signature eclairs and tarts
glisten in glass cases, and the millefeuilles are made
to order for perfect freshness. The chocolate ganaches
include Menthe Amante, a two-phase taste sensation
that finishes with mint leaves bursting on the tongue.
One part of the vast space is given over to a tearoom,
and a spiral staircase leads to the *ateliers*.

★ Jean-Paul Hévin

3 rue Vavin, 6th (01.43.54.09.85/www.
jphevin.com). M° Notre-Dame-des-Champs
or Vavin. **Open** 10am-7.30pm Tue-Sat. Closed
Aug. **Credit** AmEx, MC, V. **Map** p405 G8.
Hévin specialises in the beguiling combination of
chocolate with potent cheese fillings, which loyal
customers serve with wine as an aperitif.
Other locations 231 rue St-Honoré, 1st
(01.55.35.35.96); 23bis av de La Motte-Picquet,
7th (01.45.51.77.48).

La Maison du Chocolat

120 av Victor-Hugo, 16th (01.40.67.77.83/
www.lamaisonduchocolat.com). M° Victor Hugo.
Open 10am-7.30pm Mon-Sat; 10am-1pm Sun.
Credit AmEx, MC, V. **Map** p400 B4.

CONSUME

Robert Linxe opened his first Paris shop in 1977, and has been inventing new chocolates ever since, using Asian spices, fresh fruits and herbal infusions. **Other locations** throughout the city.

Patrick Roger
108 bd St-Germain, 6th (01.43.29.38.42/www.patrickroger.com). M° Odéon. **Open** 10.30am-7.30pm Mon-Sat. **Credit** MC, V. **Map** p408 H7.
Roger is shaking up the art of chocolate-making. Whereas other *chocolatiers* aim for gloss, Roger may create a brushed effect on hens so realistic you almost expect them to lay (chocolate) eggs.
Other locations 491 rue de Rennes, 6th (01.45.44.66.13); 199 rue du Fbg-St-Honoré, 8th (01.45.61.11.46); 45 av Victor-Hugo, 16th (01.45.01.66.71).

Richart
258 bd St-Germain, 7th (01.45.55.66.00/www.richart.com). M° Solférino. **Open** 10am-7pm Mon-Sat. **Credit** AmEx, MC, V. **Map** p405 F6.
Each chocolate *ganache* has an intricate design, packages look like jewel boxes, and each purchase comes with a tract on how best to savour the stuff.

Drinks

Les Caves Augé
116 bd Haussmann, 8th (01.45.22.16.97/www.cavesauge.com). M° St-Augustin. **Open** 1-7.30pm Mon; 9am-7.30pm Tue-Sat. Closed Mon in Aug. **Credit** AmEx, MC, V. **Map** p401 E3.
The oldest wine shop in Paris – Marcel Proust was a regular customer – is serious and professional.

Les Caves Taillevent
199 rue du Fbg-St-Honoré, 8th (01.45.61.14.09/www.taillevent.com). M° Charles de Gaulle Etoile or Ternes. **Open** 10am-7.30pm Tue-Sat. Closed 1st 3wks Aug. **Credit** AmEx, DC, MC, V. **Map** p400 D3.
Choose from half a million wines to go with your meal at the nearby Taillevent restaurant (*see p198*).

Julien, Caviste
50 rue Charlot, 3rd (01.42.72.00.94). M° Filles du Calvaire. **Open** 9am-1.30pm, 3.30-7.30pm Tue-Sat; 10.30am-1.30pm Sun. Closed 3rd wk Aug. **Credit** AmEx, MC, V. **Map** p402 L5.
Julien promotes the small producers he has discovered, and often holds wine tastings on Saturdays.

★ Lavinia
3 bd de la Madeleine, 1st (01.42.97.20.20/www.lavinia.fr). M° Madeleine. **Open** 10am-8pm Mon-Sat. **Credit** AmEx, DC, MC, V. **Map** p401 G4.
Lavinia stocks a broad selection of French alongside many non-French wines; its glassed-in *cave* has everything from a 1945 Mouton-Rothschild at €22,000 to trendy and 'fragile' wines for under €10.

▶ *Have fun tasting wine with the dégustation machines on the ground floor, which allow customers to taste a sip of up to ten different wines each week for €10.*

Legrand Filles et Fils
1 rue de la Banque, 2nd (01.42.60.07.12/www.caves-legrand.com). M° Bourse. **Open** 11am-7pm Mon; 10am-7.30pm Tue-Fri; 10am-7pm Sat. Closed Mon in July & Aug. **Credit** AmEx, MC, V. **Map** p402 H4.
Fine wines and brandies, teas and *bonbons,* and a showroom for regular wine tastings.

Ryst Dupeyron
79 rue du Bac, 7th (01.45.48.80.93/www.dupeyron.com). M° Rue du Bac. **Open** 12.30-7.30pm Mon; 10.30am-7.30pm Tue-Sat. Closed 2wks Aug. **Credit** AmEx, MC, V. **Map** p405 F7.
The Dupeyrons have been selling armagnac for four generations, and still have bottles from 1868. Treasures here include 200 fine Bordeaux wines and an extensive range of vintage port.

Global

Les Délices d'Orient
52 av Emile-Zola, 15th (01.45.79.10.00). M° Charles Michels. **Open** 8.30am-9pm Tue-Sun. **Credit** MC, V. **Map** p404 B8.
Shelves groan under stuffed aubergines, halva, falafel and all manner of Middle Eastern delicacies.
Other locations 14 rue des Quatre-Frères-Peignot, 15th (01.45.77.82.93).

Izraël
30 rue François-Miron, 4th (01.42.72.66.23). M° Hôtel de Ville. **Open** 9.30am-1pm, 2.30-7pm Tue-Fri; 9.30am-7pm Sat. Closed Aug. **Credit** MC, V. **Map** p409 K6.
A Marais fixture, this narrow shop stocks spices and other delights from Mexico, Turkey and India.

★ Jabugo Ibérico & Co
11 rue Clément-Marot, 8th (01.47.20.03.13). M° Alma Marceau or Franklin D. Roosevelt. **Open** 10am-9pm Mon-Fri; 10am-8pm Sat. **Credit** AmEx, DC, MC, V. **Map** p400 D4.
Spanish hams here have the Bellota-Bellota label, meaning that the pigs have been allowed to feast on acorns. Manager Philippe Poulachon compares his cured hams (€98 a kilo) to the delicacy of truffles.
▶ *Restaurant Bellota-Bellota (18 rue Jean-Nicot, 7th, 01.53.59.96.96) also sells hams at its adjoining épicerie.*

Markets

The city council has made markets more accessible to working people by extending their opening hours. There are now more than 70 markets in Paris. The city council's website (www.paris.fr) has full details of each one; below is a selection of the best.

Marché Anvers

Pl d'Anvers, 9th. M° Anvers. **Open** 3-8pm Fri. **Map** p402 J2.

An afternoon market that adds to the village atmosphere of a peaceful *quartier* down the hill from Montmartre. Among its highlights are regional vegetables, hams from the Auvergne, lovingly aged cheeses and award-winning honey.

★ Marché Bastille

Bd Richard-Lenoir, 11th. M° Richard-Lenoir. **Open** 7am-2.30pm Thur; 7am-3pm Sun. **Map** p403 M5.

One of the biggest markets in Paris. A favourite of political campaigners, it's also a great source of local cheeses, farmers' chicken and excellent fish.

Marché Batignolles

Rue Lemercier, 17th. M° Brochant. **Open** 8.30am-1pm, 3.30-8pm Tue-Fri; 8.30am-8pm Sat; 8.30am-3pm Sun. **Map** p401 F1.

Batignolles is more down to earth than the better-known Raspail organic market, with a quirky selection of stallholders, many of whom produce what they sell. Prices are higher here than at ordinary markets, but the goods are worth it.

Marché Beauvau

Pl d'Aligre, 12th. M° Ledru-Rollin. **Open** 9am-1pm, 4-7.30pm Tue-Sat; 8.30am-1.30pm Sun. **Map** p407 N7.

This market is proudly working class. Stallholders do their utmost to out-shout each other, and price-conscious shoppers don't compromise on quality.

★ Marché Monge

Pl Monge, 5th. M° Place Monge. **Open** 7am-2.30pm Wed, Fri; 7am-3pm Sun. **Map** p406 K8.

This pretty, compact market is set on a leafy square. It has a high proportion of producers and is much less touristy than nearby rue Mouffetard.

Marché Président-Wilson

Av Président-Wilson, 16th. M° Alma-Marceau or Iéna. **Open** 7am-2.30pm Wed; 7am-3pm Sat. **Map** p400 C5.

A classy market attracting the city's top chefs, who snap up ancient vegetable varieties.

Saxe-Breteuil

Av de Saxe, 7th. M° Ségur. **Open** 7am-2.30pm Thur; 7am-3pm Sat. **Map** p405 E8.

Saxe-Breteuil has an unrivalled setting facing the Eiffel Tower, as well as the city's most chic produce. Look for farmer's goat's cheese, rare apple varieties, Armenian specialities, abundant oysters and a handful of dedicated small producers.

Fauchon.

Pâtisseries

Arnaud Larher
*53 rue Caulaincourt, 18th (01.42.57.68.08/
www.arnaud-larher.com). M° Lamarck
Caulaincourt.* **Open** 10am-7.30pm Tue-Sat.
Credit MC, V. **Map** p401 H1.
Look out for the strawberry-and-lychee flavoured
bonheur and the chocolate-and-thyme *récif*.

Finkelsztajn
*27 rue des Rosiers, 4th (01.42.72.78.91/
www.laboutiquejaune.com). M° St-Paul.* **Open**
10am-7pm Mon, Wed-Sun. Closed 15 July-
15 Aug. **Credit** (€20 minimum) AmEx, MC, V.
Map p409 L6.
This motherly, yellow-fronted shop, in business
since 1946, stocks dense Jewish cakes filled with
poppy seeds, apples or cream cheese.

Gérard Mulot
*76 rue de Seine, 6th (01.43.26.85.77/
http://gerard-mulot.com). M° Odéon.* **Open**
6.45am-8pm Mon, Tue, Thur-Sun. Closed Easter
& Aug. **Credit** V. **Map** p408 H7.
Gérard Mulot rustles up stunning pastries. Try the
mabillon: caramel mousse with apricot marmalade.
Other locations 93 rue de la Glacière, 13th
(01.45.81.39.09).

★ Pierre Hermé
*72 rue Bonaparte, 6th (01.43.54.47.77). M°
Mabillon, St-Germain-des-Prés or St-Sulpice.*
Open 10am-7pm Tue-Fri, Sun; 10am-7.30pm
Sat. Closed 1st 3wks Aug. **Credit** AmEx, DC,
MC, V. **Map** p405 G7.
Pastry superstar Hermé attracts connoisseurs from
St-Germain and afar with his seasonal collections.
Other locations 4 rue Cambon, 1st
(01.58.62.43.17); 185 rue de Vaugirard,
15th (01.47.83.89.96).

Treats & *traiteurs*

Da Rosa
*62 rue de Seine, 6th (01.45.21.41.30/www.
restaurant-da-rosa.com). M° Odéon.* **Open**
10am-11pm daily. **Credit** AmEx, MC, V.
Map p408 H7.
José Da Rosa sourced ingredients for top restaurants
before filling his own shop with Spanish hams,
Olivier Roellinger spices and Luberon truffles.

Dammann Frères
*15 pl des Vosges, 4th (01.44.54.04.88/
www.dammann.fr). M° St-Paul.* **Open** 11am-7pm
daily. **Credit** AmEx, DC, MC, V. **Map** p409 L6.
Dammann Frères, fine tea importers since 1825,
have finally opened their own boutique, a wonderful den of a place with a beamed roof and mahogany
shelves displaying hundreds of their exquisite black

INSIDE TRACK
FOODIE SHOPPING

www.edible-paris.com
Time Out's own Rosa Jackson leads
tours or can prepare you a personalised
foodie itinerary.

www.visiterungis.com
How to visit the largest wholesale food
market in the world.

boxes. The 'orgue à thés' allows you to sniff the aromas of 160 blends. A small tin of loose tea or 24 tea
bags costs €7 and they also sell traditional oriental
iron teapots, all attractively gift-wrapped.

Fauchon
*26 & 30 pl de la Madeleine, 8th (01.70.39.38.00/
www.fauchon.com). M° Madeleine.* **Open** *No.26*
8am-9pm Mon-Sat. *No.30* 9am-9pm Mon-Sat.
Credit AmEx, MC, V. **Map** p401 F4.
The city's most famous food shop is worth a visit,
particularly for the beautifully packaged gift items.

★ Hédiard
*21 pl de la Madeleine, 8th (01.43.12.88.88/
www.hediard.fr). M° Madeleine.* **Open** 8.30am-
9pm Mon-Sat. **Credit** AmEx, DC, MC, V.
Map p401 F4.
Hédiard's charming shop dates back to 1880, when
they were the first to introduce exotic foods to Paris,
specialising in rare teas and coffees, spices, jams and
candied fruits.
▶ *Pop upstairs for a cuppa in the shop's posh
tearoom, La Table d'Hédiard.*
Other locations throughout the city.

Huilerie Artisanale Leblanc
*6 rue Jacob, 6th (01.46.34.61.55/www.huile-
leblanc.com). M° St-Germain-des-Prés.* **Open**
noon-7pm Tue-Fri; 10am-7pm Sat. Closed 2wks
Aug. **No credit cards. Map** p405 H6.
The Leblanc family started making walnut oil before
branching out to press pure oils from hazelnuts,
almonds, pine nuts, grilled peanuts and olives.

Première Pression Provence
*3 rue Antoine Vollon, 12th (01.53.33.03.59/
www.premiere-pression-provence.com). M° Ledru
Rollin.* **Open** 11am-2.30pm, 3.30-7pm Tue-Fri;
10.30am-7pm Sat. **Credit** AmEx, MC, V. **Map**
p407 N7.
Première Pression Provence is L'Occitan creator
Olivier Baussan's latest project, where you are
encouraged to taste spoonfuls of single-producer
olive oil to educate your palate about the nuances of
vert, mûr and *noir* (known as the '*fruités*'). Two
dozen small producers send their oils direct from

CONSUME

their Provençal olive groves to the boutique near the Marché d'Aligre, where they are sold in aluminium cans with colour-coded labels.
Other locations 9 rue des Martyrs, 9th (01.48.78.86.51).

Torréfacteur Verlet
256 rue St-Honoré, 1st (01.42.60.67.39/www. cafesverlet.com). M° Palais Royal Musée du Louvre. **Open** 9.30am-6.30pm Mon-Sat. Closed Aug. **Credit** MC, V. **Map** p401 G5.
Eric Duchaussoy roasts rare coffee beans to perfection – sip a cup here or take some home to savour.

GIFTS
Florists

★ Culture(s)
46 rue de Lancry, 10th (01.48.03.58.71). M° Jacques Bonsergent or République. **Open** 11am-2pm; 3-7pm Tue-Sat. **Credit** AmEx, MC, V. **Map** p402 L4.
In a loft-style studio, this unusual florist combines exotic flowers, trees and garden themed items, such as floral printed rain hats. Truly original.

Au Nom de la Rose
87 rue St-Antoine, 4th (01.42.71.34.24/www. aunomdelarose.fr). M° St-Paul. **Open** *Sept-July* 10am-9pm daily. *Aug* 10am-9pm Mon-Sat. **Credit** AmEx, DC, MC, V. **Map** p409 L7.
Specialising in roses, Au Nom can supply a bouquet, as well as rose-based beauty products and candles.
Other locations throughout the city.

Gifts & eccentricities

Arty Dandy
1 rue de Furstemberg, 6th (01.43.54.00.36/www. artydandy.com). M° Mabillon. **Open** 10am-7pm Mon-Sat. **Credit** AmEx, MC, V. **Map** p408 H7.
'Dandyism is the last spark of heroism amid decadence,' said Baudelaire. Taking this as its motto, Arty Dandy is a concept shop that embraces the surreal, the tongue-in-cheek and the poetic – an R.MUTT sticker to create your own Duchampian loo, and the 'Karl who?' bag (which KL himself has been carrying) are instant pleasers. More sublime offerings include Jaime Hayon's 'Lover' figurines and Sebastien Le Gal watercolours. There are also Alchimie anti-ageing products.

★ Diptyque
34 bd St-Germain, 5th (01.43.26.77.44/www. diptyqueparis.com). M° Maubert Mutualité. **Open** 10am-7pm Mon-Sat. **Credit** V. **Map** p405 G6.
Diptyque's divinely scented candles are the quintessential gift from Paris. They come in 48 different varieties and are probably the best you'll ever find. *Photos p269.*

Galeries Laffitte
27 rue Laffitte, 9th (01.47.70.38.83). M° Notre-Dame-de-Lorette. **Open** 9am-7pm Mon-Fri; 10am-6.30pm Sat. **Credit** MC, V. **Map** p402 H3.
The basement houses a regular *papeterie* filled with pens and notebooks, and the ground floor has art supplies and a selection of gifts, from quality leather bags to Italian pastel-coloured diary covers.

★ Sennelier
3 quai Voltaire, 7th (01.42.60.72.15/www. magasinsennelier.fr). M° St-Germain-des-Prés. **Open** 2-6.30pm Mon; 10am-12.45pm, 2-6.30pm Tue-Sat. **Credit** AmEx, DC, MC, V. **Map** p405 G6.
Old-fashioned colour merchant Sennelier sells oil paints, watercolours and pastels, rare pigments, primed canvases, varnishes and paper.
Other locations 4bis rue de la Grande-Chaumière, 6th (01.46.33.72.39).

HEALTH & BEAUTY
Cosmetics

★ L'Artisan Parfumeur
24 bd Raspail, 7th (01.42.22.23.32/www. artisanparfumeur.com). M° Rue du Bac. **Open** 10.30am-7.30pm Mon-Sat. **Credit** AmEx, DC, MC, V. **Map** p405 G7.
Among scented candles, potpourri and charms, you'll find the best vanilla perfume Paris can offer – Mûres et Musc, a bestseller for two decades.
Other locations throughout the city.

By Terry
21 & 36 galerie Véro-Dodat, 1st (01.44.76.00.76/ www.byterry.com). M° Palais Royal Musée du Louvre. **Open** 10.30am-7pm Mon-Sat. **Credit** AmEx, MC, V. **Map** p402 H5.
Terry de Gunzburg, who earned her reputation at Yves Saint Laurent, offers made-to-measure 'haute couleur' make-up by skilled chemists and colourists combining high-tech treatments and handmade precision. There's prêt-à-porter, too.
Other locations 30 rue de la Trémoille, 8th (01.44.43.04.04); 10 av Victor-Hugo, 16th (01.55.73.00.73).

Détaille 1905
10 rue St-Lazare, 9th (01.48.78.68.50/www. detaille.com). M° Notre-Dame-de-Lorette. **Open** 11am-2pm, 3-7pm Tue-Sat. **Credit** MC, V. **Map** p401 H3.
Step back in time at this shop, opened, as the name suggests, in 1905 by war artist Edouard Détaille. Six fragrances (three for men and three for women) are made from century-old recipes.

Editions de Parfums Frédéric Malle
37 rue de Grenelle, 7th (01.42.22.76.40/ www.editionsdeparfums.com). M° Rue du Bac

CONSUME

or *St-Sulpice*. **Open** 1-7pm Mon; 11am-7pm Tue-Sat. **Credit** AmEx, DC, MC, V. **Map** p405 F6.
Choose from a range of eight perfumes by Frédéric Malle, former consultant to Hermès and Lacroix. Carnal Flower by Dominique Ropion is seduction in a bottle.
Other locations 21 rue du Mont-Thabor, 1st (01.42.22.77.22); 140 av Victor-Hugo, 16th (01.45.05.39.02).

★ Galerie Noémie

92 av des Champs-Elysées, 8th (01.44.76.06.26/ www.galerienoemie.com). M° George V. **Open** 11am-7pm Mon-Thur; 11am-9pm Fri, Sat. **Credit** AmEx, DC, MC, V. **Map** p402 J5.
You can tell owner Noémie is a painter by the way all the make-up is set out in palettes. Little pots of gloss (starting from €7.50) in myriad colours triple as lip gloss, eyeshadow or blusher. Check out Noemie's blog at http://blog.galerienoemie.com.
Other locations Galeries Lafayette, 40 bd Haussmann, 9th (01.42.82.34.56).

Guerlain

68 av des Champs-Elysées, 8th (01.45.62.52.57/ www.guerlain.com). M° Franklin D. Roosevelt. **Open** 10.30am-8pm Mon-Sat; 3-7pm Sun. **Credit** AmEx, DC, MC, V. **Map** p401 E4.
The golden oldie of luxury beauty products and scents is looking as ravishing than ever. Head to the first floor to get the full measure of the history behind the house that created the mythic Samsara, Mitsouko and L'Heure Bleue.

★ Salons du Palais-Royal Shiseido

Jardins du Palais-Royal, 142 galerie de Valois, 1st (01.49.27.09.09/www.salons-shiseido.com). M° Palais Royal Musée du Louvre. **Open** 10am-7pm Mon-Sat. **Credit** AmEx, DC, MC, V. **Map** p401 H5.
Under the arcades of the Palais-Royal, Shiseido's perfumer Serge Lutens practises his aromatic arts. A former photographer at Paris *Vogue* and artistic director of make-up at Christian Dior, Lutens is a maestro of rare taste. Bottles of his concoctions – Tubéreuse Criminelle, Rahat Loukoum and Ambre Sultan – can be sampled by visitors. Look out for Fleurs d'Oranger, which the great man defines as the smell of happiness. Many of the perfumes are exclusive to the Salons; prices start at around €100.
Other locations 2 pl Vendôme, 1st (01.42.60.68.61); 29 rue de Sèvres, 6th (01.42.22.46.60); 66 bd du Montparnasse, 15th (01.43.20.95.40).

Sephora

70 av des Champs-Elysées, 8th (01.53.93.22.50/ www.sephora.fr). M° Franklin D. Roosevelt. **Open** *Sept-June* 10am-midnight Mon-Thur, Sun; 10am-1am Fri, Sat. *July, Aug* 10am-1.30am daily. **Credit** AmEx, DC, MC, V. **Map** p401 E4.

The flagship of the cosmetic supe. houses 12,000 brands of scent and sk. Blanc (14 cour St-Emilion, 12th, 01.40.02.) tures beauty products in a minimalist interio.
Other locations throughout the city.

Salons & spas

Anne Sémonin

Le Bristol, 108 rue du Fbg-St-Honoré, 8th (01.42.66.24.22/www.hotel-bristol.com). M° Champs-Elysées Clemenceau or Miromesnil. **Open** 10am-8pm Mon-Sat; by appointment Sun. **Credit** AmEx, DC, MC, V. **Map** p401 E3.
Facials involve delicious concoctions of basil, lavender, lemongrass, ginger and plant essences. Also on offer are reflexology and a selection of massage styles, from Thai to ayurvedic. Body treatments cost from €70 to €210. Sémonin's renowned seaweed skincare products and essential oils are also on sale.
Other locations 2 rue des Petits-Champs, 2nd (01.42.60.94.66).

Appartement 217

217 rue St-Honoré, 1st (01.42.96.00.96/ www.lappartement217.com). M° Tuileries. **Open** 10am-7pm Tue-Sat. **Credit** AmEx, DC, MC, V. **Map** p401 G5.
Opened by Stéphane Jaulin, the former beauty director of Colette, a beautiful feng-shuied Haussmannian apartment is the setting for facials using organic beauty guru Dr Hauschka's products and ayurvedic or deep tissue massages. The water has been decalcified, electrical currents are insulated, and the silky-soft kimonos are made from organic wood pulp.

Les Bains du Marais

31-33 rue des Blancs-Manteaux, 4th (01.44.61.02.02/www.lesbainsdumarais.com). M° St-Paul. **Open** *Men* 10am-11pm Thur; 10am-8pm Fri. *Women* 11am-8pm Mon; 10am-11pm Tue; 10am-7pm Wed. *Mixed (swimwear required)* 7-11pm Wed; 10am-8pm Sat; 10am-11pm Sun. Closed Aug. **Credit** AmEx, MC, V. **Map** p409 K6.
This hammam and spa mixes the modern and traditional (lounging beds and mint tea). Facials, waxing and essential oil massages (€70) are also available. The hammam and standard massage are €35 each.

★ Hammam de la Grande Mosquée

1 pl du Puits-de-l'Ermite, 5th (01.43.31.38.20/ www.la-mosquee.com). M° Censier Daubenton. **Open** *Men* 2-9pm Tue; 10am-9pm Sun. *Women* 10am-9pm Mon, Wed, Sat; 2-9pm Fri. **Credit** MC, V. **Map** p406 K9.
The authentic hammam experience in this beautiful 1920s mosque has become popular with *parisiennes*, so avoid the weekends when the volume of traffic makes it less relaxing than it should be. Follow a

ʒe (exfoliation with a
The hammam is €15,
10. Swimwear is com-
e is also available.

re
.02.31.05/www.
cq. **Open** *Women*
om Sun. *Mixed*
(swimwear required) ___)pm Sat. **Credit**
MC, V. **Map** p403 N5.

This hammam is hard to beat – spotless mosaic-tiled surroundings, flowered sarongs and a relaxing pool. The exotic 'Forfait florale' option (€139) will have you enveloped in rose petals and massaged with *huile d'Argan* from Morocco, and the more simple hammam and *gommage* followed by mint tea and pastries is €39. Plan to spend a few hours here, as the soft-voiced staff take things at their own pace.

Spa Nuxe

32 rue Montorgueil, 1st (01.55.80.71.40/www. nuxe.com). M° Les Halles. **Open** 9am-9pm Mon-Fri; 9am-7.30pm Sat. **Credit** AmEx, MC, V. **Map** p402 J4.

This luxurious day spa housed in stone vaults with wooden cabins and safari-style tents offers massages and skin treatments using Nuxe's gentle, plant-based products. The facials, where you undress completely, begin with a short foot, tummy and neck message for total relaxation; from €70.

HOUSE & HOME
Antiques & flea markets

No trip to Paris is complete without a visit to one of the city's flea markets. The enormous **Marché aux Puces de Clignancourt** has an unrivalled abundance of junk and genuine design classics; in town, traditional antiques can be found in the **Louvre des Antiquaires**, and around Carré Rive Gauche (6th), Village Suisse and rue du Fbg-St-Honoré (1st). You'll find art deco in St-Germain-des-Prés, and retro by rue de Charonne (11th). For books, look at the **bouquinistes** (*see p241*).

INSIDE TRACK
BESPOKE SHOPPING

www.priceparis.com
Let ex-model Heather Price become your style guru for the day.

www.parisbao.com
Paris By Appointment Only is New Yorker Zeva Bellel's quirky guide to everything hand-crafted and made-to-measure.

Louvre des Antiquaires

2 pl du Palais-Royal, 1st (01.42.97.27.27/ www.louvre-antiquaires.com). M° Palais Royal Musée du Louvre. **Open** 11am-7pm Tue-Sun. Closed Sun in July & Aug. **Credit** varies. **Map** p406 H5.

This upmarket antiques centre houses 250 antiques dealers: perfect for Louis XV furniture, tapestries, porcelain, jewellery, model ships and tin soldiers.

Marché aux Puces d'Aligre

Pl d'Aligre, rue d'Aligre, 12th. M° Ledru-Rollin. **Open** 7.30am-1.30pm Tue-Sun. **Map** p407 N7.
The only flea market in central Paris, Aligre stays true to its junk tradition with a handful of *brocanteurs* peddling books, phone cards, kitchenware and oddities at what seem to be optimistic prices.

★ Marché aux Puces de St-Ouen

Av de la Porte de Clignancourt, 18th. M° Porte de St-Ouen or Garibaldi. **Open** 7am-7.30pm Mon, Sat, Sun.
See p249 **Profile**.

Marché aux Puces de Vanves

Av Georges-Lafenestre & av Marc-Sangnier, 14th. M° Porte de Vanves. **Open** 7am-7.30pm Sat, Sun.
Vanves is the smallest and friendliest of the Paris flea markets, and infinitely more tranquil than its much bigger sister at Clingancourt. It's a favourite with serious collectors, so arrive early for the best pick of decent vintage clothes, dolls, costume jewellery and silverware, although not much in the way of furniture.

Le Village St-Paul

Rue St-Paul, rue Charlemagne & quai des Célestins, 4th. M° St-Paul. **Open** 10am-7pm Mon-Sat. **No credit cards. Map** p409 L7.
This colony of antiques sellers, housed in small, linking courtyards, is a source of retro furniture, kitchenware and wine gadgets.

Design & interiors

The vast **Lafayette Maison** (*see p239*) offers a selection of current design and homeware. Also great for modern furniture is the bi-annual **Les Puces du Design** (*see p279*) every June and October.

★ A La Providence
(Quincaillerie Leclercq)

151 rue du Fbg-St-Antoine, 11th (01.43.43.06.41). M° Ledru-Rollin. **Open** 9.30am-12.30pm, 2.30-6pm Tue-Sat. **Credit** V. **Map** p407 N7.

Step into the past at this museum-piece *quincaillerie* whose 170-year-old wooden cabinets are filled with knobs, locks and other brass accoutrements for dolling up or restoring old furniture and doors.

Diptyque. See p266.

Newly crafted by artisans, the pieces look authentically antique, and there is also an expensive range of glass and crystal doorknobs. The charming couple who run it are former flight attendants.

Astier de Villatte
173 rue St-Honoré, 1st (01.42.60.74.13/www. astierdevillatte.com). M° Palais Royal Musée du Louvre. **Open** 11am-7.30pm Mon-Sat. Closed 3wks Aug. **Credit** AmEx, MC, V. **Map** p401 G4.
Once home to Napoleon's silversmith, this ancient warren now houses ceramics inspired by 17th- and 18th-century designs, handmade by the Astier de Villatte siblings in their Bastille workshop.

Byzance Home
129 rue de Turenne, 3rd (01.42.77.89.42). M° Filles du Calvaire. **Open** 11am-1pm, 2-7pm Tue-Sat. **Credit** AmEx, DC, MC, V. **Map** p409 L5.
In a cool loft space, interior designer Soraya Belhadia displays her *coups de coeur* for the home. Italian designers are in the majority, with Zanotta pouffes, Lana leather chaise longue from Palomba and one-off marquetry chest by Camobio. There's lighting, smaller objects such as Byzance scented candles, and a kitchen full of covetable gadgets. Belhadia also exhibits art and sculpture, such as Serge Van de Put's animal sculptures made of bicycle tyres.

★ Caravane Chambre 19
19 rue St-Nicolas, 12th (01.53.02.96.96/www. caravane.fr). M° Ledru-Rollin. **Open** 11am-7pm Tue-Sat. Closed 2wks Aug. **Credit** AmEx, MC, V. **Map** p407 M7.

This offshoot of Françoise Dorget's original Marais shop has goodies such as exquisite hand-sewn quilts from west Bengal, crisp cotton and organdie tunics, Berber scarves, lounging sofas and daybeds.
Other locations 6 rue Pavée, 4th (01.44.61.04.20); 22 rue St-Nicolas, 12th (01.53.17.18.55).

Christian Liaigre
42 rue du Bac, 7th (01.53.63.33.66/www. christian-liaigre.fr). M° Rue du Bac. **Open** 10am-7pm Mon-Sat. Closed 3wks Aug. **Credit** AmEx, MC, V. **Map** p405 G6.
This French interior decorator fitted out Marc Jacobs' boutiques. His showroom displays his elegant lighting and furniture designs.
Other locations 61 rue de Varenne, 7th (01.47.53.78.76).

Christophe Delcourt
47 rue de Babylone, 7th (01.42.71.34.84/ www.christophedelcourt.com). M° Jacques Bonsergent. **Open** 9am-noon, 1-6pm Mon-Fri. Closed Aug. **Credit** AmEx, DC, MC, V. **Map** p401 G4.
Christophe Delcourt's handsome art deco-influenced, geometrical lights and furniture are given a contemporary spin by their combination of stained wood and black steel.

CSAO
9 rue Elzévir, 3rd (01.42.77.66.42/www.csao.fr). M° St-Paul. **Open** 11am-7pm Mon-Sat; 2-7pm Sun. **Credit** AmEx, DC, MC, V. **Map** p409 L6.

This boutique offers African craftwork created according to fair trade principles. The artisans often fashion their objects out of recycled materials, such as the funky furniture constructed from tins.

★ Designpack Gallery

24 rue de Richelieu, 1st (01.44.85.86.00/ www.designpackgallery.fr). M° Palais Royal Musée du Louvre. **Open** 10am-7pm Mon-Fri; 11am-7pm Sat. **Credit** MC, V. **Map** p401 H5.

Too much packaging? Not according to Fabrice Peltier who is passionate about the art of *emballage*, to the extent of opening his own gallery-boutique not far from the Musée des Arts Décoratifs. Once a Tetrapak designer, he now recycles his own used packaging into desirable objects: red plastic bottles become lighting and clothes hangers, and bottle tops are melted down to become a multi-coloured armchair. African tin trinkets, Austrian vases made from cut-down bottles, and other ingenious recycling from around the world is also on sale, along with a library of books about packaging and themed exhibitions on packaging past and present.

★ FR66

25 rue de Renard, 4th (01.44.54.35.36/www. fr66.com). M° Hôtel de Ville. **Open** 10am-7pm Mon-Sat. Closed 2-3wks Aug. **Credit** AmEx, MC, V. **Map** p406 K6.

Somewhere between a gallery and a shop, this two-level experimental space accommodates contemporary artists and designers who produce exciting and original products for the home.

Galerie Patrick Seguin

5 rue des Taillandiers, 11th (01.47.00.32.35/ www.patrickseguin.com). M° Bastille or Ledru-Rollin. **Open** 10am-7pm Tue-Sat. Closed 2wks Aug. **Credit** AmEx, DC, MC, V. **Map** p407 M7.

Seguin specialises in French design from the 1950s: items by Jean Prouvé and Charlotte Perriand are on display in a showroom designed by Jean Nouvel.

Sentou Galerie

26 bd Raspail, 7th (01.45.49.00.05/www.sentou. fr). M° Pont Marie. **Open** 2-7pm Mon; 10am-7pm Tue-Sat. **Credit** AmEx, MC, V. **Map** p409 K7.

A trend-setting shop for colourful tableware and furniture: painted Chinese flasks, vases and so on. **Other location** 29 rue François-Miron, 4th (01.42.78.50.60).

Silvera

41 rue du Fbg-St-Antoine, 11th (01.43.43.06.75/ www.silvera.fr). M° Bastille or Ledru-Rollin. **Open** 10am-7pm Mon-Sat. Closed 2wks Aug. **Credit** AmEx, MC, V. **Map** p407 M7.

The former Le Bihan was taken over by Silvera in 2005 and is now a three-floor showcase for modern design. Look out for furniture and lighting from Perriand, Pesce, Pillet, Morrison, Arad and others.

Other locations 47 rue de l'Université, 7th (01.45.48.21.06); 58 av Kléber, 16th (01.53.65.78.78); 41 av de Wagram, 17th (01.56.68.76.00

Talents – Création Contemporaine

1bis rue Scribe, 9th (01.40.17.98.38/www.ateliers dart.com). M° Opéra. **Open** 11am-7pm Mon-Sat. **Credit** AmEx, MC, V. **Map** p401 G4.

This contemporary showroom for 70 creators affiliated to the craftworkers' federation Ateliers d'Art de France is a pure white gallery-style space where you'll find one-off designs in furniture, lighting, glass, ceramics and jewellery. If you want something made to measure they can put you in touch with the individual designers.

Other locations 22 & 26 av Niel, 17th (01.48.88.06.58); 4 rue de Thorigny, 3rd (01.42.78.67.74).

Kitchen & bathroom

Bains Plus

51 rue des Francs-Bourgeois, 4th (01.48.87.83.07). M° Hôtel de Ville. **Open** 2-7pm Mon, Sun; 11am-7.30pm Tue-Sat. **Credit** AmEx, MC, V. **Map** p409 K6.

This is the ultimate gentlemen's shaving shop: stock includes duck-shaped loofahs, seductive dressing gowns, chrome mirrors, bath oils and soaps.

★ E Dehillerin

18 rue Coquillière, 1st (01.42.36.53.13/www. e-dehillerin.fr). M° Les Halles. **Open** 9am-12.30pm, 2-6pm Mon; 9am-6pm Tue-Sat. **Credit** MC, V. **Map** p402 J5.

Suppliers to great chefs since 1820, this no-nonsense warehouse stocks just about every kitchen utensil ever invented. A saucepan from Dehillerin is for life.

Laguiole Galerie

1 pl Ste-Opportune, 1st (01.40.06.09.75/ www.forge-de-laguiole.com). M° Châtelet. **Open** 10.30am-7pm Mon-Sat. **Credit** MC, V. **Map** p406 J6.

Philippe Starck designed this chic boutique, a showcase for France's classic knife, the Laguiole.

MUSIC & ENTERTAINMENT

★ Crocodisc

40-42 rue des Ecoles, 5th (01.43.54.47.95/ www.crocodisc.com). M° Maubert Mutualité. **Open** 11am-7pm Tue-Sat. Closed 2wks Aug. **Credit** MC, V. **Map** p408 J7.

The excellent albeit expensive range includes rock, funk, African, country and classical, in the form of new and second-hand vinyl and CDs. For jazz and blues, try sister shop Crocojazz.

Other locations Crocojazz, 64 rue de la Montagne-Ste-Geneviève, 5th (01.46.34.78.38).

CONSUME

Fnac Forum
Levels -1 to -3, Porte Lescot, Forum des Halles, 1st (08.25.02.00.20/ticket office 08.92.68.36.22/www. fnac.com). M° Les Halles. **Open** 10am-8pm Mon-Sat. **Credit** AmEx, MC, V. **Map** p402 J5.
Fnac is a supermarket of culture: books, DVDs, CDs, audio kit, computers and photographic equipment. Most branches stock everything; others specialise, such as Fnac Music at 4 place de la Bastille. All branches operate as a concert box office.
▶ *Get discounts on large purchases by signing up for Fnac membership.*
Other locations throughout the city.

Monster Melodies
9 rue des Déchargeurs, 1st (01.40.28.09.39). M° Les Halles. **Open** noon-7pm Mon-Sat. **Credit** MC, V. **Map** p402 J5.
The owners are very willing to help you hunt down your treasured tracks – and with more than 10,000 second-hand CDs of every variety, that's just as well.

Sony Style
39 av George V, 8th (www.boutiquegeorge5.fr). M° George V. **Open** 10.30am-7.30pm Mon-Sat. **Credit** AmEx, DC, MC, V. **Map** p400 D4.
Sony's first European concept store has hit Paris, bringing high-tech gadgets and zen decor together in an *hôtel particulier*. Phones, cameras, computers and Playstations are all here, and the latest innovations from Japan are beamed in on big screens to let you know what the future holds. The store also offers a range of personal services including free IT coaching in a swanky training suite.

Virgin Megastore
52-60 av des Champs-Elysées, 8th (01.49.53.50.00/www.virginmega.fr). M° Franklin D. Roosevelt. **Open** 10am-midnight Mon-Sat; noon-midnight Sun. **Credit** AmEx, DC, MC, V. **Map** p401 E4.
The luxury of perusing CDs and DVDs till midnight makes this a choice spot, and the listening posts let you sample any CD by scanning its barcode. Tickets for concerts and sports events are available here too. This main branch has the best selection of books.
Other locations Carrousel du Louvre, 99 rue de Rivoli, 1st (01.44.50.03.10); 5 bd Montmartre, 2nd (01.40.13.72.13); 15 bd Barbès, 18th (01.56.55.53.70).

Musical instruments

Paris Accordéon
80 rue Daguerre, 14th (01.43.22.13.48/www. parisaccordeon.com). M° Denfert Rochereau or Gaîté. **Open** 9am-1pm, 2.30-7pm Tue-Fri; 9am-noon, 1-6pm Sat. **Credit** AmEx, MC, V. **Map** p405 G10.
Accordions, from simple squeezeboxes to beautiful tortoiseshell models, second-hand and new.

SPORT & FITNESS
Unless you're in the market for specialised equipment, you'll find what you want at **Go Sport** (www.go-sport.com) or the excellent **Décathlon** (www.decathlon.fr).

Citadium
50-56 rue de Caumartin, 9th (01.55.31.74.00/ www.citadium.com). M° Havre Caumartin. **Open** 10am-8pm Mon-Wed, Fri, Sat; 10am-9pm Thur. **Credit** AmEx, DC, MC, V. **Map** p401 G3.
Cultish emporium of sporting goods, from hip watches to cross-country skis, on four themed floors. Labels include Nike, Burton and North Face.

Nauti Store
40 av de la Grande-Armée, 17th (01.43.80.28.28/ www.nautistore.fr). M° Argentine. **Open** 10.30am-2pm, 3-7pm Mon-Sat. **Credit** DC, MC, V. **Map** p400 C3.
This shop stocks a vast range of sailing clothes and shoes from labels such as Helly Hansen, Musto, Aigle and Sebago.

René Pierre
35 rue de Maubeuge, 9th (01.44.91.91.21/www. rene-pierre.fr). M° Poissonnière. **Open** 10am-1pm, 2-6.30pm Mon-Sat. **Credit** MC, V. **Map** p402 H3.
France's finest table-football tables, ready for free delivery as far as Calais for UK buyers.

TICKETS
The easiest way to reserve and buy tickets for concerts, plays and matches is from a **Fnac** store (*see above*). You can also reserve on www.fnac.com or by phone (08.92.68.36.22). **Virgin** (*see above*) has teamed up with Ticketnet to create an online ticket office (www.virginmega.fr). Tickets can also be purchased by phone (08.25.12.91.39) and sent to your home for a €5.50 fee.

TRAVEL AGENTS
Nouvelles Frontières
13 av de l'Opéra, 1st (01.42.61.02.62/www. nouvelles-frontieres.fr). M° Pyramides. **Open** 9am-9pm Mon-Sat; 9am-7pm Sun. **Credit** V.
Agent with 16 branches in Paris.
Other locations throughout the city.

Thomas Cook
38 rue de Wagram, 8th (08.26.82.67.77/www. thomascook.fr). M° Opéra. **Open** 9am-10pm Mon-Sat. **Credit** AmEx, DC, MC, V.
Travel agent with more than 30 branches in and around Paris.
Other locations throughout the city.

CONSUME

Arts & Entertainment

Galerie Emmanuel Perrotin. *See p302.*

Calendar

Nude cycling? Inflatable cinema? Paris is packed with possibilities.

Paris is bursting with culture, from film festivals to world music. During summer, classical music moves outdoors, with many urban parks turning into alfresco concert venues. Among them is the lovely Parc Floral de Paris, which holds weekend concerts throughout the warmer months.

However, there are also plenty of less highbrow diversions in the city, especially at Paris-Plage, the beach on the Seine. Elsewhere, Solidays, Rock en Seine, Festival des Inrockuptibles and the Techno Parade all attract top acts. And if sports fans don't manage to get tickets for the French Open or the Six Nations, there's always the Marathon de Paris and the finale of the Tour de France – crowd-pulling events for which tickets aren't required.

SPRING

Six Nations
Stade de France, 93210 St-Denis (08.92.70.09.00/ www.stadedefrance.fr). RER B La Plaine Stade de France or RER D Stade de France St-Denis. **Admission** varies. **Date** Feb-Mar.
Brits and Celts invade Paris for three big rugby weekends in spring. Log on to www.rbs6nations. com at least three months in advance to be in with a chance of getting tickets. A date for rugby fans' diaries: France play England at the Stade de France on 20 March 2010.

Fashion Week
Various venues (www.modeaparis.com). **Date** Mar, July, Oct & Jan.
Paris presents its haute couture and prêt-à-porter collections at a variety of venues across town, but to invited guests only.

Le Printemps des Poètes
Various venues (01.53.80.08.00/www.printemps despoetes.com). **Date** 8-21 Mar 2010.
The 2010 edition of this popular national poetry festival focuses on the contribution of female poets through the ages.

Printemps du Cinéma
Various venues (www.printempsducinema.com). **Date** end Mar.
Film tickets at a variety of cinemas all across the city are cut to a bargain €3.50 for this popular three-day film bonanza.

★ Banlieues Bleues
Various venues in Seine-St-Denis (01.49.22.10.10/ www.banlieuesbleues.org). **Admission** €14-€20. **Date** Mar-Apr.
An annual five-week festival of French and international jazz, blues, R&B, soul, funk, flamenco and world music.
▶ *For more on music festivals in and around Paris, see p323.*

Le Chemin de la Croix
Square Willette, 18th (01.53.41.89.00). *Mº Abbesses or Anvers.* **Date** Good Friday.
A crowd of pilgrims follows the Archbishop of Paris from the bottom of Montmartre up to Sacré-Coeur as he performs the Stations of the Cross.

Foire du Trône
Pelouse de Reuilly, 12th (www.foiredutrone.com). *Mº Porte Dorée.* **Admission** free; rides €1.50-€4. **Date** Apr-June.
France's biggest funfair runs for nearly nine weeks, with a perfect mix of stomach-churning rides, bungee jumping and candyfloss. Noon to midnight daily.

★ Marathon de Paris
Av des Champs-Elysées, 8th, to av Foch, 16th (01.41.33.15.68/www.parismarathon.com). **Date** 11 Apr 2010.
One of the world's most picturesque marathons, with 35,000 runners heading from the Champs-Elysées along the Right Bank to the Bois de Vincennes, and back along the Left Bank to the Bois de Boulogne. The 2010 half-marathon takes place on 14 March.

Paris Bike Days

Parc Floral de Paris, Bois de Vincennes, 12th (www.parisbikedays.com). Mº Porte Dorée. **Date** mid Apr. *See p277* **Pedal Power**.

Foire de Paris

Paris-Expo, pl de la Porte de Versailles (01.49.09.60.00/www.foiredeparis.fr). Mº Porte de Versailles. **Admission** €12; €7 reductions; free under-7s. **Date** 29 Apr-9 May 2010.
This enormous lifestyle fair includes world crafts and foods, plus the latest health and house gizmos.

Fête du Travail

Date 1 May.
May Day is strictly observed. Key sights (the Eiffel Tower aside) close, and unions march in eastern Paris via Bastille. Sweet-smelling posies of lily of the valley (*muguet*) are sold on every street corner.

Printemps des Musées

Various venues (www.printempsdesmusees. culture.fr). **Date** early May.
For one Sunday in May, selected museums are free.

La Fête des Enfants du Monde

Various venues (www.koinobori.org). **Date** early May-June.
A Franco-Japanese festival with shows, exhibitions and concerts.

★ La Nuit des Musées

All over France (www.nuitdesmusees.culture.fr). **Admission** free. **Date** mid May.
For one night, museums open their doors late for special events and entertainment.

Art St-Germain-des-Prés

Various venues (www.artsaintgermain despres.com). **Admission** free. **Date** mid May.

Nicknamed the 'block party', Art St-Germain-des-Prés sees almost 50 galleries get together to showcase their top artists, with red carpets spread outside each gallery. The galleries are mostly concentrated on rue de Seine, rue des Beaux-Arts, rue Visconti, rue Guénégaud and rue Mazarine.

Quinzaine des Réalisateurs

Forum des Images, Porte St-Eustache, Forum des Halles, 1st (01.44.89.99.99/www.quinzaine-realisateurs.com). Mº Les Halles. **Admission** €5.50. **Date** May, June.
The Cannes Directors' Fortnight sidebar comes to Paris; 2009 was the 30th anniversary of this festival of screenings and events.

French Tennis Open

Stade Roland-Garros, 2 av Gordon-Bennett, 16th (01.47.43.48.00/www.frenchopen.org). Mº Porte d'Auteuil. **Admission** €21-€75. **Date** 23 May-6 June 2010.
The glitzy Grand Slam tournament, whose tricky clay courts have been the downfall of many a champion, always attracts a selection of showbiz stars. Roger Federer and Svetlana Kuznetsova are the defending champions in 2010.

Le Printemps des Rues

Various venues (01.47.97.36.06/www.leprintemps desrues.com). **Admission** free. **Date** late May.
This annual two-day street-theatre festival has an experimental vibe.

Foire St-Germain

Pl St-Sulpice & venues in St-Germain-des-Prés, 6th (01.43.29.61.04/www.foiresaintgermain.org). Mº St-Sulpice. **Admission** free. **Date** late May-July.
St-Germain-des-Prés lets its hair down for a month of concerts, theatre and workshops.

SUMMER

Festival de St-Denis

Various venues in St-Denis (01.48.13.12.10/ www.festival-saint-denis.com). Mº St-Denis Basilique. **Admission** €9-€55. **Date** June-July.
The Gothic St-Denis basilica and other historic buildings in the neighbourhood host four weeks of top quality classical concerts.

Fête du Vélo

Across Paris (www.feteduvelo.fr). **Date** early June. *See p277* **Pedal Power**.
▶ *To hire a bike or learn more about the Vélib free bike scheme, visit www.velib.paris.fr.*

Prix de Diane Hermès

Hippodrome de Chantilly, 16 av du Général-Leclerc, 90209 Chantilly (03.44.62.41.00/ www.france-galop.com). **Admission** €8; €4 reductions; free under-18s. **Date** early June.

ARTS & ENTERTAINMENT

The French Derby draws the crème de la crème of high society to Chantilly, sporting silly hats and keen to have a flutter at this handsome racecourse next to the famous château and stables.

★ Fête de la Musique
All over France (01.40.03.94.70/www.fetede lamusique.fr). **Admission** free. **Date** 21 June.
Free gigs (encompassing all musical genres) take place across the country as part of this festival on the summer solstice.

★ Gay Pride March
Information: Centre Gai et Lesbien (01.43.57.21.47/www.inter-lgbt.org). **Date** 27 June 2010.
Outrageous floats and flamboyant costumes parade towards Bastille; then there's an official fête and various club and nightlife events.
► *For more information on gay events and venues in Paris, see pp306-312.*

Festival Chopin à Paris
Orangerie de Bagatelle, Parc de Bagatelle, Bois de Boulogne, 16th (01.45.00.22.19/www.frederic-chopin.com). M° Porte Maillot, then bus 244. **Admission** €16-€37. **Date** June, July.
Candlelit evening recitals of Chopin's works are held in the Bagatelle gardens.

★ Paris Jazz Festival
Parc Floral de Paris, Bois de Vincennes, 12th (39.75/www.parisjazzfestival.com). M° Château de Vincennes. **Admission** Park €5; €2.50 reductions; free under-7s. **Date** June, July.
Two months of free jazz weekends at the Parc Floral.

Solidays
Longchamp Hippodrome (01.53.10.22.22/www. solidays.com). M° Porte Maillot. **Admission** Day €25. Weekend €45. **Date** end June.
A three-day music festival, for the benefit of AIDS charities. The 2009 event saw performances from the likes of Manu Chao, the Ting Tings and Friendly Fires. *See also p323.*

Paris Cinéma
Various venues (01.55.25.55.25/www.paris cinema.org). **Admission** varies. **Date** early July.
Premieres, tributes and restored films make up the diverse programme at the city's excellent summer film-going initiative.

Miss Guinguette
41 quai Victor Hugo, Ile du Martin-Pêcheur, 94500 Champigny-sur-Marne (information 01.49.83.03.02/www.guinguette.fr). RER Champigny-sur-Marne. **Admission** €7. **Date** 14 July.
A contest to find the light-footed queen of the open-air dancehall scene at this river island venue.

Le Quatorze Juillet (Bastille Day)
All over France. **Date** 14 July.
France's national holiday commemorates the storming of the Bastille in 1789. The evening before the holiday, Parisians dance at place de la Bastille. At 10am on the 14th, crowds line up along the Champs-Elysées as the President reviews a full military parade. By night, the Champ de Mars fills for the fireworks display.

★ Le Tour de France
Av des Champs-Elysées, 8th (01.41.33.15.00/ www.letour.fr). **Date** 25 July 2010.
See p277 **Pedal Power.**

Etés de la Danse
Grand Palais, Av Winston Churchill, 8th (08.92.68.71.00/www.lesetesdeladanse.com). M° Champs-Elysées Clemenceau or Franklin D. Roosevelt. **Tickets** €24-€65. **Date** early-late July.
A three-week festival featuring an impressive line-up of both classical and contemporary dance.

Paris, Quartier d'Eté
Various venues (01.44.94.98.00/www. quartierdete.com). **Admission** free-€15.
Date mid July-mid Aug.
A series of classical and jazz concerts, dance and theatre performances in outdoor venues.

★ Paris-Plage
Pont des Arts to Pont de Sully (08.20.00.75.75/ www.paris.fr). M° Châtelet, Hôtel de Ville, Louvre Rivoli, Pont Marie, Sully Morland. **Admission** free. **Date** mid July-mid Aug.
Palm trees, huts, hammocks and around 2,000 tonnes of fine sand on both banks of the Seine bring a seaside vibe to the city. Not only this, there's a floating pool and lending library too.

Le Cinéma en Plein Air
Parc de la Villette, 19th (01.40.03.75.75/ www.villette.com). M° Porte de Pantin.
Admission €2. **Date** mid July-end Aug.
A themed season of films screened under the stars on Europe's largest inflatable screen.

Festival Classique au Vert
Parc Floral de Paris, Bois de Vincennes, 12th (01.45.43.81.18). M° Château de Vincennes.
Admission €5; €2.50 reductions; free under-7s.
Date Aug, Sept.
Classical recitals in a park setting every weekend throughout August and September.

Fête de l'Assomption
Cathédrale Notre-Dame de Paris, pl du Parvis Notre-Dame, 4th (01.42.34.56.10). M° Cité/ RER St-Michel Notre-Dame. **Admission** free.
Date 15 Aug.

Pedal Power

From the yellow jersey to no jersey at all.

Thanks to Mayor Delanoë's eco-friendly policies, the bike has enjoyed a major boom in Paris – and it's now the focus of several annual festivals in the city. The **Fête du Vélo** (*see p275*) in June is a celebration of urban riding with thousands of cyclists invited to meet up at various points in the suburbs and pedal to Paris en masse. The result is what the organisation calls '*la convergence*', with a procession of two-wheelers meeting up for a huge picnic in the city centre. Throughout the two-day festival visitors can also try out rollerblading, as well as bicycles specially designed for children and people of reduced mobility.

Launched in 2009, **Paris Bike Days** (*see p275*) is all about getting people on bikes – of every type. This spring festival, based in the Bois de Vincennes, allows visitors to try out racers on closed roads and mountain bikes on specially designed forest trails, as well as on a bump-filled 'pump track'. There's also a range of BMX, trial and electric bikes available for test spins. Once you've found the right bike, you can buy it onsite, sign up for a club or splash out on a cycling holiday. There are also shows by leading BMX and trial riders.

The ultimate spectacle in cycling is reserved for the end of July when the world's biggest bike race, the **Tour de France** (*see p276*), arrives in Paris. After three weeks of racing, the battle for the leader's famed yellow jersey is all but over, and the final stage usually climaxes in a mass sprint with everyone finishing together. It's an incredible spectacle as the riders propel themselves at speeds of up to 65 km/h (40mph) around nine laps of a four-mile finishing circuit that takes in the Champs-Elysées and Tuileries area. Make sure you turn up early for a front-row spot.

The capital's least conventional bike event is **Cyclonudie**, when cyclists come together to ride nude or semi-nude through the streets of Paris. According to the organisers, the aim is to demonstrate the fragility of the cyclist in the face of cars and trucks. Sadly, in recent years all those bums on seats have prompted a number of arrests for indecent exposure, leaving the long-time organiser to drop out. Keep tuned for news of a new backer in 2010.

ARTS & ENTERTAINMENT

Tour de France.

Techno Parade.

A national holiday. Notre-Dame becomes a place of religious pilgrimage for Assumption Day.

★ Rock en Seine
Domaine National de St-Cloud (08.92.68.08.92/ www.rockenseine.com). M° Porte de St-Cloud. **Admission** *Day €42. 3 days €98.* **Date** end Aug.
Three days, three stages, and one world-class line-up of rock and indie groups. Oasis, The Prodigy and Faith No More all made an appearance in 2009. *See also p323.*

AUTUMN

Jazz à la Villette
Parc de la Villette, 211 av Jean-Jaurès, 19th (01.44.84.44.84/www.jazzalavillette.com). M° Porte de Pantin. **Admission** €12-€30.
Date early Sept.
The first fortnight in September brings one of Paris's best jazz festivals, including the new series of Jazz for Kids concerts.

Festival Paris Ile-de-France
Various venues (www.festival-ile-de-france.com). **Tickets** varies. **Date** early Sept-mid Oct.
Classical, contemporary and world music festival set in various venues around Paris.

Techno Parade
www.technoparade.fr. **Date** mid Sept.
The Saturday parade (finishing at Bastille) marks the start of electro music fest Rendez-vous Electroniques.

Journées du Patrimoine
All over France (08.20.20.25.02/www.journees dupatrimoine.culture.fr). **Date** mid Sept.

Embassies, ministries, scientific establishments and corporate headquarters open their doors to the public, allowing for some fascinating glimpses of their interiors. The festive Soirée du Patrimoine takes place on the first Journée. Get *Le Monde* or *Le Parisien* for a full programme.

★ Festival d'Automne
Various venues. Information: 156 rue de Rivoli, 1st (01.53.45.17.00/www.festival-automne.com). **Admission** €3-€60. **Date** mid Sept-late Dec.
Founded in 1972, this major annual arts festival focuses on bringing challenging contemporary theatre, dance and modern opera to Paris. It is intent on bringing non-Western culture into the French consciousness.

★ Nuit Blanche
Various venues (39.75/www.paris.fr). **Admission** free. **Date** early Oct.
One of the city's most distinctive festivals offers culture by moonlight – from 7pm to 7am – as galleries and museums host special after-dark installations, and swimming pools, bars and clubs stay open late into the night.

INSIDE TRACK CLOSING TIME

On public holidays (*jours fériés*; see p275), you can expect the banks, many museums, most businesses and some restaurants to close, with those remaining open often charging a premium; public transport runs a Sunday service.

Prix de l'Arc de Triomphe

Hippodrome de Longchamp, Bois de Boulogne, 16th (01.49.10.20.30/www.prixarcde triomphe.com). M° Porte d'Auteuil, then free shuttle bus. **Admission** €8; €4 reductions; free under-18s. **Date** early Oct.
France's richest flat race attracts the elite of horse racing for a weekend of pomp and ceremony.

Mondial de l'Automobile

Paris-Expo, pl de la Porte de Versailles (01.56.88.22.40/www.mondial-automobile.com). M° Porte de Versailles. **Admission** €12; €6.45 reductions; free under-10s. **Date** 2-17 Oct 2010.
Cutting-edge vehicle design from all over the world.

Fête des Vendanges de Montmartre

Rue des Saules, 18th (01.30.21.48.62/ www.fetedesvendangesdemontmartre.com). M° Lamarck Caulaincourt. **Date** mid Oct.
Paris's local wine festival takes place in Montmartre. Although the vines produce an average of just 1,000 bottles a year, the modest harvest is the pretext for a long weekend of Bacchanalian street parties.

Les Puces du Design

Quai de la Loire, 19th (01.53.40.78.77/ www.pucesdudesign.com). M° Jaurès. **Admission** free. **Date** mid Oct & June.
Having moved to the up-and-coming end of the canal, this weekend-long fair specialises in modern and vintage furniture, and design classics.

FIAC

Various venues (01.47.56.64.20/www.fiacparis. com). **Admission** €25; €12.50 reductions. **Date** mid Oct.
The Louvre and the Grand Palais are the two venues for this week-long international contemporary art fair.

★ Festival des Inrockuptibles

Various venues (01.42.44.16.16/www.lesinrocks. com). **Admission** varies. **Date** early Nov.
This festival, curated by popular music mag *Les Inrockuptibles*, boasts top international indie, rock, techno and trip hop acts. Bill-toppers in 2009 included La Roux, Passion Pit and Bat for Lashes.

Armistice Day

Arc de Triomphe, 8th. M° Charles de Gaulle Etoile. **Date** 11 Nov.
To commemorate French combatants who served in the World Wars, the President lays wreaths at the Tomb of the Unknown Soldier under the Arc de Triomphe. The *bleuet* (a cornflower) is worn.

Fête du Beaujolais Nouveau

Various venues (www.beaujolaisgourmand.com). **Date** late Nov.
The third Thursday in November sees cafés and wine bars buzz as patrons assess the new vintage.

THE BEST MUSIC FESTIVALS

For a touch of jazz
Jazz à la Villette. *See p278.*

For riverside rock
Rock en Seine. *See p278.*

For outdoor orchestra
Festival Classique au Vert. *See p276.*

WINTER

Africolor

Various venues in suburbs, including Montreuil, St-Denis & St-Ouen (01.47.97.69.99/www.africolor. com). **Admission** €5-€15. **Date** late Nov-late Dec.
A month-long African music festival.

Paris sur Glace

Pl de l'Hôtel de Ville, 4th; M° Hôtel de Ville. Pl Raoul Dautry, 15th; M° Montparnasse Bienvenüe. Pl de la Bataille de Stalingrad, 19th; M° Stalingrad. Information: 39.75/www.paris.fr. **Admission** free (skate hire €6). **Date** Dec-Mar.
These locations are turned into outdoor ice rinks.

Noël (Christmas)

Date 24, 25 Dec.
Christmas is a family affair in France, with a dinner on Christmas Eve (*le Réveillon*), normally after mass. Usually the only bars and restaurants open are the ones in the city's main hotels.

★ New Year's Eve/New Year's Day

Date 31 Dec, 1 Jan.
Jubilant crowds swarm along the Champs-Elysées. Nightclubs and restaurants hold expensive New Year's Eve soirées,and on New Year's Day the Grande Parade de Paris brings floats, bands and dancers.

Fête des Rois (Epiphany)

Date 6 Jan.
Pâtisseries sell *galettes des rois*, cakes with a frangipane filling in which a *fève,* or tiny charm, is hidden.

Mass for Louis XVI

Chapelle Expiatoire, 29 rue Pasquier, 8th (01.42.65.35.80). M° St-Augustin. **Date** Jan.
On the Sunday closest to 21 January – the anniversary of the beheading of Louis XVI in 1793 – right-wing crackpots mourn the end of the monarchy.

Nouvel An Chinois

Around av d'Ivry & av de Choisy, 13th. M° Porte de Choisy or Porte d'Ivry. Also av des Champs Elysées, 8th. **Date** 14 Feb 2010.
Lion and dragon dances, and lively martial arts demonstrations to celebrate the Chinese New Year.

ARTS & ENTERTAINMENT

Cabaret, Circus & Comedy

Roll up, roll up for clowns, cancan and café-théâtre.

True to their reputation, Paris's traditional cabarets still cater (surprisingly well) to the throngs of tourists and businessmen who come for an eyeful of boob-bouncing, posh nosh and champers. If the get-your-glitz-out-for-the-boys genre isn't your cup of tea, then a Gallic giggle is still to be had in old-fashioned *café-théâtres*, where songs and sketches accompany dinner and a bottle of plonk.

Perhaps the biggest change on Paris's entertainment circuit is the success of *le stand-up*. It hit town in a big way in 2008 thanks to comedian Jamel Debbouze, who opened **Le Comedy Club** – a launch pad for new French stand-up comics and a spinoff from his TV show *Le Jamel Comedy Club*, and the trend looks set to stay. If French isn't your forte, though, fear not: veteran Anglo venue **Laughing Matters** (105 rue du Faubourg-du-Temple, 10th, 01.53.19.98.88, www.anythingmatters.com) still provides belly laughs in English with comedy acts from across the Channel, the US and Australia. Circus-wise, Paris can do no wrong: the Parc de la Villette alone hosts several avant-garde extravaganzas, so whether you're looking for ringmaster-led acts, acrobatics or clowns, you'll be lapping it up big-top style throughout the year.

ARTS & ENTERTAINMENT

CABARET & CAFE-THEATRE

The year the Eiffel Tower raised its final girders (1889), the Moulin Rouge was raising something of its own: skirts. The risqué *quadrille réaliste* (later dubbed the cancan) became such a trademark that 120 years later, busty babes are still slinking across the stages of Paris. These days, cabaret is an all-evening extravaganza. Male dancers and magicians complement the foxy foxtrots; the dancing is perfectly synchronised, the costumes beautiful and the whole caboodle now perfectly respectable.

Cabaret

Crazy Horse Saloon
12 av George V, 8th (01.47.23.32.32/www.crazy horse.fr). M° Alma Marceau or George V.
Shows 8.15pm, 10.45pm Mon-Fri, Sun; 7pm,

9.30pm, 11.45pm Sat. **Admission** *Show only* €80-€100. *Show* (incl champagne) €100-€155; €50-€60 reductions. **Credit** AmEx, DC, MC, V. **Map** p400 D4.

More risqué than the other cabarets, the Horse, whose *art du nu* was invented in 1951 by Alain Bernadin, is an ode to feminine beauty: lookalike dancers with provocative names like Flamma Rosa and Nooka Caramel, and identical body statistics (when standing, the girls' nipples and hips are all the same height) move around the stage, clad only in rainbow light and strategic strips of black tape. In their latest show, Désirs, the girls put on some tantalising numbers, with titles such as 'God Save Our Bare Skin' (a sexy take on the Changing of the Guards) and the sensual 'Vestel's Desire'.

▶ *Dinner before or after the show can be arranged for €175-€205 per person (show included) at Fouquet's, Devez, Chez Francis or Bateaux Parisiens.*

Le Lido

116bis av des Champs-Elysées, 8th (01.40.76.56.10/www.lido.fr). M° Franklin D. Roosevelt or George V. **Lunch** 1pm. **Matinée** 3pm Tue, Sun (once a mth, dates vary). **Dinner** 7pm. **Shows** 9.30pm, 11.30pm daily. **Admission** *Matinée show* (incl champagne) €80. *Lunch & matinée show* (incl champagne) €115 Tue; €125 Sun. *9.30pm show* (incl champagne) €100; €20 reductions. *11.30pm show* (incl champagne) €90; free under-12s. *Dinner & show* €140-€280; €30 reductions. *Show & backstage tour* €110-€120. **Credit** AmEx, DC, MC, V. **Map** p400 D4.

This is the largest cabaret of all: high-tech touches optimise visibility, and chef Philippe Lacroix provides fabulous gourmet nosh. On stage, 60 Bluebell Girls and a set of hunky dancers slink around, shaking their bodies with sequinned panache in breathtaking scenes. For a special treat, opt for the brand new 'behind the scenes' tour which, before the show, takes you into the heart of the action past the costume rooms and the machines that operate the fountains and ice-rink.

▶ *For a glam night, opt for premier service (€280) with free cloakroom, the best tables in the house and free water and coffee with your meal.*

Moulin Rouge

82 bd de Clichy, 18th (01.53.09.82.82/www.moulin-rouge.com). M° Blanche. **Dinner** 7pm. **Shows** 9pm, 11pm daily. **Admission** *9pm show* (incl champagne) €102. *11pm show* (incl champagne) €92. *Dinner & show* €150-€180. *Show only* 9pm €90, 11pm €80. **Credit** AmEx, DC, MC, V. **Map** p401 G2.

Toulouse-Lautrec posters, glittery lampposts and fake trees lend tacky charm to this revue, which celebrated its 120th birthday in 2009. On stage, 60 Doriss dancers cavort with faultless synchronisation. Costumes are flamboyant and the *entr'acte* acts funny. The downer is the space, with tables packed in like sardines. There's also a twice-monthly matinée: lunch and show €130, show only €100.

★ Paradis Latin

28 rue Cardinal Lemoine, 5th (01.43.25.28.28/www.paradislatin.com). M° Cardinal Lemoine. **Dinner** 8pm. **Show** 9.30pm daily. **Admission** *9.30pm show* (incl champagne) €85. *Dinner & show* €123-€179. **Credit** AmEx, DC, MC, V. **Map** p406 K8.

This is the most authentic of the cabarets, not only because it's family-run (the men run the cabaret, the daughter does the costumes), but also because the clientele is mostly French, something which has a direct effect on the prices (this is the cheapest revue) and the cuisine, which tends to be high quality. Show-wise you can expect the usual fare: generous doses of glitter, live singing and cheesy *entr'acte* acts performed in a stunning belle époque room. There's also a twice-monthly matinée: lunch and show €95.

Café-théâtre

Les Blancs Manteaux

15 rue des Blancs-Manteaux, 4th (01.48.87.15.84/www.blancsmanteaux.fr). M° Hôtel de Ville. **Shows** from 7pm daily (phone for details). **Admission** *Show* €20; €17 students, under-25s; *2 shows* €34 (except Sat). *Dinner & 1 show* €40. **No credit cards.** **Map** p409 K6.

For the last 38 years, this Marais institution has been launching new talent with weekly comedy platforms. With a dinner-and-show ticket, you can dine on Thai cuisine at nearby Suan Thai.

Chez Michou

80 rue des Martyrs, 18th (01.46.06.16.04/www.michou.com). M° Pigalle. **Dinner** 8.30pm daily. **Shows** 10.30pm approx. **Admission** *Show* €40. *Dinner & show* €105 (incl wine). **Credit** MC, V. **Map** p402 H2.

Drag, sparkling costumes, good food and wine: Michou's show is not quite as 'blue' as his azure attire suggests. Book ahead if you want to dine.

Le Grenier

3 rue Rennequin, 17th (01.43.80.68.01/www.legrenier-dinerspectacle.com). M° Ternes. **Shows** from 7.30pm daily. **Admission** *Show* €16 Mon-Fri, Sun; €18 Sat. *Dinner & show* €27-€70 Mon-Fri; €32-€85 Sat, Sun. **Credit** MC, V. **Map** p400 D2.

If you fancy being entertained while you eat, consider the 'Loft', which still retains the allure of an old *café-théâtre* with an eclectic line-up of stand-up comedians, *chansonniers* and magic acts all on the same bill.

★ Au Lapin Agile

22 rue des Saules, 18th (01.46.06.85.87/www.au-lapin-agile.com). M° Lamarck Caulaincourt. **Shows** 9pm-2am Tue-Sun. **Admission** *Show* (incl 1 drink) €24; €17 reductions (except Sat & public hols). **No credit cards.** **Map** p402 H1.

The prices have gone up and they sell their own compilation CDs, but that's all that seems to have changed since this quaint, pink bar first opened in 1860. Tourists now outnumber the locals, but the Lapin harbours an echo of old Montmartre.

ARTS & ENTERTAINMENT

THE BEST STAGES

For big tops
Cirque Pinder. *See p283.*

For no tops
Crazy Horse Saloon. *See left.*

For belly laughs
Le Comedy Club. *See p283.*

Discover the city from your back pocket

Essential for your weekend break, 25 top cities available.

Le Petit Casino
17 rue Chapon, 3rd (01.42.78.36.50/www.lepetit casino.fr). M° *Arts et Métiers.* **Dinner** 8pm. **Shows** 9pm, 10.30pm daily (times may vary). **Admission** *Show* (2 acts) €20. *Dinner* €16 (€32 Sat & public hols). **Credit** MC, V. **Map** p406 K5.
Up-and-coming talents find precious stage space in this traditional *café-théâtre* devoted to one-man shows and cheap 'n' tasty nosh.

COMEDY & FRINGE THEATRE
Le Bout
62 rue Pigalle, 9th (01.42.85.11.88/www.lebout. com). M° *Pigalle.* **Shows** daily, times vary. **Admission** €16; €10 reductions. *2 shows* €20. **No credit cards. Map** p402 H2.
This *café-théâtre* school has been cramming them into its 40-seater venue since 1999. In line with current trends, one-man shows take pride of place.

★ Café de la Gare
41 rue du Temple, 4th (01.42.78.52.51/www. cdlg.org). M° *Hôtel de Ville.* **Shows** 9pm Mon, Tue, Sun; 7pm, 8.30pm, 10pm Wed-Sat. **Admission** €20-€24; €10-€20 reductions. **Credit** MC, V. **Map** p406 K6.
Running since 1968, the most famous fringe theatre in Paris has 300 stage-hugging seats and hosts quality French stand-up and raucous comedies.

Caveau de la République
1 bd St-Martin, 3rd (01.42.78.44.45/www. caveau.fr). M° *République.* **Shows** 8.30pm Thur-Sat; 3.30pm Sun. Closed Aug. **Admission** €34.50 Mon-Fri; €40.50 Sat, Sun & public hols. €18-€21.50 reductions. **Credit** MC, V. **Map** p402 L4.

INSIDE TRACK LE STAND-UP

One of the most successful stand-up comedians around is **Florence Foresti**. Her new one-woman show, Motherfucker, an ode to motherhood, has taken France by storm (in theatres across the country until June 2010, www.florenceforesti.com). Another big name is **Gad Elmaleh**, whose Papa est en Haut show draws on his life in Morocco, Canada and France (at the Palais des Sports until 24 April 2010, www.palaisdessports.com). Also keep your eyes peeled for the short but enormously talented **Krystoff Fluder** (occasionally known to don a goblin costume in the Harry Potter movies) who lights up the stage with his offbeat portrayal of President Sarkozy and hilarious situation sketches (look him up on Facebook for upcoming dates).

This traditional *chanson* venue has been churning out political-satirical songs and sketches for more than a century. Nowadays stand-up comedy is the main draw, and the laughs are mostly wrung from current scandals. Five artists perform each night.

Le Comedy Club
42 bd de Bonne Nouvelle, 10th (08.11.94.09.40/ www.lecomedyclub.fr). M° *Bonne Nouvelle.* **Shows** days vary. **Admission** €15-€25. **Credit** MC, V. **Map** p402 J4.
Jamel Debbouze, the comic known for his one-man shows and films such as *Le Fabuleux Destin d'Amélie Poulain*, gives the chuckle trade a helping hand with this theatre. Tuesdays and Wednesdays (7.30pm) are open mic nights. Saturdays are for the confirmed mirth merchants of Jamel's TV show.

★ Le Point Virgule
7 rue Ste-Croix-de-la-Bretonnerie, 4th (01.42.78.67.03/www.lepointvirgule.com). M° *Hôtel de Ville.* **Shows** *Mon-Wed, Sat, Sun* times vary. **Admission** €18; €14 reductions. *2 shows* €29, *3 shows* €39. *Children's show* €12; €10 children. **No credit cards. Map** p409 K6.
This small Marais theatre has become the ultimate launch pad for up-and-coming comedians, with shows, a *café-théâtre* school and an annual comedy festival in September.

CIRCUS
★ Cirque d'Hiver Bouglione
110 rue Amelot, 11th (01.47.00.28.81/www. cirquedhiver.com). M° *Filles du Calvaire.* **Shows** *Late Oct-late Feb* days vary. **Admission** €10-€48. **Credit** AmEx, MC, V. **Map** p409 L5.
This circus has been in the same family for decades. It now has a new façade to match its revamped interior, and crowds flock for its twice-yearly seasons which include tigers, horses and very silly clowns.

Cirque Pinder
Pelouse de Reuilly, Bois de Vincennes, 12th (01.45.90.21.25/www.cirquepinder.com). M° *Porte de Charenton or Porte Dorée.* **Shows** *Mid Nov-mid Jan* 2.30pm, 5.30pm, 8.45pm daily. **Admission** €15-€50; free under-2s. **Credit** AmEx, DC, MC, V.
Big cats are the stars of the show, but horses, elephants and monkeys also make Pinder the most traditional travelling circus in France.

Espace Chapiteaux
Parc de La Villette, 19th (01.40.03.75.75/ www.villette.com). M° *Porte de la Villette.* **Shows** days vary. **Admission** varies. **Credit** MC, V. **Map** p403 inset.
This big top hosts companies such as Cirque Plume, Centre National des Arts du Cirque and aerialists Les Arts Saut.

Children

We love Paris in the playtime.

French must indeed be the language of love – the country has one of the highest birth rates in Europe; vindication, many say, of the country's family-friendly policies. Most Parisians have to raise their children in gardenless apartments, so the city powers ensure there is plenty of provision for youngsters to expend their energy outside the home: every arrondissement has spaces with playgrounds, and in the big parks like the **Jardin du Luxembourg** and **Buttes-Chaumont**, pony rides, sandpits, swings, puppet shows and boating ponds spice up the childhood of many a young Parisian. Museums and other attractions don't ignore their younger visitors either, with events, workshops and child-focused exhibits.

ARTS & ENTERTAINMENT

Paris's museums and other attractions cater to children as well as adults, and also offer blissful opportunities to offload your kids on to someone else with children's workshops, held on Saturdays and Wednesdays during the school year, and daily during school holidays. If your children don't speak French, you can usually request an English speaker in advance. To find out what's coming up, contact the individual museums or check out www.commeundimanche.com, www.lamuse.net and www.paris.fr. Listings magazines like *Pariscope, L'Officiel des Spectacles, Figaroscope* (with Wednesday's *Le Figaro*) and Télérama's *Sortir* all have kids' sections too; and the free bi-monthly magazine *Paris-Mômes* is distributed with daily newspaper *Libération* in toy shops and public libraries.

Sightseeing with children can be made easier with planning. Queues at prime spots like the **Eiffel Tower** (*see p145*), **Louvre** (*see p59*) and the towers at **Notre-Dame** (*see p56*) are less disheartening in the morning. One of the most exciting ways for the family to take in the city is from a boat on the Seine; the hop-on hop-off waterborne Batobus (*see p365*) links eight prime sights, including the Eiffel Tower and Jardin des Plantes.

GETTING AROUND

One word of advice: walk whenever possible. The métro is difficult to negotiate with babies and toddlers. Two of you might manage a pushchair, but lone travellers won't and passers-by are notoriously selfish about helping out. If your babe is small enough for a baby carrier, it will save you a lot of hassle when navigating the tight turnstiles and never-ending staircases. Also try to travel between 10.30am and 5pm to avoid the crowds. The driverless line 14 (St-Lazare to Olympiades) is a big hit with kids, who can sit at the front and peer down the tunnel as the train advances; the mostly overground lines six (Nation to Charles de Gaulle Étoile) and two (Nation to Porte Dauphine) offer attractive city views; a number of RER stations have lifts, although they are frequently broken.

Buses, on the other hand, are easier thanks to priority seats near the front for passengers with young children; many, such as nos.24, 63 and 95 (www.ratp.fr), pass numerous sights. Three- to 11-year-olds qualify for a half-price *carnet* (a book of ten tickets) for all transport, including the Montmartrobus minibus and Montmartre funicular. Taxi drivers will usually take a family of four (charging €1 to carry a pushchair and a little extra for the fourth person). If you're stuck, try G7 taxis (01.47.39.47.39), which has an English-speaking booking line.

For older kids, the recent addition of extra cycle paths across the centre (especially along the Seine, up the Canal St-Martin and along the Canal de l'Ourcq) makes a spin *en famille* an enjoyable way to get around the city while seeing the sights. Short distances are easily covered using the city's **Vélib** self-service scheme (www.velib.fr; *see p367*). For day-long fun try **Vélo et Chocolat** (75 quai Seine, 19th, 01.46.07.07.87); **Cyclo Pouce** (38 quai de Marne, 19th, 01.42.41.76.98), which provides baby seats and equipment for disabled children; or **Paris à Vélo c'est Sympa** (22 rue Alphonse Baudin, 11th, 01.48.87.60.01,www.parisvelosympa.com). For a day out in beautiful surroundings, the Bois de Vincennes in the east and the Bois de Boulogne in the west provide woodlands, picnic areas, boating lakes and lawns.

EATING OUT

Affordable **Chartier** (7 rue du Fbg-Montmartre, 9th, 01.47.70.86.29, www.restaurant-chartier.com) is always a fun place to take kids, with its belle epoque dining room and waiters clad in black and white. **Tokyo Eat** at the Palais de Tokyo (13 av du Président-Wilson, 16th, 01.47.20.00.29, www.palaisdetokyo.com) is good too, with wacky decor and round, family-sized tables. For a simple snack along the lines of boiled egg and soldiers you can't beat **Coco & Co** (11 rue Bernard Palissy, 6th, 01.45.44.02.52, www.cocoandco.fr), which serves only egg dishes, in an egg-themed dining room. The restaurants on the Cour St-Emilion near Parc de Bercy are all good for traffic-free outdoor eating, and if you fancy browsing for baby clothes while slurping on a hot coffee, the **Poussette Café** (6 rue Pierre Sémard, 9th, 01.78.10.49.00, www.lepoussettecafe.com) is a haven, with parking space for buggies and milk-warming facilities.

BABIES & TODDLERS

Always pack a portable changing mat. A facility worth remembering is the WC chalet in the Jardin du Luxembourg, where €0.60 gives you access to loos with a padded changing table; the **Galeries Lafayette** and **Printemps** (for both, *see p239*) department stores have clean, well-equipped nappy changing facilities, as does the **Poussette Café** (*see above*). Breastfeeding in public is more common than ever, but still often frowned upon, so take a scarf for places where modesty is essential, or choose a quiet corner.

A city break with tots in tow doesn't have to mean missing out on the city's galleries and museums. Almost all of the main attractions have child-friendly activities or green spaces nearby – handy as a reward for good behaviour. There's a carefully tended garden by Notre-Dame, and the dignified **Musée Rodin** (*see p143*) has outdoor distractions such as a sandpit to dig in, a sculpture-filled garden to explore (free entry to parents with a pushchair) and a tempting ice-cream stand. And if the heady heights of the Eiffel Tower prove too daunting, more down-to-earth amusements can be found at the adjacent Champ de Mars, with its play areas and seasonal donkey rides; or there are old-style merry-go-rounds by the river.

BABYSITTING

Many hotels can organise babysitting (ask when you reserve). The **American Church in Paris** (65 quai d'Orsay, 7th, 01.40.62.05.00, www.acparis.org) has a noticeboard displaying ads from English-speaking babysitters and au pairs; **Baby Sitting Services** (01.46.21.33.16, www.babysittingservices.com) can organise babysitting at short notice.

MUSEUMS & SIGHTSEEING

Most museums offer children's workshops (in French) on Wednesday afternoons, at weekends and in the holidays. At the **Louvre** (*see p59*) the programme for kids varies from learning about facial expressions in paintings to Egyptian sculpture. Next door, the **Musée des Arts Décoratifs** (*see p71*) offers hands-on art workshops for ages four to 14s and special tours (tailored to different age groups). The **Palais de Tokyo** (*see p87*) has inventive 'Tok Tok' story-reading for three- to five-year-olds, workshops for five- to seven-year-olds and family visits (4.30pm Sun), often led by notable contemporary artists. The **Musée Rodin** (*see p143*) runs children's clay workshops. In July and August the place to be with little kids is the **Musée Jacquemart-André** (*see p88*), which runs a Family Fun programme (2.30-5.30pm daily), where kids aged seven to 11 are given a games book to guide them through the museum and get to dress up in old-fashioned costumes. Under-18s (and under 25s from the EU) get free admission to the national museums, including the Louvre, Musée d'Orsay, Centre Pompidou, Musée du Quai Branly and Musée Rodin.

★ Centre Pompidou – Galerie des Enfants

Rue St-Martin, 4th (01.44.78.12.33/www.centrepompidou.fr/enfants). M° Hôtel de Ville or Rambuteau/RER Châtelet Les Halles. **Open** *Museum* 11am-9pm Mon, Wed-Sun (until 10pm Thur). *Workshops* most Wed & Sat afternoons

INSIDE TRACK HELPING HAND

For English-speaking mothers or mothers-to-be, Message (www.messageparis.org) is a support network offering advice, classes and a handy book, *ABCs of Motherhood in Paris* (€25 non-members, €20 members).

ARTS & ENTERTAINMENT

& school hols. **Admission** *Museum* €10-€12; free under-18s (under-25s from EU countries). *Workshops* €10 (1 child & 1 adult). **Credit** MC, V. **Map** p402 K5.

In this ground-floor gallery, wonderfully thought out exhibitions conceived by top artists and designers introduce children to interesting aspects of modern art, design and architecture. Kids are kept enthralled with interactive elements and the opportunity to touch. There are also hands-on workshops for six- to 12-year-olds, and family workshops one Sunday afternoon a month. Audio guides for six- to 12-year-olds can also be hired for €4. Outside, look for the colourful Stravinsky fountain on the south side, designed by Niki de Saint Phalle and Jean Tinguely.

Cité de l'Architecture
Palais de Chaillot, 1 pl du Trocadéro, 16th (01.58.51.52.00/www.citechaillot.fr). M°
Trocadéro. **Open** 11am-7pm Mon, Wed-Sun (until 9pm Thur). **Admission** €8; €5 reductions; free under-18s (under-25s from EU countries). **Credit** MC, V. **Map** p400 B5.

Over 850 life-size copies of France's architectural treasures (including portions of great cathedrals such as Chartres) make for a fascinating visit for children of all ages. To help them understand the exhibits, colourful interactive games are dotted around the permanent displays, so they can try their hand at architecture and learn the concepts of Romanesque and Gothic as they create fantastical animal heads, design stained-glass windows or build a Romanesque arch. On Saturdays at 2pm, three- to seven-year-olds can have a go at doing some building themselves with wooden blocks. Entry is €8 and you don't need to reserve (just turn up about 30 minutes beforehand).

Etoiles du Rex
1 bd Poissonnière, 2nd (01.45.08.93.58/www.le grandrex.com). M° Bonne Nouvelle. **Open** 10am-7pm Wed-Sun (tours leave every 5mins); daily during school holidays. **Admission** €9.80; €8 under-12s. **Credit** AmEx, MC, V. **Map** p402 J4.

The slick but cheesy 50-minute backstage tour of the glorious art deco Grand Rex cinema is a treat for any kids with acting aspirations – plus they've just dropped the prices. Be prepared to ham your heart out when, propelled by automatic doors, lifts and mystery voices, you visit the projection room, climb behind the giant screen and are thrust into a whirlwind of sound dubbing, special effects and an audition for *King Kong*.

Grévin
10 bd Montmartre, 9th (01.47.70.85.05/ www.grevin.com). M° Grands Boulevards. **Open** 10am-6.30pm (last admission 5.30pm) Mon-Fri; 10am-7pm (last admission 6pm) Sat, Sun & hols. **Admission** €20; €12-€17 reductions; free under-6s. **Credit** AmEx, DC, MC, V. **Map** p402 H4.

This kitsch version of Madame Tussauds is a hit with kids, who can have their photo taken alongside waxworks of showbiz stars and personalities like football star Zinédine Zidane, Brigitte Bardot, the Queen and Barack Obama. Great historical moments, such as Neil Armstrong walking on the moon, are re-enacted in the 'snapshots of the 20th century' area, a small gallery at the top of a spiral staircase near the end shows how waxworks are made, and an impressive hall of mirrors (designed by France's fetish illusionist Arturo Brachetti and with music by Manu Katche) plunges you into scenes such as an Aztec temple. On Wednesdays, Saturdays and Sundays during termtime there are special children's guided tours (French only) for seven- to 12-year-olds (€15).

Musée des Arts et Métiers
60 rue Réamur, 3rd (01.53.01.82.00/www.arts-et-metiers.net). M° Arts et Métiers. **Open** 10am-6pm Tue, Wed, Fri-Sun; 10am-9.30pm Thur. **Admission** €6.50; free under-26s, 1st Sun of mth & after 6pm Thur. *Audio guides* €5. **Credit** V. **Map** p402 K5.

Abbot Grégoire founded this fascinating museum in the 18th century as 'a store for useful, new inventions'. Today it thrills budding scientists, mechanics, astronomers, pilots or kids simply curious about the world around them with highlights that include Foucault's original pendulum, used by physician Léon Foucault in 1851 to make the rotation of the earth visible to the human eye; Clément Ader's Avion III, officially the world's first working plane (1897); and Henry Ford's 'T' model car.

Musée des Egouts
Entrance opposite 93 quai d'Orsay, by Pont de l'Alma, 7th (01.53.68.27.81). M° Alma-Marceau/ RER Pont de l'Alma. **Open** *May-Sept* 11am-5pm Mon-Wed, Sat, Sun. *Oct-Apr* 11am-4pm Mon-Wed, Sat, Sun. **Admission** €4.30; €3.50 reductions; free under-5s. **Credit** MC, V. **Map** p400 D5.

Not half as revolting as it sounds, the sewer museum retraces the history of all 2,100km (1,305 miles) of Paris's underworld through a genuinely fascinating series of films, exhibits and a trip through the tunnels. During bad weather, visiting times may change or the museum may close as sudden surges in water can make the sewers dangerous.

Musée de la Magie
11 rue St-Paul, 4th (01.42.72.13.26/www.musee delamagie.com). M° St-Paul or Sully-Morland. **Open** 2-7pm Wed, Sat, Sun (extra hours & days in school hols). **Admission** €9; €7 reductions. **No credit cards. Map** p409 L7.

Small kids love the distorting mirrors and putting their hands in the lion's mouth at this museum of magic and curiosities, housed in vaulted cellars. A short magic show is included in the visit – it's in French, but rabbits out of hats translate pretty well

Profile Disneyland Paris

A slice of pure Americana in the French countryside.

With two parks to explore (Parc Disneyland and the special effects-oriented Parc Walt Disney Studios), as well as the Disney Entertainment Village (restaurants, bars and nightclubs), numerous hotels, and restaurants, the whole adventure can seem daunting. Here, we pick out some of the best bits for kids of all ages, as well as rides, restaurants and hotels for the whole family.

FOR YOUNG CHILDREN

Little ones get a kick out of Fantasyland, in the main Parc Disneyland, where the Cheshire Cat and the wicked Queen of Hearts await in Alice's Curious Labyrinth. It's a Small World takes you on a musical adventure past automated toy soldiers and animals. Meanwhile, over in Discoveryland, kids love helping Buzz save the world from little green men in the delightfully noisy Buzz Lightyear Laser Blast.

FOR OLDER CHILDREN (AND DAREDEVILS OF ALL AGES)

Disney's latest adrenalin ride, the Twilight Zone Tower of Terror (Walt Disney Studios, Production Courtyard) takes the brave to the top of an old Hollywood hotel, before sending them plummeting down a 13-storey lift shaft; and the Rock 'n' Roller Coaster in the Back Lot takes off at mega speed, before hurtling round hairpin turns and loops to the funky rhythm of Aerosmith.

FOR ALL THE FAMILY

Without doubt, the best family ride is the Pirates of the Caribbean in Parc Disneyland's Adventureland, where you will experience a ghostly pirate attack. Also fun is Star Tours, a Star Wars adventure in Discoveryland that sees you dodging objects and flying at top speeds to destroy the Death Star. And Moteurs Action, Stunt Show Spectacular! – in Walt Disney Studios Back Lot – leaves you marvelling at the stunts of a live film shoot.

EATING

For Tex-Mex food accompanied by a Wild West extravaganza, head to Buffalo Bill's Wild West Show in the Disney Village (€60 adults; €40 3-11s). Back in the main parks, the Auberge de Cendrillon in Fantasyland is swish, French and expensive (over €30), but it's the best restaurant around. For something cheaper, Walt's (in Main Street USA) offers a good choice of meats and salads (around €20); or, for a quick hot dog *à l'Américaine*, head for Coolpost in Adventureland (€5).

SLEEPING

If you plan to stay on site, Sequoia Lodge has a shuttle service to and from the park and an indoor swimming pool with waterslides (from €180 family room). Hôtel Cheyenne lets kids play at cowboys and Indians in the outside play area, equipped with tepees (from €150 family room); and the Davy Crockett Ranch, a short drive away, has an adventure playground in the forest (from €150 family room).

TOP TIPS

A Fastpass ticket, for the most popular rides, gives a time you can board without queuing.

Disneyland really works its magic at Christmas and Halloween.

Some rides have height restrictions – check beforehand.

INSIDE TRACK FARM FUN

Reserved for school classes during the week, Paris's very own farmyard, the **Ferme de Paris** (Rte du Pesage, 12th, www.paris.fr) in the Bois de Vincennes, is a real hit with kids at weekends. Inhabitants include friendly cows, sheep, rabbits and hens.

into any language. There's a great automated museum too, where 100 mechanical toys move into action before your kids' eyes.

Musée de la Musique

Parc de la Villette, 221 av Jean-Jaurès, 19th (01.44.84.45.00/www.cite-musique.fr). M° Porte de Pantin. **Open** noon-6pm Tue-Sat; 10am-6pm Sun. **Admission** €8; free under-18s. **Map** p403 inset.

This innovative music museum houses a gleamingly restored collection of instruments from the old Conservatoire, interactive computers and scale models of opera houses and concert halls. Visitors are supplied with an audio guide in a choice of languages, and the musical commentary is a joy, playing the appropriate instrument as you approach each exhibit. Once a month there are free active workshops for children over eight, who can try singing, conducting an orchestra or testing a musical instrument in the company of a musicologist (you need to reserve well in advance).

★ Musée National de la Marine

Palais de Chaillot, 17 pl du Trocadéro, 16th (01.53.65.69.69/www.musee-marine.fr). M° Trocadéro. **Open** 10am-6pm Mon, Wed-Sun. **Admission** €7; €5 reductions; free under-18s (under-25s from EU countries). **Credit** *Shop* MC, V. **Map** p400 B5.

Sail your family back in time through 400 years of French naval history. Highlights include the *Océan*, a 19th-century sailing vessel equipped with an impressive 120 cannons; a gilded barge built for Napoleon; and some extravagant, larger-than-life figureheads, from serene-faced angels to leaping seahorses. There are also dozens of model boats, dating from the 18th to the 20th century, and several old-fashioned divers' suits.

★ Muséum National d'Histoire Naturelle

36 rue Geoffroy-St-Hilaire, 2 rue Bouffon, 57 rue Cuvier, 5th (01.40.79.30.00/www.mnhn.fr). M° Gare d'Austerlitz or Jussieu. **Open** *Nov-Mar* 10am-5pm Mon, Wed-Sun. Grande Galerie de l'Evolution 10am-6pm Mon, Wed-Sun. *Apr-Oct* 10am-6pm Mon, Wed-Sun. *Both* Last admission 45mins before closing. **Admission** *Grande*

Galerie de l'Evolution €9; €7 reductions; free under-26s. *Galeries de Paléontologie et d'Anatomie Comparée & Galerie de Minéralogie et de Géologie* €7; €5 reductions; free under-4s. *Combined 2-day ticket for all sites* €25; €20 reductions. **Credit** MC, V. **Map** p406 K9.

At the Natural History Museum's Grande Galerie de l'Evolution, stuffed creatures parade majestically through their various habitats. Animals of all kinds teach children about the diversity of nature and, in the endangered and vanished section (where a dodo takes pride of place), about the importance of protecting them. Also in the Jardin des Plantes complex are the small Ménagerie zoo (*see right*), separate pavilions containing hunks of meteorites and crystals in the Galerie de Minéralogie et de Géologie, and the bony remains of fish, birds, monkeys, dinosaurs and humans in the Galerie de Paléontologie et d'Anatomie Comparée.

Musée de la Poupée

Impasse Berthaud, 3rd (01.42.72.73.11/ www.museedelapoupeeparis.com). M° Rambuteau. **Open** 10am-6pm Tue-Sun. **Admission** €8; €3-€5 reductions; free under-3s. **No credit cards. Map** p406 L7.

This small, private museum and doll hospital enchants little girls with its collection of some 400 dolls (mostly of French origin) and their accompanying accessories and pets, which are arranged in thematic tableaux. A few teddies and quacking ducks are thrown in for young boys, and storytelling sessions and workshops (along the lines of making doll's clothes or miniature food for dolls' houses) are held at 2.30pm on Wednesdays (in French, reserve in advance; €8-€13).

Musée National de la Marine.

★ Stade de France

Guided visits via entrance Porte H, Stade de France, Seine St-Denis (01.55.93.00.00/tours 08.92.70.09.00/www.stadefrance.fr). M° St-Denis Porte de Paris/RER Stade de France St-Denis. **Tours** *French* every 2hrs 11am-5pm daily (every hr from 10am Apr-Aug). *English* 10.30am, 2.30pm daily. **Admission** €12; €8 reductions; free under-6s. **Credit** AmEx, DC, MC, V.

Football- and rugby-crazy kids will absolutely love the behind-the-scenes tours of France's handsome national sports stadium. After a quick scan of the museum (photos, football shirts, electric guitars from the rock stars who also play here), the tour begins by sitting in the stands and ends with a runout through the tunnel to the sound of applause. On the way, you can visit the changing and shower rooms and learn about the on-site hospital and prison cells. On match or concert days, tours are not available.

AQUARIUMS & ZOOS

Cinéaqua

2 av des Nations Unies, 16th (01.40.69.23.23/ www.cineaqua.com). M° Trocadéro. **Open** *Apr-Sept* 10am-7pm daily. *Oct-Mar* 10am-6pm daily. **Admission** €19.50; €12.50-€15.50 reductions; free under-3s. **Credit** MC, V. **Map** p400 B5.

Paris's first 'ocean entertainment centre' is a hybrid aquarium-cinema complex containing over 500 species of fish, invertebrates, sharks and coral, and several cinema screens. There are kids' clubs, with face-painting and games, from 1pm to 5pm on Wednesday, Saturday and Sunday, plus a touch pool offering the chance to stroke carp and sturgeon.

Ménagerie du Jardin des Plantes

57 rue Cuvier, 5th (01.40.79.37.94/www.mnhn.fr). M° Gare d'Austerlitz, Jussieu or Place Monge. **Open** 9am-6pm daily. **Admission** €8; €6 reductions; free under-4s. **Credit** AmEx, MC, V. **Map** p406 K8.

Heads rolled during the Terror, leaving many an aristocratic collection of exotic animals without a home. This *ménagerie* became the solution in 1794. Nowadays, its inhabitants include vultures, monkeys, orang-utans, ostriches, flamingos, a century-old turtle, plus another one rescued from the sewers, a lovely red panda and lots of satisfyingly scary spiders and snakes. There's a petting zoo with farm animals for small kids, and older ones can zoom in on microscopic species in the Microzoo.

Palais de la Porte Dorée
Aquarium Tropical

293 av Daumesnil, 12th (01.53.59.58.60/ www.aquarium-portedoree.fr). M° Porte Dorée. **Open** 10am-5.15pm Tue-Fri; 10am-7pm Sat, Sun. **Admission** €4.50-€6.50; €6-€8 1 adult with 1 or 2 children under 12; €3-€5 reductions; free under-4s. **No credit cards**.

The basement of this art deco palace, built for the Colonial Exhibition in 1931, contains the small but much-loved city aquarium and its crocodiles, brought from Dakar in 1948; other watery residents include cuttlefish, sharks, and luminous deep-water species. ▶ *The Palais de la Porte Dorée is also home to the new Cité Nationale de l'Histoire de l'Immigration (see p108).*

Parc de Thoiry

78770 Thoiry-en-Yvelines (01.34.87.53.76/ www.thoiry.net). 45km (28 miles) west of Paris; by car A13, A12, then N12 towards Dreux until Thoiry. **Open** *July, Aug* 10am-7pm daily. *Sept-June* 10am-5pm Mon-Sat; 10am-6pm Sun. **Admission** *Safari park, park & château* €25; €18-€22 reductions; free under-3s. **Credit** MC, V.

As well as a beautiful château, the Parc de Thoiry houses one of Europe's first animal reserves. Follow the long safari park trail, accessible only by car, and see zebras rub their noses over your windscreen and bears amble down tracks. In the adjoining zoo, rarities include Siberian lynx and Tonkean macaques.

PERFORMING ARTS & SPORTS

When school's out on Wednesday afternoons, at weekends and during holidays, fairytales, fables and folk stories keep children entertained at the city's theatres and *café-théâtres*. The varied programme at the **Théâtre Dunois** (7 rue Louise-Weiss, 13th, 01.45.84.72.00, www. theatredunois.org) is almost entirely geared towards children. For children's theatre in an unusual setting, the **Abricadabra Péniche-Antipod** (opposite 55 quai de Seine, 19th, 01.42.03.39.07, http://abricadabra.nerim.net, closed July, Aug) is a riverboat on the Canal de l'Ourcq with an appealing programme.

In general, children's films are dubbed into French, but you can see VO (*version originale*) screenings of the latest Hollywood hits at most venues across town. Keep a lookout for kids' showings on Wednesdays and Saturday afternoons at the Cinémathèque Française and L'Ecran des Enfants (Oct-June 2.30pm Wed) for under-13s at the **Centre Pompidou** (*see p98*). The IMAX cinema in La Villette's **Géode** (*see p295*) will keep kids enthralled too.

Each winter, France's traditional circuses come to town, complete with big cats, clowns and horses, and set up on the Pelouse de Reuilly; the **Cirque Bouglione** (*see p283*), meanwhile, occupies the gorgeous Cirque d'Hiver with its annual extravaganza. Your brood can even learn tightrope walking, juggling and numerous other circus sports between April and September on Wednesdays (daily during spring and summer holidays) at the **Chapiteau d'Adrienne** (62 rue René-Binet, 18th, 01.43.31.80.69, www.chapiteau-adrienne.fr, admission €5).

ARTS & ENTERTAINMENT

Waterbabies can choose between 38 public pools (www.paris.fr), including the floating **Piscine Josephine-Baker** (*see p341*), moored on the Seine and filled with purified water pumped from the river; the art nouveau **Piscine de la Butte-aux-Cailles** (*see p340*), with indoor and outdoor pools fed by artesian wells; and the recently restored **Espace Sportif Pailleron** (32 rue Edouard Pailleron, 19th, 01.40.40.27.70), near Buttes-Chaumont, which has two pools and an ice rink (rollerskating in summer). At the indoor **Aquaboulevard** (*see p340*), over-threes can splash down different slides and ride the waves. Bathing caps are obligatory everywhere.

Patinoire Sonja Henie

Palais Omnisports de Paris-Bercy (01.40.02.60.60/www.bercy.fr). Mᵒ Bercy. **Open** *Sept-mid June* 3-6pm Wed; 9.30pm-12.30am Fri; 3-6pm, 9.30pm-12.30am Sat; 10am-noon, 3-6pm Sun. **Admission** €3-€6. **No credit cards. Map** p407 N9.
Bercy's Omnisports arena contains an ice rink, open on Wednesdays and weekends for skaters of all levels. Teenagers can also skate until late on Fridays and Saturdays, when disco lights colour the ice and music pumps out.

PARKS & THEME PARKS

Disneyland Paris/ Walt Disney Studios Park

Marne-la-Vallée (08.25.30.60.30/from UK 0870 503 0303/www.disneylandparis.com). 32km E of Paris. RER A or TGV Marne-la-Vallée-Chessy. By car, A4 exit 14. **Open** *Disneyland Paris* Sept-mid July 10am-8pm Mon-Fri; 9am-8pm Sat, Sun. Mid July-Aug 9am-11pm daily. *Studios Park* Winter 10am-6pm Mon-Fri; 9am-6pm Sat, Sun. Summer 9am-7pm daily. **Admission** *1 park* €51; €43 reductions; free under-3s. *1-day hopper (both parks)* €62; €54 reductions. *2-day hopper (both parks)* €112; €95 reductions; free under-7s. **Parking** €8. **Credit** AmEx, MC, V. *See p287* **Profile.**

Jardin d'Acclimatation

Bois de Boulogne, 16th (01.40.67.90.82/www. jardindacclimatation.fr). Mᵒ Les Sablons. **Open** *May-Sept* 10am-7pm daily. *Oct-Apr* 10am-6pm daily. **Admission** €2.90; €1.45 reductions; free under-3s. **Credit** (€15 minimum) MC, V.
Founded in 1860, this amusement park and garden has animals, a Normandy-style farm and an aviary, as well as boat rides, a funfair with mini rollercoasters, flying chairs, the Enchanted House for children aged two to four and two playgrounds. There's also a place to steer radio-controlled boats and mini golf. Many of the attractions cost €2.90 a go; others are free. A miniature train runs from Porte Maillot

through the Bois de Boulogne to the park entrance, and has space for pushchairs (€2.70 return; €4.15-€5.60 with entry included).

Jardin du Luxembourg

Main access 2 rue Auguste Compte, 6th. Mᵒ Odéon/RER Luxembourg. **Open** *Summer* 7.30am-dusk daily. *Winter* 8am-dusk daily. **Map** p408 H8.
The 25-hectare park is a prized family attraction. Kids come from across the city for its pony rides, ice-cream stands, puppet shows, pedal karts, sandpits, metal swingboats and merry-go-round. The playground has an entrance fee.

★ Parc Astérix

60128 Plailly (08.26.30.10.40/www.parcasterix.fr). 36km N of Paris. By coach from the Louvre or RER Roissy-Charles de Gaulle 1 (check website for times or call 08.26.30.10.40). By car, A1 exit Parc Astérix. **Open** *Apr-June* 10am-6pm daily. *July, Aug* 9.30am-7pm daily. *Sept-mid Nov* 10am-6pm Wed, Sat, Sun. Closed mid Nov-Mar except Christmas hols. **Admission** €39; €29 reductions; free under-3s. **Parking** €8. **Credit** MC, V.
The park is split into Ancient Greece, the Roman Empire, the Land of the Vikings and the indomitable Gaulish Village. Thrill-seekers can defy gravity on Goudurix, Europe's largest rollercoaster, while younger kids get wet on the Grand Splatch log flume. For some serious handshaking, Astérix, Obélix and friends wander around and a jamboree of live acts pumps up the pace. The park's newest attraction is Le Défi de César, a virtual reality ride.

Parc des Buttes-Chaumont

Rue Botzaris, rue Manin, rue de Crimée, 19th. Mᵒ Buttes Chaumont. **Open** *Oct-Apr* 7am-8.15pm daily. *May, mid Aug-Sept* 7am-9.15pm daily. *June-mid Aug* 7am-10.15pm daily. **Map** p407 N2.
This area, which was formerly mined for gypsum, was turned into a sumptuous park under Napoleon III. Spectacular in every way (including the views over Paris), it is a family magnet with Punch and Judy stands, pony rides, sandpits, waterfalls, picnic and games areas and drinks stands.

★ Parc de la Villette

Av Corentin-Cariou, 19th (01.40.03.75.75/www.villette.com). Mᵒ Porte de la Villette. Av Jean-Jaurès, 19th. Mᵒ Porte de Pantin. **Map** p403 inset.
Aside from a children's science museum, a music museum, an IMAX cinema, theatres, concert and exhibition venues, the city's former abattoir district is now made up of a succession of gardens and playgrounds. Jardin des Voltiges has climbing ropes and balancing games, and the modern Jardin des Dunes et Vents has pedal windmills, waves of bouncy tubes and giant hamster wheels. The little known Jardins Passagers (open after 3pm Apr-Sept) is a collection of gardens that teach children about flora and fauna; some even have beehives.

Dance

Take your pick – top-class ballet or Seine-side salsa.

Paris is home to a thriving dance scene, a rich programme of major international companies and plenty of home-grown talent. In 2010, the **Théâtre de la Ville** and **Théâtre National de Chaillot** will see the return of such luminaries as Akram Khan and William Forsythe. There's no shortage of ballet productions at the **Théâtre du Châtelet** and **Palais Garnier**, with the world premiere of Angelin Preljocaj's *Siddharta* on the bill in April. And the **Festival d'Automne** will again feature an impressive line-up of innovative dance.

There's even more of interest outside the centre of town. As the HQ for over 600 regional companies, the **Centre National de la Danse** in Pantin reaches out to its audience with a well-devised series of performances, and smaller dance 'laboratories' such as Ménagerie de Verre and Regard du Cygne showcase new work by smaller companies. Dance centres and festivals in the *banlieue* are also determined to draw audiences to their suburban locations, with a distinct mix of styles and cultures.

INFORMATION AND RESOURCES

For listings, *see Pariscope* and *L'Officiel des Spectacles*. For events coverage, look out for two monthlies: *La Terrasse* (distributed free at major dance venues) and the glossy *Danser*.

For shoes and equipment, **Sansha** (52 rue de Clichy, 9th, 01.45.26.01.38, www.sansha.com) has a good reputation, and **Repetto** (22 rue de la Paix, 2nd, 01.44.71.83.12, www.repetto.com) supplies the Opéra with pointes and slippers; **Menkes** (12 rue Rambuteau, 3rd, 01.40.27.91.81, www.menkes.es) sells serious flamenco gear as well as outsize glam-rock boots.

FESTIVALS

The year starts with **Faits d'Hiver** (01.42.74.46.00, www.faitsdhiver.com) and hip hop festival **Suresnes Cités Danse** (01.46.97.98.10, www.theatre-suresnes.fr) in January. May and June bring with them the **Rencontres Chorégraphiques de Seine-St-Denis** (01.55.82.08.01, www.rencontres choregraphiques.com), the **IRCAM Agora** festival (01.44.78.48.16, www.ircam.fr) and **Onze Bouge** (01.53.27.13.68, www.festival onze.org). The **Rencontres de la Villette**

(01.40.03.75.75, www.rencontresvillette.com) dishes up street dance at various suburban locations every October. You'll also find smaller dance festivals at the **Maison des Arts de Créteil**, and at the **Ménagerie de Verre** in the 11th. *See also pp274-279* Calendar.

Les Etés de la Danse

1 pl du Châtelet, 1st (01.40.28.28.40/www.chatelet-theatre.com). M° Châtelet. **Date** early-late July. Founded in 2005, this festival puts the spotlight on one company or choreographer, with three weeks of performances. The 2010 edition focuses on great dancers of the 20th century with connections to Russia, such as Ninette de Valois and Rudolf Nureyev. Shows are accompanied by workshops and activities.

THE BEST STAGES

For cutting-edge moves
Maison des Arts de Créteil. *See p292.*

For experimental dance
Festival d'Automne. *See p292.*

For big-name ballet
Palais Garnier. *See p292.*

★ Festival d'Automne

*Information: 156 rue de Rivoli, 1st
(01.53.45.17.00/www.festival-automne.com).*
Date *mid Sept-late Dec.*
For nearly 40 years, the Festival d'Automne has shown the way forward in the performing arts. With a focus on leading French experimental companies, the festival also invites big-name choreographers from around the world. Highlights in 2009 included Merce Cunningham's *Nearly Ninety*, a dramatic giant-scale work.

Paris Quartier d'Eté

01.44.94.98.00/www.quartierdete.com.
Date *mid July-mid Aug.*
This popular summer festival features eclectic programmes and free outdoor performances in Paris and around its outskirts. Public rehearsals and talks give audiences the chance to meet prestigious international choreographers.

MAJOR DANCE VENUES

Centre National de la Danse

*1 rue Victor-Hugo, 93507 Pantin
(01.41.83.27.27/box office 01.41.83.98.98/
www.cnd.fr). Mº Hoche/RER Pantin.* **Open**
Box office 10am-7pm Mon-Fri. **Admission**
€6-€14. **Credit** AmEx, MC, V.
This centre first opened its door in 2004, with the mission to bridge the divide between stage and spectator. It invites audiences to its quarterly 'Grandes leçons de danse', contemporary dance master classes. It also offers an expertly curated selection of performances presented in the studios, exhibitions, and a phenomenal archive of films and choreographic material.

Maison des Arts de Créteil

*Pl Salvador-Allende, 94000 Créteil
(01.45.13.19.19/www.maccreteil.com).
Mº Créteil-Préfecture.* **Open** *Box office* 1-7pm
Tue-Sat. Closed mid July-Aug. **Admission**
€8-€30. **Credit** MC, V.
With over 300 performances a year and a newly added third stage, this suburban arts centre is a vibrant hub of artistic creation, featuring an eclectic programme of theatre, dance, music and digital art. Don't miss the International Exit Festival of contemporary dance, which runs from 18 to 28 March in 2010.

★ Palais Garnier

*Pl de l'Opéra, 9th (08.92.89.90.90/from
abroad 01.71.25.24.23/www.opera-de-paris.fr).
Mº Opéra.* **Open** *Box office* 10.30am-6.30pm
Mon-Sat. *Telephone bookings* 9am-6pm
Mon-Fri; 9am-1pm Sat. Closed 15 July-end
Aug. **Admission** €7-€172; €5 reductions
(90mins before show). **Credit** AmEx, MC, V.
Map p401 G4.
The Ballet de l'Opéra National de Paris manages to tread successfully between classics and new productions, between the Opéra Bastille and lavish Palais Garnier. Highlights in 2010 include the world premiere of Angelin Preljocaj's *Siddharta* in conjunction with composer Bruno Mantovani and visual artist Claude Lévêque.

Théâtre du Châtelet

*1 pl du Châtelet, 1st (01.40.28.28.40/www.
chatelet-theatre.com). Mº Châtelet.* **Open** *Box
office* July, Aug 1-6pm daily. Sept-June 11am-
7pm daily. **Admission** €10-€95. **Credit** AmEx,
MC, V. **Map** p402 J6.

Ménagerie de Verre.

This classical music institution is strengthening its reputation in other live artistic disciplines. The new dance season features a diverse line-up, including a series of performances in April 2010 by Christopher Wheeldon's Morphoses ballet company.

Théâtre National de Chaillot

1 pl du Trocadéro, 16th (01.53.65.30.00/ www.theatre-chaillot.fr). M° Trocadéro. **Open** *Box office* 11am-7pm Mon-Sat; 1-5pm Sun. *Phone bookings* 11am-7pm Mon-Sat. Closed July, Aug. **Admission** €27.50-€35; €12-€29 reductions. **Credit** MC, V. **Map** p400 C5.

Chaillot's three auditoriums range from cosy and experimental to a vast 2,800-seater amphitheatre. The 2010 dance programme includes the French premiere of William Forsythe's *I Don't Believe in Outer Space*.

★ Théâtre de la Ville

2 pl du Châtelet, 4th (01.42.74.22.77/www. theatredelaville-paris.com). M° Châtelet. **Open** *Box office* 11am-8pm Mon-Sat. *Telephone bookings* 11am-7pm Mon-Sat. Closed July, Aug. **Admission** €13-€26; €8-€12 reductions. **Credit** MC, V. **Map** p406 J6.

This leading venue has nurtured long-standing collaborations with international choreographers. The 2010 programme will see a new piece by Akram Khan, fresh from his collaboration with Juliette Binoche in 2009, as well as a new work by the innovative, Belgium-based Peeping Tom company.

▶ *Some performances take place at sister venue Théâtre des Abbesses (31 rue des Abbesses, 18th).*

OTHER DANCE VENUES

L'Etoile du Nord

16 rue Georgette-Agutte, 18th (01.42.26.47.47/ www.etoiledunord-theatre.com). M° Guy Môquet. **Open** *Box office* 2-6pm Mon-Fri. Closed July, Aug. **Admission** €14; €8-€10 reductions. **Credit** V.

This smaller venue splits its programme between theatre and contemporary multimedia dance. The Avis de Turbulences festival (end May-mid June) features a decent selection of mixed bills.

Ménagerie de Verre

12-14 rue Léchevin, 11th (01.43.38.33.44/ www.menagerie-de-verre.org). M° Parmentier. **Open** *Box office* 2-6pm Mon-Fri. Closed July, Aug. **Admission** €13; €10 reductions. **No credit cards. Map** p403 N5.

This multidisciplinary hothouse is rooted in the avant-garde, with contemporary dance and classes given by a succession of guest teachers.

★ Regard du Cygne

210 rue de Belleville, 20th (01.43.58.55.93/ bookings 09.71.34.23.50/www.leregardu cygne.com). M° Télégraphe. **Open** *Box office*

1hr before show. Closed Aug. **Admission** free-€15. **No credit cards. Map** p403 Q3.

This pared-down studio in Belleville is a great place to get a taste of the alternative dance scene.

▶ *The Spectacles Sauvages nights allow unknowns to show a ten-minute piece to the public, while the Rencontres focus on the work of a particular artist and are open to all, free of charge.*

Théâtre de la Bastille

76 rue de la Roquette, 11th (01.43.57.42.14/ www.theatre-bastille.com). M° Bastille or Voltaire. **Open** *Box office* 10am-6pm Mon-Fri; 2-6pm Sat. Closed July, Aug. **Admission** €22; €13-€14 reductions. **Credit** MC, V. **Map** p407 M6.

This small theatre showcases innovative contemporary dance and drama pieces. Worth checking out in April 2010 is a performance of Daniel Léveillé's *Amour, Acide et Noix*.

DANCE CLASSES

Dance classes are available to suit all tastes and levels. The open-air dancing on the banks of the Seine is particularly popular in summer.

Centre de Danse du Marais

41 rue du Temple, 4th (01.42.77.58.19/ www.parisdanse.com). M° Hôtel de Ville or Rambuteau. **Open** 9am-9pm Mon-Fri; 9am-8pm Sat; 9am-7pm Sun. **Classes** €18. **Map** p402 K5.

There's a huge choice of classes here, with big-name teachers such as belly dance star Leila Haddad and ballet's Casati-Lazzarelli team. The five-class 'sampler' pass is a good deal at €72.

★ Studio Harmonic

5 passage des Taillandiers, 11th (01.48.07.13.39/ www.studioharmonic.fr). M° Bastille. **Open** *Office* 10am-5pm Mon-Fri. *Classes* 9.30am-10pm Mon-Fri; 9am-7.30pm Sat. Closed 3wks Aug. **Classes** €15-€16. **Map** p407 M7.

The rising star among Paris's dance schools. Studio Harmonic's claim to fame is the trademark Ragga Jam class – created by Laure Courtellemont – which combines ragga, dancehall, African dance and hip hop.

Film

Business is booming in the cradle of European cinema.

This is where it all began, in the basement of a chic café in 1895; the Lumière brothers were from Lyon, but the city in which they chose to launch their cinematograph had to be Paris. Over a century later filmgoing is still a central part of Paris life, with more tickets per head bought here than anywhere else in Europe; in any given week, the choice of films to watch exceeds 350 (more still, if you count the programmes of the regular festivals), and the range of screening venues is a rich mix of glitzy modern multiplexes and doughty historic *art et essai* cinemas that attract loyal and discerning audiences. What's more, cinema tickets are much cheaper in Paris than in London or New York.

MOVIEGOING IN PARIS

Happily, the rise of the multiplex hasn't meant a reduction in the choice and variety of films on offer. In Paris, multiplexes regularly show films from Eastern Europe, Asia and South America, and countless independent cinemas continue to screen a hugely eclectic assortment of cult, classic and just plain obscure films. As well as retrospectives and cut-price promotions, there are often visits from directors and stars.

Local interest is strong enough to sustain several monthly movie magazines and there's a decent selection of specialist film bookshops, such as **Contacts**, in the city. Launched in 2007, the annual **Salon du Cinéma** gives film buffs a chance to visit mocked-up movie sets and meet world-renowned directors and actors. Finally, French DVD labels produce some of the most expertly curated discs in the world. At **Fnac** and **Virgin Megastore** (for both,

see p271), you're more than likely to find American and British titles otherwise unavailable in the US or UK.

INFORMATION AND TICKETS

New releases hit the screens on Wednesdays. Hollywood is well represented, of course, but Paris audiences have a balanced cinematic diet that satisfies their appetite for international films as well as shorts and documentaries. On top of this there are the 150-plus annual releases funded or part-funded with French money (the French film industry is still the world's third largest, after the US and India).

For venues, times and prices, consult one of the city's two main weekly listings magazines: *L'Officiel des Spectacles* and *Pariscope*. *Films nouveaux* are new releases, *Exclusivités* are the also-showing titles, and *Reprises* means rep. For non-francophone flicks, look out for two letters somewhere near the title: VO (*version originale*) means a screening in the original language with French subtitles; VF (*version française*) means that it has been dubbed into French.

Buy tickets in the usual way at the cinema – for new blockbusters, it pays to buy at least one screening in advance. You can also call **AlloCiné** (08.92.89.28.92, www.allocine.fr). Online booking may entail a fee. Seats are often discounted by 20 to 30 per cent at Monday or Wednesday screenings, and the Mairie sponsors cut-price promotions throughout the year.

If you're in town for longer than a couple of weeks, you it might find it worth your while

INSIDE TRACK
SEATS ON THE CHEAP

For €19.80 a month, the **UGC/MK2 Illimité** card (*see p295*) offers film buffs unlimited screenings at any UGC or MK2 venue, as well as some independents. Also now available, at €35 a month, is the Illimité 2 card, which is valid for two people.

to pick up a *carte illimité*, a season ticket that allows unlimited viewing: every multiplex chain offers one.

CINEMAS

Giant screens & multiplexes

La Géode
26 av Corentin-Cariou, 19th (08.92.68.45.40/ www.lageode.fr). M° Porte de la Villette. **Admission** €10.50; €9 under-25s. **Credit** MC, V. **Map** p403 inset.
The IMAX cinema at the Cité des Sciences occupies a shiny geodesic sphere. The vast hemispheric screen lets you experience 3D plunges through natural scenery, and animated adventures where figures zoom out to grab you.

★ Le Grand Rex
1 bd Poissonnière, 2nd (08.92.68.05.96/ www.legrandrex.com). M° Bonne Nouvelle. **Admission** €7.50-€9; €6-€7.20 students, over-60s, under-12s. *Les Etoiles du Rex tour* €9.80; €8 under-12s. **Credit** MC, V. **Map** p402 J4.
With its wedding-cake exterior, fairy-tale interior and the largest auditorium in Europe (2,750 seats), this listed historical monument is one of the few cinemas to upstage whatever it screens. Its blockbuster programming (usually in French) is suited to its vast screen; it also hosts concerts and rowdy all-night compilation events. There are six smaller screens too.
▶ *The Etoiles du Rex tour is a 50-minute, SFX-laden taste of movie magic.*

Max Linder Panorama
24 bd Poissonnière, 9th (01.48.24.00.47/ www.maxlinder.com). M° Grands Boulevards. **Admission** €9; €7 Mon, Wed, Fri, students (except weekends), under-12s. **Credit** MC, V. **Map** p402 J4.

This state-of-the-art cinema, with THX surround sound and an 18m (60ft) screen, is named after the dapper French silent comedian who owned it between 1914 and 1925. The walls and 700 seats are all black to prevent even the tiniest twinkle of reflected light distracting the audience from what's happening on the screen. Look for all-nighters and one-off showings of rare vintage films or piano-accompanied silents.

★ MK2 Bibliothèque
128-162 av de France, 13th (08.92.69.84.84/ www.mk2.com). M° Bibliothèque François Mitterrand or Quai de la Gare. **Admission** €10; €7 students and over-60s (except weekends); €5.90 under-18s; €19.80 monthly pass. **Credit** MC, V. **Map** p407 M10.
The MK2 chain's flagship offers an all-in-one night out: 14 screens, three restaurants, a bar open until 5am at weekends and two-person 'love seats'. A paragon of imaginative programming, MK2 is growing all the time; it has added ten more venues in town, including two situated along the Bassin de la Villette with decent waterside cafés attached. For details of the Illimité season ticket, *see p294* **Inside Track**.

UGC Ciné Cité Bercy
2 cour St-Emilion, 12th (08.92.70.00.00/ www.ugc.fr). M° Cour St-Emilion. **Admission** €10.20; €7 students, over-60s (except Sat & Sun before 7pm); €5.90 under-18s; €19.80 monthly pass. **Credit** MC, V. **Map** p407 P10.
This ambitious 18-screen development screens art movies as well as mainstream fodder, also and hosts regular meet-the-director events. The UGC's other branch, the 19-screen UGC Ciné Cité Les Halles (7 place de la Rotonde, Nouveau Forum des Halles, 1st, 08.92.70.00.00) serves the same mix of cinema and events.

ARTS & ENTERTAINMENT

Forum des Images. *See p296.*

ARTS & ENTERTAINMENT

Showcases

Auditorium du Louvre

Musée du Louvre, 99 rue de Rivoli, 1st (01.40.20.55.55/www.louvre.fr). M° Palais Royal Musée du Louvre. **Admission** €9; €4 under-26s; free under-18s. **Credit** MC, V. **Map** p402 H5.
This 420-seat auditorium was designed by IM Pei, as part of the Mitterrand-inspired renovation of the Louvre. Film screenings are often related to the exhibitions; silent movies with live music are regulars.

Centre Pompidou

Rue St-Martin, 4th (01.44.78.12.33/www.centre pompidou.fr). M° Hôtel de Ville or Rambuteau. **Admission** €6; €4 students. **Credit** MC, V. **Map** p406 K6.
The varied programme here features themed series, experimental and artists' films, and a weekly documentary session. This is also the venue for the Cinéma du Réel festival in March (www.cinereel.org).

Le Cinéma des Cinéastes

7 av de Clichy, 17th (08.92.68.97.17/www.cinema-des-cineastes.fr). M° Place de Clichy. **Admission** €8.70; €6.90 students, under-12s, over-60s. **Credit** MC, V. **Map** p401 G2.
Done out to evoke the studios of old, this three-screen showcase of world cinema holds meet-the-director sessions and festivals of classic, foreign, gay and documentary films. Also offers a monthly pass.

★ La Cinémathèque Française

51 rue de Bercy, 12th (01.71.19.33.33/www.cinematheque.fr). M° Bercy. **Admission** *Films* €6.50; €5 students, 18s-26s; €3 under-18s; free for members. *Exhibitions* €2.50-€9. *Membership* €10/month. **Credit** MC, V. **Map** p407 N9.
Relocated to Frank Gehry's striking, spacious cubist building, the Cinémathèque Française now boasts four screens, a bookshop, a restaurant, exhibition space and the Musée du Cinéma, where it displays a fraction of its huge collection of movie memorabilia. In the spirit of its founder Henri Langlois, the Cinémathèque hosts retrospectives, cult movies, classics, experimental cinema and Q&A sessions.

Forum des Images

2 Grande Galerie, Porte St-Eustache, Forum des Halles, 1st (01.44.76.63.00/www.forum desimages.net). M° Les Halles. **Open** 1-9pm Tue-Sun. Closed 2wks Aug. **Admission** (per day) €5; €4 under-12s. Membership available (€84-€132 per year). **Credit** AmEx, MC, V. **Map** p402 J5.
Partly a screening venue for old and little-known movies, and partly an archive for every kind of film featuring Paris. Today the Forum's collection numbers over 6,500 documentaries, adverts, newsreels and films, from the work of the Lumière brothers to 21st-century reportage. They have all been painstakingly digitised. *Photo p295.*

Arthouses

Accattone

20 rue Cujas, 5th (01.46.33.86.86). M° Cluny La Sorbonne/RER Luxembourg. **Admission** €7; €6 Wed, students, under-20s (except Fri nights and weekends). **No credit cards. Map** p408 J8.
Named after Pasolini's first film, this tiny Latin Quarter cinema has a clear preference for old Italian arthouse. That said, there's still plenty of room on the rolling weekly programme for the likes of Buñuel, Oshima, Roeg and Ken Russell.

Action

Action Christine *4 rue Christine, 6th (01.43.25.85.78/www.actioncinemas.com). M° Odéon or St-Michel.* **Admission** €8; €6 students, under-20s. **No credit cards. Map** p408 J7.
Action Ecoles *23 rue des Ecoles, 5th (01.43.25.72.07). M° Maubert Mutualité.* **Admission** €8; €6 students, under-20s. **No credit cards. Map** p408 J8.
Grand Action *5 rue des Ecoles, 5th (01.43.54.47.62/www.legrandaction.com). M° Cardinal Lemoine.* **Admission** €8.50; €6.50 students, under-20s. **No credit cards. Map** p406 K8.
A Left Bank stalwart, the Action group is renowned for screening new prints of old movies. It's heaven for anyone who's nostalgic for Tinseltown classics and quality US independents.

★ Le Balzac

1 rue Balzac, 8th (01.45.61.10.60/www.cinema balzac.com). M° George V. **Admission** €9; €7 Mon, Wed, students, under-18s, over-60s; €5 under-12s. **No credit cards. Map** p400 D4.
Built in 1935 and boasting a mock ocean-liner foyer, Le Balzac scores highly for design and programming. Jean-Jacques Schpoliansky, the manager, is often found welcoming punters in person. The Balzac awards prizes according to audience votes.

Le Champo

51 rue des Ecoles, 5th (01.43.54.51.60/www.lechampo.com). M° Cluny La Sorbonne or Odéon. **Admission** €7.50; €6 last screening Wed & Sun, students, under-20s; €5 first screening. **No credit cards. Map** p408 J7.
The two-screen Champo has been in operation for nearly seven decades, a venerable past recognised in 2000 when it was given historic monument status. In the 1960s it was a favourite haunt of *nouvelle vague* directors such as Claude Chabrol.

Le Cinéma du Panthéon

13 rue Victor-Cousin, 5th (01.40.46.01.21/www.whynotproductions.fr/pantheon). RER Luxembourg. **Admission** €7; €5.50 Mon, Wed, students, 13-18s; €4 under-13s. **Credit** MC, V. **Map** p408 J8.

Celluloid City

If Paris feels eternally familiar, thank the movies.

Les Amants du Pont Neuf.

You're in film-set Paris the second you get off the train. The Gare du Nord featured in Orson Welles's *F for Fake*, and umpteen other flicks; and as for the Eiffel Tower, it has made more celluloid appearances than it has rivets. Here we pick out a few of the capital's star turns.

Hôtel du Nord
(Marcel Carné, 1938)
The Hôtel du Nord is, thanks to Carné's film, a national monument: it, and the adjacent iron footbridge and chunk of Canal St-Martin, were re-created in the studio by celebrated production designer Alexandre Trauner. On the bridge, national icon Arletty gives suitor Louis Jouvet the brush-off with the immortal '*Atmosphère! Est-ce que j'ai une gueule d'atmosphère?*'

Les 400 Coups
(François Truffaut, 1959)
Tearaway kid Antoine Doisnel (Jean-Pierre Léaud in his first role) gets around large parts of Paris, helping to launch the Nouvelle Vague on the way. His troubles start when he catches his mum in an adulterous clinch on place de Clichy.

Baisers Volés
(François Truffaut, 1968)
The opening shot – a slow pull back from the entrance to the old Cinémathèque – is probably the cinephile's ultimate Paris-on-film moment. The further adventures of Antoine Doisnel include a stint as a hotel watchman at 39 avenue Junot.

Les Ripoux
(Claude Zidi, 1984)
Loveably roguish cop Philippe Noiret teaches scrupulous rookie Thierry Lhermitte the fine art of police corruption on their Barbès beat. Free meals at the local bistro, a gratis *gigot* from the butcher and some buckshee shades from a market stall under the *métro aérien* are all in a day's work.

Les Amants du Pont Neuf
(Leos Carax, 1991)
The *folie de grandeur* that was this story of down-and-out romance (starring Juliette Binoche and Denis Lavant) was, like *Hôtel du Nord*, filmed on another mocked-up bridge – the Pont Neuf, reconstructed on a lake near Montpellier at budget-bursting cost.

La Fille sur le Pont
(Patrice Leconte, 1999)
Circus knife-thrower Daniel Auteuil saves Vanessa Paradis from drowning after she throws herself off the passerelle Debilly in Leconte's sumptuous modern fairytale. Don't feel tempted to copy her: the Seine is nothing like as clean as the underwater footage suggests.

Le Fabuleux Destin d'Amélie Poulain
(Jean-Pierre Jeunet, 2001)
Amélie's Montmartre stamping ground included her place of employment, the Café des Deux Moulins at 15 rue Lepic. The place is now a tourist attraction, although its owners have so far resisted the temptation to rename it Café Amélie.

To celebrate its centenary in 2007, the city's oldest surviving movie house opened a tearoom with interior design by Catherine Deneuve. The Cinéma du Panthéon continues to screen new, often obscure international films and hosts meet-the-director nights and discussions.

★ Le Denfert

24 pl Denfert-Rochereau, 14th (01.43.21.41.01/ www.allocine.fr). Mº Denfert Rochereau/RER Denfert Rochereau. **Admission** €7.30; €5.80 Mon, Wed, students, over-60s; €4.60 under-15s. **No credit cards. Map** p405 H10.

This charming little cinema offers a nicely eclectic repertory selection that ranges from François Ozon and Hayao Miyazaki to shorts and animation, as well as new-release foreign films.

L'Entrepôt

7-9 rue Francis-de-Pressensé, 14th (01.45.40.07.50/www.lentrepot.fr). Mº Pernety or Plaisance. **Admission** €7; €5.60 students, over-60s; €4 under-12s. **No credit cards**. **Map** p405 F10.

A diverse array of documentaries, shorts, gay cinema and productions from developing nations are more common here than mainstream stuff.

Images d'Ailleurs

21 rue de la Clef, 5th (01.45.87.18.09/www. imagesdailleurs.net). Mº Censier Daubenton. **Admission** €6; €5.50 concessions; €4.70 under-12s, for all Mon. **No credit cards.** **Map** 406 K9.

Opened back in 1990, the Images d'Ailleurs cinema focuses on cinematic works from Africa and other rare movie treats.

Le Mac Mahon

5 av Mac-Mahon, 17th (01.43.80.24.81/ www. cinemamacmahon.com). Mº Charles de Gaulle Etoile. **Admission** €6.50; €4.50 students. **No credit cards. Map** p400 C3.

This single-screen, 1930s-era cinema has changed little since its 1960s heyday (tickets are still, delightfully, of the tear-off variety), when its all-American programming fostered the label '*macmahonisme*' among the buffs who haunted the place. Americana still makes up the bulk of what's on the screen.

Le Nouveau Latina

20 rue du Temple, 4th (01.42.78.47.86/www. lelatina.com). Mº Hôtel de Ville. **Admission** €8; €6.50 Mon, Tue, students, under-20s. **No credit cards. Map** p406 K6.

The exciting programming at this flag-bearer for Latin cultures runs the gamut from Argentinian to Romanian films. Latin dance features at the €17 film-dinner-dancing deals on Monday and Wednesday evenings.

★ La Pagode

57bis rue de Babylone, 7th (01.45.55.48.48). Mº St-François-Xavier. **Admission** €8.50; €7 Mon, Wed, students, under-21s. **No credit cards. Map** p405 F7.

This glorious edifice is not, as local legend might have it, a block-by-block import, but a 19th-century replica of a pagoda by a French architect. Renovated in the late 1990s, this is one of the loveliest cinemas in the world.

Studio 28

10 rue Tholozé, 18th (01.46.06.36.07/www. cinemastudio28.com). Mº Abbesses or Blanche. **Admission** €7.50; €6.30 students, under-18s. **No credit cards. Map** p401 H1.

Studio 28 was the venue for the first screening of Buñuel's scandalous *L'Age d'Or*, and this historic cinema also features in the more heartwarming *Amélie*. It offers a decent repertory mixture of classics and recent movies, complete with Dolby sound and a rather civilised bar for a pre- or post-screening tipple.

Studio Galande

42 rue Galande, 5th (01.43.54.72.71/www.studio galande.fr). Mº Cluny La Sorbonne or St-Michel. **Admission** €7.80; €6 Wed, students. **No credit cards. Map** p408 J7.

Some 20 different films are screened in subtitled versions at this venerable Latin Quarter venue every week: international arthouse fare, combined with the occasional instalment from the *Matrix* series.

La Pagode.

INSIDE TRACK TUBE TAKES

The métro is, perhaps unsurprisingly, a popular Paris film location. These days, nearly all métro scenes in movies and advertising are shot in a disused station on line 3bis, **Porte des Lilas – Cinéma**, which is kept in working order by the RATP and hired out to production companies. It's currently open to the public only for the **Journées du Patrimoine** (*see p278*), but the Paris authorities are studying a proposal to dig a new tunnel linking line 3bis and 7bis, which would see Porte des Lilas – Cinéma returned to active transport duty in 2013.

▶ *On Fridays and Saturdays, fans of* The Rocky Horror Picture Show *turn up in drag, equipped with rice and water pistols.*

Festivals & events

The city plays host to a range of film festivals, some of them free, some taking place outdoors. *See also pp274-79* **Calendar**.

★ Salon du Cinéma
Parc des Expos, Porte de Versailles, 15th (www.salonducinema.com). M° Porte de Versailles. **Date** Jan.
This event features behind-the-scenes reconstructions of movie sets, allowing the public to watch the work of make-up artists, cameramen and stuntmen.

Festival International de Films de Femmes
Maison des Arts, pl Salvador-Allende, 94040 Créteil (01.49.80.38.98/www.filmsdefemmes. com). M° Créteil-Préfecture. **Date** Mar or Apr.
A selection of retrospectives and new international films by female directors.

Printemps du Cinéma
Various venues (www.printempsducinema.com). **Date** Mar.
Three days of bargain €3.50 entry films at cinemas all across Paris.

Côté Court
Ciné 104, 104 av Jean-Lolive, 93500 Pantin (01.48.91.24.91/www.cotecourt.org). M° Eglise de Pantin. **Date** June.
A great selection of new and old short films shown at Ciné 104 and a handful of neighbouring venues.

Paris Cinéma
Various venues (01.55.25.55.25/www.paris cinema.org). **Date** July.

The eighth edition off the capital's flagship festival is taking place in 2010, complete with official competitions and attendant stars.

★ Cinéma au Clair de Lune
Various venues (01.44.76.63.00/www.forum desimages.net). **Date** Aug.
Night-time films on giant open-air screens in squares and public gardens around town: a party atmosphere is guaranteed.

★ L'Etrange Festival
Forum des Images, for listing see p296 (01.44.76.63.00/www.etrange festival.com). **Date** Sept. **Map** p404 J5.
Explicit sex, gore and weirdness in the screenings and 'happenings' at this annual feast of all things unconventional draw large crowds.

La Master Class
Forum des Images (see p296). **Date** monthly throughout the year. **Map** p404 J5.
A global choice of new independent features, documentaries and short films.

BOOKSHOPS

Cinédoc
45-53 passage Jouffroy, 9th (01.48.24.71.36/ www.cine-doc.fr). M° Grands Boulevards. **Open** 10am-7pm Mon-Sat. **Credit** V. **Map** p402 J4.
Finding what you're looking for isn't easy in this narrow bookshop. Ask the staff or take pot luck among the old photos, film magazines and books.

Ciné Reflet
14 rue Monsieur le Prince, 6th (01.40.46.02.72). M° Odéon. **Open** 1-8pm Mon-Sat; 3-7pm Sun. **Credit** MC, V. **Map** p408 H7.
This sprawling shop is well stocked with old photos, posters, and new and second-hand books. The strong English-language selection includes the *Time Out Film Guide* and magazines like *Sight & Sound*.

★ Contacts
14 rue St-Sulpice, 6th (01.43.59.17.71/www. medialibrairie.com). M° Odéon. **Open** 10am-7pm Mon-Sat. **Credit** MC, V. **Map** p408 H7.
Truffaut's favourite *librairie* has been selling books on film for over 40 years. The stock is well organised, with a large and up-to-date selection of English-language titles. You'll also find *Film Comment* and *American Cinematographer*, plus a few videos.

Scaramouche
161 rue St-Martin, 3rd (01.48.87.78.58). M° Rambuteau. **Open** noon-1pm, 2.30-8pm Mon-Sat. **Credit** MC, V. **Map** p402 K5.
This shop covers cinema and *gestuelle* (mime and puppetry). There's a wide range of film titles in English, plus lots of publicity photos and portraits.

ARTS & ENTERTAINMENT

Galleries

Head to the Marais for the bigger picture.

Paris has been buffered from the worst excesses of the art world bubble. While lamentably few French artists have broken on to the international scene – Laurent Grasso, Philippe Parreno, Sophie Calle and Mathieu Mercier are a few exceptions – and most only attain relatively modest prices that would make Russian oligarchs, YBAs and the new Chinese millionaires snigger, contemporary art is currently *à la mode* in both public and private institutions, from installations at the Louvre or Musée Bourdelle to the annual show at Galeries Lafayette or the new prize awarded by the Hôtel Meurice.

Beyond the Marais powerhouses of Yvon Lambert, Chantal Crousel and Emmanuel Perrotin, brave new galleries continue to open and Paris remains a good place to discover a broad spectrum of international art.

GALLERIES IN PARIS

The commercial gallery scene is principally centred on the northern Marais. Across the river, the staid St-Germain-des-Prés scene has been revitalised by **Galerie Kamel Mennour** and **in situ Fabienne Leclerc**, joining a more staid modern art selection and galleries specialising in modern design. In the 13th arrondissement, the area around rue Louise-Weiss has never quite fulfilled its promise of becoming Paris's Chelsea: spaces are too small and quality too varied. Even so, **Air de Paris** and **Art:Concept** are usually worth a look. At the opposite end of the spectrum, the Champs-Elysées area is home to a handful of galleries presenting big bankable names, among more classic *antiquaires*, tribal and early 20th-century art.

The **Galeries Mode d'Emploi** leaflet (also online at www.fondation-entreprise-ricard.com) provides detailed weekly listings, as does **www.paris-art.com**. At *vernissage* time, usually Saturday evenings, the city's artists, collectors, critics and curators do the rounds of what's opening. Most galleries close from mid July to late August and at Christmas.

FAIR'S FAIR

The city's assorted art fairs are a good place to get an overview of the gallery scene. **FIAC** (Foire International d'Art Contemporain;

www.fiac.com), now split between the Grand Palais and the Cour Carrée du Louvre, is the most prestigious, with a mix of French and foreign galleries, plus a presentation of the shortlisted artists for the annual Prix Marcel Duchamp, awarded by collectors' association ADIAF to an artist working in France. **Slick** (www.slick-paris.com), which moved in 2009 to 104 (www.104.fr), focuses on young galleries, and is heavy on photography, graffiti art and simple spleen, followed in November by **Paris Photo** (www.parisphoto.fr) in the Carrousel du Louvre. Springtime sees **Art Paris** (www.artparis.fr) and the **Pavillon des Arts et du Design** (www.padparis.net), which mixes 20th-century design and fine art, and the specialist **Salon du Dessin Contemporain** (www.salondudessincontemporain.com) contemporary drawing fair.

BEAUBOURG & THE MARAIS

FAT Galerie

1 rue Dupetit-Thouars, 3rd (01.44.54.00.84/ www.fatgalerie.com). Mº Temple. **Open** 11am-7pm Tue-Sat. **Map** p409 L5.

Making their mark in the cluster of new galleries in the Haut Marais, Aurélia Lanson and Séverine van Warsch alternate shows by emerging artists – wall drawings by Cyprien Chabert, painter Lili Phung – with unusual furniture and objects by upcoming designers.

★ Galerie Alain Gutharc

7 rue St-Claude, 3rd (01.47.00.32.10/www.
alaingutharc.com). M° St-Sébastien Froissart.
Open 11am-1pm, 2-7pm Tue, Wed, Fri, Sat;
11am-1pm, 2-8pm Thur. **Map** p409 L6.
The last of the Bastille galleries has now moved to
the Marais. Gutharc talent-spots young French
artists, often giving them a first gallery show, and
also presents an annual art-design crossover.
Among recent discoveries, check out the dreamily
surreal paintings of Marlène Mocquet.

Galerie Almine Rech

19 rue de Saintonge, 3rd (01.45.83.71.90/
www.galeriealminerech.com). M° Filles
du Calvaire. **Open** 11am-7pm Tue-Sat.
Map p409 L5.
Continuing the rue Louise Weiss exodus, Almine
Rech has returned to the Marais. Spread over two
floors, her new gallery has more of an apartment feel
in which to show off big international names. Among
regulars are light installations by James Turrell, neo-
minimalists John McCracken and Anselm Reyle, the
eclectic clowning of Ugo Rondinone and powerful
films by French artist Ange Leccia.

Galerie Anne Barrault

22 rue St-Claude, 3rd (01.44.78.91.67/
www.galerieannebarrault.com). M° St-Sébastien
Froissart. **Open** 11am-7pm Tue-Sat.
Map p408 L6.
After initially concentrating on photography,
notably the provocative feminist stagings by
Katharina Bosse, Barrault now presents a wider
range of media, often with a strong graphic edge.

Galerie Anne de Villepoix

43 rue de Montmorency, 3rd (01.42.78.32.24/
www.annedevillepoix.com). M° Rambuteau.
Open 10am-7pm Mon-Sat. **Map** p402 K5.
As well as pieces by international names as
Doug Aitken and Erwin Wurm, Galerie Anne de
Villepoix features distinctive and varied talents on
the French scene, such as the bravura monochrome
paintings by Ming, witty conceptual pieces by
Franck Scurti and a politically loaded take on art
history by Kader Attia.

Galerie Chantal Crousel

10 rue Charlot, 3rd (01.42.77.38.87/www.
crousel.com). M° Filles du Calvaire. **Open**
11am-1pm, 2-7pm Tue-Sat. **Map** p409 L5.
Crousel celebrated the 25th anniversary of her
gallery with a move to this space in rue Charlot's
burgeoning design and fashion scene. She was the
first in France to show work by Mona Hatoum and
Tony Cragg. Hot younger talents include Rikrit
Tiravanija and Thomas Hirschhorn, as well as
Anri Sala and Melik Ohanian, two of France's most
exciting video artists, and Cuban duo Jennifer Allora
and Guillermo Calzadilla.

★ Galerie Chez Valentin

9 rue St-Gilles, 3rd (01.48.87.42.55/www.
galeriechezvalentin.com). M° Chemin Vert.
Open 11am-1pm, 2-7pm Tue-Sat. **Map** p409 L6.
Chez Valentin is a gallery at the experimental cutting edge, and shows here tend to be radically conceptual but often fun: look for pseudo-documentaries
by video-maker Laurent Grasso, photos by Nicolas
Moulin, installations by Pierre Ardouin and projects
by former Prix Duchamp winner Mathieu Mercier.

Galerie Daniel Templon

30 rue Beaubourg, 3rd (01.42.72.14.10/
www.danieltemplon.com). M° Rambuteau.
Open 10am-7pm Mon-Sat. **Map** p402 K5.
A Paris institution since the 1960s and conveniently
located opposite the Centre Pompidou, Galerie T
mainly shows paintings – wall-friendly items for
wealthy private collectors. Jean-Michel Alberola,
Gérard Garouste, Philippe Cognée and Vincent Corpet
all feature on the list, along with the American David
Salle and German expressionist Jonathan Meese.

Window Dressing

Art from a different angle.

Squashed in between bistro tables,
galleries and a wing of the art school
on a St-Germain side street, **Pièce
Unique** (4 rue Jacques Callot, 6th,
01.43.26.54.58, www.galeriepiece
unique.com) is indeed unique: a
shopfront space where a single specially
created artwork is displayed in the
window to catch the attention not just
of the art world cognoscenti but also of
casual passers-by – the *vitrine* remains
illuminated until 2am. Since opening
in 1991, it has presented one-offs by
artists as prestigious as Sol LeWitt,
Robert Longo, Maurizio Nannucci and
Dennis Oppenheim, with the latest
searing self-portrait from nonagenarian
Louise Bourgeois kicking off the autumn
2009-2010 season.

Over in the 13th, meanwhile, the
Random Gallery (between 28 and 32
rue Louise-Weiss, 13th; www.random-
gallery.com), which focuses on
experimental work by young artists,
is even more marginal: it is literally
the space between two of the galleries
on the rue Louise-Weiss strip. There is
no visible means of entry, but the site-
specific installations can be spied on
through a circular porthole in the wall of
galleries Air de Paris and Praz-Devallade
on either side.

★ **Galerie Dominique Fiat**
16 rue des Coutures-St-Gervais, 3rd
(01.40.29.98.80/www.galeriefiat.com).
M° St-Sébastien Froissart. **Open** 11am-7pm
Tue-Sat. **Map** p409 L6.
Fiat is part of a dynamic new generation of galleries.
Shows have included the word games and art world
parodies by novelist and artist Thomas Lélu (who
renamed the gallery Galerie Dominique Fiat Panda
for the occasion) and structures by Laurent Saksik.

★ **Galerie Emmanuel Perrotin**
76 rue de Turenne & 10 impasse St-Claude,
3rd (01.42.16.79.79/www.galerieperrotin.com).
M° St-Sébastien Froissart. **Open** 11am-7pm
Tue-Sat. **Map** p409 L5.
Now installed in an elegant Marais *hôtel particulier*,
Perrotin is one of the sharpest figures in town: not
content with owning a gallery in Miami and a glossy
magazine, he has recently jumped on the design
bandwagon with shows by Robert Stadler and Eric
Benqué. As well as the quirky Japanese set of
Takashi Murakami, Mariko Mori et al, and big
French names such as Sophie Calle, Xavier Veilhan,
Prix Marcel Duchamp winner Tatiana Trouvé and
Bernard Frize, he also features the radical Austrian
collective Gelatin.

Galerie Les Filles du Calvaire
17 rue des Filles du Calvaire, 3rd
(01.42.74.47.05/www.fillesducalvaire.com).
M° Filles du Calvaire. **Open** 11am-6.30pm
Tue-Sat. **Map** p408 L5.
Les Filles du Calvaire is based in spacious premises
in a two-storey glass-roofed industrial building in
the Marais, with an offshoot in Brussels. Shows
tend to concentrate on geometrical abstraction, featuring artists such artists as Olivier Mosset and James
Hyde, along with photography and installation.

Galerie Frédéric Giroux
8 rue Charlot, 3rd (01.42.71.01.02/www.
fredericgiroux.com). M° Filles du Calvaire.
Open 11am-7pm Tue-Sat. **Map** p408 L5.
Worth a look for some intriguing figures on the
French scene, including Delphine Kreuter, Rebecca
Bournigault and the sand-covered polystyrene
forms of Vincent Beurin.

Galerie Karsten Greve
5 rue Debelleyme, 3rd (01.42.77.19.37/www.
galerie-karsten-greve.com). M° St-Sébastien
Froissart. **Open** 11am-7pm Tue-Sat. **Map**
p409 L5.
The Cologne gallery's smart Paris outpost is the
venue for retrospective displays of top-ranking
artists: think big names rather than risk taking. Jannis
Kounellis, Louise Bourgeois, Pierre Soulages, John
Chamberlain and Dubuffet have all featured here.

★ **Galerie Laurent Godin**
5 rue du Grenier-St-Lazare, 3rd (01.42.71.10.66/
www.laurentgodin.com). M° Rambuteau. **Open**
11am-7pm Tue-Sat. **Map** p402 K5.
After running a public space in Lyon, Laurent Godin
has quickly made a name with his Paris gallery,
which features a diverse cross-generational mix,
ranging from New York neo-Pop artist Haim
Steinbach and waste-paper expert Wang Du to
promising installations by young French artist
Vincent Olinet.

Galerie Magda Danysz
78 rue Amelot, 11th (01.45.83.38.51/www.
magda-gallery.com). M° Filles du Calvaire. **Open**
11am-7pm Tue-Fri; 2-7pm Sat. **Map** p402 L5.
Magda Danysz has moved into a three-storey space
near the Cirque d'Hiver on the fringes of the Marais,
aiming to make contemporary art accessible. She

Galerie Emmanuel Perrotin.

has a taste for artists influenced by graffiti and animation, as well as the hybrid art-design-science output of the Ultralab cooperative.

Galerie Marian Goodman
*79 rue du Temple, 3rd (01.48.04.70.52/
www.mariangoodman.com). M° Rambuteau.*
Open 11am-7pm Tue-Sat. **Map** p409 K6.
The veteran New York gallery owner can be counted on to pull out the stops with impressive shows from a roster of big international names, such as Gerhard Richter, William Kentridge and Steve McQueen, presented in a lovely 17th-century mansion.

Galerie Michel Rein
*42 rue de Turenne, 3rd (01.42.72.68.13/www.
michelrein.com). M° Chemin Vert.* **Open** 11am-
7pm Tue-Sat. **Map** p409 L6.
Although hampered by lack of space, Rein presents interesting multidisciplinary artists, such as Fabien Verschaere, Dora Garcia and Saadane Afif, and has recently picked up some of the talents from eastern Europe, such as Dan Perjovschi and Mark Raidpere.

Galerie de Multiples
*17 rue St-Gilles, 3rd (01.48.87.21.77/www.galerie
demultiples.com). M° Chemin Vert.* **Open** 2-7pm
Tue-Sat. **Map** p409 L6.
Artist Mathieu Mercier was one of the founders of this gallery, dedicated to producing '*multiples*' (limited edition prints and artists' objects). Shows can take the form of anything from posters to soup ladles or pieces inspired by rock music.

Galerie Nelson-Freeman
*59 rue Quincampoix, 4th (01.42.71.74.56/www.
galerienelsonfreeman.com). M° Hôtel de Ville or
Rambuteau.* **Open** 11am-1pm, 2-7pm Tue-Sat.
Map p406 J6.

A tie-up with New York dealer Peter Freeman has given a more North American slant to the Nelson stable, although it continues to show big European names, such as photographer Thomas Ruff and Pedro Cabrita Reis, as well as representing late Fluxus maverick Robert Filliou.

Galerie Polaris
*15 rue des Arquebusiers, 3rd (01.42.72.21.27/
www.galeriepolaris.com). M° St-Sébastien
Froissart.* **Open** 1-7pm Tue-Fri; 11am-1pm,
2-7pm Sat. **Map** p409 L6.
Polaris occupies an old gym and shows artists mainly working in photo and video, such as Stéphane Couturier, known for his stunning, flattened perspective images of building sites.

★ Galerie Schleicher + Lange
*12 rue de Picardie, 3rd (01.42.77.02.77/www.
schleicherlange.com). M° Filles du Calvaire.*
Open 2-7pm Tue-Sat. **Map** p409 L5.
Shows put on by these two young Germans focus on artists yet to exhibit in Paris, alternating between upcoming London-based talents, such as Zoe

---

INSIDE TRACK VERNISSAGE

Timing your trip to Paris with a night of *vernissages* (private views) gives a taste not only of the art on offer but also of the personalities who frequent the art scene. The big rendezvous of the year is **Art St-Germain-des-Prés** (www.artsaint germaindespres.com) at the end of May. Nicknamed the 'block party', it sees almost 50 galleries get together to showcase their top artists.

Mendelson, and discoveries from eastern Europe. They also host Vidéo Surveillance, an occasional programme of video screenings.

Galerie Thaddaeus Ropac
7 rue Debelleyme, 3rd (01.42.72.99.00/ www.ropac.net). M° Filles du Calvaire. **Open** 10am-7pm Tue-Sat. **Map** p409 L5.
Ropac's main base is in Salzburg, but he also runs this attractive Paris gallery, featuring American Pop and neo-Pop by Warhol, Tom Sachs and Alex Katz, along with European artists such as Ilya Kabakov, Sylvie Fleury and Gilbert & George.

★ Galerie Yvon Lambert
108 rue Vieille-du-Temple, 3rd (01.42.71.09.33/ www.yvon-lambert.com). M° Filles du Calvaire. **Open** 10am-1pm, 2.30-7pm Tue-Fri; 10am-7pm Sat. **Map** p409 L5.
Lambert celebrated 30 years in the business in 2006, and remains a powerhouse of the French scene, with plenty of big-name stuff, a New York offshoot and a personal collection granted museum status in Avignon. The gallery includes a dedicated area for video installations, and the main space shows leading international names – American bigwigs Andres Serrano, Sol LeWitt, Nan Goldin and Jenny Holzer, plus next-generation artists Douglas Gordon and Jonathan Monk. The street-front art bookshop has a window showcase and basement gallery for younger talents.

Galerie Zürcher
56 rue Chapon, 3rd (01.42.72.82.20/www.galerie zurcher.com). M° Arts et Métiers. **Open** noon-7pm Tue-Sat. **Map** p402 K5.
Among the Chinese wholesalers north of Beaubourg, Zürcher shows emerging artists with a fresh take on painting and video: Marc Desgrandschamps, Camille Vivier and Elisa Sighicelli. Mathilde Rosier and Eléonore de Montesquiou are also featured.

THE CHAMPS-ELYSEES & NORTHERN PARIS

Galerie Jérôme de Noirmont
38 av Matignon, 8th (01.42.89.89.00/www. denoirmont.com). M° Miromesnil. **Open** 11am-7pm Mon-Sat. **Map** p401 E4.
In a chic space near the Elysées Palace, Noirmont puts on eye-catching shows featuring big names

---

INSIDE TRACK ART CRAWL

The **Navette de l'Art** ('art bus'; 01.47.00.90.85, www.art-process.com, €35-€50, reservations essential) gives a monthly insider's tour of new galleries, private collections and alternative spaces.

---

such as AR Penck, Jeff Koons, Shirin Neshat, Bettina Rheims, Fabrice Hyber, kitsch duo Pierre et Gilles, and art-world personalities Eva and Adèle.

Galerie Lelong
13 rue de Téhéran, 8th (01.45.63.13.19/ www.galerie-lelong.com). M° Miromesnil. **Open** 10.30am-6pm Tue-Fri; 2-6.30pm Sat. Closed Aug. **Map** p401 E3.
If you hanker after Miró, Tàpies, Bacon or Kounellis, Lelong is a safe bet, with its selection of bankable, postwar international names.

Russian Tea Room
1 av Trudaine, 9th (01.45.26.04.60/www. russiantearoom.fr). M° Anvers. **Open** 2-7pm Tue-Sat. **Map** p402 J2.
The Russian Tea Room was set up in 2004 to promote Russian art in Europe and opened its gallery space in 2007. Exhibitions focus mainly on the young post-*perestroika* generation with an emphasis on gritty photography.

ST-GERMAIN-DES-PRES

Galerie Denise René
196 bd St-Germain, 7th (01.42.22.77.57/www. deniserene.com). M° Rue du Bac or St-Germain-des-Prés. **Open** 10am-1pm, 2-7pm Tue-Sat. Closed Aug. **Map** p406 G6.
Denise René has remained committed to kinetic art, Op art and geometrical abstraction by Soto et al, ever since Jean Tinguely first presented his machines here in the 1950s.
Other locations 22 rue Charlot, 3rd (01.48.87.73.94).

Galerie G-P et N Vallois
36 rue de Seine, 6th (01.46.34.61.07/ www.galerie-vallois.com). M° Mabillon or Odéon. **Open** 10.30am-1pm, 2-7pm Mon-Sat. **Map** p408 H7.
Interesting conceptual work in all media includes the likes of American provocateur Paul McCarthy, Turner Prize winner Keith Tyson and a clutch of French thirty- and fortysomethings, including Alain Bublex and Gilles Barbier, as well as veteran *affichiste* Jacques Villeglé.

Galerie Kamel Mennour
47 rue St-André-des-Arts, 6th (01.56.24.03.63/ www.galeriemennour.com). M° Odéon or St-Michel. **Open** 11am-7pm Tue-Sat. **Map** p408 H7.
After bursting on to the St-Germain art scene with shows by fashion photography crossovers David LaChapelle and Ellen von Unwerth and filmmaker Larry Clark, and introducing emerging artists Kader Attia and Adel Abdessemed, Mennour has confirmed his presence on the gallery scene with a move to these grand new premises in a *hôtel particulier*. Recent shows by an impressive cross-generational

Galerie Kamel Mennour.

stable have included Daniel Buren, Claude Lévêque, France's representative at the 2009 Venice Biennale, and Huang Yong-Ping.

Galerie Lara Vincy
47 rue de Seine, 6th (01.43.26.72.51/www.lara-vincy.com). M° Mabillon, Odéon or St-Germain-des-Prés. **Open** 2.30-7pm Mon; 11am-1pm, 2.30-7pm Tue-Sat. **Map** p408 H7.
Liliane Vincy, daughter of the founder, is one of the few characters to retain something of the old St-Germain spirit and a sense of 1970s Fluxus-style happenings. Interesting theme and solo shows include master of the epigram Ben, as well as text-, music- and performance-related pieces.

Galerie Loevenbruck
40 rue de Seine, 6th (01.53.10.85.68/www.loevenbruck.com). M° Mabillon or Odéon.
Open 2-7pm Tue-Sat. **Map** p408 H6.
Loevenbruck has injected a dose of humour into St-Germain with artists – Virginie Barré, Bruno Peinado and Olivier Blankaert, and Philippe Mayeux – who treat conceptual concerns with a light touch and graphic talent.

★ in situ Fabienne Leclerc
6 rue du Pont-de-Lodi, 6th (01.53.79.06.12/www.insituparis.fr). M° Odéon or St-Michel.
Open 11am-7pm Tue-Sat. **Map** p408 H6.
Fabienne Leclerc consistently impresses with the quality of installations from a set of highly individual artists, including Mark Dion, known for his interest in zoology and classification, Indian star Subodh Gupta and video maestro Gary Hill.

13TH ARRONDISSEMENT
Air de Paris
32 rue Louise-Weiss, 13th (01.44.23.02.77/www.airdeparis.com). M° Chevaleret. **Open** 11am-7pm Tue-Sat. **Map** p407 M10.
This gallery shows experimental, neo-conceptual and chaotic material. A hip international stable of artists includes Liam Gillick, Carsten Höller, Sarah Morris and Philippe Parreno.

★ Art:Concept
16 rue Duchefdelaville, 13th (01.53.60.90.30/www.galerieartconcept.com). M° Bibliothèque François Mitterrand or Chevaleret. **Open** 11am-7pm Tue-Sat. **Map** p407 M10.
Despite its cramped conditions, Art:Concept manages to present some interesting, electic work. Look out for constructions by Richard Fauguet, as well as installations by Michel Blazy, whose favourite materials include the likes of shaving foam, spaghetti and dog biscuits.

Jousse Entreprise
24 & 34 rue Louise-Weiss, 13th (01.53.82.10.18/www.jousse-entreprise.com). M° Bibliothèque François Mitterrand or Chevaleret. **Open** 11am-7pm Tue-Sat. **Map** p407 M10.
Philippe Jousse presents contemporary artists – such as Matthieu Laurette, Frank Perrin and challenging video artist Clarisse Hahn – alongside 1950s avant-garde furniture by Jean Prouvé, lights by Serge Mouille and ceramics by Georges Jouve, which are also shown at sister design gallery at 18 rue de Seine in the 6th.

Gay & Lesbian

Let's paint this town pink.

Paris is home to a thriving LGBT community, visibly involved in every walk of life – right at the top of the tree sits openly gay mayor Bertrand Delanoë, who came out two years before running for office. Local gays and lesbians say that they encounter very little, if any, discrimination in their day-to-day lives, and feel integrated into mainstream society. However, the annual **Gay Pride March,** held on the last Sunday in June, is a powerful reminder of what the gay rights movement has accomplished over the last 30 years, and of what is yet to be achieved.

GETTING OUT AND ABOUT

Gays and lesbians live in every part of the city, but **Beaubourg** and the **'gay Marais'** are particularly gay-friendly. Most of the dedicated venues are to be found in the area bounded by rue des Archives, rue Vieille-du-Temple and rue Ste-Croix-de-la-Bretonnerie. A light lunch, coffee or cocktail at a neighbourhood café will provide ample opportunity to check out the talent, and a casual stroll through the nearby streets will introduce you to a seductive selection of shops. Fetishists, funky fashionistas, bohemians and bibliophiles will each find a boutique to suit their fancy. A good place to start is **Les Mots à la Bouche**, where you can peruse the international gay and lesbian press or pick up a few of the free monthly magazines listing the hottest events.

In the evening, kick off the action at a café or a restaurant before moving on to the bars and clubs, which don't really get going until after midnight. Start by mixing it up at **Le Mixer** or the nearby red hot **Raidd Bar**. The majestic **Bains Douches** (*see p330*), the club DJ David Guetta calls home, and the **Queen** on the Champs-Elysées remain clubbing institutions, as does the smaller and more intimate **L'Insolite**. The popular **La Scène Bastille** (*see p330*) is a relatively new trendsetter; on the other side of the coin is the oldest gay club in Paris, **Le Club 18**, which is always fun and still draws a great crowd, and the always surprising **Le Tango**. Lesbians can find a few nice bars of their own on rue du Roi de Sicile, or chill at the popular and friendly **Chez Moune** near Pigalle.

Information and resources

Magazines *Têtu* (www.tetu.com) and *Préf* (www.prefmag.com) report on goings-on in gay life and have text in English; *La Dixième Muse* (www.ladixiememuse.com) provides similar information for lesbians. There are also several free bi-weekly publications, distributed in gay bookshops, bars and clubs; the most useful are *2 X-Paris* (www.2xparis.fr), *Tribumove* (www.tribumove.com) and *AgendaQ*. And for the girls, there's *Barbi(e)turix* (www.myspace.com/barbieturix). Two excellent and informative websites provide regularly updated listings (in English) of all things gay and lesbian in the city: www.paris-gay.com and www.gayvox.com.

Centre Gai et Lesbien

63 rue Beaubourg, 3rd (01.43.57.21.47/ www.centrelgbtparis.org). M° Arts et Métiers or Rambuteau. **Open** 6-8pm Mon; 3-8pm Tue, Thur; 2-8pm Wed; 12.30-8pm Fri, Sat; 4-7pm Sun. *Library* 2-6pm Tue, Wed; 4-6pm Fri; 5-7pm Sat. **Map** p402 K6.

After many years on rue Keller, the Centre Gai et Lesbien has moved into more centrally located digs in the Marais. In addition to providing information on topics ranging from the sociopolitical (if you don't know what rights gays and lesbians have or don't have in France, you can find out all you need to know here) to the biomedical (the latest developments in the treatment of HIV, where to get tested for free), this multifunctional centre and library also hosts meetings for a variety of support groups and associations.

Inter-LGBT

c/o Maison des Associations du 3ème, boîte 8, 5 rue Perrée, 75003 Paris (01.72.70.39.22/ www.inter-lgbt.org). **Map** p409 L5.

The Interassociative Lesbienne, Gaie, Bi & Trans is an umbrella group of 50 LGBT associations. It organises the Printemps des Assoces in the Espace des Blancs Manteaux (48 rue Vieille-du-Temple, 4th) every April and the annual Gay Pride March.

SOS Homophobie

01.48.06.42.41/www.sos-homophobie.org. **Open** 6-10pm Mon, Wed, Fri; 8-10pm Tue, Thur; 2-4pm Sat; 6-8pm Sun.

Victims of and witnesses to homophobic crimes and discrimination can report them to this confidential service, which offers support and publishes an annual report on homophobia.

GAY PARIS

Bars & cafés

Le Bear's Den

6 rue des Lombards, 4th (01.42.71.08.20/ www.bearsden.fr). M° Châtelet or Hôtel de Ville. **Open** 4pm-2am Mon-Thur, Sun; 4pm-5am Fri, Sat. **Credit** MC, V. **Map** p406 J6.

The Bear's Den is a friendly local for bears, muscle bears, chubbies and their admirers. Visit the website for details on comically named theme nights such as 'Charcuterie'.

▶ *Bears, wolves and men who love hairy men also gather at the nearby Wolf; see p308.*

★ Le Café Arena

29 rue St-Denis, 1st (01.45.08.15.16). M° Châtelet. **Open** 9am-6am daily. **Credit** MC, V. **Map** p406 J5.

This bar-restaurant has a great terrace for people-watching and friendly staff; it's still the hottest rendezvous in Les Halles.

Café Cox

15 rue des Archives, 4th (01.42.72.08.00/ www.cox.fr). M° Hôtel de Ville. **Open** 1pm-2am daily. **No credit cards**. **Map** p409 K6.

Beefy, hairy, shaven-headed men congregate on the pavement in front of Café Cox for post-work drinks, before moving on to more intimate surroundings.

Le Duplex

25 rue Michel-le-Comte, 3rd (01.42.72.80.86/ www.duplex-bar.com). M° Hôtel de Ville or Rambuteau. **Open** 8pm-2am Mon-Thur, Sun; 8pm-4am Fri, Sat. **Credit** V. **Map** p409 K5.

This small bar caters to a thirtysomething crowd. It's a popular meeting place for various gay associations, with friendly staff and local art on the walls.

Eagle

33bis rue des Lombards, 1st (01.42.33.41.45). M° Les Halles. **Open** 6pm-4am Mon-Thur; 6pm-6am Fri, Sat; 5pm-4am Sun. **No credit cards**. **Map** p402 J6.

Formerly the London, this old bar has found new life, becoming a hit with bears, daddies, leathermen and the men who admire them. Have tea and cake on the patio early on, a shot of Jack at the bar later, or penetrate deeper and enjoy the disco backroom.

Etamine Café

13 rue des Ecouffes, 4th (01.44.78.09.62/ www.etamine-cafe.com). M° St-Paul. **Open** 11am-midnight Tue-Sun. **Credit** AmEx, MC, V. **Map** p409 K6.

This simple but delicious café is located very close to the lesbian bars of the Marais, and offers a contemporary and inventive twist on old classics. Excellent food, affordable prices, good atmosphere.

★ L'Interface Bar

34 rue Keller, 11th (01.47.00.67.15). M° Bastille or Ledru-Rollin. **Open** 3pm-2am Mon-Thur, Sun; 3pm-4am Fri, Sat. **No credit cards**. **Map** p407 M6.

ARTS & ENTERTAINMENT

Le Mixer. *See p308.*

The small, unpretentious Interface is on the trendy and *très* gay rue Keller. Friendly staff cater mostly to thirtysomethings; this is a great place in which to start the evening before heading off to the Scène nightclub around the corner or the hardcore Keller leather bar down the road.

Le Mixer

23 rue Ste-Croix-de-la-Bretonnerie, 4th (01.48.87.55.44). Mº Hôtel de Ville. **Open** 5pm-2am daily. **Credit** AmEx, MC, V. **Map** p409 K6.
A mixed, young and carefree crowd gathers at this watering hole for cocktails before heading off to the clubs. DJs spin techno and house to energise the crowd. Some nights are strictly for girls. *Photo p307.*

★ Open Café

17 rue des Archives, 4th (01.42.72.26.18/ www.opencafe.fr). Mº Hôtel de Ville or Rambuteau. **Open** 11am-2am Mon-Thur, Sun; 11am-4am Fri, Sat. **Credit** MC, V. **Map** p409 K6.
Cruise and be cruised in the café everybody visits at some point in the evening. Great staff and prompt service help. Pop out on to the terrace, and enjoy the people-watching at any time of the day or night.

★ Le Quetzal

10 rue de la Verrerie, 4th (01.48.87.99.07). Mº Hôtel de Ville. **Open** 5pm-5am daily. **Credit** MC, V. **Map** p409 K6.
This bar is considered to be one of the 'musts' of the Marais, as it's often filled with hot men and a few drag queens who help to keep things lively. You might be able to find some action in the small dark space upstairs.

Raidd Bar

23 rue du Temple, 4th (01.42.77.04.88/www. raiddbar.com). Mº Hôtel de Ville. **Open** 5pm-5am daily. **Credit** (min €10) MC, V. **Map** p406 K6.
The Raidd is standing room only at street level, with another bar down below. The hot, herculean bartenders take turns in the wall-mounted shower for nightly shows and the dancefloor is jam-packed.

★ Wolf

37 rue des Lombards, 1st (01.40.28.02.52/ www.wolfparis.com). Mº Les Halles. **Open** 5pm-2am daily. **No credit cards. Map** p402 J6.
Popular with bears, wolves, otters and a variety of other species, mostly on the hairy side. Everyone is welcome, though, and the ambience is laid-back.

Restaurants

Le Bar à Manger (BAM)

13 rue des Lavandières-Ste-Opportune, 1st (01.42.21.01.72). Mº Les Halles. **Open** noon-5pm, 7-11pm Tue-Sat. **Credit** MC, V. **Map** p408 J6.

Excellent, creative cuisine in a pleasant, relaxed setting. There are *prix fixe* menus available at lunch (€18) and dinner (€29).

Le Gai Moulin

10 rue St-Merri, 4th (01.48.87.06.00/www.le-gai-moulin.com). Mº Hôtel de Ville. **Open** noon-midnight daily. **Credit** MC, V. **Map** p406 K6.
One of the oldest gay-run restaurants in Paris, the Gai Moulin opened its doors in 1981 and recently moved a few doors down from its original location (now a smaller café, Le Petit Canaillou, run by the same team). The owner is famously convivial, creating a lovely, friendly atmosphere. On Tuesdays a pianist belts out French songs, and it's not uncommon for the whole room to sing along.

Le Kofi du Marais

54 rue Ste-Croix-de-la-Bretonnerie, 4th (01.48.87.48.71). Mº Hôtel de Ville. **Open** noon-11pm daily. **Credit** AmEx, MC, V. **Map** p406 K6.
Modern, simple cooking with an American twist is the speciality here. Club sandwiches, burgers and salads are menu staples. Prices are reasonable and the service is good too.

★ Aux Trois Petits Cochons

31 rue Tiquetonne, 2nd (01.42.33.39.69/ www.auxtroispetitscochons.fr). Mº Etienne Marcel. **Open** 7.30pm-midnight. **Credit** MC, V. **Map** p406 J5.

Le Quetzal.

This gay-owned, gay-run restaurant serves up traditional French cuisine with a contemporary twist. The three-course menu (€33) changes daily and is based on the freshest ingredients available. It's a very popular place, so booking is recommended.

▶ If it's too busy, try sister restaurant Pig'z, 5 rue Marie Stuart, 2nd (01.42.33.05.89).

La Victoire Suprême du Coeur
27-31 rue du Bourg-Tibourg, 4th (01.40.41.95.03/www.vscoeur.com). M° Hotel de Ville. **Open** noon-3pm, 6.30-11pm daily. **Credit** MC, V. **Map** p409 K6.
Set on a supremely cute street in the heart of the Marais, this gay-friendly restaurant finally gives Parisians a decent vegetarian option, serving up traditional dishes with a veggie twist (mushroom roast, seitan burger).

Ze Restoo
41 rue des Blancs-Manteaux, 3rd (01.42.74.10.29). M° Rambuteau. **Open** 7pm-1am Mon-Sat. **Credit** AmEx, MC, V. **Map** p409 K6.
This restaurant has become a popular place in which to eat with friends before heading out for a fun-filled evening. There's a very relaxed atmosphere, with good service and imaginative dishes.

Clubs

As well as the venues listed below, a mixed but increasingly gay crowd mingles at **Les Bains Douches** (*see p330*), **Nouveau Casino** (*see p329*) and **La Scène Bastille** (*see p330*). Most gay clubs are very hetero-friendly.

★ Le Club 18
18 rue de Beaujolais, 1st (01.42.97.52.13/ www.club18.fr). M° Palais-Royal or Pyramides. **Open** midnight-dawn Fri-Sun. **Admission** (incl 1 drink) €10. **Credit** *Bar* MC, V. **Map** p402 H5.
The oldest gay club in Paris attracts a young and beautiful clientele. It is not very big, and the decor isn't all that great, but the music is fun and there's a very laid-back vibe. Everyone is here to dance and have a good time.

Le CUD Bar
12 rue des Haudriettes, 3rd (01.42.77.44.12/ www.cud-paris.com). M° Rambuteau. **Open** 4pm-7am daily. **Credit** MC, V. **Map** p409 K5.
Upstairs is a laid-back bar, but downstairs in the old cellar is a dancefloor that can get very crowded, especially after 2am. The crowd is a mixed bunch, and it's popular with the bears.

Les Follivores & les Crazyvores
Bataclan, 50 bd Voltaire, 11th (01.43.14.00.30/ www.follivores.com). M° Oberkampf. **Open** 11.30pm-dawn. **Admission** (incl 1 drink) €17. **Credit** V. **Map** p407 M5.

Going Straight
Integrate to accumulate.

The economic crisis hasn't spared Paris's LGBT community, with several venues closing down – gone, among others, are Pulp, Le Deep, Nyx, Entre Deux Eaux and Sauna Bastille. And while a couple of new venues have opened, all in all the scene has shrunk. But the good news is that the old standbys are just as crowded as ever, and those LGBT-owned businesses that have weathered the crisis are thriving. Why? Because businesses have managed to integrate themselves so successfully that they are now attracting a significant non-LGBT clientele. You're as likely to find as many breeders as gays posing at the Open Café or Queen, eating in restaurants like Aux Trois Petits Cochons, and browsing in stores like Les Dessous d'Apollon and Boy'z Bazaar. And while purists worry that that LGBT businesses are losing their special character, most entrepreneurs are delighted and see this phenomenon as a sign of real integration into city life, leaving one wondering if labels like 'LGBT owned and operated' or 'gay-friendly' even matter any more. This quiet revolution is not only proof that the free market does not discriminate, but it's also providing a much-needed service to the heterosexual community: after all, somebody has to teach straight men how to dress with style.

Twice a month, the Bataclan concert hall transforms itself into a club to host these two hugely popular parties. Crazyvores features music from the 1970s and '80s, and at Follivores the DJs spin gay classics from all eras mixed up with cutting-edge techno. These are big events with exuberant crowds; the drag queens put on their best ball-gowns and biggest wigs, and the men sport their tightest tops. Great fun.

L'Insolite
33 rue des Petits-Champs, 1st (01.40.20.98.59/ www.insolite-club.fr). M° Pyramide. **Open** 11pm-5am Mon-Thur, Sun; 11pm-7am Fri, Sat. **Admission** free Wed, Thur, Sun; €10 (incl 1 drink) Fri, Sat. **Credit** *Bar* MC, V. **Map** p401 H4.
Hidden away underneath an old courtyard, this small club is a fun and friendly nightspot; the music tends to major in '80s disco hits and new wave, with a few more recent club hits thrown in for good measure.

ARTS & ENTERTAINMENT

Queen

102 av des Champs-Elysées, 8th *(01.53.89.08.90/www.queen.fr). M° George V.* **Open** midnight-7am Mon-Thur, Sun; midnight-8am Fri, Sat. **Admission** €15 Mon-Thur, Sun; €20 Fri, Sat. **Credit** *Bar* AmEx, MC, V. **Map** p400 D4.

One of the oldest and largest clubs, Queen's main gay nights are Saturday@Queen and Overkitsch on Sundays in the summer months, but every night is a little gay. Big-name DJs often spin here to a crowd peppered with VIPs.

★ Le Tango (La Boîte à Frissons)

13 rue au Maire, 3rd (01.42.72.17.78/www. *boite-a-frissons.fr). M° Arts et Métiers.* **Open** 8pm-2am Thur; 10.30pm-5am Fri, Sat; 6-11pm Sun. **Admission** €8; free Thur. **Credit** V. **Map** p409 K5.

Wacky crowd, Madonna songs and accordion tunes. At the Friday and Saturday Bal de la Boîte à Frissons, couples dance the foxtrot, tango, madison or *guinguette* in the early part of the evening, followed after midnight by music of every variety except techno. This unusual old dance hall never fails to entertain.

Sex clubs & saunas

Le Bunker

150 rue St-Maur, 11th (01.53.36.78.87/www. *bunker-cruising.com). M° Goncourt.* **Open** 4pm-2am Mon-Thur; 4pm-3.30am Fri; 4pm-4.30am Sat; 4pm-1am Sun. **Admission** €7.50; €6 under-26s. **Map** p403 M4.

This cruising club, located not far from the Oberkampf bar district in a remote corner of the 11th, is the hottest in Paris. It features all-naked and underwear-only nights during the week, and hardcore themes at the weekend. Friday is a very popular night, as is the first Saturday of the month, when Le Bunker hosts its S&M 'Red and Black Night' – not for the faint-hearted.

Le Dépot

10 rue aux Ours, 3rd (01.44.54.96.96/www. *suncity.fr). M° Etienne Marcel.* **Open** 2pm-8am Mon-Sat; 2-9pm Sun. **Admission** €7.50 before 11pm, €10 after 11pm Mon-Thur, Sun; €13 (incl 1 drink) Fri, Sat. **Credit** MC, V. **Map** p402 K5.

A very busy dance club upstairs with a labyrinthine maze of cubicles, glory holes and darkrooms downstairs. The glory days of this glory hole are gone now, but it still draws a crowd, particularly on the weekends. Pickpockets work the darkrooms, so be careful.

★ IDM

4 rue du Fbg-Montmartre, 9th (01.45.23.10.03/ *www.idm-sauna.com). M° Grands Boulevards.* **Open** noon-1am Mon-Thur, Sun; noon-2am Fri, Sat. **Admission** *Before 9.30pm* €20;

€13 under-35s; €10 under-30s. *After 9.30pm* €10; €5 under-30s. **Credit** MC, V. **Map** p402 J4.

The city's best gay sauna has three levels and plenty of cabins and corridors to prowl. The wet sauna is on two levels, and the small relaxation pool and showers are always at the perfect temperature. A few times a month, there are also performances by drag queens and other singers.

Next

87 rue St-Honoré, 1st (www.lenext.fr). M° Les *Halles.* **Open** noon-3am Mon-Thur; non-stop Fri-Sun. **Admission** €7 before 7pm; €10 (incl 1 drink) after 7pm; €6 (incl 1 drink) under-26s. **Credit** MC, V. **Map** p402 J5.

This hot sex club is located in one of the chicest parts of the capital. It doesn't really get going until after many clubs have closed, and at 6am on a Sunday morning it's probably the hottest, hardest place in town. The bar upstairs is a nice place to mingle before heading downstairs to the sexy labyrinth.

Le QG

12 rue Simon le Franc, 4th (01.48.87.74.18). *M° Rambuteau.* **Open** 5pm-8am Mon-Fri; 2pm-7am Sat, Sun. **Credit** MC, V. **Map** p406 K6.

This bar is well known among those who enjoy the harder gay scene. Upstairs is a simple bar, but downstairs is where the real action is, with a very well equipped backroom/dungeon. It's a small place and gets crowded at weekends.

Sun City

62 bd de Sébastopol, 3rd (01.42.74.31.41/ *www.suncity.fr). M° Etienne Marcel.* **Open** noon-6am daily. **Admission** €18 Mon-Fri; €19.50 Sat, Sun; €11 under-26s. **Credit** MC, V. **Map** p402 J5.

Owned and operated by the Dépot team (*see above*), this Bollywood-themed venue is the largest gay sauna in Europe, with a small pool, large steam room, gym and bar. The clientele is very good looking and knows it, so there's a lot of attitude.

Shops & services

Boy'z Bazaar

5 rue Ste-Croix-de-la-Bretonnerie, 4th *(01.42.71.67.00/www.boyzbazaar.com).* *M° Hôtel de Ville or St-Paul.* **Open** 2-10pm daily. **Credit** AmEx, MC, V. **Map** p409 K6.

Some of the city's trendiest clothes for nightclubbers, fashionistas and urban hipsters, in the heart of the gaybourhood.
Other locations 5 rue des Guillemites, 4th (01.42.71.63.86).

Les Dessous d'Apollon

15 rue du Bourg-Tibourg, 4th (01.42.71.87.37/ www.lesdessousdapollon.com). M° Hôtel de Ville or St-Paul. **Open** noon-7.30pm Tue-Fri; 11am-8pm Sat; 2-7pm Sun. **Credit** AmEx, DC, MC, V. **Map** p409 K6.
Probably the most extensive selection of underwear – ranging from the functional to the downright eccentric – that you'll ever encounter, plus T-shirts and accessories.

IEM

16 rue Ste-Croix-de-la-Bretonnerie, 4th (01.42.74.01.61/www.iem.fr). M° Hôtel de Ville. **Open** 1-8pm Mon-Thur; 1-10pm Fri, Sat; 3-7pm Sun. **Credit** AmEx, MC, V. **Map** p403 M4.
This sex hypermarket caters for those keen on the harder side of gay life. Videos, clothes and gadgets can all be found, and there are leather and rubber goods upstairs.
Other locations 43 rue de l'Arbre Sec, 1st (01.42.96.05.74).

★ Legay Choc

45 rue Ste-Croix-de-la-Bretonnerie, 4th (01.48.87.56.88/www.legaychoc.fr). M° Hôtel de Ville. **Open** 8am-8pm Mon, Tue, Thur-Sun. **No credit cards.** **Map** p409 K6.
Run by two brothers (one gay, one straight) whose surname just happens to be Legay, this Marais *boulangerie* and *pâtisserie* is very popular. The pastries are delightful, and the lunch-hour sandwiches are generous, so expect lengthy queues. A satellite store, serving only sandwiches, is at 17 rue des Archives (01.48.87.24.61).
► *For that special occasion, a penis-shaped loaf can be made to order.*

★ Les Mots à la Bouche

6 rue Ste-Croix-de-la-Bretonnerie, 4th (01.42.78.88.30/www.motsbouche.com). M° Hôtel de Ville or St-Paul. **Open** 11am-11pm Mon-Sat; 1-9pm Sun. **Credit** AmEx, MC, V. **Map** p409 K6.
An institution in the Marais, this bookshop has a large selection of gay fiction, non-fiction, magazines, and English-language books.

Nickel

48 rue des Francs-Bourgeois, 4th (01.42.77.41.10/ www.nickel.fr). M° Hôtel de Ville or Rambuteau. **Open** 11am-7.30pm Mon, Tue, Fri, Sat; 11am-9pm Wed, Thur. **Credit** AmEx, MC, V. **Map** p406 L6.
Body and skincare treatments, strictly for men. A one-hour facial is €48-€77, a manicure €21 and an hour-long massage €48-€69. Staff are adept, friendly and knowledgeable.

Plus Que Parfait

23 rue des Blancs-Manteaux, 4th (01.42.71.09.05). M° Hôtel de Ville or St-Paul. **Open** 3-8pm Mon; noon-8pm Tue-Sat; 3-7pm Sun. *Clothes deposit* Mon-Fri. **Credit** MC, V. **Map** p409 K6.
This *dépôt vente*, where pristine, second-hand designer clothing is sold on commission, is a veritable treasure trove of men's fashion finds.

Space Hair

10 rue Rambuteau, 3rd (01.48.87.28.51). M° Rambuteau. **Open** noon-10pm Mon; 10am-10pm Tue-Sat; 11.30am-8pm Sun. **Credit** MC, V. **Map** p409 K6.
Space Hair is divided into two salons, Cosmic and Classic, with a 1980s kitsch feel, late opening hours and cute stylists; it's best to book ahead.

Where to stay

Hôtel Central Marais

2 rue Ste-Croix-de-la-Bretonnerie, 4th (01.48.87.56.08/www.hotelcentralmarais.com). M° Hôtel de Ville or St-Paul. **Rates** €89 single or double; €109 triple; €7 breakfast. **Credit** MC, V. **Map** p409 K6.

Legay Choc.

If location and affordable rates are more important than plush surroundings, this aptly named hotel is a good bet. The barmen of the Central bar (located below the hotel) act as receptionists from 5pm until 2am, and can keep you updated on the local nightlife.

Hôtel Duo
11 rue du Temple, 4th (01.42.72.72.22/www.duo paris.com). M° Hôtel de Ville. **Rates** €200-€340 double. **Credit** AmEx, DC, MC, V. **Map** p406 K6.
The mixed but very gay-friendly Duo is a stylish place to rest your head. What's more, it has helpful staff at the reception – a rarity in this trendy area.

LESBIAN PARIS

Famous club Pulp is much missed, but the girlie scene continues to flourish, especially near the corner of rue du Roi de Sicile and rue des Ecouffes in the Marais. Most of the bars welcome men accompanied by women, but a few are women only. Some girl-only parties are staged at clubs such as **Le Tango** (*see p310*); see the free monthly magazine *Barbi(e)turix* for listings.

Le 3W Kafé
8 rue des Ecouffes, 4th (01.48.87.39.26). M° St-Paul. **Open** 6pm-2am daily. **Credit** MC, V. **Map** p409 K6.
A convivial place where beautiful women go to have a drink, meet other women and listen to good music. There's a small dance space in the basement, and a number of theme nights every month. The three Ws stand for 'women with women'.

★ La Champmeslé
4 rue Chabanais, 2nd (01.42.96.85.20/www.la champmesle.com). M° Bourse or Pyramides. **Open** 4pm-4am daily. **Credit** MC, V. **Map** p402 H4.
This veteran girlie bar remains a popular venue for lesbian locals and visitors. Beer is the drink of choice; pull up a seat and enjoy the regular cabaret nights.

Chez Moune
54 rue Pigalle, 9th (01.45.26.64.64/www. chezmoune.com). M° Pigalle. **Open** 10.30pm-late Tue-Sat. **Credit** MC, V. **Map** p401 H2.
Probably the oldest lesbian cabaret in Paris, Chez Moune opened in 1936 and still has nightly shows. Saturdays are traditionally women only, but in the last year other phallo-friendly dance parties and cabaret shows have occasionally been held.

Le Day Off
10 rue de l'Isly, 8th (01.45.22.87.90/www.leday off.com). M° Gare St-Lazare. **Open** 11am-3pm, 5pm-3am Mon-Fri. **Credit** MC, V. **Map** p401 G3.
An apt name for this weekday-only pub-restaurant – heavy drinking enjoyed by work-weary lesbians. It gets crowded in the early evening.

Dollhouse
24 rue du Roi de Sicile, 4th (01.40.27.09.21/ www.dollhouse.fr). M° St-Paul. **Open** 2-8pm Mon, Sun; 1-8pm Tue-Sat. **Credit** MC, V. **Map** p409 L6.
This store, located close to 3W, specialises in lingerie and gadgets for girls. Upstairs you'll find a selection of sophisticated and sexy underwear; head downstairs for the sexcessories.

Les Jacasses
5 rue des Ecouffes, 4th (01.42.71.15.51). M° St-Paul. **Open** 6pm-2am daily. **Credit** MC, V. **Map** p409 K6.
This new, relaxed bar for women, just around the corner from the girlie bars on rue du Roi de Sicile, makes a welcome addition to the neighbourhood.

O'Kubi Caffé
219 rue St-Maur, 10th (01.42.01.35.08/ www.okubicaffe.com). M° Goncourt. **Open** 6pm-2am Tue-Sat; noon-11pm Sun. **Credit** MC, V. **Map** p403 M3.
O'Kubi recently celebrated its second anniversary and continues to grow in popularity. It also has a bar and serves light food.

★ Le Rive Gauche
1 rue du Sabot, 6th (01.40.20.43.23/www.lerive gauche.com). M° St-Germain-des-Prés. **Open** 11pm-dawn Fri, Sat. **Admission** €10-€15. **No credit cards. Map** p405 G7.
This weekend women-only nightclub is one of the hottest places on the lesbian scene. The decor is '70s and the music eclectic.

Le So What!
30 rue du Roi de Sicile, 4th (no phone). M° St-Paul. **Open** 5pm-2am Tue-Fri; 5pm-4am Sat, Sun. **Credit** MC, V. **Map** p409 L6.
This site's previous occupant, the Nyx, went out of business last year and was quickly replaced by the So What! bar. It is primarily a girlie bar, but everyone's welcome. Recent theme nights have included live rock and drag queens.

Le Troisième Lieu
62 rue Quincampoix, 4th (01.48.04.85.64). M° Rambuteau. **Open** 6pm-2am Mon-Sat. **Credit** MC, V. **Map** p406 K5.
Elaborate *tartines*, delicious desserts and strong drinks are the fare at this lesbian-run bar and restaurant. Despite its militant subtitle ('Cantine des Ginettes Armées'), the vibe is jovial. There are also areas devoted to music and dancing.

Unity Bar
176-178 rue St-Martin, 3rd (01.42.72.70.59/ http://unity.bar.free.fr). M° Rambuteau. **Open** 4pm-2am daily. **No credit cards. Map** p402 K5.
This ladies-only bar is more butch than lipstick, with pool tables and a good beer selection.

Music

From Early Music to electro, via jazz, rap and chanson.

While Carla Bruni may have done wonders for raising the profile of French music with her winsome folky pop, and Sarkozy's son is also in the business as a hip hop producer, there is much more to the French music scene than pure political connections. The big news in the world of classical music is the construction of the Philharmonie, a prestigious new concert venue for the city. Paris's vibrant opera scene continues to thrill, jazz is enjoying a mini revival, talented new rock bands are emerging, as are venues to accommodate them, and *chanson* is managing to reinvent itelf for a 21st-century audience. Musically speaking, this town is jumping.

ARTS & ENTERTAINMENT

Classical & Opera

After years of argument and controversy, a muddy patch near the Cité de la Musique is tangible evidence that construction of the much-vaunted **Philharmonie** has finally begun. And architect Jean Nouvel's 2,400-seat concert hall is set to open on time in 2012. The Philharmonie will give the city a major venue for the symphonic repertoire, as well as hosting jazz and world music.

Across the city at the **Opéra de Paris**, the top job of director has just passed to Nicolas Joel, who was previously in charge of the Capitole in Toulouse – a choice guaranteed to please conservative operagoers, but frustrate modernist fans of the outgoing Gerard Mortier, whose controversial new productions infuriated and thrilled in equal measure. Those in search of the avant-garde will, however, be comforted by the ongoing success of the **Ensemble Intercontemporain**, and the important role that **IRCAM** continues to play in contemporary musical creation in Europe, forming exciting young composers such as Bruno Mantovani.

Although the Philharmonie is being built as a home for the **Orchestre de Paris** and its new musical director Paavo Järvi, it will also provide a welcome alternative to the **Maison de Radio France**, which is currently the permanent home of the estimable **Orchestre Philharmonique de Radio France** and the **Orchestre National de France**.

A success story of recent seasons has been the return to glory of the **Opéra Comique**. Under the direction of Jérôme Deschamps, the house has rediscovered a specifically French repertoire – figures like Hérold and Grétry, as well as their Baroque predecessors and contemporary successors, can now be seen in a perfect setting. There's disappointment, though, at the **Châtelet**, where Jean-Luc Choplin's popular programming is faltering – this season's *The Sound of Music* may please retro musical lovers, but is indicative of a general lack of musical beef.

Early Music is an abiding passion. The quest for authenticity and period instruments now extends to Mozart and even early Romantic music. **Les Arts Florissants**, under the

About the authors

Stephen Mudge *is the French correspondent for* Opera News, *and also writes about music and food for* Time Out *and the BBC.*

Anna Brooke *lives in Paris and is a regular contributor to* Time Out's *Paris publications.*

INSIDE TRACK
CLASSICAL CUTS

Many venues and orchestras offer cut-rate tickets to students under 26 an hour before curtain-up. For the Fête de la Musique (21 June) all events are free, and year-round freebies crop up at the Maison de Radio France and the Conservatoire de Paris, as well as in certain churches.

Franco-American William Christie, and Jean-Claude Malgoire's ensemble based in the north of France take up the vanguard for their performances of Lully and Rameau. The younger generation of Christophe Rousset and glamorous Emmanuelle Haïm are respected international figures in the field, and it could be argued that French musicians now hold European supremacy in this repertoire.

There's plenty of Early Music going on in the churches too. The **Festival d'Art Sacré** (01.44.70.64.10) presents church music in authentic settings in the run-up to Christmas; **Les Grands Concerts Sacrés** (01.48.24.16.97) and **Musique et Patrimoine** (01.42.50.96.18) also offer concerts at various churches. Music in Notre-Dame cathedral is taken care of by **Musique Sacrée Notre-Dame** (01.44.41.49.99, tickets 01.42.34.56.10), while the excellent **Académie Vocale de Paris** (01.70.32.39.92) gives a concert every Saturday in the Eglise Saint-Merry.

The main musical provider in summer is the **Paris Quartier d'Eté** festival (01.44.94.98.00, www.quartierdete.com), with concerts in gardens across the city. The **Festival de Saint-Denis** (01.48.13.06.07, www.festival-saint-denis.com) also offers top names in a spectacular setting, while the candlelit **Chopin Piano Festival** in the Jardin de Bagatelle in the Bois de Boulogne (01.45.00.22.19, www.frederic-chopin.com) looks all set to celebrate the composer's upcoming bicentenary (*see p315* When Chopin Met Sand).

INFORMATION AND TICKETS

For listings, see *L'Officiel des Spectacles* or *Pariscope*. Monthly magazines *Le Monde de la Musique* and *Diapason* also list classical concerts, while *Opéra* magazine provides good coverage of all things vocal. Look out too for *Cadences* and *La Terrasse*, two free monthlies distributed outside concerts.

ORCHESTRAS & ENSEMBLES

★ Les Arts Florissants

01.43.87.98.88/www.arts-florissants.com.
William Christie's 'Arts Flo' remains France's leading Early Music group and his conducting of Rameau and Lully have become benchmarks of Baroque performance. This season the group celebrates its 30th birthday with concerts across the capital and much authentic jubilation. The Jardin des Voix continues to play an important role in supplying the burgeoning Early Music scene with exciting young talent.

Ensemble Intercontemporain

01.44.84.44.50/www.ensembleinter.com.
Glamorous Finnish conductor Susanna Mälkki is the musical director of this bastion of contemporary music founded by, and still often conducted by, Pierre Boulez. The exacting standard of the 31 soloists is beyond reproach, and the ensemble has an enviable international reputation, making it one of the most poular on the Paris music scene. This season it is kept busy in the capital with the Tristan Murail retrospective and, more predictably, Boulez.

Ensemble Orchestral de Paris

08.00.42.67.57/www.ensemble-orchestral-paris.com.
The greatly respected John Nelson has been replaced by Joseph Swensen, who becomes the principal guest conductor of this chamber orchestra for the next two seasons. The orchestra struggles to find its specificity in a competitive field, but this season the ensemble is heading out for mini stays in popular areas of the city in an admirable quest to try and attract new audiences.

Orchestre Colonne

01.42.33.72.89/www.orchestrecolonne.fr.
Sometimes found at the Salle Gaveau (*see p317*), this orchestra – led by composer Laurent Petitgirard – has intelligent programming, with every concert teaming a contemporary work with more popular repertoire. The excellent series of *concerts éveil* continues to provide bargain tickets for parents and children, making an ideal introduction to classical music.

Orchestre Lamoureux

01.58.39.30.30/www.orchestrelamoureux.com.
This worthy orchestra, which made the first recording of Ravel's *Boléro*, remains woefully underfunded, and its concert appearances in the capital are sparse. But musical director Yutaka Sado is a fine conductor, and his programming is uncompromising and prepared to take on the challenge of new and unusual repertoire.

Orchestre National de France

01.56.40.15.16/www.radiofrance.fr.
Daniele Gatti is now firmly in charge of France's leading orchestra, bringing along his own brand of warm Italianate theatricality, in sharp contrast to his predecessor, veteran Kurt Masur, and his more structured Germanic approach. Gatti is not afraid of a direct comparison, as his Mahler at the Châtelet showed.

★ Orchestre de Paris

01.42.56.13.13/www.orchestredeparis.com.
Many consider this orchestra to be the finest in France, and music director Christoph Eschenbach has done a lot to raise the standard of performance; his successor in 2010 is to be Paavo Järvi. For his last season Eschenbach completes his Mahler cycle and heads a programme of music that marks his time both as conductor and pianist. A magnificent series of piano concertos with some of the finest soloists in the world reaches a climax in June 2010

When Chopin Met Sand

Love and loss in 19th-century Paris.

The year 2010 is the bicentenary of Frédéric Chopin's birth in Poland, but it was Paris that played the leading part in his life story, and the city is celebrating with an exhibition and concerts at the Cité de la Musique (*see p316*), and programming at the annual summer piano festival in the Jardin de Bagatelle (*see p276*). The composer's relationship with the French capital and the writer George Sand are intriguing subjects, combining scandal, tragedy and genius among the world of the 19th-century Romantics.

When Chopin arrived in Paris in 1831, he lived in cramped accommodation at 27 rue Poissonière, where, according to the already delicate composer, 'everyone envies my view but nobody my stairs'. In 1836 he met George Sand at a salon hosted by the mistress of Franz Liszt, Countess Marie d'Agoult. At first he did not take much to the stern figure of Sand, but he invited her to a soirée where both he and Liszt played, and Sand lit up a fat cigar. Repelled yet fascinated by Sand's outspoken ideas, Chopin began an 11-year liaison with the writer, which, despite a brief romantic interlude, was predominantly based around a mother-son relationship.

Hoping to strengthen him, Sand carted the sickly Frédéric off to Mallorca, with her two children from a previous marriage, to spend a perishing winter in the monastery at Valldemossa. After a stay on Sand's estate in Nohant, the couple returned to Paris, where Chopin left his apartment and moved into Sand's house at 16 rue Pigalle, where they lived together with her children. In 1842, they moved to the area known as La Nouvelle Athènes, a popular haunt of the Romantics, where they occupied adjacent apartments on place d'Orléans.

The author nursed and cajoled her swooning composer, but by 1847 the relationship had run its course. Sand had always had a confrontational relationship with her daughter Sandrine, and when Chopin supported her marriage to the sculptor Auguste Clésinger, the fragile quartet was permanently fractured. Sand saw the possibility of literary copy in the relationship and wrote a fictionalised account, *Lucrezia Floriani* (1846), where maternal love triumphs over romantic love.

A broken Chopin continued composing until his death from tuberculosis two years later in an apartment on place Vendôme. He is buried in Père-Lachaise cemetery; his last published work was a cello and piano sonata suffused with a sense of tragedy and regret. As Franz Liszt was reported to have said when Sand brusquely summoned the composer to light her cigar: 'Pauvre Frédéric...'

ARTS & ENTERTAINMENT

Chopin and Sand.

with Radu Lupu and Nikolaï Lugansky. Pierre Boulez also returns for a series of concerts to trace his musical roots.

Orchestre Pasdeloup

01.42.78.10.00/www.concertspasdeloup.com.
The Pasdeloup is the oldest orchestra in Paris, but the time when it premiered works by major composers including Ravel and Bizet has long passed. Patrice Fontanarosa's theme for this season is *'lumière'* and the orchestra attempts to shed light on a repertoire of essentially popular classical masterpieces performed to a reasonable standard.

Orchestre Philharmonique de Radio France

www.radiofrance.fr.
Musical director Myung-Whun Chung remains one of the most underrated conductors in France, but his performance at last summer's Chorégies d'Orange and his concerts for the celebration of the Messiaen centenary should have earned him new respect. The standard of the orchestra is traditionally considered to lag behind that of the Orchestre National.

VENUES

Auditorium du Louvre

Entrance through Pyramid, Cour Napoléon, Musée du Louvre, rue de Rivoli, 1st (01.40.20.55.55/reservations 01.40.20.55.00/ www.louvre.fr). M° Palais Royal Musée du Louvre. **Box office** 9am-5.30pm Mon, Wed-Fri. Closed July, Aug. **Admission** €8-€30. **Credit** MC, V. **Map** p401 H5.
The Auditorium du Louvre packs in a full season with chamber music, lunchtime concerts and music on film. This season is divided into themed groups, presenting mainly young artists performing a wide range of music, including a strong emphasis on Russian artists for the France-Russie year in 2010.

Châtelet – Théâtre Musical de Paris

1 pl du Châtelet, 1st (01.40.28.28.40/ www.chatelet-theatre.com). M° Châtelet. **Box office** 11am-7pm Mon-Sat; 1hr before performance Sun. **By phone** 10am-7pm Mon-Sat. Closed July, Aug. **Admission** €10-€122.50. **Credit** AmEx, DC, MC, V. **Map** p408 J6.
Jean-Luc Choplin has radically changed the programming of this bastion of Paris music-making. An attempt to rediscover the theatre's popular roots has been achieved at the expense of traditional fine music subscribers. *The Sound of Music* may guarantee full houses, but it's unlikely that classical music fans will be tempted. The general impression is of programming that has been slimmed down for financial reasons, with even the previously vibrant concert programme looking threadbare. The performances of Scott Joplin's second opera, *Treemonisha*, look tempting, though.

★ Cité de la Musique

221 av Jean-Jaurès, 19th (01.44.84.45.00/ www.cite-musique.fr). M° Porte de Pantin. **Box office** noon-6pm Tue-Sun. **By phone** 11am-7pm Mon-Sat; 10am-6pm Sun. **Admission** €25-€30. **Credit** MC, V. **Map** p403 inset.
The energetic programming here features a vast non-classical repertoire that includes world music and jazz. Concerts are frequently grouped into series with a pedagogic aim: the bicentenary of Chopin's birth in 2010 is celebrated with an exhibition and a series of concerts, which makes a welcome change from programming that tends to concentrate on the Baroque and the contemporary.
► *The Conservatoire (209 av Jean-Jaurès, 19th, 01.40.40.45.45) hosts world-class performers and professors, and features many free concerts.*

IRCAM

1 pl Igor-Stravinsky, 4th (01.44.78.48.43/ www.ircam.fr). M° Hôtel de Ville. **Map** p406 K6.
The underground bunker next to the Centre Pompidou, set up in 1969 by the avant-garde composer Pierre Boulez to create electronic microtonal music for the new century, is looking less redundant nowadays with a full programme of courses and conferences. Not many concerts take place in the building itself, but IRCAM sponsors concerts with a modernist theme across the city. See the website for concert venues, and details of courses.

Maison de Radio France

116 av du Président-Kennedy, 16th (01.56.40.15.16/information 01.42.30.15.16/ www.radiofrance.fr). M° Passy/RER Avenue du Pdt Kennedy. **Box office** 11am-6pm Mon-Sat. **Admission** €5-€55. **Credit** AmEx, DC, MC, V. **Map** p404 A7.
State-owned radio station France Musique broadcasts a broad range of classical concerts from this comfortless cylindrical building on the banks of the Seine. The main stage (the Salle Olivier Messiaen) may be charmless, but the quality of music-making from the Orchestre National de France and the Orchestre Philharmonique de Radio France makes up for much. The Passe Musique offers under-26s admission to four concerts for €18, or a year of concerts for €99. Watch out for free events here, as well as the enterprising Présences contemporary music festival, which this year took place over two weekends in Paris and a week in Shanghai.

Musée National du Moyen Age

6 pl Paul-Painlevé, 5th (01.53.73.78.16/ www.musee-moyenage.fr). M° Cluny La Sorbonne. **Admission** €16; €13 reductions. **Credit** AmEx, MC, V. **Map** p408 J7.
The museum presents a worthy programme of medieval concerts in which troubadours reflect the museum's collection. There are also occasional 45- minute *heures musicales* in a similar style.

Musée d'Orsay

62 rue de Lille, 7th (01.40.49.47.57/www.musee-orsay.fr). M° Solférino/RER Musée d'Orsay.
Admission €6-€32. **Credit** MC, V. **Map** p405 G6.
The museum runs a full series of lunchtime and evening concerts. The lunchtime concerts at 12.30pm concentrate on promising young artists – this year celebrating the bicentenary of the birth of Liszt. Evening concerts are more prestigious, with a series based on the musical implications of *Crime and Punishment*, culminating in a playful concert by Dame Felicity Lott and Ann Murray accompanied by Graham Johnson in June 2010.

Opéra National de Paris, Bastille

Pl de la Bastille, 12th (08.92.89.90.90/from abroad 01.71.25.24.23/www.operadeparis.fr). M° Bastille. **Box office** (130 rue de Lyon, 12th) 10.30am-6.30pm Mon-Sat. *By phone* 9am-6pm Mon-Fri; 9am-1pm Sat. **Admission** €5-€196. **Credit** AmEx, MC, V. **Map** p409 M7.
It is never going to be a beautiful building, but when the restoration of the falling fascia tiles is completed, it may at least become a safe one. The unfinished *salle modulable*, the unflattering acoustics and the miles of corridors combine to create an atmosphere more akin to an airport than an opera house, but the standard of performance is what matters and the Bastille looks set for some exciting evenings under new director Nicolas Joel. The forging of a new production of Wagner's Ring cycle begins with *Das Rheingold* in March 2010, followed by *Die Walküre* at the end of May, conducted by new musical director Philippe Jordan and staged by Günter Krämer.

★ Opéra National de Paris, Palais Garnier

Pl de l'Opéra, 9th (08.92.89.90.90/from abroad 01.71.25.24.23/www.operadeparis.fr). M° Opéra. **Box office** 10.30am-6.30pm Mon-Sat. *By phone* 9am-6pm Mon-Fri; 9am-1pm Sat. **Admission** €7-€172. **Credit** AmEx, MC, V. **Map** p401 G4.
The Palais Garnier, with its ornate, extravagant decor and ceiling by Marc Chagall, is the jewel in the crown of Paris music-making, as well as a glistening focal point for the Right Bank. The Opéra National often favours the high-tech Bastille (*see above*) for new productions, but the matchless acoustics of the Palais Garnier are superior to the newer Bastille's, and they will surely be shaken by the Paris premiere of Philippe Fénelon's thunderous new *Faust* in March 2010. A gentler repertoire includes a new production of Rossini's *La Donna del Lago* in June starring Joyce DiDonato.

Péniche Opéra

Facing 46 quai de la Loire, 19th (01.53.35.07.77/ reservations 01.53.35.07.77/www.peniche opera.com). M° Jaurès or Laumière. **Box office** 10am-7pm Mon-Fri; 2-7pm Sat. **Admission** €12-€24. **Credit** MC, V. **Map** p401 M1.

The Péniche Opéra is an enterprising, barge-based company that produces chamber-scale shows and concerts, directed by the indefatigable Mireille Larroche. Programming ranges from Baroque rarities to contemporary creations via charming revue-style shows. This is one Paris institution that deserves to be kept afloat.

Salle Cortot

78 rue Cardinet, 17th (01.47.63.85.72). M° Malesherbes. **No box office. Admission** phone for details. **Map** 401 E2.
This intimate concert hall in the Ecole Normale de Musique has excellent acoustics for chamber music and master classes, which are often free of charge.

Salle Gaveau

45 rue La Boétie, 8th (01.49.53.05.07/www.salle gaveau.com). M° Miromesnil. **Box office** 10am-6pm Mon-Fri. **Admission** €10-€100. **Credit** MC, V. **Map** p401 E3.
An ideal venue for chamber music, the Salle Gaveau seems to be passing through one of the least productive stages of its history. The top-quality chamber music that used to be the hall's core repertoire is a rarity. Too many variety shows and dark evenings make for sorry reading.

Salle Pleyel

252 rue du Fbg-St-Honoré, 8th (01.42.56.13.13/ www.sallepleyel.fr). M° Ternes. **Box office** noon-7pm Mon-Sat. *By phone* 11am-7pm Mon-Sat; 11am-5pm Sun. **Admission** €10-€160. **Credit** MC, V. **Map** p400 D3.
Home to the Orchestre de Paris, the restored concert hall looks splendid. If the improved acoustics are only partially successful, the venue has nevertheless regained its status as the capital's leading concert hall for large-scale symphonic concerts, and should keep it until the completion of the city's new concert hall in 2012. Soloists read like a who's who of classical music, and this season includes an interesting series entitled Pollini Perspectives, which gives the great pianist free musical rein.

La Sorbonne

Amphitheatre Richelieu, 17 rue de la Sorbonne, 5th (01.42.62.71.71/www.musiqueensorbonne.fr). M° Cluny La Sorbonne or Odéon. **Box office** by phone or at the door. **Admission** €18-€40. **Credit** MC, V. **Map** p408 J7.
The lecture theatre of the university continues with a series of ambitious concerts featuring the orchestra and chorus of the Sorbonne. Standards waver but the setting is impressive.

★ Théâtre des Bouffes du Nord

37bis bd de la Chapelle, 10th (01.46.07.34.50/ www.bouffesdunord.com). M° La Chapelle. **Box office** 11am-6pm Mon-Sat. **Admission** €10-€26. **Credit** MC, V. **Map** p402 K1.

ARTS & ENTERTAINMENT

Théâtre National de l'Opéra Comique.

This elegant theatre directed by Micheline Rozan and Peter Brook boasts one of the most imaginative programmes of chamber music in the capital. Adventurous programming this year includes an evening of festive music from 17th-century Istanbul, Müsennâ, and the return of veteran harpsichordist Gustav Leonhardt.

Théâtre des Champs-Elysées
15 av Montaigne, 8th (01.49.52.50.50/ www.theatrechampselysees.fr). M° Alma Marceau. **Box office** 1-7pm Mon-Sat. *By phone* 10am-noon, 2-6pm Mon-Fri. **Admission** €5-€160. **Credit** AmEx, MC, V. **Map** p400 D5.

This beautiful art nouveau theatre, with bas-reliefs by Bourdelle, hosted the scandalous première of Stravinsky's *Le Sacre du Printemps* in 1913. This is the final season for director Dominique Meyer, who is leaving for the Vienna Opera; his successor Michel Franck takes over in 2010. It remains the favourite venue for visiting foreign orchestras. The prestigious line-up of visiting maestros includes Lorin Maazel, Riccardo Muti and Christian Thielemann, as well as Covent Garden's musical director Antonio Pappano. Staged performances include Mozart's Da Ponte operas, conducted with an eye for authenticity by Jean-Claude Malgoire, as well as Handel's *Semele* and Cavalli's *La Calisto*, under the baton of Early Music specialist Christophe Rousset. Operatic superstar tenors Roberto Alagna and Jonas Kaufmann will give recitals, and instrumentalists include former Leeds Piano Prize winner Michel Dalberto and fellow French pianist Alexandre Tharaud. Cellist Jean-Guihen Queyras will play the complete Bach suites.

Théâtre National de l'Opéra Comique
Pl Boieldieu, 2nd (01.42.44.45.40/www.opera-comique.com). M° Richelieu Drouot. **Box office** 11am-7pm Mon-Sat; 11am-5pm Sun. *By phone* 11am-7pm Mon-Sat; 11am-5pm Sun **Admission** €6-€115. **Credit** AmEx, DC, MC, V. **Map** p402 H4.

Its promotion to national theatre status has brought this jewel box of a theatre back to life and the opening seasons, exploring a specifically French repertoire often ignored by the larger houses, have been welcomed with enthusiasm by press and public alike. After his triumphant *Carmen* last season, Sir John Eliot Gardiner has been invited back to conduct Debussy's *Pelléas et Mélisande* in a production by Stéphane Braunschweig: one of the most important operas of the 20th century returns to the theatre where it was first staged in 1902.

Théâtre du Tambour-Royal
94 rue du Fbg-du-Temple, 11th (01.48.06.72.34/ tambour.royal.monsite.wanadoo.fr). M° Belleville or Goncourt. **Box office** 6.30-8pm Tue-Fri; 3-8pm Sat, Sun. *By phone* 10am-8pm Mon-Sat. **Admission** €16-€21. **Credit** MC, V. **Map** p403 M4.

This charming venue is where Maurice Chevalier launched his career. Its programming includes occasional concerts of light repertoire and revue-style shows, including the popular Best of Mozart, but expectations should not be raised too high.

Théâtre de la Ville
2 pl du Châtelet, 4th (01.42.74.22.77/www.theatre delaville-paris.com). M° Châtelet. **Box office** 11am-7pm Mon; 11am-8pm Tue-Sat. **Admission** €12-€17. **Credit** MC, V. **Map** p408 J6.

Programming in this vertiginous concrete amphitheatre, hidden behind a classical façade, features hip chamber music outfits such as the Kronos and Takács Quartets and Early Music pioneer Fabio Biondi. Soloists this season include guitarist Filomena Moretti, violinist Frank-Peter Zimmermann and tenor Werner Güra.

▶ *The season here spills over to performances at Les Abbesses (31 rue des Abbesses, 18th), which shares the same phone number and box office hours, but is closed on Mondays.*

Rock, Roots & Jazz

Paris's music scene is bubbling with talent, and the recent emergence of some great new bands speaks volumes about the creativity of today's up-and-coming artists. Manufactured creations from TV shows such as *Star Academy, La Nouvelle Star*, and in 2010, a French version of *The X Factor,* tend to top the pop charts, but there is still plenty of space for real sounds.

The capital is overflowing with authentic concert venues, from monster stadiums to intimate bars and jazz clubs, and venues like **Nouveau Casino** and **L'International** give precious stage space to those on the way up the musical ladder, although much-loved indie and electro venue **La Flèche d'Or** closed its doors in April 2009 (the neighbours were complaining about the noise). However, it's set to reopen in 2010 under new management – rumour has it that it's a joint venture between the Bataclan and Mama Shelter hotel just opposite.

Chanson française is still going strong, helped by the revival of **Les Trois Baudets**, a government-subsidised *chanson* hall in the heart of Pigalle – French law dictates that 40 per cent of music broadcast in France must be in the French language.

Jazz is having a mini revival too: after the disappearance of old flames like Le Slow Club (once one of the most famous jazz joints in Europe), Le Bilboquet and Les 7 Lézards, a handful of new joints have opened up, while flagship clubs **Au Duc des Lombards**, **New Morning** and **Le Sunset/Le Sunside** continue to book top-notch acts from around the globe.

Paris is also a European leader for world music, particularly African and Arab acts. And don't forget that every 21 June, the whole city turns into one giant music venue for the **Fête de la Musique** (*see p276*), when a party in the street is guaranteed.

INFORMATION AND RESOURCES

Website www.gogoparis.com selects regular concert highlights and also features a decent gig list for the coming months, with all information provided in English and French;

www.infoconcert.com is also well worth a look. The weekly magazine *Les Inrockuptibles* is a valuable resource. Alternatively, try reliable, bi-monthly gig bible *Lylo*, free in bars and branches of Fnac. The **Fnac** and **Virgin Megastore** ticket offices (for both, *see p271*) also display details of up-and-coming concerts. For reduced tickets try www.billetreduc. com. Depending on your tastes (and your French) radio can be useful for tip-offs: Nova (101.5FM) does electro, lounge and world; TSF (89.9FM) and FIP (105.1FM) cover jazz; and Le Mouv' (92.1FM) and OuiFM (102.3FM) are for rock fans.

Venue box offices are usually closed in the daytime, and most venues take a break in August. Prices for gigs vary according to a group or artist's pulling power, but several excellent venues, like La Bellevilloise, host regular free nights – ideal if you're feeling adventurous and/or are on a budget. For concerts, it's best to turn up at the time stated on the ticket: strict noise curfews mean that start times are adhered to pretty closely.

ROCK & POP
Stadium venues

Palais des Congrès
Porte Maillot, 17th (www.viparis.com). M° Porte Maillot. **Open** times vary. **Credit** MC, V. **Map** p400 B2.
The sound and the views are good wherever you sit in this state-of-the-art amphitheatre. The likes of Tori Amos, Cliff Richard and 'Sex Bomb' Tom Jones graced the stage in 2009.

Palais Omnisports de Paris-Bercy
8 bd de Bercy, 12th (08.92.39.01.00/www. bercy.fr). M° Bercy. **Box office** 11am-6pm Mon-Sat. **Credit** AmEx, DC, MC, V. **Map** p407 N9.
The traditional venue for rock and pop behemoths: Tina Turner, Muse and Lenny Kravitz were among the big draws last year, and Mika's The Boy Who New Too Much tour calls in here in 2010.

Zenith
211 av Jean-Jaurès, 19th (www.zenith-paris. com). M° Porte de Pantin. **Open** times vary. **Credit** MC, V. **Map** p403 inset.
State-of-the-art sound and credible bands make this the large venue of choice. Pete Doherty and the Pixies played here last year.

Bar and club venues

Le Bataclan
50 bd Voltaire, 11th (01.43.14.00.30/www. le-bataclan.com). M° Oberkampf. **Open** times vary. **Credit** MC, V. **Map** p403 M5.

ARTS & ENTERTAINMENT

Channel Hopping

English is the new French.

Neimo.

For many British music fans the only French sounds worth listening to are by electro whizzes Daft Punk and Air; or, more recently, songstress **Camille** (www.camille-music.com), with her album *Music Hole*. So what's the key to their success? The quality of their music? Almost certainly. But could it also have something to do with their language of choice?

The French language is all well and good when Carla's singing *chanson*, but for serious pop-rock nothing can beat English lyrics. And the latest *bébés rockeurs* to hit France's rock scene are inclined to agree. **Neimo** (www.myspace.com/neimo) is one of the hottest English-speaking French rock bands around. Having nailed a cute, punky, Strokes-esque formula (accent and all), they're delivering it liberally across Europe, especially in Germany where they have their biggest following. 'If you want to sing rock 'n' roll you have to sing in English,' says lead singer Bruno Alexandre. 'The rhythm of the French language doesn't really suit rock. French sounds poetic: that's why *chanson française* is so text-oriented, with the music merely a frame for the words. Rock, on the other hand, is about the music – you can get away with "yeah, yeah" and still sound cool.'

One group sounding particularly cool with their 'yeah, yeah' is **ED-ÄKE** (pronounced 'ead-ache, www.myspace.fr/edake), whose funky music – an energetic mix of metal and Foo Fighters-like melody – is taking France by storm. **Pet Trap** (www.myspace.com/pettrap) is another hip new group to look out for in 2010, with fresh electronic sound, vaguely influenced by Primal Scream, Depeche Mode and the Pixies. And debut album *Revolver* from **Pop de Chambre** (www.myspace.com/popdechambre) has just enough accent to remind you that it's French and just the right dose of creativity (a mix of Renaissance-style chamber music and Kinks-like rock) to make you want to go out and buy it.

This distinctive venue, fashioned like a Chinese pagoda with a distinctive multi-coloured façade, first opened in 1864 and remains admirably discerning in its booking of rock, world, jazz and hip hop acts.

Batofar
Opposite 11 quai François-Mauriac, 13th (09.71.25.50.61/www.batofar.org). Mº Bibliothèque François-Mitterrand or Quai de la Gare. **Open** 9pm-late Wed-Sat. **Admission** €5-€20. **Credit** MC, V. **Map** p407 N10.
This enduringly hip party boat lays on DJs, rappers and assorted underground noise-merchants for the benefit of an up-for-it crowd. It comes into its own in the summer, when the terrace opens at 7pm.
▶ *For more on Batofar's club nights, see p328.*

★ La Cigale/La Boule Noire
120 rue de Rochechouart,18th (La Cigale 08.92.70.08.40/La Boule Noire 01.49.25.81.75/ www.lacigale.fr/www.laboule-noire.fr). Mº Anvers
or Pigalle. **Open** times vary. **Credit** MC, V. **Map** p402 J2.
Easily one of Paris's finest venues, the lovely, horse-shoe-shaped theatre La Cigale is linked to more cosy venue La Boule Noire, good for catching cult-ish visiting indie and rock acts (many from the UK).

Les Disquaires
6 rue des Taillandiers, 11th (www.myspace.com/ goldrushcrew). Mº Bastille. **Open** 7pm-late daily. **Admission** free. **Credit** MC, V. **Map** p407 M6.
This party bar provides live pop, rock, DJs and electro to a hip crowd of thirtysomethings bent on partying like they were 20 again. It's a fine spot for discovering underground Paris sounds.

Elysée Montmartre
72 bd de Rochechouart, 18th (01.44.92.45.36/ www.elyseemontmartre.com). Mº Anvers. **Open** *Bar* 11am-midnight daily. *Concerts* times vary. **Credit** *Bar* MC, V. **Map** p402 J2.

ARTS & ENTERTAINMENT

The Elysée still hosts enduring party night Le Bal (*see p328*), but mostly reserves its stage for mid-sized alternative rock and electronic acts, plus a handful of disco old-timers and the occasional headliner.

★ L'International
5-7 rue Moret, 11th (01.49.29.76.45/www.linternational.fr). M° Ménilmontant. **Open** 2pm-2am Tue-Sat; 6pm-midnight Sun. **Concerts** 8pm, 10pm daily. **Admission** free. **Credit** MC, V. **Map** p403 N4.
This concert-bar is a breath of fresh air, with free entry and a string of on-the-up bands playing to hip indie crowds every night of the week. Once a month there's an after-party until 4am.

Mains d'Oeuvres
1 rue Charles-Garnier, 93400 St-Ouen (01.40.11.25.25/www.mainsdoeuvres.org). M° Garibaldi or Porte de Clignancourt. **Open** *Bar* 9.30am-midnight daily. *Concerts* 8.30pm, days vary. **Admission** €10. **Credit** *Bar* MC, V.
A hub for fringe musical and performance activity just outside Paris, the Mains d'Oeuvres is a huge former leisure centre for car factory workers that specialises in leftfield electro, rock mavericks and multimedia artists. It also frequently hosts the Festival des Attitudes Indé (end Sept-early Oct) – an indie music festival for up-and-coming bands.

La Maroquinerie
23 rue Boyer, 20th (01.40.33.35.05/www.la maroquinerie.fr). M° Gambetta. **Open** *Box office* (in person only) 2.30-6.30pm Mon-Fri. **Concerts** 8pm Mon-Fri. Closed Aug. **Credit** MC, V. **Map** p403 P4.
Literary discussion and rock 'n' roll coexist at this happening locale. It's home to the Inrocks Indie Club nights, featuring up-and-coming rock acts, but there are still traces of its world music roots.

★ La Mécanique Ondulatoire
8 passage Thière, 11th (01.43.55.16.74/www.myspace.com/lamecanique). M° Bastille or Ledru Rollin. **Open** 6pm-2am Mon-Sat. **Concerts** from 8pm Tue-Sat. **Admission** €4-€7. **Credit** MC, V. **Map** p407 M7.
Cementing Bastille's status as Paris's prime hangout for rockers, this exciting venue has three levels and alternates eclectic DJs with live acts in the cellar, plus there's jazz on Tuesday nights. *Photo p322.*

Le Motel
8 passage Josset, 11th (01.58.30.88.52/www.myspace.com/lemotel). M° Ledru Rollin. **Open** 6pm-1.45am Tue-Sun. Closed Aug. **Credit** MC, V. **Map** p407 M7.
This most Anglophile of Paris bars, with Stone Roses and Smiths posters adorning the walls, manages to fit plenty of live bands, including some of the best new local talent, on to its tiny stage.

La Maroquinerie.

La Mécanique Ondulatoire. *See p321.*

Nouveau Casino
109 rue Oberkampf, 11th (01.43.57.57.40/
www.nouveaucasino.net). Mº Ménilmontant,
Parmentier or St-Maur. **Open** *Concerts* times
vary. **Credit** *Bar* MC, V. **Map** p403 N5.
A bankable and loveable, albeit rather commercial,
venue run by the adjacent Café Charbon, with fab
gigs and club nights featuring rock, dub and garage,
plus reasonable drinks prices.

Olympia
28 bd des Capucines, 9th (08.92.68.33.68/www.
olympiahall.com). Mº Opéra. **Open** *Box office*
10am-9pm Mon-Sat; 10am-7pm Sun. *Concerts* times
vary. **Credit** AmEx, DC, MC, V. **Map** p401 G4.
The Beatles, Frank Sinatra, Jimi Hendrix and Edith
Piaf have all performed here, as did Jacques Brel.
Now it's mainly a home for nostalgia and *variété*,
with a smattering of contemporary sounds.

O'Sullivans by the Mill
92 bd de Clichy, 18th (01.53.09.08.49/www.
osullivans-pubs.com). Mº Blanche. **Open** noon-
5am Mon-Thur; noon-6am Fri-Sun. **Concerts**
times vary. **Credit** MC, V. **Map** p401 G2.

This Irish chain bar is all about late, late nights, with
grizzly weekend rock gigs that last until sunrise,
DJs and open mic nights the first Wednesday of
the month. Thursday's Funked Up (11pm-5am)
night is always wild.

★ Point Ephémère
200 quai de Valmy, 10th (01.40.34.02.48/
www.pointephemere.org). Mº Jaurès or Louis
Blanc. **Open** noon-2am daily. *Concerts*
8.30pm daily. **Credit** AmEx, DC, MC, V.
Map p403 Q5.
This converted warehouse is a classy affair, bringing together up-and-coming local rock, jazz and
world gigs with a decent restaurant, dance and
recording studios and exhibitions.
► *Point Ephémère is the sister venue to Mains*
d'Oeuvres (see p321).

Le Reservoir
16 rue de la Forge-Royale, 11th (01.43.56.39.60/
www.reservoirclub.com). Mº Faidherbe Chaligny
or Ledru-Rollin. **Open** 8pm-5am Tue-Sat;
11.30pm-4.30pm Sun. **Admission** free-€12.
Credit AmEx, DC, MC, V. **Map** p407 N7.

This classy, Anglo-inspired venue hosts regular club nights and live indie acts, as well as low-key performances from larger acts. It also serves a decent 'jazz brunch' on Sundays.

La Scène Bastille

2bis rue des Taillandiers, 11th (01.48.06.50.70/ www.la-scene.com). M° Bastille. **Open** midnight-6am Wed-Sun. *Concerts* 7.30-10.45pm Mon-Fri. Closed Aug. **Admission** free-€20. **Credit** MC, V. **Map** p407 M7.
This beautifully designed bar offers you the option of chilling out in alcoves or joining the kids to groove to hip hop, funk and jazz.

Le Trabendo

211 av Jean-Jaurès, 19th (01.49.25.89.99/ www.trabendo.fr). M° Porte de Pantin. **Open** times vary. **Credit** MC, V. **Map** p403 inset.
This quirky spot in the 19th has carved out a niche in all things alternative, from post-rock to drum 'n' bass, avant-garde hip hop to modern jazz.

Le Who's Bar

13 rue du Petit Pont, 5th (01.43.54.80.71/ www.myspace.com/whosbar). M° St-Michel. **Open** 6.30pm-5.30am daily. **Admission** free. **Credit** MC, V. **Map** p408 J7.
With Picasso-style frescoes all over the walls and a nightly programme of live pop and rock, this is St-Michel's hippest music bar. Expect live acoustics on weekdays and harder all-round rock at weekends.

CHANSON

Chez Adel

10 rue de la Grange-aux-Belles, 10th (01.42.08.24.61). M° Jacques Bonsergent. **Open** noon-midnight Tue-Sun. *Concerts* 5pm Tue-Sun. **Admission** free. **Credit** MC, V. **Map** p402 L3.
Patron Adel is probably the most renowned *chanson* café owner in Paris, and this fine den of kitsch attracts countless devotees with its repertoire of *chanson* and Eastern European sounds.

**INSIDE TRACK
GET IN ON THE ACT**

Paris is home to three noteworthy rock festivals. The first, **Sous la Plage** (www.souslaplage.com), is free and takes place at Paris-Plage (*see p276*) from early July to mid September. **Solidays** (*see p276*), in mid July, features electro and dub, and leans more towards Gallic sounds than its more international rival **Rock en Seine** (*see p278*), which takes place in late August and hosted big-name bands such as The Prodigy and Faith No More in 2009.

★ La Bellevilloise

19-21 rue Boyer, 20th (01.46.36.07.07/www.la bellevilloise.com). M° Gambetta or Ménilmontant. **Open** 5.30pm-2am Wed-Fri; 11am-2am Sat, Sun. **Admission** free. **Credit** MC, V. **Map** p403 P4.
Is there anything Paris's former co-operative doesn't do? There's food, drinks, DJs and live music – lashings of it, not only in the downstairs concert hall but in the Oliviers restaurant and upstairs bar too. Music is eclectic, but there's a folky, world music bent.

Le Limonaire

18 Cité Bergère, 9th (01.45.23.33.33/http:// limonaire.free.fr). M° Grands Boulevards. **Open** 7pm-2am Mon; 6pm-2am Fri-Sun. *Concerts* 10pm Tue-Sat; 7pm Sun. Closed Mon, Sun in July & Aug. **Credit** MC, V. **Map** p402 J4.
Serious *chanson* takes the limelight and performances vary from piano-led *chansonniers* to cabaret. Arrive at 8pm if you want to eat.

Au Magique

42 rue de Gergovie, 14th (01.45.42.26.10/ www.aumagique.com). M° Pernety. **Open** 8pm-2am Wed-Sun. *Concerts* 9.30pm Wed, Thur; 10pm Fri, Sat. **No credit cards**. **Map** p405 F10.
Artiste-in-residence Marc Havet serenades punters with politically incorrect *chanson* at weekends; you can also expect poetry events and exhibitions of photos and paintings.

Sentier des Halles

50 rue d'Aboukir, 2nd (01.42.61.89.96/ www.sentierdeshalles.fr). M° Sentier. **Open** 7pm-midnight Tue-Sat. *Concerts* 8-10pm Tue-Sat. Closed Aug. **No credit cards**. **Map** p402 J4.
Le Sentier has developed beyond its traditional *chanson* base to embrace a variety of modern styles plus the occasional stand-up act.

Les Trois Baudets

64 bd de Clichy, 18th (01.42.62.33.33/www. lestroisbaudets.com). M° Pigalle. **Open** 6pm-1.30am Tue-Sat; 10.30am-5pm Sun. Closed Aug. **Admission** €5-€20. **Credit** MC, V. **Map** p401 H2.
All dolled up in black and red, with a 250-seater theatre, an enviable sound system, two bars and a restaurant, this new concert hall encourages *chanson française* and other musical genres (rock, electro, folk and slam) – as long as they're in French. *Photo p325.*

★ Le Vieux Belleville

12 rue des Envierges, 20th (01.44.62.92.66/ www.le-vieux-belleville.com). M° Pyrénées. **Open** *Concerts* 9pm Thur-Sat. Closed mid Aug. **Credit** MC, V. **Map** p403 N4.
If you're looking for an authentic Belleville rendezvous, there's no better location than this old-style café with terrace, where the traditions of accordion music and croaky-voiced *chanson* endure.

WORLD & TRADITIONAL

Cité de la Musique

221 av Jean-Jaurès, 19th (01.44.84.44.84/
www.cite-musique.fr). M° Porte de Pantin.
Open noon-6pm Tue-Sat; 10am-6pm Sun.
Concerts Tue-Sat (times vary). **Admission**
€18-€40. **Credit** MC, V. **Map** p403 inset.
This Villette museum/concert complex welcomes
prestigious names from all over the globe, and also
does a fine line in contemporary classical, avant-jazz
and electronica.

Institut du Monde Arabe

1 rue des Fossés-St-Bernard, 5th
(01.40.51.38.38/www.imarabe.org). M° Jussieu.
Open 10am-6pm Tue-Sun. *Concerts* usually
8.30pm Fri, Sat. **Admission** varies. **Credit**
MC, V. **Map** p409 K7.
This huge, plush auditorium attracts some of the
biggest names in the world of Arab music. The first
half of 2010 (until May) is devoted to Les Musicales,
a festival of Palestinian music and its influences.

Le Kibélé

12 rue de l'Echiquier, 10th (01.48.24.57.74/
www.kibele.fr). M° Bonne Nouvelle. **Open** noon-
2pm, 7pm-midnight Mon-Sat. *Concerts* 9.30pm
Mon-Sat. **Admission** free-€5. **Credit** AmEx,
MC, V. **Map** p402 K4.
Music from across the Mediterranean and beyond in
an intimate vaulted cellar, with a decent Turkish
restaurant overhead. Before the concerts, other acts
such as one-man shows take to the stage from 7.30pm.

Musée Guimet

6 pl d'Iéna, 16th (01.56.52.53.00/www.guimet.fr).
M° Iéna. **Open** 10am-6pm Wed-Mon. *Concerts*
8.30pm some Thur, Fri & Sat. **Admission** €16;
€10 reductions. **Credit** MC, V. **Map** p404 C5.
Indian and Asian music by visiting troupes, as well
as dance and theatre, takes pride of place in the
auditorium of the Musée Guimet.

Satellit' Café

44 rue de la Folie-Méricourt, 11th
(01.47.00.48.87/www.satellit-cafe.com).
M° Oberkampf, Parmentier or St-Ambroise.
Open *Bar* 8pm-1am Tue, Wed; 8pm-3am or 5am
Thur; 10pm-6am Fri, Sat; 6pm-2am Sun. *Club*
11pm-6am Thur-Sat. *Concerts* 9pm Tue-Thur.
Admission €10 concerts; €12 club; €8
reductions. **Credit** *Bar* MC, V. **Map** p403 M5.
This bar lends its sound system to all things global,
but the focus is on traditional African music mixed
in with the occasional bit of Bollywood.

★ Théâtre de la Ville

2 pl du Châtelet, 4th (01.42.74.22.77/
www.theatredelaville-paris.com). M° Châtelet.
Open *Box office* 11am-7pm Mon-Sat. *Concerts*
8.30pm Mon-Fri; 5pm Sun. **Admission** varies
(usually €12-€25). **Credit** MC, V. **Map** p408 J6.
Music and dance of the highest order can be found
here, with jazz and music from just about anywhere
you can think of (Iraq, Japan, Thailand, Brittany)
amid the classical recitals.

JAZZ & BLUES

Ateliers de Charonne

21 rue de Charonne, 11th (01.40.21.83.35/www.
ateliercharonne.com). M° Charonne or Ledru-
Rollin. **Open** 7pm-1am Tue-Sat. **Admission**
free. *Dinner* €35. **Credit** MC, V. **Map** p407 M7.
This spanking new jazz club is the place to see the
rising stars of gypsy jazz (*jazz manouche*). If you
want to grab a good spot near the front of the stage,
reserve for dinner and the show.

Autour de Midi-Minuit

11 rue Lepic, 18th (01.55.79.16.48/www.autour
demidi.fr). M° Blanche. **Open** noon-2.30pm, 7pm-
late Tue-Sun. *Concerts* 9pm Tue; 9.30pm Wed;
10pm Fri-Sat; 7pm Sun. **Admission** free-€5.
Credit MC, V. **Map** p401 H2.
The Tuesday night *boeuf* (jam session) is always
free, as are many other concerts – some by big
names like Laurent Epstein, Yoni Zelnik and Bruno
Casties. The upstairs restaurant serves reasonably
priced French classic cuisine.

Le Baiser Salé

58 rue des Lombards, 1st (01.42.33.37.71/
www.lebaisersale.com). M° Châtelet. **Open**
Chanson concerts 7pm daily. *Jazz concerts*
10pm daily. **Admission** *Chanson* €13; €8
in advance. *Jazz* €12-€25. **Credit** AmEx, DC,
MC, V. **Map** p406 J6.
The 'Salty Kiss' divides its time between passing
chanson merchants, world artists and jazzmen of
every stripe, from trad to fusion.

Caveau de la Huchette

5 rue de la Huchette, 5th (01.43.26.65.05/
www.caveaudelahuchette.fr). M° St-Michel.
Open *Concerts* 10.15pm-2.30am Mon-Wed,
Sun; 10.15pm-6am Thur-Sat. **Admission** €12
Mon-Thur, Sun; €14 Fri, Sat; €10 reductions.
Credit MC, V. **Map** p408 J7.
This medieval cellar has been a mainstay for over
60 years. Jazz shows are followed by early-hours per-
formances in a swing, rock, soul or disco vein.

Caveau des Oubliettes

52 rue Galande, 5th (01.46.34.23.09/www.caveau
desoubliettes.fr). M° St-Michel. **Open** 5pm-4am
daily. *Concerts* 10pm daily. **Admission** free.
Credit MC, V. **Map** p408 J7.
A foot-tapping frenzy echoes in this medieval
dungeon, complete with instruments of torture, a
guillotine and underground passages. Mondays are

Pop Rock Jam nights with the JB Manis Trio, Tuesdays are Jazz Jam Boogaloo nights with Jeff Hoffman, and there are various other jam sessions during the rest of the week.

★ Au Duc des Lombards
42 rue des Lombards, 1st (01.42.33.22.88/ www.ducdeslombards.com). M° Châtelet. **Open** *Concerts* 8pm Mon-Sat. Closed mid Aug. **Admission** €19-€25. **Credit** MC, V. **Map** p406 J6.
This venerable jazz spot goes from strength to strength, attracting a high class of performer and a savvy crowd. Check out the *'bon plans'* section of the website, which offers reduced-price tickets for certain concerts.

Lionel Hampton Jazz Club
Hôtel Méridien Etoile, 81 bd Gouvion-St-Cyr, 17th (01.40.68.30.42/www.jazzclub-paris. com). M° Porte Maillot. **Open** *Concerts* 10pm-2am Mon-Sat; 12.30pm Sun. **Admission** (incl 1 drink) €26. **Credit** MC, V. **Map** p400 B2.
This hotel venue has a strong US bias, with lots of R&B and gospel, but native acts get a look in as well. It's not particularly progressive, but classy nonetheless (and the cocktails are great).

★ New Morning
7-9 rue des Petites-Ecuries, 10th (01.45.23.51.41/ www.newmorning.com). **Open** 8pm daily. *Concerts* 9pm daily. **Admission** €15-€25. **Credit** MC, V. **Map** p402 K3.
One of the best places to see the latest cutting-edge jazz exponents, with a policy that also embraces *chanson*, blues, world music and sophisticated pop.

Le Petit Journal Montparnasse
113 rue du Commandant René-Mouchotte, 14th (01.43.21.56.70/www.petitjournal-montparnasse. com). M° Gaîté or Montparnasse-Bienvenüe. **Open** 8pm-2am daily. *Concerts* 10pm Mon-Sat. **Admission** (incl 1 drink) €25; €15 reductions; €60 dinner. **Credit** MC, V. **Map** p405 F9.
A two-level jazz brasserie with New Orleans sound, big bands, Latin and soul-gospel.

Le Sunset/Le Sunside
60 rue des Lombards, 1st (Sunside 01.40.26.21.25/ Sunset 01.40.26.46.60/www.sunset-sunside.com). M° Châtelet. **Open** *Concerts* 9pm, 10pm daily. **Admission** €8-€30. **Credit** MC, V. **Map** p406 J6.
A split-personality venue, with Sunset dealing in electric groups and Sunside hosting acoustic performances. Their renown pulls in big jazz names.

Le Swan Bar
165 bd de Montparnasse, 6th (01.44.27.05.84/ www.swanbar.fr). M° Raspail or Vavin. **Concerts** 7.30pm & 9.30pm Tue-Sat. **Admission** varies. **Credit** MC, V. **Map** p405 H9.
A modern, American-style jazz bar for traditional jazz, torch songs and jamming. Occasional classical and tango concerts are thrown in for good measure.

Théâtre du Châtelet
1 pl du Châtelet (01.40.28.28.40/www.chatelet-theatre.com). M° Châtelet. **Open** times vary. **Admission** €25-€150. **Credit** AmEx, DC, MC, V. **Map** p406 J6.
This venerable theatre and classic music hall has another life as a jazz and *chanson* venue, with performances by top-notch international musicians.

ARTS & ENTERTAINMENT

Les Trois Baudets. *See p323.*

Nightlife

Slow and low, that is the tempo.

When it comes to hardcore clubbing, the French capital is no longer a global challenger – serious nighthawks migrated long ago to more happening cities such as London, New York and Berlin, and the best Paris party experiences tend to be reserved for those connected enough to be in the know or on the guestlist. In addition, the ban on all-you-can-drink events in 'open bars', which was introduced in early 2009 in an effort to prevent binge drinking, has dealt a further blow to the city's late-night revellers. However, all is not lost after dark: the city is fighting back with a string of great new venues aimed at a more laid-back crowd.

ABOUT THE SCENE

Ritzy places such as the **VIP Room** and **Le Baron** are still the talk of the town, but more low-key indie venues such as **Panic Room** and **Le Truskel** are pulling in a diverse crowd – with the emphasis far more about having fun than posing.

Another new nightlife twist is the recent wave of designer-led hotel cocktail bars, which are attracting some big-name DJs. **Mama Shelter** (*see p174*), which created a huge buzz when it opened in 2008, may be famous for its great design by Philippe Starck, but it's also picking up style points for its music selection; the **Hôtel Ritz** (*see p157*) boasts some of the finest resident DJs in the bar on weekends; the **Murano Urban Resort** (*see p170*) hosts Lucky Star on Thursday nights, when a famous French actor and/or singer takes over the deckst; and the **Kube Hotel** (*see p169*) has daily DJ sets.

THE BEST NEW VENUES

For indie tunes
Panic Room. See p328.

For nicotine nights
Chacha Club. See p327.

For cool cabaret
Le Régine. See p329.

August is traditionally the time when most Paris clubs shut down. But one beacon of summer light is Ed Banger Records, which has been throwing amazing parties instead (*see p332* **Pedro Winter**). Look out for more brilliant August action in 2010.

Finally, bear in mind that Parisians tend to go out late and most venues will be empty before midnight. Look out for flyers, join the MySpace and Facebook groups of your favourite venues, and most importantly, make friends with people in the places you go to: it's the best way to hear about cool parties coming up. In Paris, it's all about scratching the glossy surface to discover the rougher, more authentic face of the city.

For listings, check www.flyersweb.com, www.novaplanet.com, www.radiofg.com and www.lemonsound.com. Radio stations FG (98.2FM) and Nova (101.5FM) also provide details on what's happening.

CLUB BARS

★ Andy Whaloo
69 rue des Gravilliers, 3rd (01.42.71.20.38/ www.myspace.com/andywhaloo). M° Arts et Métiers. **Open** 5pm-2am Tue-Sun. **Admission** free. **Drinks** €3-€12. **Credit** AmEx, MC, V. **Map** p409 K5.
Owned by the people behind Momo and Sketch in London, Andy Whaloo serves sumptuous snack food and is tastefully decorated with Moroccan artefacts. The seating is made from upturned paint cans, and the DJs play everything from hip hop to techno, stepping up the volume as the night progresses.

★ Baxo

*21 rue Juliette Dodu, 10th (01.42.02.99.71/
www.baxo.fr). M° Colonel Fabien.* **Open** 9am-
3pm, 7pm-2am Mon-Fri; 5pm-2am Sat, Sun.
Admission free. **Drinks** €3-€10. **Credit**
MC, V. **Map** p403 M3.

A spanking new hybrid venue that triples as a
restaurant, bar and DJ lounge for an übercool, bobo
clientele. Friday nights are for resident DJs, and
Saturdays bring live bands and guest splicers. The
food is satisfyingly innovative.

Café Chéri(e)

*44 bd de la Villette, 19th (01.42.02.02.05).
M° Belleville.* **Open** 8am-2am daily. **Admission**
free. **Drinks** €2.80-€7. **Credit** MC, V.
Map p403 M3.

A popular DJ bar, especially in summer, when fashionistas flock to the terrace. Live music is played from
Thursdays to Saturdays after 10pm. Expect anything
from DJ Jet Boy's electro punk to rock, funk, hip hop,
rare groove, indie, dance, jazz and '80s classics.
▶ *Café Chéri(e) is also a chic daytime venue.*

★ Chacha Club

*47 rue Berger, 1st (01.40.13.12.12/www.
chachaclub.fr). M° Châtelet.* **Open** 8pm-5am
Mon-Sat. **Admission** varies. **Drinks** €4-€12.
Credit MC, V. **Map** p402 J5.

Paris's fetishistic obsession with the cigarette has
produced a new nightlife phenomenon: the fumoir.
The Chacha Club was the first high-profile establishment to open one, and it forms just one of the
sexy attributes of this hot haunt near Les Halles that
is attracting a spectacularly good-looking clientele
through its doors. In the style of a private club,
but with no membership requirement (only a trio
of exacting 'physionomists' stand at the door), it
combines restaurant, bar and club in a suite of intimate rooms with subdued lighting and seductive,
1930s-inspired decor.

Dépanneur Lounge

*27 rue Fontaine, 9th (01.44.53.03.78). M°
Blanche or Pigalle.* **Open** 10am-2am Mon-Thur;
4am-2am Fri-Sun. **Admission** free. **Drinks**
€2-€8.90. **Credit** MC, V. **Map** p401 H2.

Just below Montmartre, but away from the seedy
Pigalle drag, this new arrival serves decent French
cuisine and cocktails by the bucket-load. As the last
dinner plates are cleared, the DJ sets up for a night
of serious splicing.

★ La Fourmi

*74 rue des Martyrs, 18th (01.42.64.70.35). M°
Pigalle.* **Open** 8.30am-2am Mon-Thur, Sun; 8am-
4am Fri, Sat. **Admission** free. **Drinks** €1.60-€8.
Credit MC, V. **Map** p402 H2.

La Fourmi is a precursor to the industrial-design,
informal, music-led bars that have sprung up around
Paris – and it's still very much a style leader, attracting everyone from in-the-know tourists to fashionable Parisians. Great throughout the day for coffees
or a beer, it has a small seating area outside and an
always busy bar with DJ decks. You can stay into
the early hours at weekends, but it's also a handy
pre-club rendezvous and flyer supplier.

Lizard Lounge

*18 rue du Bourg-Tibourg, 4th (01.42.72.81.34/
www.cheapblonde.com). M° Hôtel de Ville or
St-Paul.* **Open** noon-2am daily. **Admission**
free. **Drinks** €6-€9. **Credit** AmEx, MC, V.
Map p409 K6.

This three-level, trendy Marais hangout has a boozer
upstairs serving beer in pint glasses, a mezzanine for

ARTS & ENTERTAINMENT

Baxo.

crowd voyeurs, and a more full-on DJ bar in the booth-filled basement – often full, due to its modest proportions. Local DJs play a variety of contemporary styles.

La Mezzanine de l'Alcazar
62 rue Mazarine, 6th (01.53.10.19.99/www.alcazar.fr). M° Odéon. **Open** 7pm-2am Wed-Sat. **Admission** free. **Drinks** €9-€13. **Credit** AmEx, DC, MC, V. **Map** p406 H7.
The stylish, Conran-owned Mezzanine is the upstairs posher sister of the Wagg, which is intended to be a clubbier venue. Naturally, both have become well-heeled hangouts, but the Mezzanine remains the venue of choice for the suited and booted.

★ Panic Room
101 rue Amelot, 11th (01.58.30.93.43). M° St-Sébastien Froissart. **Open** 6pm-2am Tue-Sat. Closed 2wks Aug. **Admission** free. **Drinks** €5-€8. **Credit** MC, V. **Map** p409 L5.
This newcomer has quickly carved out a niche on the rock scene, and it's not nearly as daunting as its name suggests. The excellent Goldrush collective has live acts and DJs blasting the sound system in the basement, while upstairs friendly barmen serve affordable cocktails behind a concrete counter. The indie crowd and occasional media celebs are loving it.

Le Troisième Lieu
62 rue Quincampoix, 4th (01.48.04.85.64/www.myspace.com/letroisiemelieu). M° Rambuteau. **Open** 6pm-5am Thur-Sat. **Admission** free. **Drinks** €2.50-€6. **Credit** MC, V. **Map** p402 K5.
Opened by Les Ginettes Armées, organisers of renowned Sunday lesbian and mixed events, the Troisième Lieu tends towards electro and house. The ground floor hosts DJs mixing eclectic sounds for chatting and relaxing to, whereas the basement is more dancefloor-oriented.

Le Wax
15 rue Daval, 11th (01.40.21.16.16/www.lewax.fr). M° Bastille. **Open** 5pm-2am Wed, Thur; 5pm-5am Fri-Sun. **Admission** free. **Drinks** €4.50-€10. **Credit** MC, V. **Map** p407 M6.
During the week, the Wax – clad in 1970s psychedelic orange – is a funky bar where DJs play groove until 2am. But at weekends it becomes a (tiny) nightclub that keeps a youthful crowd awake until 5am with house and electro.

Le Zèbre de Belleville
63 bd de Belleville, 20th (01.43.55.55.55/www.lezebre.com). M° Belleville. **Open** times vary. **Admission** €6-€15. **Drinks** €5-€10. **No credit cards. Map** p403 N4.
This stylish cabaret/theatre bar is used by Dan Ghenacia and the Freak 'n' Chic posse for buzzy after-parties on Sundays. It's usually a more traditional circus and cabaret venue; check flyers for event information.

COOL CLUBS

★ Bateau Concorde Atlantique
Port de Solférino, 23 quai Anatole-France, 7th (01.47.05.71.03/www.bateauconcorde atlantique.com). M° Assemblée Nationale/RER Musée d'Orsay. **Open** 11pm-5am Mon-Fri; 5pm-5am Sat; 6pm-5am Sun. Closed mid Sept-mid June. **Admission** free-€10. **Drinks** €5-€8. **Credit** MC, V. **Map** p401 F5.
With its terrace and voluminous dancefloor, this two-level boat is a clubbing paradise in the summer. The celebrated Respect crew held a popular, fondly remembered Wednesday night here, and are still involved in putting on parties at the venue, alongside other cool crews like Ed Banger.

★ Batofar
Opposite 11 quai François-Mauriac, 13th (09.71.25.50.61/www.batofar.org). M° Quai de la Gare. **Open** 11pm-6am Mon-Sat; 6am-noon 1st Sun of mth. **Admission** €5-€12. **Drinks** €3.50-€8. **Credit** MC, V. **Map** p407 N10.
In recent years the Batofar has gone through a rapid succession of management teams, with varying levels of success. The current managers have helped revive the venue's tradition of playing cutting-edge music, including electro, dub step, techno and dancehall nights featuring international acts. It's also a destination for early-morning clubbers determined to shun their beds.

Le Divan du Monde
75 rue des Martyrs, 18th (01.42.52.02.46/www.divandumonde.com). M° Abbesses or Pigalle. **Open** 8pm-2am Tue-Thur; 7.30pm-5am Fri, Sat. **Admission** €6-€30. **Credit** AmEx, MC, V. **Map** p402 H2.
After a drink in the seriously cool Fourmi opposite, pop over to the Divan for one-off parties and regular events. The upstairs specialises in VJ events, and downstairs holds dub, reggae, funk and world music club nights.

Elysée Montmartre
72 bd de Rochechouart, 18th (01.44.92.45.36/www.elyseemontmartre.com). M° Anvers. **Open** midnight-6am Fri, Sat. **Admission** €10-€15. **Drinks** €4-€10. **Credit** *Bar* MC, V. **Map** p402 J2.
A gig venue and club, the Elysée hosts big nights by outside promoters, such as Open House, Panik and Nightfever, for young clubbers.

Le Folie's Pigalle
11 pl Pigalle, 9th (01.48.78.55.25/www.lefolies pigalle.com). M° Pigalle. **Open** midnight-dawn Mon-Thur; midnight-noon Fri, Sat; 6pm-midnight Sun. **Admission** €20 (incl 1 drink); €7 Sun eve. **Drinks** €10. **Credit** AmEx, MC, V. **Map** p402 H2.

DJ Busy P.

The racy Folie's Pigalle's programme has everything from dancehall and hip hop to techno and electro, go-go dancers, striptease shows and Paris's only transsexual spectacle on Sunday evenings.

Le Gibus

18 rue du Fbg-du-Temple, 11th (01.47.00.78.88/ www.gibus.fr). M° République or Temple. **Open** midnight-6am Fri, Sat. **Concerts** 8-11.30pm Fri. **Admission** €5-€20. **Drinks** €3-€8. **Credit** *Bar* MC, V. **Map** p402 L4.
A famous 1980s punk venue, Le Gibus has gone through plenty of style changes during its life. Today it takes in R&B, reggae, '80s pop and hip hop, plus the occasional *striptease mixte*.

Le Glaz'art

7-15 av de la Porte de la Villette, 19th (01.40. 36.55.65/www.glazart.com). M° Porte de la Villette. **Open** 8.30pm-2am (sometimes 5am) on concert nights (check programme on website). **Admission** €8-€15. **Drinks** €3-€8. **Credit** MC, V. **Map** p403 inset.
This converted coach station is way out to the north-east, but its strong DJ nights and live acts pull punters in from central Paris. Dub step, breakbeat, electro and drum 'n' bass nights have made the venue a magnet for breaks fans.

Mains d'Oeuvres

1 rue Charles-Garnier, 18th (01.40.11.25.25/ www.mainsdoeuvres.org). M° Garibaldi. **Open** times vary. **Admission** €5-€15. **Drinks** €2-€5. **Credit** *Bar* MC, V.
A rehearsal space and live venue for new bands. Occasionally the whole building is turned into a club venue, with rooms devoted to different music styles. Look for flyers or keep an eye on the website.

Nouveau Casino

109 rue Oberkampf, 11th (01.43.57.57.40/ www.nouveaucasino.net). M° Parmentier. **Open** midnight-5am Wed-Sat. **Admission** €5 before 1am, €10 after. **Drinks** €5-€10. **Credit** *Bar* MC, V. **Map** p403 M5.
Conveniently surrounded by the numerous bars of rue Oberkampf and tucked behind the legendary Café Charbon, Nouveau Casino is a concert venue that also hosts some of the city's liveliest club nights. Local collectives, international names and record labels, such as Versatile, regularly host nights here; it's well worth checking the website for one-offs and after-parties.

★ Point Ephémère

200 quai de Valmy, 10th (01.40.34.02.48/www. pointephemere.org). M° Jaurès or Louis Blanc. **Open** 10am-2am daily. **Admission** varies. **Drinks** €3-€7. **Credit** AmEx, DC, MC, V. **Map** 402 L2.
This hunk of Berlin in Paris was only ever meant to be temporary, but thankfully it's still around. An uncompromising programming policy delivers some of the best electronic music in town; there's also a restaurant and bar with decks and a gallery, and terrace space by the canal in summer.

Red Light

34 rue du Départ, 15th (01.42.79.94.53/www. enfer.fr). M° Edgar Quinet or Montparnasse Bienvenüe. **Open** midnight-11am Fri, Sat. **Admission** (incl 1 drink) €20-€25. **Drinks** from €10. **Credit** MC, V. **Map** p405 F9.
The former Enfer ('Hell') remains a trance, techno and house dynamo with local and global DJs spinning to a young, up- for-it, often gay, well-groomed crowd. Expect a mixture of local and international DJs.

★ Le Régine

49 rue de Ponthieu, 8th (01.43.59.21.13/ www.leregine.com) M° St-Philippe-du-Roule. **Open** 11pm-6am Tue-Sat. **Admission** free-€10. **Drinks** €8-€12. **Credit** MC, V. **Map** p401 D4.
Régine was once a key figure on the Paris nightlife scene, and the club she created is now experiencing a rejuvenation thanks to the team behind Paris Paris. The revamped club fits right into the burlesque cabaret trend, with crazy performers, a musical mishmash, live acts on Wednesdays, and lines of cool kids at the door dying to join the A-listers inside.

ARTS & ENTERTAINMENT

★ Rex

5 bd Poissonnière, 2nd (01.42.36.10.96/
www.rexclub.com). M° Bonne Nouvelle. **Open**
11.30pm-6am Wed-Sat. **Admission** free-
€15. **Drinks** €5-€15. **Credit** *Bar* MC, V.
Map p402 J4.

The Rex's new sound system puts over 40 different
sound configurations at the DJ's fingertips, and has
proved to be a magnet for top turntable stars. Once
associated with iconic techno pioneer Laurent
Garnier, the Rex has stayed at the top of the Paris
techno scene, and occupies an unassailable position
as the city's serious club music venue.

La Scène Bastille

2bis rue des Taillandiers, 11th (01.48.06.50.70/
www.la-scene.com). M° Bastille. **Open** 7.30pm-
midnight Mon-Thur; 7.30pm-6am Fri-Sun. Closed
Aug. **Admission** €12. **Drinks** €4-€9. **Credit**
Bar MC, V. **Map** p407 M7.

This tastefully decorated club-bar-restaurant complex holds regular rock concerts, as well as club
events most Thursdays to Saturdays. The programming here changes constantly, so check what's on.
Popular gay nights too.

Showcase

Below Pont Alexandre III, 8th (01.45.61.25.43/
www.showcase.fr). M° Champs-Elysées Clemenceau.
Open 10pm-dawn Fri, Sat; 11am-3pm Sun.
Admission free-€15. **Drinks** €3.50-€8.
Credit MC, V. **Map** p401 E5.

This vast venue, in converted boat hangars below
Pont Alexandre III, is where music-crazed insomni-
acs come on weekends to discover up-and-coming
bands and dance until daybreak.

▶ *Sunday brunches here are a hit with families.*

★ Le Social Club

142 rue Montmartre, 2nd (01.40.28.05.55/
www.parissocialclub.com). M° Bourse or Grands
Boulevards. **Open** 11.30pm-3am Wed; 11pm-6am
Thur-Sat. **Admission** free-€12. **Drinks** €4-€10.
Credit AmEx, MC, V. **Map** p402 J4.

Set right in the hub of the city's club activity around
Grands Boulevards, this electro venue has some of
the hippest acts from the French and international
scene, thanks to its owner's multidisciplinary career
as a producer and founder of the record label
Uncivilized World.

INSIDE TRACK GETTING HOME

The last métro leaves at around 12.30am
(an hour later on Fridays and Saturdays),
and the first one gets rolling at 5.30am.
Between those times, you'll have to take
a night bus, taxi or Vélib (but don't drink
and ride).

Wagg

62 rue Mazarine, 6th (01.55.42.22.01/www.
wagg.fr). M° Odéon. **Open** 11.30pm-6am Fri,
Sat; 3pm-midnight Sun. **Admission** €12 Fri,
Sat; €12 Sun (incl drink). **Drinks** €7-€10.
Credit AmEx, DC, MC, V. **Map** p406 H7.

Refurbished as part of the Conran makeover of the
Mezzanine upstairs, Wagg went through a period of
attracting big-name DJs, but has settled down as
home to a well-to-do Left Bank crowd. Expect funk,
house and disco, plus salsa lessons on Sundays.

GLITZY CLUBS

★ Les Bains Douches

7 rue du Bourg-l'Abbé, 3rd (01.53.01.40.60/
www.lesbainsdouches.net). M° Etienne Marcel.
Open midnight-6am Wed-Sun (restaurant from
8pm). **Admission** €10-€20. **Drinks** €8-€10.
Credit AmEx, DC, MC, V. **Map** p402 J5.

Once a global leader, Les Bains Douches lost its way
in the 1990s, relying on its reputation to pull in
tourists. This all changed recently, and now local
star DJs like Busy P and international names such
as Erol Alkan grace its decks. The clientele is
increasingly, but not yet exclusively, gay.

▶ *There's a fancy restaurant here that serves a*
decent €39 set menu.

Le Baron

6 av Marceau, 8th (01.47.20.04.01/www.club
lebaron.com). M° Alma Marceau. **Open** times
vary. **Admission** free. **Drinks** from €10.
Credit MC, V. **Map** p400 D5.

This small but supremely exclusive hangout for the
international jet set used to be an upmarket brothel,
and has the decor to prove it. It only holds 150, most
of whom are regulars you'll need to befriend in order
to get past the door. But if you manage to get in,
you'll be rubbing shoulders with celebrities and
super-glossy people.

Le Cab

2 pl du Palais-Royal, 1st (01.58.62.56.25/www.
cabaret.fr). M° Palais Royal Musée du Louvre.
Open 11.30pm-5am Wed-Sat. *Restaurant*
7.30-11.30pm Tue-Sat. **Admission** free Tue,
Wed; €20 Thur-Sat. **Drinks** €13. **Credit** AmEx,
MC, V. **Map** p402 H5.

Le Cab is owned by the management behind Club
Mix and Queen, and R&B and commercial house
dominate the playlist. The doormen are tough, and
if they don't like you, you won't get in (unless you've
booked for dinner).

MadaM

128 rue La Boétie, 8th (01.53.76.02.11/www.
madam.fr). M° Franklin D. Roosevelt or George
V. **Open** 7pm-2am Thur; midnight-6am Fri, Sat;
10.30pm-4am Sun. **Admission** free. **Drinks**
€20. **Credit** AmEx, DC, MC, V. **Map** p401 E4.

Showcase.

MadaM's late-night sessions (kicking in at 4am at weekends) are renowned for the young, moneyed crowd they attract. The music is mainly electro and house (French), with several up to date international tunes thrown in for good measure.

★ Le Magnifique

25 rue de Richelieu, 1st (01.42.60.70.80/ www.lemagnifique.fr). M° Palais Royal-Musée du Louvre. **Open** 7pm-4am daily. **Admission** free. **Drinks** €14-€35. **Credit** AmEx, DC, MC, V. **Map** p401 H5.

Named after a 1970s film starring Jean-Paul Belmondo, this snazzy cocktail bar is a real retro treat. The decor, dominated by wood, dark leather and animal furs, is elegant, with a hint of porno chic that leaves you picturing Warhol and his posse partying in a corner. The place comes to life after midnight, when the bar turns into a club with a soundtrack of dancefloor-fillers from the past three decades. The fantastic cocktail menu, a selection of sushi (€8-€30) and the separate fumoir add to the appeal.

Le Montana

28 rue St-Benoît, 6th (01.44.39.71.00). M° St-Germain-des-Prés. **Open** 11pm-6am Mon-Sat. **Admission** free. **Drinks** €10-€15. **Credit** AmEx, DC, MC, V. **Map** p408 H7.

It's hard to believe any place could out-hype Le Baron, and yet this exclusive club manages it. Revamped by über-cool graphic artist André, Le Montana is a VIP magnet – Lenny Kravitz, Vanessa Bruno and Kate Moss have all hit the floor here since the relaunch. The biggest challenge is getting through the door.

VIP Room

188 rue de Rivoli, 1st (01.58.36.46.00/www. viproom.fr). M° Palais-Royal or Tuilleries. **Open** midnight-5am Tue-Sun. **Admission** free. **Drinks** €20. **Credit** AmEx, DC, MC, V. **Map** p401 H1.

The VIP has moved from its Champs-Elysées address into the former Scala nightclub, but other than that, nothing has changed. It's still a hit with the people who also enjoy the VIP's sister venues in Cannes and St Tropez during the summer, and the music is still dance-oriented.

MAINSTREAM CLUBS

Club Med World

39 cour St-Emilion, 12th (08.10.81.04.10/ www.clubmedworld.fr). M° Cour St-Emilion. **Open** 11pm-2am Tue-Thur; 11.30pm-6am Fri, Sat. **Admission** €15 Tue-Thur; €20 Fri, Sat; free for women. **Drinks** €9. **Credit** AmEx, MC, V. **Map** p407 N10.

Part of a massive conference, restaurant and club complex in the Bercy Village, Club Med World hosts popular disco, salsa and '80s nights at weekends.

I Love Opéra

5 av de l'Opéra, 1st (01.75.43.50.50/www.ilove opera.fr). M° Pyramides. **Open** *Bar* 6pm-midnight daily. *Restaurant* 8pm-midnight daily. **Admission** free. **Drinks** €8-€25. **Credit** AmEx, MC, V. **Map** p401 H5.

I Love Opéra is having trouble attracting the glitterati of its previous incarnation, Paris Paris,

Interview Pedro Winter

Do believe the hype.

Pedro Winter might just be the coolest Parisian in the world. Hooked by the rave scene of the early 1990s, he launched his own Hype parties at the Folies Pigalle in 1995, aged 20. Then he met two young guys who were starting a band and agreed to become their manager. The duo gained international stardom as Daft Punk, and the rest is history. Winter – who also produces tracks under the name Busy P – left Daft Punk in 2008 to focus on his record label, Ed Banger Records, and has since signed a string of outstanding newcomers, including the electro/pop/rock band Justice, his most successful act to date. The label also throws amazing parties. In 2009, the theme was Eté d'Amour, a series of 'erotic parties' on board Bateau Concorde Atlantique with DJ sets led by Pedro himself.

Pedro Winter.

Your Ed Banger parties are not only redefining the shape and sound of Parisian nightlife, they've also become a worldwide phenomenon. How did you reach such cult status?
When I started Ed Banger Records in 2003, I think I arrived at a good time. Club kids were fed up with boring electronic acts, and indie kids wanted to have more fun and stage dive. We managed to unite them all in clubs again and make it crazy. Our sound speaks to both worlds. We mix the energy.

What makes a good Ed Banger party?
It's not something you can really create. There is no recipe, and that's why they're so good. But as with everything, things will change, so I keep telling my crew to enjoy them as much as they can. We are now only doing two or three parties a year in Paris. We need to be careful not to do too many.

What's your view of Paris nightlife?
Paris's nightlife is still very 'meet 'n' greet', but there is a new wave of cool little clubs opening up. I like Social Club (*see p330*), a 600-capacity venue filled with young clubbers. It's always packed and wild, and the music is fresh. They've done a really good job. Also good are Le Baron (*see p330*) and Le Montana (*see p331*).

What's Ed Banger got planned for 2010?
We plan on doing more Ed Banger stages at festivals. It's a good way to present our artists and to invite friends like Erol Alkan, Boys Noize or 2ManyDjs. We call it 'Backstage on Stage', and we party as much as the people in the crowd. As for the label, we are finishing Uffie's first album, and hoping to release it at the end of 2009. SebastiAn is also working on his first LP, ready for early 2010. DJ Medhi just delivered a first compilation of his best remixes. And me, Busy P, I'm finishing my new single 'All You Can Dance'.

What do you think of the new British electro acts making it into the mainstream?
I saw Hot Chip live and I was blown away. They are amazing, but everybody knows that. The latest UK act I love is Harmonic 313 on Warp Records. It's so English, kind of like electronica dubstep.

but it's getting there with a chic pink, black and white dining room (menus from €36) open all day, after-work cocktail parties (from 6pm), and nightly clubbing with house, R&B, rock and hip hop.

La Loco
90 bd de Clichy, 18th (01.53.41.88.89/www. laloco.com). Mᵒ Blanche. **Open** 9pm-6am daily. **Admission** €10-€20. **Drinks** €6-€8. **Credit** MC, V. **Map** p401 G2.

La Loco has a substantial and youthful following taking advantage of its three dancefloors, which offer different musical genres: house, dance, hip-hop and chart music on weekend nights, and metal and goth concerts during the week.

★ Mix Club
24 rue de l'Arrivée, 15th (01.56.80.37.37/ www.mixclub.fr). Mᵒ Montparnasse Bienvenüe. **Open** 11pm-6am Wed-Sat; 5pm-1am Sun. **Admission** €12-€20. **Drinks** €8. **Credit** MC, V. **Map** p405 F8.

The Mix has one of the city's biggest dancefloors. Regular international visitors include Erick Morillo's Subliminal and Ministry of Sound parties, and in-house events include David Guetta's 'Fuck Me I'm Famous', 'Hipnotic' and 'One Night With Paulette', plus just about everyone else who's big in France – or anywhere else in the world, for that matter.

Queen
102 av des Champs-Elysées, 8th (01.53.89.08.90/ www.queen.fr). Mᵒ George V. **Open** 11pm-5am Mon; midnight-6am Tue-Thur, Sun; midnight-8am Fri, Sat. **Admission** €15 Mon-Thur, Sun; €20 Fri, Sat. **Drinks** €10. **Credit** *Bar* AmEx, MC, V. **Map** p400 D4.

Once the city's most fêted gay club and the only venue that could hold a torch to the Rex, with a roster of top local DJs holding court, Queen's star faded a little in the early noughties but is now starting to shine more brightly again. Last year it introduced more themed nights, and still packs 'em in seven nights a week.
▶ *For more on Queen's gay nights, see p312.*

WORLD, JAZZ & ROCK 'N' ROLL

Le Cabaret Sauvage
59 bd Macdonald, 19th (01.42.09.03.09/ www.cabaretsauvage.com). Mᵒ Porte de la Villette. **Open** 11pm-dawn, days vary. **Admission** €10-€20. **Drinks** €4-€8. **Credit** AmEx, MC, V. **Map** p403 inset.

A stylish, big top-shaped venue that's taken over by outside promoters for occasional club nights. There often used to be a world music element, but recently electronic and drum 'n' bass nights have begun to be held here, and, since the demise of Pulp, techno label Kill the DJ has started using the venue. Check the website for details of one-off nights.

La Chapelle des Lombards
19 rue de Lappe, 11th (01.43.57.24.24/ http://chapelle.lombards.free.fr). Mᵒ Bastille. **Open** 11.30pm-6am Tue-Sun. **Admission** free Mon-Wed, Sun; €15 Thur; €20 Fri, Sat (free for women Tue-Thur & before midnight Fri). **Drinks** €6-€12. **Credit** MC, V. **Map** p407 M7.

With Afrojazz and Latino bands and DJs providing the music, Latinos and Africans lead the dancefloor in this popular world music venue. Note: smart dress only.

★ Favela Chic
18 rue du Fbg-du-Temple, 11th (01.40.21.38.14/ www.favelachic.com). Mᵒ République. **Open** 8pm-2am Tue-Thur; 8pm-4am Fri, Sat. **Admission** free Tue-Thur; €10 (incl 1 drink) Fri, Sat. **Drinks** €6-€19. **Credit** MC, V. **Map** p402 L4.

Past the usually steely-faced door attendants, the Brazilian-themed Favela Chic attracts an up-for-it, international and invariably dressy crowd for some serious samba and other full-on Latin dancing. There are decent DJs, live acts, and Brazilian food and drinks too. The opening of a sister bar in London's Shoreditch has seen the Favela Chic brand expand into other forms of music, such as disco punk and electro.

La Java
105 rue du Fbg-du-Temple, 10th (01.42.02.20.52/ www.la-java.fr). Mᵒ Belleville or Goncourt. **Open** 9pm-3am Wed, Thur; 11pm-6am Fri, Sat; 2pm-2am Sun. **Admission** €5-€10. **Drinks** €3-€7. **Credit** MC, V. **Map** p403 M4.

Tucked inside the crumbling, disused Belleville market, La Java plays rock, salsa and world music, with live bands every weekend.

★ New Morning
7-9 rue des Petites-Ecuries, 10th (01.45.23.51.41/ www.newmorning.com). Mᵒ Château d'Eau. **Open** times vary. **Admission** approx €10. **Drinks** €3-€7. **Credit** MC, V. **Map** p402 K3.

Jazz fans crowd into this hip, no-frills joint to natter, drink and boogie to the consistently excellent live music. Low key it may be but it's still worth looking out for the occasional A-lister – the likes of Spike Lee and Prince have been known to grace the New Morning with their presence.

Toro
74 rue Jean-Jacques-Rousseau, 1st (01.44.76.00.03/www.toroparis.com). Mᵒ Les Halles. **Open** *DJ sets* 10pm-2am Thur-Sun. **Admission** free. **Tapas** €5. **Drinks** €8-€10. **Credit** AmEx, MC, V. **Map** p402 J5.

This recently opened, no-frills tapas bar hides a small but wonderfully wacky dancefloor down in the basement where DJs mix up house music with flamenco tunes.

ARTS & ENTERTAINMENT

Sport & Fitness

Action for all, from the Paris marathon to Paris St-Germain.

Every year, Paris hosts some 600 sports events, including 170 at national or international level. Its 366 sports complexes include 32 stadiums, 38 swimming pools and 43 tennis centres. These municipal facilities are doted with generously subsidised tariffs, while world-class professional venues enjoy heavy investment. Current projects include an extensive revamp for Roland Garros, home to the French tennis open, a major expansion of rugby's Stade Jean-Bouin, and the reopening of the legendary art-deco swimming pool, the Piscine Molitor.

SPECTATOR SPORTS

The national stadium is the 80,000-capacity **Stade de France** (*see p289*), served by stations on the RER B (La Plaine Stade de France) and RER D (Stade de France St-Denis) lines just one stop from the Gare du Nord. It was built for the 1998 football World Cup and staged the final, in which France beat Brazil 3-0 to claim the title for the first time. As well as top football matches, it hosts home legs for rugby's Six Nations and international athletics meetings.

Indoor events, including judo, basketball, handball and tennis, take place at the **Palais Omnisports de Paris-Bercy** (8 bd de Bercy, 12th, 08.92.39.01.00, www.popb.fr, M° Bercy). The **Stade Roland Garros** (Porte des Mousquetaires, 2 av Gordon-Bennett, 16th, 01.47.43.48.00, www.fft.fr/rolandgarros, M° Porte d'Auteuil) stages the French tennis open; the **Parc des Princes**, home of Paris St-Germain football club, also hosts rugby and other sporting events.

Despite recent doping scandals, the three-week **Tour de France** (www.letour.fr) is still a national festival, and huge crowds flock to the Champs-Elysées every July to welcome the riders home. The 2009 race was won by Spaniard Alberto Contador, with seven-time winner Lance Armstrong making a successful comeback in third place. For details of this and other major sporting events, *see pp274-279* **Calendar**.

Tickets for many sports are sold online at www.ticketnet.fr, and at branches of **Fnac** and **Virgin Megastore** (for both, *see p271*). For football and rugby internationals held at the Stade de France, contact the respective national associations (www.fff.fr, www.ffr.fr). The influential daily newspaper *L'Equipe* offers excellent press coverage (in French) of all major sports events.

Basketball

Paris-Levallois Basket
Stade Coubertin, 82 av Georges-Lafont, 16th (01.46.10.93.60/www.parislevallois.com). M° Porte de St-Cloud. **Tickets** from €6.
Credit MC, V.
Palais des Sports Marcel-Cerdan, 141 rue Danton, 92300 Levallois (01.46.17.06.30/ www.parislevallois.com). M° Pont de Levallois. **Tickets** from €6. **Credit** MC, V.
PL was born in 2007 following the merger of the region's two biggest clubs, Paris Basket Racing and Levallois Sporting Club Basket. The plan to create a superpower fell flat when the club was relegated to the Pro B league (second division) in its first season, but it has since climbed back into Pro A. Games are played at the Paris and Levallois sites.

Football

Paris St-Germain
Stadium *Parc des Princes, 24 rue du Commandant-Guilbaud, 16th (01.47.43.71.71/ tickets & information 32.75/www.psg.fr). M° Porte de St-Cloud.* **Tickets** €25-€100.
Credit MC, V.
Shops *27 av des Champs-Elysées, 8th (01.56.69.22.22). M° Franklin D. Roosevelt.*
Open 10am-10pm Mon-Thur; 10am-midnight

Fri, Sat; noon-8pm Sun. **Credit** AmEx, MC, V.
Parc des Princes. **Open** 10am-7pm Mon-Sat &
2hrs after game on match days. **Credit** AmEx,
MC, V.

A group of donors set up PSG by amalgamating
local clubs in 1970. During the 1980s and '90s, the
club won silverware aplenty, but its star has since
faded. Nonetheless, a positive season in 2009 saw
PSG vying for the French title before losing out to
Bordeaux in the final weeks.

▶ *For tickets, book online and pick them up from
any branch of Fnac (see p271).*

Horse racing

The full racing schedule, the *Calendrier
des Courses*, is published by *France Galop*
(www.france-galop.com). For information on
trotting, France's most popular form of racing,
consult www.cheval-francais.com. Tickets are
€1.50-€8 (free for under-18s). All betting is
done with the state-owned PMU, whose website
(www.pmu.fr) provides details of races and
odds. *Paris Turf* (www.paris-turf.com) is a
useful source of tips.

Hippodrome d'Auteuil
*Route des Lacs, 16th (01.40.71.47.47).
Mº Porte d'Auteuil.*
Steeplechasing in the Bois de Boulogne. The biggest
event is the Gras Savoye Grand Steeplechase de
Paris on the last Sunday in May.

★ Hippodrome de Chantilly
*16 av du Général-Leclerc, 60500 Chantilly
(03.44.62.44.00). Train from Gare du Nord.*
Flat racing 40km (25 miles) from Paris. The fashion
parade turns out in force for the Prix de Diane in
June; the full length of the course is used for the Prix
du Jockey Club the weekend before.

Hippodrome d'Enghien
*Pl André-Foulon, 95230 Soissy-sous-
Montmorency (01.34.17.87.00). Train from
Gare du Nord.*
Steeplechasing and floodlit trotting at this course
18km (11 miles) north of Paris.

★ Hippodrome de Longchamp
*Rte des Tribunes, 16th (01.44.30.75.00).
Mº Porte d'Auteuil then free bus.*
Flat racing in the Bois de Boulogne. This course
hosts the racing season's most fashionable social
event, the Prix de l'Arc de Triomphe Lucien
Barrière. Women in wild hats get in for free.

Hippodrome de Maisons-Laffitte
*1 av de la Pelouse, 78602 Maisons-Laffitte
(01.39.12.81.70). RER Maisons-Laffitte
then bus.*
Flat racing.

Hippodrome de Paris-Vincennes
*2 route de la Ferme, 12th (01.49.77.14.70).
Mº Château de Vincennes/RER Joinville-le-Pont
then free bus.*
Trotting in the Bois de Vincennes. Floodlights on
winter evenings add to the atmosphere.

Hippodrome de St-Cloud
*1 rue du Camp Canadien, 92210 St-Cloud
(01.47.71.69.26). RER Rueil-Malmaison.*
Flat racing.

Rugby

★ Stade Français Paris
*Stade Jean-Bouin, 26 av du Général-Sarrail,
16th (01.40.71.71.00/www.stade.fr). Mº Porte
d'Auteuil.* **Tickets** €5-€42. **Credit** AmEx,
MC, V.
Stade Français are one of the top teams in France.
Home matches tend to take place on Saturday
evenings. Note that the stadium is due to undergo
major work in 2010-11, and home matches will be
played at alternative venues.

ACTIVITIES & TEAM SPORTS

The Mairie manages many of the facilities
across the capital, ensuring very reasonable
entry prices. For details, consult its free annual
Parisports: Guide du Sport à Paris or view the
online version at www.sport.paris.fr. If you're
looking for sportswear and equipment, head for
the excellent **Décathlon** (www.decathlon.fr) or
Go Sport (www.go-sport.com) chain stores.

Some venues require proof of health
insurance, ID and passport-sized photos
for membership. Note that joining a club or
taking part in a competitive event (even a
fun run) usually requires a medical certificate
from a doctor.

All-round sports clubs

The **Standard Athletic Club** (route
Forestière du Pavé de Meudon, 92360 Meudon-
la-Forêt, 01.46.26.16.09, www.standac.com) is
a private sports club that welcomes English
speakers. Full membership costs €830 per

year. There are tennis and squash courts, a heated outdoor pool and workout facilities.

Local multi-sports clubs include **Lagardère Paris Racing** (01.45.67.55.86, www.lagardere parisracing.com), **ASPTT de Paris** (01.58.14.21,80, www.asptparis.com), **Paris Université Club** (01.44.16.62.62, www.puc.asso.fr) and **Stade Français** (01.40.71.33.33, www.stadefrancais.com).

American football

There are about 15 teams in the suburbs, plus 'no-tackle' flag football teams for men and women, and cheerleader squads. Contact the **Fédération Française de Football Américain** (01.43.11.14.70, www.fffa.org).

Athletics & running

Paris has plenty of municipal tracks, open to individual runners for a modest monthly subscription; for details pick up the *Guide du Sport* (*see p335*). Joggers use the banks of the Seine and the parks (Jardin du Luxembourg, Tuileries and Parc de la Villette), as well as the expansive Bois de Boulogne and Bois de Vincennes. The Paris Marathon takes place in April (*see p274-279* **Calendar**), and other classic road races include the Paris half-marathon in March and the Paris-Versailles in September (www.parisversailles.com). The **Hash House Harriers** organise weekly runs. Log on to parishhh.free.fr for details.

Baseball, softball & cricket

Most Paris teams practise in the Bois de Vincennes. The **Fédération Française de Baseball, Softball et Cricket** (01.44.68.89.30, www.ffbsc.org) has details. An English expat runs the **Château de Thoiry Cricket Club** (78770 Thoiry, 01.34.87.55.70, www.thoiry cricket.fr), 40km (25 miles) from Paris. **Paris University Club** (01.44.16.62.62, www.puc baseball.com) has baseball teams for all ages.

Basketball

Free practice courts are dotted around the city's parks and gardens, while almost every municipal sports centre has a club. Contact the **Fédération Française de Basketball** (01.53.94.25.00, www.basketfrance.com) for details.

Boules, pool & bowling

Boules or *pétanque* pitches are scattered all over Paris. Contact the **Fédération Française de Pétanque** (04.91.14.05.80, www.petanque.fr). Some pool venues require ID or a passport.

Bowling Mouffetard

73 rue Mouffetard, 5th (01.43.31.09.35/ www.bowlingmouffetard.fr). M° Place Monge. **Open** 3pm-2am Mon-Fri; 10am-2am Sat, Sun. **Admission** €3.20-€5.90 per set. *Shoe hire* €2. **Credit** AmEx, MC, V. **Map** p406 K9.
Centrally located venue with eight bowling lanes and pool tables.

Cercle Clichy Montmartre

84 rue de Clichy, 9th (01.48.78.32.85/ www.academie-billard.com). M° Place de Clichy. **Open** 11am-6am daily. **Admission** *Pool* from €12/hr. *Billiards* from €12/hr. **Credit** (€25 minimum) MC, V. **Map** p401 G2.
Historic venue decorated with frescoes, offering a huge bar and pool tables aplenty. No under-18s.

Climbing

To use any municipal climbing wall, you will need to obtain a personal ID card. Take a photo, your passport, proof of valid insurance and the fee (€4 per month) to the centre you want to use. For the real thing, try the superb boulder formations in the Forêt de Fontainebleau; **Grimporama** (www.grimporama.com) has full details, including maps, on its website. The **Club Alpin du pays de Fontainebleau** (01.64.22.67.18, caf77.free.fr) organises group climbs and weekend outings.

Centre Sportif Poissonnier

2 rue Jean-Cocteau, 18th (01.42.51.24.68). M° Porte de Clignancourt. **Open** 7am-10pm Mon-Sat; 8am-6pm Sun. **Admission** free. **No credit cards**.
The largest of the six municipal walls in Paris.

★ MurMur

55 rue Cartier-Bresson, 93500 Pantin (01.48.46.11.00/www.murmur.fr). M° Aubervilliers–Pantin Quatre Chemins. **Open** 9.30am-11pm Mon-Fri; 9.30am-6.30pm Sat, Sun. **Admission** €8-€15; €4-€7.50 reductions. *Joining fee* €15. **Credit** AmEx, MC, V.
One of Europe's best climbing walls, with 1,550sq m (16,000sq ft) of wall.
▶ *MurMur also has a wall at Issy-les-Moulineaux (see website for details).*

Cycling

City cycling is growing in popularity, thanks to Mayor Delanoë's expansion of bike lanes and the Vélib initiative. The **Fédération Française de Cyclisme** (01.49.35.69.00, www.ffc.fr) has details of the many local cycle clubs. The **Stade Vélodrome Jacques-Anquetil** (Bois de Vincennes, 12th, 01.43.68.01.27) is regularly open to amateur cyclists, and the circuits by the Hippodromes at **Vincennes** and **Longchamp** (*see p335*) attract large groups of road cyclists. **Mieux se Déplacer à Bicyclette** (01.43.20.26.02, www.mdb-idf.org) organises free rides for members (€30 per year).

Mountain biking (VTT, or *vélo tout terrain*) is popular in the many forests on the outskirts of Paris, including the Forêt de Montmorency in the north and the Fôret de Meudon in the south.

Buzibi
67 rue de Croulebarbe, 13th (01.47.07.16.75/www. buzibi.fr). M° Corvisart. **Open** 2-7pm Mon; 10am-7pm Tue-Sun. **Credit** MC, V. **Map** p406 K10.
A specialist electric bike shop. Buy, rent or get repairs.

★ Gepetto & Vélos
59 rue du Cardinal-Lemoine, 5th (01.43.54.19.95/ www.gepetto-velos.com). M° Cardinal Lemoine. **Open** 9am-1pm, 2-7.30pm Tue-Sat; 10am-7pm Sun. **Credit** MC, V. **Map** p406 K8.

And They're Off

Paris's best bets for a day at the races.

The Paris region is home to some of France's most prestigious racecourses. Just east of the centre, the **Hippodrome de Vincennes** (*see p335*) is the temple of French trotting, and hosts the prestigious Prix d'Amérique Marionnaud, also dubbed the 'world harness racing championship'. Founded in 1920, the race brings together 18 of the world's best trotters to compete for a €1m purse. Drivers sit behind the horse in two-wheeled carts called sulkies, occasionally using a long whip to direct their steed. With pom-pom girls and acrobats also on the bill, this January fixture is known for its festive vibe.

Arc de Triomphe at **Longchamp**.

The classier end of the racing scene is showcased at the world-famous Prix de l'Arc de Triomphe, held on the first Sunday of October at **Longchamp** (*see p335*) in the Bois de Boulogne. With a prize fund of €4m, the 'Arc' is Europe's richest race, and attracts the world's best thoroughbreds for its flagship flat race. In the reserved enclosures elegant dress is de rigueur, but many spectators in the main grandstand also choose to dress up. Given the entry fee of just €8, there's certainly room to budget for a posh hat. Choose the right one and you may even win a prize. Since 2001, the 'Chapeaux de l'Arc' has been awarded to women sporting the most spectacular headwear, with prizes given for both professionally designed hats and DIY creations. Expect tough competition, though. Longchamp also hosts the Grand Prix de Paris on 14 July, France's big national holiday. As a flat race, it's an important rendezvous for three-year-old thoroughbreds before the season's big autumn meetings. Entry is free and the evening ends with some suitably spectacular Bastille Day fireworks.

The region's other major flat race venue is **Chantilly** (*see p335*), some 25 miles north of Paris. In June, the Prix du Jockey Club attracts leading colts, while the Prix de Diane is for fillies. The leafy surroundings make first-class picnicking territory for a dressy crowd. Steeplechasing, meanwhile, is showcased at **Auteuil** (*see p335*), also in the Bois de Boulogne. The prestigious Grand Steeple-Chase de Paris in May features a challenging course with some 23 obstacles over its 5.8km (3.5-mile) length.

Betting for all races is done via the state-owned PMU. Odds (*la côte*) can be consulted on monitors, while tips should be garnished from the *Paris Turf* newspaper (www.paris-turf.com). To place a bet at the counters, announce the number of your horse, the amount you're betting and the type of bet. The simplest bets on a single horse are *gagnant* (to win) or *placé* (in the first three, or first two if there are fewer than eight starters). If you're confident of picking the top two or three horses (without stating the order), ask for *couplé gagnant* or *trio gagnant* respectively. For major money gains, though, try your luck at predicting the finishing order of the top three (*tiercé*), four (*quarté*) or even five (*quinté*).

Rents, sells and repairs all types of bicycles.
Other locations 46 rue Daubenton, 5th
(01.43.37.16.17).

Vélo Bastille

*22 rue Alphonse Baudin, 11th (01.48.87.60.01/
www.parisvelosympa.com). M° Richard Lenoir.*
Open 9.30am-1pm, 2-6pm Mon, Wed-Fri;
9am-1pm, 2-7pm Sat, Sun. **No credit cards**.
Map p406 L7.
Vélo Bastille offers repairs, rentals and guided
cycling tours of the city.

Diving

Courses for the French diving licence are
offered at the **Club de Plongée du 5ème**
(www.clubdeplongeedu5.org), which makes use
of a nearby swimming pool and runs trips to
the Med. **Bleu Passion** (94 bd Poniatowski,
12th, 01.43.45.26.29, www.bleu-passion.fr) runs
a diving school and sells equipment.

Fencing

For a list of clubs, consult www.escrime-ffe.fr.
The fencing section at the **Lagardère Paris
Racing** (5 rue Eblé, 7th, 01.45.67.55.86,
www.lagardereparisracing.com) is suitable for
leisure or competition, with 12 fencing masters
and 18 pistes. All levels and ages are welcome.

Fitness clubs

Club Med (www.clubmedgym.fr) dominates
the health club scene, with 22 branches in
Paris and the western suburbs, including five
Waou Clubs with spa facilities. Single visits
cost €26, and annual memberships start at
€805. Other leading fitness centres include
Vit'Halles (*see below*) and **Forest Hill**
(www.forest-hill.com).

The non-profit **La Gym Suédoise**
(01.45.00.18.22, www.gymsuedoise.com) holds
one-hour gym sessions in ten locations across
Paris. Membership is €75-€125 per term, or
€10 per session. Unlike most gyms, it runs
free trials at specified locations.

There are free weekly 'Sport Nature' sessions
of outdoor stretching, aerobics and running, set
up by the Mairie at 13 locations around town.
Check the annual *Guide du Sport* (*see p335*)
or visit www.sport.paris.fr.

Club Quartier Latin

*19 rue de Pontoise, 5th (01.55.42.77.88/www.
clubquartierlatin.com). M° Maubert Mutualité.*
Open 9am-midnight Mon-Fri; 9am-7pm Sat,
Sun. **Admission** *Pool* from €4.20. *Gym* from
€20; from €16 reductions. **Credit** MC, V.
Map p406 K7.

Home to the Pontoise pool (*see p341*), this venerable
centre off boulevard St-Germain houses no-frills fitness facilities, and has a room for step, aerobics,
stretching and yoga classes. There's a sauna too.

★ Espace Vit'Halles

*48 rue Rambuteau, 3rd (01.42.77.21.71/
www.vithalles.com). M° Rambuteau.* **Open** 8am-
10.30pm Mon-Fri; 9am-10pm Sat; 10am-7pm Sun.
Admission €25/day. **Credit** AmEx, MC, V.
Map p406 K5.
This sunken-level health club has Technogym fitness machines, a sauna and some of the best classes
in the city, particularly for step and spinning; the
classes cost extra.

Football

For information on the local amateur leagues,
contact the **Ligue Ile-de-France de
Football** (01.42.44.12.12, paris-idf.fff.fr).
To join a weekend kickabout, try the Bois de
Boulogne near Bagatelle, the Bois de Vincennes
or the Champ de Mars.

Jorkyball 92

*51 blvd de la Liberté, 92320 Chatillon
(01.40.84.01.01/www.jorkyball92.com).
M° Châtillon-Montrouge.* **Open** 10am-midnight
Mon-Fri; 10am-8pm Sat, Sun. **Admission** €40/hr
for a court. **Credit** MC, V.
Invented in France, Jorkyball is a form of two-on-
two football heavily influenced by squash. It's
played on artificial turf and this centre on the southern outskirts of Paris boasts eight courts. Footwear
is available to rent for €2.

Golf

The suburbs are full of courses suitable for all
levels and budgets. Contact the **Fédération
Française de Golf** (01.41.49.77.00,
www.ffgolf.org) for more information.

Golf du Bois de Boulogne

*Hippodrome d'Auteuil, 16th (01.44.30.70.00/
www.golfduboisdeboulogne.fr). M° Porte
d'Auteuil.* **Open** *Mid Sept-Apr* 8am-8pm daily.
May-mid Sept 8am-9pm daily. **Admission** €5.
Credit AmEx, MC, V.
This municipal site has putting greens and a practice area complete with bunkers and water obstacles.
Lessons are available from €30 for 30 minutes. It's
closed on horse-racing days, so check beforehand.

Golf National

*2 av du Golf, 78280 Guyancourt (01.30.43.36.00/
www.golf-national.com). RER St-Quentin-en-
Yvelines then taxi.* **Open** 8am-7pm Mon-Fri;
8am-8pm Sat, Sun. **Admission** €25-€120;
annual membership from €550. **Credit** MC, V.

This is the home of the French Open. There are two 18-hole courses and one nine-hole course.

Horse riding

To enjoy the horse-riding trails in the Bois de Boulogne or the Bois de Vincennes, you need to join a riding club such as **La Société d'Equitation de Paris** (Centre Hippique du Bois de Boulogne, 16th, 01.45.01.20.06, www.equitation-paris.com), the **Centre Hippique du Touring** (Bois de Boulogne, 16th, 01.45.01.20.88, www.chtcf.com) or the **Cercle Hippique du Bois de Vincennes** (8 rue de Fontenay, 94130 Nogent-sur-Marne, 01.48.73.01.28, www.chbv.fr). Beginners can learn at the **Club Bayard Equitation** in the Bois de Vincennes (Centre Bayard, UCPA Vincennes, 12th, 01.43.65.46.87, www.clubbayard.com). During July and August, you can have one-off lessons (€23) or take a special five-day course for €300. Out near Versailles, the **Haras de Jardy** (boulevard de Jardy, 92430 Marnes-la-Coquette, 01.47.01.35.30, www.haras-de-jardy.com) is open every day and offers lessons by the hour for all ages, with no membership fee. Leisurely rides in the forests of Fontainebleau are run by **La Bleausière** (06.82.01.21.18, la.bleausiere.free.fr).

Ice skating

The most popular open-air skating rink is the free one in front of the Hôtel de Ville, which is open from December to February. Smaller wintertime rinks are also erected at the Tour Montparnasse and Bibliothèque François Mitterrand. *See also pp274-279* **Calendar**.

Patinoire de Boulogne

1 rue Victor-Griffuelhes, 92100 Boulogne-Billancourt (01.46.08.00.88/www.patinoire boulogne.com). M° Marcel Sembat. **Open** 3-6pm Wed; 10.30am-1pm, 3-6pm, 9pm-midnight Sat; 10am-1pm, 3-6pm Sun (open daily during school hols). **Admission** €5.50; €4.60 reductions. **No credit cards.**
Year-round indoor rink with free skate rental.

Patinoire Pailleron

32 rue Edouard-Pailleron, 19th (01.40.40.27.70/ www.pailleron19.com). M° Bolivar. **Open** noon-1.30pm, 4-10pm Mon, Tue, Thur; noon-10pm Wed; noon-1.30pm, 4pm-midnight Fri; noon-midnight Sat; 10am-6pm Sun. **Admission** €4-€6; €3-€4 reductions. **No credit cards.** **Map** p403 N2.
Reopened in 2006, this rink is part of a renovated art deco sports complex. Skaters can sign up for hockey and dance lessons on the ice.

Patinoire Sonja Henie

Palais Omnisports de Paris-Bercy (01.40.02.60.60/ www.bercy.fr). M° Bercy. **Open** *Sept-mid June* 3-6pm Wed; 9.30pm-12.30am Fri; 3-6pm, 9.30pm-12.30am Sat; 10am-noon, 3-6pm Sun. **Admission** €3-€6. **No credit cards. Map** p407 N9.
Protection, helmets and skates for hire (€3).

In-line skating

You can hire skates from **Nomades** (37 bd Bourdin, 4th, 01.44.54.07.44, www.nomadeshop.com). For lessons for all ages, try the **Roller Squad Institute** (01.56.61.99.61, www.rsi.asso.fr). And for impressive in-line skating and skateboard acrobatics, head for **Rollerparc Avenue** (100 rue Léon-Geffroy, 01.47.18.19.19) in Vitry-sur-Seine, or the **Espace Glisse de Paris** (*see below*).

Rowing & watersports

Paris residents can row, canoe and kayak for free on Saturdays at the **Base Nautique de la Villette** (41bis quai de la Loire, 19th, 01.42.40.29.90). Reserve a week in advance and bring along proof of residence, two photos and a swimming certificate (obtainable at any pool). You can go waterskiing and wakeboarding at the **Club Nautique du 19ème** (Bassin de Vitesse de St-Cloud, 92100 Boulogne-Billancourt, 01.42.03.25.24). Serious rowers can join the annual Traversée de Paris. Contact the **Ligue Ile-de-France d'Aviron** (94736 Nogent-sur-Marne, 01.48.75.79.10). For a leisurely paddle, hire a boat at Lac Daumesnil or Lac des Minimes in the Bois de Vincennes, or at Lac Supérieur in the Bois de Boulogne.

Rugby

For a good standard of play, try the **Athletic Club de Boulogne** (Stade du Saut du Loup, av de la Butte-Mortemart, 16th, 01.41.10.25.30, www.acbb.fr), which fields two teams. The **British Rugby Club of Paris** (58-60 av de la Grande Armée, 17th, 01.40.55.15.15, www.brfcparis.com) fields two teams in the corporate league.

Skateboarding

In 2008, the Mairie inaugurated the **Espace Glisse de Paris** (*see p340*), doubtless hoping to reduce skateboarding in public places. Nonetheless, the most popular skateboarding spots remain the riverfront courtyard at the **Palais de Tokyo**, known as 'Le Dôme', and the ledges and steps at **Trocadéro**.

La **Défense** tends to be full of security guards, but is still worth exploring for smooth marble, ledges and rails; the **Palais Omnisports de Paris-Bercy** (*see p334*) has vast ledges and some almighty gaps.

A more relaxed scene is to be found at the **place des Innocents** (by the Forum des Halles, 1st), which has low ledges and smooth ground, and at the **Opéra Bastille** (11th), which has small steps. For equipment and advice, try **Street Machine** at Les Halles (12 rue des Halles, 1st, 01.40.26.47.90, www.streetmachine.fr).

Cosanostra Skatepark
18 rue du Tir, 77500 Chelles (01.64.72.14.04/ www.cosanostraskatepark.net). RER Chelles-Gournay. **Open** *July, Aug* 2-8pm Mon-Wed, Sat; 2-11pm Thur, Fri; 2-7pm Sun. *Sept-June* 4-11pm Tue, Thur, Fri; 2-8pm Sat; 2-7pm Sun. **Admission** €6. *Season ticket* €274; €258 under-13s. **No credit cards**.
A huge indoor street course and micro-ramp, which hosts international competitions.

★ Espace Glisse de Paris
Stade des Fillettes, 54bis bd Neyn, 18th (01.55.26.97.92/ www.egp18.com). M° Porte de la Chapelle. **Admission** free.
Opened in 2008, this covered complex provides urban sports fans with a vast space. There are bowls and street furniture, plus a funbox and beginners area. Different time slots are allocated for skaters, bladers and BMXers, so check ahead. Equipment can be hired on site.

Squash

No membership is necessary to play squash at the **Club Quartier Latin** (*see p338*), which charges €20-€30 per match (racket rental from €2.50). The **Standard Athletic Club** (*see p335*) also rents squash courts to members or on payment of a €185 seasonal fee.

Squash Montmartre
14 rue Achille-Martinet, 18th (01.42.55.38.30). M° Lamarck Caulaincourt. **Open** 10am-11pm Mon-Fri; 10am-7pm Sat, Sun. **Admission** from €11. **Credit** V.
Period memberships are available at this club, as well as equipment hire.

Swimming

Pools are plentiful and cheap. Most require a swimming cap and ban bermudas, and many are open late. Swimming to music is integral to **Nuit Blanche** in October (*see p278*). Times given below may change during school and national holidays.

Piscine Pontoise Quartier Latin.

Aquaboulevard
4 rue Louis-Armand, 15th (01.40.60.10.00/ www.aquaboulevard.com). M° Balard. **Open** 9am-11pm Mon-Thur; 9am-midnight Fri; 8am-midnight Sat; 8am-11pm Sun. **Admission** *6hrs* €20-€25; €12 reductions. **Credit** AmEx, MC, V. **Map** p404 A10.
With year-round summer temperatures, this water park under a giant atrium is great fun for kids. An extra charge gets you a steam bath and three saunas.

Piscine Butte-aux-Cailles
5 pl Paul-Verlaine, 13th (01.45.89.60.05). M° Place d'Italie. **Open** 7-8am, 11.30am-1.30pm, 4.30-6.30pm Tue; 7am-7pm Wed; 7-8.30am, 11.30am-6.30pm Thur, Fri; 7-8am, 10am-6pm Sat; 8am-5.30pm Sun. **Admission** €3; €1.70 reductions. **Credit** AmEx, MC, V.
This listed complex, built in the 1920s, has one main indoor pool and two outdoor pools (open in the summer). The water is a temptingly warm 28°C, thanks to the natural sulphurous spring.

Piscine Georges-Vallerey
148 av Gambetta, 20th (01.40.31.15.20). M° Porte des Lilas. **Open** 11.45am-1.30pm Mon; 11.45am-1.30pm, 5.15pm-10pm Tue, Thur; 10am-1pm, 2-7pm Wed; 9am-5pm Sat, Sun. **Admission** €3; €1.70 reductions. **Credit** (€15 minimum) MC, V.

Built for the 1924 Olympics, this complex features a retractable Plexiglas roof, a 50m pool (often split into two 25m pools) and one for kids.

★ Piscine Josephine-Baker
Quai François-Mauriac, 13th (01.56.61.96.50).
Mº Quai de la Gare. **Open** 7-8.30am, 1-9pm Mon;
1-11pm Tue, Thur; 7-8.30am, 1-9pm Wed, Fri;
11am-8pm Sat; 10am-8pm Sun. **Admission** €3;
€1.70 reductions. **Credit** MC, V. **Map** p407 M10.
Moored on the Seine by the Bibliothèque Nationale, the pool is back to shipshape, apparently cured of the technical problems that plagued it since opening a few years ago. The revamped complex boasts a 25m main pool (with sliding glass roof), a paddling pool and café, and a busy schedule of exercise classes.

Piscine Keller
14 rue de l'Ingénieur Keller, 15th (01.45.71.81.00).
Mº Charles Michels. **Open** noon-10pm Mon;
7-8.30am, noon-10pm Tue, Thur; 7am-2pm Wed;
noon-10pm Fri; 9am-9pm Sat; 9am-7pm Sun.
Admission €3; €1.70 reductions. **Credit** V.
Map p404 B8.
Fully renovated in 2008, this 50m pool features a retractable roof and uses an innovative, chlorine-free water treatment method. Lane-swimming is prioritised, and there's a 15m pool for kids.

Piscine Nakache
4-12 rue Dénoyez, 20th (01.58.53.57.80). Mº
Belleville. **Open** 7-8am, 11.30am-1.30pm, 4.30-6pm Tue, Fri; 7am-6pm Wed; 7-8.30am, 11.30am-1.30pm, 4.30-10pm Thur; 7-8am, 7am-6pm Sat; 8am-6pm Sun. **Admission** €3; €1.70 reductions.
No credit cards. Map p403 N4.
Opened in 2009, the city's newest swimming complex boasts two pools (25m and 12.5m) and a children's paddling pool, all treated with ozone rather than chlorine. There's also a gym and sauna, plus a mysterious sound artwork by Melik Ohanian in the changing rooms.

★ Piscine Pontoise Quartier Latin
18 rue de Pontoise, 5th (01.55.42.77.88/www.
clubquartierlatin.com). Mº Maubert Mutualité.
Open 7-8.30am, 12.15-1.30pm, 4.30-10pm Mon;
7-8.30am, 12.15-1.30pm, 4.30-7pm Tue, Thur;
7-8.30am, 11.30am-7.30pm Wed; 7-8.30am, 12.15-1.30pm, 4.30-8pm Fri; 10am-7pm Sat; 8am-7pm Sun. *Night swimming* 8.15-11.45pm Mon-Fri.
Admission €4.20; €2.40 reductions; €10 for all 9-11.45pm. **No credit cards. Map** p406 K7.
A beautiful art deco pool with two mezzanine levels. It has private locker rooms, plus night swimming to underwater music. Small fee for lockers.

Piscine Suzanne-Berlioux
Forum des Halles, 10 pl de la Rotonde, 1st
(01.42.36.98.44). Mº Les Halles. **Open** 11.30am-11pm Mon; 11.30am-10pm Tue; 7-8.15am,

10am-11pm Wed; 11.30am-10pm Thur, Fri;
9am-7pm Sat, Sun. **Admission** €4; €3
reductions. **Credit** (€8 minimum) MC, V.
Map p402 J5.
Although usually pretty busy, this 50m pool with its own tropical greenhouse is good for lane swimming. There are no lockers, so you need to check in belongings with the attendants. It reopened in 2008 after renovation.

Tennis & table tennis

The six tennis courts at the **Jardin du Luxembourg** (01.43.25.79.18) are convenient, but there's a better selection at the **Centre Sportif La Faluère** (113 route de la Pyramide, 12th, 01.43.74.40.93) in the Bois de Vincennes.

To find public table tennis in parks around town, consult the *Guide du Sport* (*see p335*).

Centre Sportif Suzanne-Lenglen
2 rue Louis-Armand, 15th (01.44.26.26.50).
Mº Balard. **Open** 7am-10pm Mon-Fri; 7am-7pm Sat, Sun. **Admission** from €3. **No credit cards. Map** p404 A10.
Fourteen courts, two of which are covered.

Club Forest Hill
4 rue Louis-Armand, 15th (01.40.60.10.00/
www.aquaboulevard.com). Mº Balard/RER Bd
Victor. **Open** 7am-midnight daily. **Admission** prices vary. **No credit cards. Map** p404 A10.
Tennis, table tennis and other racquet sports at most of the dozen branches in and around Paris.

Triathlon

The multi-discipline effort of triathlon (swim, bike, run) is one of Europe's fastest growing sports, and the Paris area hosts some of the biggest clubs. The Paris Triathlon (www.triathlondeparis.fr) offers a short distance event for beginners, with the main race comprising a 1.5km swim in the Seine, a 40km bike leg around the Bois de Boulogne, and a 10km run in the Hippodrome de Longchamp. For details of local clubs, contact the Ligue Ile de France de Triathlon (www.idftriathlon.com).

> **INSIDE TRACK**
> **GAME, SET, MATCH**
>
> If you fancy a rally or two, the **Paris Tennis** system (www.tennis.paris.fr) allows you to register a password and reserve a court online for €7.50 per hour, €14 for indoor courts.

ARTS & ENTERTAINMENT

Theatre

The stars are coming out to play.

France's actors are still battling it out since the government reduced theatre subsidies, making it increasingly difficult for unknown thesps to earn a decent living. Fortunately for us, though, the show must go on, and it does with a jam-packed 2010-11 season marked by old regulars like Molière and Feydeau, foreign musicals, plus a flood of 'serious' international and home-grown productions, some of which include French stars – making them sure-fire crowd pleasers. It's a full house in the city of lights, from Peter Brook to the *banlieue* fringe.

PARIS IN STAGES

Paris's stages continue to go global. British-born Peter Brook is the stalwart English-language provider at the **Théâtre des Bouffes du Nord**, although he does tremendous credit to French classical repertoire too. Villette's **Le Tarmac** theatre (Parc de la Villette, behind the Grand Halle, 19th, 01.40.03.93.90, http://letarmac.fr) houses the TILF (Théâtre International de Langue Française), the only theatre in France dedicated to the Francophone world, welcoming visiting troupes from Africa, Asia and Canada; and on the other side of the *Périph*, the **MC93 Bobigny** hosts international companies performing in their own tongues.

After the huge success of Tennessee Williams's *Baby Doll* last year at the **Théâtre de l'Atelier** (1 place Charles-Dullin, 18th, 01.46.06.49.24, www.theatre-atelier.com), translations of English and American plays remain in vogue. Several theatres have hopped on the bandwagon, with Hitchcock's *Les 39 Marches* (The 39 Steps) playing at the

Théâtre de la Bruyère (5 rue de la Bruyère, 9th, 01.48.74.76.99, www.theatrelabruyere.com), to be followed by another Tennessee Williams classic, *A Streetcar Named Desire*, starring silver-screen beauty Isabelle Huppert, at the **Odéon, Théâtre de l'Europe** (also known for its multitude of European-language plays). Meanwhile, Shakespeare's *Cymbeline* gets an airing at the MC93 Bobigny.

Aside from Huppert at the Odéon, this year's celebrity draws are Audrey Tautou – aka Amélie Poulain – in Henrick Ibsen's *Maison de Poupée* (A Doll's House) at the **Théâtre de la Madeleine**, and ex-Bond Girl Carole Bouquet in Marivaux's *La Fausse Suivante* at **Les Bouffes du Nord** in April and May.

On the musicals front, the **Théâtre du Châtelet** is pioneering the art form, with blockbusting musicals fresh from London's West End. After *The Sound of Music* in early 2010 comes Stephen Sondheim's *A Little Night Music* in February, and the great *Les Misérables* in May (in English).

If singing and dancing are too light-hearted for you, get serious at the **Comédie Française** on the Right Bank, which continues to uphold the classics with flair. Or, for something wholly experimental, try Ionesco's absurdist *La Cantatrice Chauve*, which has been playing non-stop since 1957 in the **Théâtre de la Huchette**. The **Théâtre National de Chaillot**, **Théâtre du Rond Point**, **Théâtre de la Ville** and **Théâtre de la Bastille** (76 rue de la Roquette, 11th, 01.43.57.42.14, www.theatre-bastille.com) all offer relentlessly new and exciting spectacles that frequently combine off-the-wall theatre

---

INSIDE TRACK
LAST-MINUTE DISCOUNTS

For cheap tickets for same-night performances try the **Kiosques de Théâtre** (www.kiosquetheatre.com) on place de la Madeleine (8th), place de Ternes (17th) and in front of the Gare Montparnasse (14th). All are open 12.30-8pm Tue-Sat, 12.30-4pm Sun.

---

with dance or music too. And in the Bois de Vincennes, a special theatre bus takes you to the **Cartoucherie**, a factory remade as a theatre commune that's home to five innovative companies, including Ariane Mnouchkine's award-winning **Théâtre du Soleil**.

ALTERNATIVE THEATRE

For a healthy dose of eccentricity, head to Paris's array of alternative venues. Most are run by diehards addressing the industry's financial shortcomings by turning any premises they can get their hands on – disused factories, squats and the like – into theatres.

The bastion of alternative theatre in the north is the **Lavoir Moderne Parisien** (35 rue Léon, 18th, 01.42.52.09.14, www.rueleon.net),

a converted washhouse whose shows often tackle themes of immigration and identity. The **Point Ephémère** (*see p322*) and its gargantuan older brother, **Mains d'Oeuvres** (*see p329*), are cool urban arts centres (in former warehouses) that stage multidisciplinary performances. **Confluences** (190 bd de Charonne, 20th, 01.40.24.16.34/http://confluences.jimdo.com) is an all-in-one cultural centre – also housed in an old warehouse – equipped with an art gallery, theatre and projection room; and **Les Laboratoires d'Aubervilliers** (41 rue Lécuyer, 93300 Aubervilliers, 01.53.56.15.90, www.les laboratoires.org) churns out some wonderful, conceptualist productions that frequently mix and match acting with the disciplines of other resident artists (video, sound, dance).

Théâtre National de Chaillot. *See p346*.

ARTS & ENTERTAINMENT

Théâtre de la Huchette. *See p346.*

SHOWS IN ENGLISH

Despite first appearances, catching a play in English in Paris is easy – when you know where to look. Aside from the Théâtre de l'Odéon, which programmes productions in English, German, Spanish and Italian, Peter Brook's Théâtre des Bouffes du Nord offers regular plays in English, and the **Théâtre de la Cité Internationale**, MC93 Bobigny and the versatile stage at the **Centre Pompidou** (pl Georges-Pompidou, 4th, 01.44.78.12.33, www.cnac-gp.com) often follow suit.

Several companies offer a range of English-language shows and English translations of French works. Local improv troupe the **Improfessionals** (www.improfessionals.com) has been treading the boards of central Paris for the last seven years, offering off-the-cuff stuff; the **Théâtre en Anglais** group (4bis rue de Strasbourg, 92600 Asnières, 01.55.02.37.87, http://theatre.anglais.free.fr) travels around France, but usually stages a well-crafted interpretation of Shakespeare's *Romeo and Juliet* at the Bataclan (50 bd Voltaire, 11th, 01.43.14.00.30, www.le-bataclan.com) for its Paris stint. Shakespeare is also performed in English every June at the Bois de Boulogne's Théâtre de Verdure du Jardin Shakespeare (01.40.19.95.33, www.jardinshakespeare.fr) by the **Tower Theatre Company** (+44 207 353 5700, www.towertheatre.org.uk).

TICKETS AND INFORMATION

For weekly listings check out *L'Officiel des Spectacles* and *Pariscope* (available from news kiosks). Tickets can be bought at the theatres, from **Fnac** or **Virgin Megastore** (for both, *see p271*) or online at www.theatreonline.com.

Check out www.theatresprives.com for half-price tickets to performances during the first week of a new show.

RIGHT BANK

Cartoucherie de Vincennes
Route du Champ de Manoeuvre, Bois de Vincennes, 12th. M° Château de Vincennes, then shuttle bus.
Théâtre de l'Aquarium *(01.43.74.99.61/ www.theatredelaquarium.com).*
Théâtre du Chaudron *(01.43.28.97.04/ www.theatreduchaudron.fr).*
Théâtre de l'Epée de Bois *(01.48.08.39.74/ www.epeedebois.com).*
Théâtre du Soleil *(01.42.74.87.63/ www.theatre-du-soleil.fr).*
Théâtre de la Tempête *(01.43.28.36.36/ www.la-tempete.fr).*
Past the Château de Vincennes in the middle of the woods, five independent theatres offer first-class, politically committed fare. This drama-lover's heaven is housed in ex-army munitions warehouses, where you will be met with home-made soup.

★ Comédie Française
All *www.comedie-francaise.fr.*
Salle Richelieu *2 rue Richelieu, 1st (08.25.10.16.80/01.44.58.15.15). M° Palais Royal Musée du Louvre.* **Box office** 11am-6.30pm daily. **Admission** €11-€37. *1hr before show* €5 for cheapest seats only; €11 under-28s (free on Mon at the door 1hr before show).
Credit AmEx, MC, V. **Map** p401 H5.
Studio-Théâtre *Galerie du Carrousel du Louvre, 99 rue de Rivoli, 1st (01.44.58.98.58/ 01.44.58.98.58). M° Palais Royal Musée du Louvre.* **Box office** 2-5pm on performance day. **Admission** €7-€17; €4-€13 reductions. **Credit** MC, V. **Map** p401 H5.
Théâtre du Vieux Colombier *21 rue du Vieux Colombier, 6th (01.44.39.87.00/ 01.44.39.87.01). M° St-Sulpice.* **Box office** 1-6pm Mon, Sun; 11am-6pm Tue-Sat. **Admission** €8-€28; €6-€14 reductions. *45 mins before show* €14 under-28s. **Credit** MC, V. **Map** p405 G7.
The gilded mother of French theatres, the Comédie Française turns out season after season of classics, as well as lofty new productions. The red velvet and gold-flecked Salle Richelieu is located right by the Palais-Royal; under the same management are the Studio-Théâtre, a black box inside the Carrousel du Louvre, and the Théâtre du Vieux Colombier. The line-up for 2010 includes Corneille's *Illusion Comique.*

★ Théâtre des Bouffes du Nord
37bis bd de la Chapelle, 10th (01.46.07.34.50/ www.bouffesdunord.com). M° La Chapelle. **Box office** 11am-6pm Mon-Sat. **Admission** €12-€26; €10-€22 reductions. **Credit** MC, V. **Map** p402 K2.

Peter Brook's playground for more than 30 years, the Bouffes du Nord treats us to an adaptation of Shakespeare's *Tempest* in 2010, directed and adapted by Brook's daughter Irena.
▶ *The Bouffes du Nord also has one of the best chamber music programmes in the capital.*

Théâtre du Châtelet
1 pl du Châtelet, 1st (01.40.28.28.40/ www.chatelet-theatre.com). M° Châtelet. **Box office** 10am-7pm Mon-Sat. **Admission** €25.50-€150. **Credit** AmEx, DC, MC, V. **Map** p408 J6.
The Châtelet is fast becoming Paris's main venue for musicals hailing from Broadway and the West End – such as *The Sound of Music* – usually performed in the original language by visiting companies. It's the only venue in Paris to offer such quality musical theatre.

Théâtre de la Madeleine
19 rue de Surène, 8th (01.42.65.07.09/ www.theatremadeleine.com). M° Madeleine. **Box office** 11am-7pm daily. **Admission** €20-€47. **Credit** MC, V. **Map** p401 F4.
The theatre where Sacha Guitry composed 24 of his plays, between 1932 and 1940, continues to contribute to France's repertoire with top-notch creations by emerging and established artists. After *Qui est Mr Schmitt?*, starring Richard Berry, in 2009, Audrey Tautou gives the stage a whirl with *A Doll's House* in 2010.

Théâtre Marigny
Av de Marigny, 8th (01.53.96.70.30/ www.theatremarigny.fr). M° Champs-Elysées Clemenceau or Franklin D. Roosevelt. **Box office** 11am-6.30pm Mon-Sat; 11am-3pm Sun. **Admission** €33-€51. **Credit** MC, V. **Map** p401 E4.
Théâtre Marigny is one of the most expensive nights out for theatregoers in Paris. But then not many other theatres can boast so much: a location off the Champs-Elysées; a deluxe interior conceived by Charles Garnier (of Opéra fame); high-profile casts and an illustrious pedigree stretching back 150 years. Productions have included the French adaptation of *Equus*; Juliette Binoche's *IN-I* had its debut here in 2009.

INSIDE TRACK ALL ABOARD

A free shuttle bus takes theatregoers to the **Cartoucherie** (*see above*) in the Bois de Vincennes. The bus leaves from the Château de Vincennes métro station; leave the station at the Bois de Vincennes exit – you'll find the bus in front of the taxi rank.

ARTS & ENTERTAINMENT

Théâtre National de Chaillot

1 pl du Trocadéro, 16th (01.53.65.30.00/
www.theatre-chaillot.fr). M° Trocadéro. **Box
office** 11am-7pm Mon-Sat. **Admission**
€17.50-€35; €9-€27 reductions. **Credit** MC, V.
Map p400 B4.
Get here early, grab a cocktail and gaze in awe at the
Eiffel Tower through the lobby window. Chaillot's
three auditoriums range from cosy and experimental
to a 2,800-seater amphitheatre. In 2010, the season is
well endowed in the dance department with performances by several visiting troupes, including William
Forsythe's *I Don't Believe in Outer Space. Photo p343.*

Théâtre du Rond Point

2bis av Franklin D. Roosevelt, 8th
(01.44.95.98.21/www.theatredurondpoint.fr).
M° Champs-Elysées Clemenceau or Franklin D.
Roosevelt. **Box office** noon-7pm Tue-Sat; noon-
4pm Sun. **Admission** €26-€33; €14 under-30s;
€24 over-60s. **Credit** MC, V. **Map** p401 E4.
More than just a theatre, this historic venue multitasks as a bookshop, tearoom and restaurant. So
once you've fed your mind on contemporary, avant-
garde and sometimes politically slanted theatre,
make a night of it and opt for dinner as well.

★ Théâtre de la Ville & Théâtre des Abbesses

01.42.74.22.77/www.theatredelaville-paris.com.
Box office 11am-7pm Mon; 11am-8pm Tue-Sat.
Admission €15-€26; €12-€14 reductions.
Credit MC, V.
Théâtre de la Ville *2 pl du Châtelet, 4th.*
M° Châtelet. **Map** p406 J6.
Théâtre des Abbesses *31 rue des Abbesses,*
18th. M° Abbesses. **Map** p402 H1.
At its two sites, the 'City Theatre' turns out the most
consistently innovative programming in Paris.
Instead of running a standard rep company, the
house imports music, dance and theatre productions.

LEFT BANK

Le Lucernaire

53 rue Notre-Dame-des-Champs, 6th
(01.45.44.57.34/www.lucernaire.fr). M° Notre-
Dame-des-Champs or Vavin. **Box office** 10am-
7pm daily. **Admission** €20-€30; €10-€15
reductions. **Credit** MC, V. **Map** p401 F4.
Three theatres, three cinemas, a restaurant and a bar
make up this versatile cultural centre. Theatre-wise,
Molière and other classic playwrights get a good
thrashing, but so do up-and-coming authors.

★ Odéon, Théâtre de L'Europe

Pl de l'Odéon, 6th (01.44.85.40.00/bookings
01.44.85.40.40/www.theatre-odeon.fr). M°
Odéon. **Box office** 11am-6.30pm Mon-Sat.
Admission €10-€30; €6-€16 reductions.
Credit MC, V. **Map** p408 H7.

In 2010 both the main Odéon and its sister theatre,
Les Ateliers Berthier (1 rue André Suarès, 17th), are
showcasing politically engaging plays about Europe
as a whole, plus the Impatience festival for young
theatre companies (17-26 June).

Théâtre de la Cité Internationale

17 bd Jourdan, 14th (01.43.13.50.50/www.
theatredelacite.com). RER Cité Universitaire.
Box office 2-7pm Mon-Sat. **Admission** €21;
€5-€14 reductions. **Credit** MC, V.
A polished, professional theatre on the campus of
the Cité Universitaire, the Théâtre de la Cité displays
an international flair worthy of its setting. In addition to the main theatre and dance season, the prestigious Ecole du Théâtre National de Strasbourg
occupies the stage for a short stint each summer.

Théâtre de la Huchette

23 rue de la Huchette, 5th (01.43.26.38.99/www.
theatrehuchette.com). M° Cluny La Sorbonne
or St-Michel. **Box office** 5-9pm Mon-Sat.
Admission €20; €15 reductions; €30 double
bill ticket. **Credit** MC, V. **Map** p408 J7.
Ionesco's absurdist classic *La Cantatrice Chauve*
(The Bald Soprano) has been playing here since
1957, running on a double bill with his *La Leçon.*
Photo p344.

BEYOND THE PERIPHERIQUE

Culture doesn't end at the city ring road. A
combination of measures designed to bring
theatre to the masses and extortionate rental
rates for independent productions inside Paris
has led to the creation of several excellent
out-of-town venues.
   In the north-east, **MC93 Bobigny** (1 bd
Lénine, 93000 Bobigny, 01.41.60.72.72, www.
mc93.com) is a slick institution dedicated to
promoting global cross-cultural exchange with
visiting companies from across France and
abroad. The **Théâtre Gérard-Philipe** (59 bd
Jules-Guesde, 93207 St-Denis, 01.48.13.70.00,
www.theatregerardphilipe.com), run by Alain
Ollivier, offers consistently good fare of an
experimental nature, including the seasonal
Et Moi Alors? festival for youngsters.
   Just beyond La Défense's lofty towers, the
Théâtre Nanterre Amandiers (7 av Pablo
Picasso, 92022 Nanterre, 01.46.14.70.00, www.
nanterre-amandiers.com, shuttle bus from RER
Nanterre-Préfécture 1hr before show) provides
an eclectic mix of probing modern theatre
(often of a sticky political nature), as well as
the great classics and occasional opera. And the
Théâtre d'Ivry Antoine Vitez (1 rue Simon
Dereure, 94200 Ivry, 01.43.90.11.11, www.theatre-
quartiers-ivry.com) has a theatre, dance studio
and auditorium, where an interesting mix of
classics and contemporary works are performed.

Escapes & Excursions

Château Royal d'Amboise. *See p360.*

Escapes & Excursions

Head out of town for châteaux and champagne by the bucketload.

The forests surrounding Paris were once the playground of royalty and aristrocracy, and their extravagant legacy is plain to see in sumptuous châteaux such as Fontainebleau and Versailles. Further afield, the vineyards of Champagne are less than an hour from the capital, and even the Med is only a few hours away by TGV.

In this chapter, divided into **Excursions** (day trips) and **Escapes** (destinations further afield), we've listed local tourist information centres, which have details about specific areas. For the main entries – cathedrals, châteaux and other big attractions – we've included details of opening times, admission and transport; but be aware that these can change without notice. Always phone in advance to check. For a list of mainline stations in Paris and their destinations, *see p366.*

Excursions

AUVERS-SUR-OISE

This rural retreat is where Van Gogh spent his last weeks. His tiny attic room at the **Auberge Ravoux** is open to the public. Other Auvers residents included fellow artists Camille Pissarro, Paul Cézanne and Charles-François Daubigny. Today you can explore the **Daubigny Museum** (Manoir des Colombières, rue de la Sansonne, 01.30.36.80.20, www.musee-daubigny. com) and his studio (61 rue Daubigny, 01.34.48.03.03, www.atelier-daubigny.com), which is still decorated with his murals.

Another attraction is the **Absinthe Museum** (44 rue Callé, 01.30.36.83.26, www.musee-absinthe.com), a rather modest collection of art and artefacts related to the notorious drink. Banned in France since 1915, the green concoction is not available at the replica café-bar upstairs.

The local artistic legacy has not been overlooked by Auvers' main historical attraction, either. The 17th-century **Château d'Auvers** (rue de Léry, 01.34.48.48.45, www.chateau-auvers.fr) features a walk-through tour with an Impressionist theme.

Auberge Ravoux
1 pl de la Mairie, 95430 Auvers-sur-Oise (01.30.36.60.60/www.maisondevangogh.fr).
Open *Mar-Oct* 10am-6pm Wed-Sun.
Admission €5. **Credit** *Shop & restaurant* AmEx, MC, V.

Where to eat & stay

You can always do as Van Gogh might have done, and dine at the **Auberge Ravoux** (*see above*). Otherwise, try **L'Impressionit' Café** (Château d'Auvers, rue de Léry, 01.34.48.48.48), which does cheap lunches. The **Hostellerie du Nord** (6 rue Général-de-Gaulle, 01.30.36.70.74, www.hostelleriedunord.fr, closed lunch Sat, dinner Mon & Sun) has chef Joël Boilleaut running the kitchen; upstairs are eight double rooms (€99-€189).

Getting there

By car
35km (22 miles) north from Paris by A15, exit 7, then N184, exit Méry-sur-Oise for Auvers.

By train
From Gare du Nord, changing at St-Ouen L'Aumone (whole journey takes about 1hr).

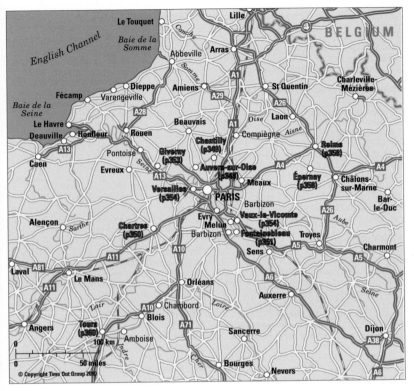

Tourist information

Office de Tourisme
Manoir des Colombières, rue de la Sansonne, 95430 Auvers-sur-Oise (01.30.36.10.06/ www.auvers-sur-oise.com). **Open** *Apr-Oct* 9.30am-12.30pm, 2-6pm Tue-Sun. *Nov-Mar* 9.30am-12.30pm, 2-5pm Tue-Sun.

CHANTILLY & SENLIS

From the 14th century until 1897, the town of **Chantilly** was the domain of the Princes of Condé, the cousins of the French kings. As well as its impressive **château**, Chantilly, with its hunting forests and prestigious horse-racing centres, has a rich equestrian history.

Much of the cream-coloured château, a fine example of French Renaissance architecture, was destroyed during the Revolution, leaving the main wing to be reconstructed in the 19th century by Henri d'Orléans, Duc d'Aumale. When the duke died in 1897, he bequeathed the Domaine de Chantilly – including the Grand Stables, the Hippodrome and the 61-square-

kilometre (23-square-mile) forest – to the Institut de France on the condition that the château be opened to the public as the **Musée Condé**, and that none of the artworks would be moved or loaned to other museums. His remarkable collection is complemented by the surrounding **park**, beautifully landscaped by André Le Nôtre (of Versailles fame).

The Grandes Ecuries ('great stables') at the château were commissioned in 1719 by Prince Louis-Henri de Bourbon (who believed he would be reincarnated as a horse). Later, they became one of Napoleon's equestrian training grounds, having suffered only light damage during the Revolution. In 1982 the great horseman Yves Bienaimé restored the stables and turned them into the **Musée Vivant du Cheval**. The Bienaimé family has also restored the **Potager des Princes**, the princes' old vegetable garden.

The **Forêt de Chantilly** is full of hiking and cycling trails. A pleasant walk of around seven kilometres (four miles) circles four small lakes, the Etangs de Commelles, and passes the Château de la Reine Blanche, a mill converted in the 1820s into a pseudo-medieval hunting lodge. For trail details, ask at the Office National des Forêts (1 av de Sylvie, 03.44.57.03.88, www.onf.fr).

Senlis, not far east of Chantilly, is known as the birthplace of the French monarchy.

Château de Chantilly/Musée Condé
Chantilly (03.44.27.31.80/www.chateaude chantilly.com). **Open** *Apr-Oct* 10am-6pm Mon, Wed-Sun. *Nov-Mar* 10.30am-5pm Mon, Wed-Sun. **Admission** *Château & park* €11; free under-18s. **Credit** MC, V.

The major attraction here is the collection of paintings and drawings at the Musée Condé. The collection includes three paintings by Raphael, and the *Très Riches Heures du Duc de Berry*, a medieval book of hours, containing the most exquisite colours imaginable. If you thought the Middle Ages was dull, think again.

★ Château park
Chantilly (03.44.27.31.80/www.chateaude chantilly.com). **Open** *Apr-Oct* 10am-8pm (last admission 6pm) Mon, Wed-Sun. *Nov-Mar* 10.30am-6pm (last admission 5pm) Mon, Wed-Sun. **Admission** *Park only* €6; free under-18s. *Combined ticket* (boat tour, carriage ride, mini-train rides) from €10. **Credit** MC, V.

The main section of the château's sprawling park, designed by royal landscape architect Le Nôtre, features traditional French formal parterres and an extensive canal system, which allows visitors to see the park from electric-powered boats. Get off the beaten path to explore the English Garden, the Island of Love, the kangaroo zoo and the original hamlet that inspired Marie-Antoinette to build her own version at Versailles.

Musée Vivant du Cheval
Les Grandes Ecuries, Chantilly (03.44.27.31.80/ www.museevivantducheval.fr). **Open** *Apr-Oct* 10am-6pm Mon, Wed-Fri; 10.30am-5.30pm Sat, Sun. *Nov-Mar* 1-6pm Mon, Wed-Fri; 1-5pm Sat, Sun. **Admission** €9; €7 reductions. **Credit** MC, V.

This museum is an interactive affair, where kids can pet the ponies and everyone gets to learn how the horses are trained to perform in the ring. It is closed for renovation until 2011.

Potager des Princes
Parc de la Faisanderie, 17 rue de la Faisanderie, Chantilly (03.44.57.39.66/www.potagerdes princes.com). **Open** *Apr-Nov* 2-7pm daily (last admission 5.30pm). **Admission** €7.50; €6.50 reductions. **Credit** MC, V.

The restored princes' kitchen garden is a 19th-century English garden with vegetable plots, trained fruit trees, a small farmyard and an open-air theatre next to the lake.

Where to eat & stay

Try the home-style cooking at **Le Goutillon** (61 rue du Connétable, 03.44.58.01.00). **La Capitainerie** (03.44.57.15.89, www.restaurant fp-chantilly.com) offers good French food in what were originally the château kitchens. To sample Chantilly whipped cream, stop for tea at **Aux Goûters Champêtres** (03.44.57.46.21, closed mid Nov-mid Mar) in the *hameau* at the château.

One of the few hotels in the town centre is the **Hôtel du Parc Best Western** (36 av du Maréchal-Joffre, 03.44.58.20.00, www.hotel-parc-chantilly.com, doubles €130-€150).

Getting there

By car
40km (25 miles) from Paris by N16 (direct) or A1 (Chantilly exit).

By train
SNCF Chantilly-Gouvieux from Gare du Nord (30mins), then 5min walk to town, 20mins to château. Some trains stop at Creil, then loop back to Chantilly.

Tourist information

Office de Tourisme (Chantilly)
60 av Maréchal-Joffre, 60500 Chantilly (03.44.67.37.37/www.chantilly-tourisme.com). **Open** *Oct-Apr* 9.30am-12.30pm, 1.30-5.30pm Mon-Sat. *May-Sept* 9.30am-12.30pm, 1.30-5.30pm Mon-Sat; 10am-1.30pm Sun.

Office de Tourisme (Senlis)
Pl du parvis Notre-Dame, 60302 Senlis (03.44.53.06.40/www.senlis-tourisme.com). **Open** *Mar-Oct* 10am-12.30pm, 2-6.15pm Mon-Sat; 10.30am-1pm, 2-6.15pm Sun. *Nov-Feb* 10am-12.30pm, 2-5pm Mon-Sat; 10.30am-1pm, 2-5pm Sun.

CHARTRES

Seen from a distance, the mismatched spires and dazzling silhouette of **Chartres cathedral** burst out of the Beauce cornfields and dominate the skyline of this modest town some 90 kilometres (56 miles) south-west of Paris. Chartres was a pilgrimage site long before the cathedral was built, ever since the Sacra Camisia (said to be the Virgin Mary's birthing garment) was donated in 876 by the king. The cathedral is one of the finest examples of Gothic architecture in the world: its doorways bristling with sculpture, along with its stained glass, embody a complete medieval world view.

The town of Chartres is an attractive tangle of narrow, medieval streets on the banks of the river Eure. Two sights merit a special mention: the **Musée des Beaux-Arts** (29 cloître Notre-Dame, 02.37.90.45.80), which houses a collection of 18th-century French paintings by Watteau and others; and the **memorial to Jean Moulin**, the legendary figure of the Resistance. A wartime prefect of Chartres until he was dismissed by the Vichy government after his refusal to co-operate with the Nazis, Moulin became de Gaulle's man in France, and died under torture in Lyon in 1943. His memorial is a ten-minute walk west of the cathedral, at the corner of rue Collin d'Arleville and boulevard de la Résistance.

★ FREE Cathédrale Notre-Dame

Pl de la Cathédrale (02.37.21.75.02). **Open** *Cathedral* 8.30am-7.30pm daily. *Tower* May-Aug 9.30am-12.30pm, 2-6pm Mon-Sat; 2-6pm Sun. Sept-Apr 9.30am-12.30pm, 2-5pm Mon-Sat; 2-5pm Sun. **Admission** *Cathedral* free. *Guided tour* €6.20; €4.20 reductions; free under-18s. **No credit cards.**

The west front, or 'Royal Portal', of this High Gothic cathedral – modelled in part on St-Denis – has three sculpted doorways. Inside, there's another era of sculpture, represented in the 16th-century scenes of the life of Christ that surround the choir. In particular, note the circular labyrinth of black and white stones in the floor. The cathedral is famed, above all, for its stained-glass windows depicting biblical scenes, saints and medieval trades in brilliant 'Chartres blue', punctuated by rich reds. During World War II the windows were removed and stored nearby for safety, only being reinstalled once the war was over. Climb the tower for a fantastic view over town and country. English-language tours by lecturer Malcolm Miller – one of the world's most knowledge-able and entertaining experts on the cathedral – take place twice daily for most of the year (noon & 2.45pm Mon-Sat, €10, €5 reductions; enquire in the gift shop. In his absence, audio-guides can be hired.

▶ *Malcolm Miller is also available for private tours of the cathedral (02.37.28.15.58, millerchartres@aol.com).*

Where to eat & stay

Tourists flock to the **Café Serpent** (2 cloître Notre-Dame, 02.37.21.68.81), in the shadow of the cathedral, but if it's full, there are plenty of easy and worthwhile options nearby. For restaurant cuisine with a riverside view, try **L'Estocade** (1 rue de la Porte Guillaume, 02.37.34.27.17, closed all day Mon & Sun eve). For fireside treats, **La Vieille Maison** (5 rue au Lait, 02.37.34.10.67, ww.lavieillemaison.fr, closed Mon & Sun) has a cosy 14th-century dining room. For a local speciality, order

some Chartres pâté at **Le Saint-Hilaire** (11 rue Pont St-Hilaire, 02.37.30.97.57).

Two perfectly serviceable chain hotels on the ring road, not far from the town centre, are the **Grand Monarque** (22 pl des Epars, 02.37.18.15.15, www.bw-grand-monarque.com, doubles €104-€180) and the more basic **Ibis Centre** (14 pl Drouaise, 02.37.36.06.36, www.ibishotel.com, doubles €79).

Getting there

By car

90km (56 miles) from Paris by A10, then A11.

By train

Direct from Gare Montparnasse (1hr).

Tourist information

Office de Tourisme

Pl de la Cathédrale, 28000 Chartres (02.37.18.26.26/www.chartres-tourisme.com). **Open** *Apr-Sept* 9am-7pm Mon-Sat; 9.30am-5.30pm Sun. *Oct-Mar* 10am-6pm Mon-Sat; 10am-1pm, 2.30-4.30pm Sun.

FONTAINEBLEAU

Home to 14 French kings since François I, Fontainebleau was once a sort of aristocratic club where gentlemen of the day came to hunt and learn the art of chivalry. The town grew up around the **château** in the 19th century, and is a pleasant place to visit.

The château is bite-sized compared to the sprawling grandeur of Versailles. The style adopted by the Italian artists brought in by François I is still visible, as are the additions by later rulers. The extensive château gardens, park and grand canal, all free for visitors to enter, are also worth exploring.

The 170-square-kilometre (66-square-mile) **Forêt de Fontainebleau** is part of the Gâtinas regional nature park, which has bizarre geological formations and diverse wildlife. It's the wildest slice of nature to be found near Paris. There are a number of well-marked trails, such as the GR1 from Bois-le-Roi train station, but more serious yompers would be better off with an official map such as the TOP25 IGN series 2417-OT, which covers the entire forest, showing climbing sites, campsites and picnic areas.

Trail maps are on sale at the **Fontainebleau tourist office**, which hires out bicycles (€19 per day) and has information on the nearby villages of Barbizon and Moret-sur-Loing. Bikes can also be hired from **La Petite Reine** (32 rue Sablons, 01.60.74.57.57, www.la-petite-reine.fr). **La Bleausière** riding school (11 allée Odette Dulac, 06.82.01.21.18, http://la.bleausiere.free.fr)

Château de Fontainebleau.

in Barbizon offers short and long guided rides for all ages and levels, throughout the year.

★ Château de Fontainebleau

Pl du Général-de-Gaulle (01.60.71.50.70/www. musee-chateau-fontainebleau.fr). **Open** *Château* Apr-Sept 9.30am-6pm Mon, Wed-Sun. Oct-Mar 9.30am-5pm Mon, Wed-Sun. *Park & gardens* Mar, Apr, Oct 9am-6pm daily. May-Sept 9am-7pm daily. Nov-Feb 9am-5pm daily. **Admission** *Château* €8; €6 reductions; free under-18s. *Park & gardens* free. PMP. **Credit** AmEx, MC, V.

The Château de Fontainebleau, a former hunting lodge, is a real mix of styles. In 1528, François I brought in Italian artists and craftsmen to help architect Gilles le Breton transform a neglected lodge into the finest Italian Mannerist palace in France. This style, noted for its grotesqueries, contorted figures and crazy fireplaces, is still visible in the ballroom and Long Gallery. Henri IV added a tennis court, Louis XIII built a double-horseshoe entrance staircase, and Louis XIV and XV added classical trimmings. Napoleon and Louis-Philippe also spent a fortune on redecoration. The château gardens include Le Nôtre's Grand Parterre and a carp pond in the Jardin Anglais. There is also an informal château park just outside.

Where to eat & stay

Rue Grande is lined with restaurants such as the stylish **Au Délice Impérial** (no.1, 01.64.22.20.70) and **Au Bureau** (no.12, 01.60.39.00.01), which has Tex-Mex specialities in a pub setting. At no.92, picnickers can find an array of local cheeses at the **Fromagerie Barthélémy** (01.64.22.21.64). For a blow-out meal, head for **Le Caveau des Ducs** (24 rue Ferrare, 01.64.22.05.05, www.caveaudes ducs.com), with its traditional French cuisine.

Some of the dozen rooms at the charming, central **Hôtel de Londres** (1 pl du Général-de-Gaulle, 01.64.22.20.21, www.hoteldelondres.com, doubles €100-€160) have balconies overlooking the château. The elegant **Hôtel Napoléon** (9 rue Grande, 01.60.39.50.50, www.hotel napoleon-fontainebleau.com, doubles €165-€260) overlooks an interior garden, and provides appropriately grand meals at its restaurant, **La Table des Maréchaux**.

Getting there

By car

60km (37 miles) from Paris by A6, then N7 (about 75mins). Be prepared for traffic jams when heading back to Paris on Sundays.

By train

Gare de Lyon to Fontainebleau-Avon (35mins), then bus AB (marked 'Château'). Ask for a 'Forfait Château de Fontainebleau' (€20.80; €7.70-€16 reductions) at the Gare de Lyon; it includes train fare, bus connection, château entrance and audio guide.

Tourist information

Office de Tourisme

4 rue Royale, 77300 Fontainebleau (01.60.74.99.99/www.fontainebleau-tourisme.com). **Open** *May-Oct* 10am-6pm Mon-Sat; 10am-1pm, 2-5.30pm Sun. *Nov-Apr* 10am-1pm Mon-Sat.

GIVERNY

In 1883, Claude Monet moved his mistress and their eight children into a quaint pink-brick house he had rented in bucolic Giverny, and spent as much time cultivating a beautiful garden here as painting the water lilies in it.

The leader of the Impressionist movement thrived on outdoor scenes, whether along the Seine near Argenteuil or by the Thames in London. Having once seen the tiny village of Giverny from the window of a train, he was smitten. By 1890 he had bought his dream home and soon had a pond dug, bridges built and a tableau of greenery created. As Monet's eyesight began to fail, he produced endless impressions of his man-made paradise, each trying to capture how the leaves and water reflected light. He died here in 1926.

Of the hundreds of tourists who visit here every day, not all are art lovers; somewhat surprisingly, there are none of his original paintings on display here (though you will see the 32 Japanese woodblock prints collected by the artist). Most of the visitors are simply here for the lilies, and a good photo opportunity.

The garden is as much a masterpiece as any of Monet's paintings, its famous water-lily pond, weeping willows and Japanese bridge still remarkably intact from the master's day; and the charming house, the **Fondation Claude Monet**, is dotted with touching mementos. But once you're back in the village, be prepared for difficulty finding a table at one of the scarce eating places, and long queues of impatient tourists almost everywhere you turn.

Get here early, or book ahead for dinner at the famous **Hôtel Baudy** museum-restaurant (81 rue Claude Monet, 02.32.21.10.03, closed Nov-Mar), where Monet's American disciples (such as Willard Metcalf and Dawson-Watson) set up their easels for several decadent years, expanding the old hotel into an *art-atelier extraordinaire*, complete with ballroom, rose garden and tennis courts – Cézanne stayed for a month. Today, it's essential to book ahead for accommodation in Giverny, but do so and you'll be first to the Monet museum in the morning. Up the road, the **Musée d'Art Américain de Giverny** (99 rue Claude-Monet, 02.32.51.94.65) houses works by the American Impressionist colony.

★ Fondation Claude Monet

84 rue Claude-Monet, 27620 Giverny (02.32.51.28.21/www.fondation-monet.com). **Open** 9.30am-6pm Tue-Sun. Closed Nov-Mar. **Admission** *House & garden* €6; €3.50-€4.50 reductions; free under-7s. **Credit** AmEx, MC, V.

Where to stay

For recommended hotels and B&Bs in the area, visit www.giverny.org. Pretty **Le Clos Fleuri** (5 rue de la Dîme, 02.32.21.36.51, www.giverny-leclosfleuri.fr, doubles €80, closed Nov-Mar) is in Giverny, close to the Musée d'Art Américain and Monet's garden.

Getting there

By car

80km (50 miles) west of Paris by A13 to Bonnières, then D201.

By train

Gare St-Lazare to Vernon (45mins), then 5km taxi ride or bus from the station.

Tourist information

Comité Départemental du Tourisme de l'Eure

3 rue du Commandant-Letellier, BP 367, 27003 Evreux (02.32.62.04.27/www.cdt-eure.fr). **Open** 9am-12.30pm, 1.30-6pm Mon-Thur; 9am-1pm, 1.30-6pm Fri.

VAUX-LE-VICOMTE

This lavish country château has a valuable lesson to teach: never, ever out-do your king. When Nicolas Fouquet (1615-80), Louis XIV's finance minister (and protégé of Cardinal Mazarin), decided to build an abode fit for his position, he had several hamlets moved away, called on three of France's most talented men (architect Louis Le Vau, painter Charles Lebrun and landscape gardener André Le Nôtre) and hired great sculptors such as Giradon, Lespagnandel and Nicolas Poussin to chip in with the decor. Its completion was celebrated in 1661 with a huge party for which Molière wrote a play and Lully composed music.

All would have gone swimmingly had it not been for one minor detail: Fouquet invited the king. Louis was disgusted at his minister's display of grandeur; soon after, Fouquet was given a show trial for the embezzlement of state funds. His personal effects were seized by the crown and he was sent into exile, dying 19 years later in prison. But Fouquet's legacy did live on, as Louis hired Le Vau, Lebrun and Le Nôtre to work their magic on Versailles.

A self-guided tour of the interior includes Fouquet's personal suite, the servants' dining room, the huge basement and wine cellar, and the copper-filled kitchen. The dome, with its unfinished ceiling – Lebrun only had time to paint the sky and one eagle before Fouquet was arreste – and the eagle are optional extras.

On the south side, a majestic staircase descends towards the gardens, divided into terraces whose boxed hedges and flowerbeds sweep into a vast expanse of lawns, grottoes, canals, lakes and fountains. Electric cars can be hired to help you cover the site. Entrance to the château includes the Musée des Equipages, where over 25 period carriages are on display in the former stables.

★ Vaux-le-Vicomte

77950 Maincy (01.64.14.41.90/www.vaux-le-vicomte.com). **Open** *Château* mid Mar-mid Nov 10am-1pm, 2-6pm daily. *Candlelight evenings* May-mid Oct 8pm-midnight Sat (July, Aug 8pm-midnight Fri). Closed mid Nov to mid Mar. **Admission** €14; €11 reductions. *Candlelight evenings* €17; €15 reductions. **Credit** AmEx, MC, V.

Getting there

By car

55km (35 miles) from Paris by A5 (direction Troyes). Exit at first toll and then follow signs.

By train

Gare de Lyon to Melun (25mins) or RER D to Melun, then 6km taxi ride.

VERSAILLES

Centuries of makeovers have made **Château de Versailles** the most sumptuously clad château in the world – a brilliant, unmissable cocktail of extravagance. Architect Louis Le Vau first embellished the original building – a hunting lodge built during Louis XIII's reign – after Louis XIV saw Vaux-le-Vicomte, the impressive residence of his finance minister, Nicolas Fouquet. André Le Nôtre turned the boggy marshland into terraces, parterres, fountains and lush groves.

After Le Vau's death in 1670, Jules Hardouin-Mansart took over as principal architect, transforming Versailles into the château we know today. He dedicated the last 30 years of

Fondation Claude Monet.

his life to adding the two main wings, the Cour des Ministres and the Chapelle Royale. In 1682 Louis moved in, accompanied by his court; thereafter, he rarely set foot in Paris. In the 1770s, Louis XV commissioned Jacques-Ange Gabriel to add the sumptuous Opéra Royal, used for concerts by the Centre de Musique Baroque (01.39.20.78.10). The expense of building and running Versailles cost France dear. With the fall of the monarchy in 1792, most of the furniture was lost – but the château was saved from demolition after 1830 by Louis-Philippe.

The **gardens** of Versailles are really works of art in themselves, their ponds and statues once more embellished by a fully working fountain system. On summer weekends, the spectacular jets of water are set to music, a prelude to the occasional fireworks displays of the Fêtes de Nuit.

Beyond the gardens are the Grand Canal and the wooded land and sheep-filled pastures of the estate's park. Outside the château gates are the **Potager du Roi** (the Sun King's vegetable garden), and stables that now house the **Académie du Spectacle Equestre**. The **Hall of Mirrors** – a 73-metre (240-foot) gallery overlooking the garden, hung with chandeliers – was commissioned in 1678 by Louis XIV and then decorated by Le Brun. It holds 357 mirrors.

In the town of Versailles, grab a *Historical Places* brochure free from the tourist office and explore. The Quartier St-Louis opposite the

Potager was developed by Louis XV around the Cathédrale St-Louis. Just off rue d'Anjou are the Carrés St-Louis, four market squares surrounded by 18th-century boutiques. North-east of the château is the Quartier Notre-Dame, part of the 'new town' designed by the Sun King himself. Eglise Notre-Dame is where members of the royal family were baptised and married. Around the corner is the Marché Notre-Dame, a market square dating back to 1671 and surrounded by restaurants and cafés. The covered market is closed on Mondays.

Académie du Spectacle Equestre

Grandes Ecuries, Château de Versailles (01.39.02.07.14/bookings 08.92.68.18.91/ www.acadequestre.fr).
Les Matinales des Ecuyers (*to watch riding practice & visit*) **Viewings** 11.15am Sat, Sun. Times vary for groups & during school hols; call for details. **Admission** €6; €5 reductions. **Credit** MC, V.
Reprise Musicale (*performance & visit*) **Performances** *Feb-Apr, mid Sept-Dec* 6pm Sat; 3pm Sun. *May-mid July* 8pm Sat; 3pm Sun. **Admission** €25; €16-€22 reductions. **Credit** MC, V.
Across from the château entrance are the Sun King's magnificent stables, restored in 2003. They house the Académie du Spectacle Equestre, which is responsible for the elaborate shows of tightly choreographed theatrics on horseback, run by famous horse trainer Bartabas.

★ Château de Versailles

78000 Versailles (01.30.83.78.00/advance tickets 08.92.68.46.94/www.chateauversailles.fr). **Open** *Apr-Oct* 9am-6.30pm Tue-Sun. *Nov-Mar* 9am-5.30pm Tue-Sun. **Admission** €13.50; €10 after 3pm; free under-18s. PMP, Passeport Versailles. **Credit** AmEx, DC, MC, V.

Versailles is a masterpiece – and usually packed with visitors. Allow yourself a whole day to appreciate the sumptuous State Apartments and the Hall of Mirrors, the highlights of any visit, and mostly accessible with a day ticket.

The Grand Appartement, where Louis XIV held court, consists of six gilded salons, all opulent examples of baroque craftsmanship. No less luxurious, the Queen's Apartment includes her bedroom, where royal births took place in view of the court. Hardouin-Mansart's showpiece, the Hall of Mirrors, where a united Germany was proclaimed in 1871 and the Treaty of Versailles signed in 1919, is flooded with natural light from its 17 vast windows. Designed to catch the last of the day's rays, it was here that the Sun King would hold extravagant receptions. Other apartments can be seen only as part of a guided tour.

Domaine de Versailles

Gardens Open *Apr-Oct* 7am-dusk daily. *Nov-Mar* 8am-dusk daily. **Admission** *Winter* free (statues covered over). *Summer* €3; €1.50 reductions; free under-10s. Passeport Versailles.
Grandes-Eaux Musicales *(01.30.83.78.88).* **Open** *Apr-Sept* Sat, Sun. **Admission** €8; €6 reductions; free under-10s. Passeport Versailles. **Credit** AmEx, DC, MC, V.
Park Open dawn-dusk daily. **Admission** free.

Sprawling across eight square kilometres (three square miles), the carefully planned gardens consist of formal parterres, ponds, elaborate statues – many commissioned by Colbert in 1674 – and a spectacular series of fountains, served by an ingenious hydraulic system only recently restored to working order. On weekend afternoons in the spring and autumn, the fountains are set to music for the Grandes Eaux Musicales – and also serve as a backdrop, seven times a year, for the extravagant Fêtes de Nuit, capturing the regal splendour of the Sun King's celebrations with fireworks, music and theatre.

INSIDE TRACK PEDAL POWER

One of the best ways to see Versailles is by bicycle. Conveniently, cycles can be hired from just outside the RER Versailles-Chantiers station (pl Raymond Poincaré, 01.39.20.16.60). Rates are €2 an hour or €12 a day.

Grand Trianon/Petit Trianon/ Domaine de Marie-Antoinette

01.30.83.78.00. **Open** *Apr-Oct* noon-7pm daily. *Nov-Mar* noon-5.30pm daily. **Admission** *Summer* €10; €6 after 4pm; free under-18s. *Winter* €6; free under-18s. PMP, Passeport Versailles. **Credit** AmEx, DC, MC, V.

In 1687 Hardouin-Mansart built the pink marble Grand Trianon in the north of the park, away from the protocol of the court. Here Louis XIV and his children's governess and secret second wife, Madame de Maintenon, could admire the intimate gardens from the colonnaded portico. It retains the Empire decor of Napoleon, who stayed here with his second Empress, Marie-Louise.

The Petit Trianon, built for Louis XV's mistress Madame de Pompadour, is a wonderful example of neo-classicism. It later became part of the Domaine de Marie-Antoinette, an exclusive hideaway located beyond the canal in the wooded parkland. Given to Marie-Antoinette as a wedding gift by her husband Louis XVI in 1774, the domain also includes the chapel adjoining the Petit Trianon, plus a theatre, a neo-classical 'Temple d'Amour', and Marie-Antoinette's fairy-tale farm and dairy, known as the Hameau de la Reine. Here, the queen escaped from the discontent of her subjects and the revolutionary fervour of Paris by pretending to be a humble milkmaid. Renovations were completed on the buildings in September 2008.

▶ *Enliven a stroll through the gardens by hiring hand-held digital PDA or iPod guides.*

Potager du Roi

10 rue Maréchal-Joffre (01.39.24.62.62/www. potager-du-roi.fr). **Open** *Nov, Dec* 10am-6pm Tue, Thur; 10am-1pm Sat. *Jan, Mar* 10am-1pm Tue, Thur. *Mar-Oct* 10am-6pm Tue-Sun. **Admission** *Tue-Fri* €4.50; €3 reductions; free under-6s. *Sat, Sun* €6.50; €3-€4.50 reductions; free under-6s. **Credit** AmEx, DC, MC, V.

The Potager du Roi, the king's vegetable garden, features 16 small squares surrounded by 5,000 fruit trees espaliered into fabulous shapes.

Where to eat & stay

Set in a building dating back to the construction of the château, **Au Chapeau Gris** (7 rue Hoche, 01.39.50.10.81, www.auchapeaugris.com, closed dinner Tue, all day Wed) is the oldest restaurant in Versailles, and serves French country cuisine under wooden beams. **Boeuf à la Mode** (4 rue au Pain, Marché Notre-Dame, 01.39.50.31.99, www.leboeufalamode-versailles.com) is an authentic 1930s brasserie serving steak and seafood specialities at mid-range prices. For a proper splurge, consider sampling **Gordon Ramsay au Trianon** (01.30.84.55.55, www.gordonramsay.com). Another long-established restaurant is the traditional

Follow the Fizz

In search of the world's most glamorous tipple.

Along the Route du Champagne, between Reims and Epernay, there are three classic circuits to discover. The Montagne de Reims and Côte des Blancs circuits are renowned for the quality of their champagnes, including several 'Grands Crus'. The nearby Vallée de la Marne circuit is where you'll find the best prices and some of the fruitiest champagnes. The circuits are well signposted from Epernay and Reims and you can also download maps from www.tourisme-en-champagne.com. The sheer number of champagne houses is astonishing, but these are our favourites:

Champagne Barnaut (Montagne de Reims)
1 pl André Collard, Bouzy (03.26.57.01.54/ www.champagne-barnaut.com).
Champagne Barnaut is one of the few houses to make red wines as well as fizz, and it makes an equally good job of both in the heart of the tiny village of Bouzy.

Champagne Charlier (Vallée de la Marne)
4 rue des Pervenches, Montigny-sous-Châtillon (03.26.58.35.18/ www.champagne-charlier.com).
A flower-clad *domaine* (best appreciated in spring and summer) that uses traditional methods to grow, press and assemble its own champagnes. Charlier's champagnes are light and fruity, including some delicious party-pink rosés, and start at around €12.70 a bottle.

Champagne Milan (Côtes des Blancs)
6 rue d'Avize, Oger (03.26.57.50.09/ www.champagne-milan.com).
If you fancy a day picking grapes during the *vendanges* (harvest) – or even a real grape-picking job – Milan is for you (enquire from July onwards). The production methods here haven't changed since 1864 and the champagnes (all Grands Crus) are mostly woody with hints of lemon.

Champagne Ployez-Jacquemart (Montagne de Reims)
8 rue Astoin, Ludes (03.26.61.11.87/ www.ployez-jacquemart.fr).
As well as being a great place to sleep off all the tastings (there are five hotel rooms), Ployez-Jacquemart has status as one of the most prestigious of the smaller producers. The pinot noir and pinot meunier grapes give the champagnes an almost nutty bouquet.

Tribaut (Vallée de la Marne)
88 rue d'Eguisheim, Hautvillers (03.26.59.40.57/www.champagne. g.tribaut.com).
Set in a chocolate-box village where Dom Pérignon created champagne as we know it, Tribaut offers panoramic views, friendly faces and a lip-smacking Grande Cuvée Spéciale (€19), as well as five other top-end champagnes.

LEONARDO DA VINC

Brasserie du Théâtre (15 rue des Réservoirs, 01.39.50.03.21), which stays open until 11.30pm for the after-show crowd from the Montansier theatre next door. You'll also find plenty of late-night bars around the Marché Notre-Dame.

The town centre has several reasonably priced hotels. One of the more historic is the **Hôtel du Cheval Rouge** (18 rue André-Chénier, 01.39.50.03.03, www.chevalrouge.fr.st, doubles €78-€98), built in Louis XIV's former stable overlooking the Marché Notre-Dame. Across from the château, the **Hôtel de France** (5 rue Colbert, 01.30.83.92.23, www.hotelfrance-versailles.com, doubles from €141) is set in an 18th-century townhouse and has period decor.

Getting there

By car
20km (12.5 miles) from Paris by A13 or D10.

By train
For the station nearest the château, take the RER C5 (VICK or VERO trains) to Versailles-Rive Gauche; or take a Transilien SNCF train from Gare St-Lazare to Versailles-Rive Droite (10mins on foot to the château).

Tourist information

Office de Tourisme
2bis av de Paris, 78000 Versailles
(01.39.24.88.88/www.versailles-tourisme.com).
Open 11am-5pm Mon, Sun; 9am-6pm Tue-Sat.

Escapes
CHAMPAGNE COUNTRY

Named after the region in which it's produced, champagne – nearly all 300 million bottles a year of it – comes from the towns of **Reims** (nasally pronounced 'Ranse') and **Epernay**, some 25 kilometres (16 miles) apart. At less than an hour by train from Paris, both are ideal destinations for a day trip or a weekend break. A tour of a champagne cellar is a big part of most visits. Most cellars give detailed explanations of how the drink is produced – from the grape varieties used to the strict name and quality controls – and guided tours finish with a sample. Don't forget your woollies when you visit, as the cellars are chilly and damp.

Epernay developed in the 19th century as expanding champagne houses moved out from Reims to acquire more space. Today, the aptly named avenue de Champagne is home to most major brands – but the best tours are at **Moët & Chandon** and **Mercier**.

In Reims, most of the major champagne houses are open by appointment only: Krug (03.26.84.44.20, www.krug.com); Lanson (03.26.78.50.50, www.lanson.fr); Louis Roederer (by appointment *and* recommendation only, 03.26.40.42.11, www.champagne-roederer.com) and Veuve Clicquot (03.26.89.53.90, www.veuve-clicquot.com). **Champagne Pommery** is set in an intriguing Elizabethan building.

Château Royal d'Amboise. *See p360.*

Home of the coronation church of most French monarchs since Clovis in 496, Reims was an important city even in Roman times. Begun in 1211, the current **Cathédrale Notre-Dame** (03.26.47.55.34, www.cathedralereims.com) has rich Gothic decoration that includes thousands of well-preserved figures on the portals. Look out, too, for the splendid stained-glass windows in the axial chapel, designed by Chagall. The statues damaged during shelling in World War I can be seen next door in the former archbishop's palace, the Palais de Tau (2 pl du Cardinal-Luçon, 03.26.47.81.79).

L'Ancien Collège des Jésuites (1 pl Museux, 03.26.35.34.71, closed Tue, Sat & Sun am) is a classic example of 17th-century baroque architecture, housing a library decorated with religious carvings and paintings by Jean Hélart.

Champagne Pommery

5 pl du Général-Gouraud, 51100 Reims (03.26.61.62.55/www.pommery.com). **Open** *Apr-mid Nov* 9.30am-7pm daily. *Mid Nov-mid Apr* (by appointment only) 10am-6pm daily. **Admission** (incl 1 glass) €12-€25. **Credit** MC, V.
Built in 1868, this unusual château was modelled on Elizabethan architecture. The visit takes place some 30m (98ft) underground, in 18km (11 miles) of tunnels linking 120 Gallo-Roman chalk quarries.

★ Mercier

68 av de Champagne, 51200 Epernay (03.26.51.22.22/www.champagne-mercier.fr). **Open** *Mid Mar-mid Nov* 9.30-11.30am, 2-4.30pm daily. *Mid Nov-mid Mar* 9.30-11.30am, 2-4.30pm Mon, Thur-Sun. **Admission** (incl 1 glass) €8.50; €4.50 reductions; free under-12s. **Credit** MC, V.
Some 7,000 tonnes of chalk were extracted to create the 18km (11 miles) of cellars at Mercier, opened in 1858. Note the 20-tonne champagne barrel at the entrance: it took 24 bulls and 18 horses to drag it all the way from Epernay to Paris for the 1889 Exposition Universelle. The interesting 45-minute underground tour takes place on a little train, and covers a stretch of tunnel that was used for mini-car races in the 1950s.

★ Moët & Chandon

20 av de Champagne, 51200 Epernay (03.26.51.20.20/www.moet.com). **Open** *Apr-mid Nov* 9.30-11.30am, 2-4.30pm daily. *Mid Nov-Mar* 9.30-11.30am, 2-4.30pm Mon-Fri. **Admission** (incl 1 glass) €14-€26; €9 reductions; free under-10s. **Credit** AmEx, DC, MC, V.
Moët & Chandon started life in 1743 as champagne supplier to Madame de Pompadour, mistress of Louis XV. It later supplied Napoleon and Alexander I of Russia. Since then it has kept pole position, with the largest domaine and more than 250 global outlets. In the hour-long tour, visitors are led through a section (under the grand house) of the 28km (17 miles) of tunnels.

Where to eat & stay

In Reims, countless cafés and brasseries line lively **place Drouet d'Erlon**, as do many hotels. If you fancy staying at a working champagne domaine, contact **Ariston Fils Champagne** (4-8 Grande-Rue, 51170 Brouillet, 03.26.97.43.46, www.champagneaspasie.com, doubles €55-€60), which has three rooms and pampers its guests. To sleep like a king, book one of the luxuriously extravagant rooms at the **Château les Crayères** (64 bd Henry Vasnier, 03.26.82.90.00, www.chateaulescrayeres.com, doubles €325-€660), a grand country-house hotel set in lush grounds.

In Epernay, **La Cave à Champagne** (16 rue Gambetta, 03.26.55.50.70) does good traditional French food, as does **Théâtre** (8 pl Pierre-Mendès-France, 03.26.58.88.19, closed dinner Tue & Sun, all Wed & 15 Feb-2 Mar, 15 July-2 Aug & 22-28 Dec). Known for its champagnes, **Les Cépages** (16 rue Fauvette, 03.26.55.16.93, closed Wed & Sun and July & Christmas) serves homely food.

Set in a 19th-century red-brick mansion, **Le Clos Raymi** (3 rue Joseph-de-Venoge, 03.26.51.00.58, www.closraymi-hotel.com, doubles €140-€160) is a cosy mix of traditional and modern. Part of the international Best Western chain, the **Hôtel de Champagne** (30 rue Eugène-Mercier, 03.26.53.10.60, www.bw-hotel-champagne.com, doubles €95-€120) is comfy enough, and the **Hôtel Kyriad** (3bis rue de Lorraine, 03.26.54.17.39, www.kyriad-epernay.fr, doubles from €69) has basic, clean rooms.

Getting there

By car
150km (93 miles) from Paris by the A4. For Epernay, exit at Château Thierry and take the N3.

By train
From Gare de l'Est, trains take about 45mins for Reims and Epernay.

INSIDE TRACK AMBOISE

A leisurely 20-minute drive east from Tours (*see right*), **Amboise** is a small town of narrow streets and quaint residences overlooking the Loire river. It is also home to two star sites: the imposing **Château Royal d'Amboise** (www.chateau-amboise.com, *photo p358*), set on a rocky spur and one of the most historically important buildings in the region; and Leonardo da Vinci's former home, the **Clos Lucé** (www.vinci-closluce.com), an exquisitely restored manor house with landscaped gardens and a museum of da Vinci's inventions.

Tourist information

Office de Tourisme (Epernay)
7 av de Champagne, 51200 Epernay (03.26.53.33.00/www.ot-epernay.fr). **Open** *Mid Apr-mid Oct* 9.30am-12.30pm, 1.30-7pm Mon-Sat; 11am-4pm Sun. *Mid Oct-mid Apr* 9.30am-noon, 1.30-5.30pm Mon-Sat.

Office de Tourisme (Reims)
2 rue Guillaume-de-Machault, 51100 Reims (08.92.70.13.51/www.reims-tourisme.com). **Open** *May-Sept* 9am-7pm Mon-Sat; 10am-6pm Sun. *Oct-Apr* 9am-6pm Mon-Sat; 10am-1pm Sun.

TOURS

Novelist Honoré de Balzac (1799-1850) once described his beloved birthplace as being 'more fresh, flowery and perfumed than any other town in the world', and Tours has a lot going for it today. In fact, it's a positively pleasant city, bursting with history, medieval quarters, a lively student population, colourful flower markets (Wednesday and Saturday on boulevard Béranger) and enticing bars and restaurants. Only an hour from Paris by TGV, it is the official gateway to the Loire Valley, and a choice place in which to refuel before overdosing on sumptuous Renaissance castles.

Sandwiched between the Loire (north) and the Cher (south) rivers, it began life as a fertile floodplain, prized by the Turones – a Celtic tribe that gave modern Tours its name. In 57 BC Julius Caesar conquered the city, modestly changing its name to Caesarodunum (Caesar's hill). Traces of the third-century Gallo-Roman city wall and amphitheatre can still be seen in the Musée des Beaux-Arts gardens (the left-hand tower of the Archbishop's palace and the curved wall to the east).

When Christianity arrived, St Martin, the founder of France's first monastery (in Ligugé in Poitou), became bishop of Tours. After his death in 397, his relics, laid to rest in the Roman **Basilique St-Martin**, were believed to have healing powers, drawing in thousands of pilgrims en route to Santiago de Compostela in Spain, and prompting the construction of Tours' medieval quarters.

Throughout the 15th and 16th centuries, the city vied with Paris as the seat of power: Charles VII, Louis XI (who established Tours' silk industry), Charles VIII and François I all cherished Tours; Henry IV preferred Paris.

The city was bombarded by the Prussians in 1870 and suffered widespread damage in World War II, especially in the historic centre, which by the 1960s was a no-go zone of crumbling masonry. Nowadays, after 40 years of regeneration, the medieval quarters

Get Away

Hop on the TGV and leave the capital far behind.

Lyon.

Thanks to the mighty TGV, you can cover a decent portion of the country in just a few hours – a godsend when you're hankering for a change of scenery. But where to go? Below are three destinations at approximately one, two and three hours from Paris by TGV; ideal weekend and day-trip getaways (www.sncf.com).

1HR 20MINS METZ
http://tourisme.mairie-metz.fr
This handsome capital of the Lorraine region is a genuine delight, with an array of French and Prussian architecture, an award-winning commitment to green, natural spaces and a convivial yet cosmopolitan atmosphere. In 2007 the TGV Est line opened, slashing journey times from Paris in half, and the new Pompidou Centre is finally set to open its doors in 2010. Coupled with existing venues such as the Arsenal and Les Trinitaires, it is set to place Metz squarely at the heart of France's cultural radar.

2HRS LYON
www.lyon-france.com
Lyon has its beautiful parts – what better place to build a city than at the confluence of two of France's most graceful rivers, the Rhône and the Saône – and its history stretches back to Roman times, but France's second-largest city is best loved

for the here and now: for food, fashion and culture. Lyon has a thriving arts scene, a fine opera house, superb shopping and, best of all, some of the country's true gourmet tables. It is also home to Renaissance architecture and a slew of museums and monuments.

3HRS 20MINS MONTPELLIER
www.ot-montpellier.fr
Montpellier is one of the best places in France to be right now. A long-term programme of renovation and innovation has helped transform this sleepy university city into a powerhouse of Mediterranean France. But it's not all about technology and transformation: Montpellier is also an ancient academic centre with a handsome medieval core, abundant gardens and a world-class museum. It's also a young city, with the under-25s making up nearly 40 per cent of the 230,000-strong population. The number of students has quadrupled in the last 20 years, maybe helped by the fact that it's within a bike ride of the Med. Talking of two wheels, bikes are a big thing in Montpellier, which now has nearly 150 kilometres (93 miles) of cycle paths linking the historic old town to the seaside at Palavas. What's more, this development is coupled with a brilliant municipal bike hire scheme.

contain some of Tours' most charming streets. Pedestrianised **place Plumereau**, with its exquisite half-timbered façades housing cafés, galleries and boutiques, is the hub of the town. Wander down lanes like rue Briçonnet to find concealed courtyards, more half-timbered houses and the occasional crooked tower. In **place de Châteauneuf**, a lone Romanesque tower is the only intact segment of the original Basilique-St-Martin, which was sacked by the Huguenots in 1562. The neo-Byzantine **Basilique St-Martin** (02.47.05.63.87) houses St-Martin's shrine further up the road, opposite the ruined vestiges.

The east of Tours is dominated by the **Cathédrale St-Gatien** (02.47.70.21.00). Work on it began on this splendid building in the 13th century and ended in the 16th century, demonstrating the French Gothic style in its entirety. The stained-glass windows inside are often compared to those of Sainte-Chapelle in Paris. Next door, the archbishop's palace and **Musée des Beaux Arts** (18 pl François-Sicard, 02.47.05.68.73, open 9am-6pm Mon, Wed-Sun) has a surprisingly rich collection of paintings by Degas, Rembrandt and Delacroix, and several sculptures by Rodin and Bourdelle. Check out the enormous 200-year-old cedar of Lebanon in the garden, the branches of which are so heavy they have to be held up.

North of here, Tours' **Château Royal** (25 av André Malraux) looks over the Loire River with dishevelled majesty. You can best take in its assorted architecture by following the river: the **Tour de Guise** (look out for machicolations and a pepper-pot roof) was a 13th-century fortress, and the 15th-century **Logis des Gouverneurs** on the quay has gable dormers and a chunk of Gallo-Roman wall at its base.

Further west, the **Eglise St-Julien** has managed to insinuate a wine museum, the **Musée des vins de Touraine** (16 rue Nationale, 02.47.21.62.20, open 9am-noon, 2-6pm Mon, Wed-Sun), into its Gothic, monastic cells. Next door, the **Musée du Compagnonnage** (8 rue Nationale, 02.47.21.62.20, open 9am-noon, 2-6pm Mon, Wed-Sun, daily mid June-mid Sept) is a dinky museum, showcasing the handiwork of master craftsmen of the guilds.

Cross over rue Nationale (the main thoroughfare and shopping district) and you'll get to the fabulous **Hôtel Goüin**, a splendid Renaissance beauty that once belonged to a rich silk merchant, and which now contains the **Musée Archéologique de la Touraine** (25 rue de Commerce, 02.47.66.22.32, open 10am-1pm, 2-6pm Tue-Sun), devoted to the history of the Touraine region. Sadly, the only place still keeping the local silk industry alive is the **Manufacture Le Manach** (35 quai

Paul Bert, 02.47.70.37.37, www.lemanach.fr, book through tourist office), on the right bank of the Loire. The weaving methods here have remained unchanged since the early 19th century, and it is one of the few manufacturers in France capable of reproducing authentic fabrics using patterns from the 17th century. Enquire at the tourist office if you fancy a visit.

Where to eat & stay

For dreamy regional dishes such as *crépine de dinde* (a giant turkey meatball cooked in red wine) and *poire tappée* (poached pear), head to **Le Petit Patrimoine** (58 rue Colbert, 02.47.66.05.81). If *moules-frites* is more your thing, the **Taverne de l'Homme Tranquille** has a large selection (22 rue du grand Marché, near pl Plumereau, 02.47.61.46.04).

For a few sneaky glasses of Touraine wine before you head back, **Au Chien Jaune** (74 rue Bernard Palissy, 02.47.05.10.17), a former brothel, is in a handy spot by the tourist office and railway station. Aside from the wine, it specialises in regional dishes.

If you're on a budget, a good, cheap option in a central location is **Hôtel Mondial** (3 pl de la Résistance, 02.47.05.62.68, www.hotel mondialtours.com, doubles €60-€90). For a touch more luxury, follow in the footsteps of Winston Churchill and try Tours' only four-star hotel, **L'Hôtel de l'Univers** (5 bd Heurteloup, 02.47.05.37.15, www. hotel-univers.fr, doubles €198-€398); or for somewhere a little more modest, with decent rooms and a pretty garden, the **Best Western Central Hôtel** (21 rue Berthelot, 02.47.05.46.44, www.bestwesterncentralhotel tours.com, doubles €76-€140), is more charming than the other chain hotels in Tours.

Getting there

By car
235km (146 miles) west from Paris by A10.

By train
From Gare Montparnasse to Tours centre (1hr).

Tourist information

Office de Tourisme
78-82 rue Bernard Palissy, 37042 Tours (02.47.70.37.37/www.ligeris.com). **Open** *Mid Apr-mid Oct* 8.30am-7pm Mon-Sat; 10am-12.30pm, 2.30-5pm Sun & bank hols. *Mid Oct-mid Apr* 9am-12.30pm, 1.30-6pm Mon-Sat; 10am-1pm Sun & bank hols.
If you're keen to see the châteaux but not to drive, the tourist office runs day trips from Paris to Azay-le-Rideau, Villandry, Chenonceau and Amboise.

Directory

Getting Around

DIRECTORY

ARRIVING & LEAVING

By air

Roissy-Charles-de-Gaulle airport
01.70.36.39.50/www.adp.fr.
Most international flights use Roissy-Charles-de-Gaulle airport, 30km (19 miles) north-east of Paris. Its two main terminals are some way apart, so check which one you need for your return flight. The terminals are linked by the CDGVAL free driverless train. The **RER B** (RATP helpline, 08.92.69.32.46, www.transilien.com) is the quickest way to central Paris (about 40mins to Gare du Nord; 45mins to RER Châtelet-Les Halles; €8.50 single). RER trains run every 10-15mins, 4.58am-11.58pm daily from the airport to Paris.
    Air France buses
(08.92.35.08.20, www.cars-airfrance.com; €15 single, €24 return, €7.50 under-11s, free under-2s) leave every 15mins, 5.45am-11pm daily, from both terminals, and stop at porte Maillot and place Charles-de-Gaulle (35-50min trip). Air France buses also run to Gare Montparnasse and Gare de Lyon (€16.50 single, €27 return, €8 under-11s, free under-2s) every 30mins (45-60min trip), 7am-9pm daily; there's a shuttle bus between Roissy and Orly (€19 (no return), €9.50 under-11s, free under-2s) every 30mins, 5.55am-10.30pm daily from Roissy; 6.30am-10.30pm Mon-Fri, 7am-10.30pm Sat, Sun from Orly. The **RATP Roissybus** (08.92.69.32.46, www.ratp.fr; €9.10) runs every 15-20mins, 5.45am-11pm daily, between the airport and the corner of rue Scribe/rue Auber (at least 45mins); buy tickets on the bus.
Paris Airports Service
is a door-to-door minibus service between airports and hotels, 24/7. The more passengers on board, the less each one pays. Roissy prices go from €26 for one person to €12.40 each for eight people, 6am-8pm (minimum €41, 4-6am, 8-10pm); book on 01.55.98.10.80, www.parisairportservice.com.
Airport Connection
(01.43.65.55.55, www.airport-connection.com; booking 7am-11pm) runs a similar service, 4am-midnight. Prices for Roissy are €27

per person, €44 for two, then €17 per extra person. A **taxi** to central Paris can take 30-60mins depending on traffic. Expect to pay €30-€50, plus €1 per item of luggage.

Orly airport
01.70.36.39.50/www.adp.fr.
Domestic and international flights use Orly airport, 18km (11 miles) south of the city. It has two terminals: Orly-Sud (mainly international) and Orly-Ouest (mainly domestic).
    Air France buses
(08.92.35.08.20, www.cars-airfrance.com; €11.50 single, €18.50 return, €5.50 under-11s, free under-2s) leave both terminals every 30mins, 6.15am-11.15pm daily, and stop at Invalides and Montparnasse (30-45mins). The **RATP Orlybus** (08.92.69.32.46, www.ratp.fr; €6.40) runs between the airport and Denfert-Rochereau every 15mins, 6am-11.50pm Mon-Fri, 6am-12.50am Sat-Sun (30min trip); buy tickets on the bus. The high-speed **Orlyval** (www.orlyval.fr) shuttle train runs every 4-7mins (6am-11pm daily) to RER B station Antony (€9.85 to Châtelet-les-Halles) getting to central Paris takes about 35mins. You could also catch the **Paris par le train** bus (€6.20) to Pont de Rungis, where you can take the RER C into central Paris. Buses run every 20mins, 4.34am-11.14pm daily from Orly-Sud; 35min trip. Orly prices for the **Paris Airports Service** and **Airport Connection** door-to-door facility (*see above*) are €25 for one person and €5-€12 each for extra passengers depending on numbers. A **taxi** into town takes 20-40mins and costs €16-€26, plus €1 per piece of luggage.

Paris Beauvais airport
08.92.68.20.66/www.aeroport beauvais.com.
Beauvais, 70km (44 miles) from Paris, is served by budget airlines such as **Ryanair** (08.92.23.23.75, www.ryanair.com). Buses (€13) leave for Porte Maillot 15-30mins after each arrival; buses the other way leave 3hrs 15mins before each departure. Get tickets from the arrivals lounge (information: 08.92.68.20.64) or buy tickets on the bus.

Major airlines

Aer Lingus
08.21.23.02.67/www.aerlingus.com.
Air France
08.20.32.08.20/www.airfrance.fr.
American Airlines *01.55.17.43.41/ www.americanairlines.fr.*
bmibaby *0044.8458.101. 100/www.bmibaby.com.*
British Airways *08.25.82.54.00/ www.britishairways.fr.*
British Midland *0044.1332.648. 181/www.flybmi.com.*
Continental *01.71.23.03.35/ www.continental.com.*
Easyjet
08.99.65.00.11/www.easyjet.com.
KLM & NorthWest
08.92.70.26.08/www.klm.com.
United
08.10.72.72.72/www.united.fr.

By car

Options for crossing the Channel with a car include: **Eurotunnel** (08.10.63.03.04, www.euro tunnel.com); **Brittany Ferries** (08.25.82.88.28, www.brittany ferries.com); **P&O Ferries** (08.25.12.01.56, www.poferries.com); and **SeaFrance** (0044.8454.580.666, www.seafrance.com).

Shared journeys

Allô-Stop *30 rue Pierre Sémard, 9th (01.53.20.42.42/www.allostop. net).* Mᵒ *Poissonnière.* **Open** 10am-1pm, 2-6pm Mon-Fri; 10am-1pm, 2-4pm Sat. **Credit** MC, V.
Call several days ahead to be put in touch with drivers. There's a fee (€5 under 250km, 155 miles; €8 over 250km), plus a contribution towards the petrol expenses, paid to the driver (from €5 under 100km, 62 miles, up to €90 for over 2,000km, 1,243 miles).

By coach

International coach services arrive at the Gare Routière Internationale Paris-Gallieni at Porte de Bagnolet, 20th. For reservations (in English), call **Eurolines** on 08.92.89.90.91 (€0.34 per min) or 01.41.86.24.21 from abroad, or visit the website, www.eurolines.fr. Fares start from €19 for a single journey from London to Paris.

By rail

From London, **Eurostar** services (01233 617 575, www.eurostar.com) to Paris depart from the dedicated terminal at St Pancras International. Thanks to the new high-speed track, the journey from London to Paris now takes 2hrs 15mins direct, slightly longer for trains stopping at Ashford and Lille. Eurostar services from the new terminal at Ebbsfleet International, near junction 2 of the M25, take 2hrs 5mins direct. Fares start at £59/€77 for a London-Paris return ticket. Passengers must check in at least 30mins before departure time. Trains arrive at Gare du Nord (08.92.35.35.39, www.sncf.fr), with easy access to public transport and taxi ranks.

  Cycles can be taken as hand luggage if they are dismantled and carried in a bike bag. You can also check them in at the Eurodispatch depot at St Pancras (Esprit Parcel Service, 08705 850 850) or Sernam depot at Gare du Nord (01.55.31.58.40). Check-in must be done 24hrs ahead; a Eurostar ticket must be shown. The service costs £20/€25.

MAPS

Free maps of the métro, bus and RER systems are available at airports and métro stations. Other brochures from métro stations are *Paris Visite – Le Guide*, with details of transport tickets and a small map, and *Plan de Paris*, a fold-out one showing *Noctambus* night bus lines. A Paris street map (*Plan de Paris*) can be bought from newsagents. The blue *Paris Pratique* is clear and compact.

PUBLIC TRANSPORT

Almost all of the Paris public transport system is run by the **RATP** (Régie Autonome des Transports Parisiens; 08.92.69.32.46, www.ratp.fr): the bus, métro (underground) and suburban tram routes, as well as lines A and B of the RER (Réseau Express Régional) suburban express railway, which connects with the métro within the city centre. National rail operator **SNCF** (08.92.35.35.35, www.sncf.com) runs RER lines C, D and E, and serves the Paris suburbs (*Banlieue*), as well as the French regions and international destinations (*Grandes Lignes*).

Fares & tickets

Paris and suburbs are divided into six travel zones; zones 1 and 2 cover the city centre. RATP tickets and passes are valid on the métro, bus and RER. Tickets and *carnets* can be bought at métro stations, tourist offices and *tabacs* (tobacconists); single tickets can also be bought on buses (€1.70). Hold on to your ticket in case of spot checks; you'll also need it to exit from RER stations.

● A single ticket *T+* costs €1.60, but it's more economical to buy a *carnet* of ten for €11.60.

● A one-day *Mobilis* pass costs from €5.90 for zones 1 and 2 to €16.70 for zones 1-6 (not including airports).

● A one-day *Paris Visite* pass for zones 1-3 is €8.80; a five-day pass is €28.30, with discounts on some attractions.

● One-week or one-month *Carte Orange* passes (passport photo needed) offer unlimited travel in the relevant zones; if bought in zones 1 or 2, each is delivered as a Navigo swipe card. A *forfait mensuel* (monthly *Carte Orange* valid from the first day of the month) for zones 1 and 2 costs €56.60; a weekly *forfait hebdomadaire* (weekly *Carte Orange* valid Mon-Sun inclusive) for zones 1 and 2 costs €17.20 and is better value than *Paris Visite* passes.

Métro & RER

The Paris **métro** is the fastest and cheapest way of getting around the city. Trains run 5.30am-12.40am Mon-Thur, 5.30am-1.30am Fri-Sun. Individual lines are numbered, with each direction named after the last stop. Follow the orange *Correspondance* to change lines. Be prepared for the fact that some interchanges, such as Châtelet-Les-Halles, Montparnasse-Bienvenüe and République, involve long walks. The exit (*Sortie*) is indicated in blue. The driverless line 14 runs from Gare St-Lazare to Olympiades. Pickpockets and bag-snatchers are rife on the network – pay special attention as the doors are closing.

  The five **RER** lines (A, B, C, D and E) run 5.30am-1am daily through Paris and out into the suburbs. Within Paris, the RER is useful for faster journeys – Châtelet-Les-Halles to Gare du Nord is one stop on the RER,

and six on the métro. Métro tickets are valid for RER journeys within zones 1 and 2.

Buses

Buses run 6.30am-8.30pm, with some routes continuing until 12.30am, Mon-Sat; limited services operate on selected lines on Sunday and public holidays. You can use a métro ticket, a ticket bought from the driver (€1.70) or a travel pass to travel on the bus. Tickets should be punched in the machine next to the driver; passes should be shown to the driver. When you want to get off, press the red request button.

Night buses

After the métro and normal buses stop running, the only public transport – apart from taxis – are the 47 **Noctilien** lines, running between place du Châtelet and the suburbs (hourly 12.30am-5.30am Mon-Thur; half-hourly 1am-5.35am Fri, Sat); look out for the Noctilien logo on bus stops or the N in front of the route number. A ticket costs €1.60 (€1.70 from the driver); travel passes are valid.

River transport

Batobus

(08.25.05.01.01/www.batobus.com). River buses stop every 15-30mins at: Eiffel Tower, Musée d'Orsay, St-Germain-des-Prés (quai Malaquais), Notre-Dame, Jardin des Plantes, Hôtel de Ville, Louvre, Champs-Elysées (Pont Alexandre III). They run Nov, Feb-mid Mar 10.30am-4.30pm; mid Mar-Apr & Sept, Oct 10am-7pm; June-Aug 10am-9.30pm. A one-day pass is €12 (€6, €8 reductions); two-day pass €16 (€8, €11 reductions); five-day pass €19 (€9, €13 reductions); season-ticket €55 (€35 reductions). Tickets can be bought at Batobus stops, online at www.batobus.com, RATP ticket offices and the Office de Tourisme (*see p381*).

Trams

Two modern tram lines operate in the suburbs, running from La Défense to Issy-Val de Seine and from Bobigny Pablo Picasso to St-Denis; a third runs between the Garigliano Bridge in the west of the city to Porte d'Ivry in the south-east. They connect with the métro and RER; fares are the same as for buses.

RAIL TRAVEL

Suburban destinations are served by the RER. Other locations farther from the city are served by the SNCF railway; the TGV high-speed train has slashed journey times and is being extended to all the main regions. There are few long-distance bus travel. Tickets can be bought at any SNCF station (not just the one from which you'll travel), SNCF shops and travel agents. If you reserve online or by phone, you can pay and pick up your tickets from the station or have them sent to your home. SNCF automatic machines (*billeterie automatique*) only work with French credit/debit cards. Regular trains have full-rate White (peak) and cheaper Blue (off-peak) periods. You can save on TGV fares by buying special cards. The *Carte 12/25* gives under-26s a 25-50 per cent reduction; even without it, under-26s are entitled to 25 per cent off. Buy tickets in advance to secure the cheaper fare. Before you board any train, stamp your ticket in the orange *composteur* machines located on the platforms, or you might have to pay a hefty fine.

SNCF reservations & tickets

National reservations/information 08.92.35.35.35 (€0.34 per min)/www.sncf.com. **Open** 7am-10pm daily. You can also dial 3635 and say 'billet' at the prompt.

Mainline stations

Gare d'Austerlitz Central and south-west France and Spain.
Gare de l'Est Alsace, Champagne and southern Germany.
Gare de Lyon Burgundy, the Alps, Provence and Italy.
Gare Montparnasse West France, Brittany, Bordeaux, the south-west.
Gare du Nord Eurostar, Channel ports, north-east France, Belgium and Holland.
Gare St-Lazare Normandy.

TAXIS

Paris taxi drivers are not known for their flawless knowledge of the Paris street map; if you have a preferred route, say so. Taxis can also be hard to find, especially at rush hour or early in the morning. Your best bet is to find a taxi rank (*station de taxis*, marked with a blue sign) on major roads, crossroads and at stations. A white

light on a taxi's roof indicates the car is free; an orange light means the cab is busy. There is a service charge of €2.20. The rates are then based on zone and time of day: **A** (10am-5pm Mon-Sat central Paris, €0.89 per km); **B** (5pm-10am Mon-Sat, 7am-midnight Sun central Paris; 7am-7pm Mon-Sat inner suburbs and airports, €1.14 per km); **C** (midnight-7am Sun central Paris; 7pm-7am Mon-Sat, all day Sun inner suburbs and airports; all times outer suburbs, €1.38 per km). Most journeys in central Paris cost €6-€12; there's a minimum charge of €6, plus €1 for each piece of luggage over 5kg or bulky objects, and a €0.70 surcharge from mainline stations. Most drivers will not take more than three people, although they should take a couple and two children. There is an additional charge of €2.95 for a fourth adult passenger.

Don't feel obliged to tip, although rounding up to the nearest euro is polite. Taxis are not allowed to refuse rides if they deem them too short and can only refuse to take you in a certain direction during their last half-hour of service (both rules are often ignored). If you want a receipt, ask for *un reçu* or *la note*. Complaints should be made to the **Bureau des Taxis et des Transports Publics**, 36 rue des Morillons, 75732 Paris Cedex 15 (01.55.76.20.05).

Phone cabs

These firms take phone bookings 24/7; you also pay for the time it takes your taxi to reach you. If you wish to pay by credit card, mention this when you order.

Airportaxis *to and from Paris airports, 01.41.50.42.50/ www.taxiparisien.fr.*
Alpha *01.45.85.85.85/ www.alphataxis.fr.*
G7 *01.47.39.47.39/ www.taxis-g7.fr.*
Taxis Bleus *08.91.70.10.10/ www.taxis-bleus.com.*

DRIVING

If you bring your car to France, you must bring its registration and insurance documents.

As you come into Paris, you will meet the Périphérique, the giant ring road that carries traffic into, out of and around the city. Intersections, leading on to other main roads, are called *portes* (gates). Driving on the Périphérique

is not as hair-raising as it might look, though it's often congested. Some hotels have parking spaces that can be paid for by the hour, day or by types of season tickets.

In peak holiday periods, the organisation Bison Futé hands out brochures at motorway *péages* (toll gates), suggesting less crowded routes. French roads are categorised as *Autoroutes* (motorways, with an 'A' in front of the number), *Routes Nationales* (national 'N' roads), *Routes Départementales* (local, 'D' roads) and rural *Routes Communales* ('C' roads). *Autoroutes* are toll roads; some sections, including most of the area around Paris, are free.

Infotrafic *08.92.70.77.66 (€0.34 per minute)/ www.infotrafic.fr.*
Bison Futé *08.00.10.02.00/ www.bison-fute.equipement.gouv.fr*
Traffic information service for Ile-de-France *08.26.02.20.22/www.securite routiere.gouv.fr.*

Breakdown services

The AA and RAC do not have reciprocal arrangements with an equivalent organisation in France, so it's advisable to take out additional breakdown insurance cover, for example with a company like **Europ Assistance** (0870 737 5720/ www.europ-assistance.co.uk). If you don't have insurance, you can still use its service (08.10.00.50.50, available 24/7), but it will charge you the full cost. Other 24-hour breakdown services in Paris include: **AB Auto** (01.45.58.49.58) and **Dan Dépann Auto** (08.00.25.10.00).

Driving tips

● At junctions where no signposts indicate right of way, the car coming from the right has priority. Many roundabouts now give priority to those on the roundabout. If this is not indicated (by road markings or a sign with the message *Vous n'avez pas la priorité*), priority is for those coming from the right.
● Drivers and all passengers must wear seat belts.
● Under-tens are not allowed to travel in the front of a car, except in baby seats facing backwards.
● You should not stop on an open road; you must pull off to the side.
● When drivers are flashing their lights at you, this often means they will not slow down and are warning you to keep out of the way.

Parking

There are still a few free on-street parking areas in Paris, but they're often full. If you park illegally, you risk getting your car clamped or towed away (*see below*). It's forbidden to park in zones marked for deliveries (*livraisons*) or taxis. Parking meters have now been replaced by *horodateurs*, pay-and-display machines, which take a special card (*carte de stationnement* at €10 or €30, available from *tabacs*). Parking is often free at weekends, after 7pm and in August.

Car hire

To hire a car, you must be 25 or over and have held a licence for at least a year. Some agencies accept drivers aged 21-24, but a supplement of €20-€25 per day is usual. Take your licence and passport with you. Bargain firms may have an extremely high charge for damage: read the small print.

Hire companies

Ada *01.48.06.58.13/ 08.25.16.91.69/www.ada.fr.*
Avis *08.21.23.07.60/ 08.20.05.05.05/www.avis.fr.*
Budget *01.53.32.79.00/ 08.25.00.35.64/www.budget.fr.*
EasyCar *01.70.61.85.52/ www.easycar.com.*
Europcar *01.53.64.16.24/ 08.25.35.83.58/www.europcar.fr.*
Hertz *01.55.31.93.21/ www.hertz.fr.*
Rent-a-Car *08.91.70.02.00/ www.rentacar.fr.*

Chauffeur-driven cars

Chauffeur Services Paris
(01.80.40.00.86/www.csparis.com). **Open** 24hrs daily. **Prices** from €125 airport transfer; €240 for 4 hours. **Credit** AmEx, DC, MC, V.

CYCLING

In 2007, the mayor launched a municipal bike hire scheme – **Vélib** (www.velib.paris.fr). There are now over 20,000 bicycles available 24 hours a day, at nearly 1,500 'stations' across the city. Just swipe your travel card to release the bikes from their stands. The *mairie* actively promotes cycling in the city and the Vélib scheme is complemented by the 400km (250 miles) of bike lanes snaking their way around Paris.

The Itinéraires Paris-Piétons-Vélos-Rollers – scenic strips of the city that are closed to cars on Sundays and holidays – continue to multiply; www.paris.fr can provide an up-to-date list of routes and a downloadable map of cycle lanes. A free *Paris à Vélo* map can be picked up at any mairie or from bike shops. Cycle lanes (*pistes cyclables*) run mostly N-S and E-W. N-S routes include rue de Rennes, av d'Italie, bd Sébastopol and av Marceau. E-W routes take in the rue de Rivoli, bd St-Germain, bd St-Jacques and av Daumesnil. You could be fined (€22) if you don't use them. Cyclists are also entitled to use certain bus lanes (especially the new ones, set off by a strip of kerb stones); look out for traffic signs with a bike symbol. Don't let the locals' blasé attitude to helmets and lights convince you it's not worth using them.

Cycles & scooters for hire

Bike insurance may not cover theft.

Freescoot *63 quai de la Tournelle, 5th (01.44.07.06.72/ www.freescoot.fr). M° Maubert Mutualité or St-Michel.* **Open** 9am-1pm, 2-9pm daily; closed Sun Oct-mid Apr. **Credit** AmEx, MC, V. Bicycles & scooters.
Left Bank Scooters *(06.82.70.13.82/www.leftbank scooters.com).* This company hires out vintage-style Vespas (from €70 per day), with delivery and collection from your apartment or hotel. Various tours also available.

WALKING

Walking is the best way to explore Paris; just remember to remain vigilant at all times. Brits should be aware that traffic will be coming from the 'wrong' direction and that zebra crossings mean very little. By law, drivers are only obliged to stop at a red traffic light – even then, many will take a calculated risk.

TOURS

Bus tours

The following companies offer hop-on, hop-off bus tours of the city with commentary. Prices are for one day.

Les Cars Rouges *01.53.95.39. 53/www.carsrouges.com.* **Tickets** €24; €12 4-11s.

Paris l'OpenTour *01.42.66. 56.56/www.pariscityrama.com.* **Tickets** €29; €15 4-11s.
Paris Vision *01.42.60.30.01/ http://fr.parisvision.com.* **Tickets** €22.

Bike tours

Fat Tire Bike Tours *01.56.58. 10.54/http://fattirebiketours.com/ paris.* **Tickets** €26; €24 reductions. Bike tours of the city, with the main tour starting at the south leg of the Eiffel Tower. Tours run daily at 11am, with a 3pm tour added in summer. Check online for full details.

Boat tours

Cruising along the River Seine is a delightful way to see Paris. The companies below all run a variety of tours on the river. Most boats depart from the quays in the 7th and 8th, and proceed to go on a circuit around the islands. Check online for full tour details and times: many companies operate more than one type of tour, though the basic tour usually runs every 20-60mins in summer. Rates are for one day only, though other tickets may be available.

Bateaux-Mouches *Pont de l'Alma, 8th (01.42.25.96.10/ www.bateaux-mouches.fr). M° Alma-Marceau.* **Tickets** €10; €5 reductions; free under-4s.
Bateaux Parisiens *Port de la Boudonnais, 7th (01.76.64.14.45/ www.bateauxparisiens.com). RER Champ de Mars.* **Tickets** €11; €5 reductions; free under-3s.
Batobus Tour Eiffel *Various stops (08.25.05.01.01/www.batobus. com).* **Tickets** €12; €6 reductions.
Vedettes de Paris *Port de Suffren, 7th (01.44.18.19.50/ www.vedettesdeparis.com). M° Bir-Hakeim.* **Tickets** €11; €5 reductions; free under-4s.
Vedettes du Pont-Neuf *Sq du Vert-Galant, 1st (01.46.33.98.38/ www.vedettesdupontneuf.com). M° Pont-Neuf.* **Tickets** €12; €6 under-12s; free under-4s.

Walking tours

Paris Walking Tours *01.48.09. 21.40/www.paris-walks.com.* **Tickets** €12; €8-€10 reductions. Led by long-term resident expats, these daily walking tours (times vary by season) explore various city locales.

DIRECTORY

Resources A-Z

TRAVEL ADVICE

For up-to-date information on travel to a specific country – including the latest on safety and security, health issues, local laws and customs – contact your home country government's department of foreign affairs. Most have websites with useful advice for would-be travellers.

AUSTRALIA
www.smartraveller.gov.au

CANADA
www.voyage.gc.ca

NEW ZEALAND
www.safetravel.govt.nz

REPUBLIC OF IRELAND
foreignaffairs.gov.ie

UK
www.fco.gov.uk/travel

USA
www.state.gov/travel

DIRECTORY

ADDRESSES

Paris arrondissements are indicated by the last two digits of the postal code: 75002 denotes the second, 75015 the 15th, and so on. The 16th arrondissement is divided into two sectors, 75016 and 75116. Some business addresses have a more detailed postcode, followed by a Cedex number, which indicates the arrondissement; *bis* or *ter* is the equivalent of 'b' or 'c' after a building number.

AGE RESTRICTIONS

For heterosexuals and homosexuals, the age of consent is 15. You must be 18 to drive, and to consume alcohol in a public place. You must be 16 to buy cigarettes.

ATTITUDE & ETIQUETTE

Parisians take manners seriously and are generally more courteous than their reputation may have led you to believe. If someone brushes you accidentally when passing, they will more often than not say *'pardon'*; you can do likewise, or say *'c'est pas grave'* (don't worry). In shops it is normal to greet the assistant with a *'bonjour madame'* or *'bonjour monsieur'* when you enter, and say *'au revoir'* when you leave. The business of *'tu'* and *'vous'* can be tricky for English speakers. Strangers, people significantly older than you and professional contacts should be addressed with the respectful *'vous'*; friends, relatives, children and pets as *'tu'*. When among themselves, young people will often launch straight in with *'tu'*.

BUSINESS

The best first stop for initiating business is the CCIP (*see p369*). Banks can refer you to lawyers, accountants and tax consultants.

Conventions & conferences

Paris is the world's leading centre for trade fairs.

CNIT *2 pl de la Défense, BP 321, 92053 Paris La Défense (01.40.68.22.22/www.viparis. com). M°/RER Grande Arche de La Défense.*
Mainly computer fairs.
Palais des Congrès *2 pl de la Porte-Maillot, 17th (01.40.68.22.22/www.palais-congres-paris.fr). M° Porte-Maillot.*
Parc des Expositions de Paris-Nord Villepinte *SEPENV 60004, 95970 Roissy-Charles-de-Gaulle (01.40.68.22.22/www. expoparisnord.com). RER Parc des Expositions.*
Trade fair centre near Roissy airport.
Paris-Expo *Porte de Versailles, 15th (01.40.68.22.22/www. viparis.com). M° Porte de Versailles.*
The city's biggest expo centre.

Courier services

ATV *08.11.65.56.05/www.atoute vitesse.com.* **Open** 24hrs daily. **Credit** MC, V.
Bike or van messengers 24/7. Rates rise after 8pm on weekdays and at weekends.
Chronopost *Customer service: 08.25.80.18.01/www.chronopost. com.* **Open** 8am-8pm Mon-Fri; 9am-1pm Sat. **Credit** MC, V.
This overnight delivery offshoot of the state-run post office is the most widely used service for parcels.

UPS *34 bd Malesherbes, 8th (08.21.23.38.77/www.ups.com). M° St-Augustin.* **Open** 8am-7pm Mon-Fri; 8am-1pm Sat. **Credit** AmEx, MC, V.
International courier services.

Secretarial services

ADECCO International *28 rue Caumartin, 9th (01.45.24.67.78/ www.adecco.fr). M° Havre-Caumartin.* **Open** 8.30am-12.30pm, 2-6.30pm Mon-Fri. International employment agency specialising in bilingual secretaries and staff. **Other locations** throughout the city.

Translators & interpreters

Documents such as birth certificates, loan applications and so on must be translated by certified legal translators, listed at the CCIP (*see p369*) or embassies. For business translations there are dozens of reliable independents.

Association des Anciens Elèves de l'Esit *01.44.05.41.46/ www.aaeesit.com.* **Open** for phone calls only, 8am-8pm Mon-Fri; 8am-6pm Sat.
A translation and interpreting co-operative whose 1,000 members are graduates of the Ecole Supérieure d'Interprètes et de Traducteurs.
International Corporate Communication *3 rue des Batignolles, 17th (01.43.87.29.29/ www.iccparis.com). M° Place de Clichy.* **Open** 9am-1pm, 2-6pm Mon-Fri.
Translators of financial and corporate documents, plus simultaneous translation.

Useful organisations

American Chamber of Commerce *156 bd Haussmann, 8th (01.56.43.45.67/www.amcham france.org). M° Miromesnil.*
Closed to the public, calls only.
British Embassy Commercial Library *35 rue du Fbg-St-Honoré, 8th (01.44.51.31.00/www.amb-grandebretagne.fr). M° Concorde.*
Open by appointment.
Stocks trade directories, and assists British companies that wish to develop or set up in France.
CCIP (Chambre de Commerce et d'Industrie de Paris) *27 av de Friedland, 8th (08.20.01.21.12/ www.ccip.fr). M° Charles de Gaulle Etoile.* **Open** 8.30am-6.30pm Mon-Fri.
A variety of services for people doing business in France and is very useful for small businesses. Pick up the free booklet *Discovering the Chamber of Commerce* from its head office. There's also a legal advice line (08.92.70.51.00, 9am-4.30pm Mon-Thur, 9am-1pm Fri).
Other locations: Bourse du Commerce, 2 rue de Viarmes, 1st (has a free library and bookshop); 2 rue Adolphe-Jullien, 1st (support for businesses wishing to export goods and services to France).
INSEE (Institut National de la Statistique et des Etudes Economiques) *Salle de consultation, 195 rue de Bercy, Tour Gamma A, 12th (08.25.88.94.52/www.insee.fr). M° Bercy.* **Open** 9.30am-12.30pm, 2-5pm Mon-Thur; 9.30-12.30pm, 2-4pm Fri.
Source of statistics relating to the French economy and society.
US Commercial Service *Postal address: US Embassy, 2 av Gabriel, 8th. Visit: US Commercial Service, NEO Building, 14 bd Haussmann, 9th (01.43.12.70.57/www.buyusa. gov/france). M° Richelieu Drouot.* **Open** by appointment 9am-6pm Mon-Fri.
Helps American companies looking to trade in France. Advice by fax and email.

CONSUMER

In the event of a serious problem, try one of the following:

Direction Départementale de la Concurrence, de la Consommation et de la Répression des Fraudes *8 rue Froissart, 3rd (39.39). M° St-Sébastien Froissart.* **Open** 9am-noon, 2-5pm Mon-Fri.

Come here to file a consumer complaint concerning problems with Paris-based businesses.
Institut National de la Consommation *80 rue Lecourbe, 15th (08.92.70.75.92/www. conso.net). M° Sèvres Lecourbe.* **Open** by phone 9am-12.30pm Mon-Fri; recorded information at other times.
Deals with questions on housing, consumer, regulatory and administrative issues.

CUSTOMS

Custom declarations are not usually necessary if you arrive from another EU country and are carrying legal goods for personal use. The amounts given below are guidelines only: if you come close to the maximums in several categories, you may still have to explain your personal habits to an interested but sceptical customs officer.

● 800 cigarettes, 400 small cigars, 200 cigars or 1kg loose tobacco.
● 10 litres of spirits (more than 22% alcohol), 90 litres of wine (less than 22% alcohol) or 110 litres of beer.
Coming from a non-EU country, you can bring:
● 200 cigarettes, 100 small cigars, 50 cigars or 250g tobacco.
● 1 litre of spirits (more than 22% alcohol) or 2 litres of wine or beer (more than 22% alcohol).
● 50g (1.76oz) of perfume.

Tax refunds

Non-EU residents can claim a refund or *détaxe* (around 12 per cent) on VAT if they spend over €175 in any one day in one shop and if they live outside the EU for more than six months in the year. At the shop concerned ask for a *bordereau de vente à l'exportation*, and when you leave France have it stamped by customs. Then send the stamped form back to the shop. *Détaxe* does not cover food, drink, antiques, services or works of art.

DISABLED TRAVELLERS

It's always wise to check up on a site's accessibility and provision for disabled access before you visit. There is general information (in French) available on the **Secrétaire d'Etat aux Personnes Handicapées** website: www.handicap.gouv.fr, telephone 08.20.03.33.33.

Association des Paralysés de France *13 pl de Rungis, 13th (01.53.80.92.98/www.apf.asso.fr). M° Place d'Italie.* **Open** 9am-12.30pm, 2-6pm Mon-Fri.
Publishes *Guide 98 Musées, Cinémas* (€3.81) listing accessible museums and cinemas, and a guide to restaurants and sights.
Fédération APAJH (Association pour Adultes et Jeunes Handicapés) *185 Bureaux de la Colline, 92213 St-Cloud Cedex (01.55.39.56.00/www.apajh.org). M° Marcel Sembat.*
Advice for disabled people living in France.
Maison Départementale des Personnes Handicapées de Paris *(08.05.80.09.09).* **Open** 9am-4pm Mon-Wed, Fri; 9am-5pm Thur.
Advice available in French to disabled persons living in or visiting Paris. The Office de Tourisme website (www.paris info.com) also provides useful information for disabled visitors.

Getting around

The métro and buses are not wheelchair-accessible, with the exception of métro line 14 (Météor), stations Barbès-Rochechouard (line 2) and Esplanade de la Défense (line 1), and bus lines 20, 21, 24, 26, 27, 29, 30, 31, 38, 39, 43, 53, 54, 60, 62, 63, 64, 80, 81, 88, 91, 92, 94, 95, 96 and PC (Petite Ceinture) 1, 2 and 3. Forward seats on buses are intended for people with poor mobility. RER lines A, B, C, D and some SNCF trains are wheelchair-accessible in parts. For a full list of wheelchair-accessible stations: 08.10.64.64.64, www.infomobi.com. All Paris taxis are obliged by law to take passengers in wheelchairs.

Aihrop *3 av Paul-Doumer, 92508 Rueil-Malmaison Cedex (01.41.29.01.29/www.adiph95.fr).* **Open** 9.30am-12.30pm, 1.30-5.30pm Mon-Fri. Closed Aug.
Transport for the disabled, anywhere in Paris and Ile-de-France; book 48 hours in advance.

DRUGS

French police have the power to stop and search anyone. It's wise to keep prescription drugs in their original containers and, if possible, to carry copies of the original prescriptions. If you're caught in possession of illegal drugs, you can expect a prison sentence and/ or a fine. *See also p370* Health.

DIRECTORY

ELECTRICITY & GAS

Electricity in France runs on 220V. Visitors with British 240V appliances can change the plug or use an adaptor (*adaptateur*). For US 110V appliances, you'll need to use a transformer (*transformateur*), available at BHV or branches of Fnac and Darty. Gas and electricity are supplied by the state-owned Electricité de France-Gaz de France. Contact EDF-GDF (08.10.01.03.33/ www.edf.fr or 08.11.01.30.00/ www.gazdefrance.com) about supply, bills, power failures and gas leaks.

EMBASSIES & CONSULATES

For a full list of embassies and consulates, see the Pages Jaunes (www.pagesjaunes.fr) under 'Ambassades et Consulats'. Consular services (passports, etc) are for citizens of that country only.

Australian Embassy *4 rue Jean-Rey, 15th (01.40.59.33.00/ www.france.embassy.gov.au). M° Bir-Hakeim.* **Open** *Consular services* 9.15am-noon, 2-4.30pm Mon-Fri; *Visas* 10am-noon Mon-Fri.

British Embassy *35 rue du Fbg-St-Honoré, 8th (01.44.51.31.00/ www.ukinfrance.fco.gov.uk). M° Concorde. Consular services: 18bis rue d'Anjou, 8th. M° Concorde.* **Open** 9.30am-12.30pm, 2.30-4.30pm Mon-Fri.
Visas: 16 rue d'Anjou, 8th (01.44.51.31.01). **Open** 9.30am-noon by phone; 2.30-4.30pm. British citizens wanting consular services (new passports, etc) should ignore the long queue stretching along rue d'Anjou for the visa department, and instead walk straight in at no.18bis.

Canadian Embassy *35 av Montaigne, 8th (01.44.43.29.00/ www.amb-canada.fr). M° Franklin D. Roosevelt.* **Open** 9am-noon, 2-5pm Mon-Fri.
Consular services: 01.44.43.29.02. **Open** 9am-noon Mon-Fri.
Visas: 37 av Montaigne, 8th (01.44.43.29.16). **Open** 8.30-11am Mon-Fri.

Irish Embassy *12 av Foch, 16th. Consulate 4 rue Rude, 16th (01.44.17.67.00/www.embassyof ireland.fr). M° Charles de Gaulle Etoile.* **Open** *Consular/visas* 9.30am-noon Mon-Fri; by phone 9.30am-1pm, 2.30-5.30pm Mon-Fri.

New Zealand Embassy *7ter rue Léonard-de-Vinci, 16th (01.45.01.43.43/www.nzembassy. com/france). M° Victor Hugo.* **Open** 9am-1pm, 2-5.30pm Mon-Fri (closes 4pm Fri). *July, Aug* 9am-1pm, 2-4.30pm Mon-Thur; 9am-2pm Fri. *Visas* 9am-12.30pm Mon-Fri. Visas for travel to New Zealand can be applied for on the website www.immigration.govt.nz.

South African Embassy *59 quai d'Orsay, 7th (01.53.59.23.23/ www.afriquesud.net). M° Invalides.* **Open** 8.30am-5.15pm Mon-Fri. *Consulate & visas* 8.30am-noon Mon-Fri.

US Embassy *2 av Gabriel, 8th (01.43.12.22.22/http://france. usembassy.gov). M° Concorde. Consulate & visas: 4 av Gabriel, 8th (08.10.26.46.26). M° Concorde.* **Open** *Consular services* 9am-12.30pm, 1-3pm Mon-Fri. *Visas* 08.92.23.84.72 or check website for non-immigration visas.

EMERGENCIES

Most of the following services operate 24 hours a day. In a medical emergency, such as a road accident, phone the Sapeurs-Pompiers, who have trained paramedics. *See also* **Health: Accident & Emergency; Doctors; Helplines.**

Ambulance (SAMU) 15
Police 17
Fire (Sapeurs-Pompiers) 18
Emergency (from a mobile phone) 112
GDF (gas leaks) 08.10.33.37.51/www.gazdefrance.fr
EDF (electricity) 08.10.33.37.51
Centre anti-poison 01.40.05.48.48

GAY & LESBIAN

For information on HIV and AIDS, *see below* **Health**. *See also pp306-312* **Gay & Lesbian**.

HEALTH

Nationals of non-EU countries should take out insurance before leaving home. EU nationals staying in France can use the French Social Security system, which refunds up to 70 per cent of medical expenses. UK residents travelling in Europe require a European National Health Insurance Card (EHIC). This allows them to benefit from free or reduced-cost medical care when travelling in a country belonging to the European Economic Area

(EEA) or Switzerland. The EHIC replaces the E111 form and is free of charge. For further information, refer to www.dh.gov.uk/travellers.

If you're staying for longer than three months, or working in France but you are still making National Insurance contributions in Britain, you will need form E128 filled in by your employer and stamped by the NI contributions office in order to get a French medical number. Consultations and prescriptions have to be paid for in full on the spot, and are reimbursed on receipt of a completed *fiche*. If you undergo treatment, the doctor will give you a prescription and a *feuille de soins* (bill of treatment). Stick the small stickers from the medication boxes on to the *feuille de soins*. Send this, together with the prescription and details of your EHIC card, to the local **Caisse Primaire d'Assurance Maladie** for a refund. For those resident in France, more and more doctors now accept the **Carte Vitale**, which lets them produce a virtual *feuille de soins* and you to pay only the non-reimbursable part of the bill. Information on health insurance can be found at www.ameli.fr. You can track refunds with Allosecu (08.11.90.09.07). See also the Ministry of Health's website at www.sante.gouv.fr.

Accident & emergency

Hospitals specialise in one type of emergency or illness – refer to the Assistance Publique's website (www.aphp.fr). In a medical emergency, call the Sapeurs-Pompiers or SAMU (*see* **Emergencies**). The following (in order of district) have 24hr accident and emergency services:

ADULTS
Hôpital Hôtel Dieu *1 pl du Parvis Notre-Dame, 4th (01.42.34.82.34).*
Hôpital St-Louis *1 av Claude-Vellefaux, 10th (01.42.49.49.49).*
Hôpital St-Antoine *184 rue du Fbg-St-Antoine, 12th (01.49.28.20.00).*
Hôpital de la Pitié-Salpêtrière *47-83 bd de l'Hôpital, 13th (01.42.16.00.00).*
Hôpital Cochin *27 rue du Fbg-St-Jacques, 14th (01.58.41.41.41).*
Hôpital Européen Georges Pompidou *20 rue Leblanc, 15th (01.56.09.20.00).*

Hôpital Bichat-Claude Bernard
*46 rue Henri-Huchard, 18th
(01.40.25.80.80).*
Hôpital Tenon *4 rue de la Chine,
20th (01.56.01.70.00).*

CHILDREN
Hôpital Armand Trousseau
*26 av du Dr Arnold-Netter,
12th (01.44.73.74.75).*
Hôpital St-Vincent de Paul
*74-82 av Denfert-Rochereau,
14th (01.58.41.41.41).*
Hôpital Necker *149 rue de Sèvres,
15th (01.44.49.40.00).*
Hôpital Robert Debré *48 bd
Sérurier, 19th (01.40.03.20.00).*

PRIVATE HOSPITALS
American Hospital in Paris
*63 bd Victor-Hugo, 92200 Neuilly
(01.46.41.25.25/www.american-
hospital.org). M° Porte Maillot,
then bus 82.* **Open** 24hrs daily.
English-speaking hospital. French
Social Security refunds only a small
percentage of treatment costs.
**Hertford British Hospital
(Hôpital Franco-Britannique)**
*3 rue Barbès, 92300 Levallois-
Perret (01.46.39.22.22/www.
british-hospital.org). M° Anatole-
France.* **Open** 24hrs daily.
Most staff here speak English.

Complementary medicine

Centre de Médecine Naturelle
*2 rue d'Isly, 8th (01.43.87.60.33).
M° St-Lazare.* **Open** by
appointment 9am-8pm Mon-Fri;
9am-1pm Sat.
Health services include acupuncture,
aromatherapy and homeopathy.

Contraception & abortion

To get the pill (*la pilule*) or coil
(*stérilet*), you need a prescription,
available on appointment from
the two places listed below, from
a *médecin généraliste* (GP) or from
a gynaecologist. The morning-after
pill (*la pilule du lendemain*) can
be had from pharmacies without
prescription but is not reimbursed.
Condoms (*préservatifs*) and
spermicides are sold in pharmacies
and supermarkets, and there are
condom machines in most métro
stations, club lavatories and on
some street corners.

**Centre de Planification et
d'Education Familiales** *27 rue
Curnonsky, 17th (01.48.88.07.28).
M° Porte de Champerret.* **Open**
9am-5pm Mon-Fri.
Free consultations on family
planning and abortion.

**MFPF (Mouvement Français
pour le Planning Familial)**
*10 rue Vivienne, 2nd
(01.42.60.93.20/www.planning-
familial.org). M° Bourse.* **Open**
2-4pm Mon; 11am-1pm Tue;
noon-3pm Thur.
Phone for an appointment for
prescriptions and contraception
advice. For abortion advice, turn up
at the centre at one of the designated
time slots (Mon & Tue). The
approach here, however, is brusque.
Other locations: 94 bd Masséna,
13th (01.45.84.28.25).

Dentists

Dentists are found in the *Pages
Jaunes* under *Dentistes*. For
emergencies, contact:

Hôpital de la Pitié-Salpêtrière
(see p370) also offers 24hr
emergency dental care.
SOS Dentaire *87 bd Port-Royal,
13th (01.43.37.51.00). M° Les
Gobelins/RER Port-Royal.*
Open *by phone* 9am-midnight.
A telephone service for emergency
dental care.

Doctors

You'll find a list of GPs in the
Pages Jaunes under *Médecins:
Médecine générale*. For a social
security refund, choose a doctor or
dentist who is *conventionné* (state
registered). Consultations cost €20
or more, of which a proportion can
be reimbursed. Seeing a specialist
costs more still.

Centre Médical Europe *44 rue
d'Amsterdam, 9th (01.42.81.93.33).
M° St-Lazare.* **Open** 8am-7pm Mon-
Fri; 8am-6pm Sat.
Practitioners in all fields; modest
consultation fees.
SOS Médecins *36.24.* House
calls cost €35 before 7pm; from
€50 after and on holidays; prices
are higher if you don't have French
social security.
Urgences Médicales de Paris
01.53.94.94.94. Doctors make
house calls for €35 during the day
(€60 if you don't have French social
security); €50/€80 until midnight;
€63.50/€90 after midnight. Some
speak English.

Opticians

Branches of **Alain Afflelou**
(www.alainafflelou.com) and
Lissac (www.lissac.com) stock
hundreds of frames and can make
prescription glasses within the

hour. For an eye test, you'll need to
go to an *ophtalmologiste* – ask the
optician for a list. Contact lenses
can be bought over the counter if
you have your prescription details.

Hôpital des Quinze-Vingts
*28 rue de Charenton, 12th
(01.40.02.15.20).*
Specialist eye hospital offers on-the-
spot consultations for eye problems.
SOS Optique
01.48.07.22.00/www.sosoptique.com.
24hr repair service for glasses.

Pharmacies

French *pharmacies* sport a green
neon cross. A rota of *pharmacies
de garde* operate at night and on
Sundays; see below for a list of
these night pharmacies. If closed,
a pharmacy will have a sign
indicating the nearest one open.
Staff can provide basic medical
services such as bandaging
wounds (for a small fee) and
will indicate the nearest doctor
on duty. *Parapharmacies* sell
almost everything pharmacies
do but cannot dispense prescription
medication. Toiletries and sanitary
products are often less expensive
in supermarkets.

**Grande Pharmacie de la
Nation** *13 pl de la Nation, 11th
(01.43.73.24.03). M° Nation.*
Open 8am-11pm daily.
Matignon *2 rue Jean-Mermoz, 8th
(01.43.59.86.55). M° Franklin D.
Roosevelt.* **Open** 8.30am-2am daily.
Pharmacie des Champs-Elysées
*84 av des Champs-Elysées, 8th
(01.45.62.02.41). M° George V.*
Open 24hrs daily.
**Pharmacie Européene de la
Place de Clichy** *6 pl de Clichy,
9th (01.48.74.65.18). M° Place
de Clichy.* **Open** 24hrs daily.
Pharmacie des Halles *10 bd de
Sébastopol, 4th (01.42.72.03.23).
M° Châtelet.* **Open** 9am-midnight
Mon-Sat; 9am-10pm Sun.
Pharmacie d'Italie *61 av d'Italie,
13th (01.44.24.19.72). M° Tolbiac.*
Open 8am-2am daily.
Pharma Presto *01.61.04.04.04/
www.pharma-presto.com.* **Open**
24hrs daily. Delivery (€40 8am-
6pm; €55 6pm-8am & weekends)
of medication.

STDs, HIV & AIDS

**Cabinet Médical (Mairie
de Paris)** *2 rue Figuier, 4th
(01.49.96.62.70). M° Pont-Marie.*
Open 9am-12.30pm, 1.30-6.30pm
Mon-Fri; 9.30-noon Sat.

Free, anonymous tests (*dépistages*) for HIV, hepatitis B and C and syphilis (wait one week for results). Good counselling service, too.

Le Kiosque Infos Sida-Toxicomanie *36 rue Geoffroy-l'Asnier, 4th (01.44.78.00.00). Mº St-Paul.* **Open** 10am-7pm Mon-Thur; 1-7pm Fri; 11am-2pm, 3-7pm Sat.
Youth association offering information and counselling on AIDS, sexuality and drugs

SIDA Info Service *08.00.84.08.00/ www.sida-info-service.org.* **Open** 24hrs daily.
Confidential AIDS information in French. English-speakers are available 2-7pm Mon, Wed, Fri.

HELPLINES

Alcoholics Anonymous in English *01.46.34.59.65/ www.aaparis.org.* A 24hr recorded message gives details of Alcoholics Anonymous meetings at the American Cathedral or American Church (*see p376*).

Allô Service Public *39.39/www.service-public.fr.* **Open** 8am-7pm Mon-Fri; 9am-2pm Sat.
A source of information and contacts for all aspects of tax, work and administration matters. They even claim to be able to help if you have problems with neighbours. The catch: you can only dial from inside France, and operators speak only French.

Counseling Center *01.47.23.61.13.*
English-language counselling service, based at the American Cathedral.

Drogues Alcool Tabac Info Service *08.00.23.13.13/ www.drogues.gouv.fr.*
Phone service, in French, for help with drug, alcohol and tobacco problems.

Narcotics Anonymous *01.43.72.12.72/www.narcotiques anonymes.org.*
The helpline is open daily 6-8pm. Meetings in English are held three times a week.

SOS Dépression *01.40.47.95.95/ http://sos.depression.free.fr.* **Open** 24hrs daily.
People listen and/or give advice to those suffering from depression. Can send round a counsellor or psychiatrist in case of a crisis.

SOS Help *01.46.21.46.46/ www.soshelpline.org.* **Open** 3-11pm daily.
English-language helpline.

ID

French law requires that some form of identification be carried at all times. Be prepared to produce your passport or **EHIC** card (*see p370*).

INSURANCE

See p370 **Health**.

INTERNET

ISPs

Free *10.44/www.free.fr.*
Neuf *08.05.70.18.01/www.neuf.fr).*
Orange *32.20/www.orange.fr.*

Internet access

Many hotels offer internet access – and an increasing number of public spaces are setting themselves up as Wi-Fi hotspots.

Milk *31 bd de Sébastopol, 1st (01.40.13.06.51/www.milklub. com). Mº Châtelet or Rambuteau/ RER Châtelet Les Halles.* **Open** 24hrs daily.
Other locations throughout the city.

LANGUAGE

See p382 **Vocabulary**; for food terms, *see p190* **Menu Lexicon**.

LEFT LUGGAGE

Gare du Nord
There are self-locking luggage lockers (6.15am-11.15pm daily) on Level -1 under the main station concourse: small (€3.50), medium (€7) and large (€9.50) for 48 hours.
Roissy-Charles-de-Gaulle airport Bagages du Monde
(01.34.38.58.90/www.bagagesdu monde.com). **Terminal 1** *Niveau Départ, Porte 14 (01.34.38.58.82).* **Open** 8am-8pm daily. **Terminal 2A** *Niveau Départ, Porte 3-4 (01.34.38.58.80).* **Open** 8am-8pm daily. **Terminal 2F** *Niveau Arrivée, Porte 4-5 (0134.38.58.81).* **Open** 7am-7pm daily.
Company with counters in CDG and an office in Paris (102 rue de Chemin-Vert, 11th, 01.34.38.58.97, open 9am-noon, 2-6pm Mon-Fri; 10am-5pm Sat). Can ship baggage worldwide, or store luggage.

LEGAL HELP

Mairies can answer some legal enquiries; ask for times of their free *consultations juridiques*.

Direction Départementale de la Concurrence, de la Consommation et de la Répression des Fraudes *8 rue Froissart, 3rd (01.40.27.16.00). Mº St-Sébastien Froissart.* **Open** 9am-noon, 2-5pm Mon-Fri.
Part of the Ministry of Finance; deals with consumer complaints.

Palais de Justice Galerie de Harlay *Escalier S, 4 bd du Palais, 4th (01.44.32.51.51). Mº Cité.* **Open** 9am-noon Mon-Fri.
Free legal consultation. Arrive early and obtain a ticket for the queue.

SOS Avocats *08.25.39.33.00.* **Open** 7-11.30pm Mon-Fri. Closed July, Aug.
Free legal advice by phone.

LIBRARIES

Every arrondissement has a free public library. To get hold of a library card, you need ID and evidence of a fixed address in Paris.

American Library *10 rue du Général-Camou, 7th (01.53.59.12.60/www.american libraryinparis.org). Mº Ecole-Militaire/RER Pont de l'Alma.* **Open** 10am-7pm Tue-Sat (shorter hours in Aug). **Admission** day pass €12; annual €100; discount for students.
A useful resource: this is the largest English-language lending library on the Continent. It receives 400 periodicals, as well as popular magazines and newspapers (mainly American).

Bibliothèque Historique de la Ville de Paris *Hôtel Lamoignon, 24 rue Pavée, 4th (01.44.59.29.40). Mº St-Paul.* **Open** 1-6pm Mon-Fri; 10am-6pm Sat. Closed 1st 2wks Aug. **Admission** free (bring passport photo and ID).
Books and documents on Paris history in a Marais mansion.

Bibliothèque Marguerite Durand *79 rue Nationale, 13th (01.53.82.76.77). Mº Tolbiac.* **Open** 2-6pm Tue-Sat. Closed 3wks Sept. **Admission** free.
40,000 books and 120 periodicals on women's history. The feminism collection includes letters of Colette and Louise Michel.

Bibliothèque Nationale de France François Mitterrand *quai François-Mauriac, 13th (01.53.79.59.59/www.bnf.fr). Mº Bibliothèque.* **Open** 10am-7pm Tue-Sat; 1-7pm Sun. Closed 2wks Sept & bank holidays. **Admission** day pass €3.30; annual €35.

Books, papers and periodicals, plus titles in English. An audio-visual room lets you browse photo, film and sound archives.

Bibliothèque Publique d'Information (BPI) *Centre Pompidou, 4th (01.44.78.12.33/ www.bpi.fr). M° Hôtel de Ville/ RER Châtelet Les Halles.* **Open** noon-10pm Mon, Wed-Fri; 11am-10pm Sat, Sun. Closed 1 May. **Admission** free.

Now on three levels, the Centre Pompidou's vast library has a huge global press section, reference books and language-learning facilities.

BIFI (Bibliothèque du Film) *51 rue de Bercy, 12th (01.71.19.32.32/www.bifi.fr). M° Bercy.* **Open** 10am-7pm Mon-Fri. 1-6.30pm Sat. Closed 2wks Aug. **Admission** €3.50 day pass; €34 annual; €15 students annual.

Housed in the same building as the **Cinémathèque Française**, this world-class researchers' and film buffs' library offers books, magazines, film stills and posters, as well as films on video and DVD.

Documentation Française *29-31 quai Voltaire, 7th (01.40.15.71.10/www.ladocumentat ionfrancaise.fr). M° Rue du Bac.* **Open** 9am-6pm Mon-Fri. Closed Aug & 1st wk Sept.

The official government archive and central reference library has information on French politics and economy since 1945.

LOCKSMITHS

Numerous round-the-clock repair services handle locks, plumbing and, sometimes, car repairs. Most charge a minimum €18-€20 call-out (*déplacement*) and €30 per hour, plus parts. Charges are higher on Sunday and at night.

Allô Serrurerie *01.40.29.44.68/ www.alloserrurerie.com.*
SOS Dépannage *08.20.22.23.33/ www.okservice.fr.*
SOS Dépannage is double the price of most services, but claims to be twice as reliable.

LOST PROPERTY

Bureau des Objets Trouvés *36 rue des Morillons, 15th (08.21.00.25.25/www.prefecture-police-paris.interieur.gouv.fr). M° Convention.* **Open** 8.30am-5pm Mon-Thur; 8.30am-4.30pm Fri. Visit in person to fill in a form specifying details of the loss. This may have been the first

lost property office in the world, but it is far from the most efficient. Huge delays in processing claims mean that if your trip to Paris is short, you may need to nominate a proxy to collect found objects after you leave, although small items can be posted. If your passport was among the items lost, you'll need to go to your consulate to get a single-entry temporary passport in order to leave the country.

SNCF lost property
Some mainline SNCF stations have their own lost property offices.

MEDIA

See also p383 **Websites**.

Magazines

Arts & listings Two modest local publications compete for consumers of basic Wednesday-to-Tuesday listings: the handbag-sized **L'Officiel des Spectacles** (€0.35) and **Pariscope** (€0.40). Look out also for **Lylo**, a free bi-monthly booklet distributed around bars and clubs, for information on gigs and DJ nights. **Technikart** tries – not entirely successfully – to mix clubbing with the arts. Highbrow TV guide **Télérama** has superb arts coverage and comes with **Sortir**, a Paris listings insert. **Les Inrockuptibles** (fondly known as *Les Inrocks*) deals with contemporary music scenes at home and abroad; it has strong coverage of film and books too.

There are specialist magazines for every interest. The choice of film-related titles, in particular, is wide, and includes long-established intellectual heavyweights **Les Cahiers du Cinéma**, **Positif** and **Trafic**, fluffy **Studio** and celebrity-heavy **Première**.

Business *Capital*, its sister magazine **Management** and weightier **L'Expansion** are the notable monthlies. **Défis** has tips for the entrepreneur; **Initiatives** is for the self-employed.

English The **Time Out Paris Visitors' Guide** is on sale in newsagents across the city. **FUSAC** (France-USA Contacts) is a small-ads magazine that lists flat rentals, job ads and appliances for sale.

Gossip The French love gossip. **Public** gives weekly celebrity updates; **Voici** is the juiciest scandal sheet; **Gala** tells much

the same stories without the sleaze. **Paris Match** is a French institution founded in 1948, packed with society gossip, celeb interviews and regular photo scoops. **Point de Vue** specialises in royalty (no showbiz fluff). Monthly **Entrevue** aims to titillate and tends toward features on nonconformist sex.

News Weekly news magazines are an important sector in France, offering news and cultural sections as well as in-depth reports; they range from respected organs **L'Express**, **Le Point** and **Le Nouvel Observateur** to the sardonic, chaotically arranged **Marianne**. Weekly **Courrier International** publishes an interesting selection of articles, translated into French, from newspapers all over the world.

Women, men & fashion **Elle** was a pioneer among women's mags and has editions across the globe. In France it's a weekly, and spot-on for interviews and fashion. Monthly **Marie-Claire** takes a more feminist, campaigning line. Both have design spin-offs (**Elle Décoration**, **Marie-Claire Maison**), and *Elle* has also spawned foodie **Elle à Table**. **DS** has lots to read and coverage of social issues. **Vogue**, bought for its fashion coverage and big-name guests, is rivalled during fashion week by **L'Officiel de la Mode**.

Meanwhile the underground prefers to buy more radical publications such as **Crash** and the new wave of fashion/lifestyle mags: **WAD** (stands for We Are Different), **Citizen K**, **Jalouse** and **Numéro**. Men's mags include the naughty-bizarre **Echo des Savanes** and French versions of lad bibles **FHM**, **Maximal** and **Men's Health**.

Newspapers

French national dailies, with relatively high prices and low print runs, are in dire straits. Only 20 per cent of France read a national paper; regional dailies dominate outside Paris. Serious, centre-left **Le Monde** is must-read material for business types, politicians and intellectuals, and despite its lofty reputation, subject matter is eclectic.

The conservative upper and middle classes go for daily broadsheet **Le Figaro**, which has a devotion to politics, shopping,

DIRECTORY

food and sport. Taken over in 2004 by the head of the Dassault defence and media group, it steers clear of controversial industrial issues. Its sales are aided by pages of property and job ads and Wednesday's **Figaroscope** Paris listings. The Saturday edition has three magazines.

Founded in the aftershocks of 1968 by a group that included Sartre and de Beauvoir, **Libération**, once affectionately known as *Libé*, is shedding readers and yet to find a modern identity. In early 2005, its staff accepted a plan for financier Edouard de Rothschild to take a 39 per cent stake in the paper – only to go on a three-day strike when he later proposed 52 job cuts across the board. It is still the preferred read of the *gauche caviar* (champagne socialists) and worth buying for news and arts coverage.

For business and financial news, the French dailies **La Tribune**, **Les Echos** and the weekly **Investir** are the tried and trusted sources. The easy-read tabloid **Le Parisien** is strong on consumer affairs, social issues, local news, events and vox pops. Downmarket **France Soir** has gone tabloid. **La Croix** is a Catholic, right-wing daily. The Communist Party **L'Humanité** (shortened to *L'Huma*) struggles on. Sunday broadsheet **Le Journal du Dimanche** comes with **Fémina** mag and a Paris section.

L'Equipe is the doyen of European sports dailies – Saturday's edition comes with a magazine. Its sister bi-weekly **France Football** is the bible of world soccer. Each was instrumental in setting up the game's top competitions during the golden age of French sports journalism after the war. **Paris-Turf** is for horse fans.

English-language papers

Paris-based **International Herald Tribune** is on sale throughout the city; British dailies, Sundays and **USA Today** are widely available on the day of issue at larger kiosks in the centre, though often without their supplements. The most popular (and many esoteric) English and US newspapers and magazines can be found in central bookshops (*see pp241-42*).

Satirical papers

Wednesday institution **Le Canard Enchaîné** is the Gallic *Private Eye* – in fact it was the

inspiration for the *Eye*. It's a broadly left-wing satirical weekly broadsheet that's full of in-jokes and breaks political scandals.

Radio

For a complete list of all Paris radio frequencies, go to www.bric-a-brac.org/radio. A mandatory state-defined minimum of 40 per cent French music has led to overplay of Gallic pop oldies and to the creation of dubious hybrids by local groups that mix words in French with a refrain in English. Trashy phone-in shows also proliferate. Frequencies are given in MHz.

87.8 France Inter Highbrow, state-run; jazz, international news and discussion slots aplenty.
90.4 Nostalgie As you'd expect.
90.9 Chante France 100 per cent French *chanson*.
91.3 Chérie FM Lots of oldies.
91.7 France Musiques State classical music channel: highbrow concerts and top jazz.
92.1 Le Mouv' New public station aimed at luring the young with pop and rock music.
93.1 Aligre From local Paris news to literary chat.
93.9 France Culture Talky state culture station.
94.8 RCJ/Radio J/Judaïque FM/Radio Shalom Shared wavelength for Jewish stations.
95.2 Ici et Maintenant/Neo New stations hoping to stir local public debate about current events.
96.0 Skyrock Pop station with loudmouth presenters. Lots of rap.
96.4 BFM Business and economics.
96.9 Voltage FM Dance music.
97.4 Rire et Chansons A non-stop diet of jokes and pop oldies.
97.8 Ado Music for teenagers.
98.2 Radio FG Beloved of clubbers for its on-the-pulse tips, this station ditched its all-gay remit back in 1999.
99.0 Radio Latina Great Latin and salsa music.
100.3 NRJ 'Energy' – geddit? National leader with the under-30s.
101.1 Radio Classique Top-notch, state-run classical music station.
101.5 Radio Nova Hip hop, trip hop, world, jazz.
101.9 Fun Radio Now embracing techno alongside Anglo pop hits.
102.3 Ouï FM Ouï will rock you.
103.9 RFM Easy listening.
104.3 RTL The most popular French station nationwide mixes music and talk programmes.

104.7 Europe 1 News, press reviews, sports, business, entertainment. Much the best weekday breakfast news broadcast, with politicians interviewed live.
105.1 FIP Traffic and weather information, what's on in Paris and a mix of jazz, classical, world and pop. 'Fipettes', female continuity announcers employed for their come-to-bed voices, are a much-loved feature.
105.5 France Info 24hr news, weather, economic updates and sports bulletins. Reports get repeated every 15 minutes: useful if you're learning French.
106.7 Beur FM North African music and discussion.

English You can receive the **BBC World Service** (648 KHz AM), with English-language news, current events, pop and drama; also on 198KHz LW, from midnight to 5.30am daily. At other times 198KHz LW carries **BBC Radio 4**, with British news, talk and *The Archers*. **RFI** (738 KHz AM; www.rfi.fr) has an English-language programme of news and music 7-8am, 2.30-3.30pm and 4.30-5pm daily. There's also the French capital's first all-English station, Paris Live (www.paris-live.com).

Television

In 2005, the choice of free TV channels in France more than doubled. Under the acronym TNT (Télévision Numérique Terrestre, or terrestrial digital television), seven new channels – available via the traditional rooftop aerial with a decoder that costs about €100, or automatically to cable and satellite customers – began broadcasting. For more information, go to www.tdf.fr or pick up a copy of weekly mag *Télérama*. The channels listed below are the six 'core' stations available on an unenhanced TV set:

TF1 *(www.tf1.fr)*. The country's biggest channel. Reality shows, soaps and football are staples.
France 2 *(www.france2.fr)*. This state-owned station mixes game shows, chat, documentaries and the usual cop series and films.
France 3 *(www.france3.fr)*. This, the more heavyweight of the two state channels, offers wildlife and sports coverage, debates, *Cinéma*

de Minuit – classic films in VO (*version originale*, or original language) – and the endearing cookery show *Bon Appétit Bien Sûr*, fronted by Joël Robuchon.

Canal+ *(www.canalplus.fr).* Subscription channel shows recent films, exclusive sport and late-night porn. A week's worth of the satirical puppets show *Les Guignols* is broadcast unscrambled on Sundays at 1.40pm.

Arte/France 5 *(www.arte-tv.com).* The intellectual Franco-German hybrid Arte shares its wavelength with educational channel France 5 (3am-7pm).

M6 *(www.m6.fr).* Dubbed US sci-fi series and made for TV movies, plus investigative reportage, popular science and kids' shows.

Cable TV & satellite France offers a decent range of cable and satellite channels but content in English is still limited. CNN and BBC World offer round-the-clock news coverage. BBC Prime keeps you up to date on *EastEnders* (omnibus Sun 2pm), while Teva supplies comedy such as *Sex and the City*.

Numericable
(39.90/www.numericable.fr). The first cable provider to offer an interactive video service via the internet.

MONEY

The amount of currency visitors may carry is not limited. However, sums worth over €7,600 must be declared to customs when entering or leaving the country.

The euro

Non-French debit and credit cards can be used to withdraw and pay in euros, and currency withdrawn in France can be used subsequently all over the euro zone. Daylight robbery occurs, however, if you try to deposit a euro cheque from any country other than France in a French bank: they are currently charging around €15 for this service, and the European parliament has backed down on its original decision that cross-border payments should be in line with domestic ones across the euro zone. This is good news for the British, though: if you transfer money from the UK to France in euros, you will pay the same charges as if Britain were within the euro zone (but it pays to watch the exchange rate carefully).

ATMs

Withdrawals in euros can be made from bank and post office automatic cash machines. The specific cards accepted are marked on each machine, and most can give instructions in English. Credit card companies charge a fee for cash advances, but rates are often better than banks.

Banks

French banks usually open 9am-5pm Mon-Fri (some close at lunch); some banks also open on Sat. All are closed on public holidays, and from noon on the previous day. Note that not all banks have foreign exchange counters. The commission rates vary between banks; the state-owned Banque de France usually offers good rates. Most banks accept travellers' cheques, but may be reluctant to accept personal cheques even with the Eurocheque guarantee card, which is not widely used in France.

Bank accounts

To open an account (*ouvrir un compte*), French banks require proof of identity, address and your income (if any). You'll probably be required to show your passport, an electricity, gas or phone bill in your name and a payslip/letter from your employer. Students need a student card and may need a letter from their parents. Of the major national banks (BNP, Crédit Lyonnais, Société Générale, Banque Populaire, Crédit Agricole), Société Générale tends to be the most foreigner-friendly. Most banks don't hand out a Carte Bleue/Visa card until several weeks after you've opened an account. A chequebook (*chéquier*) is usually issued in about a week. Payments made with a Carte Bleue are debited directly from your current account, but you can arrange for purchases to be debited at the end of every month. French banks are tough on overdrafts, so try to anticipate any cash crisis in advance and work out a deal for an authorised overdraft (*découvert autorisé*) or you risk being blacklisted as '*interdit bancaire*' – forbidden from having a current account – for anything up to ten years. Depositing foreign currency cheques can be slow, so try to use wire transfer or a bank draft in euros to receive funds from abroad.

Bureaux de change

If you happen to be arriving in Paris early in the morning or late at night, you will be able to change money at the **American Express** bureaux de change in terminals 1 (01.48.16.13.26), 2A, 2B, 2C and 2D (01.48.16.48.40) and 2E (01.48.16.63.81) at Roissy, and at Orly Sud (01.49.75.77.37); all open 6.30am-11pm daily. **Travelex** (*see p376*) has bureaux de change at the following train stations:

Gare Montparnasse *01.42.79.03.88.* **Open** 8am-6.30pm daily.
Gare du Nord *01.42.80.11.50.* **Open** 6.30am-10pm daily.

Credit cards

Major international credit cards are widely used in France; Visa (more commonly known in France as *Carte Bleue*) is the most readily accepted. French-issued credit cards have a security microchip (*puce*) in each card. The card is slotted into a reader, and the holder keys in a PIN to authorise the transaction. Non-French cards work, but generate a credit slip to sign. In case of credit card loss or theft, call one of the following 24hr services which have English-speaking staff:

American Express *01.47.77.70.00.*
Diners Club *08.20.82.05.36.*
MasterCard *01.45.67.84.84.*
Visa *08.92.70.57.05.*

Foreign affairs

American Express *11 rue Scribe, 9th (01.47.77.70.00/www.american express.com). M° Opéra.* **Open** 9am-6.30pm Mon-Sat. Travel agency, bureau de change, *poste restante* (you can leave messages for other card holders), card replacement, travellers' cheque refund service, international money transfers and a cash machine for AmEx cardholders.

Barclays *6 rond-point des Champs-Elysées, 8th (08.10.09.09.09/ www.barclays.fr). M° Franklin D. Roosevelt.* **Open** 9.15am-4.30pm Mon-Fri. Barclays' international Expat Service handles direct debits, international transfer of funds, and so on.

Citibank *15 rue Paul Cézanne, 8th (01.70.75.50.50/www.citibank.fr). M° St-Philippe-du-Roule.* **Open** 10am-5.30pm Mon-Fri.

DIRECTORY

Bank clients get good rates for international money transfers, preferential exchange rates and no commission is charged on travellers' cheques.

Travelex *52 av des Champs-Elysées, 8th (01.42.89.80.33/ www.travelex.com/fr).* M° *Franklin D. Roosevelt.* **Open** 9am-10.30pm daily.

Travelex issues travellers' cheques and insurance and also deals with bank transfers.

Western Union Money Transfer *www.westernunion.com.* Many post offices in the city (*see below*) provide Western Union services. Transfers from abroad should arrive within 15 minutes; charges paid by the sender.

Tax

French VAT (*taxe sur la valeur ajoutée* or TVA) is arranged in three bands: 2.1 per cent for items of medication and newspapers; 5.5 per cent for food, books, CDs and DVDs; and 19.6 per cent for all other types of goods and services (the TVA for restaurants has been lowered from 19.6 per cent to 5.5 per cent).

NATURAL HAZARDS

Paris has no natural hazards as such, though in recent years the town hall has produced evacuation plans to cover flooding.

OPENING HOURS

Standard opening hours for shops are 9 or 10am to 7 or 8pm Monday to Saturday. Some shops are closed on Monday. Shops and businesses often close at lunchtime, usually 12.30-2pm; many shops close in August. Sunday opening is found in the Marais, on the Champs-Elysées, at Bercy Village and in the Carrousel du Louvre, although this may change – President Sarkozy is currently trying to extend Sunday trading. Most areas have a local grocer that stays open into the night and will often open on Sundays and public holidays too.

24hr florist Elyfleur *82 av de Wagram, 17th (01.47.66.97.19).* M° *Wagram.* **Credit** MC, V.
24hr garage Shell *6 bd Raspail, 7th (01.45.48.43.12).* M° *Rue du Bac.*
This garage has an extensive array of everyday supermarket products on sale from the Casino chain. No alcohol sold 10pm-6am.

24hr newsagents include: *33 av des Champs-Elysées, 8th,* M° *Franklin D. Roosevelt. 2 bd Montmartre, 9th,* M° *Grands Boulevards.*
Late-night tabacs Le Brazza *86 bd du Montparnasse, 14th (01.43.35.42.65).* M° *Montparnasse-Bienvenüe.* **Open** 6am-2am daily.
La Favorite *3 bd St-Michel, 5th (01.43.54.08.02).* M° *St-Michel.* **Open** 7am-2am daily.

POLICE

The French equivalent of 999 or 911 is **17** (**112** from a mobile), but don't expect a speedy response. That said, the Préfecture de Police has no fewer than 94 outposts in the city. If you're assaulted or robbed, report the incident as soon as possible. You'll need to make a statement (*procès verbal*) at the *point d'accueil* closest to the site of the crime. To find the nearest, call the Préfecture Centrale (08.91.01.22.22) or go to www.prefecture-police-paris. interieur.gouv.fr. Stolen goods are unlikely to be recovered, but you'll need a police statement for insurance.

POSTAL SERVICES

Post offices (*bureaux de poste*) are open 8am-7pm Mon-Fri; 8am-noon Sat, apart from the 24-hour post office listed below. Details of all branches are included in the phone book: under 'Administration des PTT' in the *Pages Jaunes*; under 'Poste' in the *Pages Blanches*. Most post offices contain automatic machines (in French and English) that weigh your letter, print out a stamp and give change, thus saving you from wasting time in an enormous queue. You can also usually buy stamps and sometimes envelopes at a tobacconist (*tabac*). For more information refer to www.laposte.fr.

Main Post Office *52 rue du Louvre, 75001 Paris, 1st (36.31).* M° *Les Halles or Louvre Rivoli.* **Open** 24hrs daily for poste restante, telephones, stamps, faxes, photocopying and a modest amount of banking operations. This is the best place to arrange to have your mail sent to if you haven't got a fixed address in Paris. Mail should be addressed to you in block capitals, followed by Poste Restante, then the post office's address. There will be a charge of €0.50 for each letter received.

RECYCLING & RUBBISH

The city has a recently established system of colour-coded domestic recycling bins. A yellow-lidded bin can take paper, cardboard cartons, tins and small electrical items; a white-lidded bin takes glass. All other rubbish goes in the green-lidded bins, except for used batteries (shops that sell batteries should accept them), medication (take it back to a pharmacy), toxic products (call 08.20.00.75.75 to have them picked up) or car batteries (take them to an official tip or return to garages exhibiting the '*Relais Verts Auto*' sign). Green, hive-shaped bottle banks can be found on many street corners. More information is available at www.environnement.paris.fr.

RELIGION

Churches and religious centres are listed in the *Pages Jaunes* under 'Eglises' and 'Cultes'. Paris has several English-speaking churches. The *International Herald Tribune*'s Saturday edition lists Sunday church services in English.

American Cathedral *23 av George V, 8th (01.53.23.84.00/ www.americancathedral.org).* M° *George V.*
American Church in Paris *65 quai d'Orsay, 7th (01.40.62.05.00/ www.acparis.org).* M° *Invalides.*
Emmanuel International Church of Paris *56 rue des Bons Raisins, Rueil-Malmaison (01.47.51.29.63/ www.eicparis.org).* RER *Rueil-Malmaison, then bus 244.*
Kehilat Gesher *10 rue de Pologne, 78100 St-Germain-en-Laye (01.39.21.97.19/ www.kehilatgesher.org).* RER *St-Germain-en-Laye.*
The Liberal English-speaking Jewish community has services in Paris and the western suburbs.
La Mosquée de Paris *2 pl du Puits de l'Ermite, 5th (01.45.35.97.33/www.mosquee-de-paris.org).* M° *Place Monge.*
St George's Anglican Church *7 rue Auguste-Vacquerie, 16th (01.47.20.22.51/www.stgeorgespari s.com).* M° *Charles de Gaulle Etoile.*
St Joseph's Roman Catholic Church *50 av Hoche, 8th (01.42.27.28.56/www.stjoeparis.org).* M° *Charles de Gaulle Etoile.*
St Michael's Church of England *5 rue d'Aguesseau, 8th (01.47.42.70.88/www.saintmichaels paris.org).* M° *Madeleine.*

RENTING A FLAT

Apartments are generally cheapest in northern, eastern and south-eastern Paris. You can expect to pay approximately €20 per square metre per month (which works out as, for example, €700 per month for a modest 35sq m apartment). Studios and one bedroom flats fetch the highest prices proportionally; the provision of lifts and cellars will also boost the rent.

Flat-hunting Given the scarcity of housing in Paris, it's a landlord's world; you'll need to search actively, or even frenetically, in order to find an apartment. The internet is a decent place to start: www.explorimmo.fr lists rental ads from *Le Figaro* and specialist real estate magazines; you can place a classified ad or check lettings on www.avendrealouer.fr. Thursday morning's *De Particulier à Particulier* (www.pap.fr) is a must for those who want to rent directly from the owner, but be warned – most flats go within hours. Fortnightly *Se Loger* (www.seloger.com) is also worth getting, though most of its ads are placed by agencies.

Landlords keen to let to foreigners advertise in the *International Herald Tribune* and English-language *FUSAC* (www.fusac.fr); rents tend to be higher than in the French press. There are also assorted free ad brochures that can be picked up from agencies. Private landlords often set a visiting time; prepare to meet hordes of other flat-seekers and have your documents and cheque book to hand.

There's also the option of flat-sharing – one that's been growing in popularity in recent years. To look for housemates, pick up a copy of *FUSAC* or browse the 3,000-odd weekly announcements found at www.colocation.fr, which also organises monthly soirée Le Jeudi de la Colocation, a chance to meet your potential future flatmates in the flesh.

Rental laws The minimum lease (*bail de location*) on an unfurnished flat is three years (though the tenant can give notice and leave before this period is up); furnished flats are generally let on one-year leases. During this period the landlord can only raise the rent by the official construction inflation index. At the end of the lease, the rent can be adjusted, but tenants

can object before a rent board. Tenants can be evicted for non-payment, or if the landlord wishes to sell the property or use it as his own residence. It is illegal to throw people out in winter.

Landlords will probably insist you present a dossier with pay slips (*fiches de paie/bulletins de salaire*) showing income equivalent to three to four times the monthly rent, and for foreigners in particular, provide a financial guarantor (someone who will sign a document promising to pay the rent if you abscond). When taking out a lease, payments usually include the first month's rent, a deposit (*caution*) of the equivalent of two months' rent, and an agency fee, if applicable.

It's customary to have an inspection of the premises (*état des lieux*) at the start and end of the rental, the cost of which (around €150) is shared by landlord and tenant. Landlords may try to rent their flats *non-déclaré* – without a written lease – and get rent in cash. This can make it hard for tenants to establish their rights – which is one reason why landlords do it.

Centre d'information et de défense des locataires *9 rue Severo, 14th (01.45.41.47.76).* *M° Pernety.* **Open** *by appointment* 10am-12.30pm, 2.30-3.30pm Mon-Thur.
Helps sort out problems with landlords, rent hikes, etc.

SAFETY & SECURITY

Beware of pickpockets, especially around crowded tourist hotspots. *See also p365* **Métro & RER** and *p376* **Police**.

SHIPPING SERVICES

Hedley's Humpers *6 bd de la Libération, 93284 St-Denis (01.48.13.01.02/www.hedleys humpers.com).* **Open** 9am-1pm, 2-6pm Mon-Fri. Closed 2wks Aug.
Specialist in transport of furniture and antiques. **In UK:** 3 St Leonards Road, London NW10 6SX (020 8965 8733). **In USA:** 21-41 45th Road, Long Island City, New York NY 11101 (1-718 433 4005).

SMOKING

Although smoking seems to be an essential part of French life (and death), the French state and public

health groups have recently waged war against the cigarette on several fronts. Smoking is now banned in all enclosed public spaces, including bars, cafés, clubs, restaurants, hotel foyers and shops, as well as on public transport. Many bars, cafés and clubs offer smoking gardens or terraces. There are also increasingly strident anti-smoking campaigns in France. Health warnings on cigarette packets are unignorable, and prices have soared.

For information about stopping smoking, contact the Tabac Info Service (39.89/www.tabac-info-service.fr). If you're a dedicated smoker, you'll soon learn that most *tabacs* close at 8pm (for a few that don't, *see p76* **Opening hours**). Some bars sell cigarettes behind the counter, generally only to customers who have a drink.

STUDY

Language

Most large multinational language schools, such as **Berlitz** (08.25.04.34.30, www.berlitz.com), have at least one branch in Paris. **Konversando** (01.47.70.21.64, www.konversando.fr) specialises in international exchanges and conversation.
Alliance Française *101 bd Raspail, 6th (01.42.84.90.00/ www.alliancefr.org). M° St-Placide.* The Alliance Française is a non-profit French-language school. Beginner and specialist courses start every month.
Ecole Eiffel *3 rue Crocé-Spinelli, 14th (01.43.20.37.41/www.ecole-eiffel.fr). M° Pernety.* Intensive classes, business French and phonetics.
Institut Catholique de Paris *12 rue Cassette, 6th (01.44.39.52.68/www.icp.fr/ilcf). M° St-Sulpice.* Courses in French culture and language. You must hold a *baccalauréat*-level qualification and be 18 or over (but you don't have to be Catholic).
Institut Parisien *29 rue de Lisbonne, 8th (01.40.56.09.53). M° Monceau.* A dynamic private school that offers courses in language, French civilisation and business French.
La Sorbonne – Cours de Langue et Civilisation *47 rue des Ecoles, 5th (01.44.10.77.00/www.ccfs-sorbonne.fr). M° Cluny-La Sorbonne/RER Luxembourg.*

DIRECTORY

Classes for foreigners ride on the name of this eminent institution. Teaching is grammar-based.
University of London Institute in Paris *9-11 rue Constantine, 7th (01.44.11.73.83/www.ulip.lon.ac.uk). M° Invalides.*
Linked to the University of London, this 4,000-student institute offers English courses for Parisians, and French courses at university level.

Specialised

Many of the prestigious Ecoles Nationales Supérieures (including film schools La FEMIS and ENS Louis Lumière) offer summer courses in addition to their full-time degree courses – ask for *formation continue*.

Adult education courses
www.paris.fr or your local mairie.
A huge range of inexpensive adult education classes is run by the city of Paris, including French as a foreign language, computer skills and applied arts.
American University of Paris *31 av Bosquet, 7th (01.40.62.07.20/ www.aup.edu). M° Ecole-Militaire/ RER Pont de l'Alma.*
International college awarding four-year American liberal arts degrees (BA/BSc).
Cordon Bleu *8 rue Léon-Delhomme, 15th (01.53.68.22.50/www.cordon bleu.edu). M° Vaugirard.*
Courses range from three-hour sessions on classical and regional cuisine to a nine-month diploma for those starting a culinary career. Bon appetit!
Ecole du Louvre *Palais du Louvre, porte Jaugard, place du Carrousel, 1st (01.55.35.18.00/www.ecole dulouvre.fr). M° Palais Royal Musée du Louvre.*
Art history and archaeology courses. Foreign students not wanting to take a degree can attend lectures.
INSEAD *bd de Constance, 77305 Fontainebleau (01.60.72.40.00/ www.insead.edu).*
Highly regarded international business school offering a ten-month MBA course in English as well as PhDs in a range of business subjects.
Parsons School of Design *14 rue Letellier, 15th (01.45.77.39.66/ www.parsons-paris.com). M° La Motte-Picquet-Grenelle.*
Subsidiary of the New York art college offering BFA programmes in fine art, photography, fashion, marketing and interior design.

Ritz-Escoffier Ecole de Gastronomie Française *38 rue Cambon, 1st (01.43.16.30.50/ www.ritzparis.com). M° Madeleine.*
Everything from afternoon demonstrations in the Ritz kitchens to diplomas. Courses are in French with English translation.

Student life

Student & youth discounts
To claim a *tarif étudiant* (around €1.50 off cinema seats, up to 50 per cent off museums and standby theatre tickets), you must have a French student card or International Student Identity Card (ISIC), available from **CROUS** (*see right*), student travel agents and the **Cité Universitaire** (*see below*). ISIC cards are valid in France only if you are under 26. Under-26s can get up to 50 per cent off rail travel on some trains with the SNCF's Carte 12/25 and the same reduction on the RATP network with the Imagine R card.

Long-term visas & housing
benefit UK and other students from the EU may stay in France for as long as their passport is valid. To also work legally during their course in Paris, they can find out more information about their rights at www.droitsdesjeunes.gouv.fr.
Foreign students from outside the EU wishing to study in Paris for longer than three months must apply for a long-term visa through the French embassy in their particular country.

Student accommodation

The simplest budget lodgings for medium-to-long stays can be found at the **Cité Universitaire** or *foyers* (student hostels). There are some 37 halls of residence set in landscaped gardens, with sports facilities and a theatre (*see below*). Another option is a *chambre contre travail* – free board in exchange for childcare, housework or English lessons; for this, look out for ads at language schools and the American Church. For cheap hotels and youth hostels, *see pp154-84*. As students often cannot provide proof of income, a *porte-garant* (guarantor) who will guarantee the payment of rent and bills is required.

Cité Universitaire *17 bd Jourdan, 14th (01.44.16.64.00/www.ciup.fr). RER Cité Universitaire.* **Open** *Offices* 8am-6pm Mon-Fri.
Foreign students enrolled on a university course, or interns who are also studying, can apply for a place at this campus of halls of residence (but be forewarned: only about ten per cent of the students who apply are actually successful). Rooms can be booked for a week, a month or for an entire academic year. Rents are approximately €300-€400 per month for a single

SIZE CHARTS

WOMEN'S CLOTHES

British	French	US
4	32	2
6	34	4
8	36	6
10	38	8
12	40	10
14	42	12
16	44	14
18	46	16
20	48	18

WOMEN'S SHOES

British	French	US
3	36	5
4	37	6
5	38	7
6	39	8
7	40	9
8	41	10
9	42	11

MEN'S CLOTHES

British	French	US
34	44	34
36	46	36
38	48	38
40	50	40
42	52	42
44	54	44
46	56	46
48	58	48

MEN'S SHOES

British	French	US
6	39	7
7.5	40	7.5
8	41	8
8	42	8.5
9	43	9.5
10	44	10.5
11	45	11
12	46	11.5

room and €200-€300 per person for a double. UK citizens must apply to the Collège Franco-Britannique, and Americans to the Fondation des Etats-Unis.

CROUS (Centre Régional des Oeuvres Universitaires et Scolaires) *39 av Georges-Bernanos, 5th (01.40.51.36.00/ 08.92.25.75.75/www.crous-paris.fr). Service du Logement: (01.40.51.35.95). RER Port-Royal.* **Open** 9am-5pm Mon-Fri.
Manages all University of Paris student residences, posts ads for rooms and has a list of hostels. Requests for rooms must be made by 1 April for the next academic year. CROUS also runs cheap canteens (listed on website) and is the clearing house for all *bourses* (grants) issued to foreign students. Call the Service des Bourses on 01.40.51.36.12.

Ethic Etapes *27 rue de Turbigo, 2nd (01.40.26.57.64/www.ethic-etapes.fr). Mº Etienne Marcel.* **Open** 9am-6pm Mon-Fri.
Operates cheap, short-stay hostels from two help centres: 5th (01.43.29.34.80); 14th (01.43.13.17.00).

Working as a student

Foreign students can legally work up to 20 hours per week. Non-EU members studying in Paris must apply for an *autorisation provisoire de travail* from the DDTEFT. The job service at CROUS (01.40.51.37.53) finds part-time jobs for students.

DDTEFT (Direction Départementale du Travail, d'Emploi et du Formation Professionelle) *109 rue Montmartre, 2nd (08.21.34.73.47/ 01.44.84.41.00/www.travail.gouv. fr). Mº Bourse.*

Useful organisations

CIDJ (Centre d'Information et de Documentation Jeunesse) *101 quai Branly, 15th (08.25.09.06.30/01.44.49.12.00/ www.cidj.com). Mº Bir-Hakeim/ RER Champ de Mars.* **Open** 10am-6pm Mon-Wed, Fri; 1-6pm Thur; 9.30am-1pm Sat.
The library here can give students advice on choices of courses and careers; the youth bureau of ANPE (Agence Nationale pour l'Emploi/ www.anpe.fr) can assist with job applications.

Maison des Initiatives Etudiantes (MIE) *50 rue des Tournelles, 3rd (01.49.96.65.30/ www.paris.fr).* **Open** 10am-10pm Mon-Fri; 2-9pm Sat.
Provides student associations with logistical assistance and Paris-based resources like meeting rooms, grants and computers. Radio Campus Paris, a radio station for students, has been broadcasting since September 2004.

Socrates-Erasmus Programme Britain: *UK Socrates-Erasmus Council, British Council, 10 Spring Gardens, London, SW1A 2BN (020 7389 4910/www.erasmus.ac.uk).* **France**: *Agence Socrates-Leonardo Da Vinci, 25 quai des Chartrons, 33080 Bordeaux Cedex (05.56.00.94.00/www.socrates-leonardo.fr).*
The international Socrates-Erasmus scheme lets EU students with reasonable written and spoken French spend a year of their degree in the French university system. Applications must be made via the Erasmus co-ordinator at your home university. Non-EU students should find out from their university whether it has an agreement with the French university system.

American students can find out more from the following organisations:

MICEFA *26 rue du Fbg-St-Jacques, 14th (01.40.51.76.96/ www.micefa.org).*
Relais d'accueil (Foreign students helpdesk) *Cité Universitaire, 17 bd Jourdan, 14th. RER Cité Universitaire. CROUS de Paris, 39 av Georges-Bernanos, 5th (01.40.51.37.35). RER Port-Royal.* **Open** *Sept-Nov* 9.15am-12.30pm, 1.15-4.30pm Mon-Fri (Cité); 9am-4.30pm Mon-Fri (CROUS).
Gives advice on housing, banking, visas, social security and university registration is available (by appointment) to foreign students at the addresses above.

TELEPHONES
Mobile phones

A subscription (*abonnement*) will normally get you a free phone if you sign up for at least one year. Two hours' calling time a month costs about €35 per month. International calls are normally charged extra – a lot extra. The three companies that rule the cell phone market in France are:

Bouygues Télécom *31.06/www.bouyguestelecom.fr.*
France Télécom/Orange *39.70/www.orange.fr.*
SFR *10.23/www.sfr.fr.*

Dialling & codes

All French phone numbers have ten digits. Paris and Ile-de-France numbers begin with 01; the rest of France is divided into four zones (02-05). Mobile phone numbers start with 06. 08 indicates a special rate (*see p380*); numbers beginning with 08 can only be reached from inside France. If you are calling France from abroad, leave off the 0 at the start of the ten-digit number. The country code is 33. To call abroad from France dial 00, then the country code, then the number. France Télécom has a useful website with information on rates and contracts: www.agence.france telecom.com.

France Télécom English-Speaking Customer Service *(08.00.36.47.75/from abroad +33 1.55.78.60.56).* **Open** 9am-5.30pm Mon-Fri.
Freephone information line in English on phone services, bills, payment, internet.

Operator services

Operator assistance, French directory enquiries *(renseignements)* 12.
To make a reverse-charge call within France, ask to make a call *en PCV*.
Airparif *01.44.59.47.64/ www.airparif.asso.fr.*
Information about pollution levels and air quality in Paris and Ile-de-France: invaluable for asthmatics.
International directory enquiries *32.12*, then country code. €3 per call.
International news (France Inter recorded message, in French), *08.92.68.10.33* (€0.34 per min).
Telegram *all languages, international 08.00.33.44.11; within France 36.55.*
Telephone engineer *10.13.*
Time *36.99.*
Traffic news *08.26.02.20.22.*
Weather *08.99.70.12.34* (€1.39 then €0.34 per min) for enquiries on weather in France and abroad, in French or English; you can also dial 08.92.68.02.75 (€0.34 per min) for a recorded weather announcement for Paris and region.

DIRECTORY

Public phones

Most public phones in Paris, almost all of which are maintained by France Télécom, use *télécartes* (phonecards). Sold at post offices, *tabacs*, airports and train and métro stations, they cost €7.50 for 50 units and €15 for 120 units. For cheap international calls, you can also buy a *télécarte à puce* (card with a microchip) or a *télécarte pré-payée*, which features a numerical code you dial before making a call; these can be used on domestic phones too. Travelex's International Telephone Card can be used in more than 80 countries (available from **Travelex** agencies, *see p376*). Cafés have coin phones, while post offices usually have card phones. In a phone box, the display screen will read 'Décrochez'. Pick up the phone. When 'Introduisez votre carte' appears, put your card into the slot; the screen should read 'Patientez SVP'. 'Numérotez' is your signal to dial. 'Crédit épuisé' means you have no more units left. Hang up ('Raccrochez') – and don't forget your card. Some public phones take credit cards. If you're using a credit card, insert the card, enter your PIN number and 'Patientez SVP' will appear.

Telephone directories

Telephone books can be found in all post offices and most cafés. The *Pages Blanches* (White Pages) list people and businesses alphabetically; the *Pages Jaunes* (Yellow Pages) list businesses and services by category order. Online versions can be found at www.pagesjaunes.fr.

Telephone charges

All local calls in Paris and Ile-de-France (to numbers beginning with 01) cost €0.11 for three minutes, standard rate and €0.04/min thereafter. This only applies to calls to other landlines. Calls beyond a 100km radius (*province*) are charged at €0.11 for the first 39 seconds, then €0.24 per minute.

International destinations are divided into 16 zones. Reduced-rate periods for calls within France and Europe are 7pm-8am during the week and all day Saturday and Sunday. Reduced-rate periods for the US and Canada are 7pm to 1pm Monday to Friday and all day Saturday and Sunday.

Cheap providers

Getting wise to the market demand, smaller telephone providers are becoming increasingly popular, as rates from giant France Télécom are not at exactly bargain-basement levels. The following can offer alternative rates for calls – although you will still need to rent your telephone line from France Télécom to use them:

AT&T Direct (local access) *08.00.99.00.11.*
Free *10.44/www.free.fr.*
With the Freebox (Free's modem for ADSL connection), €29.99 per month gets you ten hours of free calls to landlines (additional calls cost €0.01 per minute), €0.19 per minute to mobiles and €0.03 per minute for most international calls.
IC Télécom *08.05.13.26.26/ www.ictelecom.fr.*
Neuf Télécom *10.23/www.neuf.fr.*
Onetel *08.92.13.50.50/ www.onetel.fr.*

Special-rate numbers

0800 Numéro Vert
Freephone.
0810 Numéro Azure
€0.11 under three minutes, then €0.04/min.
0820 Numéro Indigo
€0.118/min.
0825 Numéro Indigo II
€0.15/min.
0836.64/0890.64/0890.70
€0.112/min.
0890.71 €0.15/min.
0891.67/0891.70 €0.225/min.
0836/0892 €0.337/min. This line is for the likes of ticket agencies, cinema and transport information.
10.14 France Télécom information; free (except from mobile phones).

TIME & SEASONS

France is one hour ahead of Greenwich Mean Time (GMT). France uses the 24hr system (for example, 18h means 6pm).

TIPPING

A service charge of ten to 15 per cent is legally included in your bill at all restaurants, cafés and bars. However, it is polite to either round up the final amount for drinks, or to leave a cash tip of €1-€2 or more for a meal, depending on the restaurant and, of course, the quality of the service.

TOILETS

The city's automatic street toilets are not really as terrifying as they look. Each loo is completely washed down and disinfected after use.

If a space age-style lavatory experience doesn't appeal, you can nip into the toilets of a café; although theoretically reserved for customers' use, a polite request should win sympathy with the waiter – and you may find you have to put a €0.20 coin into a slot in the door-handle mechanism, customer or not. Fast-food chain toilets often have a code on their toilet doors that is made known to paying customers only.

TOURIST INFORMATION

Espace du Tourisme d'Ile de France Carrousel du Louvre, 99 rue de Rivoli, 1st (www.nouveau-paris-ile-de-france.com). M° Palais Royal Musée du Louvre or Pyramides. Open 8.30am-7pm Mon-Fri. This is the information showcase for Paris and the Ile-de-France.
Maison de la France 20 av de l'Opéra, 1st (01.42.96.70.00/ www.franceguide.com). M° Opéra or Pyramides. **Open** 10am-6pm Mon-Fri; 10am-5pm Sat.
The Maison de la France is the state organisation for tourism in France: information galore.
Office de Tourisme et des Congrès de Paris 25 rue des Pyramides, 1st (08.92.68.30.00 recorded information in English & French/www.parisinfo.com). M° Pyramides. **Open** 9am-7pm daily. Information on Paris and the suburbs, shop, bureau de change, hotel reservations, phonecards, museum cards, travel passes and tickets. Multilingual staff.
Other locations: *Gare de Lyon* 20 bd Diderot, 12th. M° Gare de Lyon. **Open** 8am-6pm Mon-Sat. *Gare du Nord* 18 rue de Dunkerque, 10th. M° Gare du Nord. **Open** 8am-6pm daily. *Montmartre* 21 pl du Tertre, 18th. M° Abbesses. **Open** 10am-7pm daily. *Porte de Versailles* 1 pl de la Porte de Versailles, 15th. **Open** 11am-7pm daily.

VISAS

EU nationals don't need a visa to enter France, nor do US, Canadian, Australian, New Zealand or South African citizens for stays of up to three months. Nationals of other countries should enquire at the nearest French embassy or consulate before leaving home. If they are travelling to France from one of the countries in the Schengen agreement (most of the EU, but not Britain or Ireland), the visa from that country should be sufficient.

EU citizens may stay in France for as long as their passport is valid. For non-EU citizens who wish to stay for longer than three months, they must apply to the French embassy or consulate in their own country for a long-term visa. For more information, contact these two offices:

CIRA (Centre Interministeriel de Renseignements Administratifs) *39.39/www.service-public.fr.* **Open** 8am-7pm Mon-Fri; 8am-noon Sat. CIRA gives advice on most French administrative procedures via its local-rate phone line.
Préfecture de Police de Paris Service Etrangers *7-9 bd du Palais, 4th (01.53.73.53.73/ www.prefecture-police-paris. interieur. gouv.fr). M° Cité.* **Open** 9am-4pm Mon-Fri. This office can provide information on residency, along with work permits for foreigners.

WEIGHTS & MEASURES

France uses only the metric system; remember that all speed limits are in kilometres per hour. One kilometre is equivalent to 0.62 miles (1 mile = 1.6km). Petrol, like other liquids, is measured in litres (one UK gallon = 4.54 litres; 1 US gallon = 3.79 litres).

WHAT TO TAKE

Binoculars for studying high-altitude details of monuments, a pocket knife with corkscrew (for improvised picnics) and – vital for getting around the city on foot – comfortable shoes.

WHEN TO GO

In July and August there are often deals on hotels and a good range of free events (such as Paris-Plage), but many family-run restaurants and shops close as the locals go off *en vacances.* Avoid October, with its fashion weeks and trade shows.

WOMEN

Though Paris is not an especially threatening city for women, the precautions you would take in

---

THE LOCAL CLIMATE

Average temperatures and monthly rainfall in Paris.

	High (°C/°F)	Low (°C/°F)	Rainfall (mm/in)
Jan	7 / 45	2 / 36	53 / 2.1
Feb	10 / 50	2 / 36	43 / 1.7
Mar	13 / 55	4 / 39	49 / 1.9
Apr	17 / 63	6 / 43	53 / 2.1
May	20 / 68	9 / 48	65 / 2.6
June	23 / 73	12 / 54	54 / 2.1
July	25 / 77	15 / 59	62 / 2.4
Aug	26 / 79	16 / 61	42 / 1.7
Sept	23 / 73	12 / 54	54 / 2.1
Oct	20 / 68	8 / 46	60 / 2.4
Nov	14 / 57	4 / 39	51 / 2.0
Dec	7 / 45	3 / 37	59 / 2.3

---

any major metropolis apply here: be careful at night in certain areas, including Pigalle, the rue St-Denis, Stalingrad, La Chapelle, Château Rouge, Gare de l'Est, Gare du Nord, the Bois de Boulogne and Bois de Vincennes. If you receive unwanted attention, a politely scathing *N'insistez pas!* (Don't push it!) will make your feelings abundantly clear. If things get too heavy, go into the nearest shop or café.

CIDFF (Centre d'Information et des Droits des Femmes et de la Famille) *165 bd Sérurier, 19th (01.44.52.19.20/www.info femmes.com). M° Porte de Pantin.* **Open** visits by appointment only. The CIDFF offers health, legal and professional advice for women.
Violence Conjugale: Femmes Info Service *01.40.33.80.60.* **Open** 7.30am-11.30pm Mon-Sat. A hotline for the victims of domestic violence, directing them towards medical aid, shelters and other services.
Viols Femmes Informations *08.00.05.95.95.* **Open** 10am-7pm Mon-Fri. Freephone service. Help and advice available, in French, to rape victims.

WORKING IN PARIS

Most EU nationals– including Irish and UK citizens – are legally entitled to work in France, but should apply for a French social security number. Some job ads can be found at branches of the French national employment bureau, the **Agence Nationale pour l'Emploi** (ANPE), or on its website (www.anpe.fr). Branches o f ANPE are also the place to sign up as a *demandeur d'emploi,* to be

placed on file as available for work and possibly to qualify for French unemployment benefits.

Britons can only claim French unemployment benefit if they were already signed on before leaving the UK. Non-EU nationals need a work permit and cannot use the ANPE network without having valid work papers.

Club des Quatre Vents *1 rue Gozlin, 6th (01.43.29.60.20/ www.cei4vents.fr). M° St-Germain-des-Prés.* **Open** 9am-6pm Mon-Fri. Provides three-month work permits for US citizens at university or recent graduates.
Espace Emploi International (OMI et ANPE) *48 bd de la Bastille, 12th (01.53.02.25.50/ www.emploi-international.org). M° Bastille.* **Open** 9am-5pm Mon, Wed-Fri; 9am-noon Tue. This organisation provides work permits of up to 18 months for Americans aged 18-35.
Language Network *01.44.64.82.23/www.thelanguage network.fr.* Helps native English speakers who wish to find work teaching.

Job ads

Help wanted advertisements sometimes appear in the *International Herald Tribune,* in *FUSAC* and on noticeboards at language schools and the **American Church** (*see p376*).

Bilingual secretarial/PA work is available for those with good written French as well as secretarial skills. If you're looking for professional work, have your CV translated, including French equivalents for any qualifications. Most job applications require a photo and a handwritten letter.

DIRECTORY

Vocabulary

In French, the second person singular (you) has two forms. Phrases here are given in the more polite *vous* form. The *tu* form is used with family, friends, children and pets; you should be careful not to use it with people you do not know sufficiently well. Courtesies such as *monsieur, madame* and *mademoiselle* are generally used more than their English equivalents.

DIRECTORY

GENERAL

● **good morning/afternoon, hello** bonjour; **good evening** bonsoir; **goodbye** au revoir
● **OK** d'accord; **yes** oui; **no** non; **how are you?** comment allez vous?/vous allez bien?; **how's it going?** comment ça va?/ ça va? (familiar)
● **sir/Mr** monsieur (M.); **madam/Mrs** madame (Mme); **miss** mademoiselle (Mlle)
● **please** s'il vous plaît; **thank you** merci; **sorry** pardon; **excuse me** excusez-moi; **I am going to pay** je vais payer
● **do you speak English?** parlez-vous anglais?; **I don't speak French** je ne parle pas français; **I don't understand** je ne comprends pas; **speak more slowly, please** parlez plus lentement, s'il vous plaît
● **it is** c'est; **it isn't** ce n'est pas; **good** bon/bonne; **bad** mauvais/ mauvaise; **small** petit/petite; **big** grand/grande; **beautiful** beau/belle; **well** bien; **badly** mal; **a bit** un peu; **a lot** beaucoup; **very** très
● **with** avec; **without** sans; **and** et; **or** ou; **because** parce que; **who?** qui?; **when?** quand?; **what?** quoi?; **which?** quel?; **where?** où?; **why?** pourquoi?; **how?** comment?; **at what time/when?** à quelle heure?
● **forbidden** interdit/défendu; **out of order** hors service (HS)/en panne; **daily** tous les jours (tlj)

ON THE PHONE

● **hello** allô; **who's calling?** c'est de la part de qui?/qui est à l'appareil?; **this is... speaking** c'est... à l'appareil; **I'd like to speak to...** j'aurais voulu parler à...; **hold the line** ne quittez pas; **please call back later** rappelez plus tard s'il vous plaît; **you must have the wrong number** vous avez dû composer un mauvais numéro

GETTING AROUND

● **where is the (nearest) métro?** où est le métro (le plus proche)?; **when is the next train for... ?** c'est quand le prochain train pour... ?; **ticket** un billet; **station** la gare; **platform** le quai; **entrance** entrée; **exit** sortie
● **left** gauche; **right** droite; **straight on** tout droit; **far** loin; **near** pas loin/près d'ici; **street map** un plan; **road map** une carte

SIGHTSEEING

● **museum** un musée; **church** une église; **exhibition** une exposition; **ticket** (*museum*) un billet; (*theatre, concert*) une place
● **open** ouvert; **closed** fermé; **free** gratuit; **reduced price** un tarif réduit

ACCOMMODATION

● **do you have a room (for this evening/for two people)?** avez-vous une chambre (pour ce soir/pour deux personnes)?; **full** complet; **room** une chambre; **bed** un lit; **double bed** un grand lit; **(a room with) twin beds** (une chambre à) deux lits; **with bath(room)/shower** avec (salle de) bain/douche; **breakfast** le petit déjeuner; **included** compris

AT THE CAFE OR RESTAURANT

● **I'd like to book a table (for three/at 8pm)** je voudrais réserver une table (pour trois personnes/à vingt heures); **lunch** le déjeuner; **dinner** le dîner

● **coffee** (espresso) un café; **tea** un thé; **wine** le vin; **beer** une bière; **mineral water** eau minérale; **tap water** eau du robinet/une carafe d'eau; **the bill, please** l'addition, s'il vous plaît

SHOPPING

● **cheap** pas cher; **expensive** cher; **how much?/how many?** combien?; **have you got change?** avez-vous de la monnaie?; **I'll take it** je le prends
● **I would like...** je voudrais...; **may I try this on?** est-ce que je pourrais essayer cet article?; **do you have a smaller/larger size?** auriez-vous la taille en-dessous/au dessus?; **I'm a size 38** je fais du 38

STAYING ALIVE

● **be cool** restez calme; **I don't want any trouble** je ne veux pas d'ennuis; **I only do safe sex** je ne pratique que le safe sex

NUMBERS

● **0** zéro; **1** un, une; **2** deux; **3** trois; **4** quatre; **5** cinq; **6** six; **7** sept; **8** huit; **9** neuf; **10** dix; **11** onze; **12** douze; **13** treize; **14** quatorze; **15** quinze; **16** seize; **17** dix-sept; **18** dix-huit; **19** dix-neuf; **20** vingt; **21** vingt-et-un; **22** vingt-deux; **30** trente; **40** quarante; **50** cinquante; **60** soixante; **70** soixante-dix; **80** quatre-vingts; **90** quatre-vingt-dix; **100** cent; **1000** mille; **10,000** dix mille; **1,000,000** un million

DAYS, MONTHS & SEASONS

● **Monday** lundi; **Tuesday** mardi; **Wednesday** mercredi; **Thursday** jeudi; **Friday** vendredi; **Saturday** samedi; **Sunday** dimanche
● **January** janvier; **February** février; **March** mars; **April** avril; **May** mai; **June** juin; **July** juillet; **August** août; **September** septembre; **October** octobre; **November** novembre; **December** décembre
● **spring** le printemps; **summer** l'été; **autumn** l'automne; **winter** l'hiver

Further Reference

BOOKS

Non-fiction

Robert Baldick *The Siege of Paris* A gripping account of the Paris Commune of 1871.
Antony Beevor & Artemis Cooper *Paris after the Liberation* Rationing, freedom, Existentialism.
NT Binh *Paris au cinéma* Attractively illustrated hardback round-up of Paris sights on film.
Henri Cartier-Bresson *A propos de Paris* Classic black and white shots by a giant among snappers.
Vincent Cronin *Napoleon* A fine biography of the emperor.
Léon-Paul Fargue *Le Piéton de Paris* The city anatomised, just before World War II.
Jean-Marie Gourio *Brèves de comptoir* An anthology of wisdom and weirdness overheard at café counters. A French classic.
Alastair Horne *The Fall of Paris* Detailed chronicle of the Siege and Commune 1870-71.
J-K Huysmans *Croquis Parisiens* The world that Toulouse-Lautrec painted.
Ian Littlewood *Paris: Architecture, History, Art* Paris's history and its treasures.
Henri Michel *Paris Allemand*; *Paris Résistant* Detailed, two-volume account of life in Paris during the Occupation.
Noel Riley Fitch *Literary Cafés of Paris* Who drank what, where.
Virginia Rounding *Les Grandes Horizontales* Entertaining lives of four 19th-century courtesans.
Simon Schama *Citizens* Epic, readable account of the Revolution.
William Shirer *The Collapse of the Third Republic* Forensic account of the reasons for France's humiliating 1940 defeat.
Thibaut Vandorselaer *Paris BD* A lovely series of walking trails around the city, illustrated entirely with 'BD' (cartoon) frames.

Fiction & poetry

Honoré de Balzac *Illusions perdues*; *La Peau de chagrin*; *Le Père Goriot*; *Splendeurs et misères des courtisanes* Much of the 'Comédie Humaine' cycle of novels is set in Paris.
Charles Baudelaire *Le Spleen de Paris* Prose poems, Paris settings.
Louis-Ferdinand Céline *Mort à crédit* Vivid, splenetic account of an impoverished Paris childhood.
Victor Hugo *Notre Dame de Paris* Romantic vision of medieval Paris. Quasimodo! Esmeralda! The bells!
W Somerset Maugham *Christmas Holiday* Young, middle-class Brit spends Christmas with a prostitute in Paris.
Gérard de Nerval *Les Nuits d'octobre* Late-night Les Halles and environs, mid 19th century.
Georges Perec *La Vie, mode d'emploi* Cheek-by-jowl life in a Haussmannian apartment building.
Raymond Queneau *Zazie dans le Métro* Paris in the 1950s: bright and very *nouvelle vague*.
Nicolas Restif de la Bretonne *Les Nuits de Paris* The sexual underworld of Louis XV's Paris.
Georges Simenon *Rue Pigalle*; *Maigret et les braves gens*, etc. Many of the famous Maigret books are set in Paris.
Emile Zola *L'Assommoir*; *Nana*; *Le Ventre de Paris* Accounts of the underside of the Second Empire from the master Realist.

The ex-pat angle

Janet Flanner *Paris Journal* Three volumes of reports on postwar Paris arts and politics, written for the *New Yorker*.
Ernest Hemingway *A Moveable Feast* Chronicle of 1920s Paris.
Henry Miller *Tropic of Cancer* Love and low life: lusty and funny.
George Orwell *Down and Out in Paris and London* Work in a Paris restaurant, hunger in a Paris hovel, suffering in a Paris hospital.

FILM

Luc Besson *Subway* Christophe Lambert goes underground.
Marcel Carné *Hôtel du Nord* Arletty stars in this poetic slice of life by the Canal St-Martin.
René Clair *Paris qui dort* Clair's surrealist silent comedy is one of the best Paris films ever made.
Louis Feuillade *Fantômas* Supervillain Fantomas repeatedly outwits Paris law enforcers in Feuillade's masterful silent serials.
Jean-Luc Godard *A Bout de Souffle* Belmondo, Seberg, Godard, the Champs-Elysées, the attitude, the famous ending. Essential.
Edouard Molinaro *Un Témoin dans la ville* Lino Ventura on the run in 1950s nocturnal Paris. Superb *noir*.
François Truffaut *Les 400 Coups* The first of the Antoine Doinel cycle.
Agnès Varda *Cléo de 5 à 7* The *nouvelle vague* heroine spends an anxious afternoon in the city.

MUSIC

Miles Davis *Ascenseur pour l'échafaud* The soundtrack to Louis Malle's film is superb after-dark jazz.
Fréhel *1930-1939* The immortal Fréhel sings of love, drugs and debauchery in true *chanson réaliste* style.
Naive New Beaters *Wallace* Great pop from a hot new Paris band.
Serge Gainsbourg *Le Poinçonneur des Lilas* Classic early Gainsbourg.

WEBSITES

www.culture.fr Current and forthcoming cultural events of all kinds, in Paris and other big French cities.
www.edible-paris.com Customised gastronomic itineraries in Paris by the editor of Time Out's *Eating & Drinking in Paris* guide.
www.gogoparis.com Online version of free monthly Anglo listings mag.
www.meteo.fr State weather forecasts.
www.pagesjaunes.fr The Paris yellow pages, with maps and multi-angle photos of every address in the city.
www.parissi.com Films, concerts and a strong calendar of clubbing events.
www.parisinfo.com Official site of the Office de Tourisme et des Congrès de Paris.
www.ratp.com Everything you'll need to know about using the buses, métro, RER and trams.
www.timeout.com/paris A pick of the best current events and good hotels, restaurants and shops.

DIRECTORY

Index

INDEX

INDEX

Get the local experience

Over 50 of the world's top destinations available.

INDEX

Advertisers' Index

Please refer to the relevant pages for contact details.

INDEX

Maps

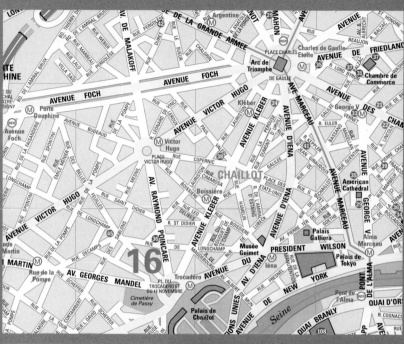

Place of interest and/or entertainment	
Hospital or college	
Railway station	
Park	
River	
Autoroute	═══
Main road	
Pedestrian road	
Arrondissement boundary...................	
Airport	✈
Church	✚
Métro station	Ⓜ
RER station	Ⓡ
Area name	**LES HALLES**
Hotel	❶
Restaurant	❶
Cafés & Bars	❶

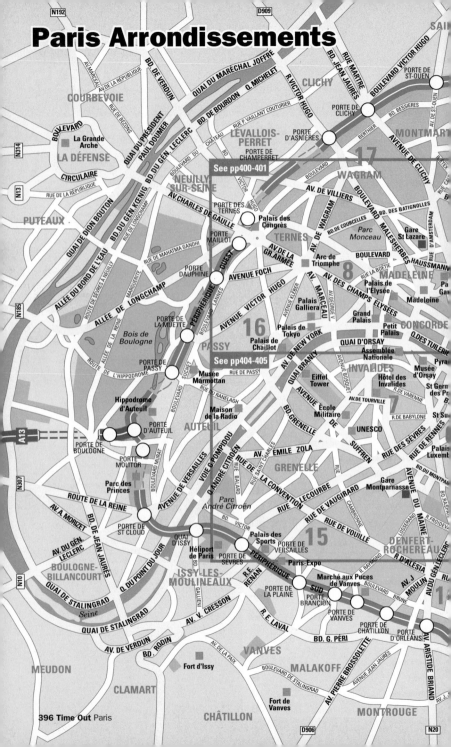

Paris Arrondissements

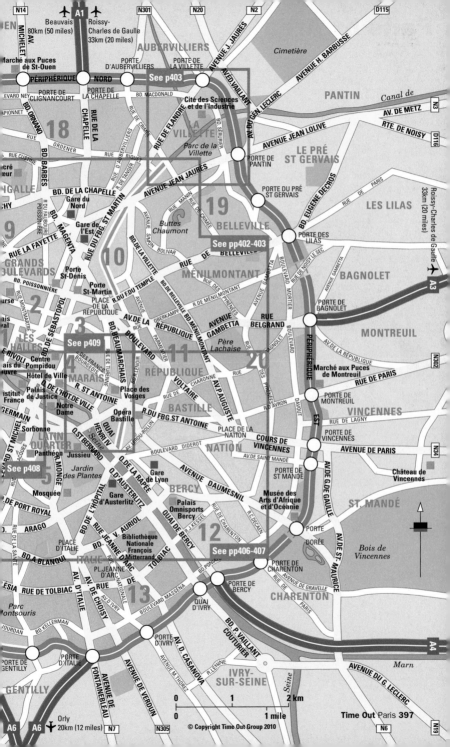

© Copyright Time Out Group 2010

Paris by Area

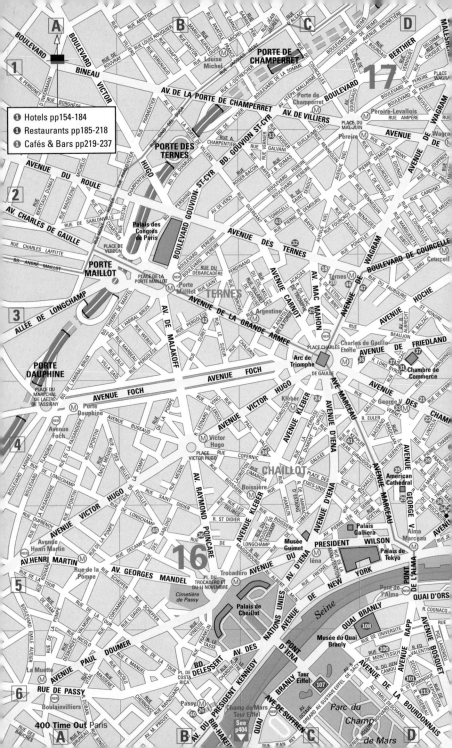

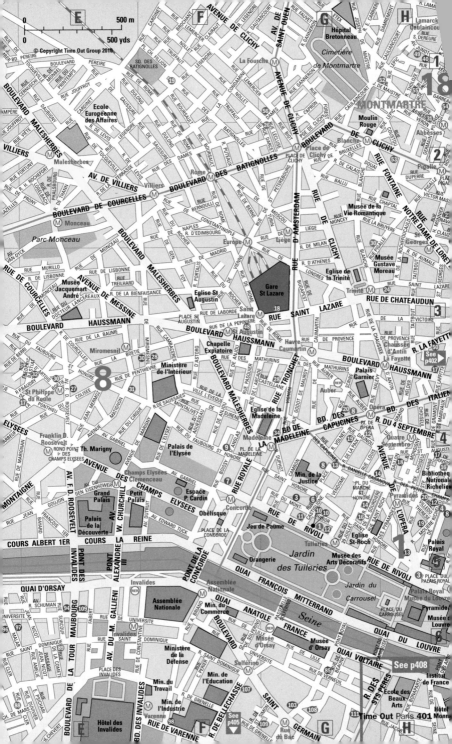

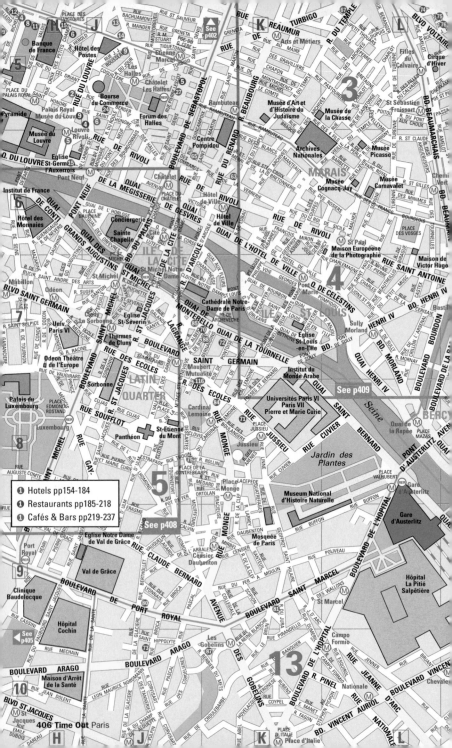

❶ Hotels pp154-184
❶ Restaurants pp185-218
❶ Cafés & Bars pp219-237

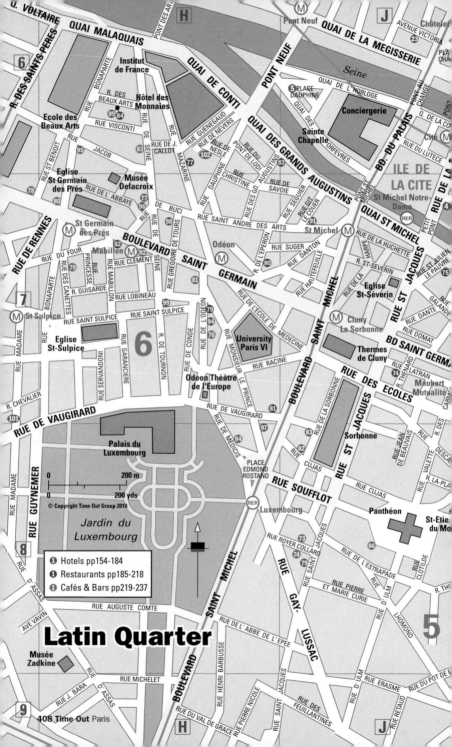

Latin Quarter

❶ Hotels pp154-184
❶ Restaurants pp185-218
❶ Cafés & Bars pp219-237

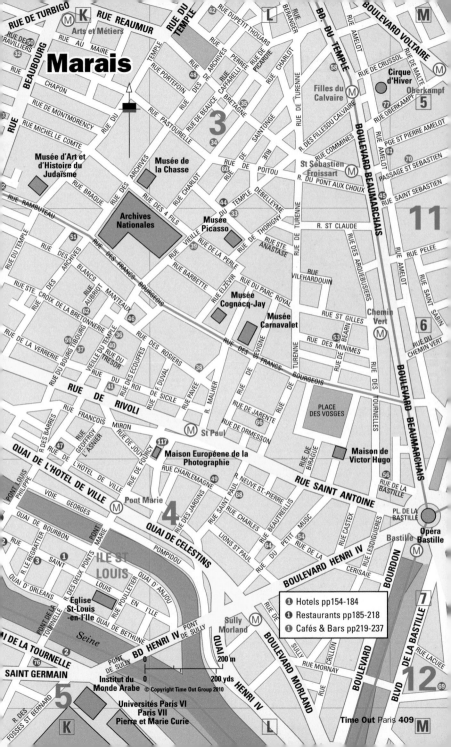

Marais

Musée d'Art et d'Histoire du Judaïsme

Musée de la Chasse

Archives Nationales

Musée Picasso

Musée Cognacq-Jay

Musée Carnavalet

St Sébastien Froissart

Cirque d'Hiver

Oberkampf

Filles du Calvaire

St Sébastien

Chemin Vert

Place des Vosges

Maison Européenne de la Photographie

Maison de Victor Hugo

St Paul

Pont Marie

Opéra Bastille

Bastille

ILE ST LOUIS

Eglise St-Louis -en-l'Ile

Sully Morland

Institut du Monde Arabe

Universités Paris VI Paris VII Pierre et Marie Curie

| ❶ Hotels pp154-184 |
| ❶ Restaurants pp185-218 |
| ❶ Cafés & Bars pp219-237 |

200 m

200 yds

© Copyright Time Out Group 2010

Street Index

STREET INDEX

STREET INDEX

Paris RER

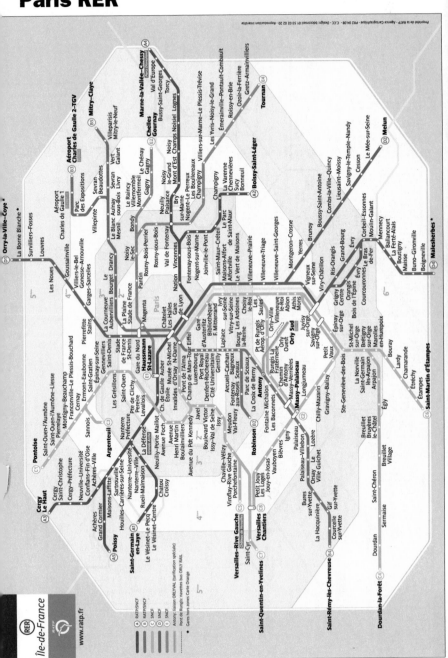

Paris Métro

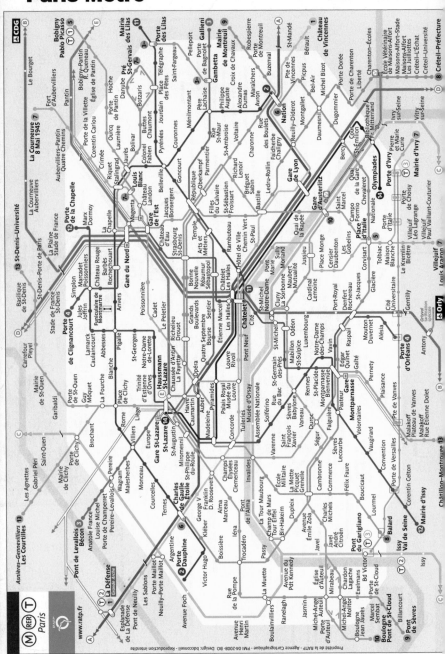